[英 汉 对 照]

西方学术经典文库

理 想 国

REPUBLIC

[古希腊]柏拉图 著

庞爔春 译

张云江 译校

(一)

九 州 出 版 社
JIUZHOUPRESS

图书在版编目(CIP)数据

理想国.2/(古希腊)柏拉图著;庞爔春译.—北京:九州出版社,2007.4

(西方学术经典文库)

ISBN 978-7-80195-568-5

Ⅰ.理…　Ⅱ.①柏…②庞…　Ⅲ.古希腊罗马哲学　Ⅳ.B502.232

中国版本图书馆 CIP 数据核字(2007)第 049105 号

理想国

作　　者　[古希腊]柏拉图　著　　庞爔春　译　张云江　译校
责任编辑　张海涛　安静
出版发行　九州出版社
地　　址　北京市西城区阜外大街甲 35 号(100037)
发行电话　(010)68992190/2/3/5/6
网　　址　www.jiuzhoupress.com
电子信箱　jiuzhou@jiuzhoupress.com
印　　刷　三河东方印刷厂
开　　本　630×970mm　1/16
印　　张　55.125
字　　数　590 千字
版　　次　2007 年 7 月第 1 版
印　　次　2007 年 7 月第 1 次印刷
书　　号　ISBN 978-7-80195-568-5/C·119
定　　价　109.00 元(全二册)

出版说明

在西方学术思想的发展流变中，出现过很多影响深远的经典著作，这些著作穿越时空，为人们长久研读，有的甚至影响了整个人类文明的发展进程。这套《西方学术经典文库》（英汉对照本），精选了其中最有代表性的一些名著，计划达到一百部，将陆续分批出版直至全部完成。

《西方学术经典文库》由多位专家学者指导分类选目，内容涵盖哲学、文学、宗教学、政治学、经济学、社会学、人类学、心理学、法学、历史学等类，注重权威性、学术性和影响性，收录了不同国家、不同时代、不同流派的诸多名著。

《西方学术经典文库》中译本译自英文原著或其他文种的英文译本，以英汉对照的形式出版，读者可以参照原文对作品有更加客观的理解，更好地把握西方学术思想的精髓。

为加以区别，原文中的英文注释，注释号用①、②……形式表示；中文译者注释则以〔1〕、〔2〕……形式表示。至于英译本中出现的原文页码和特殊索引等问题，中文译者在"译者后记"中将予以解释、说明。另外，在英文原著中，有一些表示着重意义的斜体或大写等字体，考虑到读者可以在对照英文阅读中看到，因此在中译文中，没有照样标出，还望读者理解。

九州出版社

Republic

By *Plato*

English Translation

By *Robin Waterfield*

本书根据 Oxford University Press 1993 年版本译出

CONTENTS

目　录

(一)

（二）

CHAPTER 1

327a Yesterday I went down to the Piraeus with Glaucon the son of Ariston to worship the goddess and also because I wanted to see how they would conduct the festival on this, its first performance. I was certainly impressed with the splendour of the procession made by the local people, but I have to say that the Thracians rose to the occasion just as well in their procession. Once our worshipping and watching
b were over, we were starting to make our way back to town, when Polemarchus the son of Cephalus spotted us from a distance setting off home, and he told his slave to run over to us and tell us to wait for him. The boy came up behind me, caught hold of my coat, and said, 'Polemarchus wants you to wait.'

I turned around and asked where his master was. 'There,' he said, 'coming up behind you. Please wait.'

'All right, we will,' said Glaucon.

c Polemarchus soon caught up with us, and so did Glaucon's brother Adeimantus, Niceratus the son of Nicias, and some others; they had all apparently been at the procession.

'Socrates,' Polemarchus said, 'it looks to me as though the two of you are setting off back to town.'

'That's right,' I replied.

'Well,' he said, 'do you see how many of us there are?'

'Of course.'

'You'd better choose, then,' he said, 'between overpowering us and staying here.'

第一章

昨天我和阿里斯同的儿子格劳孔一起下去到比雷埃乌斯敬 327a
拜女神，同时也因为我想去看看他们在这种场合是如何庆祝节日的，这是它的第一次演出。当地人的壮观游行给我留下了深刻的印象，但我不得不说色雷斯人在游行中的相机表现也很不错。我们敬拜并看完表演之后，就开始赶路回城，这时，凯发卢斯的儿子 b
玻勒玛库斯从远处看见我们，于是他吩咐他的家奴赶上我们，告诉我们等他一下。那家奴从后面追上我，抓住我的外套，说："玻勒玛库斯请你们等一下。"

我转过身问他的主人在哪儿。"在那儿，"他说，"正在你们后面朝这里来呢。请等等吧。"

"好，我们等等吧。"格劳孔说。

玻勒玛库斯很快就赶上我们了，还有格劳孔的兄弟阿狄曼 c
图，尼西亚斯的儿子尼克拉图，以及其他一些人；显然，他们刚刚都在游行队伍里。

"苏格拉底，"玻勒玛库斯说，"我看你们两个好像是要动身回城去吧？"

"对啊。"我回答说。

"好吧，"他说，"你看见我们有几个人吗？"

"当然看到了。"

"那么，你最好做一个选择，"他说："或者打败我们，或者留在这儿。"

'Well, there *is* one further possibility,' I pointed out. 'We might convince you to let us leave.'

'Can you convince people who don't listen?' he asked.

'Impossible,' Glaucon replied.

'Then I think you should know that we won't be listening to you.'

328a 'Anyway,' Adeimantus added, 'don't you realize that there's going to be a horseback torch-race this evening for the goddess?'

'Horseback?' I said. 'That's unusual. Do you mean there'll be a horse-race in which they'll carry torches and pass them on to one another?'

'Precisely,' Polemarchus said. 'And they're also putting on an all-night celebration, which should be worth seeing. We're going to go out to watch it after dinner, and lots of young men will be there too,
b whom we shall be talking to. So you must do as we suggest and stay.'

'It looks as though we'd better stay,' said Glaucon.

'Well, if you think so,' I said, 'then that's what we should do.'

So we went to Polemarchus' house, and there we found his brothers Lysias and Euthydemus, and also Thrasymachus of Chalcedon, Charmantides of Paeania, and Cleitophon the son of Aristonymus. Polemarchus' father Cephalus was in the house too; I thought
c he looked very old, but then I hadn't seen him for quite a while. He was sitting on a chair with a cushion, and wearing a chaplet, since he had just been making a ritual offering in the courtyard. Some other chairs had been placed in a circle there, so we sat down beside him.

As soon as Cephalus saw me, he said hello and then went on, 'Socrates, unfortunately for us, you're not in the habit of coming down to the Piraeus. You should, you know. I mean, if I still had the strength to make the journey up to town easily, you wouldn't have to come here, because I'd be visiting you. But as things are, you should come here more often. In my

“嗯，还有一种可能性，”我指出，“我们也许可以说服你让我们走。”

“你能说服不听说话的人吗？”他问道。

“不可能。”格劳孔回答道。

“那么我想你应该知道我们是不会听你说的。”

“不管怎么说，”阿狄曼图补充说，“你们难道不知道今晚将有 328a
一场献给女神的马背上的火炬接力赛吗？”

“马背上？”我说，“那倒是不寻常。你是说会有一场赛马，在赛马中他们会拿着火把相互传递吗？”

“正是，”玻勒玛库斯说，“并且还要加上整晚的庆祝，应该值得一看吧。晚饭后我们将去看看，也会有很多年轻人在那里，我
们会和他们聊聊。所以你务必照我们的建议留下来。” b

“看来我们最好还是留下来吧。”格劳孔说。

“好吧，如果你这么想的话，”我说，“那么我们就这么办吧。”

于是我们就去了玻勒玛库斯的家，在那里我们看到了他的兄弟吕西阿斯和欧绪德谟，有卡尔色顿的塞拉西马库斯，培阿尼亚的卡尔曼提德，还有阿里斯托尼姆的儿子克利托丰。玻勒玛库斯的父亲凯发卢斯也在家；我觉得他看起来很苍老了，不过我也有
很长一段时间没有见到他了。他正坐在一张带靠垫的椅子上，头 c
戴花冠，因为他刚在庭院里做完祭献仪式。还有些其他椅子在院内被摆成一圈，所以我们就在他旁边坐下。

凯发卢斯一看到我就向我打招呼，然后继续说：“苏格拉底，对我们来说不幸的是，你不是常来比雷埃乌斯。你知道你是应该来的。我的意思是说，如果我仍旧有力气出行而轻松地赶到城里的话，你就不必非到这里来了，因为我会去拜访你。但实际情况

d case, you see, declining interest in physical pleasures is exactly
matched by increasing desire for and enjoyment of conversation. So
please do as I ask: by all means spend time with these young men
who are your companions, but treat us too as your friends—as your
very close friend—and come here to visit us.'

'I certainly will, Cephalus,' I replied. 'I do in fact enjoy talk-
e ing with very old people, because I think we ought to learn from
them. They've gone on ahead of us, as it were, on a road which we
too will probably have to travel, and we ought to find out from them
what the road is like—whether it is rough and hard, or easy and
smooth. And I'd be especially glad to ask you your opinion about it,
since you've reached the time of life the poets describe as being "on
the threshold of old age". Is it a difficult period of one's life, would
you say, or what?'

329a 'Of course I'll tell you my opinion, Socrates,' he said. 'You
see, it's not uncommon for some of us old men of approximately the
same age to get together (and so vindicate the ancient proverb!).
These gatherings are invariably used for grumbling, by those who miss
the pleasures of youth. They remind themselves of their love lives,
drinking, feasting, and the like, and consequently complain of having
been robbed of things that are important and claim that in those days
they used to live well, whereas nowadays they aren't even alive. Oth-
b ers bleat about how their families treat old age like dirt; in fact, this is
the main reason they go on and on about all the evils for which old age
is responsible. But to my mind, Socrates, they are holding an inno-
cent responsible. If old age were to blame, then I too would have had
the same experiences as them at least as far as old age is concerned—
and so would everyone else who has reached this age. But in the past
I, at any rate, have met others like myself who do not feel this way.
In particular, I was once with Sophocles the poet when someone
c asked him, "How do you feel about sex, Sophocles? Are you still
capable of having sex with a woman?" He replied, "Be quiet,

是,你该常来这里。对我来说,你知道,对于肉体快乐的兴趣在削 d
减,对于交谈的期望和享乐在相应增加。所以请满足我的请求:一定要花些时间在这些年轻人身上,他们是你的伙伴啊,但你还要把我们当作你的朋友,当作非常亲密的朋友,并常常来这看看我们。”

“我当然会,凯发卢斯,”我回答说,“实际上我乐于和年寿已
高的人谈话,因为我认为我们应该向他们学习。这好比是在一条 e
路上,他们已经走在了我们前面,这路也许是我们也要走的,而我们应该从他们那里了解路况怎样——它是崎岖艰难的,还是轻松平坦的。故我尤其高兴听听你对这条路的想法,因为你已经到了诗人所谓的‘老年门槛’的年纪了,这是否是人生中一段艰难的时光呢,还是别的什么,你想说说吗?”

“我当然会告诉你我的想法,苏格拉底,”他说。“你知道,我 329a
们几个年纪相仿的老人聚会不是不寻常的,(这正应了那句古话!)这些聚会免不了被那些失去了年轻时代快乐的人用来抱怨。他们回想起从前他们自己的爱情生活、宴饮及诸如此类,结果就抱怨自己被夺走了种种重要的东西,并且声称在那些日子里他们总是过得很舒适,但是现在的日子甚至就不是在生活。还有些人
喃喃怨诉亲人们是如何地轻贱老年;实际上,这就是他们将不断 b
遭受的所有不幸归咎于老年的主要理由。但在我看来,苏格拉底,他们所归于的责任是清白的。如果要归咎于老年,那么就老年这一点来说,我也会有与他们同样的感受,并且其他到了这个年纪的人也都会这样。然而,不管怎样,我从前所遇到的和我相仿的其他一些人并不这样觉得。尤其是有一次我和诗人索福克
勒斯在一起,有人问他:‘索福克勒斯,你在性方面怎么啦?你还 c
有能力和女人做爱吗?’他回答说:‘别提了,朋友!让我倍感欣慰

man! To my great delight, I have broken free of that, like a slave
who has got away from a rabid and savage master " I thought at the
time that this was a good response, and I haven't changed my mind. I
mean, there's no doubt that in old age you get a great deal of peace
and freedom from things like sex. When the desires lose their intensi-
ty and ease up, then what happens is absolutely as Sophocles de-
d scribed freedom from a great many demented masters. However, the
one thing responsible for this, and for one's relationship with relatives
as well, is not a person's old age, Socrates, but his character. If
someone is self-disciplined and good-tempered, old age isn't too much
of a burden; otherwise, it's not just a question of old age, Socrates
such a person will find life difficult when he's young as well.'

e I was filled with admiration for him and his words, and because I
wanted him to continue, I tried to provoke him by saying, 'Cepha-
lus, I think that most people would react to what you're saying with
scepticism; they'd think that you're finding old age easy to bear not
because of your character, but because of your great wealth. The rich
have many consolations, they say.'

'You're right,' he said, 'they are sceptical. And they do have
a point, though not as important a point as they imagine. The story a-
bout Themistocles is relevant here—how when the man from Seriphus
330a was rudely saying that his fame was due not to his own merits but to
his city, he replied, "It's true that I wouldn't have become famous if I
were a Seriphian, but it's also true that you wouldn't if you were an A-
thenian." The same principle applies to people who aren't rich and are
finding old age hard to bear. It's true that a good man wouldn't find
old age particularly easy to bear if he were poor, but it's also true that
a bad man would never be content with himself even if he were

的是我已经摆脱那种事情了，就像一个从狂暴野蛮的主人那里获得自由的奴隶一样。'当时我想那是一个很好的回答，并且我至今也还没有改变我的想法。我的意思是，毫无疑问，到了老年，你获得了巨大的平静安宁，并且从性之类的事情上解脱开来。当欲望失去了它们的强度而缓和时，那么所发生的就绝对如同索福克勒斯所描述的那样，是从很多疯狂的奴隶主那里解脱出来了。然而
造成上述现象及他们与亲戚的这种关系的原因，并不是人们的年 d
老，苏格拉底，而是人的性格。如果一个人有自制力和好脾气，那么年老并不是一个过于沉重的负担；否则，这并不仅仅是年龄老了的问题，苏格拉底——这类感到年老是过于沉重的负担的人，在他年轻时，他会发现生活也是难以忍受的。"

我对他和他的话充满了崇敬，为了想让他继续说下去，我试
着激发他，就说："凯发卢斯，我觉得大多数人听了你的话以后会 e
持怀疑态度；他们会认为你觉得老年好过并不是因为你的性格，而是因为你的巨大财富。有钱人有很多的安慰，他们说。"

"你说得对，"他说，"他们是会怀疑的。他们的确有些道理，虽然这道理并没有他们所想的那么重要。这里有个关于塞米司托克勒[1]的故事——当塞利福斯人粗暴无礼地说，他的名誉并不
是由于他的功绩而是由于他是雅典人时，他回答说：'的确，如果 330a
我是塞利福斯人，那么我便不会成名，但即使你们是雅典人，你们也不会成名。'同样的道理也适合于那些既不富有又觉得老年很难受的人。确实的，一个良好的人如果是贫穷的，那么他也不会觉得年老很容易忍受，但这也是确实的，一个不良的人，即使他很

---

〔1〕 塞米司托克勒，古希腊雅典著名政治家。

wealthy.'

'Did you inherit most of your wealth, Cephalus,' I asked, 'or did you make it yourself?'

b 'What's that you say, Socrates?' he asked. 'Make it myself? As a businessman, I come between my grandfather and my father. My grandfather (after whom I'm named) inherited assets approximately equal to what I have now, and increased them considerably; my father Lysanias, however, decreased them to less than they are now. It'll make me happy if I leave these sons of mine not less, but a little more than I inherited.'

'I'll tell you why I asked,' I said. 'It was because I got the im-
c pression that you don't particularly care for money, and this is usually the mark of someone who hasn't made it himself, whereas people who have made it themselves are twice as attached to it as anyone else. Poets are attached to their own compositions, fathers to their sons; in the same way, businessmen are concerned about money not only because it's useful (which is why everyone else is interested in it), but also because it is the product of their own labours. This makes them irritating to be with, since money is the only thing they're prepared to think highly of.'

'You're right,' he said.

d 'Yes,' I said. 'But there's another question I wanted to ask you. What do you think is the greatest benefit you've gained from being rich?'

'Something which many people might find implausible,' he answered. 'You see, Socrates, when thoughts of death start to impinge on a person's mind, he entertains fears and worries about things which never occurred to him before. In the past he used to laugh at the stories that are told about what goes on in Hades—about how someone who has done wrong here is bound to be pun-
e ished there—but now they trouble his mind, in case they might be

富有,他也是决不会满足于自身的。"

"凯发卢斯,你的大部分财产是继承来的,还是自己赚来的?"我问道。

"苏格拉底,你说什么呀?"他问道。"我自己赚?作为一个商 b
人,我介于我的祖父和我的父亲之间。我的祖父(我被取名为和他同名)继承了大致相当于我现在所拥有的财产,并大大地增加了这些财产;然而我的父亲吕珊尼阿斯却让它们缩减到比现在还少。我能把这些财产留给儿子们,并且也不比我继承来的少,也许还能多一些,我就满足了。"

"告诉你,我之所以这样问你,"我说,"是因为我觉得你并不
是特别计较金钱,而这通常是那些自己不赚钱的人的标志,相反, c
那些自己赚钱的人却是像其他人一样更加贪爱金钱。诗人们爱恋他们自己的诗作,父亲们爱他们的儿子;同样,商人们关心金钱并不只是因为它有用(而这是所有其他人对金钱感兴趣的原因),更因为它是他们自己劳动的成果。这使得他们和人打交道时让人难受,因为金钱是他们乐意尊敬的唯一事物。"

"你说得对。"他说。

"是啊,"我说,"但还有个问题我想问你。你认为你从财富中 d
所获得的最大益处是什么?"

"某些事很多人可能会觉得难以相信,"他回答说,"你知道的,苏格拉底,当死亡的想法开始侵入一个人的头脑之中,他就怀有了对以前在他身上从未发生过的事情的恐怖与烦恼。过去他可是对听来的有关哈德斯[1]那里发生的故事——一个在此世作恶的人是怎样必定会在那里遭到惩罚——嗤之以鼻的,但是现在这
些故事却使他的心情烦扰痛苦起来,万一它们可能是真的呢?这 e

〔1〕 哈德斯:希腊神话中主宰阴间的冥王。

true. This might be due to the weakness of old age or it might be because, now that he's closer to the next world, he sees it more clearly; the result is that he becomes filled with anxiety and fear, and starts to make calculations and to see if he has wronged anyone in any way. Anyone who discovers that during his life he has committed a lot of crimes wakes up constantly in terror from his dreams, as children do,
331a and also lives in dread; on the other hand, anyone who is aware of no wrong in himself faces the future with confidence and optimism which, as Pindar says as well, "comforts him in old age". To my mind, Socrates, he expresses it beautifully when he says that anyone who has spent his life behaving morally and justly has "Sweet hope as a companion, joyfully fostering his heart, comforting him in old age—hope which steers, more than anything else does, men's fickle intention." This is incredibly well put. And this is the context in which I value the possession of money so highly—at least for a decent, orderly
b person. I mean, the possession of money has a major role to play if one is to avoid cheating or lying against one's better judgement, and also avoid the fear of leaving this life still owing some ritual offerings to a god or some money to someone. It serves a lot of other purposes too, but all things considered I'd say that for an intelligent person, Socrates, wealth is particularly useful in this far from insignificant context.'

c 'A thoroughly commendable sentiment, Cephalus,' I said. 'But what about this thing you mentioned, doing right? Shall we say that it is, without any qualification, truthfulness and giving back anything one has borrowed from someone? Or might the performance of precisely these actions sometimes be right, but sometimes wrong? This is the kind of thing I mean. I'm sure everyone would agree that if you'd borrowed weapons from a friend who was perfectly sane, but he went insane and then asked for the weapons back, you shouldn't give them back, and if you were to give them back you wouldn't be doing right, and neither would someone who was ready to tell the whole truth to a person like that.'

d 'You're right,' he agreed.

或许是因为年老体弱,或是因为现在他更接近另一个世界而看得更加清楚了;结果是,他变得充满焦虑和恐惧,并开始做些盘算,看看他是否曾以任何方式伤害过别人。那些发现在其一生中作恶多端的人,会像孩子一样频频从恶梦中醒来,并且生活于恐惧
之中;另一方面,一个问心无愧的人则自信而乐观地面对未来,就 331a
像品达所说的,'这在老年给他以安慰。'在我看来,苏格拉底,他说的好极了,他说高尚而正义地生活的人有'甜蜜的希望做伴侣,来陶然滋养他的心灵,慰藉他的垂暮之年——它比其他任何东西更能驾驭人们那变幻莫测的心意'。这无疑是说得很好的。在这种情况下,我高度肯定拥有财富,至少是对那些正派规矩的人而
言的。我的意思是,拥有财富的一个主要作用就是有了它,人们 b
就能避免违背良知的欺骗或撒谎,并在结束此生时,也避免了因为还欠着应献给神的一些祭品或者某人的一些钱财而产生的不安。财富也还有许多其他用途,但全面地考虑,我得说,苏格拉底,对于一个明智的人来说,比起其他一些无关紧要的情况来说,财富在这种情况下是尤其有用的。"

"你的想法十分令人钦佩,凯发卢斯,"我说,"不过,说到行为 c
正当,它又是什么呢?我们能毫无限制条件地说它就是讲诚信、把借来的东西归还给人家吗?还是说这样做有时候是对的,而有时候是错的呢?这正是我要说的意思。要是有人向他头脑完全正常的朋友借了武器,而之后他疯了,且想要回武器,我确信所有人都会同意不该把武器归还给他,而如果你还给他武器,那就是不正当的,而如果有谁准备将整个真实情况都告诉那样的一个
人,也是不正当了。" d

"你说得对,"他同意道。

'It follows that this isn't the definition of morality, to tell the truth and to give back whatever one has borrowed.'

'Yes, it is. Socrates,' Polemarchus interjected. 'At least, it is if we're to believe Simonides.'

'Well now,' said Cephalus, 'I shall pass the discussion on to you two, since it's time for me to attend to the ceremony.'

'And shall I be your heir?' asked Polemarchus.

'Of course,' he said with a chuckle, and promptly left for the ceremony.

e 'Well then,' I told him, 'now that you've inherited the discussion, tell us what it is that Simonides says which you think is an accurate statement about morality.'

'That it is right to give anyone back what you owe them,' he said. 'In my opinion, this is a fine remark.'

'Well,' I said, 'it isn't easy to disagree with Simonides: he's a clever man—superhumanly so. But while *you* may understand what he means by this, Polemarchus, I don't, I mean, he obviously doesn't mean what we were talking about a moment ago, the returning of something one has been lent to someone insane who's asking for it
332a back. And yet something lent is owed, wouldn't you say?'

'Yes.'

'And if the person asking for it back is insane, it's inconceivable that it should be given back, isn't it?'

'True,' he replied.

“据此推论，那么说实话并把借来的任何东西归还，并不就是正义[1]的定义。”

“不对，那就是定义，苏格拉底，”玻勒马库斯插话说。“至少，如果我们相信西蒙尼德的话。”

“好吧，”凯发卢斯说，“现在我把讨论交给你们两人，因为现在我得去参加典礼了。”

“要我接替你吗？”玻勒玛库斯问道。

“当然，”他微笑着说，于是就很快离开参加典礼去了。

“那么好吧，”我对他说，“现在你承接下了讨论，告诉我们西蒙尼德说了什么，让你觉得这就是对正义的准确表述。” e

“欠人什么还人什么，就是正义的，”他说，“我认为这话说得很好。”

“是啊，”我说，“我们难以对西蒙尼德表示异议：他是一个聪明人，超出一般人的聪明。但你也许明白他这么说是什么意思呢，玻勒玛库斯啊，而我却不太清楚，我的意思是说，他说的显然不是我们刚才谈到的那个意思，即把一个疯子索还的东西还给他。可是借了东西就是欠债了，你不是这样说吗？” 332a

“是的。”

“那么如果索还的人是疯子，还要把武器还给他，那就是不能想象的，不是吗？”

“说得对，”他回答道。

---

〔1〕 这个英译本中的Morality，指的就是柏拉图在《理想国》中讨论的“正义”。柏拉图将正义分成两个部分来讨论：城邦中的正义和人灵魂中的正义。两者是相对应的。柏拉图认为对于一个好（善）的城邦而言，它应该具有智慧、勇敢、自制和正义四种美德，其中正义是高处于前三者的，因为无论智慧、勇敢还是自制都有做得是否合适的问题，这就是正义和非正义的问题。同样，灵魂中的四种美德也是与城邦中的美德相对应的。本英译者将正义翻译为morality似乎意义于过宽泛，因此，中译本统一翻译成“正义”。

'Then apparently it wasn't this, but something else, that Simonides meant by the assertion that it is right to give back what is owed.'

'Yes, of course it was something else,' he said. 'His view is that friends owe friends good deeds, not bad ones.'

'I see,' I said. 'So if someone gives money back to someone who lent it to him, and this repayment and returning turns out to be
b harmful, and both the giver and the receiver are friends, then this is not a case of giving back what is owed: is this Simonides' meaning, according to you?'

'Yes, exactly.'

'Now, should we give back what is owed to our enemies?'

'Oh, yes,' he said. 'What is owed to them—yes, absolutely. And what an enemy owes an enemy, I think, is also what is appropriate—something bad.'

'There was apparently a certain obscurity, then, in Simonides'
c definition of morality,' I remarked. 'How typical of a poet! Although, as it turns out, he meant that it is right to give back to people what is appropriate for them, he called it what is owed to them.'

'I'm surprised you thought any different,' he said.

'But listen,' I said, 'suppose he were asked, "So, Simonides, take the art that we know as medicine. What is it? What does it give that is owed and appropriate, and to what does it give it?" What do you suppose his reply to us would be?'

'Obviously,' he answered, 'he'd reply that it is the art of giving drugs, food, and drink to bodies.'

'What about cookery? What art do we say it is? What does it

“那么西蒙尼德断言归还亏欠的东西是正义，就显然不是这个意思，而有别的意思。”

“是的，当然有别的意思，”他说，“他的观点是朋友把好事归于朋友，而不是坏事儿。”

“我明白了，”我说，“如果有人把钱还给借钱给他的人，而同时这种偿还与归还等于损害他，并且出借者和归还者都是朋友， b
那么这就不算是归还所亏欠的东西的例子：按你的看法，这是西蒙尼德的意思吗？”

“确实是的。”

“那么，我们是否应该把欠我们的敌人的东西还给他们呢？”

“哦，是的，”他说，“亏欠他们的东西——是的，绝对是。而一个敌人亏欠一个敌人的东西，我想，也是适合双方身份的——一些有害的东西。”

“这样看来，西蒙尼德对正义的定义显然还有些模糊之处。”
我评论道，“多典型的一个诗人啊！虽然像那句话所表明的那样， c
他的意思是说，把适合他们的东西归还才是正确的，而他却将其称为亏欠他们的东西。”

“我很惊讶你的想法如此特别。”他说。

“但是注意，”我说，“假如他被人问道：‘那么，西蒙尼德，举我们知道的技术如医学为例。它是什么？它所提供的，亏欠且适合的东西是什么？医学又将它提供给什么东西呢？’你猜想他给我们的回答会是怎样的呢？”

“显然，”他回答说，“他会回答说那就是向身体提供药物、食物和饮料的技艺。”

“烹调术又如何呢？我们说它是什么技艺呢？它所提供的亏

d give that is owed and appropriate, and to what does it give it?'

'It gives taste to cooked food.'

'All right. So which art—the art of giving what to what—might we call morality?'

'In order to be consistent with what was said earlier, Socrates,' he replied, 'it has to be the art of giving benefit and harm to friends and enemies respectively.'

'So Simonides claims that morality is doing good to one's friends and harm to one's enemies, does he?'

'I think so.'

'Now, where sickness and health are concerned, who is best able to do good to his friends and harm to his enemies when they aren't well?'

'A doctor.'

e 'And where the risks of a sea voyage are concerned, when friends are on board a ship?'

'A ship's captain.'

'And what about a moral person? In which walk of life or for what activity is he best able to benefit his friends and harm his enemies?'

'In fighting against enemies and in support of friends, I'd say.'

'All right. Now, my dear Polemarchus, a doctor is no use unless people are ill.'

'True.'

'And a captain is no use unless people are on a sea voyage.'

'Quite so.'

'Is a moral person, then, no use to anyone who is not at war?'

'No, I don't agree with that.'

'So morality is useful during times of peace too?'

欠与适合的东西是什么呢,又是将它提供给什么东西了呢?”

“为烹饪的食物提供美味。” d

“好。那么何种技术——将什么提供给什么的技术——我们可以叫做正义呢?”

“为了与前面所说的保持一致,苏格拉底,”他回应说,“这肯定是一种分别施惠朋友、损害敌人的技艺。”

“那么西蒙尼德宣称的正义就是施惠他的朋友、损害他的敌人,对吗?”

“我想是这样的。”

“那么,在关乎疾病和健康方面,谁最能施惠他的朋友,损害他的敌人,当他们都不太好的时候?”

“医生。”

“那么当海上航行遇险而朋友还在甲板上的时候呢?” e

“一艘船的船长。”

“那么一个正义之人又如何呢?何种行业或曰从事何种活动的人,是最能施惠其朋友并损害其敌人的人呢?”

“我得说是在对敌作战和支援朋友的时候。”

“很好。我亲爱的玻勒玛库斯,要是没有人生病,那医生就没有什么用处。”

“对。”

“要是没有人出海,那船长也没有什么用。”

“说得很对。”

“那么,对于不打仗的人来说,正义的人是否就没用了呢?”

“不,我并不同意这种说法。”

“在和平时期正义也是有用的吗?”

333a 'Yes.'

'And so is farming. Yes?'

'Yes.'

'To provide us with crops?'

'Yes.'

'And shoemaking too?'

'Yes.'

'To provide us with shoes, I imagine you'd say?'

'Exactly.'

'All right, then. What can we use morality for? What does it provide us with? What would you say morality is good for in times of peace?'

'For business contracts, Socrates.'

'By business contracts do you mean when people enter into association with one another, or what?'

'Yes, when people enter into association with one another.'

b 'So when there's a move to make in backgammon, is it a moral person, or an expert backgammon player, who is a good and useful associate?'

'An expert backgammon player.'

'And when it's a question of the positioning of bricks and stones, is a moral person a better and more useful associate than a builder?'

'Not at all.'

'Well, what kind of association is it that people enter into for which a moral person is a better associate than a builder or a musician? I mean, analogously to how a musician is better than a moral person when it comes to an association over melodies.'

'An association involving money, in my opinion.'

'Yes, Polemarchus, but what about when money is put to use?

“是的。” 333a

“那么耕作的技艺也是有用的,是吗?”

“是的。”

“为了给我们提供农作物?”

“是的。”

“那制鞋的技艺也有用吗?”

“是的。”

“我想你会说是为了提供给我们鞋子,是吗?”

“确实会这样说。”

“那么好吧。我们把正义用作什么目的呢?它为我们提供了什么呢?你觉得正义在和平时期有什么用呢?”

“在订立商业契约的时候有用,苏格拉底。”

“你所说的商业契约意思是指与别人建立合作,还是别的什么意思?”

“是的,就是与别人建立合作的意思。”

“那么在下双陆棋的时候,谁是良好而有用的合作伙伴,是正 b
义的人呢,还是高明的棋手?”

“高明的棋手。”

“在使用砖头和石头的时候,正义的人是比泥瓦匠更好并更有用的合作者吗?”

“绝不是。”

“那么,在哪类合作上,正义的人是比泥瓦匠或乐师更好的合作者呢?我的意思是,依此类推,在奏乐方面的合作,乐师是比正义的人更好的合作者。”

“依我看来,这是一种牵涉到金钱的合作。”

“是的,玻勒马库斯,但是当金钱拿去使用的时候又如何呢?

When you jointly need to buy or sell a horse, for instance, then I
c suppose an expert in horses is a better associate, don't you think?'

'I suppose so.'

'And if you need to buy or sell a ship, then it's a shipwright or a sailor?'

'You could be right.'

'For what joint usage of money, then, is a moral person more useful than anyone else?'

'When we want to put it on deposit and have it in safe keeping, Socrates.'

'You mean when you don't want to put it to use, but just to have it in store?'

'Yes.'

d 'So morality is useful in relation to money at precisely the time when money is not in use?'

'So it seems.'

'Furthermore, when a pruning-knife needs to be kept safe, then morality is useful (whether you're on your own or have an associate); but when it needs using, then it's viticulture that is useful. Yes?'

'I suppose so.'

'And would you also say that when a shield or a lyre needs to be protected and kept unused, then morality is useful, whereas when they need using, then military or musical expertise is useful?'

'Of course.'

'In every instance, then, morality is useless when anything is being used, and useful when anything is not being used.'

'So it seems.'

e 'Morality can't be a very important thing, then, can it, my

比如，当你们需要一起买马或卖马的时候，那么我想善相马者就是一个更好的合作者，不是吗？” c

“我想是这样的。”

“如果你们需要买船或卖船，那么造船匠或水手就是更好的合作者？”

“可以这么说吧。”

“那么在共同花钱方面，正义的人是否比别的任何人都要更为有用呢？”

“在我们想妥善保管钱财的时候，苏格拉底。”

“你的意思是说，当你们不想花钱，而只是想把它存起来的时候？”

“是的。”

“那么，准确地说，正义是在不使用钱财的时候才是有用的吗？” d

“看来是这样的。”

“进一步说，当修枝剪存需要放起来的时候，那时正义才是有用的（无论是对自己还是对合作者）；而当它需要被使用的时候，栽培法才是有用的，是吗？”

“我认为是这样的。”

“那么，你是否也说当盾牌或竖琴需要被收起来不用的时候，正义才是有用的，而当需要使用它们的时候，军事或音乐的技艺才是有用的？”

“那当然。”

“那么从所有例子来看，当某事物被使用的时候，正义就没用，而某事物不被使用的时候，正义才有用。”

“看来如此。”

“那就住口吧，我的朋友，如果正义只是对无用的对象有用的 e

friend, if it is useful for useless objects. And there's another point for us to consider. In a fight—a boxing-match or any other kind of fight—isn't it the person who is expert at hitting who is also expert at protecting himself?'

'Yes.'

'And isn't it the person who knows how to give protection from a disease who is also the expert at secretly inducing the disease?'

'I would say so.'

334a 'Moreover, it's one and the same person who's good at protecting an army and at stealing the enemy's plans and outwitting the rest of his projects, isn't it?'

'Yes.'

'So anything one is good at protecting, one is also good at stealing.'

'So it seems.'

'If a moral person is good at protecting money, therefore, he's also good at stealing it.'

'That's what the argument suggests, anyway,' he said.

'Morality has been exposed, then,' I said. 'A moral person is a
b kind of thief, apparently. You probably got this notion from Homer. He speaks warmly of Autolycus, Odysseus' grandfather on his mother's side, and also says that he surpassed everyone "at theft and perjury". So the view that morality is a kind of stealing is yours, Homer's, and Simonides'—with the qualification that it must be done to benefit friends and harm enemies. Was this what you meant?'

'It most certainly was not,' he said, 'but I'm no longer sure what I meant. I do still think this, however—that morality lies in helping one's friends and harming one's enemies.'

c 'When you say "friends", do you mean those who appear to a

话,那么它就不会是一种非常重要的东西了。而对于我们来说还有另外一个观点需要考虑。在一场搏斗中——一场拳击比赛或者其他任何种类的搏斗——一个在打斗上内行的人,在保护自己方面不是也很内行吗?”

“是的。”

“一个知道如何保护自己免于疾病的人,难道不也就是善于秘密传播疾病的人吗?”

“是这样。”

“并且,善于保护自己军队的人,和善于盗窃敌人的计划并在
其它部署上以智取胜的人,也就是同一个人,不是吗?” 334a

“是的。”

“这么说来,善于保护的人也就是善于偷窃的人。”

“看起来是这样的。”

“如果一个正义的人是善于保管钱财的,所以他就也是善于盗窃钱财的。”

“无论如何,那就是这个论证所推论出的。”他说。

“那么,正义就被揭示出来了,”我说,“很明显,一个正义之人
似乎就是一种盗贼。这种想法你可能是从荷马那里得来的。他 b
热情地说起奥德修斯的外祖父奥托吕科,并还说他‘在偷窃和作伪证方面’超过任何人。所以你、荷马和西蒙尼德的观点是认为正义就是一种偷窃——条件是它必须施惠朋友并损害敌人。你说的是这个意思吗?”

“当然不是这个意思,”他说,“但我对自己的意思都不再确信了。然而,我还是这么认为的,正义在于帮助他的朋友并损害他的敌人。”

“当你说‘朋友’的时候,你是指那些看上去是好人的人,还是 c

person to be good, or those who genuinely are good (even if they don't appear to be)? And likewise for enemies.'

'It seems plausible to suggest', he said, 'that one treats as friends those one regards as good, and as enemies those one regards as bad.'

'Isn't It common to make mistakes about this, and think that people are good when they aren't, and vice versa?'

'Yes.'

'When this happens, then, doesn't one regard good people as enemies and bad people as friends?'

'Yes.'

'But all the same, in these circumstances it's right for one to help bad people and harm good people, is it?'

d 'Apparently.'

'But good people are moral and not the kind to do wrong.'

'True.'

'On your line of reasoning, then, it's right to harm people who do no wrong.'

'Not at all, Socrates,' he said. 'My reasoning must be flawed, I suppose.'

'It's right to harm wrongdoers, then,' I said, 'and to help those who do right?'

'That sounds better.'

'But since there are lots of people who are completely mistaken,
e Polemarchus, then it will commonly turn out to be right for people to harm friends (whom they regard as bad) and to help enemies (whom they regard as good). And in affirming this, we'll be contradicting what we said Simonides meant.'

'Yes,' he said, 'that is a consequence of what we're saying. Let's change tack, however: we're probably making a wrong assump-

指那些即使看上去不是但却是真正的好人呢？同样，敌人指的又是什么意思？”

他说：“看来有些道理的是这样的说法：一个人把他认为善良的人当作朋友，而把那些他认为邪恶的人当作敌人。”

“把并不好的人当做好人，把并不坏的人当做坏人，犯这种错误不也是常见的吗？”

“是的。”

“那么这种情况发生时，人们不是把好人当做敌人，把坏人当做朋友了吗？”

“是的。”

“但是在这些情况下，对于一个人而言，去帮助坏人而伤害好人仍旧是正义的，是这样吗？”

“显然是的。” d

“但好人都是道德的，并且不是那种为非作歹的人。”

“对啊。”

“那么按照你的推理，去伤害那些不做坏事的人就是正确的了。”

“根本不是，苏格拉底，”他说，“我想我的推理一定有误。”

我说：“那么，正义是否就是损害做坏事的人，并且帮助那些做正义之事的人？”

“那样说更好些。”

“然而由于有很多人都完全弄错了，玻勒玛库斯，这样一来， e
人们伤害朋友（他们认其为坏人）并帮助敌人（他们认其为好人），这倒通常成为正义的了。要是承认这一点的话，我们就会与我们说过的西蒙尼德的意思相反。”

“是的，”他说，“那是从我们的讨论中得出的一个结论。让我

tion about friends and enemies.'

'What assumption, Polemarchus?'

'That someone who appears good is a friend.'

'What shall we change that to instead?' I asked.

'That someone who doesn't just appear good, but actually *is*
335a good, is a friend; and that someone who seems good, but actually isn't, is an apparent friend, not a genuine one. And the same goes for enemies.'

'So on this line of reasoning, it's a good man who is a friend, and a bad man who is an enemy.'

'Yes.'

'You're telling us, then, that our original description of morality, when we said that it was right to do good to a friend and harm to an enemy, was incomplete. Now you want us to add that it is right to do good to a friend, provided he is good, and to harm an enemy, provided he is bad. Is that right?'

b 'Yes,' he said, 'I think that's a good way to put it.'

'Can a moral person harm *anyone*?' I asked.

'Yes, he can,' he replied. 'He has to harm bad men, people who are his enemies.'

'When horses are harmed, do they improve or deteriorate?'

'Deteriorate.'

'In respect of a state of goodness for dogs or of a state of goodness for horses?'

'In respect of a state of goodness for horses.'

'So the same goes for dogs too: when they are harmed, they deteriorate in respect of what it is to be a good dog, not in respect of what it is to be a good horse. Is that right?'

'No doubt about it.'

c 'And where people are concerned, my friend, shouldn't we say that when they're harmed they deteriorate in respect of what it is to be a good human?'

们还是改换一下思路:我们可能对朋友和敌人做了错误的假设。”

“什么假设,玻勒玛库斯?”

“把那些看起来好的人当做朋友。”

“我们该怎么来进行改变呢?”我问道。

“把那些不仅看起来好的人,并且也真正好的人当做朋友;那些看起来是好但实际上并不好的人是表面上的朋友,而不是真正的朋友。对敌人也一样。” 335a

“所以根据这样的推理,朋友就是好人,敌人就是坏人。”

“是的。”

“那么你是在告诉我们,我们原本关于正义的描述(即我们说,对朋友做有益的事情而对敌人加以伤害,是正确的),是不完善的。现在你要我们补充上,对一位朋友做有益的事情,倘若他是好人,并且伤害一个敌人,倘若他是一个坏人。是这样吗?”

“是,”他说,“我想这么说是对的。” b

“一个正义的人能损害任何人吗?”我问道。

“是, 他能,” 他回答说,“他必须损害那些作为他敌人的坏人。”

“当马受到伤害时,它们变好了还是变坏了?”

“变坏了。”

“说的是狗的品状还是马的品状?”

“马的品状。”

“所以狗也一样:当它们受到伤害时,它们是在作为好狗的品状方面变坏了,而不是在作为好马的品状方面。是那样吗?”

“毫无疑问。”

“我的朋友,考虑到人的时候,当人受到伤害时,我们是否应当说他们在作为好人的品状方面变坏了?” c

'Yes.'

'And isn't a moral person a good human?'

'There's no doubt about that either.'

'It necessarily follows, Polemarchus, that people who are harmed become less moral.'

'So it seems.'

'Now, can musicians use music to make people unmusical?'

'Impossible.'

'Can skilled horsemen use their skill to make people bad horsemen?'

'No.'

'So can moral people use morality to make people immoral? Or
d in general can good people use their goodness to make people bad?'

'No, that's impossible.'

'I imagine this is because cooling things down, for instance, is not the function of warmth but of its opposite.'

'Yes.'

'And moistening things is not the function of dryness but of its opposite.'

'Yes.'

'So harming people is not the function of a good person, but of his opposite.'

'I suppose so.'

'And is a moral person a good person?'

'Of course.'

'It is not the job of a moral person, then, Polemarchus, to harm a friend or anyone else; it is the job of his opposite, an immoral person.'

'I think you're absolutely correct, Socrates,' he said.

e 'So the claim that it's right and moral to give back to people

"是的。"

"正义的人难道不就是好人吗?"

"那也毫无疑问。"

"玻勒玛库斯,结论必然是:受到损害的人变得不那么正义了。"

"看起来是这样。"

"那么,音乐家们会用乐曲让人们听起来刺耳吗?"

"不可能。"

"熟练的骑手能用他们的技艺使得人骑术很差吗?"

"不能。"

"那么正义的人能用正义而使得人不正义吗?或一般说来,好人能用他们的德性而使人变坏吗?" d

"不能,那不可能。"

"我这样想是因为,比如说,使东西降温并不是热的作用,而是它的对立者。"

"是的。"

"使东西潮湿不是干燥的作用,而是它的对立者。"

"是的。"

"所以损害人不是一个好人的作用,而是他的对立者才这样。"

"我想是的。"

"一个正义的人就是好人吗?"

"当然。"

"那么,玻勒玛库斯,损害朋友或别人就不是正义之人做的事;是他的对立者,即不义者干的事。"

"苏格拉底,我认为你说得绝对正确。"他说。

"所以,认为把亏欠别人的归还给别人就是正义和道德的主 e

what they are owed—if this is taken to mean that a moral person owes harm to his enemies and help to his friends—turns out to be a claim no clever person would make. I mean, it's false: we've found that it is never right to harm anyone.'

'I agree,' he said.

'You and I will join forces, then,' I said, 'to combat anyone who asserts that it is the view of Simonides or Bias or Pittacus or anyone else who is so sublimely clever.'

'Yes,' he said, 'I'm ready to play my part in the battle.'

336a 'Do you know whose view I think it is,' I said, 'that it's right to help one's friends and harm one's enemies?'

'Whose?' he asked.

'I think it was Periander or Perdiccas or Xerxes or Ismenias of Thebes or someone else like that—a rich man who fancied himself to be vastly powerful.'

'You're quite right,' he said.

'All right,' I said. 'Now that we've found that being moral and doing right don't consist in this, can we come up with an alternative definition?'

b Now, Thrasymachus had often made as if to interrupt us in mid-sentence and pounce on the argument, but he'd always been restrained by his neighbours, who had wanted to hear the discussion out. But when we did come to a break, and I'd asked this question, he could no longer remain silent: like a wild animal, he crouched and hurled himself at us as if to tear us apart.

Polemarchus and I were terrified and panic-stricken, but Thra-
c symachus bellowed out for all to hear, 'What a lot of drivel, Socrates! Why are you deferentially bowing and scraping to each other like simpletons? If you really want to know what morality is, then don't just ask questions and look for applause by refuting any and every answer you get, because you've realized that it's easier to ask questions than

张——如果它被理解为正义之人就是损害他的敌人和帮助他的朋友的话——就表明它不是一个聪明人所会做出的主张。我的意思是,这么讲是错误的:我们已经发现损害任何人都绝不是正确的。”

“我同意。”他说。

“那么你和我会通力合作,”我说,“去反对任何维护西蒙尼德、彼阿斯、彼塔库斯,或者其他任何也是如此绝顶聪明者的观点的人。”

“是的,”他说,“我已经准备好加入战斗。”

“帮助一个人的朋友和损害一个人的敌人是正当的,”我说, 336a
“你知道我认为这是谁的观点吗?”

“谁的?”他问道。

“我想是佩里阿德、佩尔迪卡、克塞尔克斯、底比斯的伊斯美尼亚或某些其他与他们类似的人——一个幻想自己掌有大权的有钱人。”

“你说得非常对。”他说。

“好吧,”我说,“既然我们已经发现正义和正当并不包含于此,那么我们能想出一个代替它的定义吗?”

这时候,塞拉西马库斯好像已经多次要在谈话中间打断我 b
们,突袭地进入争论中来,但总是被他邻座的人所制止,他们想听我们把话说完。但当我们刚停下来,我想问那个问题时,他再也不能保持沉默了:他像一只蜷伏已久的野兽,猛地向我们扑来,好像要把我们扯开似的。

玻勒玛库斯和我受到了惊吓而惊慌失措,塞拉西马库斯还是对着所有听着的人咆哮道:“苏格拉底,你们尽是胡说八道!为什么你们像傻瓜一样毕恭毕敬地相互奉承?如果你真想知道正义 c
是什么,就不要只是问问题并通过反驳所得到的任何答案而寻求赞许,因为你早已意识到提问比回答问题要容易。不许这样。把

it is to answer them. No, state an opinion yourself: say what you
d think morality is. And make sure you state your view clearly and precisely, without saying that it is duty or benefit or profit or gain or advantage; I won't let you get away with any rubbish like that.'

I was scared stiff at his words, and l looked at him in fear. I think that if I hadn't seen him before he saw me, I'd have been unable to speak. But in fact I had got in the first look, when he originally began
e to get furious at the discussion, and so I was able to respond to him. 'Thrasymachus,' I said, trembling with fear, 'please don't be cross with us. If Polemarchus and I are going wrong anywhere in the course of investigating the ideas, I assure you that we don't mean to. You can imagine that, if we were looking for money, we wouldn't under any circumstances choose to defer to each other in the course of the search and ruin our chances of finding it. It is morality we are looking for, however, and this is more valuable than pots of money; so you shouldn't think that we'd be so stupid as to give in to each other and not do our level best to discover it. Believe me, Thrasymachus, we're doing all we can. If we lack competence—which I suppose is the case—then pity is a far more reasonable feeling for you experts to
337a have for us than impatience.'

He erupted into highly sarcastic laughter at my wobds and said, 'God, there goes Socrates again, pretending to be an ignoramus! I knew this would happen; I even told the others here some time ago that you wouldn't be prepared to express opinions, and would feign ignorance and do anything rather than answer a question put to you.'

'That's because you're clever, Thrasymachus,' I said. 'You were well aware of the fact that if you were to ask someone what twelve is, and were to add as a rider to the question, "And just make
b sure you avoid saying that twelve is two times six, or three times four, or six times two, or four times three. I won't let you get away with any nonsense like that"—well, I'm sure it was obvious to you that no one would answer a question phrased like that. But suppose this person said, "What do you mean, Thrasymachus? You don't want me to give

你自己的观点提出来:说说你所认为的正义是什么。一定要做到
把你的观点说得清晰、准确些,不要说它是职责、好处、利益、收益 d
或益处;我不会让你用那些垃圾一样的东西蒙混过去的。”

我被他的话吓得僵直,害怕地看着他。我想要不是自己在他
看见我之前看见过他,我早已说不出话了。不过,当他一开始对
谈话感到恼怒的时候,实际上我就一眼看到他了,所以我还能回
应他。“塞拉西马库斯,”我战战兢兢地说,“请不要对我们发脾 e
气。如果玻勒玛库斯和我在探讨理念的过程中有任何错误的话,
我向你保证我们并非是有意的。你能想象得出,如果我们是在寻
找金钱,那么在寻找过程中,在任何情况下,我们都不会选择因彼
此顺从而丧失掉自己找到金钱的机会的。这是比一罐罐的金钱
还有价值的东西;那么你不应该认为我们愚蠢到向对方屈服而不
去努力发现它。相信我,塞拉西马库斯,我们正在尽我们最大的努力
啊。如果我们缺乏能力——我想就是这种情况——那么,对于你这
样的能手,为我们感到的是同情而非不耐烦,这才是更加合理的。” 337a

他听了我的话,便发出一阵嘲讽的笑声,说道:“神啊,苏格拉
底又来了,他装作一个无知者!我料到会这样;我甚至之前就告
诉过在这里的其他人,说你不会准备说出你的想法,并且佯装无
知,宁可做任何事情,就是不愿回答向你提出的问题。”

“那是因为你聪明,塞拉西马库斯,”我说,“你很清楚这样一
个事实,如果你问别人十二是多少,并在问题上附加说:‘一定要
避免说十二就是二乘以六,或三乘以四,或六乘以二,或四乘以 b
三。我不会让你用那些废话蒙混过去的。’那么,我想你很明白,
是没有人能够回答像那样提出来的一个问题的。但假如这人说:
‘塞拉西马库斯,你这是什么意思?你不让我用你提到的任何答

any of the answers you've mentioned? But what if twelve really is one of those things, Thrasymachus? Shall I still avoid that answer— that is, not tell the truth? Or what would you have me do?" How would you respond to this?'

c 'Well,' he said, 'it's not as if the two cases were similar.'

'Why not?' I replied. 'Anyway, even if they aren't, and it's only that the person you've asked thinks they are, do you think that makes any difference? Won't he still state his opinion, whether or not we rule it out?'

'That's what you're going to do as well, is it?' he asked. 'Respond with one of the answers I ruled out?'

'I wouldn't be surprised if I decided to do that, once I'd looked into the matter,' I said.

d 'What if I were to demonstrate that there's another answer you can give about morality,' he asked, 'which isn't any of those answers and is better than any of them? What penalty would you expect?'

'The penalty which is appropriate for ignorance, of course,' I said, 'which is learning from an expert. That's the penalty I expect.'

'Don't be naive,' he said. 'You can't just learn: you must pay for it too.'

'If I ever have the money, I will,' I said.

'He has it,' said Glaucon. 'We'll all help Socrates out financially, so as far as the money is concerned, Thrasymachus, go ahead and speak.'

e 'Oh yes, sure!' he said. 'So that Socrates can get his way and not make any claims himself, while he attacks and criticizes someone else's claims.'

'That's because I have no choice, Thrasymachus,' I explained. 'How can anyone express a view when he's not only ignorant, but also admits his ignorance? Moreover, when he's been forbidden to men-

案回答吗？但，塞拉西马库斯，要是十二真的是那些答案中的其中一个呢？我依然要回避那个答案，也就是说，不要说出真理来吗？或者，你要我怎么做呢？'对此你会如何作答？" c

"喔，"他说，"这两种情形好像并不相似。"

"为什么不相似？"我回应说，"不管怎样，即使它们不相似，只要你问的那个人认为相似就行了，你觉得有区别吗？无论我们是否将之排除，他难道不还是说出他的想法吗？"

"这也就是你将要做的，不是吗？"他问道，"用我已排除掉的某个答案来回答吗？"

"一旦我对该问题有所观察，我还是决定那样去做的话，也并 d
不是什么令人惊讶的事情啊。"我说。

"如果我能证明你能提出关于正义的另外一种答案，那又将如何？"他说，"这个答案不是上述任何答案中的一种，并且比它们中的任何一个都更令人满意。你希望接受什么样的处罚？"

"当然是适合于无知的惩罚了，"我说，"就是向一位行家学习。这是我想要受的惩罚。"

"别天真了，"他说，"你不能只是学习；你还必须为此出点钱。"

"要是我有钱，我会的。"我说。

"他有的，"格劳孔说，"在钱的方面，我们都会在经济上帮助苏格拉底的，塞拉西马库斯，你就继续说吧。"

"哦，好吧，"他说，"那么苏格拉底可以采取他的方式了，自己 e
不做任何主张，而攻击和批评别人提出来的主张。"

"那是因为我别无选择，塞拉西马库斯，"我解释说，"当一个人无知并且也承认自己无知的时候，他如何能表述自己的看法呢？更何况，他可能会有的任何想法都被一位相当有才能的人给

tion any opinion he might happen to hold by a man of considerable
338a calibre? No, it's you who ought to speak, really, since you do claim to have knowledge and to be able to express it. So please do what I'm asking: if you state your view, you'll be doing me a favour, and also generously teaching Glaucon here and all the others too.'

My words prompted Glaucon and the others to urge him to do what I was asking, and although it was clear that Thrasymachus wanted to be heard (since he thought he had an impressive position to state, which would win him acclaim), yet he continued to dissemble and to argue that it should be me who stated my position. Eventually,
b however, he gave in, and then added, 'Now you can see what Socrates is good at—he refuses to do any teaching himself, but he goes around learning from other people and doesn't even give them thanks in return.'

'You're quite right to say that I learn from other people, Thrasymachus,' I said, 'but quite wrong to say that I don't repay them with gratitude. I pay what I can—and compliments are all I can give, since I don't have money. If I think someone has a good idea, I'm quick to applaud it—as you'll find out very soon when you tell us your opinion, since I'm sure it will be a good one.'

c 'All right, then, listen to this,' he said. 'My claim is that morality is nothing other than the advantage of the stronger party... Well, why aren't you applauding? No, you won't let yourself do that.'

'First I need to understand your meaning,' I told him. 'I don't yet. You say that right is the advantage of the stronger party, but what on earth do you mean by this, Thrasymachus? Surely you're not claiming, in effect, that if Poulydamas the pancratiast is stronger than us and it's to his advantage, for the sake of his physique, to eat beef, then this food is advantageous, and therefore right, for us too, who
d are weaker than him?'

'Foul tactics, Socrates,' he said, 'to interpret what I say in the way which allows you unscrupulously to distort it most.'

禁止了呢？不，实际上应该说话的人是你，因为你确在宣称有知识并且能把它说出来。所以请应允我的请求：如果你说出了你的 338a 观点，那么你将帮了我一个忙，并且也还能慷慨地让在这里的格劳孔以及其他人得以领教。”

我的话使得格劳孔和其他人催促他满足我的请求，虽然塞拉西马库斯显然想让大家听他说（因为他认为自己已有了一个能为他赢得喝彩的深刻观点），但他还是继续装模作样并争论说，应该说出观点的人是我。但最后，他放弃了，并补充说：“现在你们看到了苏格拉底所擅长的伎俩了——他自己拒绝教别人，却到处向 b 别人学习，甚至不向他们道声谢以示回报。”

“塞拉西马库斯，你说得非常对，我是向别人学习，”我说，“但说我对他们不满怀感激作为回报，那就大错特错了。我尽力答谢——我所能给的唯有赞美，因为我没钱。如果我认为某人有个好见解，我很快就会对其表示赞扬——等你告诉我们你的想法，你就会发现这一点的，因为我确信那将是个好想法。”

“那么，好吧，听着，”他说。“我的主张是，正义非是别物，而 c 是强者的利益……嗯，你为什么不鼓掌欢迎啊？不，你是不想让自己这样做吧。”

“首先我得搞明白你的意思，”我对他说，“我还没明白。你说正义就是强者的利益，但，塞拉西马库斯，你这说的到底是什么意思？实际上你说的应该不是这样的意思吧：如果运动健将布利达马比我们健壮，而吃牛肉有利于他的体格，那么这种食物对我们这些比他弱的人也是有益的，由此也是正义的吗？” d

“卑鄙的伎俩，苏格拉底，”他说，“你竟用这种方式理解我说过的话，以便你不知羞耻地尽可能地曲解它。”

‘No, you’ve got me wrong, Thrasymachus,’ I said. ‘I just want you to explain yourself better.’

‘Don’t you know, then,’ he said, ‘that some countries are dictatorships, some are democracies, and some are aristocracies?’

‘Of course I do.’

‘And that what has power in any given country is the government?’,

‘Yes.’

e ‘Now, each government passes laws with a view to its own advantage: a democracy makes democratic laws, a dictatorship makes dictatorial laws, and so on and so forth. In so doing, each government makes it clear that what is right and moral for its subjects is what is to its own advantage; and each government punishes anyone who deviates from what is advantageous to itself as if he were a criminal and a wrongdoer. So, Socrates, this is what I claim morality is: it is the same in every country, and it is what is to the advantage of the
339a current government. Now, of course, it’s the current government which has power, and the consequence of this, as anyone who thinks about the matter correctly can work out, is that morality is everywhere the same—the advantage of the stronger party.’

‘Now I see what you mean,’ I said. ‘And I’ll try to see whether or not your claim is true. Your position too, Thrasymachus, is that morality is advantage—despite the fact that you ruled this answer out for me—except that you immediately add “of the stronger party”.’

‘Hardly a trivial addition,’ he said.

b ‘Whether or not it is important isn’t yet clear. What *is* clear is that we must try to find out whether your claim is true. The point is that I agree that morality is some kind of advantage, but you are qualifying this and claiming that it is the advantage of the stronger party; since I haven’t made up my mind about this qualified version, we must look into the matter.’

‘Go ahead,’ he said.

‘All right,’ I said. ‘Here’s a question for you: you’re also clai-

“不是的，塞拉西马库斯，你误解我的意思了，”我说，“我只是想让你把你自己的意思解释得更加清楚些。”

他说：“那么，难道你不知道有些城邦是僭主制的，有些是民主制的，还有些是贵族制的吗？”

“我当然知道。”

“任何城邦的掌权者不就是统治者吗？”

“是的。”

“现在，每个统治者都按照自己的利益来制定法律：民主制的 e
制定民主的法律，僭主制的制定独裁的法律，如此等等。通过这样做，每个统治者都向被他们统治的人宣布，正义和德道就是对统治者自己有利；而每个统治者将那些违背他们利益的人当做罪犯和犯错者加以惩罚。所以，苏格拉底，这就是我所说的正义：它在
每一个城邦都是一样的，它就是有利于现行的统治者的利益。现 339a
在，当然是现行统治者掌权，其结论就像一个对此事加以正确思考过的人所得出的那样，即，正义到处都一样——就是强者的利益。”

“现在我明白你的意思了，”我说，“我还要尽力想想你的观点是否正确。塞拉西马库斯，你的观点是正义就是利益——尽管事实上你为我排除了这个答案——此外你直接加上了‘强者的’。”

“恐怕是一个微不足道的补充。”他说。

“这个补充是否重要还不清楚。清楚的是我们必须尽力考察一下你的主张是否正确。关键是我同意正义是某种益处，但你对此加以了限制，并主张正义是强者的利益；因为我还没有弄明白这个经过限定的说法，所以我们必须加以考察。”

“那就开始吧。”他说。

“那好，”我说，“有个问题想问问你：我想，你同样主张服从统

ming, I assume, that obedience to the government is right?'

'Yes, I am.'

c 'And is the government in every country infallible, or are they also capable of error?'

'They are certainly capable of error,' he said.

'So when they turn to legislation, they sometimes get it right, and sometimes wrong?'

'Yes, I suppose so.'

'When they get it right, the laws they make will be to their advantage, but when they get it wrong, the laws will be to their disadvantage. Is that what you're saying?'

'Yes.'

'And you're also saying that their subjects must act in accordance with any law that is passed, and that this constitutes doing right?'

'Of course.'

d 'Then it follows from your line of argument that it is no more right to act to the advantage of the stronger party than it is to do the opposite, to act to their disadvantage.'

'What are you saying?' he asked.

'Exactly the same as you, I think; but let's have a closer look. We're agreed that sometimes, when a government orders its subjects to do things, it is utterly mistaken about its own best interest, but that it's right for the subjects to act in accordance with any order issued by the government. Isn't that what we agreed?'

'Yes, I suppose so.'

e 'Then you must also suppose', I continued, 'that you have agreed that it is right to do things which are not to the advantage of the government and the stronger party. When the rulers mistakenly issue orders which are bad for themselves, and since you claim that it is right for people to act in conformity with all the government's orders, then, my dear Thrasymachus, doesn't it necessarily follow that it is right to do the opposite of what your position affirmed? I mean, the

治者是正义的?”

“是的,我是这样想的。”

“那么每一个城邦的统治者都不会犯错,还是也会犯错?” c

“他们当然会犯错。”他说。

“那么当他们立法时,有时候做得对,有时候做得不对吗?”

“是的,我想是这样。”

“当他们做对时,他们所立的法律会对他们有利,但当他们做错时,法律会对他们不利。你说的是这个意思吗?”

“是的。”

“你也说他们的臣民必须遵守所立的任何法律,并且这样才算做的对?”

“当然。”

“那么从你的论证思路中就不难得出这样一个观点,为了强者的利益做事,并不比反其道而行之,即损害他们的利益做事更为正当。” d

“你说什么?”他问道。

“我想,这正是你的意思;但我们还是仔细看看吧。我们都同意,有些时候,当一个政府命令它的臣民做事情时,关于它自身最大利益之所在,竟完全搞错了,但是对于它的臣民来说,遵从政府发布的任何命令行事,就是正当的。那不是我们都同意的吗?”

“是的,我想是这样。”

“那么你必然同样想到,”我继续说道,“你已经承认,所做事情并不符合政府及强者的利益,它仍旧是正当的。如果统治者错误地发布了对其自身不利的命令,而且由于你宣称,对于人民来说,遵照政府所有的命令行事就是正当的,那么,我亲爱的塞拉西马库斯,不就必然会推论出,反汝断然支持之道而行之,不也是对 e

weaker party is being ordered to do what is disadvantageous to the stronger party, obviously.'

340a 'Yes, Socrates,' said Polemarchus, 'that's perfectly clear.'

'Of course,' Cleitophon interrupted, 'if you're going to act as a witness for Socrates.'

'There's no need for a witness,' Polemarchus replied. 'Thrasymachus himself admits that rulers sometimes issue orders which are bad for themselves, and that it's right for people to carry out these orders.'

'That's because Thrasymachus maintained that it was right to carry out the rulers' instructions, Polemarchus.'

'Yes, Cleitophon, and he also maintained that right is the ad-
b vantage of the stronger party. And once he'd affirmed both of these propositions, he also agreed that sometimes the stronger party tells the weaker party, which is subject to it, to do things which are disadvantageous to it. And from these premisses it follows that morality is no more what is advantageous to the stronger party than it is what is disadvantageous to the stronger party.'

'But,' Cleitophon said, 'what he meant by the advantage of the stronger party was what the stronger party *thinks* is to its advantage. This is what he was maintaining the weaker party ought to do, and this is what he was maintaining morality is.'

'But that's not what he said,' Polemarchus remarked.

c 'Never mind, Polemarchus,' I said. 'If this is what Thrasymachus is saying now, then let's accept it as his view. But do please tell me, Thrasymachus: *did* you mean to define morality as what appears to the stronger party to be to its advantage, whether or not it really is to its advantage? Is that how we are to understand your meaning?'

'Absolutely not!' he protested. 'Do you suppose I would describe someone who makes mistakes as the stronger party when he is making a mistake?'

'Yes,' I replied, 'I did think you were saying this, when you agreed that rulers are not infallible, but also make mistakes.'

的吗？我的意思是说，很明显，弱者是被命令去做那些对于强者不利的事情。”

“是的，苏格拉底，”玻勒玛库斯说，“那十分清楚。” 340a

“当然，”克利托丰插嘴说，“要是你准备为苏格拉底作见证。”

“不需要见证人，”玻勒玛库斯回应说，“塞拉西马库斯自己都承认，统治者有时会发布对自己有害的命令，并且人民去执行这些命令就是正当的。”

“玻勒玛库斯，那是因为塞拉西马库斯主张，履行统治者的命令是正当的。”

“是的，克利托丰，他还主张正义就是强者的利益。一旦他同
时肯定了这两个命题，还同意有时候强者会命令弱者，即被统治 b
者，去做对他不利的事。从这些前提得出：正义不过就是对强者有利的东西，也是对强者不利的东西了。”

“但是，”克利托丰说，“他所说的强者的利益是指强者自己认为对他有利的。这就是他主张弱者所应该做的，并且这是他所主张的正义。”

“但那不是他所说的。”玻勒玛库斯指出。

“没关系，玻勒玛库斯，”我说，“如果这就是塞拉西马库斯现 c
在所要说的，那么我们就把它作为他的观点。但，塞拉西马库斯，一定请你告诉我：你是否想把正义定义为强者以为有利于自己的东西，而不管是否真的对自己有利？我们那样的理解是你的意思吗？”

“绝对不是！”他抗议道，“你认为当他们犯错时我会把这些犯错的人当做强者吗？”

“是的，”我回答说，“当你承认统治者并非一贯正确，而是也会犯错误，我确实认为你说的就是这个意思。”

d ‘That's because you're a bully in discussions, Socrates,’ he said. ‘I mean, to take the first example that comes to mind, do you describe someone who makes mistakes about his patients as a doctor in virtue of the fact that he makes mistakes? Or do you describe someone who makes mistakes in his calculations as a mathematician, at precisely the time when he is making a mistake, and in virtue of the mistake that he is making? It's true that the expression is in our language: we say that a doctor or a mathematician or a teacher makes
e mistakes; but in fact, in my opimon, to the extent that each of them is what we call him, he never makes mistakes. And the consequence of this is that, strictly speaking—and you're the stickler for verbal precision—no professional makes mistakes: a mistake is due to a failure of knowledge, and for as long as that lasts he is not a professional. Professional, expert, ruler—no ruler makes a mistake at precisely the time when he is ruling, despite the universal usage of expressions like "The doctor made a mistake" or "The ruler made a mistake". So, when I stated my position to you recently, you should appreciate that I too was speaking like that; but the most precise formulation is in fact
341a that a ruler, to the extent that he is a ruler, does not make mistakes; and in not making mistakes he passes laws which are in his best interest; and any subject of his should act in conformity with these laws. Consequently, as I said in the first place, my position is that morality is acting to the advantage of the stronger party.’

‘Well, Thrasymachus,’ I said, ‘so you think I'm a bully, do you?’

‘Yes, I do,’ he said.

‘And that's because you think my questions were premeditated attempts to wrong you?’

b ‘I'm certain of it,’ he said. ‘And you won't gain any advantage from it, firstly because I'm aware of your unscrupulous tactics, and secondly because as long as I am aware of them, you won't be able to use the argument to hatter me down.’

‘My dear Thrasymachus,’ I protested, ‘the idea would never even occur to me! But we must make sure that this situation doesn't arise again, so please would you make something perfectly clear? is it, according to you, the ruler and the stronger person in the loose sense,

“那是因为在讨论中你是一个无赖，苏格拉底，”他说。“我的 d
意思是，就拿我首先想到的例子来说吧，某人对他的病人看错了
病，你能根据他犯错误这一事实而将其称为医生吗？或者某人在
他的计算中出现了失误，那么你能恰巧当他出现失误的时候，并
根据他刚出现的失误而将其称为数学家吗？在我们的语言中确
实有那样的表达：我们说医生、数学家或教师犯了错；但事实上，
在我看来，就我们称呼他的意义上说来，他是不会犯错的。其结 e
果便是，严格地说——你是个用词苛求准确的人——没有行家会
犯错：错误是由于缺乏知识，要是一直那样的话，他就不是一个行
家了。行家、专家、统治者——虽然‘医生犯错’或‘统治者犯错’
这样的用法普遍，但是没有统治者正好在他统治的时候犯错。所
以当我刚才向你表述我的观点时，你应该明白我也是以那种方式
说的；但最准确的表述实际上应该是，统治者只要还是统治者就
不会犯错误；在不犯错误的情况下，他制定了对他最有利的法律； 341a
而受他统治的人应该遵守这些法律。由此，就像我一开始所说的
那样，我的观点是，正义就是为了强者的利益做事。”

“好吧，塞拉西马库斯，”我说，“那么你认为我是一个无赖吗？”

“是的，我是这么认为的。”他说。

“那是因为你认为我提的问题是预谋好引你犯错的吧？”

“对此我很确信，”他说，“你不会从中得到任何好处的，因为
首先我意识到了你的无赖手段，其次因为我一旦意识到它们，你 b
就不能用论证来打败我了。”

“我亲爱的塞拉西马库斯，”我辩解道，“我甚至连这样的想法都没有！但我们必须使这样的情况不会再发生，那么你能做些彻底的澄清吗？按你的意思，正是这统治者和强者（在宽泛意义上

or in what you were just calling the precise sense, whose interest, since he is the stronger party, it is right for the weaker party to act in?'

'I'm talking about the ruler in the most precise sense possible,' he replied. 'You can do anything you like, as far as I'm concerned, so try your unscrupulous and bullying tactics on that, if you can! But you don't stand a chance.'

c 'Do you think I'm crazy enough to try to shave a lion and bully Thrasymachus?' I asked.

'Well, you tried just now,' he said, 'even though you're a non-entity at that too.'

'That's enough of that sort of remark,' I said. 'But let's take this doctor you were talking about a short while ago—the one who's a doctor in the strict sense of the term. Is he a businessman, or someone who attends to sick people? Think about the genuine doctor, please.'

'He attends to sick people,' he replied.

'What about a ship's captain? Is the true captain in charge of sailors or a sailor?'

'In charge of sailors.'

d 'In other words, we shouldn't take any account of the fact that he is on board a ship and describe him as a sailor. I mean, it isn't because he's on a ship that he's called a captain, but because of his expertise and because he has authority over the sailors.'

'True,' he said.

'Now, does each of the various parties in these situations have a particular advantage to gain?'

'Yes.'

'And isn't it the case,' I went on, 'that the *raison d'être* of a branch of expertise is to consider the welfare and interest of each party and then procure it?'

'Yes, that is what expertise is for,' he answered.

'Is there anything which is in the interest of any branch of expertise except being as perfect as possible?'

或你刚才在严格意义上所称者），由于他是强者，故弱者为其利益做事就是正当的？”

“我是在可能的最严格的意义上谈论统治者的，”他回答说，“把你的伎俩都耍出来吧，在我面前试试你的无赖、霸道的招数，看你能不能！但你是办不到的。”

“你以为我疯了，想虎口捋须，欺负你塞拉西马库斯吗？”我问道。 c

“哟，你才刚刚试过呢，”他说，“尽管你在那方面也是一个不值一提的家伙。”

“好了，不说那种话了，”我说，“让我们在严格意义上谈谈你刚才提到的医生吧。他是商人，还是照顾病人的人？请你考虑一下真正的医生。”

“他是照顾病人的人。”他说。

“那么船长呢？一个真正的船长是领导水手的人还是一名水手？”

“领导水手的人。”

“换句话说，我们不应该因为他在船上这个事实就把他当做 d
水手。我的意思是说，他不是因为在船上而被称为船长，而是因为他的专业技艺和他在水手面前的权威。”

“对。”他说。

“那么，在这些情况下，各种不同的团体是否各有各的特殊利益可得呢？”

“是的。”

我继续说：“每门技艺存在的理由，就是关切并谋求各自的好处和利益，难道不是吗？”

“是的，专业技艺就是为了这个。”他回答说。

“除了尽可能完善之外，还有什么是专业技艺的好处呢？”

e ‘I don’t understand the question.’

‘For instance,’ I said, ‘suppose you were to ask me whether it’s enough for the body just to be the body, or whether it needs anything else. I’d reply, “There’s no doubt at all that it needs something else. That’s why the art of medicine has been invented, because the body is flawed and it isn’t enough for it to be like that. The branch of expertise has been developed precisely for the purpose of procuring the body’s welfare.” Would this reply of mine be correct, do you think, or not?’ I asked.

‘Yes, it would,’ he said.

342a ‘Well now, is medicine itself flawed? Are all branches of expertise imperfect? For instance, eyes need sight and ears need hearing, and that’s why they need a branch of expertise to consider their welfare in precisely these respects and to procure it. Is expertise itself somehow inherently flawed as well, so that each branch of expertise needs a further branch to consider its welfare, and this supervisory branch needs yet another one, and so on *ad infinitum*? Or does every
b art consider its own interest and welfare? Or is the whole question of it, or another art, being needed to consider its welfare in view of its flaws irrelevant, in the sense that no branch of expertise is flawed or faulty in the slightest, and it’s inappropriate for any branch of expertise to investigate the welfare of anything other than its own area of expertise? In other words, any branch of expertise is flawless and perfect, provided it’s a genuine branch of expertise—that is, as long as it wholly is what it is, nothing more and nothing less. Please consider this issue with the same strict use of language we were using before, and tell me: am I right or not?’

‘I think you’re right,’ he said.

c ‘It follows, then,’ I said, ‘that medicine does not consider the

“我不理解这个问题。” e

“比如，”我说，“假设你问我，对于身体来说，仅仅是身体是否就够了，或者它是否还需要其他的东西。我会回答说：‘毫无疑问身体还需要其他东西。这就是医术被发明出来的原因，因为身体是有缺陷的，它像那个样子并非就足够了。这一专业技术学科得以精确发展的目的，就在于获得身体的利益。’你认为我的回答是正确的还是错误的？”我问道。

“是对的。”他说。

“那么好吧，医术自身有缺陷吗？所有的专业技艺的分科是 342a
否都是不完善的？比如说，眼睛需要视力，耳朵需要听力，这就是为什么恰恰在这些方面它们还需要一门专业分科来关切并谋求它们的利益。是不是专业技术自身不明原委地本来就存有缺陷，所以每一门专业分科又都需要更细的一门分科来细想它的利益，而这门专管的分科仍需要另外一门分科，如此等等无限类推下去呢？还是说每一门技艺都考虑自身的好处和利益？或者说，整个问题是，每一种技艺都或者需要另一种技艺来考虑其利益，而这 b
另一种技艺的缺欠是与其不相干的？在此意义上，专业分科是没有多少缺陷或错误的，而且任何一门专业分科去考察其他任何别物的利益而不考察自身专业领域内事物的利益，则是不恰当的？换句话说，任何专业分科都是无缺陷和完善的，倘若它是一门真正的专业分科的话——也就是说，只要它完全是它所是，不多也不少。请用与我们使用过的同样严格的用语加以考虑，并告诉我：我说得对不对？”

“我认为你说得对。”他说。

“那么，由此推出，”我说，“医术并不考虑医术之利，而是考虑 c

welfare of medicine, but the welfare of the body.'

'Yes,' he said.

'And horsemanship considers the welfare of horses, not of horsemanship. In short, no branch of expertise considers its own advantage, since it isn't deficient in any respect: it considers the welfare of its area of expertise.'

'So it seems,' he said.

'But surely, Thrasymachus, the branches of expertise have authority and power over their particular areas of expertise.'

He gave his assent to this with extreme reluctance.

'So no branch of knowledge considers or enjoins the advantage
d of the stronger party, but the advantage of the weaker party, which is subject to it.'

Eventually, he agreed to this too, although he tried to argue against it. Once he'd agreed, however, I said, 'Surely, then, no doctor, in his capacity as doctor, considers or enjoins what is advantageous to the doctor, but what is advantageous to the patient? I mean, we've agreed that a doctor, in the strict sense of the term, is in charge of bodies, not a businessman. Isn't that what we agreed?'

He concurred.

'And a ship's captain too is, strictly speaking, in charge of sailors, not a sailor?'

He agree.

e 'So since captains are like this and wield authority in this way, they won't consider and enjoin the interest of the captain, but what is advantageous to the sailor, the subject.'

He reluctantly agreed.

'Therefore, Thrasymachus,' I said, 'no one in any other kind

身体之利。”

“是的。”他说。

“马术考虑的是马的利益，而不是马术的利益。总之，没有专业分科是关切自身的利益的，因为它在任何方面都没有缺陷：它考虑的是它的专业技艺领域对象的利益。”

“看起来如此。”他说。

“但是，塞拉西马库斯，这些专业分科必定是对它们专业的特别领域拥有权威和能力的。”

他非常勉强地同意了这个说法。

“所以知识的分科所考虑或规定的，不是强者的利益，而是臣服于强者的弱者利益。” d

虽然他尽力反驳，但最终他对此也表示同意了。然而他一旦同意，我便说：“那么医生，在其医生职位上，考虑或规定的当然不是医生的利益，而是病人的利益吧？我的意思是，我们已经赞同，是医生（就该词的严格意义而言），而不是商人，对身体负责。这不是我们赞同的吗？”

他同意。

“那么，严格地说，也是一艘船的船长，不是一名水手，要对水手们负责，是不是？”

他同意。 e

“由此，因为船长就是这样的并在这一方面发挥支配权，那么他们所考虑和规定的，就不是船长的利益，而是水手、他的下属的利益了。”

他勉强同意。

“所以，塞拉西马库斯，”我说，“任何其他掌权者，在其统治者

of authority either, in his capacity as ruler, considers or enjoins his own advantage, but the advantage of his subject, the person for whom he practises his expertise. Everything he says and everything he does is said and done with this aim in mind and with regard to what is advantageous to and appropriate for this person.'

343a Once we'd reached this point in the discussion, it was perfectly clear to everyone that the definition of morality had been turned upside down. Thrasymachus didn't respond to my last remarks, but instead said, 'Tell me, Socrates, do you have a nurse?'

'What?' I asked. 'Shouldn't you come up with some response rather than this question?'

'The point is,' he said, 'that she takes no notice of your runny nose and lets it dribble on when it needs wiping, when you can't even tell her the difference between sheep and shepherd.'

'I haven't the faintest idea what you're getting at,' I said.

b 'What I'm getting at is your notion that shepherds or cowherds consider what is good for their sheep or their cows, and fatten them up and look after them, with any aim in mind other than what is good for their masters and for themselves; and also at your supposition that the attitude which people with political authority—who are the real rulers—have towards their subjects differs in the slightest from how one might feel about sheep, and that what they consider day and night
c is anything other than their own advantage and how to gain it. You're so far off understanding right and wrong, and morality and immorality, that you don't even realize that morality and right are actually good for someone else—they are the advantage of the stronger party, the ruler—and bad for the underling at the receiving end of the orders. Nor do you realize that the opposite is true for immorality: the wrongdoer lords it over those moral simpletons—that's what they are, really—while his subjects do what is to his advantage, since he is stronger, and make him happy by doing his bidding, but don't further their own happiness in the slightest.

职位上,考虑或规定的不是自身的利益,而是他的下属的利益,为了他们,他操持他的专业。他所说的每一句话、他所做的每一件事情,都是依着心中这一目的而说而做,并且要考虑到,对这种人来说,什么是有利的和适合的。”

我们的讨论进行到这里,大家都很明白,正义的定义已经颠倒过来了。塞拉西马库斯没有回答我最后的那些话,而是说:“告诉我,苏格拉底,你有女仆吗?” 343a

“什么?”我问道,“怎么不回答问题,反而问这种问题?”

他说:“问题是她没在意你流着鼻涕,当它应该被擦的时候还听任它流淌,那时你甚至还不能告诉她羊和牧羊人有什么区别。”

“我对你所说的话一点也不理解。”我说。

“我要说的是,你以为牧羊人或放牛郎想着他们的羊、他们的牛的利益,养肥它们,照看它们,而心中不想着他们的主人和他们自己的利益;你还以为拥有政治权力的人——真正的统治者——对其臣民的态度与人们对待羊的态度没有多少区别,他们日夜所想的任何事情都不是他们自己的利益和怎样获得这利益。你远没有理解对与错、正义与非正义,你甚至没有明白正义与正当,事实上就是对其他人有益——它们是强者亦即统治者的利益——而对接受最终命令的下属却是有害的。你也没有搞明白,对于不正义而言,相反的情形也是正确的:作恶者作威作福,欺凌那些道德傻瓜——实际上他们就是这个样子的——他的臣民为了他的利益做事,因为作恶者更强大,而且要按他的吩咐去做来取悦他,但一点儿都不能增加他们自己的幸福。 b

d 'You fool, Socrates, don't you see? In any and every situation, a moral person is worse off than an immoral one. Suppose, for instance, that they're doing some business together, which involves one of them entering into association with the other: by the time the association is dissolved, you'll never find the moral person up on the immoral one—he'll be worse off. Or again, in civic matters, if there's a tax on property, then a moral person pays more tax than an immoral one even when they're both equally well off; and if there's a hand-
e out, then the one gets nothing, while the other makes a lot. And when each of them holds political office, even if a moral person loses out financially in no other way, his personal affairs deteriorate through neglect, while his morality stops him making any profit from public funds, and moreover his family and friends fall out with him over his refusal to help them out in unfair ways; in all these respects, however, an immoral person's experience is the opposite.

344a 'I'm talking about the person I described a short while ago, the one with the power to secure huge advantages for himself. This is the person you should consider, if you want to assess the extent to which immorality rather than morality is personally advantageous—and this is something you'll appreciate most easily if you look at immorality in its most perfect form and see how it enhances a wrongdoer's life beyond measure, but ruins the lives of his victims, who haven't the stomach for crime, to the same degree. It's dictatorship I mean, because whether it takes stealth or overt violence, a dictator steals what doesn't belong to him—consecrated and unconsecrated objects, private possessions, and public property—and does so not on a small
b scale, but comprehensively. Anyone who is caught cormmitting the merest fraction of these crimes is not only punished, but thoroughly stigmatized as well: small-scale criminals who commit these kinds of

“头脑简单的苏格拉底，难道你没有看出来吗？在任何 d
的、在每一种的情况下，一个正义的人要比一个不正义的人处境差。举个例子说，假如他们一起做生意，一个人和另一个人合伙，到散伙时，你绝不会发现正义的人比不正义的人占优，他会吃亏。或再举一例，在公民事务上，如果要征财产税，那么一个正义的人支付的比一个不正义的人要多，甚至是当他们俩同样富裕的时候也是这样；而如果有钱可分，那
么一个人什么都得不到，而另一个得了很多。当他们都担任 e
公职时，即使正义的人没有其他经济损失，他的个人事务也会因为疏忽而搞得一团糟，而他的正义阻碍了他从公共财产中获得利益，此外，因为拒绝徇私帮助他的亲人和朋友们，所以他们也和他疏远了；然而，在所有这些方面，一个不正义的人的遭遇则相反。

“我指的是刚才所说的利用权力为自己谋取巨大好处
的人。如果你想要评定个人不正义比正义所获取利益的范 344a
围与程度有多大，那么这便是你应该考虑的人——而如果你着眼于不正义的极端形式，看到它是如何极度地增益了作恶者的生活，并在同等程度上毁掉了他的受害者，即那些不想作恶的人的生存状态，那么这也是你最容易意识到的事情了。我指的就是僭主，因为无论暗偷还是明抢，不管是圣物还是俗物，不管是私产还是公产，僭主把这些不属于他们的东西不是偷走一点点，而是通通偷走。任何犯
了此类小罪的人则不仅要受罚而且还要名誉扫地，犯了这 b
些罪的小偷小盗被称为圣物盗窃者、拐骗者、盗贼、小偷、抢劫犯。另一方面，当有人剥夺了公民们的财产，并进而

crimes are called temple-robbers, kidnappers, burglars, thieves, and robbers. On the other hand, when someone appropriates the assets of the citizen body and then goes on to rob them of their very freedom and enslave them, then denigration gives way to congratulation, and it
c isn't only his fellow citizens who call him happy, but anyone else who hears about his consummate wrongdoing does so as well. The point is that immorality has a bad name because people are afraid of being at the receiving end of it, not of doing it.

'So you see, Socrates, immorality—if practised on a large enough scale—has more power, licence, and authority than morality. And as I said at the beginning, morality is really the advantage of the stronger party, while immorality is profitable and advantageous to oneself.'

d After flooding our ears, like an attendant in the baths, with this torrential gush of words, Thrasymachus was thinking of leaving. No one there would let him go, however: they forced him to stay and justify what he'd been saying. I myself was particularly insistent. 'My dear Thrasymachus,' I said, 'you surely aren't thinking of leaving? You can't just pelt us with words, so to speak, and then leave before adequately demonstrating—or before finding out yourself—whether or not they're true. Or do you think that what you're attempting to define
e is a trivial matter, and not how anyone can live his life in the most rewarding manner?'

'Am I disagreeing with you?' Thrasymachus protested.

'You do give that impression,' I replied, 'unless it's just us you don't care about in the slightest, and you don't spare a thought for whether our ignorance of what you're claiming to know will make us
345a live better or worse lives. No, Thrasymachus, please do your best to enlighten us too: it won't turn out badly for you to do so many of us a favour. I'll tell you my position: I'm not convinced. I do not think that immorality is more profitable than morality, not even if it is given free rein and never prevented from getting its own way; and even if I grant you your immoral person , Thrasymachus , with the power to do

剥夺了公民们的自由并且奴役他们时，恶名反而让位于祝贺，
不光是他同城的市民祝他幸福，其他任何听到了他的滔天罪 c
行的人也会祝福他。关键在于，不正义之所以有坏名声，那是
因为人们害怕由之而来的后果，而不是不敢去做。

“所以你看，苏格拉底，不正义——如果足够心狠手辣地加以
践行的话——就会比践行正义拥有更多的权力、法律特许以及威
望。所以就像我在开头说过的，正义实际上就是强者的利益，而
不正义则使自己有利可图、有便宜可占。”

就像澡堂里的伙计，塞拉西马库斯用他的高谈阔论浇灌了 d
我们的耳朵后就想着要离开了。然而，在座的没有人想让他走。
他们强迫他留下并要他为所说的话作解释。我自己非常坚持他
留下。我说：“我亲爱的塞拉西马库斯，你不会考虑一定要离开
吧？你不能刚刚用可以说是疾言利辞攻击了我们一番，然后在
充分证明——或者说在你自己查明——这些言论是否正确之前
就离开吧。或者你认为刚才试图阐述的内容都是些鸡毛蒜皮的
小事儿，而不关乎任何一个人怎样才能以一种最有获益的方式
过活吗？” e

“我非要和你吵架吗？”塞拉西马库斯抗议道。

我回答说：“你的确给我们有那种印象，除非你最不在乎的就
是我们，并且你也不想想，我们对你的主张的一无所知，会使我们
的生活会变好还是变差。不，塞拉西马库斯，请你尽量开导我们
吧：帮我们那么多人 一个忙，这对你不会有什么坏处的。我会告 345a
诉你我的立场：我没有被你说服。即使不义者并非得以自由地从
不受阻地行事，我也并不认为不正义比正义更为有益；塞拉西马
库斯，即使我承认你所谓的不正义的人使用他的权力去作恶，无

wrong either by stealth or by brute force, for my part I'm still not con-
b vinced that it is more profitable than morality. It's possible that someone else here feels the same, and that I'm not alone; so, Thrasymachus, you must come up with a good enough argument to convince us that rating morality higher than immorality is a mistake.'

'How do you expect me to do that?' he asked. 'If what I've just been saying doesn't convince you, what else can I do? Do you want me to spoonfeed the argument into your mind?'

'No, I certainly don't want you to do that,' I said. 'Above all, I'd like you to be consistent; or if you do change your mind, I'd like you to do so openly, without trying to deceive us. What's happening,
c you see, Thrasymachus—I mean, we haven't completed our investigation of what you were saying before—is that although you started by trying to define the true doctor, you didn't maintain the same level of precision when you subsequently turned to the true shepherd. You don't think that the reason a shepherd, in his capacity as shepherd, herds sheep is what is best for the sheep; you think he's like a dinner-guest when a meal is due, and is interested only in indulging him-
d self—or alternatively that he behaves like a businessman rather than a shepherd, and is interested only in making money. But of course the sole concern of shepherding is to procure the best for what is in its charge, since its own best state has been sufficiently procured, as we know, as long as it wholly and entirely is shepherding. The same reasoning, I thought, was what compelled us not long ago to conclude that all authority (whether political or non-political), *qua* authority,
e considers what is best for nothing except its subjects, its wards. But do you think that people with political authority—the 'real' rulers—exercise authority willingly?'

'I most definitely do not *think* so,' he replied. 'I'm absolutely certain of it!'

论是偷偷摸摸地还是凭蛮力硬干，对我来说，我还是对不正义比正义更有益的说法不信服。可能这儿的其他人也有同感，可能并 b
不止我一个人；这样，塞拉西马库斯，你必须拿出充足的理由来使我们相信把正义置于比不正义更高的地位是个错误。”

“你希望我怎么说服你？”他问道，“如果我刚才说的都不能使你信服，我还能怎么做？难道你希望我用勺子把论据喂到你的脑袋里面去吗？”

“不，我当然不是要你那样做，”我说，“首先，我想你得前后一致；或者如果你改变主意，我想你要光明正大地改，不要试图欺骗我们。塞拉西马库斯，你看，现在要说的是——我意思是，我们还没有完成对刚才你说的问题的探究，——虽然你开始试图定义真 c
正的医生，问题是当你后来转向真正的牧羊人时，你没有保持同等层面的严格性。你没有想到这样一个推论，一个牧羊人，就其作为牧羊人的职能而言，把羊赶在一起放牧，对羊而言就是最大的利益；你认为他像是一个被邀请来吃大餐的饕餮之徒，一门心思想着的只是满足自己的食欲——或者换个说法，你认为他的行为像是一位商人，而不是一个牧羊人，一门心思想着的就是赚钱。 d
但是，理所当然地，牧羊唯一关心的就是获得其主管事物的最大利益，因为就像我们知道的那样，它自身的最佳状态，只是在它完完全全表现牧羊的技艺的时候而得以充分的获得。我想是同样的理由促使我们不久前得出的结论说，所有真正的统治者（无论是政治上的还是非政治上的），作为统治者，所考虑的无非就是受他统治和保护的人的最大利益。但你认为那些拥有政治权力的 e
人——即“真正”的统治者——他们会心甘情愿地履行职权吗？”

“我确信他们不愿意，”他回答道，“对此我完全确定。”

'But, Thrasymachus,' I said, 'don't you realize that no other form of authority is willingly exercised by its holder? People demand wages, on the grounds that the power isn't going to benefit *them*, but those who are in their charge. I mean, tell me this: when we want to
346a distinguish one branch of expertise from another, don't we do so by distinguishing what it is capable of doing? And please, Thrasymachus, make sure that your reply expresses what you really believe; otherwise, we won't make any progress.'

'Yes, that's how we distinguish it,' he said.

'And doesn't every branch of expertise have its own particular benefit to bestow as well, rather than one which it shares with other branches of expertise? For instance, medicine confers health, naval captaincy confers safety at sea, and so on.'

'Yes.'

b 'And isn't an income conferred by expertise at earning money? I mean, this is what it is capable of doing. You surely don't identify medicine and captaincy, do you? We must do as you suggested and make precise distinctions, so if a ship's captain recovers from illness because seafaring is good for him, does this lead you to call what he does medicine?'

'Of course not,' he said.

'Nor, I imagine, if someone recovers from illness while earning money, do you describe moneymaking skill as medical skill.'

'Of course not.'

'Well, suppose someone earns money while restoring health? Does this make you describe medicine as moneymaking?'

c 'No.'

'We've agreed that every branch of expertise has its own particular benefit to bestow, haven't we?'

“但是，塞拉西马库斯，”我说，“难道你没有意识到没有什么形式的权力是其掌握者所情愿操持的吗？人们做事要钱，理由是权力并不将利益带给他们，而是带给受他们管理的人。我的意思是，告诉我：当我们要把一种专业技艺和另一种专业技艺相区分的时候，我们这样做，难道不就是依据于对它们的功能的区分吗？ 346a
塞拉西马库斯，请你保证你回答的是你确实相信的；否则，我们就不能取得任何进展了。”

“是的，我们就是那样区分的。”他说。

“是否每门专业技艺自身也有其所能提供的特殊的好处，而不是与其他技艺一同提供一种好处？比如，医术提供健康，航海的技艺提供航海安全，如此等等。”

“是的。”

“赚钱的技艺所提供的不就是赚来的钱吗？我的意思是说， b
这就是它的功能。你当然不会把医术和航海术等同，是吗？我们必须像你所建议的那样做出准确的区分，所以如果一个船长恢复了健康是因为航海有益于他，你就把这称作医术吗？”

“当然不能。”他回答说。

“我想也不能。假如有人赚钱而恢复了健康了呢？你能把医术说成是赚钱的技巧吗？”

“当然不能。” c

“那么，设想某人在恢复他人健康同时赚了钱，你能将医术说成是赚钱之术吗？”

“不能。”

“我们已经同意，每门专业分科自身都有其所能提供的特殊的好处，不是吗？”

'Yes, I grant you that,' he said.

'So if there's any benefit which the practitioners of every branch of expertise share, then obviously this benefit must come from something which is the same for all of them, and which they all equally make use of, over and above making use of their own particular expertise.'

'I suppose so,' he said.

'And it's our view that practitioners of branches of expertise benefit by earning money because they make use of the skill of moneymaking in addition to their own particular skill.'

He reluctantly agreed.

d 'It follows that no one benefits, in the sense of earning money, as a result of practising his own branch of expertise. Instead, given that our enquiry has to be conducted with precision, we should say that medicine creates health, while moneymaking creates an income, and that building creates a house, while moneymaking may accompany building and create an income, and so on for the other branches of expertise: each of them has its own job to do and benefits what is in its charge. But leaving wages aside, is there any benefit which a practitioner gains from his expertise?'

'Apparently not,' he said.

e 'And what about when he works for free? Does he in fact fail to confer any benefit at that time?'

'No, I think he does.'

'So, Thrasymachus, it's now clear that no branch of expertise or form of authority procures benefit for itself; as we were saying some time ago, it procures and enjoins benefit for its subject. It considers the advantage of its subject, the weaker party, not that of the stronger party. That, my dear Thrasymachus, is why I was proposing just now
347a that no one willingly chooses authority and the task of righting other

“是的，我承认。”他说通。

“所以如果有一种使每种专业分科的工匠都享有好处的技艺，那么很明显，这种好处除了来源于他们各自所使用的特殊技艺之外，必定来源于某种对他们所有人来说是相同的并且都同样使用的东西。”

“我想是这样。”他说。

“我们的观点就认为，专业分科的执业者因赚钱而受益，是因为他们在其各自的独特技术之外，还利用了赚钱的技术。”

他勉强同意。

“从赚钱的角度看来，可以得出：没有人能从他自身的专业技 d
艺实践中获得利益。要是我们严格地加以探讨的话，我们倒是应该说，医术产生健康，而赚钱的技艺产生报酬，建筑术产生房屋，而赚钱的技艺可以伴随着建筑术创造收入，其他的专业技艺也是如此：每门技艺各司其职并从它的掌管对象中得到利益。但是除了工钱，工匠还能从他的技艺中获得任何好处吗？”

“显然不能。”他说。

“那么他工作而又赚不来钱又当如何呢？当时他岂不是实际
上没有得到任何的利益吗？” e

“是的，我想他不能。”

“那么，塞拉西马库斯，这就清楚了，没有一种专业技艺或统治形式是为了自身谋利益的；就像我们以前的某个时间说过的那样，它为它的支配对象谋利益。它关心的是它的支配对象的利益，即弱者的利益而非强者的利益。我亲爱的塞拉西马库斯，那就是我刚才为什么提议说，没有人心甘情愿地选择职权，选择纠
正其他人们错误这桩苦差事的原因；他们对此要求回报，因为任 347a

people's wrongs; they ask to be paid for it, because anyone who works properly with his expertise consistently fails to work for his own welfare, and also fails to legislate for his own welfare when he gives instructions as a professional. It isn't *his* welfare, but that of his subject, which is his concern. This presumably explains why it is necessary to pay people with money or prestige before they are prepared to hold authority, or to punish them if they refuse.'

'What do you mean, Socrates?' asked Glaucon. 'I recognize your two modes of payment, but I don't know what punishment you are referring to and how it replaces payment.'

b 'Then you don't know what kind of payment is needed to induce truly excellent people to be prepared to rule,' I said. 'Don't you realize that to say that someone is interested in prestige or money is thought—and rightly thought—to be insulting?'

'Yes, I know that,' he said.

'Well,' I explained, 'that's why neither money nor prestige tempts good people to accept power. You see, if they overtly require money for being in charge, they'll be called hired hands, and if they covertly make money for themselves out of the possession of power, they'll be called thieves; and they don't want either of these alternatives. On the other hand, they won't do it for prestige either, since they aren't ambitious. So one has to pressurize them and threaten
c them with punishment, otherwise they'll never assume power; and this is probably the origin of the conventional view that it's shameful to *want* to take power on, rather than waiting until one has no choice. The ultimate punishment for being unwilling to assume authority oneself is to be governed by a worse person, and it is fear of this happening, I think, which prompts good men to assume power occasionally. On these occasions, they don't embark upon government with the expectation of gaining some advantage or benefit from it: their attitude is that they have no choice in the matter, in the sense that they haven't
d been able to find people better than themselves, or even their e quals , to Whom they might entrust the task . The chances are that

何一心使用他的技艺的人总会疏忽了为自己谋利益，并且当他职
业性地给出指示时，他也疏于考虑自己的利益。他所考虑的不是
他自己的利益而是他的支配对象的利益。这或许能解释为什么
在人们准备掌权之前有必要给予他们以金钱或名誉的报酬，如果
他们拒绝，那么就惩罚他们。”

“苏格拉底，你说的是什么意思？”格劳孔问道，“我明白金钱
和名誉这两种报酬，但我不知道你指的惩罚是什么，它又是怎样
代替了报酬的。”

“那么你不知道引诱真正优秀的人乐意去管理需要什么
样的报酬吧，”我说，“你难道没有察觉到，说某人醉心于名利， b
那就会被认为是——并且是实实在在地被认为——遭到了侮
辱吗？”

“是的，我知道。”他说。

“那么，”我解释说，“那就是为什么金钱和名誉都不能诱使良
善之人接受权力的原因。你看，要是他们公开地对管理工作索要
报酬的话，他们就会被称为雇工，而要是他们偷偷地以权谋私，他
们就会被称为窃贼；这两者，他们一个都不想要。另一方面，他们
也不会为了名誉而接受权力，因为他们没有野心。所以人们只好
对他们施加压力，并用惩罚胁迫他们，否则，他们才不会担任什么 c
官职呢；这可能就是传统观念的来源吧，这种观念认为：想要掌
权，而不是等到无可选择才掌权，是可耻的。对自己不愿意掌权
的最终的惩罚，将是被一个比他差的人统治，我想正是对此事的
担心才偶尔促使好人掌权。在这些情况下，他们担任公职并不是
希望谋取一些好处，或从中获得利益：对于此事，他们是觉得没有
选择的余地，因为他们找不到比他们更优秀的或甚至与他们同等 d

were a community of good men to exist, the competition to avoid power would be just as fierce as the competition for power is under current circumstances, in such a community, it would be glaringly obvious that any genuine ruler really is incapable of considering his own welfare, rather than that of his subject, and the consequence would be that anyone with any sense would prefer receiving benefit to all the problems that go with conferring it. So anyway, I utterly disagree with Thrasymachus' assertion that morality is the advantage of the stronger
e party; but we've examined that topic enough for the time being.'

'Thrasymachus' current claim, however, is that a life of crime is better than a life of integrity, and this seems to me to be a far more important assertion. Do you have a preference, Glaucon?' I asked. 'Which view do you think is closer to the truth?'

'I think a moral life is more rewarding.'

348a 'Did you hear Thrasymachus' recent long list of the advantages of an immoral life?' I asked.

'I did,' he answered, 'but I'm not convinced.'

'Shall we try to convince him, then, if we possibly can, of the falsehood of his claim?'

'Yes, of course, let's,' he said.

'Well,' I said, 'if we counter his claim by drawing up an alternative list of all the advantages of morality, and then he responds to that, and we respond to his response, we'll find ourselves in the posi-
b tion of having to add up advantages and measure the lengths of our respective lists, and before we know it we'll need jurors to adjudicate for us. On the other hand, if we conduct the investigation as we did just now, by trying to win each other's consent, then we'll be our own jurors *and* claimants.'

'Quite so,' he said.

优秀的、对其可以委以信任的人了。要是有一个由好人组成的城邦存在,那么避免不当官的竞争就会和当前的争相当官的竞争一样激烈,在这样的城邦显而易见的是,任何真正的统治者都不会考虑自己的利益,而是考虑受他统治之人的利益,结果就是任何正常的人都愿意受人之惠而不愿意授惠于人。所以无论如何,我都全然不同意塞拉西马库斯的论断:正义是强者的利益;但我们 e
对这个主题的研讨暂时是足够了。"

"然而塞拉西马库斯现在的说法是,罪恶的生活要比正直的生活好,这在我看来是一个非常重要的论断。格劳孔,你喜欢哪种?"我问道,"你觉得哪种观点更接近真理?"

"我觉得一种正义的生活更加有益。"

"你听到塞拉西马库斯刚才那一长串有关不正义生活的利益
的话了吗?"我问道。 348a

"我听到了,"他回答说,"但我并不信服。"

"那么,如果可能的话,我们要力图说服他,让他觉得自己的说法是错误的吗?"

"是的,当然,来吧。"他说。

"那么,"我说,"如果我们通过画一张列举所有正义好处的可供选择的表单来反对他的主张,然后他作出回应,而我们又对他的回应作出回应,我们就会发现,我们的任务是必须添加好处,并且要衡量各自所列举的表单的长度,那么在我们知道孰优孰劣之 b
前,我们就需要评委为我们加以裁定。另一方面,如果我们像刚才所做一样,通过力求赢得对方的赞同,来进行这项探究,那么我们就既是自己的法官又是申辩者。"

"说得很对。"他说。

'Which plan do you like, then?' I asked.

'The latter,' he said.

'All right, then, Thrasymachus,' I said, 'let's go back to the beginning. Could you please confirm for us that your claim is that perfect immorality is more profitable than perfect morality?'

c 'Yes, that's my claim,' he said, 'and I've explained why too.'

'And here's another question about them: do you think that one of them is a good state and the other is a bad one?'

'Of course.'

'That is, morality is a good state, and immorality a bad one?'

'Don't be so naïve, Socrates,' he said. 'Would I say that when I'm claiming that it's immorality which is profitable, not morality?'

'What *is* your position, then?'

'The opposite of what you said,' he replied.

'That morality is bad?'

'No, it's sheer simplicity.'

'So you're saying that immorality is duplicity, are you?'

d 'No, it's sound judgement,' he said.

'Do you really think that criminals are clever, good people, Thrasymachus?'

'Yes, if their criminality is able to manifest in a perfect form and they are capable of dominating countries and nations. I suppose you think I was talking about pickpockets. Actually,' he added, 'activities like that are rewarding too, if you can get away with them, but they're insignificant—unlike the ones I've just mentioned.'

e 'Yes, I see what you mean,' I said. 'But I'm surprised you count immorality as a form of goodness and cleverness, and morality

“那么你喜欢哪种计划呢?”我问道。

“后者。”他说。

“那么好吧,塞拉西马库斯,”我说,“让我们回到开头。你能让我们确信你的主张就是完全的不正义比完全的正义要更加有益吗?”

“是的,那就是我的主张,”他说,“而且我也已经解释过了为什么是这样。” c

“关于它们还有一个问题:你会把其中的一个称作善,另一个称作恶吗?”

“当然。”

“就是说,正义是善而不正义是恶吗?”

“苏格拉底,你别这么幼稚了,”他说,“当我说不正义是有利的而正义无利可图时,我还会那样说吗?”

“那么你的观点是什么?”

“与你说的相反。”他回答说。

“那么,正义是恶吗?”

“不,它是纯粹的头脑简单。”

“那么你说的不正义就是口是心非,不是吗?” d

“不是,不正义是正确的判断。”他说。

“塞拉西马库斯,你真的认为罪犯是聪明的好人吗?”

“是的,如果他们的罪行能表现出一种完美的形式,并且他们能够统治城邦和国家的话。我想你认为我说的是小偷小摸,”他补充道,“实际上要是你能够让他们逃脱,那么,像那样的活动也是有得益的,只是微不足道罢了——不像我刚才提到的那些。”

“是的,我明白你的意思,”我说。“但是你将仁慈善良与聪明机灵包含在不正义的名目下,而将其反道纳入正义名目下,这还 e

as the opposite.'

'Nevertheless, that's exactly what I do.'

'You've come up with a rather intractable idea this time,' I commented. 'It's not easy to know how to respond to it. If you were proposing that immorality is profitable, but also conceding (as others do) that it's contemptible and bad, then our conversation could proceed against a background of convention. However, since you've made the enterprising suggestion that it's to be classified along with goodness and cleverness, you're obviously going to say that it is a
349a fine, effective quality, and will attribute to it all the other properties which we tend to ascribe to morality.'

'Your prophecy couldn't be more accurate,' he said.

'All the same,' I said, 'I mustn't be put off. I must continue with the discussion and carry on with the investigation, as long as I feel that you're speaking your mind. I mean, I get the impression, Thrasymachus, that now you aren't toying with us in the slightest, but are expressing your beliefs about the way things truly are.'

'What does it matter to you whether or not it's what I believe?' he said. 'Why don't you just tackle what I'm saying?'

b 'It doesn't matter to me at all,' I said. 'But here's another question I'd like you to try to answer, over and above what you've already said. Do you think a moral person would wish to set himself up as superior to another moral person?'

'Of course he wouldn't,' he replied. 'Otherwise he wouldn't be the civilized simpleton he is.'

'Well, would he want to set himself up as superior to moral behaviour?'

'Again, no,' he replied.

'Would he, or would he not, want and intend to set himself up as superior to an immoral person?'

'He would intend to,' he replied, 'but he wouldn't be able to.'

是很让我吃惊的。”

“然而我的确就是那样划分的。”

“这次你提出了一个颇为棘手的想法,”我评说道,“要懂得如何回答它,可是不简单。如果你提出不正义是有利的,但同时又像别人一样同意它是卑鄙的、坏的,那么我们的谈论按常理还可以继续下去。然而,因为你大胆地说要把不正义划分到和美德、智慧一起,那么你显然就想说不正义是好的、卓越的,并把所有其 349a
他我们倾向归之于正义的性质也归之于它。”

“你的预言真是再准不过了。”他说。

我说:“我还是不可被阻遏。我必须继续讨论,进行探讨,只要我觉得你在说心里话。塞拉西马库斯,我的意思是,我有印象,现在你一点都没有和我们在开玩笑,而是在说你所真信的事情。”

“我所信或不信,这对你有什么重要关系吗?”他说,“为什么不是仅仅来应对我所说的呢?”

“这和我完全无关,”我说,“但除了你已经说过的之外,我这 b
里还有个问题想问问你。你认为一个正义的人会希望在地位权威上高过另一个正义之人吗?”

“他当然不会,”他回答说,“否则他就不是现在这个受过教化的傻瓜了。”

“那么,他会想要在正义行为上使自己处在比他人优越的位置上吗?”

“还是不会的。”他回答道。

“他会不会希望并打算在正义行为上使自己处在比不义之人优越的位置上呢?”

“他倒是打算这样做,”他回答说,“但是他做不到。”

'I'm not asking whether he'd be able to do it,' I said. 'My
c question is: isn't it the case that a moral person does not intend or wish to set himself up as superior to another moral person, but only to an immoral person?'

'That's correct,' he said.

'What about an immoral person? Does he want to set himself up as Superior to a moral person and to moral behaviour?'

'Of course,' he replied. 'He wants to gain the upper hand in everything.'

'So will an immoral person also try to set himself up as superior to another immoral person and to immoral behaviour? In short, will he struggle to gain the upper hand over everyone else in everything?'

'Yes.'

'Let's put it this way,' I said. 'A moral person doesn't set himself up as superior to people who are like him, but only to people who are unlike him; an immoral person, on the other hand, sets himself
d up as superior to people who are like him as well as to people who are unlike him.'

'You couldn't have put it better,' he said.

'Now, an immoral person is clever and good, and a moral person is neither clever nor good. Isn't that right?'

'Yes, you've put that well too,' he said

'So is it the case that an immoral person also *resembles* a clever, good person, while a moral person does not?' I asked.

'Naturally,' he replied. 'Since that's the type of person he is, then of course he resembles others of the same type; and of course a moral person does not resemble them.'

'Fine. So each of them is of the same type as people he resembles?'

'That goes without saying,' he said.

“我不是在问他是否能做到，”我说，“我的问题是：一个正义之人并不打算或希望使自身处在比另一个正义之人优越的位置上，而只是想比一个不义之人优越，情况是这样的吗？” c

“那是对的。”他说道。

“那么一个不义之人又如何呢？他也希望使自身处在比一个正义之人以及某种正义行为更优越的位置上吗？”

“当然，”他回答道，“他想在每一件事情上都占上风。”

“所以一个不义之人，也会尽量使自身处在比另一个不义之人与不义行为更优越的位置上吗？简而言之，他要尽力使得自己对每个人并在每一件事情上都占上风吗？”

“是的。”

“让我们这样说吧，”我说道，“一个正义之人不会使自身处在比其同类之人更优越的位置上，而只是比不同之人更优越；另一方面，一个不义之人，则无论是与其同不同类，他都将使自身处在更优越的位置上。” d

“你说得再好不过了。”他说。

“那么，一个不义的人是既聪明又善良的，而正义之人既不聪明也不善良。难道不是那样吗？”

“是的，你也说得太好不过了。”他说。

“所以情况就是不义之人与聪明的好人相似，而正义之人与之不相似，对吗？”我问道。

“当然，”他回答。“因为他就是那类人，所以他当然就与其他同类相似；而一个正义之人当然就与他们不相似。”

“很好。那么他们中的每一个人都与同类相似？”

“那就不必说了。”他说。

e ‘All right, Thrasymachus. Do you acknowledge that some people are musical and some aren't?’

‘I do.’

‘Which ones are clever and which aren't?’

‘The musical ones are clever, of course, and the unmusical ones aren't.’

‘And if someone is clever at something, isn't he also good at it, and bad at it if he isn't clever at it?’

‘Yes.’

‘And doesn't the same apply to medicine?’

‘Yes.’

‘Do you think, then, Thrasymachus, that when a musical person is tuning a lyre—tightening and slackening the strings— he would want to set himself up as superior to, and gain the upper hand over, another musical person?’

‘No, I don't think so.’

‘As superior to an unmusical person, then?’

‘Inevitably,’ he said.

350a ‘And what about a doctor? Do you think that in dietary matters he would have the slightest desire to set himself up as superior to another doctor or to medical practice?’

‘Of course not.’

‘But as superior to non-medical people and practice?’

‘Yes.’

‘Consider any instance of knowledge or ignorance. Do you think that the actions or words of anyone who is knowledgeable in anything are motivated by a desire to surpass the actions or words of another person with the same knowledge? Don't you think that his actions and

“好吧，塞拉西马库斯。你承认有些人懂音乐而有些人不懂音乐吗？” e

“承认。”

“哪类人聪明，哪类人不聪明？”

“当然是懂音乐的人聪明，不懂音乐的人不聪明。”

“那么如果某人在某方面很聪明，他难道不是也擅长此道，却在他不够聪明的方面束手束脚吗？”

“是的。”

“那么同样的不也适合于医术吗？”

“是的。”

“那么，塞拉西马库斯，你认为当一个精通音乐的人在给一架里拉调音时——拉紧和松弛琴弦——他会想要使自身处在另一位精通音乐的人之上，并占他的上风吗？

“不，我不这样认为。”

“那么会想胜过不懂音乐的人吗？”

“必定。”他说。

“那么医生又会如何呢？你认为在饮食方面他会有一点点愿望想胜过别的医生或医疗践习吗？” 350a

“当然不会。”

“但会想胜过不懂医术的人和活动吗？”

“会的。”

“来考虑一些有关有知与无知的事例吧。你认为，任何一个在任何事上都富有见识的人，其行为举止或言谈辞令有没有受到一种渴望的推动，这种渴望便是想要超胜另一位同样富有见识的人的行为举止或言谈辞令？难道你不认为他的举止言谈，

words would be identical to those of someone like him in the same circumstances?'

'Yes, I suppose that's bound to be the case,' he said.

'What about an ignoramus? Wouldn't he try to set himself up as
b superior to knowledgeable people and to ignorant people equally?'

'I suppose so.'

'A knowledgeable person is clever, isn't he?'

'Yes.'

'And a clever person is good?'

'Yes.'

'So it's if someone is good and clever that he won't want to set himself up as superior to people who are like him, but only to people who are unlike him and have nothing in common with him.'

'So it seems.'

'If someone is bad and ignorant, however, he'll want to set himself up as superior to people who are like him as well as to people who are unlike him.'

'I suppose so.'

'Well, Thrasymachus,' I said, 'we found that it was an immoral person who sets himself up as superior to people who are like him as well as to people who are unlike him, didn't we? Isn't that what you said?'

'I did,' he replied.

c 'And a moral person won't set himself up as superior to people who are like him, but only to people who are unlike him?'

'Yes.'

'It follows,' I said, 'that it is a moral person who resembles a clever, good person, and an immoral person who resembles a bad, ignorant person.'

都会和那些像他一样处在同样情况下的一些人的举止言谈完全相同吗？”

“是的，我想肯定是这样的，”他说道。

“一个不学无术的笨蛋又会怎样呢？难道他不是尽力想使自己处在比博学的人优越的位置上，而且同样也比无知的人优越吗？” b

“我想是这样的。”

“博学之人是聪明的，不是吗？”

“是的。”

“聪明之人是好人吗？”

“是的。”

“所以一个人若是既聪明又好，那么他就不会想胜过和他相类似的人，而只想比那些与他不相似的并且与他毫无共同点的人更优越。”

“看起来如此。”

“然而，如果他既邪恶又无知，那么他就会既想要胜过与他相似的人，也想胜过与他不相似的人。”

“我想是这样的。”

“那么，塞拉西马库斯，”我说，“我们发现正是不正义的人才会想胜过那些与他相似的人，并且也想胜过与他不相似的人，不是吗？那不是你说过的吗？”

“我这样说过。”他回答道。

“一个正义之人不会使自身处在另一位与之相类似的人之上，而是在那些不与之相类似的人之上，是不是这样呢？” c

“是的。”

“以此得出，”我说，“正是正义之人才与聪明的好人相似，而不正义的人与无知的坏人相似。”

'It looks that way.'

'And we agreed that each of them is of the same type as people he is like.'

'Yes, we did.'

'We've proved, then, that it is a moral person who is good and clever, whereas an immoral person is ignorant and bad.'

Now, although Thrasymachus did concede all these points, it
d wasn't as easy as I'm making it sound by describing it: he was hauled along with great reluctance, sweating profusely (since it was the hot season). And I also saw then something I'd never seen before—a red-faced Thrasymachus.

'So anyway, we agreed that morality was a good state and was knowledge, and that immorality was a bad state and was ignorance.' Next I said, 'All right. We may have settled that issue, but we also have before us the claim that immorality is effective. Do you remember, Thrasymachus?'

'Yes, I remember,' he replied. 'But I'm not satisfied with the statements you've just been making. I could address them, but I'm sure that if I did, you'd claim that I was holding forth like an orator.
e So either let me say what I want and for as long as I want, or go on with your questions, if you insist on doing that, and I'll go on saying "All right" and nodding and shaking my head as if I were listening to old women telling stories.'

'But you must never go against what you actually believe,' I said.

'Why shouldn't I?' he said. 'It makes you happy. You won't let me speak—do you want more from me than that?'

'No, not at all,' I replied. 'If you'll do what you said, that's fine, and I'll ask the questions.'

'Go ahead, then.'

'Well, here's the question I was getting at just now; I think it's
351a the logical next one for our investigation. When morality is compared

“看来是这样。”

“而我们同意他们中的每一个人都与同类相似。”

“是的，我们同意。”

“那么我们就证明了，一个正义之人才是善良而聪明的，相反，一个不正义的人却是无知而邪恶的。”

现在，塞拉西马库斯虽然勉强承认了所有这些观点，但并不是如我现在所描述的那么容易：他非常不情愿地被拽着走，由于天热，他满身是汗。我也看到了某些我从未看到过的情形——塞拉西马库斯脸红了。 d

“所以无论如何，我们承认正义就是善良，就是有识，而不正义就是邪恶，就是无知。”随后我说：“好吧，这点我们可以解决了，但在我们面前还有这么一种主张，即不正义是强有力的。塞拉西马库斯，你还记得吗？”

“是的，记得。”他回答说，“但我对你刚才的说法还是不满意。我会把它们说出来，但要是这样做，我想你肯定会说我雄辩地像个演说家。所以，要么让我想说什么就说什么，要么你继续问你 e
的问题，如果你还是那样坚持的话，我会继续说‘好吧’，或点头或摇头，就像听一个老妇人讲故事。”

“但你决不能违背你的真实想法啊。”我说。

“为什么不可以？”他说，“让你高兴呀。你不让我说话——除此之外，你还想从我这得到什么？”

“不，根本不是这样，”我回答说，“如果你按你说的话去做就好，我要提问了。”

“那就问吧。”

“好吧，那我就提刚才提过的那个问题；我想这就是按我们探讨的次序所要提的问题。拿正义与不正义相比时，关于正义我们 351a

with immorality, what do we learn about morality? I mean, the suggestion was made that immorality is more powerful and more effective than morality; but the fact that we've now established that morality is a good state and is knowledge will make it easy to prove, I think, that it's also more effective than immorality, given that immorality is ignorance, as everyone knows by now. However, I don't want our investigation to be couched in such abstract terms, Thrasymachus, but rath-
b er as follows: would you agree that it is wrong for a community to undertake the domination of other communities, to deprive other communities of their freedom, and to keep a number of other communities subservient to itself?'

'Of course it is,' he said. 'And the better the community—the more perfectly irnmoral—the more it will act in exactly that way.'

'I appreciate that this is your position,' I said, 'but what I'm doing is exploring an aspect of it and asking whether a community which is stronger than another community will retain its power if it doesn't have morality, or whether it can do so only if it has morality.'

'If your recent assertion was correct,' he replied, 'that moralityc is knowledge, then it will take morality; but if I'm right, it takes immorality.'

'Thrasymachus,' I said, 'I'm really pleased that you're not just nodding and shaking your head, but are giving these excellent answers.'

I'm doing it to make you happy,' he said.

'Thank you. You'll carry on making me happy if you answer this question of mine. Do you think that a community or an army or pirates or thieves or any other band which forms for the purpose of wrongdoing would be capable of doing anything if the members of the band wrong one another?'

d 'Of course not,' he said.

'But if they don't wrong one another, then they stand a better chance of success?'

'Yes.'

知道了些什么？我的意思是，先前说过，不正义比正义要更强大、更有力；但我们现在已经证明正义是善良和知识，我想这个事实让我们容易证明：如果不正义就是无知，那么正义就还是比不正义更强有力，就像大家现在所知道的一样。但，塞拉西马库斯，我不想在我们的探讨中使用如此抽象的说法，而应该这样理解：一
个城邦征服其他城邦，剥夺它们的自由并且让其他城邦臣服于自 b
己，你会同意那个城邦是不正义的吗？”

“当然是，”他说，“一个城邦越是优秀——越是近乎完全的不正义——它就越会完全地那样做。”

“我明白了，这是你的立场，”我说道，“但我所做的就是探究问题的一个方面，并询问一下，一个比另一城邦更强大的城邦，如果没有正义，其强力是否还能保持得住，或者说，是不是只有在其有正义的情况下才能保持得住其强力。”

他回答说：“如果你刚才的说法是正确的，正义就是知识，那 c
就要正义；但如果我是对的，那就要不正义。”

“塞拉西马库斯，”我说，“我非常高兴，你不仅点头、摇头，还做了这些很好的回答。”

“我这样做是为了让你开心。”他说。

“谢谢你。如果你回答我的这个问题的话，那就还会让我高兴的。一个城邦或一支军队或一群盗贼，或其他为了做坏事的团体，如果团体内的成员相互作恶，你认为他们会做成什么事吗？”

“当然不会。”他说。 d

“但如果他们不相互作恶，那么他们是否就有更大的成功可能了呢？”

“是的。”

'Because immorality makes for mutual conflict, hatred, and antagonism, while moral behaviour makes for concord and friendship. Is that right?'

'I'll grant you that: I don't want to quarrel with you,' he said.

'Thank you, Thrasymachus. Now here's another question for
e you. If it's a function of immorality to generat hatred in its train, then whenever it arises among people—people from any walk of life—won't it make them hate one another and clash ewith one another and be incapable of doing things together?'

'Yes.'

'What about when it arises between two people? Won't it make them quarrel with and feel hatred and hostility towards not only each other but also moral people?'

'It will.'

'And, Thrasymachus, if immorality arises within a single person, it won't lose its power, surely, will it? Won't it retain it in an undiminished form?'

'I dare say it does,' he said.

'Evidently, then, its power is twofold. First, its occurrence makes things incapable of co-ordinated action, because of their inter-
352a nal conflict and dissension; second, as well as generating internal hostility, it generates hostility between them and anything which is completely different from them—that is, anything which is moral. And this is the case whether it arises in a community, a family, an army, or anything else. Isn't this right?'

'Yes.'

'And when it arises within a single individual, it will, I suppose, produce exactly the same results—the results it is inherently bound to have. First, it will make him incapable of action, because of internal dissension and discord ; second , as well as generating in

“因为不正义造成了相互冲突、仇恨和对抗，而正义的行为有助于和谐和友谊。是那样吗？”

“我承认你的说法：我不想和你争吵。”他说。

“谢谢你，塞拉西马库斯。现在还有个问题要问你。如果不正义的一个作用就是到处制造仇恨，那么当它在人们当中——无论在哪个阶层的人当中——产生时，它不就会使他们相互仇恨、相互冲突而不能一起行动了吗？” e

“是的。”

“那么当它在两个人之间产生的时候又如何呢？它不就会使他们发生争吵，仇恨，相互怀有敌意，不光是在他们之间，而且对正义之人也会这样吗？”

“会这样。”

“那么，塞拉西马库斯，如果不正义在一个人身上产生，它不会丧失掉它的力量，肯定不会，对不对？它还会以一种毫无减少的形式保持下来，不是吗？”

“我敢说它会保留下来。”他说。

“那么，它的力量显然是双重的。首先，它的出现会使事情由于冲突和争端而不能相互协调；其次，在产生内部敌对的同时，还 352a
造成它们与那些完全不同的事情的敌对——也就是和任何正义的事物敌对。无论不正义出现于城邦、家庭、军队还是其他地方，情况都是这样。这不对吗？”

“对的。”

“那么当不正义在单个人身上产生的时候，我想不正义会产生完全一样的效果——这些效果是必定会产生的。首先，它会使人由于内在的争端和不和谐而不能行动；其次，在产生内在的敌

ternal hostility, it will generate hostility between him and moral people. Right?'

'Yes.'

'Now, my friend, aren't the gods moral beings?'

'I dare say,'

b 'Therefore, an immoral person will be an enemy of the gods, Thrasymachus, and a moral person will be in their favour.'

'That's right, indulge yourself,' he said. 'And don't worry: I won't contradict what you're saying. I mean, I don't want to fall out with our friends here.'

'All right, then,' I went on. 'You'll treat me to all the food I still need to be satisfied, if you continue to answer my questions as you have been just now. I mean, we've found that moral people are more expert at getting things done, are better at it, and are more capable of it, and that immoral people are not capable of acting together at all. Moreover, if we ever claim that immoral people have been effective and have performed
c some concerted action together, then we are not telling the whole truth, because if they were absolutely immoral, they'd have been at one another's throats; there was obviously a degree of morality in them, which enabled them to refrain from wronging one another as well as their victims and which allowed them to do what they did. Immorality had only half perverted them when they embarked upon their misdeeds, since people who are rotten through and through and are perfectly immoral are perfectly incapable of doing anything either. I now see that all this is correct, and that your original
d position was quite wrong.'

'However, we must also look into the postponed issue of whether moral people have a better and a more fulfilled life than immoral people. I must say that at the moment it does look to me as though they do, on the basis of what we've been saying. All the same, we must look more closely at the matter, since what is at stake is far from insignificant: it is how one should live one's life.'

'Go ahead with your investigation, then,' he said.

'All right,' I said. 'Tell me, please: do you think that a horse has a function?'

对的同时,它还会使他产生与正义之人的敌对。是这样的吗?"

"是的。"

"那么,我的朋友,诸神不是正义者吗?"

"我敢说是的。"

"所以,塞拉西马库斯,不正义的人是诸神的敌人,而正义之 b
人则受诸神的喜爱。"

"好吧,随你怎么说,"他说,"别担心:我不会反驳你说的。我的意思是,我不想和这里的朋友闹翻。"

"那么好吧,"我继续说,"如果你继续还像刚才那样回答我的问题,那么你将会为我提供所有我需得以满足的食物。我的意思是说,我们已经发现正义之人在做事情上更加内行,更加擅长并且更加能干,而不正义之人根本不能进行合作。此外,如果我们
说不正义之人有所成效并完成了某些共同的协作,那么我们也没 c
有完全说得真切,因为要是他们是绝对不正义的话,他们就早已相互残杀了;在他们之中显然有一定程度的正义,使得他们在加害敌人时避免相互作恶,从而让他们完成他们所做的事。当他们实施罪行时,不正义只是部分地败坏了他们,因为彻头彻尾堕落之人以及完全不义者,随便哪一个都做不成任何事情。我现在知道了所有这些都是正确的,而你原来的观点是完全错误的。"

"然而,我们还必须来考察一下这个被拖延的话题,正义之人的生活是否就比不正义之人的生活更加幸福美好。根据我们已经说过的话,我要说现在事情是显而易见的。同样,我们必须仍然对之加以仔细的考察,因为恐怕这个问题远非不重要:这就是人们应该如何生活。"

"那么,就开始你的探讨吧。"他说。

"好吧,"我说,"请告诉我:你认为马有功用吗?"

e ‘Yes.’

‘And would you say that a horse’s function, or anything else’s function, is what can be done only with that thing, or can be done best only with that thing?’

‘I don’t understand,’ he said.

‘Look at it this way: can you see with anything except eyes?’

‘Of course not.’

‘And can you hear with anything except ears?’

‘No.’

‘Would it be right, then, for us to say that these are their functions?’

‘Yes.’

353a ‘Now, you could cut a vine-twig with a shortsword or a cobbler’s knife or plenty of other things, couldn’t you?’

‘Of course.’

‘But I should think that the best tool for the job would be a pruning-knife, the kind made especially for this purpose.’

‘True.’

‘Shall we say that this is its function, then?’

‘Yes.’

‘No doubt you can now see the point of the question I asked a moment ago, whether the function of anything is what it alone can do, or what it can do better than anything else.’

b ‘Yes, I can,’ he said. ‘And I agree that this is anything’s function.’

‘All right,’ I said. ‘Now, don’t you think that anything which has been endowed with a function also has a state of being good? Let’s go back to the same examples. We’re saying that eyes have a function?’

‘Yes.’

“有的。” e

“那么马的作用或其他任何东西的作用，就是指只能用它才行，或是指用它能做得最好，你会这么说吗？”

“我不理解。”他说。

“那就这样来考虑：除了用眼睛看，你还能用什么看呢？”

“当然不能。”

“那么除了用耳朵听，你还能用什么听呢？”

“没有。”

“那么我们说这些是它们的功能，对吗？”

“是的。”

“那么，你可以用匕首、凿子或种种其他东西来修剪葡萄藤， 353a
不是吗？”

“当然。”

“但我认为干这个活的最好的工具是修枝刀，它是专门为此制造的。”

“对的。”

“那么，我们会说修剪葡萄就是修枝刀的功能吗？”

“是的。”

“毫无疑问，现在你能理解我刚才所问的意思了吧，即任何事物的功能，是否就是指只有用它才行，或是指用它能比用别的东西更好。”

“是的，我能（理解），”他说，“我同意这就是一件事物的功能。” b

“那好，”我说，“现在你难道不认为，被赋予功用的事物也就有了一种品质吗？让我们回到原先的例子吧。我们说眼睛有一种功能，是吗？”

“是的。”

'And do eyes also have a state of being good?'

'Yes, that too.'

'And do ears have a function?'

'Yes.'

'And a state of being good as well?'

'Yes, that too.'

'And does the same go for everything else?'

'Yes.'

c 'Now then, could eyes do a good job if they weren't in their own special good state, but were instead in a bad state?'

'Of course not,' he replied. 'I suppose you mean if they were blind instead of capable of seeing.'

'I mean whatever their good state is,' I said. 'You've answered a question I haven't yet asked. At the moment I'm asking only whether it is thanks to its own special state of goodness that anything with a job to do performs its function well, and thanks to badness that it does its job badly.'

'Well, that's true,' he said.

'And in the absence of their goodness, will ears do their job badly?'

'Yes.'

'And so on, on the same principle, for everything else?'

d 'I think so.'

'All right, now here's the next point to think about. Does the mind have a function—something you couldn't do with anything else? Consider, for instance, management, the exercise of authority, planning, and so on: would it be right for us to ascribe them to anything except the mind or to say that they were the particular province of anything except the mind?'

'No.

'And what about one's way of life? Won't we say that this is a

"眼睛也有一种品质吗?"

"是的,也有。"

"耳朵有一种功能吗?"

"是的。"

"品质也有吗?"

"是的,也有。"

"对所有其他事物也一样吗?"

"是的。"

"如果眼睛不具有它们特定的品质而是损坏了,那么它们还能正常使用吗?" c

"当然不能,"他回答道,"我想你的意思是它们瞎了看不见东西了。"

"我说的是它们的任何品质,"我说,"你已经回答了一个我还没问的问题。现在我只是问,是否由于其自身特定的品质,事物才很好地发挥了它的功能,而由于缺陷,事物则发挥不了它的功能。"

"哦,说得对。"他说。

"缺乏了耳朵的品质,就发挥不了它们的功能吗?"

"是的。"

"同样的道理,对于其他任何事物也是一样吗?" d

"我想是的。"

"好吧,现在接下来考虑这个问题:心智有你不可用其他东西代替的功能吗?考虑一下,比如说,管理、统治、计划等等:除了心智,我们还能把它们归于其他东西吗,或者,除了心智外还能说它们是其他东西的专门功能吗?"

"不能。"

"那么一个人的生活方式怎样呢?难道我们不能说这就是心

function of the mind?'

'Absolutely,' he said.

'And do we also think that the mind has a good state?'

'Yes.'

e 'Will the mind, then, Thrasymachus, ever perform its functions well in the absence of its own special goodness? Or is that impossible?'

'Yes, it's impossible.'

'Therefore, management and authority will inevitably be handled badly by a bad mind, whereas a good mind will do all these things well.'

'Inevitably.'

'Now, we agreed that morality is a good mental state, and that immorality is a bad state.'

'We did.'

'So a moral mind and a moral person will live a good life, and an immoral person will live a bad life.'

'Apparently,' he said, 'on your line of reasoning.'

'Now, anyone who lives a good life is happy and fulfilled, and anyone who doesn't is the opposite.'

'Of course.'

354a 'Therefore, a moral person is happy, whereas an immoral person is unhappy.'

'I dare say,' he said.

'Now, no one is well off because they're unhappy, but because they're happy.'

'Of course.'

'Therefore, my dear Thrasymachus, immorality is never more rewarding than morality.'

智的功能吗?”

“肯定能。”他说。

“我们也认为心智有其品质吗?”

“是的。”

“那么,塞拉西马库斯,心智没有了它自身的特别的品质还会 e
很好地发挥功能吗? 或者说那是不可能的?”

“是的,这不可能。”

“所以,管理或统治必然被一个邪恶的心智弄糟,而一个善良的心智会把所有这些事情处理得很好。”

“必然这样。”

“现在我们承认,正义就是一种善的精神状态,而不正义则是一种恶的精神状态。”

“我们承认。”

“所以,一个正义的精神和一个正义的人会过一种善的生活,而一个不正义的人则会过一种恶的生活。”

“很显然是这样,”他说,“按照你的推论。”

“那么,生活得好的人就是快乐充实的,而生活得不好的人则相反。”

“当然。”

“所以,正义之人是快乐的,而不正义之人是不快乐的。” 354a

“我敢这么说。”他说。

“那么,人们之所以百事安顺,不是因为其不快乐,而是因为其快乐。”

“当然。”

“所以,我亲爱的塞拉西马库斯,不正义绝不比正义更有益。”

'There's your treat, Socrates,' he said, 'for this festival of Bendis.'

'And the meal was provided by you, Thrasymachuso,' I said,
b since you were kind to me and stopped being cross. I've not had a proper meal, however—but that's my fault, not yours, l think I've behaved like those gluttons who can't wait to taste every dish that's served up, before they've given themselves a proper chance to enjoy the previous one. l gave up before we discovered what we set out to discover—the nature of morality—and I embarked instead on an investigation into whether it was a bad state and ignorance, or whether it was knowledge and a good state; then later, when the idea cropped up that immorality was more profitable than morality, I couldn't resist turning to that next. Consequently, the effect of our discussion on me has been ignorance. I mean, if I don't know what morality actually
c is, it's going to be difficult for me to know whether or not it is good, and whether its possession makes someone unhappy or happy.'

“有对你的招待，苏格拉底，“他说道，”为了这次的本迪斯节日。”

“那么膳食是你准备的了，塞拉西马库斯，”我说道。“因为你对我很好，也不再对我发火了。然而我并没有吃好——但那是我的过错，不是你的错。我想我像那些贪吃者一样，还没细细品尝 b
前一道菜就等不及地尝遍端上来的所有菜。在发现我们一开始想要发现的东西——正义的本性——之前我就放弃了，改而开始探讨正义是否是邪恶和无知，是否是知识和善良；之后又出现了不正义比正义更有益的说法，我就禁不住转到这个问题上了。由此，对我来说，讨论的结果是一无所知，我的意思是说，如果我不知道正义究竟是什么，那么，要知道它是否是善的，以及拥有它是 c
否让人不快乐或快乐，这对我来说将是困难的。”

CHAPTER 2

357a At this point, I thought I'd be exempt from further talking, but apparently that was only the preamble. You see, it's not in Glaucon's nature to cut and run from anything, and on this occasion he refused to accept Thrasymachus' capitulation, but said, 'Socrates, do you
b want us *really* to be convinced that in all circumstances morality is better than immorality or merely to pretend to be?'

'If it were up to me,' I replied, 'I'd prefer your conviction to be genuine.'

'Well,' he remarked, 'your behaviour is at odds with your wishes, then. I mean, here's a question for you. Don't you describe as good something which is welcomed for its own sake, rather than because its consequences are desired? Enjoyment, for instance, and all those pleasures which are harmless and whose future consequences are only enjoyable?'

'Yes,' I agreed, 'good seems to me the right description for that situation.'

'And what about things which are welcome not just for their own sakes, but also for their consequences? Intelligence, sight, and health, for instance, are evidently welcomed for both reasons.'

'Yes,' I said.

c 'And isn't there, in your experience,' he asked, 'a third category of good things—the category in which we find exercise, medical treatment, and any moneymaking job like being a doctor? All these things are regarded as nuisances, but beneficial, and are not welcomed for their
d own sakes, but for their financial rewards and other consequences.'

第二章

到这时候，我还以为我可以不用再谈论了，但那显然才只是 357a
一个开场白呢。你看，向任何事情退却不是格劳孔的性格，于是
在这样的场合，他拒绝接受塞拉西马库斯的投降，而是说："苏格
拉底，在任何情况下正义都比不正义要好，你希望我们真的被说
服了，还是仅仅装作被说服了？" b

"如果我能胜任的话，"我回答道，"我宁愿你们是真的被说服了。"

"唔，"他评论说，"那么，你的行为可是和你的愿望不一致呢。我的意思是，这儿有个问题想请教你。你描述的善事，之所以为人乐意接受，是因为其自身的原因，而不是因为渴慕其结果，不是这样吗？例如快乐，以及所有那些愉悦、满足等，都是不会造成伤害的，其以后的结果也只有愉快与享受，难道不是这样吗？"

"是的，"我同意说，"在我看来，善就是描述那种情形的。"

"那么，是否有那样一些东西，我们喜爱它们，不仅仅是出于 c
它们自身，也是出于它们的后果？比如，才智、视力和健康，就显
然由于两种原因而受人喜爱的。"

"是的。"我说。

"那么，根据你的经验，"他问道："就没有第三种善的事情吗？在
这其中，我们发现有像医生那样的运动、医疗和任何的赚钱工作呢。
所有这些事情都被认为是麻烦的，但又是有益的，它们不是因为其自
身而为人所喜爱，而是因为它们带来的经济上的回报和其他结果。" d

'Yes,' I agreed, 'there is this third category as well. What of it?'

'To which category do you think morality belongs?' he asked.

358a 'In my opinion,' I replied, 'it belongs in the best category—the category which anyone who expects to be happy should welcome both for its own sake and for its consequences.'

'That's not the usual view,' he said, 'which consigns morality to the nuisance category of things which have to be done for the sake of financial reward and for the prospect of making a good impression, but which, taken in isolation, are so trying that one should avoid them.'

'I'm aware of this view,' I said, 'and it's the reason why Thrasymachus has been running morality down all this time, and praising immorality. But I'm slow on the uptake, apparently.'

'All right, then,' he said, 'listen to what I have to say too,
b and see if you agree with me. The point is that Thrasymachus gave up too soon, in my opinion: you charmed him into docility as if he were a snake. The arguments that have been offered about both morality and immorality leave *me* unsatisfied, however, in the sense that I still want to hear a definition of them both, and to be told what the effect is of the occurrence of each of them in the mind—each of them in isolation, without taking into consideration financial reward or any other consequence they might have.

'So if it's all right with you, what I'll do is revive Thrasyma-
c chus' position. First, I'll explain the usual view of the nature and origin of morality; second, I'll claim that it is only ever practised reluctantly, as something necessary, but not good; third, I'll claim that this behaviour is reasonable, because people are right to think that an immoral person's life is much better than a moral person's life.

'Now, I don't agree with any of this, Socrates, but I don't know what to think. My ears are ringing from listening to Thrasymachus and

“是的，”我同意说，“是还有第三种。它是什么？”

“你认为正义属于哪一种？”他问道。

“在我看来，”我回答说，“它属于最好的一种，任何期望得到快乐 358a
的人，都应该既因为它自身原因，又因为它带来的结果而欣然接受它。”

“那可不是通常的观点，”他说道，“通常的观点是把正义划归为令人讨厌的那一类事情的范畴之中，对这类事情，人们是因为经济上的回报以及有获得好名声的期望，才不得不去做的，但是孤立隔绝地来看正义，那真是太费劲、太令人难受了，因而人们会尽量远离它们。”

“我了解这种观点，”我说，“那就是为什么塞拉西马库斯总是贬低正义、颂扬不正义的原因。但我显然有点愚钝，学不了他。”

“那么好吧，”他说，“也听听我说的吧，看是否你同意我的说 b
法。依我看，关键是塞拉西马库斯认输太早：你好像对他使用了符咒，使他顺从得像一条蛇一样。但是，已经提出的关于正义与不正义的论点，是不能令我满意的，在理智上，我仍希望听一听有关二者的定义，并希望能被告知，它们中的每一种，当在心灵中发生或出现的时候，其作用或效果是什么——所谓‘它们中的每一种’，是在孤立隔绝意义上而言的，不要考虑其经济上的回报，或它们可能带来的其它任何结果。

“所以如果你同意的话，那么我会重申一下塞拉西马库斯的
观点。首先，我会解释正义的本性与起源的一般看法；其次，我会 c
说，人们只是把正义当做必要之物才不情愿地实行，而非把它当作善；第三，我会说这种做法是有道理的，因为人们有理由认为不正义之人的生活比正义之人的生活要好得多。

“苏格拉底，现在我不同意这些说法，但我不知道如何思考。我的耳朵塞满了塞拉西马库斯和无数其他人的说法，但还没有听

countless others, but I've never yet heard the kind of support for morality, as being preferable to immorality, that I'd like to hear, which is a hymn to the virtues it possesses in and of itself. If I can get this from anyone, it'll be you, I think. That is, why I'll speak at some length in praise of the immoral life; by doing so, I'll be showing you the kind of rejoinder I want you to develop when you criticize immorality and commend morality. What do you think of this plan?'

'I thoroughly approve,' I replied. 'I mean, I can't think of another topic which any thinking person would more gladly see cropping up again and again in his conversations.'

e 'That's wonderful,' he said. 'Well, I promised I'd talk first a-
bout the nature and origin of morality, so here goes. The idea is that
although it's a fact of nature that doing wrong is good and having
wrong done to one is bad, nevertheless the disadvantages of having it
done to one outweigh the benefits of doing it. Consequently, once
people have experienced both committing wrong and being at the re-
ceiving end of it, they see that the disadvantages are unavoidable and
359a the benefits are unattainable; so they decide that the most profitable
course is for them to enter into a contract with one another, guaran-
teeing that no wrong will be committed or received. They then set a-
bout making laws and decrees, and from then on they use the terms
"legal" and "right" to describe anything which is enjoined by their
code. So that's the origin and nature of morality, on this view: it is a
compromise between the ideal of doing wrong without having to pay for
it, and the worst situation, which is having wrong done to one while
lacking the means of exacting compensation. Since morality is a com-
promise, it is endorsed because, while it may not be good, it does
b gain value by preventing people from doing wrong. The point is that
any real man with the ability to do wrong would never enter into a
contract to avoid both wronging and being wronged: he wouldn't be so
crazy. Anyway, Socrates, that is what this view has to say about the
nature and origin of morality and so on.

'As for the fact that morality is only ever practised reluctantly,
by people who lack the ability to do wrong—this would become partic-
c ularly obvious if we performed the following thought-experiment. Sup

到我所愿听的那种认为正义比不正义更可取的赞成之声,它是称扬正义自身的及其所具有的诸优点的赞美诗。如果我能从谁那里听 d
到的话,那我想就是从你这里了。这就是为什么我尽力赞美不正义的生活的原因;我这样做是为了向你提供一种批驳的靶子,想让你在批评不正义和颂扬正义的时候对此加以发挥。你同意这个打算吗?"

"我完全同意,"我回答说,"我的意思是说,我再也想不出还有什么其他论题,能使得任何善于思想的人乐于一遍一遍地看到它在其对话中出现了。"

"那太好了,"他说,"好吧,我首先要来说正义的本性和起源, e
那现在就开始吧。这种观点是,作恶便是善,遭受作恶便是恶,尽管自然的事实便是如此,但是对于一个个体而言,受恶的损害超过作恶的得益。因此,一旦人们既作过恶,又承受过恶果,他们就会明白,遭受作恶的损害是不可避免的,而作恶的利益是难以获得
的;所以他们觉得对他们最有利的就是相互订立契约,确保既不作恶, 359a
也不遭受作恶。随后他们就开始制定法律和律令,从那时起,人们用'合法'、'正义'来描述守法的行为。所以那就是正义的起源和本性,由此看来:它是在作恶而不用为此付出代价的想法,和受到了损害而得不到赔偿的最坏情形,这两者之间的折中。因为正义是一种折中,所以大家表示赞同并不是因为它好,而是因为它能防止人们因作恶而
获利。问题是任何真正有能力作恶的人,是决不会订立契约,来防止 b
作恶并避免遭受作恶的:他不会那么愚蠢。苏格拉底,无论怎样吧,这就是我要说的关于正义本性和起源等等的观点。

"至于这样一种事实:即从来都只是那些没有能力去作恶的人,才会勉勉强强地实行正义,如果我们进行以下的思想试验,那
么这一点就会变得尤其明显。假如我们给正义和不正义两种人 c

pose we grant both types of people—moral and immoral—the scope to do whatever they want, and we then keep an eye on them to see where their wishes lead them. We'll catch our moral person red-handed: his desire for superiority will point him in the same direction as the immoral person, towards a destination which every creature naturally regards as good and aims for, except that people are compelled by convention to deviate from this path and respect equality.

'They'd have the scope I'm talking about especially if they acquired the kind of power which, we hear, an ancestor of Gyges of
d Lydia once acquired. He was a shepherd in the service of the Lydian ruler of the time, when a heavy rainstorm occurred and an earthquake cracked open the land to a certain extent, and a chasm appeared in the region where he was pasturing his flocks. He was fascinated by the sight, and went down into the chasm and saw there, as the story goes, among other artefacts, a bronze horse, which was hollow and had windows set in it; he stooped and looked in through the windows and saw a corpse inside, which seemed to be that of a giant. The corpse was naked, but had a golden ring on one finger; he took the
e ring off the finger and left. Now, the shepherds used to meet once a month to keep the king informed about his flocks, and our protagonist came to the meeting wearing the ring. He was sitting down among the others, and happened to twist the ring's bezel in the direction of his body, towards the inner part of his hand. When he did this, he be-
360a came invisible to his neighbours, and to his astonishment they talked about him as if he'd left. While he was fiddling about with the ring again, he turned the bezel outwards, and became visible. He thought about this and experimented to see if it was the ring which had this power; in this way he eventually found that turning the bezel inwards made him invisible and turning it outwards made him visible. As soon as he realized this, he arranged to be one of the delegates to the king; once
b he was inside the palace, he seduced the king's wife and with her help assaulted and killed the king, and so took possession of the throne.

'Suppose there were two such rings, then—one worn by our moral person, the other by the immoral person. There is no one, on this view,

为所欲为的机会，然后我们观察他们的欲望会把他们引向何方。我们就会发现，我们的正义之人正在犯罪：他对于成为优越者的渴慕会将其引向如同不义之人一样的方向，引向一个共同的目标，那是每一个动物本能地认作有价值的、并一直企图实现的目标，除非人们为习俗与惯例所强迫，而从这条道路上走开，才会考虑到人人平等的问题。

"我所说的尤其是指他们能得到那样的机会，即我们听到过
的吕底亚人吉格斯的祖先曾得到过的那种。他是当时吕底亚王 d
手下的牧羊人。有一次，一场巨大的暴风雨突然来临，地震使大
地裂开，在他放羊的地方，大地出现了一道裂口。他为这一景象
迷住了，便下到裂缝里察看，就像故事所说的，他在众多的东西当
中看到了一匹空心并且身上有窗户的铜马；他弯下身，从窗户里
看进去，看到里面有具尸体，看起来像个巨人。这具尸体除了在
指头上有一枚金戒指外什么都没有；他取下了戒指就离开了。当 e
时牧羊人总是每月聚会一次并向国王报告羊群的情况，我们的主
人公也戴着戒指来参加聚会。他坐在他们中间时无意中把对着
他身体的宝石往手心侧转了一下。这时，邻座的人就看不见他
了，并且让他惊异的是，他们谈论他时，就以为他已经离开了。当 360a
他再次拨弄戒指，把宝石向外转时，就变得可见了。他想试试，看
看这枚戒指是否有这种力量；以此方式，他最终发现把宝石向内
转就会使他不可见，把宝石向外转就会使他可见。他一认识到这
点，就设法让自己成为国王的使者；一进入王宫，他就勾引王后， b
在她的协助下袭杀了国王，篡夺了王位。

"假设有两枚这样的戒指，一枚给正义之人戴着，另一枚给不正义之人戴着。在这种情况下，没有人能有足够坚强的意志保持

who is iron-willed enough to maintain his morality and find the
strength of purpose to keep his hands off what doesn't belong to him,
when he is able to take whatever he wants from the market-stalls with-
out fear of being disccovered, to enter houses and sleep with whomever
c he chooses, to kill and to release from prison anyone he wants, and gen-
erally to act like a god among men. His behaviour would be identical to
that of the other person: both of them would be heading in the same di-
rection.

'Now this is substantial evidence, it would be claimed, that mo-
rality is never freely chosen. People do wrong whenever they think
they can, so they act morally only if they're forced to, because they
regard morality as something which isn't good for one personally. The
d point is that everyone thinks the rewards of immorality far outweigh
those of morality—and they're right, according to the proponent of
this view. The sight of someone with that kind of scope refusing all
those opportunities for wrongdoing and never laying a finger on things
that didn't belong to him would lead people to think that he was in an
extremely bad way, and was a first-class fool as well—even though
their fear of being wronged might make them attempt to mislead others
by singing his praises to them in public.

e 'That's all I have to say on this. As for actually assessing the
lives of the people we're talking about, we'll be able to do that cor-
rectly if we make the gap between a moral person and an immoral per-
son as wide as possible. That's the only way to make a proper assess-
ment. And we should set them apart from each other by leaving their
respective immorality and morality absolutely intact, so that we make
each of them a consummate professional. In other words, our immoral
person must be a true expert. A top-notch ship's captain, for in-
stance, or doctor, recognizes the limits of his branch of expertise and
361a undertakes what is possible while ignoring what is impossible; moreo-
ver, if he makes a mistake, he has the competence to correct it. E-
qually, our immoral-person must get away with any crimes he under-
takes in the proper fashion, if he is to be outstandingly immoral; get-
ting caught must be taken to be a sign of incompetence, since the ac

他的正义,并找出强有力的理由坚持不碰不属于他的东西,如果
他在市场上能拿走任何他想要的东西而不用害怕被发现,也能入
室与他所想要的任何人同睡,杀害或从监狱释放任何他想杀害或 c
释放之人,总之,就像一个人间之神。他的行为会与另一个人一
样:他们两个都朝着同样的方向走。

“现在相当明确的是,人们会说正义不是自由选择的。无论
何时,只要人们认为自己能够,他们就会作恶,所以他们履践正
义,只是因为被迫如此,因为他们把正义当作对个人来说是没什
么益处的东西。关键是所有人都认为不正义的报偿要远远超过
正义的报偿——根据这个观点的支持者的说法,他们是对的。拥 d
有上述那种机会的某人,如果拒绝了所有那些作恶的良机,而绝
不染指不属于他的任何一件东西,那么在世人眼里又如何呢?人们
会把他当成一个倒霉蛋,而且还是一个第一流的大傻瓜——尽管出
于害怕遭受恶作的畏惧会使得他们公开颂扬他,以企图误导他人。

“那就是所有我必须要说的。至于对我们所说的人的生活作
出真正的评判,若是在正义之人和不正义之人之间划一道尽可能 e
大的鸿沟,我们就能作出正确的评断。那是我们作出恰当评判的
唯一方法。我们应该将他们相互分开,而对他们各自的不正义和
正义决不加干涉,那样我们就使他们各自成为完全的自身。换句
话说,我们的不正义之人必须是个真正的专业者。比如说,一个
一流的船长或医生,知道他的专业技艺的限度,承担起可能做得
到的事情,忽视掉不可能做到的事情;此外,如果他犯了错,他有 361a
能力纠正。同样,我们说的那个不正义之人,如果是个一流的不
正义之人的话,那他必定能以恰当的方式逃脱他所犯的罪行;被
抓肯定会被看作无能的标志,因为极度的不正义就是给人以正义

me of immorality is to give an impression of morality while actually
being immoral. So we must attribute consummate immorality to our
consummate criminal, and if we are to leave it intact, we should have
b him equipped with a colossal reputation for morality even though he is
a colossal criminal. He should be capable of correcting any mistakes
he makes. He must have the ability to argue plausibly, in case any of
his crimes are ever found out, and to use force wherever necessary,
by making use of his courage and strength and by drawing on his fund
of friends and his financial resources.

'Now that we've come up with this sketch of an immoral person,
we must conceive of a moral person to stand beside him—someone
who is straightforward and principled, and who, as Aeschylus says,
wants genuine goodness rather than merely an aura of goodness. So we
must deprive him of any such aura, since if others think him moral,
c this reputation will gain him privileges and rewards, and it will be-
come unclear whether it is morality or the rewards and privileges
which might be motivating him to be what he is. We should strip him
of everything except morality, then, and our portrait should be of
someone in the opposite situation to the one we imagined before. I
mean, even though he does no wrong at all, he must have a colossal
reputation for immorality, so that his morality can be tested by seeing
whether or not he is impervious to a bad reputation and its conse-
quences; he must unswervingly follow his path until he dies—a saint
d with a lifelong reputation as a sinner. When they can both go no fur-
ther in morality and immorality respectively, we can decide which of
them is the happier.'

'My dear Glaucon,' I said, 'I'm very impressed at how indus-
triously you're ridding each of them of defects and getting them ready
for assessment. It's as if you were working on statues.'

'I'm doing the best I can,' he replied. 'And now that we've es-
tablished what the two of them are like, I'm sure we won't find it diffi-
cult to specify what sort of life is in store for either of them. That's

的印象，而事实上却是不正义的。所以我们必须把极度的不正义给予我们最极端的罪犯，并且如果我们不加干涉，我们应该让他拥有巨大的正义的名声，虽然他是个大罪犯。他应该能够纠正他 b
所犯的任何错误。万一他的什么犯罪行为最终被人揭发出来，那么他应该有能耐列举理由以证明自己的清白，而且花言巧语，说的头头是道，并在任何必要的情况下利用势力，如利用自己的勇气与意志力，并利用朋友对他的支持，以及他的财力资源等。

“既然我们已经描绘了不正义之人的大致轮廓，我们也必须想出一个正义之人来和他做对比——就像埃斯库罗斯所说的，一个正直的、有原则的并且想要真正的善而非仅仅伪善的人。所以我们必须把任何这类伪善外表从他身上去掉，因为要是别人认为他是正义的，这种名声会给他带来特权和回报，这就会让人搞不 c
清是正义还是那些回报和特权驱使他成为他这样。那么我们应该从他身上去掉除正义之外的一切，然后我们应该把他刻画成这样一个人，他处于与我们先前所想象的完全相反的处境中。我的意思是，虽然他完全没有做过什么恶事，他也必须背上巨大的不正义的名声，这样，他的正义就能通过看他是否不为坏名声及其后果所动而得到考察，他必须义无返顾地走他的道路，直到死为止——一个一生都背着罪名的圣者。当他们两人都分别无法再更 d
加正义或不正义的时候，我们就能确定他们中的哪一个是幸福的。”

“我亲爱的格劳孔啊，”我说，“我对你怎样勤勉地为他们各自去除缺点和对他们评判所做的准备印象很深。那就好像你在雕刻一尊塑像一样。”

“我尽力而为，”他回答说，“现在我们已经树立了他们两种人的形象，我确信我们说出他们各自所过的是什么样的生活就不难

e what I must do, then—and if my words are rather coarse, Socrates, please remember that the argument is not mine, but stems from those who prefer immorality to morality.

'Here's what they'll say: for a moral person in the situation I've described, the future holds flogging, torture on the rack, imprisonment in chains, having his eyes burnt out, and every ordeal in the
362a book, up to and including being impaled on a stake. Then at last he'll realize that one's goal should be not actual morality, but the appearance of morality. In fact, that phrase of Aeschylus' has far more relevance for an immoral person, in the sense that, as they will claim, it is really an immoral person who wants genuine immorality rather than merely an aura of immorality, because his occupation takes account of the way things are and his life is not concerned with appearances. He
b is the one who "reaps the harvest of wise plans which grow in his mind's deep furrow" —and what he plans is first to use his reputation for morality to gain control over his country, and then to marry a woman from any family he wants, to have his children marry whomever he wants, to deal and do business with whomever he wants, and, over and above all this, to secure his own benefit by ensuring that his lack of distaste for crime makes him a financial profit. If he's challenged privately or publicly, he wins the day and comes off better
c than his enemies; because he gains the upper hand, he gets rich; he therefore does good to his friends and harm to his enemies, and the religious rites he performs and the offerings he makes to the gods are not just adequate but magnificent; his service to the gods and to the men he favours is far better than a moral person's; and consequently it is more appropriate for the gods to smile on him rather than on a moral person, and more likely that they will. And this, Socrates, is why both gods and men provide a better life for an immoral person than for a moral person, according to this view.'

了。那就是我必须做的——苏格拉底,要是我的话说得太粗了, e
就请你记住那个论证不是我的,而是来自于那些认为不正义比正义要好的人。

“这就是他们会说的:对于处在我已描述过的处境下的正义之人来说,等待他的将是鞭打、刑具上的折磨、枷锁下的囚禁、眼
睛被烙瞎,以及每一项见诸书册的严酷考验,直到包括被钉上火 362a
刑柱的惩罚。那么他最终会认识到,一个人的目标不应该是真正的正义,而是正义的外表。实际上,对于一个不义之人而言,埃斯库罗斯的说法倒是再中肯不过了,在某种意义上,就像他们会主张的,正是一个真正的不义之人,需要真正的不正义,而不仅仅是一个不正义的光环,因为他的职业要考虑的便是如何将此厚黑之道发扬光大,而且他的生活也不需要顾忌什么外在形象。他是一个‘城府很深、心机很重的人,在其心地中生长的是老谋深算,从
这儿收获的是精明的主意’——他的计划便是,首先利用其正义 b
之令誉,而获致其国家操控之权,然后与任何来自他所想要的家族中的女子结婚,让子女与任何他看中的家族联姻,与任何他所愿意的人打交道、做买卖,除了所有这些之外,通过确保自己丧尽天良,他便可大发其财,从而保证了自己的利益。要是他私下或是公开地受到挑衅,他(总会)获胜并且要占对手的便宜;因为他占了上风,所以就变得富有;因此他施惠于他的朋友,加害于他的
敌人,他所做的宗教祭献仪式和向诸神所奉的牺牲就不只是充足 c
了,而是丰盛;他给诸神以及给其喜爱之人提供的服务,也远远比一个正义之人所能提供的丰厚;因此,他也比一个正义之人更能让诸神有理由并乐意青睐他。这样看来,这就是为什么无论是诸神还是凡人都对不正义之人提供了一种比正义之人更优越之生活的理由。”

d After Glaucon's speech, l was intending to make some reply to what he'd been saying, but his brother Adeimantus asked, 'Surely you don't consider that an adequate treatment of the issue, do you, Socrates?'

'Why shouldn't I?' I said.

'It's precisely the most important point which has been omitted,' he said.

'Well,' I said, 'as the saying goes, a man and his brother should stick together. So if Glaucon here has left anything out, you should back him up. As far as I'm concerned, however, even what he's already said is enough to floor me and make me a totally ineffective ally of morality.'

e 'Rubbish,' he said. 'But don't let that stop you listening to what I have to say as well. In order to clarify Glaucon's meaning, we also have to go into the arguments for the opposite of his point—the arguments in favour of morality and against immorality. As you know, fathers point out to their sons the importance of morality and impress it upon them (as every guardian impresses it upon his ward) by singing
363a the praises not of morality itself but of the good reputation it brings. The inducement they offer is that power, good marriage, and all the things Glaucon mentioned a moment ago come to someone who is thought to be moral as a result of this reputation: if a moral person gets them, it is because he is well thought of.

'They have more to say about the consequences of reputation. They adduce being well thought of by the gods, and then they have benefits galore to talk of, all the ones the gods are said to award to just people. There are, for instance, the statements of noble Hesiod and of Homer. Hesiod says that the gods make "oaks bear acorns on
b their outsides and bees in their centres" for moral people; and he says that "their woolly sheep are weighed down by their fleeces", and that they gain many other advantages. Homer makes very similar claims: "As of some righteous king," he says, "who pleases the gods by upholding justice, and the dark earth bears wheat and barley, the trees hang heavy with fruit, the sheep steadily give birth, and the

在格劳孔发言之后，我正想对他所说的话作一些回应，但他 d
的兄弟阿狄曼图问道："苏格拉底，你一定不会认为对这个问题做
了充分讨论，是吗？"

"为什么我不会？"我说。

"正是最重要的一点被遗漏掉了。"他说。

"好吧，"我说，"俗话说，兄弟同心。所以如果格劳孔在这里
有什么遗漏的，你应该给他补上。然而，就我而言，他所说的话已
足以难住我，使我完全不能成为正义的支持论者。"

"都是些胡言乱语罢了，"他说，"但不要让那些话阻碍了你听 e
我也要说的话。为了澄清格劳孔的意思，我们也不得不考察与他
的观点相反的那些论证——这些论证赞成正义并且反对不正义。
就如你所知道的，父亲为儿子指出正义的重要性，并使他们牢记
它（就像监护人叮嘱受监护人一样），但不是通过对正义自身高唱 363a
赞歌，而是赞扬正义所带来的好名声。它们所带来的激励就是权
力、好的婚姻，以及不久前格劳孔所提到的所有那些东西，这些就
是那被认为是正义之人由于他们的正义之名所得到的东西：如果
正义之人得到了它们，那是因为他的好名声。

"他们对于名声所带来的后果还有更多的话要说。他们引证
了诸神带来的好名声，他们还谈了很多好处，还说所有那些诸神
赐予的好处都是给正义之人的。比如，高贵的赫西俄德和荷马就
有这样的说法。赫西俄德说，诸神为了正义之人而使'橡树开花
结果，蜜蜂在其中采蜜'；他说：'绵羊身上长着厚厚的羊毛，'人们 b
得了许多的好处，荷马做了非常类似的表述：'如同一位有德的国
王，'他说，'他执法公允，黝黑的土地载承小麦与大麦，树木垂
挂累累硕果，羊群不断繁衍，大海产出鱼群，以这些而使诸神

c sea-waters yield fish."

'Musaeus and his son claim that the gods give moral people even more exciting advantages. Once they've transported them, in their account, to Hades and got them reclining on couches for the party they've laid on for just people, they next have them spending eternity wearing chaplets on their heads and drinking, on the assumption that
d the best possible reward for goodness is perpetual intoxication. Others have the gods' rewards for morality lasting even longer: they say that the legacy left behind by a person who is just and keeps his promises is that his children's children are better people.

'These, and others like them, are the glowing terms in which they speak of morality. As for unjust and immoral people, they bury them in Hades in a kind of mud and force them to carry water in sieves, and they make sure that while they remain alive they are thought badly of; and they claim that all the punishments which Glaucon specified for people who, despite being moral, are thought to be immoral are destined for immoral people. They have no novel punishments to add to this list, however.

'Anyway, that's how morality is commended and immorality condemned. But there's also another point for you to take into consideration, Socrates. It's the sort of thing ordinary people say to one another
364a about morality and immorality, but it occurs in the poets as well. They all unanimously go on and on about how self-discipline and morality may be commendable, but are also difficult and troublesome, whereas self-indulgence and immorality are enjoyable and easily gained, and it's only in people's minds and in convention that they are contemptible. They also say that, on the whole, immorality is more rewarding than morality; and whereas they're perfectly ready to admire bad men, if they're affluent and powerful in other respects as well, and to award them political office and personal prestige , they have disrespect and

高兴。'〔1〕 c

"穆塞乌斯和他的儿子宣称诸神甚至给正义之人更令人兴奋的好处。从前他们在谈话中把正义之人带到冥界,让他们躺着,享受按照他们的说法,一旦诸神将正义之人送至哈德斯之处,他们便会被邀至专门为正义之人聚会而设置的长榻之上,然后他们头戴花冠,手捧酒杯,亦饮亦咏,以消永昼,并假设,对仁慈善良而言,最好的奖赏可能便是永远的陶醉。其他人则认为,诸神对道德的奖赏持续得甚至更为久远:他们说,一个既公正而又恪守然 d
诺的人,其身后的遗泽是,他的子子孙孙蕃衍生息、道德卓越。

"这些,以及其它类似的言辞,便是他们谈及正义时洋溢着热情与欢快的语言。而对于不公正、不正义之人而言,诸神则将他们埋在哈德斯那里的某种泥浆之中,并强迫他们用筛子去打水,而且诸神还保证,这些不义之人还活着的时候已经臭名远扬了;他们宣称,那些格劳孔所说的正义之人因被当作不义之人而所受之惩罚,也注定是给这些不义之人的。不过,他们在这列表中没有加上奇异的惩罚。

"不管怎样,那就是正义者如何得到颂扬、不正义者如何得到谴责的情形。但是,苏格拉底,还有一点是你要考虑的。这种关于正义和不正义话题是一般人相互之间谈论的,但诗人们也谈论。他们都总是众口一词,说自律和正义是如何如何的好,但也 364a
是困难和令人讨厌的,但是自我放纵和不正义却是令人愉快和容易获得的,它们只是在人们的心里和习俗上才是可鄙的。他们还说,总的看来,不正义比正义更有利;如果坏人富有并在其他方面还掌有大权,那么他们完全乐于赞扬坏人,授予他们以官职和个人特

〔1〕《奥德赛》第19卷109~13。

look down on people who are in any way powerless or are poor, even
b while admitting their moral superiority to the others.

'The most astonishing thing of all, however, is what gets said about the gods and goodness—that the gods often assign misfortune and a terrible life to good people, and the opposite to the other type of person. Beggar-priests and soothsayers knock on the doors of wealthy households and try to persuade the owners that (as long as there's some enjoyable feasting involved) the gods have granted them the power to use rituals and spells to expiate any sin committed by a per-
c son or by any of his ancestors, and that if anyone has an enemy he'd like to hurt, then it'll cost hardly anything to injure him—and it makes no difference whether the target is a moral or an immoral person—by means of certain incantations and formulae, since they can persuade the gods, they say, to do their bidding.

'The poets are called on to support all these claims. Some people concede that vice involves nothing arduous, on the grounds that
d "There's no difficulty in choosing vice in abundance: the road is smooth and it's hardly any distance to where it lives. But the gods have put sweat in the way of goodness", and a long, rough, steep road. Others cite Homer in support of the idea that humans can influence the gods, pointing out that he too said, "Even the gods themselves can be moved by entreaty: men appeal to them by means of rites and softly spoken prayers, libations and sacrifices, and influence
e them, when a crime has been committed and a wrong has been done." They come up with a noisy mob of books written by Musaeus and Orpheus (who are descended from the Moon and the Muses, they say), which are source-books for their rituals; and they convince whole countries as well as individuals that there are in fact ways to be free and cleansed of sin. While we remain on earth, this involves rit-
365a uals and enjoyable diversions, which also work for us after we have died and which they call initiations. These initiations, they say, free us from all the terrors of the other world, but ghastly things await any-

权，却看不起在任何方面都没有权力的人或穷人，即使承认他们道德方面超过别的人。 b

“然而最令人震惊的事情是他们对于诸神和善良的说法——诸神常常把不幸和苦难的生活给予善良之人，而把相反的东西给予另一种人。像乞丐一样卑贱可怜的牧师与占卜者们，‘朝扣富儿门，暮随肥马尘’（只要主人能给他们提供一些可大快朵颐的盛宴就行啦），他们努力让主人相信，诸神已经授予他们能力，他们可以用宗教仪式与咒语来消除个人或其所有祖先犯下的任何罪孽，而且如果某人有一个敌人想要损伤之而后快，那么这也费不 c
了什么事——至于要损伤的目标，才不管他是一个正义之人还是一个不义之人呢——而其手段仍旧是某些咒语与仪式，因为按照其说法，他们可以说服诸神按照他们的命令办事。

“他们请来诗人来为所有他们的说法所辩护。有人认为作恶并不困难，因为‘邪恶泛滥，作恶不难：道路平坦，离之亦不远。但 d
诸神在正义之路上挥洒汗水，’并且正义之路是一条漫长、崎岖、艰难的路。其他人则引用荷马支持人能影响诸神的说法，指出他也说过：‘即使诸神也能被哀求所感动：当一桩罪行已经犯下，一件大错已经铸成，人们可以通过宗教仪式、轻声祷告、奠酒祭神、献祭牺牲等手段，向诸神祈求宽恕，并影响他们。’他们拿出一大堆由穆塞乌斯和奥尔菲斯写成的聒噪之辞（他们说，这两个人可 e
是月亮女神和缪斯女神的后裔呢），并将其著作当成他们宗教仪轨的源卷。并且他们不但使一些人，而且使整个城邦都相信确实有从罪恶中解脱和净化的方法。当我们还在世的时候，这就包括祭献和欢快的娱乐，这些对我们死后也还是有效用的，他们将之 365a
称为入会仪式。他们说，这些仪式使我们免除对另一个世界的所

one who didn't take part in the rituals.

'This, my dear Socrates,' he went on, 'is the kind of thing that gets said—and at this kind of length—about how highly gods and men regard virtue and vice. Can we tell what the effect of being exposed to all this is on a young mind which is naturally gifted and is capable of working out, as a result of flitting (so to speak) from one idea to another and dipping into them all, what type of person he has to be and
b what road he has to take to have as good a life as possible? He would probably follow Pindar and ask himself, "Is it honesty or crooked deceit that enables me to scale the higher wall" and so live my life surrounded by secure defences? What I hear is people telling me that, unless I also gain a reputation for morality, my actually being moral will do me no good, but will be a source of private troubles and public punishments. On the other hand, an immoral person who has managed to get a reputation for morality is said to have a wonderful life. There-
c fore, since the experts tell me that "Appearance overpowers reality" and is responsible for happiness, I must wholeheartedly devote myself to appearance. I must surround myself with an illusion of goodness. This must be my front, what people see of me, but behind me I must have on a leash that cunning, subtle fox of which Archilochus, the greatest of all experts, speaks. Someone might object, "But it's not easy to cloak one's badness for ever." That's because no important project is easy, we shall reply; nevertheless, everything we hear
d marks this as the road to take if we are to be happy. To help us with our disguise, we shall form clubs and pressure-groups, and we can acquire skill at political and forensic speaking from teachers of the art of persuasion. Consequently, by a combination of persuasion and brute force, we shall dominate others without being punished for it.

'"But you can't hide from the gods, or overpower them." "Well, suppose there are no gods, or suppose they aren't bothered in the slightest about human affairs: then why should we in our turn
e bother about hiding from them? On the other hand, if the gods do exist, and

有恐惧,而对那些不祭献的人,则有恐怖的东西在等待他们。

"我亲爱的苏格拉底,"他继续说,"人们用这些冗长的话谈论崇高的诸神和人们是如何对待美德与邪恶的。我们能说说所有这些对年轻人的心灵有什么影响吗?他们的心灵是有天赋的,能够进行周密思想的,它能够从一个观念走到另一个观念,并且大体全部地了解它们,之后的结果是决定他要成为什么样的人,走什么样的道路以尽可能地获得正义的生活。他或许会像品达一样 b
问自己:'诚实正直还是坑蒙拐骗能使我步步高升',并由此能使我安度一生呢?我听到人们告诉我,除非我也得到正义之名,否则我实际的正义不会给我带来好处,反而将是遭受个人不幸和公众惩罚的根源。另一方面,一个能够得到正义之名的不正义之人,则被认为会过上精彩的生活。因为,自从有个中高人告诉我说,'外表胜过真实',而且这便是幸福的原因之后,我便全心全意地投身于正义外表的伪装之中。我要使自己周围环绕着一层仁慈善良的假象。这便是我在人前的形象,是人们用眼睛观察到的我的形象,但是在背后,我必须像个中最厉害的高人阿基洛库斯所说的那样, c
要以皮带约束、控住一只狡猾、诡秘的狐狸。也许会有人反对说,'但是,一个人老是用外衣遮蔽住他的恶劣,可也是一件大不易的事情啊。'我们则会回答说,那是因为没有一件重要的事业是不费吹灰之力就能完成的;尽管如此,我们耳闻目睹的每一件事情都昭示我们,如果想要获得幸福,这便是前行的道路。为了用我们的伪装帮助我们,我们会组成俱乐部以及压力集团,而且我们还可以从精通说服艺术的教师那里学到政治与法庭演讲的技巧。由此,通过将说服技术与野蛮、残忍的暴力结合起来,我们就能支配、统治他人,而不会为此受到惩罚。

"'但是你们隐瞒不了诸神,也不能制服、压倒他们。''是的, d
但是让我们假设一下吧,假设诸神并不存在,或者假设他们一点儿也不会干扰人类的事务,那么为什么我们应该为想着要隐瞒他

do care for us, then our only sources of knowledge and information about them are tradition and the poets who have described their lineage. And these are precisely the people who are telling us that the gods can be persuaded and influenced by ' rites and softly spoken prayers' and offerings. Their credibility in one respect stands or falls with their credibility in the other respect. So if we listen to them, our course is to do wrong and then make offerings to the gods from the
366a proceeds of our crimes. The point is that if we behave morally, then the most that we'll avoid is being punished by the gods, but we'll also pass up the opportunity for making a profit from our immorality; if we are immoral, however, we'll not only get rich, we'll win the gods over with our entreaties and get off scot-free, for all the crimes we commit and wrong we do."

'"But we'll pay in Hades for the crimes we've committed here on earth—or if we don't ourselves, then our children's children will." He'll think about it and then reply, "No, my friend, we won't. Initiations are very effective and the gods whose domain is exoneration have a great deal of power: that is the message we are given by very impor-
b tant countries and by the offspring of the gods, who have become poets and the gods' interpreters, and who reveal that this is so."

'Is there any argument left, then, which might persuade us not to choose out-and-out immorality, but to prefer morality? I mean, if we combine immorality with a fraudulent, but specious, facade, then we can do as we please in this world and in the next, in the presence of both gods and men. This is what both ordinary people and out-
c standing people are telling us. So after all these arguments, Socrates, is there any strategy to enable someone With potential—whether it is due to mental attributes or wealth or physique or lineage—to be prepared to rate morality highly, rather than laugh when he hears it

们而自寻烦恼呢？另一方面，如果诸神的确存在，而且也愿意为我们操心，那么我们关于他们的知识、信息的唯一来源都是口传的，或诗人们写成的，他们已经描述了诸神的血统世系。也恰恰是这些人们告诉我们说，诸神是可以由"宗教仪式、轻声祷告"以及献祭牺牲而被说服、影响的。他们话语的可信性，在一个方面得以确立，抑或不能确立，但在另一方面仍然可以获得其可信性。
所以如果我们听他们的，我们的方针便是去作恶，然后再从我们 336a
的恶行收益中拿出一部分向诸神献祭牺牲。关键是，如果我们行为正义，那么最好的结局也只是免于诸神的惩罚，但是我们也就拒绝了从不义中获利的机会；而如果我们不义，那么我们不仅会发财致富，而且还可以用祈求将诸神争取到我们这一边来，对于我们所犯下的累累罪行以及所做下的恶事，也能够安然逃脱而逍遥法外。'

"'但在哈德斯那里我们会为我们在此世所犯的罪行而付出代价——或者不是我们自己的话，那么我们的子子孙孙都会（为此付出代价）。'他想了想，回答说：'不，我的朋友，我们不会的。为死者赎罪的方法非常灵验，而且负责赦罪的神灵本事也很大：这是非常伟大的城邦和诸神的后裔所传递给我们的信息，他们就
是诗人和诸神的信使，他们所启示的就是这样的。' b

"那么还有什么理由能说服我们不选择完全的不正义而选择正义呢？我的意思是说，如果我们能够将不正义与一种实际上的奸诈狡猾而且外表上的美观正派结合起来，那么无论此世还是来世，无论在诸神面前还是在人面前，我们就能为所欲为。无论是普通人还是杰出人物们对我们都是这么说的。所以，苏格拉底，
根据所有这些论证，还有办法能让任何有潜力的人——无论是在 c
智力上的、财力上的、体力上的还是出身上的——听到赞扬正义

being praised?

'I tell you, if there's anyone who can not only refute the arguments I've been stating, but is also secure in his knowledge that morality is best, then what he feels for immoral people is not anger but a large measure of forgiveness. He knows that people abstain from wrong either because, by divine dispensation, they instinctively find it distasteful, or because of some realization they've come to, and that
d otherwise no one chooses to be moral, although people find fault with immorality when cowardice or old age or some other form of weakness prevents them from doing wrong. This is obviously the case: the first of these people to gain power is the first to behave immorally—and as immorally as he possibly can.

'One thing is responsible for all this, and it is the same thing which constituted the starting-point of this whole discussion. Both Glaucon and I, Socrates, are saying to you, "My friend, we can start with those original heroes whose writings are extant and end with our contemporaries, but we find that not a single one of you self-styled supporters of morality has ever found fault with immorality or commen-
e ded morality except in terms of the reputation, status, and rewards which follow from them. What each of them does on its own, however, and what the effect is of its occurrence in someone's mind, where it is hidden from the eyes of both gods and men, has never been adequately explained either in poetry or in everyday conversation; nor has it ever been proven that the worst possible thing that can occur in the mind is immorality, and that morality is the best. If this is how all of
367a you had approached the matter from the outset, and if you had started trying to convince us when we were young, then we wouldn't now be defending ourselves against one another's wrongdoing, but everyone would be his own best defender, since he'd be afraid that if he did wrong he'd be opening his doors to the worst of all possible residents."

'That, Socrates, is what Thrasymachus—though he's not the only one, of course—might say on the subject of morality and immorality, and he'd probably have even more to add. Now, I think he's

时也准备高赞正义而不嘲笑呢?”

“我告诉你,如果有什么人,他不仅反驳我刚才阐述的观点,而且还根据他的学问确信正义就是最好的,那么他对于不义的人们的感受就不会是愤怒,而是一种深刻的宽恕之情。他知道,人们避免为非作歹,或者是因为神圣的教规,他们本能地感觉到正义堕落是令人讨厌
的,或者是因为他们达到了某种精神境界,否则,没有人会选择成为正 d
义的人,尽管当人们因为怯懦、年老或其他某种形式的虚弱而不能为非作歹时,他们也会批评不义。这是一个很明显的事实:那些首先获得权力的人,也便是最早行为不义的人——而且是尽其所能地不义。

“之所以是这样,是因为整个讨论都是以同一件事开头的。苏格拉底,格劳孔和我都对你说:‘我的朋友啊,我们可以从那些
其著作保留至今的最早的杰出人物开始,直到我们的同时代人为 e
止,但是我们发现你自称的正义倡导、拥护者中,除了对名声、地位及从中得到的收益进行毁誉之外,还没有哪个曾经批评过不义或赞扬过正义呢。但是,义与不义就其自身而言是什么,它们存在于人心时会有什么样的影响,当人所不知、神所未见时它藏匿何处,关于上述这些问题,无论是在诗歌中还是在日常谈话中,可都从来没有得到过充分
的说明呢;也从来没有谁证明说,在心灵中发生的可能最有害的事情 367a
就是不义,而正义则是最有益的。如果你们全体从一开始就在这个问题上作如是处理,还有如果在我们还小的时候你们就开始设法来说服我们,那么我们现在就用不着防卫自身以免于彼此的不道德行为了,而每个人都会是他自己最好的道德防卫者,因为他会害怕,如果他做了坏事,他就为所有可能的最糟糕居民打开了方便之门。’

“苏格拉底,这便是塞拉西马库斯——当然,尽管不止他一人——对于义与不义这一话题可能要说的话吧。而且他可能还有

crudely misrepresenting their functions, but the reason I've taken his argument as far as I can is, to he perfectly candid, because I want to
b hear you making the opposite claims, It's not enough just to demonstrate that morality is better than immorality. Why does one of them, in and of itself, make anyone who possesses it bad, while the other one, in and of itself, makes him good? And, as Glaucon suggested, don't bring reputation into it. You see, if you leave them with reputations which genuinely reflect their natures, and don't attribute to each of them reputations which fail to do justice to them, then we'll accuse you of praising a reputation for morality rather than morality itself, and of criticizing a reputation for immorality rather than immorality it-
c self; and we'll claim that what you're recommending is being immoral and getting away with it, and that you actually agree with Thrasymachus that morality is good for someone else—that it is the advantage of the stronger party—while it is immorality that is to one's own advantage and profit, but is disadvan-tageous to the weaker party.

'So, since it is your expressed opinion that morality is one of those paramount good things which are worth having not just for their consequences, but also and especially for themselves (like sight,
d hearing, intelligence—health, of course—and any other good things which are not just thought to be worth while, but are inherently so), then this is the aspect of morality which you should pay tribute to. You should show how morality is worth while in and of itself for anyone who possesses it and how immorality harms him, and leave others to praise rewards and reputations. I mean, I can accept the fact that others praise morality and criticize immorality in these terms, by eulogizing or abusing their reputations and rewards, but I won't put up
e with that from you (unless you insist), because this and this alone is what you've spent your whole life investigating. So it's not enough just to demonstrate that morality is better than immorality: show us why one of them, in and of itself, makes anyone who possesses it good, whether or not it is hidden from the eyes of gods and men, while the other one, in and of itself, and whether or not it is hidden from the eyes of gods and men, makes him bad.'

更多的话要说呢。现在我想,他可能因为缺乏知识或技巧而对正义
与不正义的作用做了不如实的说明,但是我已经尽我所能将其论辩
的理由说明白了,坦白地说,我这样做是因为我想听听你所做的反 b
驳。仅仅证明正义比不义好是不够的。为什么其中一个就其本身
来说会为它的拥有者带来坏处,而另一个就其本身来说会为它的拥
有者带来好处?像格劳孔建议的一样,不要把名声牵涉进去。你知
道,如果你不把歪曲它们本性的名声撇开而把虚假的东西掺杂进去
的话,那么我们就会指责你所赞美的东西是正义的名声而非正义自
身,批评你所赞美的东西是不正义的名声而非不正义自身;我们会
认为你所赞成的是做不正义的事情,并且能逃脱,而你实际上同意 c
塞拉西马库斯的说法,认为正义就是对他人有利,也就是说,正义是
强者的利益,而不正义有利于自己的利益和好处,但对弱者不利。

“由此,因为你清楚地说过,正义是最大的好事,值得拥有它不
仅是由于它的后果,而且也尤其是由于它自身,就像视力、听力、智
力,当然还有健康以及其他好的东西,它们并不只是由于人们的意
见,而且还因为它自身就值得拥有,那么,你应该加以颂扬的就是正 d
义的这一面。你应该宣扬正义自身和对它的拥有者的好处以及不
正义自身和对它的拥有者的害处,而让别人去赞扬回报和名声吧。
我的意思是说,我还能接受这样的事实,即别人以赞扬或贬低其名
声和回报的方式去颂扬正义、谴责不正义,但我不能忍受你那样做,
除非你坚持(要那样),因为正是这个问题,也唯有这个问题,是你毕
生探索的。所以仅仅证明正义比不正义好还是不够的:还要告诉我 e
们为什么其中之一就其自身而言造成了它的拥有者的好,无论其是
否藏匿而不让诸神和人的眼睛看见,而为什么另一个就其自身而言
却造成拥有者的坏,无论其是否藏匿而不让诸神和人的眼睛看见。”

CHAPTER 3

Now, I've always admired Glaucon's and Adeimantus' temperaments, but I was particularly delighted with them on this occasion,
368a once I'd heard what they had to say. 'Like father, like sons,' I remarked. 'The first line of the elegiac poem which Glaucon's lover composed when you distinguished yourselves at the battle of Megara wasn't wrong in addressing you as "sons of Ariston, godlike offspring of an eminent sire". I think this is quite right: "godlike" is certainly the word for your state, if you can speak like that in support of immorality, and yet remain unconvinced that it is better than morality. I *do*
b think that you really are unconvinced; my evidence is what I know of your characters from other occasions. If I'd had to judge from your words alone, I would have doubted it. But it's precisely because I don't doubt it that I'm in a quandary. On the one hand, I can't come to the assistance of morality, since I am incompetent—as is proven by the fact that although I thought the points I'd made to Thrasymachus had shown that morality was better than immorality, you weren't satisfied. On the other hand, I can't not come to morality's assistance, since I'm afraid that it might actually be sacrilegious to stand idly by while morality is being denigrated and not try to assist as long as one has
c breath in one's body and a voice to protest with. Anyway, the best thing is for me to offer it whatever help I can.'

Glaucon and the others begged me to do everything I could to help; they implored me not to abandon the discussion, but to make a thorough enquiry into the nature of both morality and immorality, and to search out the truth about their expediency. I told them what occurred to me: 'We're undertaking an investigation which, in my opin-
d ion, requires care and sharp eyesight. Now, we're not experts,' I pointed out, 'so I suggest we conduct the investigation as follows.

第三章

我总是钦佩格劳孔和阿狄曼图的性情,但现在听了他们说的话之后,在这一点上我就尤其感到高兴。“有其父必有其子啊,” 368a
我说,“你们在麦加拉战役中获胜后,格劳孔的情人所写的那首哀歌的第一句说得还不错:‘阿里斯同之子,杰出祖辈的神一般的子嗣。’我想这句话说得很对:‘神一般的’这个词当然也适合于你们,如果你说赞成不正义,却仍不信服于不正义比正义要好。我确实认为你真的不信服;我依据的是在其他场合下你们的性格。 b
如果一定要我从你们说的话加以判断的话,我也会怀疑的。但那正是因为我越相信就越不知如何是好。另一方面,我不能协助正义,因为我没有能力——就像事实所证明的,虽然我的认为正义比不正义要好的观点反驳了塞拉西马库斯,但你们还是不满意。另一方面,我也不是不能协助正义,因为当正义受到玷污时,要是我一息尚存,还能发出反抗的声音,而站在一旁,不提供帮助,我想这恐怕就是真的有罪的,所以我最好尽我所能提供帮助。” c

格劳孔和其他人求我在力所能及的事情上帮助他们;他们恳求我不要放弃讨论,而要对正义和不正义的本性进行彻底的考察,并寻找到关于它们与目的相称的事实来。我告诉他们我所想到的:“在我看来,我们所进行的研究需要细心和敏锐的目光。现在我们还没有这个能力,”我指出说,“所以我建议按以下的方式来探究。假设我们非常近视,还要求我们从很远的地方看微小的 d

Suppose we were rather short-sighted and had been told to read small writing from a long way off, and then one of us noticed the same letters written elsewhere in a larger size and on a larger surface: I'm sure we'd regard this as a godsend and would read them there before examining the smaller ones, to see if they were really identical.'

'Of course we would,' said Adeimantus. 'But how is this analo-
e gous to our investigation into morality, Socrates, in your view?'

'I'll tell you,' I replied. 'Wouldn't we say that morality can be a property of whole communities as well as of individuals?'

'Yes,' he said.

'And a community is larger than a single person?'

'Yes,' he said.

'It's not impossible, then, that morality might exist on a larger scale in the larger entity and be easier to discern. So, if you have
369a no objection, why don't we start by trying to see what morality is like in communities? And then we can examine individuals too, to see if the larger entity is reflected in the features of the smaller entity.'

'I think that's an excellent idea,' he said.

'Well,' I said, 'the theoretical observation of a community in the process of formation would enable us to see its morality and immorality forming too, wouldn't it?'

'I should think so,' he said.

'And once the process is complete, we could expect to see more easily what we're looking for?'

b 'Yes, much more easily.'

'Are we agreed, then, on the necessity of trying to see this plan through? I'm asking because I think it'll take a lot of work. So are you sure?'

'Yes, we are,' said Adeimantus. 'Please do what you're proposing.'

'Well,' I said, 'a community starts to be formed, I suppose,

字,然后我们中有一个人发现同样的字用大号字体写在别的较大的地方:我确信我们一定会把这当作神的馈赠,在看小字之前会先看那里的大字,看看它们是否真的相同。”

“我们当然会的,”阿狄曼图说,“但是,苏格拉底,按你的看
法,这与我们对于正义的研究相类似吗?” e

“我会告诉你的,”我回答说,“我们难道不能说正义是城邦的性质也是个人的性质吗?”

“是的。”他说。

“城邦不是比单个人大吗?”

“是的。”他说。

“那么,在大的东西上存在着更多的正义并且更容易辨认,这
不是不可能的。所以要是你不反对,我们为什么不先从城邦中的
正义开始考察呢？然后我们再去考察个人的正义,看看大的东西 369a
特征是否就在小的东西里得到了反映。”

“我觉得这是个绝好的想法。”他说。

“好吧,”我说,“在形成过程中对城邦进行理论性的考察也会让我们看到正义和不正义的产生,不是吗?”

“我想应该是这样的。”他说。

“一旦我们完成了这个过程,我们是否就有希望更加容易看到我们所要寻求的东西呢?”

“是的,要容易得多。” b

“那么,我们同意必须力求彻底理解我们的计划吗？我这样问是因为我想它会花去很多工夫。你们确定要这样做吗?”

“是的,我们确定,”阿狄曼图说,“就按你说的做。”

“那么,”我说,“我假设一个城邦开始产生了,当个人发现他

when individual human beings find that they aren't self-sufficient, but that each of them has plenty of requirements which he can't fulfil on his own. Do you have an alternative suggestion as to why communities are founded?'

'No,' he said.

c 'So people become involved with various other people to fulfil various needs, and we have lots of needs, so we gather lots of people together and get them to live in a single district as our associates and assistants. And then we call this living together a community. Is that right?'

'Yes.'

'And people trade goods with one another, because they think they'll be better off if each gives or receives something in exchange, don't they?'

'Yes.'

'All right, then,' I said. 'Let's construct our theoretical community from scratch. Apparently, its cause is our neediness.'

'Of course.'

d 'And the most basic and most important of our needs is that we are provided with enough food for existence and for life.'

'Absolutely.'

'The second most important is our need for somewhere to live, and the third is our need for clothing and so on.'

'True.'

'All right,' I said. 'How will our community cope with all this provisioning? Mustn't one member of it be a farmer, another a builder, and another a weaver? Is that all the people we need to look after our bodily needs? Shall we add a shoemaker to it as well?'

'Yes.'

'And there we'd have our community. Reduced to its bare essentials, it would consist of four or five people.'

e 'So it seems.'

们不是自足的，而是他们每人都有许多他们自己不能满足的需求。对于为何城邦建立，你还有别的说法吗？”

“没有。”他说。

“所以人们开始与各种别的人相联系以满足各种不同的需要，而 c
我们有许多需求，所以我们使很多人聚集生活在一定的区域内，把他们当作我们的伙伴和帮手。然后我们把这种聚居称作城邦。是吗？”

“是的。”

“人们相互之间做买卖，因为他们认为有进有出相互交换有助于自己，不是吗？”

“是的。”

“那么好吧，”我说，“让我们从头开始，建造我们理论上的城邦吧。从表面上看，它的原因似乎是我们的需要。”

“当然。”

“我们最基本和最重要的需要就是提供给我们生存和生活所 d
需的足够的食物。”

“毫无疑问。”

“第二重要的是我们需要住房，第三就是对于衣着的需要，如此等等。”

“对的。”

“那么，”我说，“我们的城邦怎么才能满足所有这些需要呢？不就是这一个成员必须是农民、另一个是瓦匠、又一个是纺织匠吗？为了照料身体的需要，那些人就够了吗？我们是否还要加上鞋匠呢？”

“是的。”

“这就是我们的城邦。加以精简也要有四五个人组成。”

“看起来是这样。” e

'Well now, should each of them make what he produces public-
ly available for everyone? For instance, although the farmer is only
one person, should he supply all four people with food? Should he
spend four times as long and work four times as hard on supplying
food and share it out, or should he ignore everyone else and spend a
quarter of his time producing only a quarter of this amount of food for
370a himself, and divide the other three-quarters between getting a house
and clothes and shoes for himself, and not have all the bother of asso-
ciating with other people, but look after his own affairs on his own?'

Adeimantus said, 'It looks as though the first alternative is simpler, Socrates.'

'That's not surprising, of course,' I said. 'I mean, it occurred
to me while you were speaking that, in the first place, different peo-
b ple are inherently suitable for different activities, since people are not
particularly similar to one another, but have a wide variety of natures.
Don't you agree?'

'I do.'

'And is success a more likely consequence of an individual working at several jobs or specializing in only one?'

'Of his specializing in only one,' he said.

'Now, here's another obvious point, I'm sure—that missing the critical opportunity has a deleterious effect.'

'Yes, obviously.'

'The reason being that the work isn't prepared to wait for the
c worker to make time for it. No, it's crucial for the worker to fall in
with the work and not try to fit it into his spare time.'

'Yes, that's crucial.'

'So it follows that productivity is increased, the quality of the products is improved, and the process is simplified when an individual sets aside his other pursuits, does the one thing for which he is naturally suited, and does it at the opportune moment.'

'Absolutely.'

“那么，他们中的每一个是否都要把他所生产的东西提供给所有人呢？比如说，虽然农民只是一个，但他是否应该提供给所有四个人食物呢？我们是否应该花四倍的时间和四倍的辛劳来供应食物与其他人共享呢？还是不考虑别人而只花四分之一的时间为自己生产四分之一量的食物，把其他四分之三的时间用来为自己造房子，做衣服，做鞋，各管各的事，与人无涉？” 370a

阿狄曼图说：“苏格拉底，看起来好像第一种方式更加简单些。”

“当然，这一点都不奇怪，”我说，“我的意思是说，你说话的时候，我就想，在最初的状况下，不同的人本来就适合不同的工作，因为人与人并不是非常的相似，而是本性上有很大的差别。你难 b
道不同意吗？”

“我同意。”

“一个人干多份工作，或是只专注于一份工作，哪一样更有可能会带来成功？”

“只专注于做一份工作。”他说。

“现在，我相信还有另一点是明显的：错过关键的机会会酿成恶果。”

“是的，显而易见。”

“因为工作是不会等着做工的人为之抽出时间来的，不会的，重要的是做工的人要全身心投入工作，而不是尽量把工作放到他
的空余时间去做。” c

“是的，那非常重要。”

“由此，当个人把其他工作放下，在恰当的时候做适合他禀赋的工作时，生产力提高了，产品质量提高了，工作流程也简化了。”

“肯定是的。”

'We need more than four citizens, then, Adeimantus, to supply the needs we mentioned. I mean, if the farmer's going to have a good
d plough, he will apparently not be making it himself, and the same goes for his hoe and all the rest of his farming implements. Moreover, the builder won't be making his own tools either, and he too needs plenty of them; nor, by the same token, will the weaver and the shoemaker. True?'

'True.'

'So plenty of other craftsmen—joiners, metalworkers, and so on—will join our little settlement and swell its population.'

'Yes.'

'It still won't be very big, though, even when we've added shepherds and other herdsmen—who are also needed, otherwise the farm-
e ers won't have oxen to plough with, and there'll be no draught-animals for them and the builders to use for pulling things, and no leather or wool for the weavers and shoemakers.'

'No,' he said, 'but it won't be small either with all that lot.'

'Now, it's practically impossible to build the actual community in a place where it will have no need of imports,' I pointed out.

'Yes, that's too much to expect.'

'Then they'll need more people, to bring in what it needs from elsewhere.'

'Yes.'

'But if their man goes empty-handed, in the sense of taking nothing with him which satisfies the requirements of the people from
371a whom they're trying to get what they need, then he'll depart empty-handed, won't he?'

'I should say so.'

'Then their home production must not only be enough to satisfy their own requirements, but must also be of a type and a quantity which satisfies the requirements of the people they need.'

“那么，阿狄曼图，我们需要超过四个人来提供我们提到的那些需求。我的意思是说，如果农民想要有好的犁的话，他显然不会自己去做，对于锄头和其他农具也是一样。此外，泥瓦匠也不 d
会去做他自己的工具，他也需要许多（别的）人；同样，纺织工和鞋匠也不会。对吗？”

“对的。”

“所以其他工匠——木匠、铁匠等等——都会加入我们的小城邦，使其人口增加。”

“是的。”

“但是即使我们把牧羊人和其他放牧的人也加上，城邦也不会很大，他们是我们所需要的人，否则农民就没有牛来耕作，没有 e
牲口为他们及泥瓦匠拖运东西，也没有提供给纺织工和鞋匠的皮毛了。”

“不是很大，”他说，“但是有了所有那些人之后城邦也就不小了。”

“把现实的城邦建立在一个不需要进口货物的地方，这实际上是不可能的。”我指出说。

“是的，确实如此。”

“那么就需要更多的人把所需的东西从别处运来。”

“是的。”

“但如果他们的人两手空空地走，也就是说他不带去任何满足那些人需要的东西，尽量换回自己所需的东西，那么他也将两 371a
手空空返回，不是吗？”

“应该说是的。”

“那么他们城邦内的产品必须不仅能够满足他们自己的需求，而且在种类和数量上也必须满足他们所需要的外邦人的需要。”

'Yes, it must.'

'So our community had better increase the number of its farmers and other craftsmen.'

'Yes.'

'And also the number of its workers, I suppose, who import and export all the different kinds of goods—which is to say, merchants. Don't you agree?'

'Yes.'

'We'll need merchants too, then.'

'Certainly.'

'And if they deal with overseas countries, then a great many
b other people will be needed—experts in all sea-related work.'

'Yes, we'll certainly need a lot of them.'

'Now, within the actual community, how will people trade their produce with one another? I mean, that was why we established an association and founded a community in the first place.'

'They'll trade by buying and selling, obviously,' he said.

'Then a consequence of this is that we'll have a market-place and coinage as a system of trading.'

'Yes.'

c 'So if a farmer or one of the other producers brings some of his produce to the market-place, but doesn't arrive at the same time as the people who want to trade with him, won't he be sitting in the market-place neglecting his own work?'

'No,' he replied, 'because there are people who notice the situation and take it on themselves to supply this service; in properly organized communities, they tend to be those who are physically the weakest and who are therefore unsuited for any other kind of work.
d Their job is to stay there in the market place and to give people who want to sell something money in exchange for their goods, and then to give goods in exchange for money to people who want to buy something.'

'So this need', I said, 'gives rise to stallholders in our community. I mean, aren't people who stay put in a market-place and do

“是的,必须满足。”

“所以我们的城邦最好还要增加农民和其他工匠的数量。”

“是的。”

“我想也还需要一些从事进口和出口工作的人,这就是说,需要商人。难道你不同意吗?”

“同意。”

“那么我们还会需要商人。”

“当然。”

“如果他们与海外的城邦做买卖的话,那么就需要一大批其他懂得航海的人。” b

”是的,我们当然需要很多那样的人。”

“那么,在现实的城邦中,人们如何将他们的产品与别人交易呢?我的意思是,那就是为什么我们首先要建立一种交往,谛造一个城邦的原因。”

“他们显然会通过买卖做交易。”他说。

“那么其结果就是,我们需要交易市场和作为交易体系的货币。”

“是的。”

“所以如果一个农民或其他生产者带着一些他所生产的东西 c
来到市场上,但与想要和他做交易的人来的不是同一个时候,那么,他不就是坐在市场里而疏忽了自己的工作?”

“不,”他回答说,“因为有人看到了这种情况就让自己来提供这种服务;在合理治理的城邦里,他们往往是身体比较虚弱因而不适合做任何其他工作的人。他们的工作就是待在市场,用钱买下那些想卖东西的人的货物,然后再卖给那些想要买东西的人。” d

“这种需要就在我们的城邦里产生了店主。”我说,“我的意思

the job of buying and selling called "stallholders", as distinct from those who travel from community to community, who are called "merchants"?'

'Yes, that's right.'

e 'I think there's another category of worker too, consisting of people who don't really deserve to join our community for their mental abilities, but who are physically strong enough to undertake hard labour. They sell the use of their strength, "pay" is the name of the reward they get for this, and that is why they're called "paid hands", I suppose, don't you?'

'Yes.'

'With paid hands as well, then, our community has reached its limit, I should think.'

'I agree.'

'Well, Adeimantus, our community has certainly grown. Is it now just right?'

'I suppose so.'

'Does it contain morality and immorality, then? If so, where and thanks to which of the people we've considered?'

372a 'I've no idea, Socrates,' he said, 'unless it has something to do with how these people treat one another.'

'You might be right,' I said. 'We must look into your idea: it deserves to be taken seriously. Let's start by considering how people who've been provided for like this will live. Surely they'll spend their time producing food, wine, clothes, and shoes, won't they? Once they've built their houses, they'll turn to production, which they'll invariably work at in the summer naked and with bare feet, and in the winter with adequate protective clothing and footwear. Their food will
b be barley meal and wheat-meal, which will sometimes be cooked and sometimes pulped, and the resulting honest fare of barley-cakes and wheat-cakes will be served up on reeds or on clean leaves, as they and their children, wearing chaplets and singing hymns to the gods, recline on carpets of bryony and myrtle and eat their fill, while drink

是说，那些待在市场里做买卖的人，不是与往来于城邦之间的那些我们称之为‘商人’的人不同吗？”

“是的，可以那样说。”

“我想还有另一种工作的人，由那些人组成，他们之所以值得进 e
入我们的城邦，并不是由于他们的智力，而是由于他们身体强壮能承担繁重的工作。他们出卖体力，‘工钱’就是称呼他们为此得到的回报的，我想他们之所以被称为‘挣工钱的’就是这个原因，不是吗？”

“是的。”

“那么我想，有了挣工钱的人，我们城邦就应该完整了。”

“我同意。”

“那么，阿狄曼图，我们的城邦当然已经形成了。现在它完备了吗？”

“我想是的。”

“那么，它包含正义和不正义吗？如果是的话，那么它们在哪儿，又要归因于我们曾考察过的哪些人呢？”

“我不知道，苏格拉底，”他说，“除非与这些人相互之间相处 372a
的方式有关。”

“你也许说得对，”我说，“我们必须考察一下你的想法：它值得加以认真的对待。让我们考察一下那些得到这些供应的人将是如何生活的。他们当然就不需要把他们的时间花在生产粮食、酿酒、做衣服和做鞋子上了，不是吗？一旦他们造完房子，他们就转向生产，他们常常在夏天赤膊光脚地工作，而在冬天则穿上防寒的衣服和鞋子工作。他们的食物是大麦片和小麦粉，有时烘 b
烤，有时做成粥，糕点和煎饼会放在芦苇或干净的树叶上，他们和孩子们戴着花冠歌颂诸神，躺在蔓草和桃金娘叶做的席子上，吃

ing wine. They'll enjoy having sex, except that concern about poverty
c or war will stop them procreating beyond their means.'

At this point Glaucon interrupted and said, 'This diet you're giving them dispenses with savouries, apparently.'

'You're right,' I said. 'I was forgetting that they'll also have savouries—salt, obviously, and olives and cheese—and they'll boil up the kinds of roots and vegetables which country stews are made of. We'll serve them with desserts too, I suppose, of figs, chick-peas, and beans; and they'll roast myrtle-berries and acorns in the fire as
d they sip their drinks. And so, it seems, their life will pass in peace and good health, and at their death in old age they will pass on a similar way of life to their offspring.'

'Socrates,' he remarked, 'isn't this exactly the fodder you'd lay on if you were devising a community for pigs?'

'What would you suggest, then, Glaucon?' I asked.

'Nothing abnormal,' he replied. 'I think they should recline on couches, if they're to be comfortable, and eat from tables, and have
e the kinds of savouries and desserts which are in current usage.'

'All right,' I said. 'I see. We're not just investigating the origins of a community, apparently, but of an indulgent community. Well, that may not be wrong: if we extend our enquiry like that, we might perhaps see how morality and immorality take root in communities. Now, I think that the true community—the one in a healthy condition, as it were—is the one we've described; but if you want us to inspect an inflamed community as well, so be it. There's no reason
373a not to. I mean, some people apparently won't be satisfied with the provisions and the lifestyle we've described, but will have all sorts of furniture like couches and tables, and a wide selection of savouries, perfumes, incense, prostitutes, and pastries. Moreover, the essential requirements can no longer be restricted to the houses and clothing and shoes we originally mentioned; no, we have to invent painting and ornamentation, and get hold of gold and ivory and so on. Don't

吃东西，喝喝酒。除了担心贫穷或战争会阻碍他们的生育之外，他们享受着性生活。” c

这时格劳孔插嘴说：“你向他们提供的饮食显然缺少调味品。”

“你说得对，”我说，“我忘了他们也要调味品——显然要有盐、橄榄和奶酪——他们会煮各种乡下炖着吃的根类和蔬菜。我想我们饭后也会给他们吃无花果、鹰嘴豆和豌豆；他们喝酒时也可以在火里烤爱神木果和橡子吃。这样，他们的生活似乎能在宁 d
静和健康中度过，在他们年老死去的时候，他们会把相似的生活传给他们的后代。”

“苏格拉底，”他评论说，“如果你是在为猪设计一个城邦，这不正是你要给的饲料吗？”

“那么，格劳孔，你有什么建议吗？”我问道。

“没什么特别的东西，”他回答说，“我想，如果他们想要舒服的话，那就躺在躺椅上，在桌边就餐，还要有各种调味品和甜食，就像现在的一样。” e

“好的，”我说，“我明白了。我们显然不只在探究一个城邦的起源，而是一个奢侈城邦的起源了。好吧，那样做也许并不坏：如果我们像那样拓展研究的话，我们或许还可以看看正义和不正义是如何植根于城邦中的。现在，我想真正的城邦——就其自身而言是处于健康状态的——就是我们所描述过的那个；但是要是你想要我们也考察一个兴奋的城邦，这样做也行。没有理由不这么做。我的意思是说，有些人显然对我们描述过的饮食和生活方式会不满足，还要诸如椅子桌子各类家具，各种调味品、香料、香水、 373a
妓女和糕点。此外，基本的需求不再局限于我们起先提到的住房、衣服和鞋子；不，我们还必须发明绘画和装饰品，拥有黄金和

you agree?'

b 'Yes,' he said.

'So we have to increase the size of our community once again. That healthy community will no longer do; it must become bloated and distended with occupations which leave the essential requirements of a community behind—for instance, with all kinds of hunters and imitators. Among the latter will be hordes of people concerned with shapes and colours, and further hordes concerned with music (poets and their dependants—rhapsodes, actors, dancers, producers), and
c manufacturers of all kinds of contraptions and all sorts of things, especially women's cosmetics. Furthermore, we'll need a larger number of workers — don't you think? —such as children's attendants, nurses, nannies, hairdressers, barbers, and savoury-cooks and meat-cooks too. And that's not the end of it: we'll need pig-farmers as well—a job which didn't exist in our previous community, since there was no need of it, but which will be needed in the present one—and huge numbers of cows and sheep, if they are to be eaten, won't we?'

"Of course.'

d ' And with this lifestyle won't we be in far greater need of doctors than we were before?'

'Yes.'

'And, of course, although the inhabitants of our former community could live off the produce of the land, the land will be too small now, don't you think?'

'I agree.'

'So we'll have to take a chunk of our neighbours' land, if we're going to have enough for our herds and our crops, won't we? And suppose they too have stopped limiting themselves to necessities and have gone in for the uncontrolled acquisition of innumerable possessions: then they'll have to take a chunk of our land too, won't they?'

'That's more or less inevitable, Socrates,' he replied.

e 'And the next step will be war, Glaucon, don't you think?'

象牙等等。你难道不同意吗?”

“同意。”他说。 b

“所以我们必须再次扩大我们的城邦。那个健康的城邦不再能承受了;它肯定要变得充斥着那些与城邦的基本需求无关的从业者,比如说,充斥着各种捕猎者和模仿者。在后者当中就有很多人从事于塑造与粉饰,也有很多人从事音乐,有诗人和他们的助手——史诗朗诵者、表演者、舞蹈者和制作者、各种新奇事物的制作者以及各种用品,尤其是妇女用品的制作者;此外,我们也需要大量做工的人,比如照看孩子的人、奶妈、保姆、美容师、理发师 c
和厨师,你不这么认为吗? 而那还没完呢:我们也还需要养猪的人——这个工作在我们以前的城邦里没有,因为我们不需要,但现在我们却需要了——还有供我们食用的大量牛羊,不是吗?”

“当然。”

“以这样的生活方式,我们对医生的需要不就比以前大得 d
多吗?”

“是的。”

“当然,虽然我们以前的城邦的居民能够依赖地里出产的东西生活,但现在土地却太小了,你不这么认为吗?”

“我同意。”

“所以如果我们没有足够的土地放牧和耕作的话,那么我们就不得不从邻邦那儿掠夺一块土地过来,不是吗? 假设他们也不满足于必需品,陷进对巨大财富的无节制的贪欲中,那么他们也不得不掠夺我们的一块土地,不是吗?”

“苏格拉底,那或多或少是不可避免的。”他回答说。 e

“格劳孔,你不认为下一步就是战争了吗?”

'I agree,' he said.

'Now, let's not commit ourselves yet to a view on whether the effects of war are good or bad,' I said. 'All we're saying at the moment is that we've now discovered the origin of war. It is caused by those factors whose occurrence is the major cause of a community's troubles, whether it's the community as a whole which is afflicted or any individual member of it.'

'Yes.'

'We need another sizeable increase in our community, then, Glaucon—an army-sized increase. We need an army to go
374a out and defend all the community's property and all the people we were talking about a moment ago against invaders.'

'But can't the inhabitants do this themselves?' he asked.

'No,' I replied. 'At any rate, they can't if the proposition we all—including you—agreed to when we were forming our community was correct. The proposition was, if you remember, that it is impossible for one person to work properly at more than one area of expertise.'

'You're right.'

'Well,' I said, 'don't you think that warfare requires expertise?'

b 'I certainly do,' he answered.

'So should we take more trouble over our shoemakers than we do over our soldiers?'

'Not at all.'

'Well now, we prohibited a shoemaker from simultaneously undertaking farming or weaving or building, but had him concentrating exclusively on shoemaking, to ensure quality achievements in shoemaking; and we similarly allotted every single person just one job—the one for which he was naturally suited, and which he was to work at all his life, setting aside his other pursuits, so as not to miss the
c opportunities which are critical for quality achievement. Isn't it crucial, however, that the achievements of warfare are of a high standard?

“我同意。”他说。

“现在，我们还不要讨论战争的后果是好是坏，”我说，“此刻我们在讨论的只是我们现在已经发现了战争的起源。无论遭受灾难的是作为整体的城邦还是成员个人，引起城邦灾难的主要原因就是这些因素，它们造成了灾难。”

“是的。”

“那么，格劳孔，在我们的城邦中还需要另一项相当大的增加——一支军队的增加。我们需要一支军队出征，保卫我们不久 374a
前提到的城邦的所有财产和所有人民，打败侵略者。”

“但是，居民难道不能自己保卫自己吗？”他问道。

“不能，”我回答说，“如果我们，包括你，在当初我们组建我们城邦时都同意那个说法是正确的，那么他们无论如何都不能。如果你还记得的话，那个说法就是，一个人精通多个专业领域是不可能的。”

“你说得对。”

“那么，”我说，“你难道不认为打仗需要专业技能吗？” b

“我认为当然需要。”他回答说。

“那么我们对于我们的鞋匠应该费更多的劳神关心，胜过对于我们的战士吗？”

“绝对不是。”

“那么现在，我们禁止鞋匠同时去务农、纺织或造房子，而是让他专门制鞋，以确保把鞋做好；我们同样把一个最适合其本性的工作分配给每一个人，让他放下其他工作，一生从事这项工作，
这样就不会错失提高质量的关键机会。然而，按高标准获胜战争 c
不是至关重要的吗？或者说，成为战士很容易，以至于任何人都

Or is soldiering so easy that someone can be expert at it while carrying on with his farming or shoemaking or whatever his profession might be, despite the fact that no one could even become a competent backgammon-player or dice-player if he took it up only in his spare time and didn't concentrate on it for years, starting when he was a young
d man? Does someone just have to pick up a shield (or whatever military implement or instrument it may be) and he instantaneously becomes a competent fighter in a heavy infantry engagement (or in what-ever form of armed conflict it may be)? This would be unique, since no other implement makes a person a craftsman or an athlete if he just holds it, and no other implement is the slightest good to anyone unless he's acquired the knowledge of how to use it and has devoted sufficient attention to it.'

'Yes,' he said, 'if tools could do that, they'd be highly prized.'

e 'Now,' I said, 'the amount of time allotted just to it, and also the degree of professionalism and training, should reflect the supreme importance of the guardians' work.'

'I certainly think so,' he said.

'And a natural talent for the job would help too, wouldn't it?'

'Of course.'

'Our job, then, if we're up to it, would seem to be to select which people and what types of person have a natural gift for protecting our community.'

'Yes, it is.'

'We've certainly taken on an awesome task, then,' I said. 'Still, we mustn't be intimidated; we must do the best we can.'

375a 'I agree.'

'Well,' I went on, 'do you think there's any difference, as far as suitability for guarding is concerned, between the nature of the best type of dog and that of a well-born young man?'

'What are you getting at?'

'That both of them have to be acutely perceptive, quick on their

能擅长于战斗，同时还做他的农活、制鞋或做他的无论何种的本职工作？就是下棋和投骰子来说吧，如果只是在业余时间而不是从小开始专注于下棋多年，那么事实就是，根本没有人会成为一名高水平的棋手或骰子玩家的。任何一个人拿起盾牌（或任何军
事器械）就能马上在重武器战斗或别的形式的武装冲突中成为一 d
名能干的战士吗？这似乎是很特别的，没有别的工具能够使人拿起来就会成为工匠或运动员，也没有别的工具对人有任何好处，除非他知道如何使用工具并给之以充分的关注。”

“是的，”他说，“如果工具可以那样做的话，那么它们就成为至宝了。”

“既然如此，”我说，“分派用来专门做此事的时间总量，还有
其专业与训练程度，应该反映出卫士工作的极端重要性。” e

“我当然是这样想的。”他说。

“天赋也有助于工作，不是吗？”

“当然。”

“那么，我们的工作，要是我们承担起来的话，看来似乎就是找出哪些人以及哪些类型的人具有保护我们城邦的天赋。”

“是的，那是我们的工作。”

“那么，我们当然就承担了一个繁重的任务，”我说，“但我们还不能退缩；我们必须尽力而为。”

“我同意。” 375a

“那么，”我继续说，“就适合保卫工作这一点来说，你认为品种最好的狗的本性和出生优越的年轻人的本性之间有什么区别吗？”

“你指的是什么意思？”

“他们都必须是感觉敏锐，跑得快，能追上任何他们感觉到的

feet (so as to chase after anything they do perceive) and strong as well, in case they have to fight someone they've cornered.'

'Yes,' he said, 'they need all these qualities.'

'And a good fighter must be brave, of course.'

'That goes without saying.'

'Now, you'll never find courage without passion, in a horse or a dog or any other creature, will you? I mean, you must have noticed how indomitable and invincible passion is. It always takes passion in
b a mind to make it capable of facing any situation without fear and without yielding, doesn't it?'

'Yes.'

'It's obvious what physical attributes a guardian must have, then.'

'Yes.'

'And the importance of a passionate temperament is also clear.'

'Again, yes.'

'Well, aren't people of this type bound to behave like brutes to one another and to the rest of their fellow citizens, Glaucon?' I asked.

'Yes, it certainly won't be easy to stop them,' he replied.

c 'However, they should really behave with civilized gentleness towards their friends and neighbours and with ferocity towards their enemies. Otherwise, it won't be a question of waiting for others to come and destroy them: they'll do the job first themselves!'

'True,' he said.

'What shall we do, then?' I asked. 'Where are we going to find a character that is simultaneously gentle and high-spirited, when gentleness and passion are opposites?'

'Yes, they do seem to be mutually exclusive.'

'And yet if a guardian is deprived of either of them he can't be a

东西，并且也强壮，能够与被他们逼入绝境的东西搏斗。”

“是的，”他说，“他们需要所有这些品质。”

“善战者当然必须勇敢。”

“那不用说。”

“那么，无论在马或狗还是别的动物身上，你绝不会发现没有血气的勇气，是吗？我的意思是说，你必须注意到血气是多么不
可抗拒和征服啊。心灵中有了血气，就有能力面对任何情况都不 b
会畏惧和屈服了，不是吗？”

“是的。”

“那么，一个卫士可能需要什么样的自然品质，也就很清楚了。”

“是的。”

“激情品性的重要性也是显而易见的。”

“也是的。”

“那么，这种类型的人对待同事及他们同一城邦中的公民的行为举止，必定会像野兽、畜牲一样残忍凶暴的，难道不是这样吗，格劳孔？”我问道。

“是的，阻止他们当然不容易。”他回答说。

“然而，他们对待朋友和邻人应该表现出真正的温和，对待敌 c
人则是凶狠。否则问题就不会是等别人来消灭他们了：他们先就把自己消灭了。”

“对的。”他说。

“那么，我们应该怎么办呢？”我问道，“既然温和与激情是相反的，那么我们去哪里寻找一个既温和又充满激情的人呢？”

“是的，它们似乎是相互排斥的。”

“然而，如果一个卫士被剥夺了两者之一的话，那么他便不是

good guardian. We seem to be faced with an impasse; it turns out

d that a good guardian is an impossibility.'

'I suppose so.'

I was stuck. I surveyed the course of the discussion and then said, 'We deserve to be stuck, Glaucon. We haven't kept to the analogy we proposed.'

'What do you mean?'

'We've overlooked the fact that the supposedly impossible type of character, which contains these opposite qualities, does exist.'

'Where?'

e 'In animals. You could find the combination primarily— though not exclusively—in the animal we used as an analogy for our guardian. I mean, as I'm sure you know, there's no creature more gentle towards people it knows and recognizes, and no creature more savage towards strangers, then the best type of dog; and this is due to its innate character.'

'Yes, I'm aware of that.'

'So it *is* a possibility, then,' I said. 'We're not looking for something unnatural in looking for a guardian of this type.'

'No, I suppose not.'

'Now, don't you think there's another quality which a would-be guardian needs as well? Don't you think that in addition to being naturally passionate he should also have a philosopher's love of knowledge?'

376a 'Why?' he asked. 'I don't see why.'

'Take dogs again,' I said. 'It's noticeable that they have a remarkable feature.'

'What?'

好卫士了。我们似乎面临着一个两难；结果就是，一个好的卫士
是不可能有的。” d

“我想是这样的。”

我被难住了。我通盘思考了一下讨论的过程，然后说：“格劳孔，我们活该被卡在这儿。因为我们没有遵循我们自己提出的类比原则。”

“你是什么意思？”

“我们忽视了这样一个事实，即那种含有对立性的、被认为不可能的秉性类型是存在的。”

“在哪里呢？”

“在动物身上。你能在我们拿来与卫士做类比的动物身上发
现原初的混合，但并不是唯独这种动物身上才有。我的意思是 e
说，正如我想你肯定知道的那样，没有比良种的狗更好、会对认识和熟悉的人温和而对陌生人凶暴的动物了；这就在于其内在的秉性。”

“是的，我知道。”

“那么，这是可能的，”我说，“我们寻找这种卫士并不是在寻找某些非自然的东西。”

“是的。我想并非在找那样的东西。”

“那么，你难道不认为还有另一种品质也是卫士所需要的吗？你难道不认为除了本性上具有激情之外，也还需要哲学家的对于知识的爱吗？”

“为什么？”他问道，“我不明白为什么。” 376a

“再拿狗来说，”我说，“它们具有一种明显的特质，这令人惊讶。”

“是什么？”

‘They get fierce with strangers even before the slightest harm has been done them, and they welcome familiar people even if they’ve never been benefited by them. Has this never struck you as surprising?’

‘I hadn’t really thought about it until now,’ he said. ‘But yes, they do clearly do that.’

b ‘But don’t you think that this feature shows how naturally smart they are and how genuinely they love knowledge?’

‘How?’

‘Because’, I explained, ‘their sole criterion for the friendlinessor hostility of what they see is whether or not they have learnt to recognize it. Now, anything that relies on familiarity and unfamiliarity to define what is congenial and what is alien must prize learning, mustn’t it?’

‘Yes,’ he said, ‘inevitably.’

‘Well,’ I went on, ‘isn’t loving learning the same thing as loving knowledge?’

‘Yes, it is,’ he said.

‘So why don’t we stick our necks out and suggest that the same
c goes for a human being too—that if he’s going to be gentle with his friends and acquaintances, he must be an innate lover of knowledge and learning?’

‘All right,’ he said.

‘Anyone who is going to be a truly good guardian of our community, then, will have a philosopher’s love of knowledge, and will be passionate, quick on his feet, and strong.’

‘Absolutely,’ he said.

“对于那些陌生人，即便他们曾经最轻微地伤害过它，它也会咆哮不已，而对于那些他熟悉的人，即便他们并没有给过它什么好处，它也会摇尾示好。这种现象从来没有让你感到惊奇吗?”

“在此之前，我从来没有真正地这样想，”他说，“但是，是的，它们的确显然是那样的。”

“但你难道不认为这个特质表明它们天性是多么聪明，是多
么真正地爱知识吗?” b

“何以见得?”

“因为，”我解释说，“它们对自己所看到的东西怀有好感还是怀有敌意的唯一标准就是它们是否已经学会认识它。那么，凭借熟悉或不熟悉来判定什么是自家的、什么是外来的，这就是热爱学习，不是吗?”

“是的，”他说，“必然是的。”

“那么，”我接着说，“热爱学习和热爱知识不就是一回事吗?”

“是的。”他说。

“那么我们为什么不大胆地说对于人类也是同样的——如果
一个人温和地对他的朋友和认识的人，那么他必须内在地热爱知 c
识和学习?”

“说得对。”他说。

“那么，任何想要成为我们城邦的真正卫士的人，必须拥有哲学家对知识的热爱，具有激情，步伐敏捷并且强壮。”

“完全正确。”他说。

CHAPTER 4

'So those are his attributes. But how are we going to bring these
people up? What education shall we give them? If we look into these
376d issues, does it further the overall purpose of our enquiry, which is to
see how morality and immorality arise in society? We have to be careful not to leave out any relevant argument or to swamp the discussion with too many topics.'

It was Glaucon's brother who said, 'I expect the consideration of these issues will substantially further it.'

'In that case, my dear Adeimantus,' I said, 'we must certainly not give up, even if the investigation turns out to be rather lengthy.'

'No, we mustn't.'

'All right, then, let's devise a theoretical education for these people, as if we were making up a story and weren't worried about time.'

e 'Yes, that's a good idea.'

'How shall we educate them, then? Or is it hard to improve on the educational system which has evolved over a long period of time? This, as you know, consists of exercise for the body and cultural studies for the mind.'

第四章

“所以这些就是他的品质。但我们如何培养他们呢？我们应该给予他们什么样的教育呢？如果我们来考察这些问题的话，那么这是否会促进我们的总体研究目标，即考察正义和不正义是如
何在城邦里产生的？我们必须小心，不要离开相关的论证或陷入 376d
太多的论题讨论中去。”

格劳孔的兄弟说：“我希望对这些问题的讨论能更接近目标。”

“那样的话，我亲爱的阿狄曼图，”我说，“即使探讨变得过于冗长，我们也一定不能放弃。”

“是，我们一定不会的。”

“那么好吧，让我们在理论上为这些人设想一种教育，就像我们在讲故事一样，而无须担心时间。”

“好的，那是个好主意。” e

“那么，我们该怎么教育他们呢？或者说，改善已经进化了很长时期的教育体系是困难的吗？就如你所知的，它包括身体的锻炼和心灵的文艺学习。”[1]

---

[1] “cultural study”译为“文艺学习”而未译为“文化学习”，是因为在古希腊，这种学习主要指音乐、诗歌等文学艺术方面的熏陶，故采此译，以下皆同。

'Yes.'

'And shall we begin the cultural programme before the physical one?'

'Of course.'

'Cultural studies include literature, don't you think?' I asked.

'I do.'

'Aren't there two kinds of literature, true and false?'

'Yes.'

377a 'Should we include both kinds in our educational system, and start with the untrue kind?'

'I don't understand what you're getting at,' he said.

'Don't you realize,' I asked, 'that we start by telling children stories which are, by and large, untrue, though they contain elements of truth? And stories precede physical exercise in our education of children.'

'True.'

'Which is why I suggested that cultural studies should be taken up before physical exercise.'

'It was a good suggestion,' he said.

'Now, do you appreciate that the most important stage of any enterprise is the beginning, especially when something
b young and sensitive is involved? You see, that's when most of its formation takes place, and it absorbs every impression that anyone wants to stamp upon it.'

'You're absolutely right.'

'Shall we, then, casually allow our children to listen to any old stories, made up by just anyone, and to take into their minds views which, on the whole, contradict those we'll want them to have as adults?'

“是的。”

“那么我们应该先从文艺的学习计划开始，然后再是体育吗？”

“当然。”

“你认为文艺学习包括故事吗？”我问道。

“我是这么认为的。”

“不是有两种故事吗，一种是真的，一种是假的？”

“是的。”

“我们应该把两种都包罗在我们的教育体系中，并从假的那 377a
种开始吗？”

“我不理解你指的是什么意思。”他说。

“你难道没有意识到，”我问道，“我们一开始向孩子讲述的故事虽然含有真的成分，但总的说来还是假的？而且在我们对孩子的教育中，故事是先于体育锻炼的。”

“对的。”

“这就是为什么我认为文艺教育应该先于身体操练的原因。”

“这是个好想法。”他说。

“那么，你是否认为任何事情最重要的阶段就是开端，尤其是
对年幼、敏感的生灵？你知道，那时最具有可塑性，他们对人们所 b
施加的印象都接受。”

“你说得完全正确。”

“那么我们应该让我们的孩子们随便去听由什么人虚构的一些古老的故事吗？我们应该将那些整体而言与我们希望孩子们将来长大后所具有的观点相抵触的观念放到他们的心灵中去吗？”

'No, we won't allow that at all.'

'So our first job, apparently, is to oversee the work of the story-
c writers, and to accept any good story they write, but reject the others. We'll let nurses and mothers tell their children the acceptable ones, and we'll have them devote themselves far more to using these stories to form their children's minds than they do to using their hands to form their bodies. However, we'll have to disallow most of the stories they currently tell.'

'Which stories?' he asked.

'If we examine the grander kind of story,' I said, 'that will give us insights into the more lightweight kind as well, because the same principle must be involved and both kinds are bound to have the same effect, don't you think?'

d 'That sounds fine to me,' he replied, 'but I don't even understand which stories you're describing as grander.'

'The ones which Hesiod, Homer, and their fellow poets tell us. In the past, it's always been the poets who've composed untrue stones to tell people, and it's no different nowadays.'

'Which stories?' he asked. 'And what's their defect, in your view?'

'There is no defect which one ought to condemn more quickly and more thoroughly,' I replied, 'especially if the lies have no redeeming feature.'

'Yes, but what *is* this defect?'

e 'Using the written word to give a distorted image of the nature of the gods and heroes, just as a painter might produce a portrait which completely fails to capture the likeness of the original.'

'Yes,' he said, 'it's quite right to find fault with that sort of thing. But how do they do that? What kinds of things do they say?'

"不,我们完全不会让他们那样的。"

"所以我们的首要工作,就是审查写故事的人的作品,采用他们写得好的所有故事,而排除其余的。我们要让保姆和母亲们向 c
她们的孩子讲述那些被采纳的故事,我们让她们用这些故事去塑造孩子们的心灵,更胜于用她们的手去塑造他们的身体。然而,她们现在讲述的大部分的故事是我们必定不允许的。"

"哪些故事?"他问道。

"如果我们研究分析较为重大的一类故事,"我说道,"那么同样也能让我们领悟较为无足轻重的故事中的一些东西,因为二者必然包含着同样的道德标准,也必定具有同样的影响,你不这样认为吗?"

"我觉得那样很好,"他回答说,"但是我甚至不知道你把哪类 d
故事称作较为重大一类的故事?"

"就是那些赫西俄德、荷马以及类似的诗人所讲述的故事。在过去,总是由诗人编造一些虚假的故事来向人们讲述,与现在没什么不同。"

"哪一类故事?"他问道,"在你看来它们的错误是什么?"

"人们应该首先迅速而彻底地谴责这一类缺点,"我回答道,"特别是如果这些谎言故事所造成的后果是无法加以挽回、弥补的话。"

"是的,但是这类缺点是什么呢?"

"使用文字扭曲诸神和英雄的本性的形象,就像画匠画出来 e
的画与原来的东西完全不像一样。"

"是的,"他说,"谴责这种事情是很对的。但他们到底是怎么做的?他们说了些什么东西?"

'First and most important, since the subject is so important,' I
378a said, 'there is no redeeming feature to the lies which Hesiod repeats, about Uranus' deeds and Cronus' revenge on Uranus. Then there are Cronus' deeds and what his son did to him. Now, I think that even if these stories are true, they oughtn't to be told so casually to young people and people who lack discrimination; it's better to keep silent, and if one absolutely has to speak, to make them esoteric secrets told to as few people as possible, who are to have sacrificed no mere piglet, but something so large and rare that the smallest conceivable number of people get to hear them.'

'Yes,' he said, 'these stories are definitely dangerous.'

b 'And we must censor them in our community, Adeimantus,' I said. 'No young person is to hear stories which suggest that were he to commit the vilest of crimes, and were he to do his utmost to punish his father's crimes, he wouldn't be doing anything out of the ordinary, but would simply be behaving like the first and the greatest gods.'

'No, I absolutely agree,' he said. 'I share your view that these stories are unsuitable and shouldn't be repeated.'

c 'And that's not all,' I said. 'The stories which have gods fighting and scheming and battling against one another are utterly unsuitable too, because they're just as untrue. If the prospective guardians of our community are to loathe casual quarrels with one another, we must take good care that battles between gods and giants and all the other various tales of gods and heroes coming to blows with their relatives and friends don't occur in the stories they hear and the pictures

“首先并且最重要的是，因为这一主题是如此的重要，”我说道，“所以赫西俄德复述的谎言所造成的恶果是无法弥补的，例如他讲述的关于乌拉诺斯[1]的事迹，还有克洛诺斯[2]向乌拉诺斯复仇的故
事。然后是克洛诺斯的行为以及他儿子对他的报复。现在，我想，即 378a
使这些故事是真实的，也不能随便地向年轻人和缺乏辨别能力的人讲述它们；最好保持沉默，如果不得不说的话，那么把它作为密传讲给尽可能少的人听，这些人所要做的献祭牺牲不仅仅是一头小猪，而是又大又稀少的东西，那么只有少得难以想象的人才能听了。”

“是的，”他说，“这些故事无疑是危险的。”

“阿狄曼图，在我们的城邦里我们必须加以审查，”我说，“年轻人 b
不可以听这些故事，这些故事教唆他们去犯下最道德败坏的罪行，让他们竭力去惩戒其父亲的罪行，而且还告诉他说，他并不是在做一件不寻常的事情，只不过仅仅像最早的、最伟大的诸神那样去做罢了。”

“是的，我完全同意，”他说，“我与你的观点一致，这些故事是不适合的，不应该讲述它们。”

“那还不是全部，”我说，“这些关于诸神相互争斗、谋算和打
斗的故事也是完全不适合的，因为它们是不真实的。如果期望我 c
们城邦的卫士厌恶彼此间随随便便就会发生的争吵的话，我们就必须要小心，不要在他们所听到的故事中、所看到的图画中，出现有关诸神与巨人之间发生战斗的内容，也不要在其中出现所有其他各种有关诸神、英雄与其亲戚、朋友互殴的传说。完全不可以

[1] 根据希腊神话的传说，乌拉诺斯是最早的至上神，是天的化身，是大地女神的儿子和配偶，希克罗比斯和泰坦们的父亲。

[2] 克洛诺斯，希腊神话中的泰坦，在被他的儿子宙斯废黜之前一直统治着宇宙。泰坦是一个巨人家族的成员，这个家族是乌拉诺斯和盖亚的子女，他们试图统治天国，但被宙斯家族推翻并取代。

they see. No, if we're somehow to convince them that fellow citizens never fall out with one another, that this is wrong, then that is the kind of story they must hear, from childhood onwards, from the
d community's elders of both sexes; and the poets they'll hear when they're older must be forced to tell equivalent stories in their poetry. But we'd better not admit into our community the story of Hera being tied up by her son, or the episode when Hephaestus is hurled away by his father for trying to save his mother from a beating, or any of the battles between the gods which Homer has in his poetry, whether or not their intention is allegorical. The point is that a young person can't tell when something is allegorical and when it isn't, and any idea admitted by a person of that age tends to become almost ineradicable
e and permanent. All things considered, then, that is why a very great deal of importance should be placed upon ensuring that the first stories they hear are best adapted for their moral improvement.'

'Yes, that makes sense,' he said. 'But suppose we were once again to be asked, in this context as well, what stories we meant, how would we respond?'

'Adeimantus,' I said, 'you and I are not making up stories at
379a the moment; we're founding a community. Founders ought to know the broad outlines within which their poets are to compose stories, so that they can exclude any compositions which do not conform to those outlines; but they shouldn't themselves make stories up.'

'You're right,' he said. 'But that's precisely the point: what are these guidelines for talking about the gods?'

'They'd be something like this,' I said. 'Whatever the type of poetry—epic, lyric, or tragic—God must of course always be portrayed as he really is.'

'Yes, he must.'

b 'Well, isn't God good, in fact, and shouldn't he be described as such?'

'Of course.'

'And nothing good is harmful, is it?'

的,如果我们想以某种方式让他们相信,市民伙伴之间从来不会发生彼此争吵之事,而且这种争吵是不道德的,那么从其孩童时期起,就要让他们聆听城邦中爷爷、奶奶们讲述的那种故事;等他们长大了,必须强制他们听到诗人在他们的诗作中讲述同样的故 d
事。然而我们最好不要允许这样的故事进入城邦:赫拉被她的儿子捆绑起来的故事,赫非斯托斯为了救他的遭打的母亲而被他父亲摔开的故事,或者在荷马诗作中的诸神间打斗的故事,无论它们的意思是否是寓言式的。关键是年轻人不能区分何时是寓言式的,何时不是寓言式的,那个年纪的人接受的想法会变得几乎是不可根除的和永恒的。考虑到所有这些事情,那么这就是为什 e
么最重要的事情在于保证他们首先听到的故事应该是最利于提高他们的品德的原因。"

"是的,那样做有道理,"他说,"但要是我们又被问到我们指的是什么故事,我们怎么回答呢?"

"阿狄曼图,"我说,"你我现在不是在编故事;我们在缔造城
邦。缔造者应该知道诗人们创作故事的总体标准,这样他们就能 379a
排除任何不符合这个标准的作品;但他们不应该自己编故事。"

"你说得对,"他说,"可关键就是这点:谈论诸神的这些标准是什么呢?"

"它们应该是这样的标准,"我说,"即任何形式的诗——史诗、抒情诗还是悲剧——神当然必须总是被刻画成他真实的样子。"

"是的,他必须那样。"

"实际上神不就是善的,并且不就应该被描写成善的吗?" b

"当然。"

"没有一样善的东西是有害的,是吗?"

'I don't think so.'

'Now, can anything harmless cause damage?'

'No, of course not.'

'Can anything incapable of causing damage do anything bad?'

'Again, no.'

'And something which never does bad couldn't be responsible for bad, could it?'

'Of course not.'

'Well now, is goodness beneficial?'

'Yes.'

'And it's responsible for doing good, then?'

'Yes.'

'So goodness is not responsible for everything: it's responsible for things that are in a good state, but bad things cannot be attributed to it.'

c 'Exactly,' he said.

'The same goes for God too, then,' I said. 'Since he is good, he cannot be responsible for everything, as is commonly said. He is responsible only for a small part of human life, and many things cannot be attributed to him—I mean, there's far more bad than good in the world. He and he alone must be held responsible for the good things, but responsibility for bad things must be looked for elsewhere and not attributed to God.'

'I think you're absolutely right,' he said.

d 'So,' I said, 'we shouldn't connive at Homer or any other poet making the stupid mistake of saying about the gods, "Two jars sit on Zeus' threshold: one is full of good destinies, but the other is full of wretched destinies", and that if Zeus mixes the two up together and-doles them out to someone, that person "sometimes meets with bad, sometimes with good", whereas if he doesn't mix them up, but allots the pernicious ones to someone in an unadulterated form, that person "is driven over the glorious earth by the evil of poverty".

“我想是没有的。”

“那么没有害的东西会产生害处吗?”

“不,当然不会。”

“不能产生坏处的东西做坏事了吗?”

“也不会。”

“不作恶的东西就不是恶的原因,是吗?”

“当然不是。”

“那么,善是有益的吗?”

“是的。”

“那么,它就是善行的原因吗?”

“是的。”

“由此,善不是一切事物的原因:它是好的事物的原因,而坏的事物则不能归咎于它。”

“完全正确。”他说。 c

“那么神也一样,”我说,“因为神是善的,所以他不能像平常人们说的那样是一切事情的原因。他只是一小部分人类生活的原因,很多事情不能归因于他——我的意思是,世上坏事比好事多得多。唯有他是好事的原因,而坏事的原因必须到别处去找而不能归因于神。”

“我认为你说得完全正确。”他说。

“所以,”我说,“我们不应该纵容荷马或任何其他诗人说
诸神的蠢话,‘宙斯的殿前放着两个罐子,一个装满好运,但另 d
一个装满厄运’,如果宙斯把两者混合在一起,再分给人,那么
那个人‘有时遇上厄运,有时遇上好运’,而要是他不将两者混
合,单单把厄运给予人时,那个人‘被迫在富饶的大地上遭受

e Nor will we connive at them claiming that "Zeus is the dispenser of
both good and evil".

'Moreover, we'll disapprove of the attribution of Pandarus' per-
jury and truce-breaking to the agency of Athena and Zeus, and of the
gods' quarrel and its resolution to Themis and Zeus; and we'll not al-
380a low the younger generation to hear the idea which Aeschylus expresses
as "When God wants to visit utter ruin on a household, he implants
the cause in men." No, if plays are composed (such as the one these
lines are from) about Niobe's afflictions, or about the trials and tribu-
lations of the descendants of Pelops, or about the Trojan War, the
playwrights must either be prohibited from saying that God was re-
sponsible for these events, or if they do attribute them to God, they
have to come up with an explanation which approximates to the one
we're looking for at the moment, and say that what God did was right
b and good, in the sense that the people in question were being pun-
ished and therefore benefited; but poets should be prohibited from
saying that these people were in a *bad* way as a result of being pun-
ished and that this was God's doing. The claim that the sinners were
badly off because they were in need of punishment, and that in pun-
ishing them God was benefiting them, is permissible; but the claim
that God, who is good, is responsible, for any instance of badness is
to be resisted as forcefully as possible by anyone who wants a well-
regulated community, until it is never spoken and never heard by any-
c one, of whatever age, whether the tale is told in verse or in prose.
And the reasons are that the voicing of these views is sacrilege, they
do us no good, and they are inconsistent with one another.'

'I approve of this law,' he said. 'I'll be right behind you when you cast your vote for it.'

'So now we have the first of the laws and guidelines which pertain to the gods,' I said. 'Any spoken words or composed works will have to conform to the principle that God is not responsible for everything, but only for good.'

'Well, I'm certainly happy with it,' he said.

贫困之恶’。我们也不能纵容他们说‘宙斯是善与恶的分发 e
者’。

“此外,我们不同意潘达洛斯的背信弃义、破坏停战是因
为雅典娜和宙斯的作用,也不同意把诸神之间的争吵和解决
归因于塞米斯和宙斯;我们不能让年轻人听到埃斯库罗斯的 380a
说法,他是这样说的:‘当神想要毁掉一个家族,他便把原因埋
在人身上。’相反,如果有人以这些诗句的形式写关于尼俄柏
的磨难,或有关佩洛普斯的后代的审判和苦难,或有关特洛伊
战争,那么就必须禁止剧作家说神是这些事情的原因,或者如
果他们真的归因于神,那么他们必须拿出一个与我们现在所
寻找的相近的解释,说神所做的是正义的、善的,是在让那些 b
人得到惩罚并由此使他们得到好处的意义上说的;但诗人应
该禁止说那些人由于神的惩罚和神的所作所为而处境悲惨。
这样的说法是允许的,即恶人处境悲惨是因为他们需要惩罚,
因为神通过惩罚而使他们受益;然而任何想治理好城邦的人,
应该极力抵制善的神是任何恶的原因这种说法,直到它不再
被任何年龄的人说起或听到,无论故事是否用韵文写的。理 c
由就是这些话是亵渎神灵的,它们对我们没有什么好处,而且
还是自相矛盾的。”

“我赞成这条法律,”他说,“你为之投票的时候我会支持你的。”

“那么现在我们有了一条关于神的法律和准则,”我说,“说出来的任何话和创作出来的任何作品,都必须符合这条原则,即神不是一切事情的原因,而只是好事的原因。”

“好的,我当然为之感到高兴。”他说。

d ‘All right, then. What about a second principle, as follows? Do you think that God is a sorcerer and can by exercising his will vary his appearance from time to time, sometimes by actually changing and transforming his appearance into a large number of forms, and at other times by deluding us into thinking that's what he's done? Or do you think he's uniform and extremely unlikely to abandon his own appearance?’

‘I'm not in a position to say just at the moment,’ he replied.

e ‘Look at it this way. Isn't it inevitable that if anything sheds its form, the change is due either to itself or to something else?’

‘Yes.’

‘Now, really good things are extremely unlikely to be altered or moved by an external agent, aren't they? For instance, a human body is altered by food, drink, and exercise, and plants are altered by the heat of the sun and by wind and phenomena like that; but the more
381a healthy and strong a thing is, the less likely it is to be altered.’

‘Of course.’

‘And the more courageous and intelligent a mind is, the less likely it is that an external agent would disturb it and alter it?’

‘Yes.’

‘Moreover, the same principle applies universally even to manufactured items, such as utensils, houses, and clothes: things which are well made and are in good condition are less likely to be altered by time and other phenomena.’

‘True.’

b ‘So anything which is in a good state—whether that is due tonature or human skill or both—can hardly be changed at all by an external agent.’

‘That sounds right.’

“那么好吧。接下来第二条原则是什么呢？你认为神是 d
魔术师，能够凭他的意愿不时地变换他的样子，有时真的把样子转变成很多形式，而有时让我们错误地相信他的所作所为？或者你是否认为他是单一的并且绝对不可能脱离他自己的样子？”

“现在我答不上来。”他回答说。

“这样来看。如果一个东西脱离了它的形式，那么不就必然
是由于自身或别的东西吗？” e

“是的。”

“那么，真正善的东西是最不可能被一个外部事物改变或推动，不是吗？比如，身体被饮食和运动所改变，植物被阳光的热量、风以及诸如此类的因素所改变；但一个东西越是健康、强壮，
它就越少可能被改变。” 381a

“当然。”

“一个灵魂越是勇敢和智慧，就越少可能被外部事物打扰和改变？”

“是的。”

“此外，同样的原则甚至还可以普遍地运用于制成品，如器具、房子和衣服：做得很好和处于良好状态下的东西，就不大可能为时间或其他因素所改变。”

“对的。”

“那么任何处于良好状态下的东西——无论是由于其本性还 b
是由于人工或者两者兼而有之——几乎不能被一个外部的东西所改变。”

“听起来是对的。”

'But God and the divine realm are of course in all respects as perfect as anything can be.'

'Of course.'

'From this point of view, then, God is extremely unlikely to have at his disposal a large number of forms.'

'Yes, extremely unlikely indeed.'

'Would he, however, change and alter himself internally, by his own resources?'

'If he changes in the first place,' he said, 'then obviously this must be how.'

'Well, does he enhance and improve himself, or does he worsen and debase himself?'

c 'If he changes,' he said, 'then it must be for the worse, since it's unthinkable that God's goodness and excellence are anything less than perfect.'

'You're absolutely right,' I said. 'And, Adeimantus, in this context, do you think that anyone—human or divine—deliberately makes himself deteriorate in any respect?'

'That's impossible,' he said.

'It is equally impossible, then,' I said, 'for God to want to change himself. Since, as we have found, the divine nature is as perfect and as good as anything could be, then any god retains his own form in a uniform, direct fashion for ever.'

'I think that's absolutely inevitable,' he said.

d 'It follows, Adeimantus,' I said, 'that none of our poets is to say, "The gods travel around human habitations disguised as all sorts of visitors from other lands." Nor are they to tell lies about Proteus and Thetis, or present Hera in a tragedy or any other kind of poem in an altered form, as a mendicant holy woman begging alms "for the life-giving children of the Argive river Inachus", or repeat the mass of other' similar lies that have

“但神和属于神的领域当然在所有方面都像任何能够完善的事物一样，是最完善的。”

“当然。”

“那么这样看来，神最不可能随意地具有多种形式。”

“是的，确实是最不可能的。”

“然而他会依靠自己而发生改变且是自身内在的改变吗？”

“如果神发生了变化，”他说，“那么显然肯定是这样改变的。”

“那么，他使自己变好提升了自己，还是使自己变坏堕落了？”

“如果他最初发生变化，”他说，“那么他肯定是变坏。” c

“你说得完全正确，”我说，“阿狄曼图，这样说来，你认为他——无论是人还是神——会有意使自己在任何方面变坏吗？”

“那不可能。”他说。

“那么神要改变自己同样也是不可能的，”我说，“因为正如我们发现的那样，神性是最完美的，任何神都单纯而永远地保持在自己的唯一的形式中。”

“我认为那是绝对必然的。”他说。

“因此，阿狄曼图，”我说，“我们的诗人中没有人可以说：‘诸 d
神装扮成各种外邦来客，环游凡人的城邦。’他们也不可以讲述关于普洛托斯和忒提斯的谎话，也不可以把悲剧或任何其他形式的诗中的赫拉说成是改变了形象，装扮成女祭司，‘为那些伊那科斯河的阿尔戈弗的给予生命的孩子们’募捐，也不可以重复讲述诸如此

e been told. Furthermore, we should neutralize the poets' influence on mothers, which makes them scare their children with terrible stories about how some gods tend to prowl around during the hours of darkness in a wide variety of unfamiliar human guises, so that we stop the mothers blaspheming against the gods, and at the same time stop them making their children too timid.'

'Yes, we should,' he said.

'But even if it isn't in the gods' nature actually to change,' I said, 'do they magically delude us into seeing them appear in all kinds of guises?'

'It's not inconceivable,' he said.

382a 'Well, would God willingly mask the truth behind appear ance and deceive us by his words or actions?' I asked.

'I don't know,' he answered.

'Don't you know that a true falsehood (if you'll allow me the phrase) is loathed by everyone, divine or human?' I asked.

'What do you mean?' he asked.

'I mean', I said, 'that no one chooses and wants to be deceived in the most important part of himself and about the most important things. The presence of falsehood there is his worst fear.'

'I still don't understand,' he said.

b 'That's because you think I'm trying to make a high-powered point,' I said. 'But all I'm saying is that no one is at all happy at being lied to and deceived in his mind about the facts; no one likes being ignorant, and the existence and presence of falsehood there are extremely unwelcome to everyone; they particularly hate it there.'

'They certainly do,' he said.

'Well, I might have been perfectly correct when I described this

类的谎言。此外,我们还要消除除掉诗人对母亲们的影响,这些 e
诗人的作品被母亲们当作可怕的故事用来吓唬她们的孩子,它们讲述的是某些神在各种人所不熟悉的面目下在黑暗中到处游荡,这样我们就能阻止母亲们亵渎神灵,同时也阻止她们使她们的孩子变得过于胆小。”

“是的,我们应该这样做。”他说。

“但是即使神的本性并不发生真正的改变,”我说,“他们也会用魔法来蛊惑我们,让我们看到他们以各种各样虚假的外貌出现吗?”

“这并不是不可想象的。”他说。

“啊,神会把真相置于表象之后,而用他的言行来欺骗我们 382a
吗?”我问道。

“我不知道。”他回答道。

“一个真正的谎言(如果你允许我用这个短语表达),是为每个人所厌恶的,无论是神还是人,你不这样认为吗?”我问道。

“你是什么意思呢?”他问道。

“我的意思是,”我说,“没有人会选择想要在自己最重要的部分,在关于最重要的事情上受到欺骗。他最怕的就是虚假。”

“我还是不明白。”他说。

“那是因为你以为我在说很深奥的意思,”我说,“然而我说的 b
意思是,没有人乐于受欺骗,在心灵中真相受到蒙蔽;没有人喜欢被愚弄,虚假的存在和出现是所有人都极其不愿意接受的;他们尤其讨厌它的存在。”

“他们当然讨厌它。”他说。

“那么,我把刚才那种状况说成是真正的虚假,也许是完全正

state a moment ago as true falsehood—the state of misapprehension caused by falsehood in the mind. I mean, a spoken lie is a kind of
c copy and subsequent reflection of the mental condition, and no pure lie, don't you think?'

'Yes.'

'Now, a genuine lie is hated by men as well as gods.'

'I think so.'

'What about a spoken lie? Aren't there occasions and situations when telling lies is helpful and doesn't therefore warrant hatred? What about when we're dealing with enemies, or with people we count as friends, but who are trying to do something bad because they've gone mad or have somehow taken leave of their senses? Isn't telling lies helpful under these circumstances as a preventative medicine? Moreo-
d ver, consider those stories we were discussing not long ago. we cannot know the truth about events in the past, so we make something up which approximates as closely as possible to the truth, and that helps us, doesn't it?'

'Yes,' he said, 'you're quite right.'

'Which of these reasons, then, makes telling lies helpful to God? Would he make up something which resembles the truth because he doesn't know the past?'

'That's a ridiculous suggestion,' he said.

'So there's nothing of the lying poet in God.'

'I don't think so.'

'Would he lie out of fear for his enemies?'

e 'Hardly.'

'Because his friends have taken leave of their senses or gone mad?'

'Anyone witless or insane is no friend of God,' he said.

'So God has no reason to lie.'

'No.'

确的——这种错误的理解是由心灵中的虚假导致的。我的意思是说,一个说出口的谎言是心灵状况的一种摹本,是其并发的一种反映,而不是一个纯粹的谎言,你不这么认为吗?” c

“是这样的。”

“那么,真正的谎言不仅为神所讨厌,而且也为人所讨厌。”

“我想是这样的。”

“言辞中的虚假呢?是否有这样的情况和场合,说谎是有帮助的,因而肯定不会引起厌恶?对付敌人的时候,或者面对我们疯了或失去了理智而想去作恶的朋友的时候呢?在这种情况下,谎言作为一种防范性的药物不是有帮助的吗?此外,想想我们不久前讨论的那些故事:我们不能知道那些过去发生的事情的真相,所以我们编造一些与真相最相近的东西,这对我们是有帮助 d
的,不是吗?”

“是的,”他说,“你说得非常对。”

“那么,什么理由使得我们说谎言对神有用呢?是否神对过去的事情无知,我们才编造一些与真相相近的东西出来?”

“那是很荒唐的假设。”他说。

“那么在神中间找不到说谎的诗人。”

“我想找不到。”

“他会害怕敌人而说谎吗?”

“几乎不会。” e

“是因为他的朋友失去了理智或变疯了吗?”

“任何傻瓜或疯子都不是神的朋友。”他说。

“所以神没有理由说谎。”

“没有。”

'So it is not in the nature of deities or gods to deceive.'

'Absolutely not,' he said.

'Whether acting or speaking, then, God is entirely uniform and truthful. He doesn't actually change himself, and he doesn't delude others either, during their sleeping or their waking hours, in how he appears or in what he says or in the signs he sends.'

383a 'Listening to you speak,' he said, 'I find myself agreeing with you.'

'So do you agree,' I said, 'that this is the second principle to which religious discussions and literature must conform—that the gods are not shape-shifting wizards and do not mislead us by lying in what they say or do?'

'I agree.'

'Although there is much to commend in Homer, then, we won't approve of the passage when Zeus sends the dream to Agamemnon. Likewise, we won't approve of the bit of Aeschylus where Thetis says that at her wedding Apollo "celebrated in song how happy my children
b would make me—how they wouldn't know sickness and would live for many long years—and went on and on about how lucky I was and how the gods smiled on me, until he made my heart glad. And since Phoebus is a god and abounds in prophetic skill, I expected his words to be true. But for all his singing, for all his sharing of our feast, for all these claims of his, it is he who has now killed my son." We'll come down hard on anyone who says anything like this about the gods: we'll
c refuse him a chorus and ban teachers from using his works to educate our children. Otherwise, our guardians won't grow up to be religious people, or to be as godlike themselves as is humanly possible.'

'I'm in complete agreement with these principles,' he said, 'and would want them enshrined as laws.'

386a 'All right, then,' I said. 'If people are going to revere the gods, respect their parents, and not belittle friendship with one anoth-

“所以欺骗不是神灵或诸神的本性。”

“绝对不是。”他说。

“那么无论是行动还是言说，神都是不变的、可信的。实际上他不会改变自己，无论别人在睡觉还是醒着，他也不会通过他的形象、话语或征兆来欺骗他们。”

“听你这样说，”他说，“我发觉自己同意你的说法。” 383a

我说：“那么你同意这就是有关神的言论和诗歌所要遵守的第二条准则——诸神不是会变形的魔术师并且不会用他们欺骗性的言行来误导我们？”

“我同意。”

“那么，虽然在荷马作品中有许多可称颂的东西，但是我们不会赞赏宙斯托梦给阿伽门农的段落。同样我们也根本不会赞同埃斯库罗斯，在他的段落里，忒提斯说阿波罗在她的婚礼
上‘颂唱：我的孩子会给我带来多么大的欢喜啊——他们不会 b
知晓病痛且会长寿——唱啊唱啊，我是多么幸运，诸神向我微笑，直到我心愉悦。福波斯是神，有很多预言的技巧，我希望他的话能成真。他为所有这些颂唱，与我们同宴共享，以及许下所有这些许诺，现在竟是他杀了我的儿子。’我们会斥责那
些对诸神说出这种话的人：我们拒绝他加入歌队，禁止教师使 c
用他的作品教育我们的孩子。否则，我们的卫士就不会成长为虔诚严谨的人，或者是成长为尽可能充满人性的像神本身一样的人了。”

“我完全赞同这些准则，”他说，“并希望把它们立为法律。”

“那么好吧，”我说，“如果人们要敬畏诸神，尊敬他们的父母， 386a
不轻视相互之间的友谊，那么显然，从他们的孩童时代起，那些有

er, then apparently those are the kinds of stories they should and shouldn't hear about the gods, from childhood onwards.'

'I'm sure we're right about this,' he said.

'What about if they are to be brave? Won't they also need stories
b which are designed to make them fear death as little as possible? I mean, don't you think that courage and fearing death are mutually exclusive?'

'Yes, I certainly do,' he answered.

'What about the idea that Hades doesn't just exist, but is terrifying? Do you think this goes with facing death fearlessly and with preferring death in battle to defeat and slavery?'

'Of course not.'

'So here's another aspect of story-telling for us to oversee, apparently. We must ask those who take on the job of telling stories not to denigrate Hades in the simple fashion they have been, but to speak well of it, because otherwise they'll not only be lying, but also not
c speaking in a way that is conducive to courage in battle.'

'Yes, we must,' he said.

'Then we'll start with the following lines,' I said, 'and delete everything which resembles them: "I'd rather be a slave labouring for someone else—someone without property, who can hardly make a living—than rule over all the spirits of the dead"; and "The vile, dank halls, which
d even the gods hate, might appear to men and gods"; and "Amazing! The soul, the likeness of a person, really does exist in Hades' halls, but it is completely witless"; and "He alone had consciousness, while the rest were darting shadows"; and "His soul flew from his body and went to Hades
387a bewailing its fate, forfeiting courage and the glory of young manhood"; and "Like a wisp of smoke, his soul went down-to the underworld with a

关诸神的故事,有的应该让他们听,有的则不应该让他们听。”

“我确信在这一点上我们是对的。”他说。

“如果想要他们勇敢,又该怎样呢?他们是否也需要一些使得他们尽可能地不畏惧死亡的故事呢?我的意思是,你难道不认为勇敢和
害怕死亡是相互排斥的吗?” b

“是的,我当然这样认为。”他回答说。

“这样的一种观念又会怎样呢,即认为地府冥王不仅存在,而且令人恐怖?你认为伴随这种观念而有的,将会是勇敢地面对死亡,以及在战争中宁愿战死也不愿失败而成为奴隶的行为吗?”

“当然不会。”

“那么显然,我们还要监视讲故事的人。我们必须要求那些以讲故事为业的人,不得把冥界自身简单地加以丑化,而要说它的好,因为要不是这样的话,他们不光是在说谎,而且在语言表述
上也无助于鼓舞战场上的勇气。” c

“是的,我们必须这样。”他说。

“那么我们从下面这些诗句开始,”我说,“删去所有类似于它们的诗句:‘我宁愿成为为别人出劳力的奴隶——纵使那人没有财产度日艰难——也不要统治所有亡故者的灵魂’;‘那连诸神都憎恶的简陋、潮湿的厅堂,可能就会暴露在人和
诸神的面前’;‘啊,灵魂鬼影确实存在于冥王的厅堂中,只是 d
全然没有了理智’;‘唯有他有意识,其余的都是飘忽的鬼影’;‘他的灵魂哀叹着它的命运,失去了勇气和年轻人的荣
美,脱离他的身体去向冥界’;‘他的灵魂像一缕烟雾恸哭着落 387a
往下面的世界’;‘就像在阴暗的洞穴深处吱吱盘旋的蝙蝠,当

shrill cry"; and"As when bats flit about squeaking in the depths of an awful cave, when one of them loses its perch on the crowded rock,
b and they cling to one another, so the flock of souls went with shrill cries." We'll implore Homer and the rest of the poets not to get cross if we strike these and all similar lines from their works. We'll explain that it's not because the line are not good poetry and don't give pleasure to most people; on the contrary, the better poetry they are, the more they are to be kept from the ears of children and men who are to be autonomous and to be more afraid of losing this freedom than of death.'

'Absolutely.'

'Now, we'd better get rid of all the frightening and terrifying names which crop up here. I mean names like Cocytus and Styx,
c ghost and wraith, and so on—all the names which are designed to make everyone who hears them shudder. In another context, they may have a useful purpose to serve; but our worry is that this shivering might make our guardians too feverish and enervated.'

'It's a legitimate worry,' he remarked.

'Should we ban them, then?'

'Yes.'

'It's names which have the opposite effect that should be used in both prose and poetry, isn't it?'

'Clearly.'

d 'Shall we also remove the passages where eminent men weep and wail in mourning, then?'

'We have to,' he said. 'It follows from what we've already done.'

'Let's see whether or not we're right to remove them,' I said. 'We can agree that one good man will not regard death as a terrible thing for another good man—a friend of his—to suffer.'

'Yes, we can.'

'So a good man won't mourn as if the other person had suffered something terrible.'

有一只从拥挤的岩壁上掉落时,其余的连连掉落一般,众灵魂也
恸哭随行。'如果我们把这些诗句以及其他类似的诗句从他们的
作品中去除,我们恳请荷马和其他诗人不要对我们发怒。我们会 b
解释说,那并不是因为它们不是好诗,没有给大多数人以快乐;相
反,越是好的诗就越是要远离儿童和成年人的耳朵,他们得成为
自主的人,并且应是害怕失去这种自由更胜于害怕死亡。"

"完全是这样的。"

"那么,我们最好去掉所有这里出现的吓人、恐怖的名词。我
说的名词指的是诸如科赛特斯河和冥河、鬼魂和幽灵等等——这
些名词都使任何听到它们的人颤栗。在别的语境中,它们也许对 c
某个目的来说是有用的;但我们担心的是这种恐惧会使得我们的
卫士过于胆怯无力。"

"这种担心有道理。"他说。

"那么,我们应该对此加以禁止吗?"

"是的。"

"应该在诗文中使用具有相反效果的名词,不是吗?"

"毫无疑问。"

"那么,我们也应该把那些涉及到杰出人物哭泣、哀痛的段落 d
删去?"

"从我们已经讨论过的来看,我们必须这样做。"他说。

"让我们来考察一下把它们删去是否正确,"我说,"我们同意,一个好人不会把另一个好人——他的一个朋友——的死亡看作是一件可怕的事情。"

"是的,我们可以同意。"

"所以一个好人不会哀痛,就好像另一个人遭受了可怕的事情。"

'No.'

'Moreover, we can also agree that a good man is preeminently capable of providing himself with a good life entirely from his own resources, and is absolutely the last person to need anyone or anything else.'

e 'True.'

'So he'd be the last person to be overwhelmed by the loss of a son or a brother or some money and so on and so forth.'

'Yes, definitely.'

'He'll also be the last person to mourn, then, when some such disaster overtakes him: no one will endure it with more equanimity than him.'

'Very true.'

'We'd be right, then, not to have famous men mourning. We can allow women to do that (as long as they aren't admirable women) and
388a any bad men there might be, so that the people we claim to be training for guardianship of our land find all that sort of behaviour distasteful.'

'That's right,' he said.

'So we have a further request to make of Homer and the rest of the poets. We'll ask them not to portray Achilles, who was the son of a goddess, "at one point lying on his side, then later on his back,
b and then on his front; and then getting to his feet and sailing, crazed with grief, over the sands of the bitter sea", or as "pouring handfuls of filthy ashes over his head", or generally as weeping and wailing to the extent and in the fashion that the poet portrays him. And we'll ask them not to have Priam, a close relative of the gods by birth, "begging, and rolling in the dung as he calls out to each man by name". We'll be even more forceful, however, in our request that they don't
c portray the *gods* lamenting and saying things like, "Oh, poor me! How wretched I am to have borne the noblest of children!"; or at the very least they ought to stop short of giving such an inaccurate portrait of the greatest of the gods that they have him saying, "Alas! The man I now see being chased around Troy is dear to me, and my heart grieves", and

"不会。"

"此外,我们也能同意,一个好人是完全能够自给自足地过上
幸福一生的,并且也绝对不依赖任何人或任何东西的。" e

"对的。"

"所以他是最不会被失去儿子、兄弟、钱财等等诸如此类东西所吓倒的。"

"对,肯定是的。"

"那么,当这样的灾难降临时,他也是最不会感到哀痛的:没有人能比他更泰然处之。"

"非常正确。"

"那么,我们不让名人哀痛是对的。我们可以允许妇人去哀
痛(只要她们不是令人赞佩的妇人),还有任何的坏蛋也可以去哀
痛,这样我们正在培养来保护我们土地的人们,才会觉得所有那 388a
些行为是令人厌恶的。"

"那样是对的。"他说。

"所以我们对荷马和其余的诗人有更多的要求。我们要求他
们不得把女神的儿子阿基琉斯描述成'他时而侧卧,时而仰卧,时
而俯卧,最后他站起来,去到海边,在那里徘徊,心神错乱,'或描
述成'他用双手抓起地上发黑的泥土,撒到了自己的头上',或就 b
像诗人那样把他描绘成饮泣悲叹。我们要求他们不要把诸神的
近亲普里亚姆描绘成'在污泥泥里翻滚乞求,呼唤着每个人的名
字'。然而我们甚至更强烈地要求他们不能描述诸神恸哭,并且
说这样的话:'哦,可怜的我啊,生了这个最高贵的孩子,我是多么
不幸啊!';或者至少他们不应该把最伟大的诸神描述得如此不准 c
确,他们说:'哎呀!我现在看见我心爱的人被追得沿特洛伊逃跑,我

d “Alas that Sarpedon, the dearest of men to me, is destined to fall at the hands of Patroclus the son of Menoetius.”

'The point is, my dear Adeimantus, that if the young men of our community hear this kind of thing and take it seriously, rather than regarding it as despicable and absurd, they're hardly going to regard such behaviour as despicable in human beings like themselves and feel remorse when they also find themselves saying or doing these or similar things. Instead, they won't find it at all degrading to be constantly chanting laments and dirges for trivial incidents, and they won't resist doing so.'

e 'You're quite right,' he said.

'And what we've just been arguing, in effect—and at the moment no one's come up with a better argument, so we should stick to this one—is that we must prevent this happening.'

'Yes, we must.'

'Now, they'd better not be prone to laughter either. I mean, the stronger the laughter, the stronger the consequent emotional reaction too—that's almost inevitable.'

'I agree,' he said.

'We should, therefore, refuse admittance to any poetry which portrays eminent humans as being overcome by laughter, and do so even more vigorously if it shows gods in that state.'

389a 'Yes, indeed,' he said.

'So we'll also reject the lines of Homer where he says about the gods, “Unquenchable laughter arose among the blessed gods as they watched Hephaestus bustling about the house.” According to your argument, we should disallow this type of passage.'

'Yes, if you want to attribute the argument to me,' he said. 'At any rate, we should disallow it.'

b 'Next, they must rate honesty highly. You see, if we were right in what we were saying a short while ago, and the gods really have no use for falsehood, although it can serve as a

心伤悲’，‘哎呀，萨耳波冬，最亲近我的人啊，注定要落入墨诺提
俄斯的儿子帕特洛克罗之手。’ d

“我亲爱的阿狄曼图，问题是如果我们城邦中的年轻人听到了这些东西并且还认真地对待，而不是把它们当作可鄙的、愚蠢的，那么他们也不会把发生在自己身上的这样的行为，看作是可鄙的，当他们发现自己说了或者做了这些或与这些类似的事情时，也不会感到悔恨。相反，他们并不觉得经常为小事哀唱挽歌是可耻的，并且他们对此也不加克制。”

“你说得非常正确。”他说。 e

“我们所讨论的恰是我们必须阻止此事的发生，事实上，此刻没有人能拿出一个更好的论证，所以我们应该坚持这个结论。”

“是的，我们必须坚持。”

“那么，他们最好也不要轻易地取笑。我的意思是，笑得越厉害，随之而来的情感反应也更强烈——那几乎是不可避免的。”

“我同意。”他说。

“因此，我们应该拒绝接受在诗歌里描绘杰出者们放声大笑不
能自制，要是甚至更加起劲地把诸神描绘成那样就更难以接受了。” 389a

“确实是的。”他说。

“所以我们也要拒绝荷马的那些关于诸神的诗句：‘看着赫非斯托斯在厅堂里奔忙，永乐诸神发出难以克制的大笑。’依据你的说法，我们不能容许这样的诗文。”

“是的，如果你想把这个说法看作是我的，”他说，“无论如何，
我们不应该容许这种说法。” b

“那么，他们必须把真实看作高于一切。你想想，如果我们不久前正谈论着的是对的，而且虚假对于诸神的确没有什么用处，虽然

type of medicine for us humans, then clearly lying should be entrusted to doctors, and laymen should have nothing to do with it.'

'Clearly,' he said.

'If it's anyone's job, then, it's the job of the rulers of our community: they can lie for the good of the community, when either an external or an internal threat makes it necessary. No one else, however, should have anything to do with lying. If an ordinary person lies
c to these rulers of ours, we'll count that as equivalent in misguidedness, if not worse, to a patient lying to his doctor about his physical condition, or an athlete in training lying to his trainer about his physical condition, or someone misleading a ship's captain, with respect to his ship or crew, by telling him lies about his own state or that of one of his fellow crewmen.'

'You're absolutely right,' he said.

d 'So if anyone else is caught lying in our community—"any artisan, whether diviner or healer of ills or carpenter"—he is to be punished on the grounds that he's introducing a practice which is just as liable to wreck and ruin a community as a ship.'

'Yes, it would,' he said, 'if what people did was influenced by what he had said.'

'Now, won't the young men of our community need self-discipline?'

'Of course.'

'And aren't the most important aspects of self-discipline, at least
e for the general rank and file, obedience to those in authority and establishing one's own authority over the pleasures of drink, sex, and food?'

'I think so.'

'So I'm sure we'll approve of the kind of thing Homer has Diomedes say—"Sit down, shut up, and listen to me"—and related passages, like "Exuding an aura of courage, the Greeks advanced in silence,

它对于我们人类能作为一剂药,那么,谎言显然应该交托给医生,一般人不应该与它有什么关联。”

“显然。”他说。

“如果说它是某个人的职责的话,那么这就是我们城邦的统治者的职责:当内外的危险使得事态本身有必要的时候,他们可以为城邦的利益而说谎。然而别的人不应该说谎。如果一般人
向我们的那些统治者说谎,那么我们会把这情况看作是一种罪 c
过,如果不是更坏的话,那也是等同于病人就他的身体状况向他的医生撒谎,或参加训练的运动员就他的身体状况向他的教练撒谎,或者某人误导船长,在船只或船员方面谎报他自己的或他的船员伙伴之一者的情况。”

“你说得完全正确。”他说。

“所以如果有任何人在我们城邦里说谎被逮住了——‘任何 d
具有专门技艺之人,无论是占卜者、疾病治疗者还是木匠’——他必要受到惩罚,因为他所带来的行为使得城邦会像船一样容易被倾覆和毁灭。”

“是的,”他说,“如果人们的行动受到了他谎话的影响,那么会的。”

“那么,我们城邦的年轻人不需要自我克制吗?”

“当然需要。”

“对于一般人来说,自我克制的最重要的方面,不就是服从统 e
治者,并且在饮酒、食色方面的快乐能加以控制?”

“我想是这样的。”

“所以我赞同荷马让狄奥墨得斯说的那些话——‘坐下来,闭上嘴,听我说’——以及相关的段落,如‘希腊人充满着勇气,默默

respecting their leaders", and so on and so forth.'

'Yes, we will.'

'Well, what about lines like "You're groggy with wine, you have
390a the eyes of a dog and the heart of a deer" and the next few lines? Are they all right? And what about all the other impertinent things people have said to their rulers in works of prose or poetry?'

'We won't approve of them.'

'That, I suppose, is because they don't encourage self-discipline in their audience, though they may well be enjoyable from another point of view. What do you think?'

'I agree,' he said.

'What about having your cleverest character saying that in his o-
b pinion the best thing in the world is when "The nearby tables are laden with bread and meat, and the steward draws wine from the mixing-bowl, brings it, and pours it into the cups"? Do you think this is the right material for a young man to hear if he is to be self-controlled? Or "There is no death worse than death by starvation, no more wretched fate to face"? And then there's the passage where, while everyone else—mortal and immortal—is asleep, Zeus stays awake to do some
c planning, but in no time at all it is driven completely out of his mind by his sexual desire, and he is so overwhelmed by the sight of Hera that he doesn't even want to go to their room, but wants to have sex with her there and then, on the ground, and he says that he's feeling more desire for her even than the first time they slept together, "without our parents knowing". And the story of how Hephaestus ensnared Ares and Aphrodite for similar reasons is equally inappropriate material for them to hear.'

'I couldn't agree with you more,' he said. 'It's quite unsuitable.'

'On the other hand,' I said, 'it's worth their paying atten-
d tion to the portrayal on stage or in writing of occasions when famous men express, by their words or actions, resistance to all kinds of temptations. For instance, there are the lines, "He struck his breast and spoke sternly to his heart: 'Patience, heart—

地行进着，敬畏他们的长官'，如此等等。"

"是的，我们赞同。"

"那么，'你是喝醉了，头上生狗眼，身上长鹿心'以及接下去的几行，这样的诗句怎么样呢？它们都是对的吗？在诗文中，所 390a
有其他人们对统治者说的无礼的话又怎么样呢？"

"我们不会赞同它们的。"

"我想那是因为他们没有在他们的听众中鼓励自制，虽然从另一个角度看它们也许会有些乐趣。你怎么认为？"

"我同意。"他说。

"让最聪明的人说的一席话怎么样呢？他认为世上最好的事情就是在'面前的餐桌上摆满了各式食品肴馔，司酒把调好的蜜
酒从调缸舀出给各人的酒杯一一斟满'的时候。一个年轻人若是 b
该有节制，那么你认为这些东西说给他听恰当吗？或者'最糟糕的死亡莫过于饿死，没有比这更不幸的命运'？还有这样一个段落，当其他每个人——可朽的凡人和不朽的神灵——都睡着时，宙斯却为了某个计划还醒着，但顷刻间他由于性欲的驱使而完全
失去了理智，他全然为赫拉的容光所倾倒，以致他甚至不想进屋， c
那时那地就想要和赫拉在地上做爱，他说他对她的欲求更甚，甚至超过了他们第一次'瞒着我们的父母同床'。赫非斯托斯如何将阿瑞斯和阿芙洛狄特捆绑起来的故事，出于类似的理由，同样不适合于他们去听。"

"我实在太同意你了，"他说，"那非常不适合。"

"另一方面，"我说，"名人们在他们的言行中抵制各种诱惑的 d
场景，倒是值得他们注意在舞台上或写作中加以刻画的。比如这些诗句：'他捶击着胸脯，严厉地对他的心说："忍耐吧，心啊——你

you've put up with worse in the past.'"'

'Absolutely,' he said.

'Then again, we shouldn't let them be mercenary or avaricious.'

'Of course not.'

e 'So they shouldn't repeat the verse "Gifts win over even gods and magnificent kings". And we won't compliment Achilles' attendant Phoenix on his restraint in advising Achilles to accept the gifts he was being offered and help the Greeks in their fight, but not to refrain from his "wrath" unless he was bribed. It will also go against our wishes and our convictions for Achilles himself to be mercenary enough to accept Agamemnon's gifts and to refuse to release a corpse until he'd been given a ransom.'

391a 'Yes, it would be wrong to approve of that kind of be-haviour,' he said.

'Now, the fact that it's Homer makes me hesitate,' I said, 'but I'm not sure it's not actually sacrilegious for us to say things like this about Achilles and accept them when others say them. The same goes also for when Achilles says to Apollo, "There's no god more baneful than you—you with your aloofness. You misled me, and I'd pay you back if I could.' We shouldn't believe that he refused to obey the riv-
b er-god either, and was ready to fight him, and that he said of his hair, which was dedicated to another river, the Spercheius, "I hereby give my hair to the hero Patroclus: may he take it with him", when Patroclus was dead—we shouldn't believe that he did this. And we'll deny the truth of the stories that he dragged Hector around Patroclus' tomb and slaughtered prisoners on his funeral pyre. And we won't allow our citizens to believe that Achilles—the child of a goddess and of Peleus
c (who was himself a model of self-discipline and a grandson of Zeus) and tutored by the sage Cheiron—was so full of turmoil that he

连过去更坏的都挺过来了。”’”

“完全是的。”他说。

“那么我们还不应该让他们贪婪或唯利是图。”

“当然不能。” e

“所以他们不应该一再地说这样的诗句‘赠礼甚至能说服诸神和伟大的君王’。而且我们不会赞同阿基琉斯的随从斐尼克斯的谨慎,他建议阿基琉斯接受赠礼,帮助希腊人作战,如果不收到贿赂就不释‘怒’。说阿基琉斯贪婪地接受了阿伽门农的赠礼,不得到赎金就拒绝放还尸首,这也是违背我们的意愿和信念的。” 391a

“是的,赞同那样的行为是错误的。”他说。

“现在,事实是荷马使得我犹豫,”我说,“叙说类似于这些关于阿基琉斯的事情或接受别人关于他们的说法对我们来说实际上并不是亵渎神灵的,对此我还不敢确信。同样的情形也在于阿基琉斯对阿波罗说:‘没有比你更毒的神了——带着你的冷漠。你将我引入迷途,我要惩罚你,如果我有力量。’我们也不应该相信他拒绝遵从河神,并且准备和 b
他战斗,以及他说到他的献给另一位河神斯佩凯乌斯的头发,当帕特洛克罗死去时,他说:‘我特此把我的头发献给英雄帕特洛克罗:愿他带着它。’——我们不应该相信他做了这些。说他拖着死去的赫克托尔环绕帕特洛克罗的坟墓,在他的火葬柴堆上屠杀俘虏,我们要否认这些故事的真实性。我们不会让我们的公民相信,阿基琉斯——他是女神和珀琉斯的儿子(珀琉斯自身是自制的榜样,是宙斯的孙子),并且得 c
到贤哲凯隆的教导——如此充满混乱以至于他害有两种相互冲突

suffered from the two conflicting diseases of mean-spirited avarice and disdain for gods and men.'

'You're right,' he said.

'Moreover,' I went on, 'we won't believe or tolerate the story about those horrific kidnap projects by Theseus and Peirithous, who
d were respectively the sons of Poseidon and Zeus; and in general, we find it unthinkable that anyone with a god as a parent, or any hero, would be unscrupulous enough to do the terrible, sacrilegious things people falsely attribute to them. No, we should force the poets to deny either that the heroes did these things or that their parents were gods, but not to say both; and they should also be forcibly prevented from trying to persuade the young men of our community that the gods are the source of evil and that the heroes are no better than ordinary
e people. We demonstrated earlier the impossibility of bad things originating with the gods; so, as we said then, these stories are not only sacrilegious, but also false.'

'Of course.'

'And they have a pernicious effect on their audience as well, in the sense that no one will find his own badness reprehensible once he's been persuaded that these things are and always have been done by "immediate descendants of the gods, close relatives of Zeus, people whose altar to Zeus, their father-protector, is high on Mount Ida, above the clouds" and "in whom the blood of deities is still fresh". That's why we must put an end to stories of this nature: if we don't,
392a they will engender in the young men of our community a casual attitude towards badness.'

'I quite agree,' he said.

'Now,' I said, 'if we want to distinguish what in literature should be allowed and what should be censored, there's one further type of writing we should still look at, isn't there? I mean, we've discussed how gods must be portrayed—and deities, heroes, and the dead.'

的疾病：卑贱的贪婪以及傲然地藐视神和人。”

“你说得对。”他说。

“此外，”我继续说，“我们不要相信和容忍那些关于忒修斯和庇里托俄斯的骇人听闻的拐骗事件的故事，他们分别是波塞冬和宙斯的儿子；总体上来说，我们觉得不可想象是：任何其父母为神 d
灵或英雄的人，会肆无忌惮到做出可怕的、亵渎神灵的那些事情来，这些事是人们错误地归结给他们的。相反，我们应该迫使诗人们要么否认是英雄做了这些事情，要么否认他们的父母是神灵，而不能两者都肯定；也应该强力禁止他们去说服我们城邦中的年轻人的企图，说诸神是恶的原因，英雄并不比一般人好。我们早先证明了恶的东西是不可能产生于诸神的；所以，就像我们当时说的那样，这些故事不光是亵渎神灵的，而且还是错误的。” e

“当然。”

“它们也在听众中产生了有害的效果，因为没有人会觉得自己的恶行要受到指责，只要他信服这些事情是并且总是由这些人干的，他们是‘诸神的直系后代，宙斯的近亲，他们向宙斯——他们的父神——所献祭的祭坛高高地在伊代山巅，云霄之上’，并且‘神灵的血液还在他们之中流淌’。这就是为什么我们必须终止这种故事的原因：如果我们不这样，它们就会在我们城邦的年轻人当中产生出一种对待恶的轻慢态度。” 392a

“我非常同意。”他说。

“那么，”我说，“如果我们想要在文学作品中区分什么是允许的，什么该受审查，那么还有另外一种类型的写作我们应该加以考察，不是吗？我的意思是说，我们已经讨论了诸神、神灵、英雄以及死者必须如何加以描述的问题。”

'Yes.'

'So wouldn't we be left with writing which has human beings as its subject?'

'Yes, obviously.'

'In fact, though, we can't evaluate this kind of writing at the moment.'

'Why not?'

'Because what we'd claim, I imagine, is that poets and prose-
b writers misrepresent people in extremely important ways, when—as they often do—they portray immoral people as happy and moral people as unhappy, and write about the rewards of undiscovered immorality and how morality is good for someone else, but disadvantageous to oneself. I suppose we'd proscribe assertions of that kind, and tell them that their poems and stories are to make the opposite points, don't you think?'

'I'm certain we would,' he said.

'Well, if you concede this, then won't I claim that you've conceded the original purpose of the enquiry?'

'Yes, I take your point,' he said.

c 'So we'll postpone our conclusion that these are the types of stories that should be told about people until we've got to the bottom of morality and found out how, given its nature, it rewards its possessor whether or not he gives an impression of morality.''

'You're quite right,' he said.

'Let's take our discussion of stories no further, then. But the next thing we should look at, in my opinion, is style. Then we'll have considered not only the content, but also the form the stories should have, and our enquiry will be complete.'

'I don't understand what you're getting at here,' said Adeimantus.

d 'But it's important that you do,' I responded. 'Maybe this

“是的。”

“那么留给我们不还有一种以人为主题的写作吗?”

“显然是的 。”

“然而,事实上我们现在还不能评价这种写作。”

“为什么不能?”

“因为我想,我们所说的是,诗人和散文作家在极其重要的方面都歪曲了人,就如他们经常做的那样,他们把不正义之人描述 b
成是幸福的,而把正义之人描述成是不幸福的,叙述那些由未被发现的不正义而得来的好处,正义如何是对别人有利而对自己不利。我想我们要禁止那种主张,并且告诉他们,他们的诗作和故事要表述相反的观点,你难道不这么认为吗?”

“我确信我们要那样做。”他说。

“好吧,如果你承认了这一点,那么我不就能说你已经承认了探究的原初目标了吗?”

“是的,我同意你的观点。”他说。

“我们只有先弄清正义的真相,并查明,就正义的本质而言, c
它是如何为正义之人赢得报答或奖赏的,而不管该正义之人是否给人一种具有正义的印象,只有这样,我们才能得出结论说,有哪种类型的关于人的故事可以讲述。”

“你说得非常正确。”他说。

“那么关于故事就不要再深入讨论了吧。在我看来,下一个我们考察的就是风格。那么我们要考察的不光是内容,还有故事所应该具有的形式,这样我们的探讨就完整了。”

“我不明白你这里所说的是什么意思。”阿狄曼图说。

“但这很重要,你要搞懂,”我回答说,“也许这样才会把事情 d

will clarify matters for you: isn't everything told by story-tellers or poets actually a narrative of events in the past, present, or future?'

'Of course,' he said.

'And don't they achieve their effect by making use either of pure narrative, or of representational narrative, or of both?'

'I'm still finding this very obscure,' he said.

'What a ridiculous teacher I seem to be!' I said. 'I don't make things plain at all. I'll stop trying to behave like a professional speak-
e er, and instead of talking in general terms, I'll take a particular example and use that to try to explain my meaning. So here's a question for you. You know the very beginning of the Iliad, where Homer has Chryses ask Agamemnon to release his daughter, and Agamemnon
393a gets annoyed, and Chryses doesn't get his way and so calls on his god to curse the Greeks?'

'Yes.'

'Well, as you know, Homer starts by speaking in his own voice and doesn't try to lead us astray by pretending that anyone else is the speaker; this goes on up to the lines "He implored all the Greeks, but especially their leaders, the two sons of Atreus." Next, however, he
b speaks in Chryses' voice and tries his very hardest to make us believe that it isn't Homer who is speaking, but the old priest. And the same method of composition is employed throughout nearly all his narrative of events in Troy and Ithaca and in the *Odyssey* in general.'

'Quite so,' he said.

'Now, the term "narrative" covers all the speeches as well as the passages in between the speeches, doesn't it?'

'Of course.'

向你说清楚:所有讲故事的人或诗人所讲的每一件事实际上不就是叙述过去、现在、将来所发生的事情吗?”

“当然。”他说。

“他们不就是通过纯粹的叙述,或模仿性的叙述,或两者兼有而实现他们的效果吗?”

“我对此还是不太清楚。”他说。

“我看上去是个多么可笑的老师啊!”我说,“我并没有使事情变得清晰。我不再试图表现得像那些擅长说话的人那样,并且不从整体上谈论事情了,我会举个别的例子,用它来尽量向你说明
我的意思。所以想问你一个问题。在《伊利亚特》的一开头,荷马 e
让克律塞斯祈求阿伽门农释放他的女儿,阿伽门农大怒,克律塞斯的要求没有得到满足, 于是他就呼告他的神去诅咒希腊人, 你
知道吗?” 393a

“知道。”

“好吧,就像你所知道的那样,荷马用他自己的话开始讲述,而并不试图通过假装有另一个说话者来误导我们;这一直进行到这些话语:‘他向所有希腊人,但特别是向他们的领袖,阿特乌斯的两位儿子祈求。’可是,接下来,他用克律塞斯的语气说话了,并
尽最大努力使我们相信不是荷马在说话,而是老祭司在说话。同 b
样的写作手法几乎应用于所有对特洛伊和伊塔卡发生的事情叙述,以及整个《奥德赛》中。”

“确实如此。”他说。

“那么,‘叙述’这个词涵盖了所有的对话以及插入对话之间的段落,难道不是吗?”

“当然是的。”

c ‘And when he assumes someone else’s voice to make a speech, don’t you think that on those occasions he does his very best to adapt his own style to whoever he tells us is about to do the talking?’

‘Yes, certainly.’

‘Now, to adapt oneself—one’s voice or one’s appearance— to someone else is to represent that person, isn’t it?’

‘Of course.’

‘So this turns out to be a case of Homer and the rest of the poets composing representational narrative.’

‘Yes.’

d ‘And if Homer were to remain undisguised throughout, then all his poetry and all his narrative would be free of representa-tion. But I don’t want you saying that you don’t understand again, so I’ll tell you how this might happen. If Homer had described Chryses as coming with his daughter’s ransom to appeal to the Greeks, but especially their kings, and had then gone on to continue speaking in his own voice rather than taking on the role of Chryses, then it would be pure narrative, not representation. It would go something like this, in my prose version—I’m no poet. “The priest came and prayed that the
e gods would allow the Greeks to take Troy and come through unscathed, and also prayed that the Greeks would accept the ransom and, out of reverence for Apollo, release his daughter. Although everyone else gave their assent and approval to what he said, Agamemnon became incensed and ordered him to leave immediately and not to return, or else he would find that his staff and its Apolline garlands were insufficient protection; he said that his daughter would grow old in Argos with him sooner than be released, and he told him to leave and not to make him angry, if he wanted to get home safe. The old
394a man was frightened by what Agamemnon had said, and left without a word, but once he was away from the encampment he prayed over and over to Apollo. He invoked the god’s titles, reminded him of all favours he had done him, and asked to be recom-pensed for any shrine he had built or ritual sacrifice he had performed which had pleased the god.

“当他以另一个人的语气在说话的时候，你难道不认为在那 c
些情况下，他要尽可能地使他自己的风格与他告诉我们要模仿的说话人相一致吗？”

“是的，当然。”

“那么使自己与别人的语气和外表相一致，就是在模仿那个人，不是吗？”

“当然是模仿。”

“所以看来情况是这样的：荷马和其他的诗人是在从事模仿性的叙述。”

“是的。”

“如果荷马自始至终都不隐藏自己，那么他所有的诗和叙述
就不会是模仿了。但我不希望你又说不明白，所以我会告诉你这 d
是如何可能的。要是荷马把克律塞斯描述为带着他女儿的赎金来向希腊人祈求，尤其是向他们的君王，然后还接着用他自己的语气说，而不是扮演克律塞斯的角色，那么就是纯粹的叙述而非模仿。我用散文来表述吧——我不是诗人。诗大致如此：‘祭司来了，祈求诸神，让希腊人攻占特洛伊并平安返回，也祈求希腊人
接受他的赎金，出于对阿波罗的敬畏，释放他的女儿。虽然所有 e
其他人表示同意并答应他的祈求，但阿伽门农勃然大怒，并命令他马上离开，不得返回，否则他会发现连权杖和桂冠都保护不了他；阿伽门农说，祭司的女儿在释放之前要和他在阿耳戈斯生活到老，他命令祭司离开，如果想平安回家的话，就不要使他恼怒。
这位老人对阿伽门农所说的话感到恐惧，就一声不响地离开了， 394a
但一旦远离了营地，他就一遍遍地向阿波罗祈祷。他呼告神的名号，求神顾念他为神做的一些劳绩，请求神回报他为取悦神而造的神

He prayed that, in recognition of these favours, the Greeks would be made to pay for his tears with Apollo's darts." That, my friend,' I con-
b cluded, "is how we get pure narrative, which is free of representation.'

'I see,' he said.

'Well,' I went on, 'do you also appreciate that we get the opposite when all the passages which the poet composed in between the speeches are excised and only the dialogue is left?'

'Yes,' he said, 'I understand this as well: this is what happens in tragedies, for instance.'

'You've grasped my meaning perfectly,' I said. 'I think I'm now getting across to you what I couldn't explain before. There are several varieties of poetry and story-telling. Some—tragedy and come-
c dy, as you say—is entirely representational; some is in the poet's own voice—you'd find this particularly in dithyrambic poetry; finally, the kind which employs both methods is what we find in epic poetry, but also in many other types of poetry too. Do you see what I mean?'

'Yes,' he said, 'and I understand what you were trying to tell me earlier.'

'Now cast your mind back to what we were saying even before that—that we had discussed the required content of stories, but still had their form to consider.'

'I remember.'

d 'What I was getting at, then, was just this: we have to decide whether to allow our poets to compose representational narratives, or to compose narratives which are partly represen-tational and partly not (and if so, we have to decide what kinds of subjects should be treated in either of these ways), or to insist that they avoid representation altogether.'

'The underlying point of your enquiry seems to me', he said, 'to be whether or not we'll allow tragedy and comedy into our community.'

'It could be,' I said, 'but it may be far broader. I certainly

龛或所行的祭献。他祈求神顾念他的劳绩，让希腊人为他的眼泪付出阿波罗之箭的代价。’我的朋友，”我总结说，“那就是我们所说的没有模仿的纯粹叙述。” b

“我明白了。”他说。

“那么，”我继续说，“你是否也明白，除去插在诗人所写的对话之间的所有段落而只剩下对话的部分，那么我们就会得到一种相反的东西吗？”

“是的，”他说，“这我也明白：比如说，这就是悲剧的写法。”

“你已经完全理解我的意思了，”我说，“现在我能够让你明白先前无法向你解释的东西了。有好几种诗歌和故事。有一些——就像你说的，悲剧和喜剧——完全是模仿性的；有一些是 c
用诗人自己的语气——你尤其可以在酒神颂歌中看到；最后，还有一类使用了两种方法，我们可以在史诗中找到，在许多其他类型的诗歌中也有。你明白我的意思吗？”

“是的，”他说，“我明白了你先前想要告诉我的意思。”

“现在再回想一下之前说过的话——我们讨论了故事所要求的内容，但还要考察它们的形式。”

“我记得。”

“那么，我要说的意思正是这个：我们得决定是否允许我们的 d
诗人使用模仿性的叙述，或者部分进行模仿性的叙述，部分不是，如果是这样的话，我们还要规定哪些主题是可以采用其中的方式的，或者坚持他们应该完全避免使用模仿。”

“在我看来，你探究的潜在含义，就是我们是否允许悲剧或喜剧进入我们的城邦。”他说。

“可以这么说，”我说，“但也许要更加宽泛。我的确还不太清

don't know yet; we must let our destination be decided by the winds of the discussion.'

'Well said,' he commented.

e 'What I want you to consider carefully, Adeimantus, is whether or not our guardians should be good at representation. Or do you think the answer follows from what we've already established—that whereas an individual can do one job well, he cannot do lots of jobs well, and if he were to try to do so, he would fail to achieve distinction in any occupation, despite undertaking a lot of them?'

'Of course it does.'

'So the same principle applies to representation too: it's impossible for a single individual to play lots of roles as successfully as he plays a single role.'

'That's right.'

395a 'It would be unreasonable, then, to expect a single individual to work at one of the commendable pursuits and at the same time play lots of parts and be good at representation. I mean, as you know, it isn't possible for the same people simulta-neously to be successful in two representational spheres at once, even when those spheres are arguably closely related. Witness, for example, the composition of comedy and the composition of tragedy. Didn't you just describe them as representational?'

'I did—and you're right: people are incapable of doing both at once.'

'And they can't be competent rhapsodes and competent actors at the same time either.'

'True.'

'In fact, the same people can't be competent comic actors and also
b competent tragic actors. These are all representational, wouldn't you say?'

'Yes.'

'And the totality of human nature seems to me, Adeimantus, to

楚;我们必须让讨论之风来决定我们的目的地。”

“说得好。”他评论道。

“阿狄曼图,我想要你仔细考虑的事情是:我们的卫士是否应 e
该善于模仿。或者说你是否觉得答案可以从我们已经确定的事情当中推出——一个人只能做好一个工作,那么他不可能做好许多个工作,而如果他想要做,那么他虽然担负了许多工作,但在任何行业中都不会取得成就?”

“当然是这样。”

“所以同样的原则也可应用于模仿:让一个人像扮演一个角色一样成功地扮演多个角色,那是不可能的。”

“说得对。”

“那么期望一个人在从事一项有价值的工作的同时扮演 395a
许多角色并且还善于模仿,这是没有道理的。我的意思是,就如你了解的那样,让同一个人同时成功地从事两个领域的模仿是不可能的,即使这两个领域按理说是非常接近的。比如悲剧的创作和喜剧的创作,就是证明。你难道不正是把两者都称为模仿吗?”

“我是把他们都称为模仿——你说得对:人不能同时做两件事。”

“他们不可能同时既是称职的朗诵者又是称职的演员。”

“对。”

“事实上,同一个人不能是称职的喜剧演员又是称职的悲剧 b
演员。这些都是模仿,难道不是吗?”

“是的。”

“阿狄曼图,在我看来,人类本性已被分割成比银子还小,以

have been broken down into even smaller slivers than this, until an individual is incapable of successfully playing more than one representational role, or of doing more than one of the actual things which the roles represent.'

'You're absolutely right,' he said.

'Our original position was that our guardians ought to be released from all other sorts of work: they are to be precision craftsmen
c of the community's autonomy, and must not engage in any work which does not tend towards this goal. If we're not to undermine this position, then, our guardians have to concentrate exclusively on this work and on this role. Any representational roles they do take on must, from childhood onwards, be appropriate ones. They should represent people who are courageous, self-disciplined, just, and generous and should play only those kinds of parts; but they should neither do nor be good at representing anything mean-spirited or otherwise contemptible, in case the harvest they reap from representation is reality. I
d mean, haven't you noticed how if repeated representation continues much past childhood, it becomes habitual and ingrained and has an effect on a person's body, voice, and mind?'

'I certainly have,' he replied.

'So,' I said, 'we won't allow people we claim to care for, and who we're saying have to be good men, to represent (despite being men) a woman, young or old, as she hurls insults at her husband, or pits herself against the gods and arrogantly imagines herself to be hap-
e py, or is gripped by catastrophe, grief, and sorrow; and it goes without saying that the same goes for representing a woman who's ill or is suffering pangs of love or labour.'

'I couldn't agree more,' he said.

'And the same prohibition applies to representing slaves of either sex going about their servile duties.'

'I agree.'

'And also, I suppose, to representing bad men who are cowards and whose conduct is the opposite of what we men-tioned a short while ago—who abuse and mock and revile one another when they're
396a drunk, or even when they're sober, or who in general, by their words

致单个人不能成功地扮演多个模仿性的角色、或多个他要模仿的现实事物。”

“你说得完全正确。”他说。

“我们原初的立场是卫士应该放弃所有其他各种工作：他们要专门从事于保卫城邦自治的工作，而不得从事任何与此目的无 c
关的工作。如果我们不想推翻这个说法的话，那么我们的卫士就得要专事这项工作和这个角色。如果一定要模仿什么的话，那么他们从小就要模仿适合他们的。他们应该模仿那些勇敢、自制、正义和慷慨的人，并且应该只是扮演这类角色；而不应该做或善于去模仿那些平庸、卑贱的东西，以防把从模仿中学来的东西付诸实践。我的意思是说，自儿时起的重复模仿会成为习惯，变得 d
根深蒂固，并对人的身体、话语和心灵造成影响，你难道没有注意到吗？”

“我当然注意到了。”他回答说。

“所以，”我说，“我们不允许那些我们声明要关心的人，和我们指望其成为好人的人，身为男人却模仿女人，无论年轻还是年老，模仿她侮辱她的丈夫，或诋毁诸神，还自大地以为自己幸福，或遭受巨大的悲伤而恸哭；更不用说去模仿病痛的或遭受爱情之 e
痛或临产之痛的女人了。”

“我非常同意。”他说。

“同样的禁令也适合于模仿男女奴隶做他们的奴隶事务。”

“我同意。”

“我想也不可模仿胆小之人和坏人，以及其行为与我们不久前所说的相对立的人——他们醉酒时，甚至在酒醒时相互辱骂、嘲笑、斥责，他们都在言行上对自己作恶也对别人作恶。此外，我确 396a

and their actions, sin against themselves and others. Moreover, I'm sure they shouldn't get into the habit of adapting their behaviour to the words and actions of mad people; they must be able to recognize madness and badness in men and women, but they mustn't do or represent any of these things.'

"You're absolutely right,' he said.

'And should they represent artisans like metalworkers,' I asked, 'or oarsmen on a trireme or the petty officers in charge of them, or the like?'

b 'There'll be no chance of that,' he said, 'since there won't even be the opportunity for any of these concerns to occupy their attention.'

'And will they represent horses neighing, bulls bellowing, rivers splashing, the sea crashing, thunderclaps, and so on and so forth?'

'No,' he said. 'We've already forbidden them to behave abnormally or like madmen.'

'So what you're saying, if I'm getting it right,' I said, 'is that there are two kinds of style, two kinds of narrative. There's one kind which a truly good person would use, when called upon to deliver a narrative; 'and then there's another, quite different kind, which would be the staple narrative method of someone who by nature and upbringing was the opposite of truly good.'

'What are they?' he asked.

'My impression', I said, 'is that when a moderate man comes in the course of a narrative to something said or done by a good man, he'll happily assume the role of that good man and read it out, He won't find representation of this kind ignominious. He'll concentrate on representing a good man who is acting reliably and in full pos-
d session of his senses, but he'll be less enthusiastic about and will tend to avoid representing a good man who has become unreliable as a result of illness, love, drink, or in general some catastrophe. However, when he comes across a degrading character, he won't be prepared to assimilate himself seriously to this inferior person, except on the few occasions when this character does something good. He'd be ashamed to do so, not only because he's untrained in representing this type of person, but also because he finds it distasteful to mould and conform himself to an inferior stamp, which his mind finds

信他们不应该在行为上养成像疯子言行一样的习惯;他们必须能够辨别男人和女人身上的疯狂和恶劣,但他们不得去做或模仿任何这些行为。"

"你说得完全正确。"他说。

"他们是否应该模仿金属制造工之类的工匠,"我说,"或一艘三排桨战舰上的划桨手,或主管他们的小官员,或者其他类似的人呢?"

"没有那种可能",他说道,"因为这些人物中的任何一种,甚
至都没有机会来引起他们的注意。" b

"他们会模仿马嘶、牛叫、大河翻腾、大海咆哮、雷鸣等等种类东西吗?"

"不会,"他说,"我们已经禁止他们行为不端或像个疯子。"

"如果我的理解没错的话,"我说,"那么你说的意思就是有两种风格,两种叙述。一种是给真正的好人讲话时使用的风格;另
一种完全不同,它主要是给那些在本性和教育上与真正的好人相 c
反的人所使用的。"

"它们是什么?"他问道。

我说:"我的印象是,一个谦逊之人来叙述一个好人的言行的时候,他会高兴地担当起那个好人的角色并把它讲述出来。他并不以这种模仿为耻。他会专注于模仿一个行为可靠、能充分自制
其感觉的好人,但当好人由于疾病、爱情、醉酒或什么灾难而变得 d
不可靠时,他就没有那么热情并且不想去模仿一个好人了。然而,当他遇到一个低劣之人,他就不会认真地去准备模仿这个比他差的人,除了在少数情况下,当这个人做了好事的时候。他羞于这样做,不只是因为他未受过模仿这类人的训练,还因为他觉得模仿低劣人物,以他们为模范是可耻的,他心底里就看不起他

e contemptible, except for fun.'

'Yes, that's likely,' he said.

'So the sort of narrative he'll use will be the kind we described a short while ago when we were discussing the Homeric epics: he'll employ the style which incorporates both representation and narrative, but the proportion of representation in the text will be small. Do you think I'm right, or am I talking nonsense?'

'What you're talking is certainly not nonsense,' he replied. 'You're describing the principle that kind of person is bound to follow when speaking.'

397a 'All right, then,' I said. 'Now, what about the other kind of person? The less good he is, the less he'll be inclined to omit any of the narrative and regard anything as degrading. We'll end up with someone who's prepared to represent anything and everything, and to do so seriously and publicly. He'll even represent sounds and noises and cries like those of the things we mentioned just now—thunder, wind and hail, axles and pulleys, trumpets, reed-pipes, wind-pipes, and every single musical instrument, and also dogs, sheep, and birds. His style will be the one which relies entirely on vocal or bodily
b representation (though it may contain a small amount of narrative), won't it?'

'Yes, it's bound to be,' he said. 'You're right again.'

'Well, that's what I meant when I said that there were two kinds of style,' I said.

'And there are,' he said.

'Now, one of them involves little variation. Suppose a suit-able musical mode and rhythm is assigned to a speaker's style: it turns out that anyone who uses this style correctly is not far off speaking in one and the same mode (given that the variation is only slight), and also
c with a rhythm that is similarly almost constant. Do you agree?'

'Yes, that's exactly how it is,' he said.

'What about the other speaker's style? Won't it be the opposite?

们，除非是开开玩笑。” e

“是的，很有可能是那样的。”他说。

“所以他使用的这类叙述，就是不久前在讨论荷马的史诗时谈到的那种：他所使用的风格融合了模仿和叙述两者，但模仿在文中的比例很小。你认为我说得对呢，还是说得没有道理？”

“你所说的当然并非没有道理，”他回答说，“那类人在说话时必定要遵守的，就是你所说的这个原则。”

“那么好吧，”我说，“那么另外一类人又怎么样呢？一个人越 397a
少良善，他就越是不会放过叙述，并把任何事物都看成低劣的。结果，他会模仿所有一切事物，并在大庭广众之下认真地对其加以模仿。他甚至会模仿我们刚才提到过的声响、噪音和哭喊——雷、风、冰雹、车轴、滑轮、喇叭、长笛和各种单个的乐器，还有狗、羊和鸟。他的风格完全依赖于对声音或形体的模仿（虽然它可能 b
包含小部分的叙述），不是吗？”

“是的，肯定是的，”他说，“你又说得很对。”

“嗯，当我说有两种风格的时候，我想说的就是这个意思。”我说。

“是有两种。”他说。

“那么，其中一种所包含的变化甚微。假设给一个说话者分派一种合适的音调和节奏：结果就是，任何正确地使用这种风格的人，说话不会离同一个音调很远（因为变化甚微），也不会离一个几乎同样不变的节奏很远。你同意吗？” c

“是的，完全是这样的。”他说。

“那么另一种说话者的风格是怎么样呢？会是相反的吗？因

For it to be used properly, won't it need every mode and every rhythm there is, since it involves every conceivable kind of variation?'

'Yes, that's an excellent description of it.'

'Now, doesn't every poet—everyone who expresses himself in any way at all, in fact—conform to one of these two styles or to one which he concocts by mixing the two together?'

'Necessarily,' he said.

d 'What shall we do, then?' I asked. 'Shall we allow all these styles into our community, or one of the two unmixed styles, or the mixed one?'

'I'd vote for the unmixed style which represents the good man,' he said.

'But the mixed style does at least give pleasure, Adeimantus; and the one which gives by far the most pleasure to children and their attendants, and the general run of people, is the one which is the opposite of your choice.'

'Yes, that's because it is very enjoyable.'

'But perhaps you'd say that it isn't compatible with our
e community's political system,' I went on, 'because each of our people has a single job to do, and therefore none of them is two-sided or many-sided.'

'That's right: it's incompatible.'

'And this was the principle which meant that ours is the only kind of community where we'll find a shoemaker who is a shoemaker and not a ship's captain as well, and a farmer who is a farmer and not a judge as well, and a soldier who is a soldier and not a businessman as well, and so on, wasn't it?'

'True,' he said.

'So it follows that were a man who was clever enough to be able

为它包含了所有想得到的变化，那么为了恰当地使用它，不就需要各种音调和节奏吗？”

“是的，这是对它的一种很精彩的形容。”

“那么，每一个诗人——事实上每一个在任何情况下完全表达自己的人——不都要遵从这两种风格中的一种，或是一种他所混合了两者的风格吗？”

“必然如此。”他说。

“那么我们该做什么？”我问道，“我们是否应该允许所有这些 d
风格都进入我们的城邦，或者没有混合的两种当中的一者，还是那种混合的风格？”

“我赞同模仿好人的那种纯粹的风格。”他说。

“但是，阿狄曼图，那混合的风格毕竟能带来快乐，给予孩子们和他们的监护人以及一般人以最大乐趣的风格，却与你所选的相反。”

“是的，那是因为它确实受人喜欢。”

“但也许你会说它与我们城邦的政治体制不相容，”我继续说，“因为我们的民众当中每人只做一种工作，所以他们中没有人是双面手或多面手。” e

“对，是不相容的。”

“这个原则意味着我们的城邦是唯一的，我们发现鞋匠就是鞋匠，而不是同时又是船长，农民就是农民，而不是同时又是法官，战士就是战士，而不是同时又是商人，如此等等，难道不是吗？”

“对的。”他说。

“所以可以说，如果有一个人，他足够聪明，能够扮演所有类

398a to assume all kinds of forms and to represent everything in the world to come in person to our community and want to show off his compositions, we'd treat him as an object of reverence and awe, and as a source of pleasure, and we'd prostrate ourselves before him; but we'd tell him that not only is there no one like him in our community, it is also not permitted for anyone like him to live among us, and we'd send him elsewhere, once we had anointed his head with myrrh and given him a chaplet of wool. Left to ourselves, however, with benefit
b as our goal, we would employ harsher, less entertaining poets and story-tellers, to speak in the style of a good man and to keep in their stories to the principles we originally estab-lished as lawful, when our task was the education of our militia.'

'Yes,' he said, 'that's certainly what we'd do, if it were up to us.'

'So now, Adeimantus,' I said, 'I should think we've exhausted the aspect of cultural studies which relates to stories and fables. I mean, we've discussed both the content and the form which the stories should have.'

'I agree,' he said.

c 'Next, we still have to discuss the procedure for staging and music,' I said.

'Evidently.'

'Well, what we have to say about them—about which types are permitted—if we are to be consistent with what has already been said, must by now be universally obvious, surely?'

Glaucon laughed and said, 'It looks as though I don't belong to this universe, then, Socrates. It's not sufficiently clear to me at the moment what we ought to say, though I have a vague idea.'

型的形象，并能表现世界上的每一种事物，这样的一个人来 398a
到我们的城邦，并想要炫耀、卖弄他的艺术作品，那么我们似乎就会把他当作崇拜和敬畏的对象，当作一种快乐的源泉，我们似乎还会跪倒在他的面前；但是与此相反，我们不仅会告诉他，在我们的城邦里没有一个像他一样的人，并且也会告诉他，任何像他这样的人，是不允许生活在我们当中的，我们会把没药抹在他头上，送他羊毛花冠之后就把他遣送到别的地方去。当我们的任务是教育我们的卫士的时候，为了给我们自己带来好处，我们会任用严肃的、朴实的诗人和讲故事之人， b
以好人的风格来讲述，使他们的故事保持与我们起初确立规范的原则相一致。”

“是的，”他说，“如果让我们来做的话，这当然是我们要做的。”

“所以现在，阿狄曼图，”我说，“我想我们已经完成了关于故事和神话的音乐方面的探讨。我的意思是说，我们已经讨论了故事所应该具有的内容及形式。”

“我同意。”他说。

“接下来我们还要讨论格律和曲调。”我说。 c

“显然。”

“如果我们要与前面已经说过的话保持一致，那么我们对于它们要说的话——关于哪些类型是允许的——现在对所有人来说必定都是显而易见的了，对吗？”

格劳孔笑了，且说：“那么，苏格拉底，看来我似乎不属于这‘所有人’之列呀。虽然我有一个模糊的想法，但此刻我还是不太清楚我们应该说些什么。”

'Well,' I said, 'I'm sure that here, in the first place, is a no-
d tion you have a perfectly adequate grasp of: that a song is a blend of three ingredients—words, music, and rhythm.'

'Yes,' he said, 'I understand that.'

'Now, surely the verbal component doesn't differ at all from words which are not part of a song, in the sense that the words still have to conform to those same principles we mentioned a moment ago and to the same style, don't they?'

'True,' he said.

'And the music and the rhythm must be in keeping with the words.'

'Of course.'

'Well, we said that laments and dirges need never be voiced.'

'That's right.'

e 'So which are the plaintive musical modes? You must tell me—you're the musician.'

'The Mixed Lydian', he replied, 'and the Taut Lydian, and any others like them.'

'We should exclude them, then,' I said. 'They don't help even women achieve the required goodness, let alone men.'

'Right.'

'Now, it's utterly inappropriate for our guardians to be drunk and soft and idle.'

'Of course.'

'Well, which modes are soft and suitable for drinking-parties?'

'There's an Ionian mode which is called "loose",' he answered, 'and another Lydian one as well.'

399a 'Can you find any use for them, Glaucon, when you're dealing with military men?'

“好吧，”我说，“首先在这里我确信你能充分地把握这个概念：一首歌曲由三个成分构成——歌词、曲调和节奏。” d

“是的，”他说，“我理解。”

“那么，歌词与没有写进曲子的词语肯定没有一点儿区别，因为词语还必须要符合那些我们不久前提到的同样的原则，也必须符合同样的风格，不是吗？”

“对。”他说。

“曲调和节奏必须适合于歌词。”

“当然。”

“那么，我们说过决不可唱哀婉悲伤的曲子。”

“对。”

“那么什么是哀婉的曲调呢？你是音乐家，你必须告诉 e
我们。”

“混合的吕底亚曲调，”他回答说，“高音吕底亚曲调以及其他与它们类似的曲调。”

“那么，我们应该摒弃它们，”我说，“它们甚至帮不了女人获得应有的善，更不用说男人了。”

“对。”

“那么，醉酒、软弱和闲散对我们的卫士来说是完全不适宜的。”

“当然。”

“那么哪些曲调是柔和的、适合于酒席的呢？”

“有一种伊奥尼亚曲调可称得上是‘散漫’，”他回答道，“另一种吕底亚曲调也是。”

“格劳孔，当你与卫士来往时，你觉得它们有什么用吗？” 399a

'None at all,' he replied. 'It looks as though you're left with the Dorian and Phrygian modes.'

'I'm no expert on the modes,' I said, 'but please leave me with a mode which properly captures the tones and variations of pitch of a brave man's voice during battle or any other enterprise he'd rather not
b be involved in—the voice of a man who, even when he fails and faces injury or death or some other catastrophe, still resists fortune in a disciplined and resolute manner. And leave me another mode which captures his voice when he's engaged in peaceful enterprises, where there's no lack of will and he can choose what to do; or when he's trying to win someone over to his point of view and is appealing to him, whether this involves praying to a god or explaining to a human being where he has gone wrong; or alternatively when he patiently submits to others' appeals or explanations or arguments, and when he has subsequently completed an action to his satisfaction, and doesn't get big-headed, but acts with self-discipline and restraint throughout and accepts whatever
c outcome there may be. Leave me these two modes, then—the voluntary and the involuntary ones— which perfectly capture the tones of self-disciplined and courageous men in failure and success.'

'But you're asking to be left with exactly the modes I just mentioned,' he said.

'We'll not need in our songs and music a wide range of notes and the full range of modes, then,' I remarked.

'No, I suppose not,' he said.

'Then we won't keep artisans to make psalteries and harps and any other instruments which are designed to produce a wide range of notes and modes.'

d 'I suppose we won't.'

'Well, will you allow into our community people who make reed-pipes or people who play them? I mean, doesn't this produce a wider range of notes than any other instrument? Don't all instruments which can play the full range of modes in fact take after the reed-pipe

“根本没用，”他回答说，“看来对你就剩下多利亚和弗里基亚曲调了。”

“我不是曲调方面的专家，”我说，“但请给我留下一种曲
调，它能恰当地符合一个勇士在战场上或在其他他不愿参与
的事件中，其声音的音调和音高的变化——甚至当他失败，面
对伤害、死亡或其他灾难，其声音依然克制而坚定地与命运抗 b
争。再留给我另一种曲调，它能符合他如是时刻的声音：他投
身和平事业，并不缺乏意志，能够选择做什么；或者，他试图用
他的观点去说服别人或向他们恳求，无论这是向神祷告还是
对人指出其过错之处；或相应地，当他耐心地接受别人的恳
求、解释或论证的时候，以及当他随后满意地完成一项行动
时，他的行为在任何情况下都是谦逊和自制的，没有一点高
傲，而是报以理解，并且满足于任何结果。留给我这两种曲调 c
吧——自愿的和不自愿的——它们完美地把握住了在失败与
成功中自制而勇敢之人的语调。”

“但你要求留下的，正好是我刚才提到的曲调。”他说。

“那么，在我们的歌曲和音乐中，就不需要宽广的音域和充分的调式了。”我说。

“我想不需要。”他说。

“那么我们不会雇用工匠制作索尔特里琴、竖琴和其他被设
计来发生宽广音域和调式的乐器。” d

“我想我们不会。”

“那么，你会允许那些制作长笛或演奏长笛的人进入我们的城邦吗？我的意思是说，它不是比其他乐器的音域更广吗？在这个方面，所有其他能够演奏全部曲调的乐器事实上不就是在模仿

in this respect?'

'Obviously they do,' he said.

'So you're left with the lyre and the cithara', I said, 'as instruments which serve some purpose in an urban setting; and then in the countryside the herdsmen can have wind-pipes.'

'That's what the argument suggests, anyway,' he said.

e 'It's not as if we were doing anything startlingly original', I
pointed out, 'in preferring Apollo and Apollo's kind of instrument to
Marsyas and his kind of instrument.'

'How interesting!' he said. 'I suppose we aren't.'

'You know what strikes me?' I said. 'Without realizing it, we've been re-purging the community of the indulgence we mentioned a while back.'

'That just shows how disciplined we are!' he said.

'All right, then, let's finish the purging. We should discuss
rhythm next, after music, and make sure we avoid chasing after com-
plexity of rhythm and a wide variety of tempos. We should try to dis-
cern the rhythms of a life which is well regulated and courageous.
When we've done so, we'll force the metre and the tune to conform to
400a the words which express such a life, rather than forcing the words to
conform to the metre and the tune. And it's up to you to tell us what
those rhythms are, just as you did with musical modes.'

'Good heavens, no!' he said. 'I can't do that. Because of
my studies, I could tell you that there are three elements of tem-
po, just as in the case of sound there are four basic constituents
of all the musical modes. But I can't tell you which rhythmic
b elements represent which lifestyle.'

'Well,' I said, 'we'll have to bring in Damon too, and consult him about which tempos suit meanness and promiscuity or derangement, and other forms of badness, and which rhythms should be reserved for the opposite qualities. I remember having heard a difficult

长笛吗?”

“它们显然在模仿。”他说。

“所以对你剩下的就是七弦琴和奇塔拉琴了,”我说,“就像在城市的配曲中为着某种效果而使用的那些乐器;而在乡下牧人们则使用短笛。”

“无论如何,那是论证所得出的。”他说。

“选择阿波罗和他的那种乐器而舍弃玛西亚和他的那种乐器,”我指出,“这看上去并不是我们的惊人首创。”

“多有趣啊!”他说,“我想并不是。” e

“你知道令我吃惊的是什么吗?”我说,“我们无意之中已经净化了我们不久前提到的奢华的城邦。”

“这正说明我们是多么有节制啊!”他说。

“那么好吧,让我们完成净化。在曲调之后我们接下来应该讨论节奏,以确保我们避免追求节奏的繁复和旋律的多变。我们应该力求明辨具有良好规律和勇气的生活之节奏。这样做后,我
们就能使节拍和调子与表达这种生活的歌词相一致,而不是强使 400a
歌词与节拍和调子相一致。该你来告诉我们了:那些节奏是什么样的,就像谈论曲调一样。”

“天哪,不!”他说,“我做不到。通过我的研究,我可以告诉你节拍有三种元素,就像声音,所有的音调都由四种基本成分构成。
但我说不出哪种节奏的元素模仿哪种生活方式。” b

“好吧,”我说,“我们还是要询问达蒙,向他请教哪种节拍适合于卑鄙、放荡、疯狂和其他类型的邪恶,哪种节奏应该留给那些相反的性质。我听到过他的一个晦涩的谈话,他把一种复合节拍说成是有军事意义的,另一种是长短格,英雄

talk of his in which he described one compound rhythm as martial, finger-like, and heroic, and he somehow divided it into ordered parts and made it equal in its rise and its fall; and, as I recall, he described an iamb as involving a short period and a long period,
c and he described a trochee too; and he assigned to all of these their long and short quantities. And I think he condemned and commended the cadences of some of these rhythms just as much as he did the rhythms themselves; or perhaps it was the combination of cadence and rhythm he was talking about—I can't say. As I said, let's put this on one side for Damon, since it would take us ages to resolve the issue. What do you think?'

'I couldn't agree more,' he said.

'But at least you're sure that grace and inelegance depend on good and bad rhythm, aren't you?'

'Of course.'

d 'Furthermore, good and bad rhythm depend, respectively, on assimilation to a good speaking style or its opposite, and the same goes for harmony and disharmony. This follows from what we were just saying—that rhythm and the harmony of music should conform to language, not vice versa.'

'Yes, they should,' he said.

'As for speaking style and language,' I said, 'they depend on a person's character, don't they?'

'Of course.'

'And everything else depends on speaking style?'

'Yes.'

'It follows, then, that good use of language, harmony, grace, and rhythm all depend on goodness of character. I'm not
e talking about the state which is actually stupidity, but which we gloss as goodness of character; I'm talking about when the mind really has equipped the character with moral goodness and excellence.'

'Absolutely,' he said.

体，而且他不知如何地把它分成了有序的部分并使它的升降
一致；如我所记得的，他描述了一种包含了短音程和长音程的
抑扬格，也描述了强弱二音节的扬抑格；他还给所有这些配上
其长和短的特征。我想他对待某些这类节拍韵律的褒贬就像 c
他对待节拍自身一样；或者也许是他所说的节拍和韵律的组
合——我说不准。就像我说的，把这个留给达蒙吧，因为解决
这问题会花去我们很长的时间。你怎么想？"

"我非常赞同。"他说。

"但至少你能确信优雅和粗俗在于好的和坏的节奏，不是吗？"

"当然。"

"此外，好的和坏的节奏分别倚赖于好或坏的言谈风格的融 d
合，对于和谐和不和谐也是同样。从我们刚才的谈话中可以得出
结论，即节奏和音调应该和语言一致，而不是相反。"

"是的，应该这样。"他说。

"至于说话的风格和语言，"我说，"它们在于一个人的品格，不是吗？"

"当然。"

"所有别的东西都在于说话风格吗？"

"是的。"

"那么，结论就是，言辞、和谐、优雅和节奏的良好运用全都取
决于品性的良好。我说的并不是实际上的头脑简单这个状态，而 e
是我们解释为品性之善的状态；我的意思是灵魂确实具有道德的
善良和完美的品质。"

"绝对如此。"他说。

'And shouldn't the young people of our community take every opportunity to cultivate these qualities, if they are to do their jobs?'

'Yes, they should.'

401a 'Now, painting and related arts, and weaving, embroidery, architecture, and the manufacture of utensils in general, and also the physical structures of creatures and plants, are all pervaded by these qualities, in the sense that they may display grace or inelegance. And inelegance, lack of rhythm, and dis-harmony are allied to abuse of language and a corrupt character, whereas their opposites are allied to and reflect a disciplined and good character.'

'Absolutely,' he said.

b 'Is it only the poets we should oversee, then, and compel to choose between imbuing their compositions with the image of goodness of character or not practising their art in our community? Don't we also have to oversee artisans in general and stop them imbuing their portraits of animals, their edifices, and whatever else they may produce, with corruption, lack of self-restraint, meanness of spirit, and inelegance, and punish failure to comply with a ban on working in our community? Otherwise, during their upbringing our guardians will be
c surrounded by the pernicious pasturage of images of badness, which will be so common that they'll often be nibbling and feeding on them, day in and day out, a little at a time, until without realizing it they'll amass badness in their minds. No, we must look for craftsmen who have the innate gift of tracking down goodness and grace, so that the young people of our community can live in a salubrious region where everything is beneficial and where their eyes and ears meet no influences except those of fine works of art, whose effect is like a breeze which
d brings health from favourable regions, and which imperceptibly guides them, from childhood onwards, until they are assimilated to, familiar with, and in harmony with the beauty of reason,'

'Yes, that would be an outstandingly fine upbringing for them,' he said.

“如果我们城邦的年轻人要做他们的工作，那么他们难道不应该抓住每个机会去接受这些品质的熏陶吗？”

“是的，他们应该这样。”

“那么，绘画和相关的工艺，纺织、刺绣、建筑以及一般的工 401a
具的制作，还有动植物的身体构造都充满了这些品质，因为它们会表现出优雅或粗俗。粗俗、缺乏节奏感以及不和谐，都跟语言的滥用、品质的败坏有关联，而与之相反，其对立的品质则与自我克制的修养及良好的性格有关联，并能够反映出这种修养与性格来。”

“完全如此。”他说。

“那么，我们是否应该只监督诗人，迫使他们作出选择，要 b
么在诗篇中培植好品质的形象，要么在我们的城邦里就不让推行他们的技艺？我们不是还要监督其他一般的工匠，阻止他们在动物的绘画、建筑，以及其他他们可能制作的东西中鼓吹堕落、缺乏自制、灵魂的卑鄙和粗俗，并且还要对不遵守者加以惩罚，禁止他们在我们的城邦里工作？否则在他们的教
育中，我们的卫士会被坏形象的毒草所包围，常常以此来喂食 c
他们，每次虽然只是一点点，但日积月累，不知不觉地在他们的心灵中就铸成了大错。相反，我们必须寻找一些艺人，他们具有追寻善和美德的天赋，那样我们城邦的年轻人就能生活于健康之乡，在那里一切都是有益的，他们的眼睛和耳朵所触及的除了精美的艺术作品外便不受其他影响，其效果就像和风从美好的地方带来健康，从小时候起就开始潜移默化引导
他们，直到他们吸收、熟悉并融合于理智之美。” d

“是的，对他们来说那会是非常好的教育。”他说。

'Now, Glaucon,' I said, 'isn't the prime importance of cultural education due to the fact that rhythm and harmony sink more deeply into the mind than anything else and affect it more powerfully than anything else and bring grace in their train? For someone who is given a
e correct education, their product is grace; but in the opposite situation it is inelegance. And isn't its importance also due to the fact that a proper cultural education would enable a person to be very quick at noticing defects and flaws in the construction or nature of things? In other words, he'd find offensive the things he ought to find offensive. Fine things would be appreciated and enjoyed by him, and he'd ac-
402a cept them into his mind as nourishment and would therefore become truly good; even when young, however, and still incapable of rationally understanding why, he would rightly condemn and loathe contemptible things. And then the rational mind would be greeted like an old friend when it did arrive, because anyone with this upbringing would be more closely affiliated with rationality than anyone else.'

'Yes,' he said, 'to my mind those are the kinds of reasons for cultural education.'

'It's analogous to the process of becoming literate, then,' I said. 'We weren't literate until we realized that, despite being few in number, the letters are fundamental wherever they occur, and until we appreciated their importance whether the word which contained them was
b great or small, and stopped thinking that we didn't need to take note of them, but tried hard to recognize them everywhere, on the grounds that literacy would elude us until we were capable of doing so.'

'True.'

'And we won't be able to tell which letters are which when

“那么，格劳孔，”我说，“文艺教育之所以如此重要，是不是归因于这样一个事实，即韵律与和声比其他任何东西都能更深刻地感发人的心灵，而且也比其他任何东西具有更强大的心灵影响力量，并能够在其训练中带来优美雅致的风度？对于受过恰当教育的人而言，他们的作品就会优雅；但在相反情况下则是粗鄙难堪的。而且，文艺教育的另一个重要原因是不是还在于，一种恰当适宜的文艺教育，能够使一个人在事物的结构或性质中，可以非常快速地察觉瑕疵与缺陷？换言之，对于他应该觉得厌恶的事物，他会感到厌恶。对于那些使他愉悦、让他开心的事物，他便会接受它们，把它们当作心灵的养分，从而变得真正美好；甚而在他年轻还未能在理智上把握原因，他也会谴责和憎恶可鄙的事物。然后等理智来了，它 402a
会像老朋友一样似曾相识，因为在这样的教育下长大的人与理智的联合要比其他任何人更加紧密。”

“是的，”他说，“在我看来这些确实是进行文艺教育的理由。”

“那么它类似于我们识字的过程，”我说，“我们只有在认识到，字母虽然在数量上很少，但无论什么情况下，只要有字词组合，它们都是最基本、最重要的，也只有意识到，包含有字母的单词无论是大的还是小的，但都是非常重要的，并 b
且不再以为我们并不需要注意它们，而是尽力在每个地方去认知它们，只有这样，我们才能识文断字，也只有我们能够如此这般地去做，并经过一番奋斗之后，读写能力才不会躲避我们了。”

“对的。”

“在我们能够认出字母本身之前，我们不会认出映在水中

they're reflected in water or a mirror either, until we can recognize the letters themselves, will we? It takes the same expertise and training, doesn't it?'

'Absolutely.'

'Then this is incredibly similar to what I've been saying. We
c won't be cultured either (and this doesn't apply only to us, but to the people we're claiming to educate for guardianship) until we recognize the types—self-discipline, courage, generosity, broadness of vision, and all the qualities which are allied and opposed to them—wherever they occur, and notice instances of their presence, whether it is the qualities themselves or their reflections that we are noticing, and don't underestimate them whether the situation in which they're occurring is great or small, but bear in mind that it takes the same expertise and training. Right?'

'Definitely,' he said.

d 'Now,' I went on, 'imagine a situation where someone combines beautiful mental characteristics with physical features which conform to the same principle and so are consistent and concordant with the beauty of his mind. Could there be a more beautiful sight for anvone capable of seeing it?'

'Hardly.'

'And the more beautiful a thing is, the more lovable it is?'

'Naturally.'

'Therefore, the more people are of this type, the more a cultured person will love them. If they're discordant, however, he will not love them.'

e 'No, he won't,' he said, 'if they have a mental defect; but if their flaw is physical, he'll put up with it and not refuse his affection.'

或镜子中的字母的,不是吗？这需要同样的专门技艺和训练,不是吗?”

“完全是这样。”

“那么这就与我们说过的极其相似了。在我们认识诸种类型
之前,我们也不会是有教养的(这不光适用于我们,而且也适用于 c
我们声明要教育成卫士的人),这些类型——自制、勇敢、慷慨、眼界开阔,以及所有与其相关联、相对立的品质——它们无论在什么地方出现,都能够识别出来;而且无论它们显现出自身的性质还是我们看到的映像,都能够发觉这些类型存在的实例;无论它们是出现在大事物中还是小事物中,都不会轻视或忽略它们,而是要牢牢记住,它都是属于同一专门技艺、同一学习训练的。对吗?”

“必定是的。”他说。

“那么,”我继续说,“设想一个情形,有人把心灵美的品质和 d
遵循同一个原则的身体特质结合起来,那么它们就与心灵之美和谐一致了。任何看到过这景象的人难道不会认为这是最美的吗?”

“那是最美的。”

“一事物越是美,它就越是可爱吗?”

“那是自然。”

“所以受过文艺教育的人就会最爱这类人,但他不会爱任何
缺乏和谐之人?” e

“不,他不会爱的,如果他们有精神上的缺陷的话,”他说,“但如果他们的缺陷是身体上的,那么他会加以容忍,不会拒绝他的爱慕。”

'I appreciate what you're saying,' I said. 'I know you are or were in love with someone like that, and I concede the point. But answer me this: can self-discipline and excessive pleasure go together?'

'Of course not,' he said. 'Pleasure deranges people just as effectively as distress.'

'Can excessive pleasure partner any of the other virtues?'

'No,'

403a 'What about promiscuity and dissoluteness?'

'Yes, they're its chief partners.'

'Can you think of any pleasure which is greater and more intense than sexual pleasure?'

'No, I can't,' he said, 'and I can't think of any pleasure which is more manic either.'

'And authentic love is a disciplined and cultured love of someone who is restrained as well as good-looking. Yes?'

'Definitely,' he said.

'Authentic love should have no involvement, then, with anything manic or anything which bears the trace of dissoluteness, should it?'

'No, it shouldn't.'

b 'Doesn't it follow, then, that lovers and their boyfriends who love and are loved authentically should have no involvement with this pleasure and should have nothing to do with it?'

'That's right, Socrates,' he said. 'They most certainly should not.'

'So you'll apparently be making a regulation in the community we're founding to the effect that although a lover can (if he can persuade his boyfriend to let him) kiss and spend time with and touch his boyfriend,

“我赞成你说的，”我说，“我知道你爱或曾爱过那样的人，我承认这一点。但请回答我：自律自制和过度地纵情享乐能相容吗？”

“当然不能，”他说，“纵情享乐就像遭受痛苦一样会令人精神错乱。”

“过度纵情享乐能伴有其他美德吗？”

“不能。” 403a

“淫乱与放荡怎么样呢？”

“是的，它们是主要的一对。”

“你能想出任何比色欲更大更强烈的快乐吗？”

“不，不能，”他说，“我想不出任何比这更疯狂的快乐了。”

“但真切的爱是一个既标致又严谨的人的有节制有教养的爱。是吗？”

“必定是的。”他说。

“那么，真切的爱不应该与任何疯狂的事物或具有淫乱迹象的事物同流合污，是吗？”

“是不应该的。”

“那么，这不就是说，爱人和其男友，[1]真切地爱着与被爱着的人，不应该参与这种快乐，并应该与之无涉吗？” b

“说得对，苏格拉底，”他说，“他们当然不应该。”

“所以，在我们正建着的城邦里，你们显然是要作出一个规定，使人做到：如果爱人能说服他的男友让他亲吻，那么他虽然能够亲吻他，花时间与他共处，并抚摸他，就像他的儿子——这就是

〔1〕 对话所涉及的是男性之间的爱慕。男友就是指相对于爱人的被爱者，以下直译为男友。

as he would his son—which is to say, for honourable reasons—still his relationship with anyone he cares for will basically be such that he nev-
c er gives the impression that there is more to it than that. Otherwise, he'll be liable to condemnation for lacking culture and moral sensibility.'

'Exactly,' he said.

'Now, do you join me in thinking that we've completed our discussion of cultural studies?' I asked. 'At any rate, we've reached a good place to finish: I mean, it's good for cultural studies to lead ultimately to love of beauty.'

'I agree,' he said.

'Well, after their cultural education, our young men should receive physical training.'

'Of course.'

'And this too should be a precise course of training which starts in childhood and continues throughout a person's life. See what you
d think too, but my thinking is that this is the way things are: I am not of the opinion that if the body is in a good condition, then this state of physical excellence makes the mind good too. I think it's the other way round: a good mind, by being in a state of excellence, allows a body to maximize its potential for physical goodness. What about you? What do you think?'

'I agree with you,' he replied.

'So if the education we've provided for the mind is adequate, then wouldn't it be best for us to leave the mind to attend to the de-
e tails of the physical training, and steer clear of a lengthy discussion by just outlining the principles?'

'Yes, certainly.'

'Now, we've already said that they should avoid getting drunk. I mean, a guardian is, of course, the last person who should get so drunk that he doesn't know where on earth he is.'

'Yes,' he said, 'because then our guardians would need guardians, and that would be ridiculous.'

说,是出于高尚的缘由——但他与他所关切之人的关系根本上就是这样的,而决不能给人一种僭越此举的印象。否则他要被谴责 c
为缺乏教养和道德感。”

“正是如此。”他说。

“那么,你同意我们已经完成了关于文艺教育的讨论?”我问道,“无论如何我们已经到此结束:我的意思是说,文艺教育最后引向对美的爱,这样很好。”

“我同意。”他说。

“那么,在文艺教育之后,我们的年轻人应该接受体育训练。”

“当然。”

“这也应当是一个从童年开始并延续终生的教育。也看看你的想法吧,但我的想法是这样的:我并不认为,如果身体出于好的 d
状态,那么身体上的良好状态也能使心灵变好。我是反过来想的:一个良善的心灵,凭着它的卓越,能使身体潜在的善最大限度地发挥出来。你呢?你是怎么想的?”

“我同意你的说法。”他回答说。

“所以如果我们给心灵提供充分的教育,那么我们最好让心灵去注意身体锻炼的细节,我们在这里仅仅略述其原则就可以了,从而避开冗长的讨论,你看如何?” e

“是的,当然。”

“那么,我们已经说过,他们应该避免醉酒。我的意思是说,卫士当然是最不应该醉酒的人,那样的话他就不知道自己究竟在哪儿了。”

“是的,”他说,“因为,那样的话,我们的卫士就会需要卫士保护他,那就很荒唐了。”

'What about their food? These men are competitors in the greatest contest of all, aren't they?'

'Yes.'

404a 'So would the condition of one of today's athletes be suitable for them?'

'Maybe.'

'But it's a sluggish condition, and makes health precarious. Can't you see how these athletes spend their lives sleeping and only need to deviate a tiny bit from their prescribed regimen to come down with serious and severe illnesses?'

'Yes, I can.'

'Then our warriors need a less crude form of training,' I said. 'It's essential for them to be as vigilant as watchdogs, with the best possible eyesight and hearing, and for their health to be not so precariously balanced that it is affected by changes in their drinking-water
b and their diet generally, and in the heat or cold of the weather, because these changes are commonly encountered during warfare.'

'I agree.'

'Doesn't it follow that the best physical training for them would be comparable in simplicity to the cultural education we described a short while ago?'

'In what sense?'

'I mean a simple and moderate form of physical training, and one designed particularly for warfare.'

'How?'

'Even Homer's a good source for the sort of thing I mean,' I said. 'As you know, when he portrays the heroes eating, he doesn't
c feed them, while they're campaigning, either on fish (despite the fact that they are in the Hellespont by the sea) or on boiled meat, but only on roasted meat. This is the diet which would be particularly

“那么他们的食物呢？这些人是最大的比赛[1]中的竞争者，不是吗？”

“是的。”

“所以某个当前的运动员的习惯会适合他吗？” 404a

“也许吧。”

“但这是一种贪睡的习惯，这会有害健康。你是否发现这些运动员把他们的生活都花在睡觉上，而只要稍稍偏离他们既定的饮食作息方式，他们就会由于严重的疾病而倒下？”

“是的，我发现了。”

“那么我们的卫士需要受到严格的训练，”我说，“对于他们来说重要的是，要像看门狗一样警觉，拥有尽可能最好的视力和听力，而且他们的健康不能是如此的不稳定，以至于会因其饮水和食物以及天气的热冷变化而受到影响，因为这些变化在战争中是 b
经常遇到的。”

“我同意。”

“这不就是说，对于他们最好的体育训练，与我们不久前所说的文艺教育很相近吗？”

“在什么意义上说？”

“我指的是一种简单而恰当的体育锻炼，是为了备战的那种体育锻炼。”

“什么样的？”

“我说的这些东西甚至在荷马诗里就有，”我说，“如你所知，当他描绘英雄们吃东西的时候，他不会给他们吃鱼（尽管事实上他们就

[1] 指战争。

convenient for soldiers, in the sense that they can cook on an open fire almost anywhere, whereas it's less easy for them to carry cooking-pots around wherever they go.'

'Quite so.'

'Nor, I think, does Homer ever mention savoury sauces. In fact, the necessity of avoiding this kind of food if you want to be physically fit is common knowledge among athletes, isn't it?'

'Yes, it is,' he said, 'and they're right to avoid it.'

d 'If you think they're right to do this, my friend, I suppose you disapprove of Syracusan rations and the wide variety of savouries that can be found in Sicily.'

'Yes, I think I do.'

'Then you also take exception to anyone having a Corinthian lady friend, if he intends to get fit.'

'Absolutely.'

'And to him enjoying the apparent delights of Attic pastries?'

'No doubt about it.'

'And the reason for your disapproval, I imagine, is because we'd be right to draw an analogy between everything that constitutes
e this kind of diet and lifestyle, and the composition of songs and ballads which use the full range of modes and rhythms.'

'Of course that would be a fair analogy.'

'Now, although in the case of music variety tends to engender lack of discipline, in the present case it engenders illness. Simplicity in music, however, engenders self-control, and sim-plicity in physical training gives rise to bodily health. Right?'

'Perfectly true,' he said.

405a 'When dissoluteness and disease proliferate in a community, then lawcourts and doctors' surgeries open up all over the place, and the professions of lawyer and doctor have high opinions of themselves,

驻扎在贺勒斯旁海岸边），也不给他们吃炖肉，而只是吃烤肉。这 c
些食物对于战士来说特别方便，因为他们几乎在任何地方都可以点火就做，而他们无论走到哪里都带着炊具就没那么容易了。”

“确实如此。”

“我想荷马甚至也不曾提到美味的调料。事实上，如果你想要身体健康，就别吃这样的食物，这是运动员的常识，不是吗？”

“是的，”他说，“他们不吃是对的。”

“我的朋友，如果你觉得他们这样做是对的，那么我想你不会 d
赞成叙拉古的食物和我们在西西里发现的各种美味。”

“是的，我想我并不赞成。”

“那么如果一个人想要健壮而又把科林斯女郎作为朋友，你也会反对这个吧？”

“完全会。”

“会赞成似乎很诱人的阿提卡糕点吗？”

“无疑不会。”

“我想你不赞成的理由是：我们可以做这样一个类比，所有组成这类饮食和生活方式的东西，就像那些使用了所有曲调和节奏
的歌曲和民谣作品一样。” e

“这的确是个很好的类比。”

“那么，就音乐来说，它的多样性会导致缺乏节制，就现在的情况看来，它产生了疾病。而音乐的质朴产生自制，身体锻炼中的质朴产生身体的健康。对吗？”

“完全正确。”他说。

“当放荡和疾病在城邦中泛滥的时候，法庭和医疗诊所就到 405a
处开张，法官和医生就趾高气扬，甚至连大部分自由人也把他们

when even large numbers of free men regard them as extremely important.'

'That's inevitable.'

'Could you produce more telling evidence of when a community's educational system is bad and contemptible than when top-notch doctors and lawyers are needed not only by low-ranking people and labourers, but also by those who pride themselves on their privileged upbringing? I mean, don't you think it's despicable, and highly
b indicative of lack of culture, to feel compelled to rely on a moral code which has been imported from others, as if they were one's masters and judges, and to lack one's own moral sense?'

'Nothing could be more contemptible,' he replied.

'Really?' I asked. 'Don't you think that it's more contemptible to waste most of one's life in the lawcourts as a prosecutor or defendant, and moreover to be so lacking in moral sensibility that one confidently preens oneself on this fact, and regards oneself as a skilful
c criminal, accomplished in every manoeuvre, in dodges and subterfuges for slipping through every loophole which enables one to avoid being punished, and to do all this for the sake of matters which are trivial and of no Importance, because one is ignorant of how much finer and better it is to arrange one's life so that one has no need of a drowsy juror?'

'Yes, you're right,' he said. 'This ranks even higher on the scale of contemptibility.'

'What about needing the art of medicine', I continued. 'for anything except serious injuries and when infected by certain of the seasonal epidemics? What about when it's needed instead because people
d are, thanks to inactivity and the diet we described, as full of fluids and gases as a marsh, and leave the ingenious Asclepiadae no choice

当作极其重要的人物。”

“那是难以避免的。”

“如果不仅是一般人需要一流的医生和法官，而且那些因自己受过特别的教育而自豪的人也需要他们，那么你还能拿出比这更有说服力的证据，来说明这个城邦的教育是坏的、可鄙的吗？我的意思是说，人们感到不得不依赖从别处舶来的道德法则，好
像它们是自己的主人和法官而缺乏他们自己的道德感，你难道不 b
认为这是可鄙的，是缺乏修养的显著表现吗？”

“没有比这更卑鄙的了。”他回答说。

“是吗？”我问道，“你难道不认为还有比这更卑鄙的事情吗？一个人或者当原告，或者当被告，将大部分生命浪费在法庭之上，此外更有如此的缺乏道德感者，竟在诉讼这类事情上胆大
妄为，沾沾自喜，认为自己是一个手段高明的罪犯，可以调动每 c
一种策略来完成诉讼，用搪塞、托辞等从法律的漏洞中逃脱，以避免被惩罚，而做所有这些事情，全都是为了微不足道、并不重要的事务，这是因为一个人并不知道如何更洁净、更恰当地安排自己的生活，如果他们知道，那就不需要那些漫不经心、迟钝懒怠的陪审员了。”

“你说得对，”他说，“这甚至是更卑鄙的。”

“对于医术的需求又如何呢，”我继续说，“除了严重的损伤以及某些季节性流行的疫疾传染之外？由于游手好闲和我们说过
的饮食作息方式，身体像一块沼泽一样充满风湿水气，使天才的 d
阿斯克勒庇俄斯们[1]没有办法，只有为他们那些腹胀、痢疾的疾

〔1〕 指医生。

but to come up with names like flatulence and catarrh for their disorders? Doesn't this strike you as contemptible?'

'Yes,' he said, 'these words certainly are really unfamiliar and odd when used as the names of diseases.'

'And I don't think they were used like that in Asclepius'
e time,' I said. 'The reason I think this is because when Eurypylus
was wounded at Troy and was treated with Pramnian wine which had
406a lots of pearl barley and grated cheese stirred in it (which is supposed
to be an inflammatory brew), Asclepius' sons didn't tick the woman
off for giving it him to drink, and didn't criticize Patroclus' treatment
of him either.'

'Well, it *was* an odd drink for someone in his condition,' he remarked.

'Not if you bear in mind the fact that doctors didn't use this
modern medical technique of pampering illness until Herodicus'
time,' I said. 'Herodicus was a physical-education instructor who be-
came chronically ill and combined the arts of physical exercise and
b medicine into a means of tormenting first and foremost himself, and
then subsequently a lot of other people.'

'How?' he asked.

'By prolonging his death,' I answered. 'Although he danced attendance on his illness, it was terminal, and there was no way he could cure himself, of course. He was so busy doctoring himself that for the rest of his life he had no time for anything else and suffered torments every time he deviated in the slightest from his usual regimen; thanks to his cleverness he reached old age, but had one foot constantly in the grave.'

'His expertise earned him a fine reward, then!' he said.

c 'A suitable one for someone who didn't realize that Asclepius'
omission of this type of medical method in the art he invented and
handed down to his successors was not due to his being ignorant and
unaware of it,' I said. 'It was because he knew that every citizen of
a well-regulated community is assigned a single job which he has to
do, and that no one has the time to spend his life ill and doctoring
himself. Ridiculously enough, it is noticeable today that while the

病创造出名字来，在这种情况下需求医疗的技艺又怎么样呢？你难道不觉得这个卑鄙吗？”

“是的，”他说，“这些疾病的名词确实很陌生古怪。”

“我想在阿斯克勒庇俄斯的时代是没有那些名词的，”我 e
说，“我的理由是这样，欧律庇卢斯在特洛伊受了伤，喝了调有
大麦粉和奶酪末的普兰那酒，这是一剂热药，阿斯克勒庇俄斯 406a
的儿子们并没有阻止那妇人给他喝，也没有指责帕特洛克罗
对他的看护。”

“对于他这种状况的人，这确实是一剂奇怪的药。”他说。

“要是你记得在希罗狄库时代之前，医生们并不使用现在的
医疗技术来治病，你就不会觉得奇怪了，”我说，“希罗狄库是一名
教练员，他渐渐地得了病，便把体育和医药的技艺结合起来，首先
折磨了自己，后来折磨了许多别的人。” b

“怎么做的呢？”他问道。

我回答说，“虽然当然没有办法治好他自己，但他照料他的不治之症，延迟了他的死亡。他是如此的忙于给自己治病以至于其余生再没有时间去做别的事情了，而且每次只要稍微偏离一点儿他自己惯常的养生法，便会遭受病苦的折磨；由于他的聪明机敏，他活到了老年，但是他常常有一只脚是踩在坟墓中的。”

“那么说他的专业技艺给了他嘉奖！”他说。

“阿斯克勒庇俄斯不把他发明的这种医术传给他的后代，不 c
是因为他的疏忽或没有意识到，对那些没有认识到这点的人，这
个嘉奖倒是合适的，”我说，“这是因为他知道，每个治理得井然
有序的城邦里的公民，都被指派做一份他应该做的工作，而没有
人会有时间把生活花在生病和治病上。十足荒唐的是，工匠阶

working class conform to this principle, people who are rich and supposedly happy do not.'

'What do you mean?' he asked.

d 'If a joiner gets ill,' I explained, 'what he expects from his doctor is an emetic drug to drink to vomit up the illness, or an aperient for his bowels, or to resort to cautery or surgery to get rid of the affliction. If he's prescribed a long course of treat-ment, and told to wrap his head in dressings and so on, then his immediate response is to say that he has no time to be ill, and that this way of life, which involves concentrating on his illness and neglecting the work he's been set, holds no rewards for him. Then he takes his leave of this type of
e doctor, returns to his usual regimen, regains his health, and lives performing his proper function; alternatively, if his body isn't up to surviving, he gets rid of his troubles by dying.'

'That's the right way for an artisan to approach medical science, I think,' he said.

407a 'Isn't that because he has a job to do,' I asked, 'and because if he doesn't do it, his life is unrewarding?'

'Obviously,' he said.

'But a rich person, by definition, has no job assigned to him such that if he were forced to abstain from it his life would become intolerable.'

'He isn't said to, anyway.'

'If you say that, then you haven't heard what Phocylides said about how as soon as one's livelihood' is secure, one should practise goodness.'

'I think one should do so even earlier,' he said.

'Let's not quarrel with him about this,' I said. 'Let's be our

层遵守这个原则，而富人和所谓的有福之人则不遵守，这点是显而易见的。”

“你说的是什么意思？”他问道。

我解释说：“如果一个木匠得了病，他所希望的就是从医生那 d
得到一份催吐剂，喝后把病吐出来，或一份通便剂，或求助于灼烧法，或者手术解除他的病痛。如果给他开了一份长长的处方，还吩咐他把头包起来等等，这样把主要精力集中于他的疾病而耽搁了他该做的工作，那么对他来说就没有什么价值了。这样他就会向这种医生告辞，回到他通常的养生习惯，重获他的健康，活下去 e
做他自己的工作；或者，如果他的身体不足以活下去，那么死了就可以摆脱他的痛苦。”

“对于一个工匠来说，我想这就是求助于医术的正确方法。”他说。

“那难道不是因为他有工作要做吗，”我问道，“因为如果他不 407a
工作，那么他的生活就没有收入来源？”

“显然。”他说。

“但是按说富人并无工作指派给他，乃至要是迫使他放弃工作，他的生活便会变得不可忍受。”

“不管怎样，他并没有被说成那样。”

“如果你那样说的话，那么你还没听过富库利德的话：一旦人的生活得到了保障，人就应该实践美德。”

“我认为人应该更早地这样做。”[1]他说。

“我们不要在这一点上与他争执吧，”我说，“让我们做自己的老

〔1〕 指在生活得到保障之前就应该实践美德。

own teachers, and find out whether a rich person ought to practise what Phocylides says and whether life becomes intoler-able for a rich person if he doesn't practise it. Let's see whether despite the fact that
b pampering an illness prevents a person applying himself to joinery and all the other branches of expertise, it is no impediment to anyone carrying out Phocylides' injunction.'

'Of course it is,' he exclaimed. 'It's hard to think of any impediment greater than this excessive attention to the body, this attempt to improve on physical exercise. It's a nuisance in the context of estate-management, of military service, and of sedentary political office too.'

'Its worst aspect, however, is ,hat it makes it difficult to study
c anything and to think and concentrate, since one is constantly worried about headaches and dizziness, and blaming philosophy for their occurrence. So if you're practising this philosophical type of goodness, then excessive attention to the body is a thorough hindrance, since it constantly makes you imagine that you're ill and you're always agonizing about your body.'

'Yes, that's likely,' he said.

'Well, shall we say that Asclepius realized this as well? He invented the art of medicine for people who are physically healthy,
d thanks to both their constitutions and their lifestyles, but who contract some isolated illness. This is the type of person and condition he had in mind. He used drugs and surgery to get rid of their illnesses, and then he told them to continue with their usual lifestyles, because he didn't want to damage the functioning of the community. However, he didn't try to use diet gradually to drain and fill bodies which were diseased to the core, and so be responsible for the person having a long and horrible life and in all probability producing children with the same afflictions. He didn't see any point in treating anyone who was
e incapable of living a normal life, because such a person does neither himself nor his community any good.'

'Asclepius was a public-spirited person, according to you,' he

师，弄清富人是否应该实践富库利德所说的话，要是富人不实践的话，生活对他来说是否变得不可忍受。虽然照料疾病妨碍了人们从事木工活或其他专业技艺，让我们来考察一下，对 b
于任何遵从富库利德的劝告的人来说，这是否没有什么妨碍。”

“当然有，”他说，“难以想象有比过度地关注身体，即试图提高身体锻炼更有害的事情了，这在家务管理、军事服务和案牍公事上都带来不少麻烦。”

“然而最坏的方面在于它使学习、思考和冥思都变得困难，因为人们常常担心头晕目眩，并把它们归咎于哲学。所以当你实践 c
这种善的哲学形式的时候，对于身体的过度的关注就完全是一个障碍，因为它常常使你设想自己有病，并且你总是为你的身体感到痛苦。”

“是的，那很有可能。”他说。

“那么我们可以说阿斯克勒庇俄斯也意识到了这一点吗？他为体质好、生活习惯好而身体健康但得了些小毛病的人，发明了医疗的技艺。他心中所设想的就是这种人和这种状况。 d
他使用药物和外科手术去除他们的疾病，然后吩咐他们照常生活，因为他不想妨害城邦的运作。然而，他并不试图对病入膏肓的身体使用节食、逐步排干或输入的方法，这样就会导致让人生活过于漫长而痛苦，还完全有可能生下遭受同样痛苦的孩子。他认为治疗不能过上正常生活的人是没有任何意义的，因为这样的人对自己没有好处，对城邦也没有任何 e
好处。”

“按你的看法，阿斯克勒庇俄斯是个具有政治头脑的人。”

remarked.

408a ‘Obviously he was,’ I said. ‘And look at his sons too: it was because this was his nature that at Troy they proved themselves to be good fighters and practised the kind of medicine I'm describing. Don't you remember how when Pandarus wounded Menelaus, “they sucked the blood” from the wound “and applied soothing medicines”, but didn't tell him (any more than they did Eurypylus) what to eat and drink after this treatment? They were acting on the assumption that the
b medicines were enough to cure men who had, before being wounded, been healthy and had led orderly lives, even if they happened to be drinking potions at that precise moment. But they didn't think that the people themselves or anyone else would gain by someone who was constitutionally sickly and who lacked self-discipline remaining alive; they didn't want to waste their art on these people or treat them, ever. if they were richer than Midas.’

‘Asclepius’ sons were very clever, according to you,’ he said.

‘Just as clever as they should be,’ I responded. ‘And yet the tragedians and Pindar don't see things the way we do, and they claim that Asclepius, despite being the son of Apollo, was bribed to treat a rich man who was already at death's door, and that this is ,why he
c was struck by lightning. However, we'll stick to the principles we formulated earlier and therefore not let them convince us of the truth of both assertions: either he was the son of a god, in which case (we'll claim) he wasn't attracted by dirty money; or he was attracted by dirty money, in which case he wasn't the son of a god.’

‘Yes, you're quite right,’ he said. ‘But here's a question for you, Socrates: surely we need to have good doctors in our community, don't we? And, I suppose, the more healthy and sick people
d they've dealt with, the more likely they are to be good. The same goes for legal experts too: it's those who've been involved with people of all sorts and characters who are most likely to be good.’

他说。

“他显然是有的,”我说,“且也看看他的儿子们吧:因为这是 408a
他们的本性,在特洛伊他们表明了自己是好战士,实践了我所说的那种医术。你难道不记得潘达洛斯伤了美尼劳时的情形:‘他们’从伤口中‘吸出淤血并敷上解痛的药物’,而没有像对待欧律庇卢斯那样吩咐他在这治疗之后吃什么、喝什么?他们那样做是因为药物对于治好那些受伤前是健康的、过着有规律的生活、甚至某些时候偶尔喝喝酒的人来说就足够了。但他们并不认为那 b
些体质上的病态之人和缺乏自制之人活着对他们自己或任何别的人会有什么好处;他们不想在把医术浪费在那些人身上或治愈他们,即使他们比弥达斯还富有。”

“按你的说法,阿斯克勒庇俄斯的儿子们非常聪明。”他说。

“他们是很聪明,”我回答说,“而悲剧作家和品达并不像我们那样看待事情,他们说阿斯克勒庇俄斯尽管是阿波罗的儿子,但却受贿去医治已经临近死亡的富人,这就是他受到闪电击打的原因。然而,我们会坚持先前所提出的原则,所以不 c
会被他们的那两种说法的真实性所说服:要么他是神的儿子,所以在这种情况下,我们会说他没有受到污秽的金钱的引诱;要么他受到了金钱的引诱,在这种情况下,他就不是神的儿子。”

“是的,你说得很对,”他说,“但有个问题,苏格拉底:在我们的城邦里,我们当然需要好医生,不是吗?我想他们越常跟健康的人和病人打交道,就越有可能是好医生。对于法官也一样:那 d
些与各种各样人打交道的人就最有可能是好法官。”

'I am certainly saying that we need good ones,' I replied. 'But do you know which ones I regard as good?'

'You'll have to tell me,' he said.

'I'll try,' I said. 'Your question combined dissimilar cases, however.'

'In what way?' he asked.

'Well, take doctors first. In order for doctors to attain perfect skill, they must not only have learnt their trade. In addition, from childhood onwards, they should have come into contact with as many bodies as they possibly could, in the worst con-dition they could find; moreover, they themselves should have contracted every single disease
e there is, and should be con-stitutionally rather unhealthy. I mean, it's not their bodies they use to treat other people's bodies, of course; if that were the case, it would be out of the question for their bodies to be bad or to get into a bad state. No, it's their minds they use to treat bodies, and it's impossible for a mind which is or has become bad to treat anything well.'

'Right,' he said.

409a 'On the other hand, Glaucon, a legal expert does use his mind to wield authority over other people's minds. And it's out of the question for a legal expert to be brought up, from childhood onwards, in the company of minds which are in a bad condition, and for his mind to have thoroughly explored the whole arena of immorality until it has become immoral itself and can quickly use itself as a criterion by which to assess the immorality of others' actions (by the analogy of a doctor using his body to assess others' illnesses). Instead, his mind must, while young, have no experience of bad characters, and must not be contaminated by them, if it's to become truly good at assessing the morality of actions in a reliable manner. This also explains why good people are, in their youth, thought by immoral people to be gul-
b lible simpletons: they don't contain within themselves standards of behaviour which are compatible with anything which is bad.'

'Yes, that's always happening to them,' he said.

“我当然认为我们需要好医生和好法官，”我回答说，“但你知道我把哪些看作是‘好的’吗？”

“你一定要告诉我。”他说。

“我来试试吧，”我说，“然而，你的问题把不同的情况混在一起了。”

“以什么方式呢？”他问道。

“好，首先来看看医生。为了让医生掌握完美的技艺，他们就不可只是学成他们的行当。此外，他们从小开始就应该尽可能多地接触一些他们能找得到的处于最坏状态的身体；他们还应该得过各种疾病并且体质应该相当糟糕。我的意思是他们当 e
然不是用他们的身体去治疗别人的身体；如果那样的话，那就根本谈不上让他们的身体变坏或变差。相反，是用他们的心灵去治疗身体的，一个坏的或已经变坏的心灵是不可能去医治任何东西的。”

“对的。”他说。

“格劳孔，另一方面，法官是用他的心灵在其他人的心灵里发 409a
挥其权威的。对于法官就不可能让他从小与坏的心灵相伴长大，也不可能让他的心灵完全探究过所有不正义的领域直到自己变得不正义，并将之作为标准去判断别人行为的不正义（就像医生不是使用他的身体去诊断别人的疾病一样）。相反，如果要变得真正善于可靠地判断行为的正义，那么当他还年轻的时候，其心灵就不可经验坏人坏事，不可受到他们的污染。这也可以解释为什么好人在其年轻时被不正义之人认为是人尽可欺的傻瓜：他们自己没有与坏事物相容的行为准则。” b

“是的，那总是发生在他们身上。”他说。

‘That’s why a young man doesn’t make a good legal expert,’ I said,‘and why advanced age is a prerequisite. A good legal expert must have been slow to learn the nature of immorality, because he’s been observing something which is not an inherent quality in his own mind, but an alien quality in other people’s minds. He must have trained himself over many years to discern its badness by making use
c of information, not his own experience.’

‘At any rate,’ he said,‘I suppose the best kind of legal expert is like that.’

‘So is a good one,’ I said,‘and that was what you were asking about. I mean, it’s a good mind that makes someone good. As for that clever paranoiac, who has done wrong himself many times and thinks of himself as smart and unscrupulous: in the company of people similar to himself, his caution—induced by his looking at the standards of behaviour he contains within himself—does make him appear clever.
d On the other hand, when he associates with good people and older people, then his excessive mistrust and his inability to recognize reliability—induced by the fact that he has no standard by which to recognize it—make him appear stupid. Since he more commonly encounters bad people than good people, however, he thinks himself clever rather than stupid, and this opinion is endorsed by others.’

‘That’s perfectly true,’ he said.

‘Our search for a good, skilful legal expert had better not end with him, then,’ I said,‘ but with the type of person we described before, because whereas a bad person can never recognize either goodness or badness, a good person will, with time and education, come to understand both goodness and badness—and therefore it is
e he, not a bad person, who acquires skill, in my opinion.’

‘And I agree with you,’ he said.

‘So at the same time as legislating for this type of legal practice in our community, you’ll also legislate for the kind of medical practice we described. These two practices will treat the bodies and minds of
410a those of your citizens who are naturally well endowed in these

“那就是为什么年轻人不会成为一名好的法律专家的原因，”
我说，“也是为什么老年是成为好法官的先决条件的原因。一名
好的法官必须慢慢地了解不正义的本性，因为他考察的是某种在
他自己的心灵中并不具有的品质，而是一种外在于他的、在别人
心灵中的品质。他必须经过多年的训练，通过知识而不是他自己
的经验来辨别邪恶。” c

“不管怎么说，”他说，“我想最好的法律专家会像是那样的。”

“这就是好的事物，”我说，“就是你在追问的东西。我的意思
是说，好的心灵使人成为好的。至于那狡诈之徒，他们自己做过多
次坏事还自认为聪明，恬不知耻：在与他同类的人群当中，他的谨
慎——从关注自身的行为准则可以看出——确实使得他显得聪明。
另一方面，当他跟好人和老人打交道时，他过度的猜疑以及认知上
的无能会使他看上去很愚蠢，所谓认知上的无能，指的是他无法认 d
清哪些人是可靠的，之所以如此，是因为事实上他并没有什么体认
可靠性的标准。然而，既然他更常遇到的是坏人而非好人，那么他
认为自己聪明而非愚蠢，这种看法也就得到别人的认同了。”

“那完全正确。”他说。

“因此，我们要找的好的熟练的法律专家最好不是后一种
人，”我说，“而是我们前面所说的那种人，因为坏人决不会辨别出
美德或邪恶，而好人，假以时间和教育，就会理解美德和邪恶——
所以在我看来正是好人，而不是坏人，才能掌握法律技术。” e

“我同意你的说法。”他说。

“所以在为这种司法活动制订法律的同时，你也要为我们说
过的医疗活动制订法律。这两种活动关切到你的那些天生就在 410a
这两方面健全的公民的身体和灵魂；至于其余的人，那些体质差

respects; as for the rest, those with a poor physical constitution will be allowed to die, and those with irredeemably rotten minds will be put to death. Right?'

'Yes, we've shown that this is the best course,' he said, 'for those at the receiving end of the treatment as well as for the community.'

'And so your young men,' I said, 'will obviously be careful about getting themselves into a position where they need legal expertise; they'll rely on that simple cultural training which, as we said, engenders self-discipline.'

'Naturally,' he said.

b 'And won't anyone culturally trained in this way who follows the same trail find, if he wants to, the form of physical exercise he's after, with the result that he'll not need doctors at all, except in emergencies?'

'I think so.'

'Now, the goal he aims for even with this physical exercise and effort is the passionate aspect of his nature. This is what he wants to wake up. This, not developing physical strength, will be the goal of his efforts, as distinct from all other athletes, who diet and train for the sake of physical fitness.'

'Definitely,' he said.

c 'Doesn't it follow, then, Glaucon,' I asked, 'that it's wrong to think that the people who are making cultural studies and physical exercise the constituents of our educational system are doing so for the purpose of using the one to look after the body and the other to look after the mind?'

'Why is it wrong?' he asked.

'It rather looks as though the mind is the main objective in both cases,' I said.

'I don't understand.'

'Haven't you noticed the psychological effect of people spending their whole lives on physical exercise, but excluding culture,' I asked, 'or the effect of doing the opposite?'

的人就让他们去死,那些心灵腐败到不可救药的地步之人要被处死。对吗?”

他说:“我们已经表明,这对于治疗的接受者和城邦来说都是最好的。”

“所以你们的年轻人,”我说,“显然要小心让自己陷入到需要法律技术的境地;如我们所说的,他们依靠简单的文艺训练就可以形成自制。”

“自然。”他说。

“任何照这样做而受到文艺训练的人,如果他想做,不就随后 b
可以照此同样做法找到体育锻炼的形式,结果是,除了在紧急场合之外,他就完全不需要医生了吗?”

“我想是这样。”

“那么,他参加体育锻炼和付出努力的主要目的是激发本性的激情。这就是他所要唤醒的。这就是他努力的目标,不是增强体力,不同于所有其他为了身体强壮而节食和锻炼的运动员。”

“说得对极了。”他说。

“那么,格劳孔,这岂不是要说,”我问道,“认为那些把文艺教育
和体育锻炼当作我们的教育体系组成部分的人是为了把一个部分用 c
做照料身体,把另一个部分用做照料心灵。这样的想法是错误的吗?”

“为什么是错的呢?”他问道。

“看起来心灵在两者中更像是主要对象呀。”我说。

“我不明白。”

“你难道没有注意到,那些把一生都花在体育锻炼而完全没有文艺教育的人,在心灵上的后果吗?”我问道,“或反过来,只受过文艺教育而忽视体育锻炼又有什么后果呢?”

'In what respect do you mean?' he asked.

d 'I mean in respect of the brutality and intractability of the one lot, and the softness and docility of the others,' I replied.

'Yes,' he said, 'I've noticed that people who engage exclusively in physical exercise end up being excessively brutal, while people who engage exclusively in cultural studies end up shamefully soft.'

'Now, brutality is a product of the passionate part of one's nature. With the correct training, this passionate part is brave; but if it is over-stretched, it becomes intractable and unmanage-able, as you can imagine.'

'I agree,' he said.

e 'And docility is an attribute of a philosophical temperament. Over-relaxation results in excessive softness, but if a philosophical temperament is properly trained it becomes docile and orderly, doesn't it?'

'Yes.'

'And we said that our guardians had to possess both characteristics.'

'Yes, they must.'

'So these two features have to fit harmoniously together, don't they?'

'Of course.'

411a 'If they do, the result is a mind which is self-controlled and courageous, isn't it?'

'Yes.'

'And if they don't, the result is a mind which is timid and insensitive?'

'Yes.'

'So when a person allows the music of culture to charm him and makes his ears a channel for his mind to be flooded with the modes we described not long ago as enchanting and soft, and the ones we described as plaintive, and spends his whole life humming and entranced by song, then at first he softens his passionate side,

“你指的哪方面?”他问道。

“我指的是,一方面是野蛮和倔强,另一方面是软弱和温柔。” d
我回答说。

“是的,”他说,“我已经注意到那些只从事体育锻炼的人最终会变得过于野蛮,而只得到文艺教育的人最终会变得过于软弱。”

“那么,野蛮是人们本性中激情部分的产物。加以正确的训练,激情的部分就会是勇敢;但要是过于放松,它就会变得如同你能想象地那样难以驯服和难以驾驭。”

“我同意。”他说。

“温顺是爱智的气质的一种特性。过度的松散导致过度的柔 e
弱,但要是爱智的气质得到恰当的训练,它就会变得温顺而井然有序,难道不是吗?”

“是的。”

“我们说过我们的卫士必须具有两种品质。”

“是的,他们必须具有。”

“所以这两种品质必须彼此和谐,难道不是吗?”

“当然。”

“要是它们彼此和谐的话,那么心灵就会自制而勇敢,难道不 411a
是吗?”

“是的。”

“要是它们彼此不相和谐的话,那么心灵就会怯懦而麻木?”

“是的。”

“所以当一个人沉湎于音乐,把自己的耳朵作为其心灵的通道,使之充满我们刚才说过的甜蜜、柔软以及那些我们认为哀婉的曲调,一生都花在婉转悠扬的曲子上,于是他开始像熔炼钢铁

like iron in a forge, and makes it useful, instead of useless and in-
b tractable; but if he goes on and on, and never lets up, but is beguiled, then the result is that he dissolves and melts his passionate side, until it becomes completely fluid and he has, so to speak, cut the sinews out of his mind and made himself a "feeble fighter".'

'Quite,' he said.

'If right from the start he was endowed with a mind which lacked passion,' I went on, 'then it doesn't take long for this to happen; but if he had a passionate mind, then he weakens the passion and destabilizes it, so that even trivial matters make it quickly blaze up and die down again. People like this have exchanged passion for peevish-
c ness and irritability, and are seething with discontent.'

'Absolutely.'

'And what about when someone puts a lot of effort into physical exercise and eats very well, but has nothing to do with culture and philosophy? At first, because he's physically fit, he gets all proud and passionate, and braver than he was before, doesn't he?'

'Yes, exactly.'

'But what if he restricts himself entirely to these activities and has absolutely no contact with the Muse of culture? The intellectual
d side of his mind is completely starved of intellectual studies and investigations, and never joins in a discussion or any other cultural activity. Won't it become weak and deaf and blind, because it never receives any stimulation or nourishment and its senses are never purified?'

'Yes.'

'Then this type of person ends up, I suppose, devoid of culture and with a hatred of rationality. He stops relying on the persuasive force of rational argument and instead, like a wild beast, uses brute
e violence to attain all his ends. He lives his life in blundering ignorance, lacking elegance or refinement.'

一样软化了他的激情,使它变得有用,而不是倔而无用;但他要是一直这样继续下去,不能适可而止,而入了迷,那么他的激情就会 b
消解,直到变得完全如水一般,即,他失去了心灵的力量而使自己成为一个‘软弱的战士’。”

“很对。”他说。

我继续说:“如果一开始就赋予其缺乏激情的心灵,那么这样的事不久就会发生;但如果他具有一个富于激情的心灵,那么削弱并动摇了他的激情,以至很小的事情就能很快使他激动起来,也能使他再次平静下来。这样的人就会易怒、容易与人吵架,并且还骄横跋扈。” c

“确实如此。”

“有的人费了很大的精力来锻炼身体,也吃得很好,但一点都不学文艺和哲学,这样的人又怎么样呢?因为一开始他身强力壮,充满自信和激情,比原先的自己还要勇敢,难道不是吗?”

“确实是的。”

“但要是他把自己完全限制于这些活动而与文艺之神毫无交往,那又怎么样呢?他的心灵中理智的部分就会完全缺乏理智的 d
学习和研究,也从不参与讨论或任何其他的文艺活动。由于它得不到任何启发和培育,其感觉能力就没有得到净化,那么它不就会变得虚弱,而且又聋又盲了吗?”

“是的。”

“我想这样的人最终会缺乏修养而又厌恶理性。他不再依赖于理性论辩的说服力,而是像野兽一样粗野地使用暴力去到达他所有的目的。他生活在粗野无知之中,而缺乏高尚和文雅。” e

‘You’re absolutely right,’ he said.

‘So in my opinion what we find is that, since we have a dual nature, God gave us two corresponding areas of expertise— culture and physical exercise—for our passionate and our philosophical aspects. He didn’t give them for the mind and the body, except incidentally;
412a the purpose was for those two aspects of our nature to fit harmoniously together by being stretched and relaxed as much as is appropriate.’

‘Yes, that seems to be so,’ he said.

‘Therefore, it isn’t the person who attunes the strings of a lyre to one another, it’s the person who makes the best blend of physical exercise and culture, and who applies them to the mind in the right proportions, whom we should really describe as a virtuoso and as having the most harmony m his life.’

‘That’s hard to deny, Socrates,’ he said.

‘So, Glaucon, we’ll always need someone of this type to oversee our community, if its political system is to remain intact, won’t we?’

b ‘Yes, that’ll be the most important of our requirements.’

“你说得完全正确。”他说。

“所以依我看来，我们的发现便是，因为我们具有一种双重的禀赋，神便为我们的热情和爱智方面提供了两种相应的专门知识领域——文艺教养与身体操练。除了偶发性、附带性的情况之外，神并不是将这两种专门知识提供给心灵与身体的；神提供这 412a
两种知识的目的是为了我们禀赋的两个方面能够和谐地组合在一起，张弛适宜，配合得当。”

“是的，看起来是这样，”他说。

“因此，并不是为七弦琴琴弦调音的人，而是将身体操练与文艺教养完美融合在一起的人，我们才真正称之为功力深厚的演奏名家，而那些以恰当比例将身体操练与文艺教养应用于心灵的人，我们则称之为生活中最和谐的人。”

“苏格拉底，那是难以否认的。”他说。

“所以，格劳孔，如果要使城邦的制度不受侵犯的话，我们就需要这样的人来监督我们的城邦，不是吗？”

“是的，那是我们最重要的需求。” b

CHAPTER 5

'So much for our educational principles. I mean, we don't have to describe in detail the guardians' dances, hunts, sporting competitions, and horse-races: it's fairly obvious that these activities must conform to the same principles, and their elucidation shouldn't cause any problems now.'

'No, I suppose they shouldn't,' he said.

'All right,' I said. 'What do we have to decide about next? Shouldn't we decide which members of this particular class will be the rulers and which will be the subjects?'

'Of course.'

412c 'It's obvious that the older ones should be the rulers and the younger ones the subjects, isn't it?'

'Yes.'

'And only the best of the older ones?'

'Yes, that's obvious too.'

'Now, the best farmers are the most accomplished farmers, aren't they?'

'Yes.'

'And in the present case, since we're after the best guardians, they must be those who are particularly good at safeguarding the community, mustn't they?'

'Yes.'

'They not only have to have the intelligence and the competence for the job, but they also have to care for the community, wouldn't you say?'

d 'Yes.'

第五章

“这就是我们教育的原则。我的意思是说,我们没必要讨论卫士们的舞蹈、狩猎、竞技和赛马的细节:这些活动显然都应该符合同一个原则,他们的教育现在应该不会有什么问题了。”

“我想应该没有什么问题了。”他说。

“很好,”我说,“我们接下来要确定什么呢?我们不是应该确定这个特殊阶层中的哪些成员会成为统治者,哪些人会成为被统治者吗?”

“当然。” 412c

“老人显然应该是统治者而年轻人应该是被统治者,不是吗?”

“对的。”

“只有老者中最优秀的人吗?”

“是的,那也是显而易见的。”

“那么,最好的农民就是最会务农的人,不是吗?”

“是的。”

“就当前的情形看,因为我们要找最好的卫士,故他们必须是那些特别擅长于保卫城邦的人,不是吗?”

“是的。”

“他们不仅是须有这职业的智慧和能力,而且他们还必须关心城邦,难道不是吗?”

“是的。” d

'Now, you care most for things that happen to be dear to you.'

'Inevitably.'

'And something is particularly dear to you if you regard your interests and its interests as identical, and if you think that your success and failure follow from its success and failure.'

'Yes,' he said.

'It follows that we should select from among the guardians men
e who particularly strike us, on investigation, as being the type to devote their whole lives to wholeheartedly doing what they regard as advantageous to the community, and to completely refusing to do anything they regard as disadvantageous to it.'

'Yes, they would make suitable rulers,' he said.

'I think we'll have to watch them at every stage of their lives, then, to make sure that they're good at safeguarding this idea and aren't magically or forcibly induced to shed and forget the notion that it's essential to do what's best for the community.'

'What do you mean by this shedding?' he asked.

'I'll explain,' I said. 'It seems to me that the departure of an idea from a person's mind can be either intentional or
413a unintentional. It's intentional if the idea is false and the person learns better, and unintentional whenever the idea is true.'

'I understand intentional loss,' he said, 'but I still don't understand unintentional loss.'

'But don't you think that the loss of good things is unintentional, while the loss of bad things is intentional?' I asked. 'And don't you think that being deceived about the truth is a bad thing, while having a grasp of the truth is good? And don't you think that having a grasp of the truth is having a belief that matches the way things are?'

“那么,你最关心的,恰好是你所珍爱之物。”

“这不可避免。”

“如果你把自己的利益和某事物的利益看作是一致的,并且你的成功和失败源于它的成功和失败,那么它就会与你关系特别密切。”

“是的。”他说。

“据此而言,我们应该经过调查,从卫士中挑选出一些男性来,他们特别给我们留下深刻印象的是,作为模范,只要他们认为是对城邦有利的事情,他们就会投入其全部的生命全心全意地去 e
做,而对那些他们认为是对城邦有危害的任何事情,他们则会完全拒绝去做。”

“是的,他们应该是合适的管理者。”他说。

“我想我们必须在他们生活的每个时期都对之加以考察,那就可以保证他们擅长捍卫这个理念,而不会受巫术和武力的引诱而排除和遗忘为城邦而鞠躬尽瘁的信念。”

“你说的‘排除’是什么意思?”他问道。

“我会解释的,”我说,“在我看来,信念之离开心灵有自愿的也有不自愿的。如果信念是虚假的并且人学得更好了,那就是自愿的,而信念要是正确的,那就是不自愿的。” 413a

“我理解自愿地失去,”他说,“但我还是不理解不自愿地失去。”

“但你难道不认为失去好的东西是不自愿的,而失去坏的东西是自愿的吗?”我问道,“你难道不认为真相受到蒙蔽是件坏事,而把握真相则是件好事吗?难道你不认为把握真相就是具有与事物相符的信念吗?”

'Yes, you're right,' he said. 'I agree that the loss of a true belief is unintentional.'

b 'So when this happens, it's the result of robbery, magic, or brute force, wouldn't you say?'

'I don't understand again,' he said.

'I suppose I am talking pompously,' I said. 'When I talk of a person being robbed of a belief, I mean that he's persuaded by an argument to change his mind, or time causes him to forget it: in either case, he doesn't notice the departure of the belief, I should think you understand now, don't you?'

'Yes.'

'And when I talk of a person being forced out of a belief, I mean that pain or suffering makes him change his mind.'

'Yes, I understand that too,' he said, 'and you're right.'

c 'And I'm sure you'd agree that anyone who changes his mind because he's been beguiled by pleasure or terrified by threats has had magic used on him.'

'Yes,' he said, 'any deception is a form of magic, I suppose.'

'As I was starting to say a moment ago, then, we must try to discover which of our guardians are particularly good at safe-guarding within themselves the belief that they should only ever pursue courses of action which they think are in the com-munity's best interests. We must watch them from childhood onwards, and set them tasks which maximize the possibility of their forgetting a belief like this and being misled; those who bear the belief in mind and prove hard to mislead are the ones we should select, while excluding the others. Do you agree?'

d 'Yes.'

'And we should also set them tough and painful assignments and ordeals, and watch for exactly the same things.'

'Right,' he said.

“你说得对，”他说，“我同意失去真实的信念不是自愿的。”

“所以当这种情况发生的时候，就是因为抢劫、巫术或暴力， b
你还会说是什么呢？”

“我又不明白了。”他说。

“我想我说得宽泛了，”我说，“当我说一个人被剥夺了信念，我的意思是说，他或者被论证所说服而改变了他的信念，或者是时间使他遗忘了：在任何一种情况下，他都没有意识到失去了信念。我想你现在应该理解了，对吗？”

“是的。”

“当我说一个人受到逼迫而放弃了信念，我的意思是说，痛苦或苦难使他改变了信念。”

“是的，我也理解了，”他说，“你说得对。”

“我确信你会同意，说一个人改变了他的信念，是因为他受到 c
快乐的引诱或威胁的恐吓而中了巫术。”

“是的，”他说，“我认为任何欺骗都是一种巫术般的迷惑。”

“那么，就如我刚才开始说的那样，我们必须尽力去发现那些特别善于捍卫自身信念的卫士，他们应该只追求最好地顾及城邦利益的事业。我们必须对之从小加以考察，给他们指派一些最有可能使他们遗忘这样的信念而被误导的任务；我们应该把那些把信念牢记在心而难以误导的人遴选出来，而排除其他人。你同意
吗？” d

“同意。”

“我们还应该指派给他们艰苦、费力的任务和严酷的考验，对其加以同样考察。”

“对的。”他说。

'Now, we'll have to invent a selection procedure for our third category, magic, as well,' I said, 'and observe how they perform. People test a foal's nervousness by introducing it to noise and commotion, and in the same way we must bring our guardians, while they're young, face to face with fear and then shift them into facing pleasure.
e People use fire to test gold, but our test must be far more thorough, and must show us how well they resist magic and whether they remain graceful whatever the situation, keep themselves and their cultural education intact, and display rhythm and harmony throughout; if they're capable of doing this, their value to themselves and to the community will he very high. Anyone who emerges without impurities from every
414a single test—as a child, as a young man, and as an adult—should be made a ruler and guardian of our community, and should be honoured in life and in death, in the sense of being awarded the most privileged of funerals and tombs. Anyone who gets corrupted, however, should be excluded. So, Glaucon,' I concluded, 'I think that this is how we should select and appoint our rulers and guardians. These are just guidelines, though: I haven't gone into details.'

'I agree,' he said. 'It must be something like this.'

b 'And we really and truly could hardly go wrong if we reserved the term "guardian" in its fullest sense for these people, who ensure that neither the desire nor the capacity for harming the community arises, whether from external enemies or from internal friends. As for the young men we've been calling guardians up to now, we should strictly call them auxiliaries and assistants of the guardians and their decision-making, don't you think?'

'Yes, I do,' he said.

'Now,' I said, 'can we devise one of those lies—the kind which crop up as the occasion demands, which we were talking about
c not long ago—so that with a single noble lie we can indoctrinate the rulers themselves, preferably, but at least the rest of the community?'

我说:“那么,让我们再设计第三种诱惑作为遴选的程序,并考察他们的表现。人们把小马带到嘈杂喧哗的地方去考验它们害不害怕,同样我们也必须让卫士在其年轻时面对恐惧,再让他们面对享乐。人们用火来考验金子,但我们的考验比这还要更加 e
彻底,他们必须向我们表明,他们如何能抵挡住诱惑,无论在什么环境下是否都能泰然不动,保持自己及他们的文艺教育不受影响,并且自始至终展示出节律与和谐;如果他们能够做到这点的话,那么他们对于自己和城邦的价值将是非常大的。任何在每个考验中都无懈可击的人——作为儿童,作为年轻人和作为成年人——都应该成为统治者和我们城邦的卫士,生前死后都应该得 414a
到荣誉,以最荣耀的葬礼和陵墓作为奖励。然而任何腐败之人都应该被排除掉,”我总结说,“所以,格劳孔,我想这就是我们如何遴选和任命我们的统治者和卫士的方法。然而这仅仅只是个大纲:我还没有涉及到细节。”

“我同意,”他说,“必须是像这样的。”

“要是我们把‘卫士’这个词的最完整的含义用于指称这 b
些人,我们确实几乎不会有什么错,他们保证不会有损害城邦的欲望和能力出现,无论是来自于外部的敌人还是内部的朋友。至于那些先前我们称之为卫士的人,我们应该在严格意义上称之为卫士及其决策的助理和帮手,你难道不这么想吗?”

“我是这样想的。”他说。

我说:“现在,我们是否能构想某个谎言——我们先前说过的应事而生的那种谎言——这样我们就能用一个高贵的谎言去说服统治者本人,至少说服城邦中的其他人?” c

'What sort of lie?' he asked.

'Nothing too outlandish,' I replied, 'just a tall story about something which happened all over the place in times past (at least, that's what the poets claim and have persuaded us to believe), but which hasn't happened in our lifetimes and I'm not sure it could, and people would need a great deal of convincing about it.'

'You seem reluctant to tell us the story,' he remarked.

'And you'll see that my reluctance was well founded', I said, 'when I do tell you-it.'

'Don't worry,' he said. 'Just talk.'

d 'What I'm saying is... I'm not sure where to find the gall or the words to tell the story... I'll be trying above all to convince the rulers themselves and the military, and secondarily the rest of the community, that all the nurture and education we provided happened to them in a kind of dream-world; in actual fact, they were at that time being formed and nurtured deep inside the earth, and their weaponry and their equipment in general were also being made there. When they
e were finished products, the earth, their mother, sent them up above ground; and now in their policy-making they must regard the country they find themselves in as their mother and their nurse, they must defend her against invasion, and they should think of the rest of the inhabitants of the community as their earth-born brothers.'

'I'm not surprised you were ashamed to tell us the lie before,' he remarked.

415a 'I had good reason,' I said. 'All the same, do please listen to the rest of the story as well. "Although all of you citizens are brothers," we'll continue the tale by telling them, "nevertheless, during the kneading phase, God included gold in the mixture when he was forming those of you who have what it takes to be rulers (which is why the rulers have the greatest privileges), silver when he was forming the auxiliaries, and iron and copper when he was forming the farmers and other workers. Now, despite the fact that in general your offspring will be similar in kind to yourselves, nevertheless, because you're all related, sometimes a silver child might be born to a gold parent, a gold one

“什么样的谎言?”他问道。

“没什么太新奇的,”我回答说,“就是关于从前到处都有的某事的传说(至少那是诗人们的说法并力图让我们相信的事情),但这种事情没有发生在我们的时代,我也不知其是否能够发生,要想让人们相信需要花费很大力气呢。”

“你好像不情愿告诉我们这个故事。”他说。

我说:“当我讲给你听的时候,你会发现我这么不情愿是有理由的。”

“不要有什么顾虑,”他说,“尽管说吧。”

“我想说的是……我不知道我是否有胆量或找得到语词来讲 d
述这个故事……我首先会尽力说服统治者本人和卫士,然后再说
服城邦里其余的人,对他们来说所有我们提供的养育和教育都是
一种梦幻;事实上,那时他们形成并滋养于深深的大地中,他们的
武器和装备也都是在那里制造的。当他们长大以后,大地母亲就 e
把他们送到地上来;现在在他们的决策中必须把他们所处的土地
看作他们的母亲和保姆,他们必须抵抗侵略,应该把城邦的其余
的居民看作是他们土地所生的兄弟。”

“我对你刚才羞于告诉我们这个谎言并不感到奇怪了。”他说。

“我自有理由,”我说,“请把剩下的故事也听完吧。‘尽管城 415a
邦里的所有人都是兄弟,’我们继续讲述这个传说,‘但神在塑造
他们的时候掺进了黄金,使他们成为统治者,这就是统治者享有
特权的原因,当他在塑造助手的时候掺进了白银,在塑造农民和
其他工匠的时候掺进了铁和铜。虽然总的来说你的后代会像你
本人,但由于你们都相互关联,所以有时黄金的父母可能生出白

b to a silver parent, and so on: any of them might be produced by any of the others. Therefore, of all his instructions to the rulers, there is none that God stresses more than this: there is no aspect of their work as guardians which they shall be so good at or dedicated to as watching over the admixture of elements in the minds of the children of the community. If one of their own children is born with a nature tinged with copper or iron, they shall at all costs avoid feeling sorry for it:
c they shall assign it the status appropriate to its nature and banish it to the workers or the farmers. On the other hand, if a child born to a worker or a farmer has a nature tinged with gold or silver, they shall honour it and elevate it to the rank of either guardian or auxiliary, because of an oracle which states that the community will be destroyed when it has a copper or iron guardian." Can you think of any tactics to make them believe this story?'

d 'No, not for this particular lot, anyway,' he said, 'but I can for the immediately succeeding generations and all the generations to follow.'

'I've got a pretty good idea of what you're getting at,' I said. 'It would help them care even more for the community and for one another. But the future of all this will be decided by popular consensus, not by us.'

'What we can do, however, is arm these earth-born men and mobilize them under the leadership of their rulers. They must go and look for the best location within the community for their barracks, a
e location from where they can control any disobedience to the laws on the part of the internal inhabitants, and repel the assault of an external enemy who falls on the community tike a wolf on a flock of sheep. When they've occupied the site, they must sacrifice to the appropriatc gods and construct shelters, don't you think?'

'Yes,' he said.

'And these shelters should provide adequate protection whatever the weather?'

银的孩子,而白银的父母可能生出黄金的孩子,如此等等:任 b
何人都可能生出任何别的种族来。所以在所有神的指示中,
神最强调的莫过于此:他们作为卫士,没有哪一方面能比如下
工作需要他们更为擅长或致力:监视城邦中的孩童们心灵中
成分的混合情况。如果他们自己的孩子中有一个生下来禀赋
杂有铜或铁,那么他们将不惜任何代价要避免对此感到惋惜:
他们应该把他放置到适合其禀赋的位置上去,把他放逐到工 c
匠和农民那去。另一方面,如果出生于工匠或农民之家的孩
子的本性中混有黄金或白银,那么他们应该珍视他,把他提升
到卫士或助手阶层,因为神谕昭示:含有铜或铁的人成了卫
士,则城邦就要毁灭。'你能想出什么办法让他们相信这个故
事吗?"

"不能,这些人无论如何都是不会相信的,"他说,"但有可能 d
让他们的后代以及所有的子嗣相信。"

"我很理解你说的,"我说,"这能帮助他们更加关心城邦并相
互关爱。但所有这些事情的前途是由大众的共同意见决定的,而
不是由我们决定的。"

"然而,我们所能做的就是,武装这些大地的子嗣,动员他们
遵循他们统治者的领导。他们必须在城邦里寻找一个最好的地
方安营扎寨,在这个地方他们能够控制内部居民的违法犯罪,也 e
能抗击如羊群中的狼一样的外部敌人攻击城邦。当他们占领了
这地方之后,就必须向合适的诸神献祭并建造住所,你难道不是
这么想的吗?"

"是这样想的。"他说。

"这些住所必须能抵御各种天气吗?"

'Of course,' he said. 'I mean, these are their living-quarters you're talking about, I think.'

416a 'Yes,' I said, 'but military quarters, not places of business.'

'Now what distinction are you getting at?' he asked.

'I'll try to explain,' I answered. 'Consider, for example, the dogs which shepherds train to act as their auxiliaries, to help them look after their flocks: there could be nothing more dreadful or despicable than for these dogs, thanks to their nature or thanks to the shepherds' training, to be capable of being influenced by indiscipline or hunger or some other bad habit to try to harm the sheep and behave like wolves rather than sheepdogs.'

'It goes without saying that this would be dreadful,' he said.

b 'So we must do everything possible to guard against the possibility of our auxiliaries treating the inhabitants of our community like that and using their greater power to behave like brutal despots rather than well-intentioned allies.'

'Yes, we must,' he said.

'Wouldn't a really excellent education have equipped them to take the maximum amount of care?'

'But they did receive an excellent education,' he said.

'That's not something we should stake our lives on, my dear
Glaucon,' I said. 'But we should stand firmly by our present posi-
c tion, that whatever constitutes a proper education, It is the chief factor in the guardians' treating themselves and their wards in a civilized fashion.'

'That's right,' he said.

'Now, doesn't it make sense to say that this education isn't all
they need? That in addition their living-quarters and their property in
general should be designed not to interfere with their carrying out their
work as guardians as well as possible or to encourage them to commit
d crimes against their fellow citizens?'

“当然，”他说，“我的意思是说，我想这些就是你说的他们生活的地方。”

“是的，”我说，“是军事场所而不是交易场所。”

“那你说有什么区别？”他问道。416a

“我会尽量解释的，”我说，“来看看牧羊人训练以作为其帮手、帮助他们照看他们羊群的狗的例子：没有比这样的狗更可恶、更卑劣了，由于它们的禀赋或者是由于牧羊人的训练，它们受到没有约束、饥饿或其他恶习的影响，便会设法伤害羊只，它们的行为就像狼而不像牧羊犬了。”

“不用说，这样一来是非常令人恐惧的。”他说。

“所以我们必须尽一切努力来预防这种可能性，即我们的从属人 b
员对待我们城邦中的居民，就像变坏了的牧羊犬对待羊只一样，又像残暴的君主运用巨大的权力为所欲为，而不像好心好意的同盟者。”

“是的，我们必须这样做。”他说。

“为他们提供一种真正卓越优秀的教育，不就可以最大限度地消除这种隐忧吗？”

“但是他们确实接受过一种卓越优秀的教育啊。”他说。

“对此我们不应该如此肯定，我亲爱的格劳孔，”我说，“但对现在我们的这个观点，我们应该坚决肯定，即：无论什么样的正确的教育制度，主要的因素都在于教育卫士以文明教养的风范对待 c
自己，对待他们所保护的人。”

“对。”他说。

“那么不就是说这种教育并不是全部？总的来说，除了应该提供给他们的住处和财物使他们尽可能地不影响从事作为卫士的工作之外，还要激励他们不要对其他公民为非作歹？” d

'Yes, it does.'

'I wonder if they'd turn out as we want if their lifestyle and living-quarters were somewhat as follows,' I said. 'See what you think. In the first place, none of them is to have any private property, except what is absolutely indispensable. In the second place, none of them is to have living-quarters and storerooms which are not able to be entered by anyone who wants to. Their provisions (which should be suitable in quantity for self-controlled and courageous warriors) are to
e be their stipend, paid by their fellow citizens for their guarding, the amount being fixed so that, at the end of a year, there is no excess or shortfall. There will be shared mess-halls for them to go to, and their lives will be communal, as if they were on campaign. We'll tell them that the permanent presence in their minds of divine gold and silver, which they were granted by the gods, means that they have no need of earthly gold and silver as well; and we'll add that it is sacrilegious for them to adulterate and contaminate that heavenly possession by owning the earthly variety, because in the past this earthly variety, which is accepted as currency by the masses, has provoked many acts
417a of desecra- tion, whereas theirs is untainted. So, unlike any of their fellow citizens, they are not permitted to have any contact or involvement with gold and silver: they are not to come under the same roof as gold and silver, or wear them on their bodies, or drink from gold and silver cups. These precepts will guarantee not only their own integrity, but also the integrity of the community which is in their safe keeping. If they do come to own land and homes and money, they will be estate-managers and farmers instead of guardians; they will become des-
b pots, and enemies rather than allies of the inhabitants of the community; they will spend their lives hating and being hated, plotting and being plotted against; they will have internal enemies to fear more, and more intensely, than their external enemies. With private property, they will be racing ever closer to the ruin of themselves and the whole community. All this confirms the importance of our stated arrangements for the guardians' living-quarters and so on,' I concluded, 'so shall we enshrine them in law, or not?'

'We certainly must,' said Glaucon.

“是的，的确如此。”

“我想知道，要想使他们成为符合我们所要求的，那么他们的
生活方式和住处是否应该如下那样。”我说，“你看怎么样？首先，
除了一些绝对必不可少的东西之外，他们中的任何人都不能拥有
私有财产。第二，他们中的任何人都不得拥有其他人想进而不能
进入的住处和库房。他们的供应品就是他们的薪金，按一个自制 e
且勇敢的卫士所需的量由别的公民供给，作为保护他们的报酬，
每年底定量发放，不多也不少。他们有共同的食堂，他们的生活
也是公有制的，就像生活在军营里一样。我们会告诉他们，在他
们的心灵中始终蕴涵着由诸神授予的神圣的金银，这就是说他们
不需要世俗的金银了；我们还会告诉他们说，把世俗的东西与神
圣的品性相混合，这样就是玷污了神圣的品性就是亵渎神灵，因
为过去这种世俗的作为流通货币使用的东西引发了诸多罪恶行
径，而他们神圣的品性则不应受玷污。所以与任何其他公民不 417a
同，他们不允许与金银有任何接触或关联：他们不能与金银同居
一室，身上不能穿金戴银，不能使用金银酒器。这些戒律不光能
确保他们自己的完善，还能确保他们所保卫的城邦的完善。要是
他们拥有了自己的土地、家园和金钱，那么他们就会成为业主和
农民，而不是卫士了；他们会成为暴君和城邦中居民的敌人，而不
是盟友了；他们的一生都会花费在仇恨和被仇恨、算计和被算计 b
上；比起外敌，他们会更惧怕内部的敌人。有了私有财产，他们就
会使自己和城邦更快地走向灭亡。所有这些都证实了我们对于
卫士的住所等等所说的安排是重要的。”我总结说，“所以，我们是
要将之制定为法律呢，还是不要呢？”

“我们当然必须这样做。”格劳孔说。

419a Adeimantus came in with an objection: 'Tell me, Socrates,' he said. 'How are you going to reply to the accusation that you're not making these men at all happy, and moreover you're making it their own fault? In a real sense, the community belongs to them, but they don't derive any benefit from the community. Others own estates, build beautiful mansions and stock them with suitable furniture, perform their own special religious rites, entertain, and of course own the items you were just talking about, gold and silver, and everything else without which happiness is, on the usual view, impossible. Instead of all this, a critic might say, their role in our community really
420a is just like that of auxiliary troops—mercenaries—with nothing to do except maintain a garrison.'

'Yes,' I agreed. 'And they don't even get paid like other auxiliary troops: they get no more than their provisions. Consequently, they can't even take a trip for personal reasons out of town if they want to, or give presents to mistresses, or spend money on anything else they might want to, as so-called happy people can. You're leaving all this out of your accusation, and plenty of other things too.'

'All right,' he said. 'Please assume that the accusation includes them.'

b 'So you're asking how we'll defend ourselves, are you?'

'Yes.'

'I don't think we need to change direction at all to come across a suitable defence,' I said. 'We'll reply that although it wouldn't surprise us in the slightest if in fact there were no people happier than these men, all the same we're not constructing our community with the intention of making one group within it especially happy, but to maximize the happiness of the community as a whole. We thought we'd be most likely to find morality in a community like ours and also immorality in
c a community with the worst possible management, and that once we'd examined them we'd reach the decision which is the original purpose

阿狄曼图提出了反对意见:“告诉我,苏格拉底,”他说, 419a
“你完全没有使这些人幸福,此外,你还把这当作咎由自取,你
如何回应这样的指责?实际上,城邦是属于他们的,但他们没
有从城邦中得到任何好处。而别人拥有地产,建造华丽的住
宅并配备了合适的家具,以自己的特殊方式进行献祭,款待宾
客,当然也有你刚才提到的那些东西,金银财物,以及其他一
切,在一般人看来没有这些东西幸福是不可能的。与此相反,
有人可能会批评说,他们在我们的城邦里实际上只扮演了类
似辅助部队——雇佣军——一样的角色,除了站岗放哨之外便
无所事事。” 420a

“是的,”我同意道,“他们甚至不像其他辅助部队一样得到报偿:除了供应品他们什么都得不到。结果,他们甚至都不能自由地由于私事而出城旅行,不能给情人送礼,也不能像那些被视为幸福的人那样想买其他东西就买。你的指责略过了所有这些,也略过了许多别的事情。”

“好吧,”他说,“就算还有这些指责吧。”

“所以你是在问我们如何为自己辩护,是吗?” b

“是的。”

“为了找到一个合适的回答,我想我们完全不需要改变方
向,”我说,“我们会回答说,如果事实上没有人比这些人更加
幸福,这一点都不令我们感到奇怪,不管怎样,我们建立我们
的城邦并不是打算让某个阶层的人格外幸福,而是为了整个
城邦的最大幸福。我认为我们最有可能在像我们这样的城邦
中找到正义,而在组织得最差的城邦中找到不正义,等我们考 c
察了它们之后,我们就能对我们探讨的原初目的作出判断了。

of our investigation. What we're doing at the moment, we think, is
forming a community which is happy as a whole, without hiving off a
few of its members and making them the happy ones; and before long
we'll be looking at a community in the opposite condition.

'Suppose we were painting a statue and someone came up and criti-
cized us for not using the most beautiful paint for the creature's most
beautiful features, because the eyes are the most beautiful part and they
hadn't been painted purple but black. It would be perfectly reasonable,
d in our opinion, for us to reply to this critic by saying, "My dear chap,
you can't expect us to paint beautiful eyes in a way which stops them loo-
king like eyes, or to do that to the other parts of the body either. Don't
you think that if we treat every single part in an appropriate fashion,
we're making the creature as a whole beautiful?" Likewise, in the pres-
ent case, please don't force us to graft the sort of happiness on to the
guardians which will make them anything but guardians. You see, we
e know we could dress our farmers in soft clothes and golden jewellery and
tell them to work the land only when they have a mind to, and we know
we could have our potters lie basking in their kiln-fire's warmth on a for-
mal arrangement of couches, drinking and feasting with their wheel beside
them as a table, and doing pottery only as much as they feel like, and
we know we could make everyone else happy in this sort of way, and so
have a community which was happy overall; but please don't advise us to
do so, because if we follow your recommendation, then our farmers won't
421a be farmers and our potters won't be potters and no one else will retain
that aspect of himself which is a constituent of a community. Now, this
isn't so important where the rest of the community is concerned. I mean,
if cobblers go to the bad and degenerate and pretend to be other than
what they are, it's not catastrophic for a community; but if the people
who guard a community and its laws ignore their essence and start to
pose, then obviously they're utterly destroying the community, despite
the fact that its good management and happiness are crucially in their
hands and their hands alone.

我想此刻我们所做的是塑造一个整体上都幸福的城邦出来，而不是划分出一部分成员让他们得到幸福；我们不久还要考察处于相反状况的城邦。

"假设我们在为雕像着色，有人走过来指责我们没有为塑像最美丽的部分涂上最美丽的颜色，因为眼睛是最美的部分，却没有给它们涂上紫色而是涂上了黑色。在我们看来，我们完全有理由如此回答这个批评：'我亲爱的朋友，你别指望我们把美丽的眼 d
睛涂得不像眼睛，对身体上别的部分我们也不会这样做。你难道不认为要是我们给每一单个部分都涂上恰当的颜色，我们就会让整个塑像变得漂亮吗？'同样，在当前的这种情况下，请不要迫使我们赋予卫士幸福，这样会让他们绝对成不了卫士。你明白，我们知道，我们是能够给我们的农民穿上柔软的衣服带上 e
黄金首饰，并且只是当他们想要做时才叫他们去干活，我们知道，我们是能够让我们的制陶匠躺在正式摆放的卧椅上围着他们的窑炉火烤暖，同时把他们旁边的陶轮当作餐桌吃吃喝喝，而且只在他们想去做陶器的时候才去做，我们知道，我们是能够以此方式让所有别的人得到幸福，由此整个城邦就都幸福了；但请不要让我们这样做，因为如果我们遵从了你的建议，那么我们的农民就不成其为农民，我们的制陶匠就不成其为制陶匠了，并且其他人也不再是成为城邦之部分的那种人 421a
了。而这要是涉及到城邦中的其他人，那还不是那么要紧。我的意思是说，如果一个补鞋匠变坏了、堕落了，想做别的活而不想做本分活了，这对于城邦来说倒还不是灾难性的；但是如果那些保卫城邦及其法律的人，虽然良好管理和幸福的关键都掌握在他们手里，并且也仅仅是在他们手里，他们却忽视了他们的本职工作，开始装模作样，那么他们显然会彻底毁了城邦。

b ‘Now, if we’re creating genuine guardians, who can hardly
harm their community, and the originator of that other idea is talking
about a certain kind of farmer and people who are, as it were, happy
to fill their stomachs on holiday, but aren’t members of a community,
then he’s not talking about a community, but something else. What
we have to consider is whether our intention in putting the guardians
in place is to maximize their happiness, or whether we ought to make
the happiness of the community as a whole our goal and should, by
c fair means and foul, convince these auxiliaries and guardians that
their task is to ensure that they, and everyone else as well, are the
best at their own jobs. Then, when the community as a whole is flour-
ishing and rests on a fine foundation, we can take it for granted that
every group within it will find happiness according to its nature.’

‘I’m sure you’re right,’ he said.

‘Well, I wonder if a closely related idea of mine will also strike you as sensible,’ I said.

‘What is it?’

d ‘That there are other factors which corrupt the rest of the workers and make them bad at their jobs.’

‘What factors?’

‘Affluence and poverty,’ I replied.

‘What do you mean?’

‘This is what I mean. If a potter gets rich, do you think he’ll still be willing to devote himself to his profession?’

‘Not at all,’ he answered.

‘He’ll become less hard-working and less conscientious than before, won’t he?’

‘Considerably less.’

‘Then he’ll be a worse potter?’

‘Again, considerably worse,’ he said.

"于是,如果我们塑造的是几乎不会损害其城邦的真正的卫士,而另一种想法的创始者所谈的,可以说却是乐于在 b
休假中满足满足口腹之欲的农民和其他一些人,而不是城邦的成员,那么他谈论的并不是城邦,而是别的什么东西。我们必须考虑任用卫士是否意在使他们的幸福最大化,或者说我们是否应该把整个城邦的幸福作为我们的目标,并且应该不择手段地使这些帮手和卫士相信,他们的任务就是确保自己及其他人全力做好本职工作。这样,当整个城邦繁荣昌盛 c
并创建出良好基础的时候,我们就可以说城邦中的每个阶层都依据其本性找到了幸福。"

"我确信你说得对。"他说。

"好吧,我想知道你是否会对我的另一个与此紧密相关的想法也觉得有理。"我说。

"是什么?"

"有一些其他原因使其余的工匠败坏并使其疏于工作。" d

"什么原因?"

"富裕和贫穷。"我回答说。

"你说的是什么意思?"

"我的意思是这样的:如果一个制陶匠变富有了,你认为他还会愿意献身于他的职业吗?"

"根本不会。"他回答说。

"与以前相比,他会变得懒惰和粗心大意,难道不是吗?"

"显然是的。"

"那么他就是个愈加差劲的制陶匠啰?"

"是的,相当差劲。"他说。

'But if he's so poor that he lacks the means to provide himself with tools and other essentials for his job, then he's going to be turning out inferior products and he'll not be able to provide his sons (or
e whoever else is apprenticed to him) with adequate training.'

'Of course.'

'Both affluence and poverty, then, are causes of degeneration in the products and the practitioners of a craft.'

'So it seems.'

'So we've come up with more things which the guardians must at all costs prevent from sneaking into the community without their noticing it.'

'What things?'

422a 'Affluence and poverty,' I said. 'The first brings indulgence, indolence, and innovation; the second entails miserliness and bad workmanship, as well as also bringing innovation.'

'Quite so,' he said. 'But, Socrates, here's a question for you. How will our community be capable of waging war if its coffers are empty, especially if it has to face an enemy who is large and wealthy?'

'Obviously it would be easier to have two such opponents ranged against us than one, relatively speaking,' I said.

b 'What are you getting at?' he asked.

'Chiefly this,' I said. 'If they do have to fight, won't it be a case of warriors versus plutocrats?'

'Yes,' he said.

'Well, Adeimantus,' I went on, 'don't you think that a single boxer who has received the best possible training can easily take on two non-boxers who are rich and fat?'

'Maybe not at the same time,' he answered.

'Not even if it were possible for him to draw back and then turn

“但要是他很穷，以至无法拥有其工作所需的工具和其他基本用具，那么他生产出的就是劣质的产品，他也无法给他的儿子（或其他任何学徒）以充分的训练。” e

“当然如此。”

“那么，富裕和贫穷都是使产品和手艺人退化的原因。”

“看来如此。”

“所以我们发现另一些事情，卫士必须尽力不让它们在其不注意的情况下悄悄地溜进城邦。”

“什么事情？”

“富裕和贫穷，”我说，“前者导致奢侈、懒惰和变革；后者包含 422a
着悲惨和低劣，也会导致变革。”

“的确如此，”他说，“但是，苏格拉底，还有个问题要问你。要是国库空空，那我们的城邦怎么有能力打仗，尤其是当它面对强大而富有的敌国的时候？”

“相对来说，不是与一个而是与两个这样的敌国作战就显然比较容易了。”我说。 b

“你说的是什么意思？”他问道。

“主要是这个意思，”我说，“如果他们要打仗，那么不就是战士与富人之间的战斗吗？”

“是的。”他说。

我继续说：“好吧，阿狄曼图，你难道不认为一个受过最好训练的拳击手能轻而易举地击败两个又富又肥、不懂拳击的人吗？”

“也许不能同时打倒。”他回答说。

“难道他先后退再反过来击败首先追上来的那个对手，也不能

c around and strike whichever opponent is bearing down on him first?' I asked. 'And what about if he could do this over and over again in the sunshine and stifling heat? Under these circumstances, couldn't he overcome even more opponents of the kind we're postulating?'

'Without a doubt,' he said. 'It wouldn't be at all surprising.'

'Well, don't you think that rich people are better and more experienced boxers than they are soldiers?'

'I do,' he replied.

'Our warriors will, then, in all likelihood, have no difficulty in taking on two or three times the number of rich opponents.'

'I'll concede the point,' he said. 'I think you're right.'

d 'All right, then. Suppose they send a herald to one of the two communities with the following true message: "We have no use for gold and silver; it is taboo for us, though not for you. Side with us in the war, and you can have the other side's assets." Do you think that anyone who received this message would choose the option of fighting tough, lean dogs rather than siding with the dogs against fat, tender sheep?'

'No, I don't. But if all the assets of all the other communities
e are gathered up by a single community, then don't you think this situation might entail some danger for our asset-free community?'

'It's naive of you to think that any community other than the one we're constructing deserves the name,' I said.

'What should I call them?' he asked.

'They should have a more capacious title,' I replied, 'since each of them is not so much a community as a great many communities, as in the game. Minimally, they contain two warring communi-
423a ties—one consisting of the rich and one of the poor. Then each of these two contains quite a number of further communities. It would be quite wrong to treat this plurality as a unity. However, if you treat them as a plurality and offer one section's assets and power and personnel to

吗?”我问道,“要是他在烈日炎炎之下反复操练也不行吗? 这样, c
他不就能够击败多个我们设想的那种对手了吗?”

“毫无疑问,”他说,“这没什么好奇怪的。”

“那么,比起战士,你难道认为富人是更优秀、经验更丰富的拳击手吗?”

“我认为战士更优秀、经验更丰富。”他回答说。

“那么,我们的战士,击败两倍或三倍富裕的对手似乎没什么困难。”

“我同意这点,”他说,“我认为你说得对。”

“那么,好吧。假设我们派一名使节到两城邦之一去,传达如 d
下实情:‘金银对于我们没有什么用处;它们对我们是禁忌,而对
你们不是。与我们一起作战吧,你们就能拥有对方的财富。’你认
为任何收到了这个消息的人,会选择与凶猛精干的狗去开战,而
不与狗结盟去和肥壮温顺的羊开战吗?”

“不,我不这样认为。但是如果所有其它城邦的全部财富都
为一个单一的城邦所聚集,那么对于我们没有财富的城邦而言, e
你不认为这种情形也许会让我们承担一些危险吗?”

“如果你认为除了我们正在建立的城邦之外的其他城邦配得上这个名字,那你就太天真了。”我说。

“我应该怎么称呼它们?”他问道。

我回答说:“它们应该使用一个更大的名称,因为其中的每一
个都有许多个城邦,而不是一个,就如游戏中的那样。它们至少
包含两个敌对的城邦——一个由富人组成,另一个由穷人组成。
这两个城邦的每一个包含许多城邦。要是把多当作一,那就犯错 423a
了。如果你把它们当作多,并把一些部分的财产、权力和人口分

another section, then you'll always have a lot of allies and few enemies. And as long as your community's administration retains its discipline and is arranged in accordance with our recent regulations, it will have no equal. I don't mean that it will merely have the reputation of having no equal, but that it really won't, even if its militia numbers no more than a thousand. You'll be hard put to find a community of this size in Greece or abroad which is actually single, though there are plenty of communities which are far larger in size and
b which might be thought to be single. Do you agree, or not?'

'I most certainly do,' he said.

'Now, this could also provide our rulers with the best criterion for deciding on the appropriate size for the community,' I said, 'and how much territory they should reserve for a community of this size, without expanding any further.'

'What criterion?' he asked.

'To allow growth as long as growth doesn't jeopardize its unity,' I said, 'but no further. This is the criterion I'm thinking of.'

c 'It's a good one,' he commented.

'So here's another instruction we'll be giving the guardians,' I said. 'They are to do everything possible to guard against the community either being small or merely appearing large, and to ensure that it is just the right size and is a unity.'

'I suppose you think that's a simple instruction for them to carry out,' he said.

'And here's an even simpler one,' I said, 'which we mentioned earlier as well. We were talking of the necessity of banishing to the other ranks any inferior child who is born to the guardians, and of
d having any outstanding child who is born to the other ranks join the guardians. And the point of this idea was that every single member of

给另一部分人，那么你总会有许多盟友，很少有敌人。只要你们的城邦依法治理并按照我们刚才提出的规则加以安排，那么它就会所向无敌。我说的所向无敌并不是仅仅指它的名声，而是说它实际上就是所向无敌，即使它的战士数目不超过千把人。你会发现，无论在希腊还是外邦，都难以找到这种规模并确实是单个的城邦，虽然有许多城邦在规模上要大得多，并且也可以被看作是 b
单个的。你同不同意？"

"我当然同意。"他说。

我说："那么，这也可以为我们的统治者提供最佳的尺度，使他们确定城邦的恰当规模，并确定应该为这种规模的城邦留出多少土地，而毋须向外扩张。"

"什么样的尺度？"他问道。

我说："让城邦扩张到以不损害它的统一为限。这就是我所谓的尺度。"

"这是个好尺度。"他评论道。 c

"所以我们要交给卫士们另一项使命，"我说，"他们要尽量防卫他们的城邦既不要太小也不能看起来太大，而要保证它的恰当大小和统一。"

"我想，让他们去实行这个使命并不难。"他说。

"这里甚至还有个更简单的，"我说，"我们先前也提到过。[1]我们说过，有必要把任何生于卫士之家的低劣儿童放逐到其他等级中去，而把任何生于其他等级的天赋优秀的儿童加入到卫士中 d
去。这种想法的用意在于城邦中的每个成员，从其他等级的人到

〔1〕 参看415b。

the community, from the other ranks as well as any of the guardians, has to dedicate himself to the single job for which he is naturally suited, because this specialization of function will ensure that every person is not a plurality but a unity, and thus that the community as a whole develops as a unity, not a plurality.'

'Oh yes, that's simpler—hardly worth mentioning!' he said.

'As a matter of fact, my dear Adeimantus,' I said, 'the instructions we're giving them are not as numerous or as difficult as they
e might seem: they're all simple, provided they follow the saying and "stick to the one thing that's important"—or rather, not important so much as decisive.'

'What is this thing?' he asked.

'Their education and upbringing,' I replied. 'If they receive a good education which makes them moderate, then they'll easily discover everything we're talking about for themselves—and everything we've missed out so far as well, such as what they are to do with their wives, and what to do about marriage and childbirth, and how all
424a these matters have to be dealt with in accordance with the proverbial saying that friends share everything they can.'

'Yes, that would be best,' he said.

'Now, provided our community's constitution is given a good initial start,' I said, 'then it'll get into a spiral of growth. I mean, a good educational system, if maintained, engenders people of good character; and then people of good character, if they in their turn receive the benefits of an education of this kind, become even better than their predecessors in every respect, but especially—as is the
b case with other creatures too—in that they produce better children.'

'Yes, that seems reasonable,' he said.

'To put it succinctly, then, the government of the community must adhere to this educational system, and make sure that its integrity is not subtly compromised; they should constantly be on their guard against innovations which transgress our

任何卫士,都必须专注于一个适合其本性的工作,因为这种分工保证了每个人不是多而是一,这样作为整体的城邦就成为一,而不是多。”

“哦,是的,道理是更简单——几乎不值得一提!”他说。

我说:“我亲爱的阿狄曼图,事实上我们交给他们的使命并不像看上去的那么多,那么难:它们都很简单,只要他们遵循老话并且‘专注于那件重要的事情’——或者,与其说是重要,不如说是 e
关键。”

“这是什么事情?”他问道。

“他们的教育和培养,”我回答说,“如果他们受了一种使之平和稳健的良好教育,那么他们会很容易明白我们谈论的每一件事情以及所有我们遗漏没谈的事情,比如说关于他们妻子的事情,关于结婚生子的事情,所有这些事情都必须依据俗话‘朋友分担
一切’来加以处理。” 424a

“是的,那是最好。”他说。

“一旦我们的城邦组织有个好的开端,”我说,“那么它就会螺旋式地运作起来。我的意思是说,一个好的教育体制,如果保留的话,便会培养出具有好品性的人;而另一方面具有好品性的人,如果他们从这种教育中得到了益处的话,甚至会在各个方面都比他们的祖辈更加优秀,尤其是他们还生出更优秀的孩子来——这
在其他动物也一样。” b

“是的,那看起来很有道理。”他说。

“那么,简而言之,城邦的管理者必须坚持这套教育体制并保证它完整而不打折扣;他们应该时常防止变革,不让其违反体育锻炼或文艺学习的规范。他们应该尽其所能小心防范这些变革,

regulations about either physical exercise or cultural studies. They should look out for these to the best of their ability, and should worry if they hear the claim that "the most popular song is the one which
c happens to be on singers' lips at the moment", in case the poet might commonly be taken to be talking not about new songs, but a new type of singing, and might be commended for doing so. This kind of thing should be frowned on, however, and it surely is not what the poet meant. The point is that caution must be taken in adopting an unfamiliar type of music: it is an extremely risky venture, since any change in the musical modes affects the most important laws of a community. This is what Damon claims, and I believe him.'

'You can count me as another convert to this view,' said Adeimantus.

d 'So now we know where the guardians should build their lookout post,' I said. 'it's in the field of music and culture.'

'Yes,' he said. 'At any rate, indiscipline can easily creep in here without being noticed.'

'Yes,' I agreed, 'because it's not taken seriously and is assumed to have no harmful effects.'

'That's because it doesn't,' he said, 'except that it gradually establishes itself and then silently seeps into people's mannerisms and habits, which become the basis from which it erupts, now enlarged, into their business dealings with one another, which in turn become the basis from which it assaults the laws and the constitution with
e gross indecency, Socrates, until it eventually throws everything into chaos in both the private and the public spheres.'

'Really?' I asked.

'I think so,' he said.

'Our original position was correct, then: the children of our community must engage in more lawful amusements right from the start, because when pastimes become lawless and children follow suit, it is im-
425a possible for them to grow into law-abiding, exemplary adults. Yes?'

如果他们听到有人说‘最受欢迎的歌曲正是歌手此时在吟唱的那
首’,他们就应该警惕,以防人们可能普遍认为诗人们谈论的不是 c
新的歌曲而是新的吟唱风格,并且这样做还可能得到赞扬。这类事情是应该警惕的,这当然也不是诗人的意图。关键是采用一个不熟悉的音乐风格的时候必须小心谨慎:这是个极大的冒险,因为任何音乐风格的改变将影响城邦的最重要的法律。这是达蒙说的,我相信他的话。”

“你可以把我算作相信这话的另一人。”阿狄曼图说。

“所以现在我们知道卫士应该在哪里布防设哨了,”我说,“就 d
在音乐和文艺方面。”

“是的,”他说,“不管怎样,在这里违规的事情很容易不知不觉地出现。”

“是的,”我同意说,“因为人们对此不加重视,以为不会产生什么有害的后果。”

“它之所以产生害果,”他说,“那是因为它是慢慢地将自己稳固起来,然后悄悄地向人们的行为习惯里渗透,并在此基础上生根、扩张,直至扩张到人与人的相互关系中去,而这又成为其肆无
忌惮地攻击法律和政治制度的基础,苏格拉底,直到它最终把公 e
共的和私人方面的所有事情都搞得一团糟。”

“真的吗?”我问道。

“我想是这样的。”他说。

“那么,我们原来的想法是对的:我们城邦的孩子们必须一开始就参加更为合法的娱乐活动,因为如果游戏活动变得不合法而孩子们还模仿,那么对他们来说,想要成长为遵守法律的、可做模
范的成年人,那就不可能了。是吗?” 425a

'Of course,' he said.

'Therefore, when children play in a proper manner right from the start, and their cultural education introduces them to the orderliness of law, there is the opposite result: lawfulness accompanies them in everything they do, guides their growth, and corrects any aspect of the community which was formerly aberrant.'

'You're right,' he said.

'And they therefore rediscover those apparently trivial rules which their predecessors had completely lost.'

'What rules?'

b 'For example, that one should be silent in the presence of people older than oneself. Younger people should also give up their seats for their elders, stand up when they enter the room, and look after their parents. Then there are the rules about hairstyle, clothing, footwear, and in general the way one presents oneself, and so on and so forth. Do you agree?'

'Yes.'

'But in my opinion only an idiot would legislate on these matters. I don't think these rules come into being, and I don't think they would remain in force either, through being formulated and written down.'

'How could they?'

c 'Anyway, Adeimantus,' I said, 'education is the factor which determines a person's subsequent direction in life. I mean, doesn't like always attract like?'

'Of course.'

'And I suppose we'd say that the final result is a single, dynamic whole, whether or not it's good.'

'Naturally,' he said.

'And that's why I for one wouldn't try to legislate further

“那是当然。”他说。

“所以，要是孩子们一开始就以恰当的方式参加游戏活动，他们的文艺教育引导他们遵纪守法，那么结果就会是相反的：法制观念就会伴随着他们所做的每件事当中，指引他们的成长，并纠正城邦中方方面面的违规行为。”

“你说得对。”他说。

“于是他们重新发现了那些被他们的祖辈完全废弃了的、看起来微不足道的规矩。”

“什么规矩？”

“比如说，一个人应该在比自己年长的人面前保持肃静，年轻
人应该为年长的人让座，当他们进屋的时候要起立，对父母行孝 b
道。还有各种关于发型、衣履以及体态举止等等的规矩。你同意吗？”

“同意。”

“但在我看来只有傻瓜才会把这些事情制定成法律。我并不认为经由系统阐释且写将下来，这些规矩便得以存在，也不认为那么一做，它们便会有了持久效力。”

“那它们怎样才能得到遵守呢？”

“阿狄曼图，”我说，“不管怎样，教育决定了他以后人生的方
向。我的意思是说，同类不总是相互激励吗？” c

“当然。”

“那么我想我们会说，最终的结果，无论它是好还是坏，都是一个单一的能动的整体。”

“那是自然。”他说。

“这就是在这个方面除了我们已经做的事情之外，不想再将

than we already have done in this area,' I said.

'It makes sense not to,' he remarked.

'Now then,' I said, 'what on earth shall we do about the world
d of the agora? I mean the commercial deals people make with one another and, of course, contracts with labourers, lawsuits for slander and assault, indictments, empanelling juries, the collecting or paying of any money due for renting space in the agora or the port, and any business which concerns the general regulation of the agora or the city or the ports or whatever. Shall we take it on ourselves to make any rules and regulations about these matters?'

'It isn't right to tell truly good men what to do,' he said. 'They
e won't have any difficulty, in the majority of cases, in finding out which matters need legal measures.'

'No, my friend, they won't,' I said, 'as long as, by God's will, the laws we've already discussed are preserved intact.'

'Otherwise,' he said, 'they'll spend their whole lives making rule after rule, and then trying to improve them, in the hope that they'll hit on a successful formula.'

'You mean they'll live like people who are ill, but lack the discipline to give up a way of life that is bad for them,' I said.

'That's it.'

426a 'And what a nice time *they* have! All their treatments get them nowhere (except that they increase the variety and seriousness of their ailments) and they're constantly expecting every medicine they are recommended to make them better.'

'Yes, that's typical of this kind of invalid,' he said.

'And here's another nice feature of theirs,' I said. 'The thing they can abide least of all is someone telling them the truth—that until they stop getting drunk, stuffing themselves, whoring, and doing no
b work , no medicine or cautery or surgery , and no spell or amulet or

之制定成法律的原因。”我说。

“不将之制定成法律是有道理的。”他说。

我说：“那么关于商业，我们到底应该怎么做呢？我指的
是人们相互之间所做的商业交易，当然，还有劳动契约，毁谤 d
与侮辱引起的诉讼，民事诉讼案件，陪审员的选举，征收或支付租用市场或港口的赋税以及任何涉及市场、城市、海港等等的一般法规。我们自己要为这些事务制定法规和制度吗？”

“吩咐真正优秀的人去做事情是不恰当的，”他说，“他们会自
己确定哪些事情需要法律手段，在大多数情况下他们并不觉得有 e
什么困难。”

“对，我的朋友，他们是不会有什么困难的，”我说，“只要神保佑我们讨论过的法律保持不变。”

“否则，”他说，“他们就会把他们的一生都用来制定一条条的法律，然后再努力加以修正，以得到一套成功的法律。”

“你的意思是说他们会活得像病人，但缺乏节制而不愿放弃对自身有害的生活方式。”我说。

“就是这样的。”

“他们活得多逍遥啊！所有对他们的治疗都无济于事，而只 426a
会使疾病变得更加复杂和严重，他们总是希望每种向他们推荐的药物都能治好他们。”

“是的，病人就是这个样子的。”他说。

“他们还有个有趣的特点，”我说，“他们最不可忍受的事情就
是别人告诉他们真相——要是他们老是吃喝玩乐、寻花问柳和无
所事事，那么无论药物、烧灼法或外科手术，还是符咒或别的什么 b

anything like that either, is going to do them the slightest good.'

'That's not at all nice,' he said. 'There's nothing nice about getting angry at good advice.'

'You don't think highly of this type of person, it seems,' I commented.

'No, I certainly don't.'

'And you also won't think highly of a whole community, then, if it carries on in the equivalent way we mentioned a moment ago. I mean, wouldn't you describe as identical the actions of all those badly governed states which forewarn their citizens not to interfere with the
c general political system and threaten with death anyone who does so, while anyone who treats them, despite the condition of their government, in a way which pleases them a great deal, and who gets into their good books by flattering them and anticipating their wishes and by being good at satisfying these wishes, is accounted and acclaimed by them a man of virtue and high skill?'

'Yes, I think they're doing exactly the same,' he said, 'and I've got nothing good to say about them at all.'

d 'And what about people who are prepared, and even determined, to look after such communities? Don't you admire their courage—and their casual attitude?'

'Yes, I do,' he replied, 'except when they're deluded into imagining that they're true statesmen simply because the masses think highly of them.'

'What do you mean?' I asked. 'Don't you feel compassion for them? I mean, do you suppose there's any way in which a man who is incapable of measuring can avoid thinking he's four cubits tall when
e others (who are just as ignorant) are frequently telling him he is?'

'No, he can't,' he said.

办法，都不会给他们带来一点点好处。”

“那根本没什么有趣的，”他说，“冲着好建议发怒，这样做没什么趣味可言。”

“看来你对这种人没什么好感。”我评论道。

“没有，当然没什么好感。”

“如果整个城邦都以我们刚才提到过的方式行事，那么你对整个城邦也不会有什么好感。我的意思是说，你将之视同为所有那些治理不善的城邦的行径，那些城邦预先告诫他们的公民不得干涉城邦的根本制度，对有如此行为之人以死相胁，然而那 c
些不管他们城邦的制度而为之服务并极力讨好他们的人，则被认为是具有德行和高超技能的人，这些人通过奉承巴结他们，迎合他们的意愿并善于满足他们的愿望而被载入史册，难道不是吗？”

“是的，我认为他们[1]做得完全一样，”他说，“我根本不会赞同他们。”

“那些准备好，甚至下定决心为这样的城邦服务的人又怎么 d
样呢？你难道不佩服他们的勇气和不计个人得失的态度吗？”

“是的，我佩服他们，”他回答说，“除非他们受到迷惑，仅仅因为受到民众的赞同而自认为是政治家。”

“你说的是什么意思？”我问道，“你难道不能同情他们吗？我的意思是说，假设一个人无论如何都不会测量尺寸，当其他同样无知的人经常对他说他有四肘尺高的时候，他还会不信吗？” e

“他不会不信的。”他说。

---

[1] 指病人和城邦一样。

'Don't be so hard on them, then: they're the nicest of people. They make the kinds of laws we mentioned a short while ago and then try to improve them, and constantly expect the next breach of contract to be the last one, and likewise for the other crimes we mentioned just now, because they are unaware that in fact they're slashing away at a kind of Hydra.'

'Yes, that's exactly what they're doing,' he said.

427a 'So I wouldn't have thought that in either a badly governed or a well-governed community a genuine legislator need occupy himself with laws and administration of this kind. In the one community they can't help and don't accomplish anything; in the other some of them will be obvious and others will follow automatically from habits the citizens will already have acquired.'

b 'Is there any legislation for us still to see to, then?' he asked.

'Not for us,' I replied, 'but Delphic Apollo still has to make the most important, valuable, and fundamental laws.'

'Which ones?' he asked.

'How to site temples, how to conduct sacrifices, and how in general to worship the gods, deities, and heroes. Then there's the burial of the dead and all the services we have to perform to propitiate those who have gone to the other world. You see, we aren't experts in
c this area, and in founding our city we won't—if we have any sense—trust anyone else's advice or consult any arbiter except our ancestral one. Apollo is, of course, the traditional arbiter in this area for the whole human race, and he performs his function as arbiter from his seat at the earth's navel.'

'That's a good idea,' he said. 'We must do as you suggest.'

"那么就不要对他们太苛刻了:他们是最有意思的人。我们刚才提到他们制定各种法律,还力图加以修正,总希望下一次违反契约会是最后一次,对于我们刚才提到的其他罪行,他们也是这样想的,因为他们没有意识到他们实际上是在砍九头怪蛇[1]的头。"

"是的,那正是他们所做的。"他说。 427a

"所以我认为无论在治理不善的城邦还是在治理有序的城邦,真正的立法者都不需要忙于法律以及管理。在其中的一个城邦里,它们帮不了什么忙,也没什么作用;而在另一个城邦里,某些法律是自明的,另一些则从公民已经具有的习惯中自动引申出来。"

"那么,我们要立法吗?"他问道。 b

"我们没什么要做的,"我回答说,"但德尔斐的阿波罗还要制定最重要、最有价值和最根本的法律。"

"哪些法律?"他问道。

"如何为神庙选址,如何献祭以及一般如何祭拜诸神、神灵和英雄,然后是如何安葬死者,以及如何举行为了安抚一个到另一个世界去的人而进行的所有仪式。你知道我们不是这方面的专家,在建立我们的城邦的时候,我们除了向我们祖传的神请教之外,便不会——如果我们有头脑的话——信任别人的任何建议或向别的权威讨教。在这方面,阿波罗当然是传说上的全人类的最 c
高权威者,他在地脐的神座上施行他最高权威的职责。"

"那是个好想法,"他说,"我们必须按你说的去做。"

---

〔1〕 Hydra,古希腊神话中的一种蛇,砍去一个头会生出两个头。

CHAPTER 6

‘So there you are, Adeimantus,’ I said. ‘Your community
427d seems to have been founded. The next thing for you to do is to get hold of a bright enough light and explore the community—you should invite your brother and Polemarchus and the rest of us to join you—to see if we can locate morality and immorality within it, discover how they differ from each other, and find out which of them is a prerequisite for happiness, whether or not its possession is hidden from the eyes of gods and men.’

‘Rubbish,’ said Glaucon. ‘You promised you'd do the investigating, on the grounds that it was sacrilegious for you not to do everything you could to assist morality.’

e ‘You're right,’ I said. ‘Thanks for the reminder. But you should still help me while I do so.’

‘We will,’ he said.

‘I think I know how we'd better conduct the search,’ I said. ‘I assume that ,if the community has been founded properly, it has everything it takes to be good.’

‘Necessarily,’ he replied.

‘Obviously, then, it has wisdom, courage, self-discipline, and morality.’

‘Obviously.’

‘And clearly, as we go about our search, we'll discover some of these elements and there'll be some we have yet to discover.’

428a ’Of course.’

‘Now, imagine any set of four things, and imagine we're exploring

第六章

“那么，阿狄曼图，”我说，“你们的城邦似乎已经建立起来了。你接下来要做的就是得到足够的光亮来探索这城邦——你应该 427d
邀请你的兄弟，玻勒玛库斯以及其他人加入你的讨论——看看在城邦之内我们是否能找到正义和不正义，发现它们彼此是怎样的不同，还要指出它们中的哪一个是幸福的必要前提，对它的拥有是否瞒得过诸神和人们的眼睛。”

“瞎说，”格劳孔说，“你许诺过要加以考察，因为你若是不尽力去帮助正义，那你就是不虔敬。” e

“你说得对，”我说，“谢谢你的提醒。但我在考察的时候你们还是应该帮助我。”

“我们会的。”他说。

“我想我知道最好怎样从事这个研究，”我说，“我假设如果我们的城邦已经恰当地建立起来了，那么它就是全善的。”

“必定如此。”他回答说。

“那么，它显然拥有智慧、勇敢、自制和正义。”

“显然是。”

“而且很清楚的是，随着我们研究的进行，我们会发现这些性质中的某一些，并且还会有一些有待我们去发现。”

“当然。” 428a

“现在，设想四种事物，并且设想我们在探究四种事物中的某

something for one of the four. Either we'd recognize it straight away and that would do the job, or we would recognize the one we're looking for by first recognizing the other three, in the sense that whatever is left is bound to be the one we're looking for.'

'Right,' he said.

'Well, we're faced with a set of four things here, so the principles of exploration are the same. Yes?'

'Obviously.'

b 'Now, the first thing which I think is visible here is wisdom. And there's a peculiarity in its case.'

'What?' he asked.

'Well, I do think that the community we've described really is wise. I mean, it's resourceful, isn't it?'

'Yes.'

'And this thing, resourcefulness, is obviously a kind of knowledge. I mean, it's not ignorance which makes people resourceful; it's knowledge.'

'Obviously.'

'Now, there are many branches of knowledge in our community, of all different kinds.'

'Naturally.'

'So is it the knowledge its carpenters have which makes thecommunity deserve to be described as wise and resourceful?'

c 'No, that only entitles us to call it good at carpentry,' he replied.

'It shouldn't be called wise, then, because of its knowledge of carpentry and because it is resourceful at ensuring the excellence of its furniture.'

'Certainly not.'

'Because it knows how to make metal implements, then, or anything like that?'

'Definitely not that either,' he said.

一种。要是我们直接发现了它,那么我们的工作就完成了,要是我们在寻找一种的时候首先发现了其余的三种,那么剩下的就一定是我们在寻找的第四种了。"

"对的。"他说。

"那么,我们在此面对四样东西,所以探究的原理是一样的。是吗?"

"显然是。"

"我认为在此第一个看到的东西是智慧。它有其奇特之处。" b

"什么奇特之处?"他问道。

"我确实认为我们描述过的城邦是确有智慧的。我指的是足智多谋,不是吗?"

"是的。"

"那么这种东西,足智多谋,明显是一种知识。我的意思是,无知不会让人们足智多谋的,让人足智多谋的是知识。"

"显然。"

"现在,在我们的城邦中有着所有不同种类的知识的许多分科。"

"的确如此。"

"那么,是由于木匠拥有的知识,才使得城邦可以称得上智慧和足智多谋吗?"

"不是,那只能让我们称其为擅长于木工。"他回答说。 c

"那么,并不能因为城邦在木工方面的博学多知、因为在保证它的木器品质优秀方面足智多谋,而称之为智慧吧。"

"当然不能。"

"那么要是懂得如何制作金属工具或类似的东西呢?"

"也绝对称不上。"他说。

'And the fact that it knows how to grow crops only entitles us to describe it as good at agriculture.'

'That's what I think.'

'All right,' I said. 'Is there a branch of knowledge which some of the inhabitants of the community we've just founded have, which
d enables it to think resourcefully about the whole community, not just some element of it, and about enhancing the whole community's domestic and foreign policies?'

'There certainly is.'

'What is it?' I asked. 'And which of the citizens have it?'

'It is guardianship,' he replied, 'and the people who have it are those rulers—the ones we not long ago called guardians in the strict sense of the word.'

'And what description does this branch of knowledge earn the community, in your opinion?'

'Resourceful and genuinely wise,' he answered.

'Now, do you think that in our community metalworkers will
e outnumber these true guardians, or the other way round?' I asked.

'There'll be far more metalworkers,' he said.

'And wouldn't these guardians be outnumbered by any of the other acknowledged categories of experts?' I asked.

'Yes, by a long way.'

'So when a community is founded on natural principles, the wisdom it has as a whole is due to the smallest grouping and section within it and to the knowledge possessed by this group, which is the authoritative and ruling section of the community. And we also find that this category, which is naturally the least numerous, is the one which
429a inherently possesses the only branch of knowledge which deserves to be called wisdom.'

'You're absolutely right,' he said.

'So we've somehow stumbled across one of the four qualities we were looking for and found whereabouts in the community it is located.'

“懂得种植庄稼也只能使我们称其为擅长农艺。”

“我想是这样的。”

“好吧，”我说，“在我们已建立的城邦里，是否某些居民拥有的一门知识，它使人们有足够的谋略来考虑整个城邦，而不是某 d
些方面，并且考虑如何改进整个城邦的对内对外政策？”

“当然有。”

“什么样的？”我问道，“哪些公民拥有这样的知识？”

他回答说：“保卫城邦的知识，拥有这种知识的人是那些统治者——不久前我们把他们称作严格意义上的卫士。”

“在你看来怎么样来描述拥有这种知识的城邦呢？”

“足智多谋和真正的智慧。”他回答说。

“那么，你认为在我们的城邦里，铁匠在数量上会超过这些真正的卫士吗，还是反过来？”我问道。 e

“铁匠要多得多。”他说。

“拥有其他知识的专业人士难道不也在数量上超过这些卫士吗？”我问道。

“是的，超过很多。”

“所以当一个城邦建立在自然律之上时，整个城邦具有的智慧，都归因于城邦中那个人数最少的团体和阶层，也归因于这个团体所拥有的知识，他们是城邦的当权者和统治者阶层。我们还发现，这类人数量自然是最少的，却天生地拥有那种唯一配称得 429a
上智慧的知识。”

“你说得非常正确。”他说。

“这样我们就找到了要寻找的四种性质中的一种，并且发现了它在城邦中的位置所在。”

'I think it's clear enough, anyway,' he said.

'Now, it's not too hard to spot courage and to see which section of the community possesses it and enables the community to be described as courageous.'

'Why?'

b 'The only feature of a community which might justify describing it as either cowardly or courageous', I answered, 'is its defensive and military arm.'

'Yes, that's the only one,' he agreed.

'The point is', I went on, 'that whether the rest of its in habitants are cowardly or brave wouldn't affect the nature of the community either way, I imagine.'

'No, it wouldn't.'

'Again, then, it is a section of a community that earns it the right to be called courageous. This section possesses the ability to re-
c tain under all circumstances the notion that the things and kinds of things to be feared are precisely those things and kinds of things which during their education the legislator pronounced fearful. Isn't this what you call courage?'

'I haven't understood your point,' he said. 'Please could you repeat it.'

'I'm saying that courage is a sort of retention,' I explained.

'What do you mean, retention?'

'I mean the retention of the notion, which has been inculcated by law through the agency of education, about what things and what kinds of things are to be feared. And by its retention "under all cir-
d cumstances" I meant keeping it intact and not losing it whether one is under the influence of pain or pleasure, desire or aversion. I can tell you what strikes me as analogous, if you like.'

'Yes, please.'

'Well,' I said, 'you know how when dyers want to dye wool purple, they first select something which is naturally white, rather than any

“无论如何,我认为这很清楚。”他说。

“现在,去寻找勇敢就不太难了,看看城邦中的哪部分人拥有它而使得城邦能够称得上勇敢。”

“为什么?”

“能使城邦称得上懦弱或勇敢的唯一标志,”我回答说,“就体 b
现在防卫部队和军事部队身上。”

“是的,唯独在他们身上。”他同意说。

“要点在于,”我继续说道,“我认为其他居民是懦弱或是勇敢,一点都不会影响到城邦的本质。”

“不会。”

“那么仍然是城邦的一个部分人使它配称得上勇敢。这部分
人在任何情况下都具有一种能力保持这信念,即,在他们的教育 c
中立法者断言一些事情和一些种类的事情是须得慎惧的,就是这些是他们所慎惧的。这不就是你说的勇敢吗?”

“我还是没理解你的意思,”他说,“你能再说一遍吗?”

“我说勇敢就是一种坚持。”我解释说。

“你说的坚持是什么意思?”

“我所说的坚持的意思,是指法律通过教育这个媒介的谆谆教导而建立起来的信念,这个信念是关于什么事情和什么种类的一些事情是要慎惧的。在‘任何情况下’都要坚持,我指的是一个人无论
是否受到痛苦或快乐、渴望或憎恶的影响,都要坚持不动摇,不抛弃 d
这个信念。我想到一个比方,如果你愿意,我可以给你说说。”

“好,请讲。”

“好吧,”我说,“你知道染色工人如果想要给羊毛染上紫色,他们首先选出质地是白的那种,而不是任何其他颜色的羊毛;然

other colour; then they subject it to a lengthy preparatory treatment designed to ensure that the colour will take as well as possible; and when
e it's in the required con-dition, they dye it. Anything dyed in this way holds its colour, and the colour can't be washed out, whether or not one uses solvent. But you know what happens to anything which isn't dyed in this way, when something of another colour is dyed, or when something white is dyed without having been treated first.'

'Yes,' he said. 'The dye washes out and they look ridiculous.'

'So I want you to imagine', I said, 'that we too were doing our best to achieve something similar, when we selected our militia and
430a put them through their cultural and physical education. You should assume that the educational programme was designed for one purpose only: to indoctrinate them so thoroughly that the laws take in them like a dye, so that their notions about what is to be feared and about everything else hold fast (which requires a suitable character as well as a suitable upbringing), with the dye being incapable of being washed out by those solvents which are so frighteningly good at scouring—pleasure, which is a more efficient cleanser than any soda and
b lye, and pain and aversion and desire, which outclass any solvent. So this ability to retain under all circumstances a true and lawful notion about what is and is not to be feared is what I'm calling courage. That's how I'll. use the term, unless you have an alternative suggestion.'

'No, I don't,' he said. 'I mean, I think your idea is that any true notion about these matters which is formed in an animal or a slave without the benefit of education is not really lawful, and I suppose you'd find some other name for it, not courage.'

'You're quite right,' I said.

c 'I accept your definition of courage, then.'

'Accept it by all means,' I said, 'but as a definition of the kind of courage a community has; then your acceptance will be all right. We'll go into the subject more thoroughly later, if you want; you see, at the moment our quarry is morality, not courage, which I think we've explored enough.'

后再进行长时间的预备性整理，为了确保把颜色最佳地染上去；满足了这些要求之后他们才染色。任何以这种方式染色的东西都能保持住它的颜色，无论是否用碱水洗，颜色都不会被洗掉。但要 e
是不以这种方式染色，那么当用其他颜色的毛来染色或者当白羊毛没有事先加以处理就染色，你知道会有什么状况发生吧。”

“知道，”他说，“染的颜色就会褪掉而看上去就很可笑了。”

“所以我想让你设想一下，”我说，“当我们遴选出我们的卫士并让他们接受文艺和体育教育的时候，我们也是尽我们所能在做类似的事情。你应该认识到教育内容只有一个目的：如同染色一 430a
样向他们彻底地灌输法律，这样他们关于可慎惧的事物以及关于其他一切事物的信念，就牢牢地固定下来了，而这需要恰当的天性和教养，这样染上的颜色就不会被褪色能力很强的碱水洗掉——快乐是一种比碱水和碱液更强的洗涤液，痛苦、憎恨和渴望也比其他任何洗涤液更强。所以这种在任何情况下都坚持一 b
种真正合法的信念，即关于什么是可怕的、什么是不可怕的信念，那就是我所谓的勇敢。我是要这样使用这个词了，除非你有别的建议。”

“我没有，”他说，“我的意思是说，对于那些在没有受过教育的动物或奴隶身上所形成的关于这些事情的真实信念，我想你不认为这些是真正合法的，并且我认为你会给它取别的名字，而不是勇敢。”

“你说得很对。”我说。 c

“我同意你对勇敢的定义。”

“务必接受它，”我说，“但要把它当作一个城邦所具有的勇敢的定义；这样你所接受的就是对的。如果你愿意，我们之后会对这个问题加以更彻底的探讨；你知道我们现在寻找的是正义而不是勇敢，对于这一点，我想我们已经说得够多的了。”

'That's fine by me,' he said.

'Well, we've still got two qualities to detect in the com-munity,' I
d said, 'self-discipline and the purpose of the whole enquiry, morality.'

'Quite so.'

'Can we somehow locate morality and not bother any more about self-discipline?'

'I don't know if we can,' he said, 'and anyway I wouldn't like morality to be discovered first if that entails dropping the search for self-discipline, I'd be grateful if you'd look for self-discipline before morality.'

'Then it's my duty to do so, of course,' I said.

e 'Go on, then,' he said.

'All right,' I said. 'From my point of view, we're faced here with a closer similarity to some kind of harmony and attune-ment than we were before.'

'Why?'

'To be self-disciplined', I replied, 'is somehow to order and control the pleasures and desires. Hence the opaque expression "self-mastery"; and there are other expressions which hint at its nature. Yes?'

'Absolutely,' he said.

'Isn't the phrase "self-mastery" absurd? I mean, anyone who is
431a his own master is also his own slave, of course, and vice versa, since it's the same person who is the subject in all these expressions.'

'Of course.'

'What this expression means, I think,' I continued, 'is that there are better and worse elements in a person's mind, and when the part which is naturally better is in control of the worse part, then we use this phrase "self-mastery" (which is, after all, complimentary). But when, as a result of bad upbringing or bad company, the smaller

“我觉得是这样的。”他说。

“那么，我们还要在城邦里寻找两种性质，”我说，“自制和整个研究的对象——正义。” d

“的确如此。”

“我们有办法找到正义而不用再理会自制了吗？”

“我不知道我们是否可以这样做，”他说，“不管怎样，如果那意味着去掉自制而不加探究的话，那么我不想首先发现正义。如果你在正义之前先找到自制，那我会很高兴的。”

“那么，这样做当然就是我的责任了。”我说。 e

“那么就继续吧。”他说。

“好吧，”我说，“在我看来，我们所面对的是比以前更接近于某种协调、和谐的东西。”

“为什么？”

我回答说：“自制就是某种对快乐和欲望的律令和控制。因此用一个含混的表达就是‘做自己的主人’；还有其他的表达说的也是这种性质，是吗？”

“绝对是的。”他说。

“‘做自己的主人’这个说法不是很荒谬吗？我的意思是说，任何作为自己主人的人当然也是自己的奴隶，反之亦然，因为在所有这些表述中说的是同一个人。” 431a

“当然是同一个人。”

“我想这个表述的意思是，”我继续说，“在一个人的心灵中有较好的部分和较差的部分，当天性较好的部分控制了较差的部分，那么我们就使用‘做自己的主人’这个说法，而这毕竟是溢美之词。但要是接受了坏的教养或与坏事物打交道，那么较小而较好

better part is defeated by the superior numbers of the worse part, then
b we use critical and deprecatory language and describe someone in this state as lacking self-mastery and discipline.'

'That sounds plausible,' he said.

'Have a look at our new community, then,' I said. 'and you'll find that the first of these alternatives is attributable to it. I mean, you must admit the justice of describing it as having self- mastery, since anything whose better part rules its worse part should be described as having self-discipline and self-mastery.'

'Yes, I can see the truth of what you're saying,' he said.

c 'Now, children, women, slaves, and (among so-called free men) the rabble who constitute the majority of the population are the ones who evidently experience the greatest quantity and variety of forms of desire, pleasure, and pain.'

'Yes.'

'Whereas simple and moderate forms, which are guided by the rational mind with its intelligence and true beliefs, are encountered only in-those few people who have been endowed with excellence by their nature and their education.'

'True,' he said.

'And is it clear to you that this is a property of your communi-
d ty, where the desires of the common majority are controlled by the desires and the intelligence of the minority of better men?'

'It is,' he said.

'So if any community deserves to be described as having mastered pleasure and desire, and as having self-mastery, it is this one.'

'Without the slightest doubt,' he said.

'So it also deserves to be called self-disciplined, doesn't it?'

'Yes, indeed,' he said.

'Moreover, it is in this community, more than in any other

的那个部分就会被较差较大的那个部分击败，那样我们就要使用批评性、贬斥性的话语，把处于这种状态的人说成是缺乏自主和 b
节制的。”

“听起来似乎是对的。”他说。

“那么，来看看我们的新城邦，”我说，“你会在这里发现那两种情况中的前一种。我的意思是说，你必须承认自己做自己的主人这种说法是正当的，因为任何较好的部分统治它的较差部分的东西，都应该被说成是具有自制和自主的。”

“是的，我认为你说的是对的。”他说。

“现在，孩子、妇女、奴隶和所谓自由民的下等人构成了城邦的大多数人口，他们显然经历着各种各样的欲望、快乐和痛苦。” c

“是的。”

“反之，那些具有才智与真正的信仰的理性头脑所引导的简朴而有节制的形式，则只能在少数一些人那里才能碰到，这些人因为其天性及后天的教育而被赋予了优秀的品质。”

“对的。”他说。

“你明白这就是你们城邦的特征，一般大众的欲望为少数优秀分子的欲望和智慧所控制？” d

“是的。”他说。

“所以如果哪个城邦配称得上是快乐和欲望的主人，并且是自主的，那么就是这个城邦了。”

“毫无疑问。”他说。

“所以它也配称得上是自制，不是吗？”

“确实是的。”他说。

“此外，比起任何其他可以设想城邦而言，只在这个城邦中统

e conceivable community, that the rulers and their subjects agree on who the rulers should be, don't you think?'

'Definitely,' he said.

'In a situation like this, then, is it the rulers or the subjects of the community who, In your opinion, possess self-discipline?'

'Both,' he replied.

'Is it clear to you, then,' I asked, 'that our recent conjecture that self-discipline resembles a kind of attunement wasn't bad?'

'Why?'

'Because unlike courage and wisdom, both of which imbued the
432a community with their respective qualities while being properties of only a part of the community, self-discipline literally spans the whole octaval spread of the community, and makes the weakest, the strongest, and the ones in between all sing in unison, whatever criterion you choose in order to assess their relative strengths—intelligence, physical strength, numerical quantity, wealth, and so on. And the upshot is that we couldn't go wrong if we claimed that self-discipline was this unanimity, a harmony between the naturally worse and naturally better elements of society as to which of them should rule both in a community and in every individual.'

'I certainly agree,' he said.

b 'All right,' I said. 'We've detected three of the qualities in our community, as far as we can tell. But there's one final way in which a community achieves goodness. What precisely is morality? I mean, morality is this missing type of goodness, clearly.'

'Clearly.'

'We must now imitate hunters surrounding a thicket, Glaucon, and make sure that morality doesn't somehow elude us and disappear into obscurity. I mean, we know it's some-where round here. Keep
c your eyes peeled and try to spot it. If you see it before I do, let me

治者和被统治者才会对谁应当统治达成一致看法，你难道不这么 e
想吗？”

“是这样想的。”他说。

“那么，在像这样的情况下，你认为是城邦的统治者还是被统治者具有自制？”

“两者都有。”他回答说。

我问道：“那么，你是否看到，我们刚才说自制类似于某种协调的揣度，这并不算错吧？”

“为什么？”

“因为不像勇敢和智慧，两者分别赋予城邦各自的性质，使之 432a
成为城邦中某一部分的特征，自制扩展到整个城邦，使最弱的、最强的和中间的都联合起来，而不管你选用什么标准去衡量他们的相对强度——智慧、体力、数量、财富等等。最终我们这样说是不会错的：就这种社会的天性较差的部分和天性较好的部分来说，它们中的哪一个应该在城邦和个人中支配两者，对此达成的一致、和谐就是自制。”

“我当然同意。”他说。 b

“好吧，”我说，“就我们能够说得出来的，我们已经在我们的城邦中发现了三种性质。但还有最后一种使城邦具有美德的性质。正义究竟是什么？我的意思是说，正义显然就是这种还未找到的美德。”

“显然。”

“格劳孔，我们现在必须像猎人搜寻树丛一样，千万别让正义在我们面前逃走消失于茫茫之中。我的意思是说，我们知道它就
在这附近。睁大你的眼睛去发现它。如果你比我先看见，就告诉 c

know where it is.'

'I wish I could,' he said. 'But in fact it would be more realistic of you to regard me as someone who follows in your footsteps and can see things only when they're pointed out to him.'

'Follow me, then,' I said, 'and pray for success.'

'1 will,' he said. 'You have only to lead on.'

'Now, we're in a rather rugged and overcast spot, it seems,' I said. 'At any rate, it's gloomy and hunting won't be easy. Still, we must carry on.'

d 'Yes, we must,' he said.

I caught a glimpse of something and shouted, 'Hurray! Glaucon, I believe we're on its trail! I don't think it will get clean away from us.'

'That's good news,' he said.

'What a stupid state to find ourselves in!' I exclaimed.

'What do you mean?'

'It looks as though it's been curled up at our feet all the time, right from the beginning, my friend, and we didn't see it, but lust made absolute fools of ourselves. You know how people sometimes go
e in search of something they're holding in their hands all the time? That's what we've been like. We've been looking off into the distance somewhere, instead of at our quarry, and that was why we didn't notice it, I suppose.'

'What do you mean?'

'I'll tell you,' I said. 'I think it's been the subject of our discussion all along and we just didn't appreciate that we were in a sense talking about it.'

'What a long preamble,' he said, 'when I'm so keen to hear what you're getting at!'

433a 'All right,' I said. 'See if you think there's anything in what I

我它在哪儿。”

“我希望我能发现，”他说，“但实际上更为实在的是你把我当做一名你的随从，能够发现你指给我看的东西就够了。”

“那么就跟着我来吧，”我说，“并祈求能成功。”

“我会的，”他说，“你只管往前走。”

“看来我们处在一个坑坑洼洼而又阴暗潮湿的地方，”我说，“无论如何，在黑暗中狩猎不是件容易事。我们还是必须继续前进。”

“是的，我们必须前进。”他说。 d

我发现了什么东西，就叫起来：“快！格劳孔，我想我们找到它的踪迹了！我想不会让它在我们眼前逃走了。”

“真是个好消息。”他说。

“我们多傻啊！”我惊叫道。

“你说的是什么意思？”

“我的朋友，它好像从一开始就一直蜷曲在我们跟前，而
我们却没有发现它，我们真是傻呀！你知道有时候人们会去
寻找某些一直握在手里的东西吗？我们就像是那样的。我们 e
在远处而不是在眼前寻找，我想，这就是我们没有注意到它的
原因。”

“你说的是什么意思？”

“我会告诉你的，”我说，“我想它一直是我们谈论的主题，但我们就是没有意识到自己在谈论它。”

“多么冗长的开场白啊！”他说，“而我是多么急切地想听你谈论它啊！”

“好吧，”我说，“那么你听听我说得是否有道理。从一起头，我 433a

say. From the outset, when we first started to found the community, there's a principle we established as a universal requirement—and this, or some version of it, is in my opinion morality. The principle we established, and then repeated time and again, as you'll remember, is that every individual has to do just one of the jobs relevant to the community, the one for which his nature has best equipped him.'

'Yes, that's what we said.'

'Furthermore, the idea that morality is doing one's own job and
b not intruding elsewhere is commonly voiced, and we ourselves have often said it.'

'Yes, we have.'

'So, Glaucon,' I said, 'it seems likely that this is in a sense what morality is—doing one's own job. Do you know what makes me think so?'

'No,' he answered. 'Please tell me.'

'We've examined self-discipline, courage, and wisdom,' I said, 'and it occurs to me that this principle is what is left in the community, because it is the principle which makes it possible for all those other qualities to arise in the community, and its continued presence allows them to flourish in safety once they have arisen. And
c we did in fact saythat if we found the other three, then whatever was left would be morality.'

'Yes, that's necessarily so,' he said.

'But if we had to decide which of these qualities it was whose presence is chiefly responsible for the goodness of the community,' I said, 'it would be hard to decide whether it's the unanimity between rulers and subjects, or the militia's retention of the lawful notion about what is and is not to be feared, or the wise guardianship which is an
d attribute of the rulers, or the fact that it is an attribute of every child, woman, slave, free person, artisan, ruler, and subject that each individual does his own job without intruding elsewhere, that is chiefly responsible for making it good.'

'Yes, of course that would be a difficult decision,' he said.

们开始建立城邦的时候，我们就设立了一个作为普遍要求的原则——在我看来这个原则或它的某些形式就是正义。就如你记得的那样，我们设立并且时常加以重申的原则就是每个人必须在城邦里担任唯一一项最合适其禀赋的工作。”

“是的，我们说过。”

“此外，经常听人说正义就是做自己的工作而不闯到别的领域去，我们也常常这样说。” b

“是的，我们说过。”

“所以，格劳孔，”我说，“这在某种意义上说就似乎是正义——做自己的工作。你知道是什么促使我这样想的吗？”

“不知道，”他回答说，“请你告诉我吧。”

我说：“我们已经考察了自制、勇敢和智慧，那么我想在城邦中剩下就是这条原则了，因为正义才使所有其他的性质得以在城邦中产生，它的持续存在使得它们产生之后能平平安安地成长。我们确实也说只要找到了其他的三个，那么剩下的就是 c
正义了。”

“是的，必然如此。”他说。

“但要是我们必须确定出这些性质中哪一个的存在是城邦完善的主要原因，”我说，“那么很难确定，是统治者和被统治者的观点一致，或者卫士坚持关于须得慎惧和不必慎惧之事情的合法信念，还是统治者的具有智慧的保卫城邦的禀赋， d
抑或是每个孩子、妇女、奴隶、自由民、匠人、统治者和被统治者的品性，即每个人做自己的工作而不闯入别的领域去，这些中什么是使城邦完善的主要原因。”

“这当然会难以确定。”他说。

'When it comes to contributing to a community's goodness, then, there's apparently a close contest between the ability of everyone in a community to do their own jobs and its wisdom, self-discipline, and courage.'

'There certainly is,' he said.

'And wouldn't you say that anything which rivals these qualities in contributing towards a community's goodness must be morality?'

e 'Absolutely.'

'See if you also agree when you look at it from this point of view. Won't you be requiring the rulers to adjudicate when lawsuits occur in the community?'

'Of course.'

'And won't their most important aim in doing so be to ensure that people don't get hold of other people's property and aren't deprived of their own?'

'Yes.'

'Because this is right?'

'Yes.'

'So from this point of view too we are agreed that morality is
434a keeping one's own property and keeping to one's own occupation.'

'True.'

'See if you agree with me on this as well: if a joiner tried to do a shoemaker's job, or a shoemaker a carpenter's, or if they swapped tools or status, or even if the same person tried to do both jobs, with all the tools and so on of both jobs switched around, do you think that much harm would come to the community?'

'Not really,' he said.

'On the other hand, when someone whom nature has equipped
b to be an artisan or to work for money in some capacity or other gets so

“要说到哪一个促成了城邦的完善,那么似乎在城邦中每个人做自己工作的能力与智慧、自制和勇敢之间有一场激烈的较量。”

“的确有一场较量。”他说。

“你难道不会说与促成城邦完善的这些品质进行较量的品质必定是正义吗?” e

“肯定是正义。”

“从这个角度来考察,看看你是否也会同意。当城邦中发生诉讼时,你们难道不是要求统治者来裁决吗?”

“当然是的。”

“他们这样做的主要目的,不就是在于确保人们不能占有别人的财产和自己的财产也不被剥夺吗?”

“是的。”

“因为这样做是正义的吗?”

“是的。”

“所以从这个角度来看,我们也同意正义就是拥有自己的财产并拥有自己的工作。” 434a

“对的。”

“在这一点上你是否也同意我:如果一个木匠去做鞋匠的活,或鞋匠去做木匠的活,或者他们交换工具或地位,或甚至同一个人试图做两份工作,交换了两个工作的所有工具以及诸如此类东西,你认为这会给城邦带来巨大的危害吗?”

“危害不是很大。”他说。

“另一方面,如果某个人其禀赋适合成为一个工匠,或凭其能力能成为商人或别的什么,但受到了他的财富、声望、力量或别的 b

puffed up by his wealth or popularity or strength or some such factor that he tries to enter the military class, or when a member of the militia tries to enter the class of policy-makers and guardians when he's not qualified to do so, and they swap tools and status, or when a single person tries to do all these jobs simultaneously, then I'm sure you'll agree that these interchanges and intrusions are disastrous for the community.'

'Absolutely.'

'There's nothing more disastrous for the community, then, than
c the intrusion of any of the three classes into either of the other two, and the interchange of roles among them, and there could be no more correct context for using the term criminal.'

'Indubitably.'

'And when someone commits the worst crimes against his own community, wouldn't you describe this as immorality?'

'Of course.'

'Then this is what immorality is. Here's an alternative way of putting it. Isn't it the case (to put it the other way round) that when each of the three classes—the one that works for a living, the auxiliaries, and the guardians—performs its proper function and does its own job in the community, then this is morality and makes the community a moral one?'

'Yes, I think that's exactly right,' he said.

d 'Let's not be too inflexible about it yet,' I warned. 'If we also conclude that this type of thing constitutes morality in the case of individual human beings as well, then we'll have no reservations. I mean, how could we under those circumstances? However, if we find that it doesn't apply to humans as well, then we'll have to take the enquiry into new areas. So let's now wind up that aspect of the enquiry which is based on the idea we had that it would be easier to detect the nature of morality in an individual human being if we first tried to observe it in something larger and to watch its operation there. We decided that the larger thing was a community, and so we
e founded as good a community as we could, because we were well aware

因素的诱惑而试图进入军人阶层，或者某个军人想进入立法者和卫士阶层，他虽然不够资格却交换了工具和地位，或者一个人想同时包揽所有工作，那么我确信你会同意，所有这些交换和僭越对于城邦来说都是毁灭性的。”

“的确如此。”

“如果三个阶层中的某一个干涉其他的两个，相互间交换角色，那么对于城邦来说没有比这更具灾难性的了，用‘犯罪’这个 c
词来形容这种状况是再准确不过的。”

“毫无疑问。”

“要是有人对自己的城邦犯了滔天大罪，你难道不会称其为不正义吗？”

“当然会这样说。”

“那么这就是不正义。这里还有另一种说法。反过来说不就是这样的吗？三个阶层中的每一个——劳动者、辅助者和卫士——都发挥其各自的作用，在城邦中做自己的工作，这就是正义，而且它造就了正义的城邦。”

“是的，我认为那很正确。”他说。 d

“我们还是不要将之说得过于僵死，”我提醒说，“如果我们能得出结论说这些因素构成了个人的正义，那么我们就没什么顾忌了。我的意思是说，在这些新的条件下是如何得出结论的？然而，要是我们发现它不适用于人，那么我们将探究新的领域。所以现在让我们结束那方面的研究，这个研究基于我们的一个想法，即认为要考察单个人的正义的本质就要先力图考察较大事物里的正义并考察其作用，这样会比较容易。我们把较大的事物确定为城邦，所以尽我们所能建立了一个最好的城邦，因为我们很 e

that it would have to be a good community for morality to exist in it. What we have to do now is apply the results we found in the case of the community to an individual. If there's a match, that will be fine; but if we find something different in the case of an individual, then we'll return to the community to test the new result. With Rick, the
435a friction of comparing the two cases will enable morality to flare up from these fire-sticks, so to speak, and once it's become visible we'll make it more of a force in our own lives.'

'That's a viable notion,' he said. 'We should do as you suggest.'

'Well,' I said, 'if a single property is predicated of two things of different sizes, then in so far as it's the same predicate, is it in fact dissimilar or similar in the two instances?'

'Similar,' he said.

b 'So in respect of the actual type of thing morality is, a moral person will be no different from a moral community, but will resemble it.'

'Yes,' he said.

'Now, we decided that a community was moral when each of the three natural classes that exist within it did its own job, and also that certain other states and conditions of the same three classes made it self-disciplined and courageous and wise.'

'True.'

c 'It follows, my friend, that we should expect an individual to have the same three classes in himself, and that the same conditions make him liable to the same predicates as the community receives.'

'That's absolutely inevitable,' he said.

'Glaucon,' I said, 'now we're faced with another simple enquiry, to see whether or not the mind contains these three features.'

'It hardly seems to me to be a simple one,' he remarked. 'But

清楚在好的城邦里才存在正义。我们所要做的就是把城邦中发现的结论应用于个人。如果相一致那就好了;但要是它在个人身上有什么不同,那么我们就要回到城邦对新结论加以检验。要是有幸的话,通过两种情形的相比进行揣摩,能使正义从这些火石 435a
中闪耀发光,也就是说,一旦它显露出来,我们就要在自己的生活中牢牢地记住它。"

"那是个可行的想法,"他说,"我们应该按你说的那样去做。"

"好吧,"我说,"如果用同一个名称去称谓两个不同大小的东西, 那么就它们拥有同一个名称来说, 两者实际上相同还是不相同?"

"相同。"他说。

"所以就正义是实际形式来看,正义之人与正义之城邦没有 b
什么区别,而是与之相像。"

"是的。"他说。

"当城邦中的三个天然的阶层各司其职,这三个阶层的某些其他状态和条件使城邦自制、勇敢和智慧,那么我们可以确定说这个城邦是正义的。"

"对的。"

"我的朋友,那就是说我们应该期待个人在其自身也具有同样的三个阶层,并且这同样的状况应使得他具有与城邦所具有的 c
同样的名称。"

"肯定是这样的。"他说。

"格劳孔,"我说,"现在我们碰上了另一个简单的问题,就是考察心灵是否具有这三种品质。"

"这对我来说几乎算不上简单,"他说,"但是,苏格拉底,也许

then it's probably a true saying, Socrates, that anything fine is difficult.'

d 'I think that's right,' I said. 'In fact, I have to tell you, Glaucon, that in my opinion we'll never completely understand this issue by relying on the kinds of methods we've employed so far in our discussion: a longer and fuller approach is needed. Still, we can hope to come up with something which is in keeping with what we've already said in the earlier stages of our enquiry.'

'Shouldn't we be content with that?' he asked. 'I for one would be satisfied with that for the time being.'

'And it'll do perfectly well for me too,' I said.

'No flagging, then,' he said. 'On with the enquiry.'

e 'Well, here's something we're bound to agree on, aren't we?'

I asked. 'That we do contain the same kinds of features and characteristics as the community. I mean, where else could it have got them from? When the general population of a community consists of people who are reputedly passionate— Thracians and Scythians, for example, and almost any northerner—it would be absurd to think that passion arises in this community from any other source. And the same
436a goes for love of knowledge, for which our country has a strong reputation; and being mercenary might be claimed to be a particular characteristic of Phoenicians and Egyptians.'

'Certainly.'

'This is a matter of fact, then,' I said, 'and it wasn't hard to discover.'

'No.'

'But here's a hard one: is there just a single thing which we use for doing everything, or are there three and we use different things for different tasks? Do we learn with one of our aspects, get worked up with another, and with a third desire the pleasures of eating, sex, and so on, or

俗话说得好,好事多磨。”

“我认为这话说得对,”我说,“事实上,我不得不告诉你,格劳孔,在我看来,依赖于到目前为止我们在谈论中所使用的方法,我 d
们是决不会完全理解这个问题的:还需要一个更长而完整的方法。但我们还是可以希望提出一些与先前在我们的研究中已经讨论过的内容相一致的东西来的。”

“我们不应该满足于此吗?”他问道,“对于我来说,我对目前的状况是满足的。”

“对我来说,我也完全满足了。”我说。

“那么不要偃旗息鼓,”他说,“继续探究下去。”

“好吧,这里有某些东西是我们肯定会同意的,不是吗?” e
我问道,“我们确实具有和城邦一样的品质和性质。我的意思是说,这些品质还能从哪里来呢?要是在城邦中的一般人里包含了那些被认为具有激情的人——比如色雷斯人、西叙亚人以及北方人——那么认为出现在城邦中的激情有其他的来源的想法是荒谬的。对于爱好知识也是一样,对此我们的城邦则有巨大的名声;而贪恋钱财可以说是腓尼基人和埃及人 436a
的特有品质。”

“的确如此。”

我说:“这是事实,是不难发现的。”

“不难。”

“但困难的是:我们做任何事情的时候使用的只是一个东西还是三个东西,还是在不同的工作中使用不同的东西?我们学习时用我们的某个部分,工作时用另一个部分,欲求食色之欢时用第三个部分,如此等等,还是在我们实际从事的每个工作中我们

b do we use the whole of our mind for every task we actually get going on? These questions won't be easy to answer satisfactorily.'

'I agree,' he said.

'Well, let's approach an answer by trying to see whether these aspects are the same as one another or are different.'

'How?'

'It's clear that the same one thing cannot simultaneously either act or be acted on in opposite ways in the same respect and in the same context. And consequently, if we find this happening in the case of these aspects of ourselves, we'll know that there are more than one of them.'

c 'All right.'

'What about this, then?'

'What?'

'Is it possible for the same thing to be simultaneously at rest and in motion in the same respect?' I asked.

'Of course not.'

'Let's take a closer look before agreeing, otherwise we'll start arguing later. My assumption is that if someone claims that a person who is standing still, but moving his hands and head, is the same person simultaneously being still and moving, we won't approve of this way of putting it, as opposed to saying that one part of him is still,
d and another part of him is moving, Yes?'

'Yes.'

'So even if the advocate of the claim were to get even more subtle and ingeniously maintain that when a top is spinning round with its peg fixed in place, then this is definitely a case of something simultaneously being still and moving as a whole, or that the same goes for anything else which spins round on one

使用的是我们的整个心灵？这些问题不会很容易就得到满意的 b
答案。”

“我同意。”他说。

“好吧，让我们力图考察这些部分是否与别的部分相等同还是相区别，以此来回答这个问题。”

“怎么做？”

“清楚的是，同一个东西显然不能同时以相反的方式在同一个方面和情境下既施动又受动。所以，要是我们在自身的这些部分中有如此情况发生，那么我们就可以知道有多个东西，而不是
其中的一个在起作用。” c

“对的。”

“那么这又怎么样呢？”

“怎么样？”

“让同一个事物在同一方面同时既静止又运动是有可能的吗？”我问道。

“当然不可能。”

“让我们在达成一致意见之前好好地考察一番，否则之后我们又会陷入争论。假设，如果有人说一个站着不动但头和手却在动的人，就是一个同时既是静止又运动的人，那么我们就不会赞同这种说法，相反，我们会说他的一部分是静止的而他的另一部
分是运动的，是吗？” d

“是的。”

“所以如果持这种说法的人，甚至更加巧妙狡猾地坚持说，陀螺的顶端固定在一个地方旋转，这就肯定是某个东西同时整个地既静止又运动的情形，对任何其他围绕着一个点旋转的东西也这

e spot, we wouldn't accept this assertion. We'll say that in this situation these objects are not still and moving in the same respects. We'll point out that they include an axis and a circumference, and that they may be still in respect of their axes (in the sense that they're not tipping over at all), but they have circular motion in respect of their circumferences; and we'll add that when one of these objects tips its upright to the right or left or front or back while simultaneously spinning round, then it has no stillness in any respect.'

'Yes, that's right,' he said.

'No assertion of this kind will put us off, then, or make us in
437a the slightest inclined to believe that the same thing could ever simultaneously be acted on or exist or act in opposite ways in the same respect and in the same context.'

'I won't be put off, anyway,' he said.

'That's as may be,' I said. 'But let's not feel compelled to have all the bother of going through every single one of these arguments and proving them false. Let's assume that we're right and carry on, with the understanding that if we ever turn out to have been mistaken, all the conclusions we draw on the basis of this assumption will be invalidated.'

'Yes, that's what we'd better do,' he said.

b 'Wouldn't you count assent and dissent,' I asked, 'seeking and avoidance, and liking and disliking, as all pairs of opposites? It'll make no difference whether you think of them as ways of acting or of being acted on.'

'Yes, they're opposites,' he answered.

'What about thirst and hunger and the desires generally,' I went on, 'and what about wishing and wanting? Wouldn't you
c say that all these things belong somewhere among the sets we've just mentioned? For example, won't you describe the mind of anyone who is in a state of desire as seeking to fulfil his desires, or as liking whatever the desired object is? Or again, to

么说,那么我们不会接受这种说法。我们会说在这种情况下,静止和运动着的不是这些物体的同一个部分。我们会指出说,它们有轴心和圆周,就它们的轴心来说,要是它们完全没有偏斜的话,那么它们是静止的,但就圆周来说它们在圆周运动;我们还要说,要是这些物体中的某一个其轴线在旋转时向前后左右偏斜的话,那么它无论如何都不是静止的了。” e

“是的,说得对。”他说。

“那么,不要让这种说法把我们搞糊涂或哪怕有一点点使我们相信,同一个东西能同时以相反的方式在同一个方面和同一种情境下受动,或者存在,或者行动。” 437a

“不管怎样,我都不会被搞糊涂的。”他说。

“尽管如此,”我说,“但我们并不是一定要费力去考察这每一个论证并证明其谬误。让我们假设我们这样做是正确的,但要知道,如果我们发现有错误,那么我们基于这个假设而得出的所有结论都要被撤消。”

“是的,我们最好那样做。”他说。

我问道:“你难道不会把赞同和反对,寻求和拒绝,喜欢和厌 b
恶都当作相对立的对子吗?无论你把它们看作施动的方式还是受动方式,其作用都没什么区别。”

“是没什么区别,它们是相反的。”他回答说。

我继续说:“那么一般来说,饥渴和欲望以及愿望和希望又怎么样呢?你难道不会说所有这些东西都要归属于某些我们刚刚提到的对子中去吗?比如说,你难道不会把某个有欲求之人的心 c
灵说成是正在寻求满足他的欲望或类似的所欲之物吗?或者再比如说,就心灵想要得到某物这层意义上来说,你不认为心灵是

the extent that it wants to get hold of something, don't you think it is internally assenting to this thing, as if in response to a question, and is longing for it to happen?'

'Yes, I do.'

'And what about the states of antipathy, reluctance, or unwillingness? Won't we put these states in the opposite category, which includes dislike and aversion?'

'Of course.'

d 'Under these circumstances, then, won't we say that there is a category which consists of the desires, and that the most conspicuous desires are the ones called thirst and hunger?'

'Yes,' he said.

'And the one is desire for drink, the other desire for food?'

'Yes.'

'Now, is thirst, in itself, the mental desire for anything more than the object we mentioned? For example, is thirst thirst for a hot drink or a cold one, a lot of drink or a little, or in short for any particular kind of drink at all? Doesn't it take heat in addition to thirst to
e give it the extra feature of being desire for something cold, and cold to make it desire for something hot? Doesn't it take a thirst which has been aggravated into becoming strong to produce the desire for a lot of drink, and doesn't it take a weak thirst to produce the desire for a little drink? The actual state of being thirsty, however, cannot possibly be desire for anything other than its natural object, which is just drink; and the same goes for hunger and food.'

'Yes,' he said. 'Each desire is for its natural object only, and the desire for an object of this or that type is a result of some addition.'

'It should be quite impossible, then,' I said, 'for anyone
438a to catch us unawares and rattle us with the claim that no one desires drink, but a good drink, and no one desires food, but good food. Everyone desires good, they say, so if thirst is a desire,

内在地认同该物，就像对一个问题的响应一样，并渴望能够遇到它？”

“我会这样认为的。”

“那么反感、不情愿、不愿意的状况又怎么样呢？我们难道不会把它们置于包括了不喜欢和厌恶的相反范畴下吗？”

“当然会。” d

“那么在这种情形下，难道我们不会说存在一类由欲望构成的范畴，其最显眼的欲望就是那被称为饥渴的欲望？”

“会这样说。”

“一个渴求饮料，另一个渴求食物？”

“是的。”

“那么就渴自身而言，它是否是一种心灵对于某物的欲求，而不是我们说的别的东西？比如说，渴望得到热的饮料还是冷的饮料，多喝一点还是少喝一点，或者简言之是对某种饮料的渴求？要是除了渴之外还有热，那么不就有另外对于冷的东西的 e
渴望，如果还有冷，那么不就有另外对于热的东西的渴望？如果渴感变得很强烈，那不就需要大量的饮料，而如果渴感不那么强烈，那么它不就需要一点点饮料就够了？然而实际渴的状态不就是对适合其本性的对象的欲求，即饮料；对于饥饿和食物也是一样。”

“是的，”他说，“每个欲望只欲求适合其本性的对象，对于这种或那种对象的欲求是某种添加的结果。”

我说：“那么这样，我们就应该不大可能被别人的说法搞糊涂 438a
了：没有人渴求饮料而不渴求好的饮料，没有人渴求食物而不渴求好的食物。他们说人人都欲求好的东西，如果渴是一种欲望，

it must be desire for a good drink or whatever; and so on for the other desires.'

'There might seem to be some plausibility to the claim,' he remarked.

'But there are only two categories of things whose nature it is to be relative,' I said. 'The first category consists, in my opinion, of things which have particular qualities and whose correlates have particular qualities; the second category consists of things which are just what they are and whose correlates are just what they are.'

'I don't understand,' he said.

'Don't you realize', I said, 'that anything which is greater is greater than something?'

'Yes.'

'Than something smaller?'

'Yes.'

'Whereas anything which is a lot greater is relative to some-thing which is a lot smaller. Agreed?'

'Yes.'

'And anything which was once greater (or will be) is relative to something which was once smaller (or will be), isn't it?'

'Of course,' he said.

c 'And the same goes for more in relation to less, and double in relation to half (and all similar numerical relations); also for heavier in relation to lighter, quicker in relation to slower, and moreover hot in relation to cold, and so on and so forth, don't you think?'

'Yes.'

'And what about the branches of knowledge? Isn't it the same story? Knowledge in itself is knowledge of information in itself (or whatever you choose to call the object of knowledge), but a particular branch of knowledge, knowledge qualified,

那么它必定欲求好的饮料什么的;对于其他欲望也是一样。”

“这些说法似乎也有些道理。”他说。

“但仅有两种事物的范畴,它们的本性是相关联的,”我说,“在我看来,第一种范畴包括有着特殊性质的事物,以及与它们相互关联的有着特殊性质的事物;第二种范畴包括仅仅 b
是其所是的事物,以及与它们相互关联的仅仅是其所是的事物。”

“我不理解。”他说。

我说:“你难道不明白,任何更大的事物就是比某物大的事物吗?”

“我明白。”

“更小的事物不也是这样吗?”

“是的。”

“任何大得多的事物是相对于某个小得多的事物而言的。同意吗?”

“同意。”

“任何曾是或将是较大的事物是相对于某个曾是或将是较小的事物而言的,不是吗?”

“当然。”他说。

“对于多相对于少,一倍相对于一半以及所有类似的数量关 c
系都是一样的;还有重相对于轻,快相对于慢,此外还有热相对于冷,如此等等,难道你不这么认为吗?”

“是这样想的。”

“各门知识又怎么样呢?不也一样吗?知识自身是对知识自身的认识,不管你想把知识的对象称作什么,但某一门知识,就其

d is knowledge of a particular qualified kind of thing. Here's an example: when the knowledge of making houses was developed, didn't it differ from the rest of the branches of knowledge and consequently gain its own name, building?'

'Of course.'

'And didn't it do so by virtue of the fact that It is a particular kind of knowledge, a kind which none of the other branches of knowledge is?'

'Yes.'

'And wasn't it when its object came into being as a particular kind of thing that it too came into being as a particular kind of knowledge? And doesn't the same go for all the other branches of expertise and knowledge?'

'Yes, it does.'

'I wonder if you've grasped my meaning now,' I said. 'You should think of this as the point I was trying to make before, when I said that there are two categories of things whose nature it is to be relative: some are only themselves and are related to objects which are only themselves; others have par-ticular qualities and are related to objects with particular qualities. I don't mean to imply that their quality

e is the same as the quality of their objects—that knowledge of health and illness is itself healthy and ill, and knowledge of evil and good is itself evil and good. I mean that when knowledge occurs whose object is not the unqualified object of knowledge, but an object with a particular quality (say, health and illness), then the consequence is that the knowledge itself also acquires a particular quality, and this is why it is no longer called just plain knowledge: the qualification is added, and it is called medical knowledge.'

'I do understand,' he said, 'and I agree as well.'

439a 'As for thirst, then,' I said, 'don't you think it finds its essential place among relative things? And what it essentially is, of course, is thirst...'

'... for drink,' he said. 'Yes, I agree.'

'So for drink of a particular kind there is also thirst of a

是知识而言,是关于某些特定事物的知识。举个例子说:当有了 d
一门建造房子的知识,那么它不是与其他门类的知识有了区别从而有了自己的名称,建筑学?"

"当然。"

"之所以这样,不就是因为它是一门特殊的知识,一门与任何其他门类的知识不同的知识吗?"

"是的。"

"不就是因为其对象是某种特殊的事物,才使得它成为一门特殊的知识吗?这对于其他分科的技艺和知识不也一样吗?"

"是这样的。"

"我想知道你现在是否明白我的意思了,"我说,"你应该把这当作我先前力图要解释的要点,有两类本质上相关联事物的范畴:一些事物仅仅是其所是并相关于仅仅是其所是的对象;另一些具有特殊的性质并且相关于具有特殊性质的对象。我并不是
说它们的性质与它们对象的性质相同——比如并非关于健康和 e
疾病的知识本身就是健康的和有病的,关于恶与善的知识本身就是恶的和善的。我的意思是说,若知识的对象不是一般知识的对象,而是具有特殊性质的对象(比如健康和疾病),那么结果就是知识自身便也获得了特殊的性质,这就是为什么不再将其称之为仅仅是一般的知识的原因:添加上了属性,它就被称作医学知识。"

"我确实理解了,"他说,"并且我也同意。"

"那么至于渴,"我说,"你难道不认为它本质上是那些有关联 439a
的事物之一吗?渴本质上当然是……"

"……与饮料相关,"他说,"是的,我同意。"

"所以如果饮料是特定的种类,那么渴也是特定的种类;但渴

particular kind; but thirst in itself is not thirst for a lot of drink or a little drink, or a beneficial drink or a harmful drink, or in short for drink of any particular kind. Thirst in itself is essentially just thirst for drink in itself.'

'Absolutely.'

'When someone is thirsty, then, the only thing—in so far as he is thirsty—that his mind wants is to drink. This is what it longs for and strives for.'

b 'Clearly.'

'So imagine an occasion when something is making it resist the pull of its thirst: isn't this bound to be a different part of it from the thirsty part, which is impelling it towards drink as if it were an animal? I mean, we've already agreed that the same one thing cannot thanks to the same part of itself simultaneously have opposite effects in the same context.'

'No, it can't.'

'As an analogy, it isn't in my opinion right to say that an archer's hands are simultaneously pushing the bow away and pulling it closer. Strictly, one hand is pushing it away and the other is pulling it close.'

'I quite agree,' he said.

c 'Now, do we know of cases where thirsty people are unwilling to drink?'

'Certainly,' he said. 'It's a common occurrence.'

'What could be the explanation for these cases?' I asked. 'Don't we have to say that their mind contains a part which is telling them to drink, and a part which is telling them not to drink, and that this is a different part and overcomes the part which is telling them to drink?'

'I think so,' he said.

'And those occasions when thirst and so on are countermanded occur thanks to rationality, whereas the pulls and

自身不是对于大量饮料和少量饮料的渴求,或有益或有害的饮料的渴求,或简言之对于某种特定饮料的渴求。渴自身本质上只是对饮料自身的渴求。”

“确实如此。”

“那么,当一个人渴的时候,就他渴来说,他的心灵唯一想要得到的东西就是饮料。这就是它希望并渴求得到的东西。” b

“显然是这样的。”

“所以设想一种情形,有某个东西使心灵抵挡住渴的诱惑:这个部分不就肯定是异于渴的部分,这个渴的部分迫使心灵像动物一样趋向饮料吗?我的意思是我们已经同意过,同一个东西不能由于自身的同一个部分而在同一个方面同时具有相反的效果。”

“对,不能具有相反的效果。”

“打个比方,我这样说是不对的:一个射手的手同时推弓又拉弓。严格说来,一只手在推弓而另一只手在拉弓。”

“我很同意你的说法。”他说。 c

“那么我们是否熟悉这样的情况,即人们虽然渴了但不想喝水?”

“当然,”他说,“这是常有的事。”

“这些事怎么解释?”我问道,“我们只能说他们心灵所包含的其中一个部分吩咐他们去喝水,一个部分吩咐他们不要去喝水,这是不是一个不同的部分并且支配了那个吩咐他们去喝水的部分呢?”

“我想是这样的。”他说。

“发生渴和其他诸如此类的欲望遭到阻止的那些情形要归因

d impulses occur thanks to afflictions and diseased stares, don't they?'

'I suppose so.'

'So it wouldn't be irrational of us to expect that these are two separate parts,' I said, 'one of which we can describe as rational, and the other as irrational and desirous. The first is responsible for the mind's capacity to think rationally, and the second—which is an ally of certain satisfactions and pleasures—for its capacity to feel Just, hunger, and thirst, and in general to be stirred by desire.'

e 'No, it wouldn't be irrational,' he said. 'This would be a perfectly reasonable view for us to hold.'

'Let's have these, then,' I said, 'as two distinct aspects of our minds. What about the passionate part, however, which is responsible for the mind's capacity for passion? Is it a third part, or might it be interchangeable with one of the other two?'

'I suppose it might be the same as the desirous part,' he said.

'But there's a story I once heard which seems to me to he reliable,' I said, 'about how Leontius the son of Aglaeon was coming up from the Piraeus, outside the North Wall but close to it, when he saw some corpses with the public executioner standing near by. On the one hand, he experienced the desire to see them, but at the same time he felt disgust and averted his gaze. For a while, he struggled and kept
440a his hands over his eyes, but finally he was overcome by the desire; he opened his eyes wide, ran up to the corpses, and said, "There you are, you wretches! What a lovely sight! I hope you feel satisfied!"'

'Yes, I've heard the story too,' he said.

'Now, what it suggests', I said, 'is that it's possible for anger to be at odds with the desires, as if they were different things.'

于理性，而发生牵引或拉动欲望的情形则要归因于痛苦和疾病，d
不是吗？"

"我想是这样的。"

我说："所以我们设想有两个部分，这种想法并非没有道理，我们把其中的一个称作理智，把另一个称作非理性和欲望。前者使心灵具有理性思考的能力，后者——它是一个由某些满足和快乐构成的联合体——使之具有感受欲念、饥渴以及一般的欲望之骚动的能力。"

"这不是没有道理的，"他说，"我们要坚持这个完全有道理的 e
观点。"

我说："那么就让我们把它们当作我们心灵中的两个不同部分吧。然而，负责心灵的热烈激越情感能力的激情部分怎么样呢？这是第三个部分呢，还是可以与另外两个中的一个相替换？"

"我想它可以与欲望的部分相等同。"他说。

我说："但我曾听说过一个故事，我想是可靠的，说的是阿格莱翁之子勒翁提乌斯，他从庇莱厄斯靠着北墙外进城去，那时他看见附近有几具被公开绞死的尸体。一方面，他感到欲望驱使他去观看，但同时他感到恶心而不想看到。他手捂着眼睛做了一会儿斗争，但最终还是被欲望所征服；他睁大了眼
睛，冲向尸体，说：'看吧！可怜虫！多美的景象啊！我希望你 440a
感到满足了！'"

"是的，我也听说过这个故事。"他说。

我说："这说的是愤怒可能与欲望并不相一致，就如同它们是两个不同的东西。"

'Yes, it does,' he agreed.

'And that's far from being an isolated case, isn't it?' I asked. 'It's not at all uncommon to find a person's desires compelling him to
b go against his reason, and to see him cursing himself and venting his passion on the source of the compulsion within him. It's as if there were two warring factions, with passion fighting on the side of reason. But I'm sure you wouldn't claim that you had ever, in yourself or in anyone else, met a case of passion siding with the desires against the rational mind, when the rational mind prohibits resistance.'

'No, I certainly haven't,' he said.

c 'And what about when you feel you're in the wrong?' I asked. 'If someone who in your opinion has a right to do so retaliates by inflicting on you hunger and cold and so on, then isn't it the case that, in proportion to your goodness of character, you are incapable of getting angry at this treatment and your passion, as I say, has no inclination to get worked up against him?'

'True,' he said.

'But suppose you feel you're being wronged. Under these circumstances, your passion boils and rages, and fights for what you regard as right. Then hunger, cold, and other sufferings make you stand firm and conquer them, and only success or death can stop it'
d fighting the good fight, unless it is recalled by your rational mind and calmed down, as a dog is by a shepherd.'

'That's a very good simile,' he said. 'And in fact the part we've got the auxiliaries to play in our community is just like that of dogs, with their masters being the rulers, who are, as it were, the shepherds of the community.'

'Yes, you've got it,' I said. 'That's exactly what I mean. But there's something else here too, and I wonder if you've noticed it as well.'

“是的，确实是这样的。”他同意说。

“这远非是仅此一例，不是吗？”我问道，“这也并非罕见：一个人的欲望迫使他违背他的理智，诅咒自己，对来自自身的强制感发脾气。就像两个战斗的盟友，激情与理智并肩作战。但我确信你不会说你在自己或别人身上曾遇到过这种情形，即激情与欲望一起反对理性心灵，而理性心灵则禁止抵抗。” b

“我确实没有遇到过。”他说。

“当你感觉你做错了的时候又怎么样呢？”我问道。“如果有某人，依你看来他有权力饿你、冻你、折磨你等等，他这样做来报复你，那么在这种情况下，与你性格之仁慈善良相称，你也就不能对这种遭遇生气、愤怒了，而且正如我说的，你的怒气也不可能逐渐积累朝他发泄出来，不是这样吗？” c

“对的，”他说。

“但是假使你感觉你被冤枉了结果会怎样。在这些境况下，你的怒火燃烧并狂暴地爆发出来，并为你所认为正确的事实而争辩、抗争。那么饥饿、寒冷以及其他苦难只会使你坚强，而且你会征服它们，并且只有胜利或死亡才能停息它为尊贵抗争而进行的战斗，除非怒火被你的理性头脑制服并平静下来，就像一条狗被一位牧人制服并平静下来一样。” d

“这是个很好的比喻，”他说，“我们让助手在城邦扮演的角色就像狗一样，他们的主人就是统治者，统治者就其自身而言是城邦的牧人。”

“是的，你完全理解了我的意思，”我说，“但这里还有别的含义，我想知道你是否也已经注意到了。”

e ‘What is it?’

‘That we're getting the opposite impression of the passionate part from what we did before. Previously, we were thinking that it was an aspect of the desirous part, but now that seems to be way off the mark, and we're saying that when there's mental conflict, it is far more likely to fight alongside reason.’

‘Absolutely,’ he said.

‘Is it different from the rational part, then, or is it a version of it, in which case there are two, not three, mental categories—the rational and the desirous? Or will the analogy with the community hold
441a good? Three classes constituted the community—the one which works for a living, the auxiliaries, and the policy-makers—so is there in the mind as well a third part, the passionate part, which is an auxiliary of the rational part, unless it is corrupted by bad upbringing?’

‘It must be a third part,’ he said.

‘Yes,’ I said, ‘*if* we find that it's as distinct from the rational part as it is from the desirous part.’

‘But that's easy,’ he said. ‘Just look at children. It's evident that from the moment of their birth they have a copious supply of pas-
b sion but I'm not convinced that some of them ever acquire reason, and it takes quite a time for most of them to do so.’

‘Yes, you've certainly put that well,’ I said. ‘And animals provide further evidence of the truth of what you're saying. Moreover, we can adduce the passage from Homer we quoted earlier: “He struck his breast and spoke sternly to his heart.” Clearly, Homer here has one
c distinct part rebuking another distinct part—the part which has thought rationally about what is better and worse rebuking the part whose passion is irrationally becoming aroused.’

‘You're absolutely right,’ he said.

‘It's not been easy,’ I said, ‘but we've made it to the other shore: we've reached the reasonable conclusion that the constituent categories of a community and of any individual's mind are identical in nature and number.’

“那是什么?” e

“我们现在得到的关于激情部分的看法与我们之前的看法相反。之前,我们认为它是欲望的一个方面,而现在大为不同,我们说,一旦有精神分歧,那么它便更可能与理性并肩作战。”

“确实如此。”他说。

“那么它就是异于理性部分的,或者它是理性的一个类型,在这种情况下就有两种而不是三种精神的范畴——理性和欲望?或者就像一个好的城邦一样?三个阶层构成了城邦——劳动者、
辅助者和统治者——精神也同样具有第三个部分,即激情部分, 441a
它是理性部分的助手,除非它受到不良教养的腐蚀?”

“肯定有第三个部分。”他说。

“是的,”我说,“如果我们发现激情就像不同于欲望部分一样,也不同于理性部分。”

“这很简单,”他说,“看看孩子。他们显然从其出生之时起就充满了激情,而我不相信其中的某些人获得了理性,对于他们中
的大多数人来说,获得理性要花相当长的时间。” b

“是的,你说的当然是对的,”我说,“动物更进一步证明了你的说法显然是正确的。此外,我们还能引证先前引用过的荷马的段落:‘他捶击胸脯责问他的心灵。’这里荷马显然是用一个特定
的部分来斥责另一个特定的部分——用理性地思考较好和较坏 c
事物的部分来斥责毫无理智地引发愤怒的部分。”

“你说得很对。”他说。

“这并不简单,”我说,“但我们还是已经到达了对岸:我们已经得出了合理的结论,构成城邦的范畴和构成任何个人精神的范畴,在性质和数量上都是一样的。”

'Yes, they are.'

'Isn't it bound to follow that the manner and cause of a community's and an individual's wisdom are identical?'

'Naturally.'

'And that the manner and cause of a community's and an
d individual's courage are identical, and that the same goes for every other factor which contributes in both cases towards goodness?'

'Inevitably.'

'So no doubt, Glaucon, we'll also be claiming that human morality is the same in kind as a community's morality.'

'Yes, that's absolutely inevitable too.'

'We can't have forgotten, however, that a community's morality consists in each of its three constituent classes doing its own job.'

'No, I'm sure we haven't,' he said.

'So we should impress upon our minds the idea that the same goes for human beings as well. Where each of the constituent parts of
e an individual does its own job, the individual will be moral and will do *his* own job.'

'Yes, we certainly should do that,' he said.

'Since the rational part is wise and looks out for the whole of the mind, isn't it right for it to rule, and for the passionate part to be its subordinate and its ally?'

'Yes.'

'Now—to repeat—isn't it the combination of culture and exercise which will make them attuned to each other? The two combined provide fine discussions and studies to stretch and educate the rational
442a part, and music and rhythm to relax, calm, and soothe the passionate part.'

“是的，是一样的。”

“这不就可以推论说，城邦的智慧和个人的智慧所具有的方式和原因是同样的吗?”

“自然是。”

“而且不是可以说，城邦的勇敢和个人的勇敢所具有的方式
和原因是同样的，并且，在这两种情况下，其他每一种有助于德性 d
的因素是同样的吗?”

“必然如此。”

“所以，格劳孔，毫无疑问，我们也会说人的正义与城邦的正义是同一类。”

“是的，那也必定绝对如此。”

“但我们不能忘记城邦的正义在于构成城邦的三个阶层各司其职。”

“我确信我们没有忘记。”他说。

“所以我们也应该记住这个说法对于人来说也是一样的。当
个人的每个组成部分各司其职的时候，个人就会是正义的，就会 e
各司其职。”

“是的，我们当然应该那样做。”他说。

“既然理智是智慧的并且顾及着整个心灵，那么不就应让它来领导，让激情服从于它并作为它的同盟吗?”

“是的。”

“现在再说一遍，不就是文艺和锻炼的共同作用使它们相
互协调吗？两者的结合提供了良好的讨论和研究以拓展和教
育理智部分，并用音乐和韵律使激情的部分得到放松、平静与 442a
缓和。”

'Absolutely.'

'And once these two parts have received this education and have been trained and conditioned in their true work, then they are to be put in charge of the desirous part, which is the major constituent of an individual's mind and is naturally insatiably greedy for things. So they have to watch over it and make sure that it doesn't get so saturated with physical pleasures (as they are called) that in its bloated and strengthened state it stops doing its own job, and tries to dominate
b and rule over things which it is not equipped by its hereditary status to rule over, and so plunges the whole of everyone's life into chaos.'

'Yes, indeed,' he said.

'Moreover, these two are perfect for guarding the entire mind and the body against external enemies, aren't they?' I asked. 'The rational part will do the planning, and the passionate part the fighting. The passionate part will obey the ruling part and employ its courage to carry out the plans.'

'True.'

c 'I imagine, then, that it is the passionate part of a person which we are taking into consideration when we describe him as courageous: we're saying that neither pain nor pleasure stops his passionate part retaining the pronouncements of reason about what is and is not to be feared.'

'That's right,' he agreed.

'And the part we take into consideration when we call him wise is that little par—this internal ruler, which made these pronouncements—which knows what is advantageous for each of the three parts and for their joint unity.'

'Yes.'

'And don't we call him self-disciplined when there's concord and attunement between these same parts that is, when the ruler and its
d two subjects unanimously agree on the necessity of the rational part being the ruler and when they don't rebel against it?'

“必定如此。”

“一旦这两个部分得到了这样的教育并被训练成做它们真正的工作，那么它们就会掌控欲望的部分，而欲望是一个人心灵的重要组成，天然就是对事物贪得无厌。所以它们必须对之加以监视，并确保它不沉溺于（人们所谓的）肉体快乐以至变得傲慢强大而不再做它自己的工作，还试图去控制和支配它本不该支配的东 b
西，以此使每个人的整个生活陷入混乱。”

“的确如此。”他说。

“此外，这两者能最好地保卫整个心灵和身体以抵抗外在的敌人，不是吗？”我问道，“理智的部分会出谋划策而激情部分进行战斗。激情部分会服从理智部分，并使用它的勇敢来完成这谋划。”

“对的。”

“那么我想，当我们描述一个人为有勇气、有胆量的时候，我们所考虑到的是其激情的部分：我们在说，无论是痛苦还是快乐， c
都不能阻止他的激情的部分保持理性关于什么须得慎惧什么不必慎惧的见解。”

“对的，”他同意道。

“而当我们称他为明察善断时，我们所考虑的是较小的部分，正是他的内在管理者做出了上述判断——它知道对于这三部分中的每一个以及对它们的联合体而言，什么是有利的。”

“是的。”

“当上述部分存在有和谐与协调的时候，也就是当管理者及两个被管理者全体一致地承认理性部分成为管理者的必然性，而 d
且当两个被管理者不再反抗理性部分的时候，我们不是宣布他是自制的吗？”

‘Yes, that’s exactly what self-discipline is, in both a community and an individual,’ he said.

‘And we’re not changing our minds about the manner and cause of morality.’

‘Absolutely not.’

‘Well,’ I said, ‘have we blunted the edge of our notion of morality in any way? Do we have any grounds for thinking that our conclusions about its nature in a community don’t apply in this context?’

‘I don’t think so,’ he replied.

e ‘If there’s still any doubt in our minds,’ I said, ‘we can eradicate it completely by checking our conclusion against everyday cases.’

‘What cases?’

‘Take this community of ours and a person who resembles it by virtue of both his nature and his upbringing, and suppose, for instance, we had to state whether, in our opinion, a person of this type would steal money which had been deposited with him. Is it conceivable to you that anyone would think our man capable of this, rather
443a than any other type of person?’

‘No one could think that,’ he said.

‘And he could have nothing to do with temple-robbery, theft, and betrayal either of his personal friends or, on a public scale, of his country, could he?’

‘No, he couldn’t.’

‘Moreover, nothing could induce him to break an oath or any other kind of agreement.’

‘No, nothing.’

‘And he’s the last person you’d expect to find committing adultery, neglecting his parents, and failing to worship the gods.’

‘Yes, of course,’ he said.

‘And isn’t the reason for all of this the fact that each of his

“是的,那确实就是个人和城邦中的自制。”他说。

“关于正义的方式和原因,我们没有改变我们的想法。”

“绝对不会。”

“那么,”我说,“我们是否在某种程度上模糊了我们对正义概念的界定?我们是否有理由认为,我们关于其在城邦中的本性所得出的结论不适用于这种情况?”

“我不这么认为。”他回答说。

“如果我们心里还有什么怀疑的话,”我说,“通过将我们的结论与日常的事例做一比照,我们就可以将其完全排除。” e

“什么事例?”

“举例来说,假设我们的这个城邦或一个在天性和教育上与之相似的人,并且我们一定要说出在我们看来一个这种类型的人是否会偷窃保存在他那里的钱财。你能想象得出有谁会认为是我们的人而不是任何别的类型的人会做出这种事情?” 443a

“没有人会那样想的。”他说。

“他与偷窃圣物、盗窃和背叛他的私人朋友、在公共领域里背叛城邦这些事无关,是吗?”

“没什么关系。”

“此外,没有什么东西能诱使他违背诺言或任何其他类型的协定。”

“是没有什么东西。”

“他绝不是你期望发现其通奸、不孝顺父母和不敬神的人。”

“当然。”他说。

“所有这些不就是因为他的每个组成部分都做自己作为统治 b

constituent parts does its own job as ruler or subject?'

'Yes, that's the only reason.'

'Do you need to look any further for morality, then? Don't you think it can only be the capacity we've come up with, which enables both people and communities to be like this?'

'I for one certainly don't need to look any further,' he said.

'Our dream has finally come true, then. We said we had a vague impression that we had probably—with the help of some god—
c stumbled across the origin and some kind of outline of morality right at the start of our foundation of the community.'

'Absolutely.'

'It turns out, then, Glaucon—and this is why it was so useful—that the idea that a person who has been equipped by nature to be a shoemaker or a joiner or whatever should make shoes or do joinery or whatever was a dreamt image of morality.'

'So it seems.'

'And we've found that in real life morality is the same kind of property, apparently, though not in the field of external activities. Its sphere is a person's inner activity: it is really a matter of oneself and
d the parts of oneself. Once he has stopped his mental constituents doing any job which is not their own or intruding on one another's work; once he has set his own house in order, which is what he really should be concerned with; once he is his own ruler, and is well regulated, and has internal concord; once he has treated the three factors as if they were literally the three defining notes of an octave—low, high, and middle—and has created a harmony out of them and however many notes there may be in between; once
e he has bound all the factors together and made himself a perfect unity instead of a plurality, self-disciplined and internally attuned: then and only then does he act—if he acts—to acquire property or look after his body or play a role in government or do some private business. In the course of this activity, it is conduct

者或被统治者的工作吗?”

“是的,那是唯一的理由。”

“那么,你需要再进一步寻找正义吗?你难道不认为这只能是我们找到的、能够使得人和城邦如此这般的能力吗?”

“我确信不需要再寻找了。”他说。

“那么,我们的梦想终于成真了。我们说过我们有个模糊的印象,我们可能已经——在某位神的帮助下——在建立城邦之初
就碰巧发现了正义的起源和某些要点。” c

“毫无疑问。”

“格劳孔,所以说——这就是它有用的原因——一个具有鞋匠、木匠或别的什么禀赋的人应该制鞋、做木工活或别的什么活,这种想法是正义的影像。”

“看来如此。”

“而且我们在实际生活中已经发现,正义具有同样种类的属性,尽管其不属于外在客观活动的领域之内。它的范围是一个人的内在心理的活动:它的确是本人的一桩事务,也是本人这个整
体的部分。当他停息其精神各组成部分的躁动,不去做不该做的 d
任何事情,或者不去打扰彼此的活动;当他将其真正应该关心的事情整理好;当他成为他自己的君主,并得到了良好的管理,而且有了内在的和谐;一旦他把三个部分就当作八音度的三个关键的音符——低音,高音,中音——从中创造出和谐,而在它们之间却还有很多音符;一旦他把所有三个部分结合在一起,使自己成为
一个完美的一而不是多,具有自制和内在的和谐:这时,且仅在这 e
时,他才能有所作为——如果他做了什么的话——去获得财富或照看他的身体或从事公共事务或做一些私人的事情。在这行为

which preserves and promotes this inner condition of his that he regards as moral and describes as fine, and it is the knowledge which oversees this conduct that he regards as wisdom; however, it is any conduct
444a which disperses this condition that he regards as immoral, and the thinking which oversees this conduct that he regards as stupidity.'

'You're absolutely right, Socrates,' he said.

'All right,' I said. 'I imagine that we'd regard as no more than the truth the claim that we had found out what it is to be a moral person and a moral community, and had discovered what morality actually is when it occurs in them.'

'Yes, we certainly would,' he said.

'Shall we make the claim, then?'

'Yes.'

'So be it,' I said. 'Next, I suppose, we should consider immorality.'

'Obviously.'

b 'Isn't it bound to involve these three factors being in conflict, intruding into one another's work, and exchanging roles, and one part rebelling against the mind as a whole in an improper attempt to usurp rulership—improper because its natural function is to be dominated unless it belongs to the ruling class? Our position, I'm sure, will be that it is disruption and disorder of the three parts along these lines that constitutes not only immorality, but also indiscipline, cowardice, and stupidity—in a word, badness of any kind.'

'Precisely,' he said.

c 'Now that morality and immorality are in plain view, doesn't that mean that wrongdoing and immoral conduct, and right conduct too, are as well?' I asked.

'Why?'

'Because their role in the mind happens to be identical to that of healthy or unhealthy factors in the body,' I said.

过程中,正是保存和提升他的这种内在状态的行为,他看作是正义的,并且将之说成是美好的,正是重视这行为的认知,他看作是明智的,然而,正是任何驱散这种状态的行为,他看作是不正义的,忽视这行为的想法,他看作是愚昧无知的。” 444a

“苏格拉底,你说得完全正确,”他说。

“好吧,”我说,“我想没有比这更正确的说法了,即我们已经发现了什么是正义之人和什么是正义之城邦,并且当正义存在于它们之中时,我们已经发现了正义究竟是什么。”

“是的,我们当然是这么想的。”他说。

“那么,我们确定可以这么说吗?”

“是的。”

“那就这样吧,”我说,“我想接下来我们应该思考不正义了。”

“显然。”

“不正义就必定是让这三个部分陷入冲突斗争、相互干涉并 b
改变角色,心灵的一部分向整个心灵造反,不恰当地试图篡夺统治权——说不恰当,是因为它天生的角色就是臣服,除非它处于统治阶级,对吗?我相信我们认为按照如此的说法,正是分裂和混乱不仅造成了不正义,而且还有不节制、怯懦、愚昧——一句话,任何的邪恶。”

“确实如此。”他说。

“既然搞清了正义和不正义,不就意味着做坏事、不正义的行 c
为,以及正义的行为也搞清楚了吗?”我问道。

“为什么?”

“因为它们在心灵中所起的作用正好与健康和不健康的因素在身体中所起的作用相同。”我说。

'In what sense?'

'Healthy factors engender health, and unhealthy ones illness.'

'Yes.'

'Well, doesn't moral behaviour engender morality, while immoral behaviour engenders immorality?'

d 'Inevitably.'

'But you create health by making the components of a body control and be controlled as nature intended, and you create disease by subverting this natural order.'

'Yes.'

'Doesn't it follow,' I said, 'that you create morality by making the components of a mind control and be controlled as nature intended, and immorality by subverting this natural order?'

'Absolutely,' he said.

'Goodness, then, is apparently a state of mental health, bloom,
e and vitality; badness Is a state of mental sickness, deformity, and infirmity.'

'That's right.'

'Isn't it the case, therefore, that goodness is a consequence of good conduct, badness of bad conduct?'

'Necessarily.'

'Now we come to what is, I suppose, the final topic. We have
445a to consider whether moral conduct, fine behaviour, and being moral (whether or not the person is known to be moral) are rewarding, or whether it is wrongdoing and being immoral (provided that the immoral person doesn't have to pay for his crimes and doesn't become a better person as a result of being punished).'

"在什么意义上说?"

"健康的因素产生健康,不健康的因素产生疾病。"

"是的。"

"那么正义的行为不就产生正义,而不正义的行为产生不正义?" d

"必定如此。"

"但是你按照自然的意图或目的,使得身体的构成部分控制、管理与被控制、被管理,藉此你产生了健康,你又通过颠倒这一自然的正常状态而生出了疾病。"

"是的。"

"依此类推,"我说,"你按照自然的意图或目的,通过使心灵的构成部分控制、管理与被控制、被管理而产生了正义,不正义则是颠倒了这一自然的正常状态获致的,难道不是这样吗?"

"确实如此。"他说。

"那么,美德似乎是一种灵魂健康、美好和生气勃勃的状态;而邪恶则是一种灵魂病态、丑陋和虚弱的状态。" e

"对的。"

"那么不就是这样:美德是好行为的结果,而邪恶是坏行为的结果?"

"必然如此。"

"现在我们进入,我认为是最后的一个话题了。我们只好判断一下,是道德行为、高雅举止,以及讲求良心(无论这个人的道德良心是否为人所知)会得到利益,还是为非作歹、本性邪恶(倘 445a
若这个不义的人不是必得因其罪行遭受报应,并且不是因受惩罚,结果变成一个更好的人)会得到利益。"

'It seems to me that it would be absurd to consider that topic now, Socrates,' he said. 'Life isn't thought to be worth living when the natural constitution of the body is ruined, even if one has all the food and drink and wealth and power in the world. So how could it be worth living when the natural constitution of the very life-force within
b us is disrupted and ruined? How could life be worth living if a person's chosen course of action is to avoid the path which will lead him away from badness and immorality and towards the possession of morality and goodness, given the evident accuracy of our descriptions of both of these states?'

'Yes, it is absurd,' I agreed. 'All the same, since we've reached a point which affords the clearest possible view of the truth of these matters, we shouldn't give up now.'

'I couldn't agree more,' he said. 'Giving up should be the last thing on our minds.'

c 'Come and join me here, then,' I said, 'and you'll see, I think, all the types of badness there are—at least, the ones that are worth seeing.'

'I'm coming,' he said. 'You have only to tell me.'

'Well,' I said, 'the impression I get from the vantage-point we've reached at this point of our discussion is that while there's only one kind of goodness, there are countless types of badness, of Which four are worth mentioning.'

'What do you mean?' he asked.

'There are probably as many types of character,' I said, 'as there are identifiable forms of political system.'

'And how many is that?'

d 'There are five types of political system,' I replied, 'and five types of character.'

'Please tell me what they are,' he said.

'All right,' I said. 'One of the forms of political system would be the one we've described. There are two possible ways of referring to it, however: if a single outstanding individual arises within the ruling class, it's called a kingship; but if there is a plurality of rulers, it's called an aristocracy.'

“苏格拉底，在我看来，考虑那样的问题会很荒谬，”他说，“当身体的天然构成遭到毁坏，那么即使人们具有世上所有的饮食、财富和权力，这样的生活也被认为是不值得过的。所以当我们自身之内的生命力的天然构成遭到瓦解和毁坏，那么怎么还值得活
下去呢？如果一个人选择的行为过程就是去回避那条会引领他 b
远离邪恶和不正义并趋向拥有正义和善良的道路，并且要是我们关于这两种状态的描述显然是准确的话，那么这生活还值得过吗？”

“是的，是很荒谬，”我同意说，“不管怎么说，因为我们已经到达了这一地步，最清楚地拥有关于这些事情的实际情况的看法，我们现在不应该放弃。”

“我完全同意，”他说，“我想放弃是最不应该的。”

“那么来吧，和我一起，”我说，“我想你会看到所有的邪 c
恶——至少看看那些值得一看的邪恶。”

“我来了，”他说，“你只管告诉我吧。”

“好吧，”我说，“从我们目前的谈论所达到的高度来说，我的印象是，美德只有一种，而邪恶的类型却数不清，其中的四种值得一提。”

“你说的是什么意思？”他问道。

“大概品性的类型有许多，”我说，“就像可确认的政体形式那样。”

“那有几个呢？”

我回答说：“有五种类型的政体和五种品性。” d

“请告诉我，它们是什么？”他说。

“好吧，”我说，“其中一种政体是我们已经说过的。然而可以用两种方式称呼它：如果由统治阶级中的一个杰出个人来掌权，这就叫王政；但如果有多个统治者，这就叫贵族政治。”

'True,' he said.

'This is the first of the types of political system I had in mind,'
e I said. 'The point is that whether there is a single ruler in the community, or whether there are more than one, they won't disturb any of the community's important laws, since they'll have been brought up and educated in the manner we've explained.'

'No, it's implausible to think that they will,' he said.

“对的。”他说。

“这是我想到的第一种政体类型，”我说，“关键在于，无论城
邦中是一个统治者，还是有多个统治者，他们都不会扰乱城邦的 e
任何重要法律，因为他们是以我们解说过的那种方式培养和教育
的。”

“是的，可以相信他们不会的。”他说。

CHAPTER 7

449a ‘So that’s the kind of community and political system—and the kind of person—I’m calling good and right. Given the rightness of this community, I’m describing all the others as bad and flawed: not only are their political systems wrong, but they also influence individuals’ characters incorrectly. And I see them as falling into four categories.’

‘What four categories?’ he asked.

I was on the point of listing them and explaining how, in my o-
b pinion, each in turn evolved out of the preceding one, when Polemarchus (who was sitting just beyond Adeimantus) reached out and got hold of Adeimantus’ cloak high up, by his shoulder. He drew Adeimantus to wards himself, leaned forward and whispered something with his mouth to his ear, so that all we heard of his words was: ‘Shall we let it drop or what?’

‘Of course not,’ Adeimantus replied—this was out loud.

‘What aren’t you going to let drop?’ I asked.

‘You,’ he said.

‘What have I done?’ I asked.

c ‘We think you’re being lazy,’ he said. ‘We think you’re doing us out of a whole aspect of the discussion, and a not unimportant aspect at that, so that you don’t have to spell out the details. You seem to think you can get away with casually saying, as if it were obvious to everyone, that where wives and children are concerned “friends share”.’

‘But that’s right, isn’t it, Adeimantus?’ I asked.

d ‘Yes,’ he replied. ‘But it still needs explaining, just as

第七章

"所以我把这类城邦和政体——和这类人——称作善和正义的。有了这城邦的正义之后,我便把所有其他的称作坏的和有缺陷的:不光是他们的政体是错误的,而且还错误地影响个人的品性。我把它们分作四类。" 449a[1]

"哪四类?"他问道。

我正要一一列举它们,并且解释在我看来每一个是如何从前一个推演出来的,那时,正坐在离阿狄曼图旁边不远的波勒玛库斯,伸出手拉拉阿狄曼图上肩的衣服。他拉阿狄曼图靠近些,侧过身去将嘴巴贴着耳朵轻声说了些什么,结果我们全都听到了他的话:"我们是要让他过关呢,还是怎么样?" b

"当然不行,"阿狄曼图大声地回答说。

"你们不想让谁过关?"我问道。

"你。"他说。

"我做了什么了?"我问道。 c

"我们认为你在偷懒,"他说,"我们认为讨论的整个部分你都在蒙混我们,对于一个很重要的部分你却没有仔细地加以讨论。你好像以为你能够随便说几句就蒙混过去,你说的和大家都明白的一样:妻子儿女也涉及到'朋友间共享'。"

"阿狄曼图,但那是对的,难道不是吗?"我问道。

"是的,"他回答说,"但还需加以解释,就像你解释所有别的 d

---

〔1〕 边页码445之后即接449,原文如此。

you've explained everything else. What makes this sharing right? I mean, there are all sorts of ways it could happen, so don't leave us guessing as to which one you have in mind. For a long time now we've been patiently expecting you to make some mention of their approach to procreation and how they'll bring up their children, and to discuss the whole issue of the sharing of wives and children, which is a subject you raised, because in our opinion, as far as society is concerned, a great deal—no, everything—hinges on whether or not it happens in the right way. That is why, when you were starting to criticize another type of political system before you'd adequately discussed
450a this issue, we made the decision you overheard—not to let you go on until you'd discussed this whole topic as well.'

'You should know that I share his view,' said Glaucon. 'This decision gets my vote too.'

'In fact, you'd better count us as unanimous about this decision, Socrates,' said Thrasymachus.

'If only you knew what you'd done, laying into me like this,' I said. 'You're touching off a huge discussion about the constitution of our community; it'll be like starting again from the beginning. And I was so pleased that I'd finished describing it, and so happy that the description I'd given had been found acceptable and allowed to stand!
b You've no idea how massive a swarm of arguments you're stirring up now with your appeals. It's because I noticed its size that I did nothing about it, to avoid all the bother it would cause us.'

'Do you think it's gold fever that's brought these people here?' demanded Thrasymachus. 'Don't you suppose they've come to hear arguments?'

'Yes,' I replied, 'but not endless ones.'

'Anyone with any sense lets only death put an end to this kind of discussion,' Glaucon said. 'Please don't spare us a thought: just perse-
c vere and explain your views on the matters we're asking about. How will our guardians share children and wives? What upbringing will they provide for young children between birth and schooling, which is regarded as the most difficult period? Please try to explain it to us.'

事物一样。为什么共享是对的？我的意思是说，这可以有各种说法，所以不要让我们猜测你心里的想法。我们一直耐心地希望你说说他们对生育的看法，他们如何培养他们的孩子，谈谈整个共妻共子的问题，这是你提出的一个问题，因为在我们看来，就社会来说，很多事情——不，是每一种事情——关键在于其发生方式是否正确。这就是为什么，当你在未对这个问题加以充分的讨论之前，就开始批评另一种政体的时候，我们做了你听到的那个决定——不能让你继续下去，直到你也讨论了这整个话题。” 450a

“你应该知道我也同意这种观点，”格劳孔说，“我也投票赞成这个决定。”

“事实上，苏格拉底，你最好把这当作我们的一致决定。”塞拉西马库斯说。

“你们如此地非难我，要是你们知道你们已经做了什么，那就好了，”我说，“你们引发了一个关于城邦体制的大讨论；这就像是又重新来一遍。当我把它说完并发现我的想法得到认可、得以成立的时候，我是多么高兴啊！你们不知道你们现在提出的这个请求会引起多么巨大的争论呀！正是因为我意识到它的规模，所以 b
我才什么都没说，避免它带给我们的所有麻烦。”

“你以为是淘金热把这些人带到这里来的吗？”塞拉西马库斯问道，“你难道不认为他们到这里来是为了听取争论的吗？”

“是这样想的，”我说，“但不是无休止的。”

“对于任何有理智的人来说，这样的讨论只有至死方休，”格劳孔说，“请不要为我们担心：对于那些问题，只管坚持把你的观点说出来。我们的卫士如何共有孩子和妻子？从出生到上学期 c
间，他们应该向这些年幼的孩子提供什么样的教育，这段时期被认为是最困难的时期？请尽量向我们解释一番吧。”

'It's not an easy matter to go into, Glaucon,' I said. 'There are plenty of reasons for misgivings—even more than in the matters we've already discussed. I mean, one might doubt the viability of the proposal, and even granting its viability, there'll be room for doubting whether it's the best course of action. That, my dear friend, is why I'm rather hesitant about addressing the topic: I'm scared of my ideas
d being thought to be wishful thinking.'

'Don't worry,' he said. 'You won't be faced with an audience of dunces or sceptics or grumblers.'

'Was that remark supposed to raise my morale, Glaucon?' I asked.

'Yes,' he answered.

'Well, it's having exactly the opposite effect,' I said. 'If I was sure I knew what I was talking about, then your attempt at encouragement would go down well. I mean, there's no danger or uncertainty when someone who knows the truth speaks among intelligent friends a-
e bout crucial matters which are close to their hearts, but when someone who is vacillating and who still hasn't formed any definite conclusions does the talking, as I am, it's a cause for alarm and caution.
451a My worry is not that I might make a fool of myself: that would be a childish worry. But I'm frightened of dragging my friends down with me when I stumble and fall short' of the truth in matters where uncertainty is the last thing one wants. I humbly beg Nemesis, Glaucon, to pardon what I'm about to say. You see, I'm sure that deceiving people about customs which are truly good and moral is more of a sin than accidentally killing someone. That is why it's preferable to take this risk when one is in the company of enemies rather than friends—and that's why I really appreciated your encouragement!'

b Glaucon smiled and said, 'Socrates, if anything nasty happens to us as a result of what you say, we'll acquit you of murder, so to speak, and find you free of all taint of deceit. So you can talk with confidence.'

'Well, it's true that in homicide cases there's a law guaranteeing

“格劳孔,这可不是件容易办到的事情,”我说,“这有许多疑点——甚至比我们已经讨论过的那些问题的疑点还要多。我的意思是说,人们可能怀疑这个建议的可行性,即使是可行的,还要怀疑这样做是否是最好的。我的好朋友,这就是我非常犹豫去谈论这个问题的原因:我怕我的观点被认为是一厢情愿的想法。” d

“别担心,”他说,“你不会面对愚蠢、满腹疑惑或牢骚的听众的。”

“格劳孔,这话是在给我鼓气吗?”我问道。

“是的。”他回答说。

“不过结果适得其反,”我说,“如果我确信自己知道要说的东西,那么你的鼓励是很好的。我的意思是,当某个知道真理的人在聪明人中间谈论他们关心的头等大事,那是没有危险和疑虑的,但如果某个像我一样犹豫不决,并且还没有得出任何确定结 e
论的人来谈论,那么这就会引起警惕和担心。我担心的不是可能 451a
受人嘲笑:这种担心是孩子气的。我怕的是当我摔了跤并且在充满疑虑的问题中迷失了真理的时候,还会把我的朋友和我一起拽倒。格劳孔,我谦卑地向涅墨西斯乞求,原谅我所要说的话。你知道,比起失手杀人,我确信在真正的善和正义的习俗上欺骗人是更大的罪恶。这就是为什么最好在敌人中间而不是在朋友中间冒这个险的原因——那是我确实感激你的鼓励的原因!” b

格劳孔笑笑说:“苏格拉底,要是由于你说的话而给我们带来坏处,我们也不会把你当作杀人犯,可以这么说,我们对你这个杀人犯无罪释放,并且裁决你没有任何因欺骗、谎言而带来的道德上的污点。这样你就可以大胆说了吧。”

“嗯,在杀人案件中倒真的有这一条规定,即任何人只要法庭

that anyone who has been acquitted is free of the taint of pollution,' I said, 'so I suppose the same rule applies here too.'

'Then there's nothing to stop you getting on with the discussion,' he said.

'We'd better backtrack, then,' I said. 'The proper time for the
c discussion may have been earlier, but we'll have to have it now. It'll probably be all right this way, though—to proceed with the women's business now that the men's business is completed and done, especially since that's what you're asking me to do. It is my opinion that there is only one correct way for people with the character and education we've described to have and deal with their children and wives, and that is if they continue in the direction we gave them at the outset. What we tried to do, as you know, was make the men in theory like guardians of a flock.'

'Yes.'

d 'So let's keep to the same path and have the women born and brought up in a closely similar way, and see whether or not it turns out right for us.'

'How?' he asked.

'Well, should female guard-dogs share with the males the guarding and hunting and whatever other duties the males might have, do you think? Or should they stay indoors, incapacitated by their bearing and rearing of whelps, while the males work and do all the overseeing of the flocks?'

e 'They should share in everything,' he said. 'The only qualification is that we're dealing with a physically weaker sex: the males are stronger.'

'Can you employ any two creatures for the same purposes if you haven't given them the same upbringing and education?' I asked.

'No.'

'Therefore, if we're going to use the women for the same purposes as the men, we have to educate them in the same way.'

宣告无罪,那么他也就免除了道德上败坏的名声,"我说,"所以我想同样的法律在这里也适用。"

"那么就没什么阻止你进行讨论了。"他说。

"那么,我们最好回过头来,"我说,"讨论的恰当时机也许在早些时候,但我们不得不现在来讨论。然而这种方式也许也是可以 c
的——既然男人的事情结束了,那么继续讨论女人的事情,尤其因为这是你们要求我做的。在我看来,对于具有那些我们描述过的品行和教育的人来说,对待他们的孩子和妻子的唯一正确的道路,就是继续向着我们开始给他们指出的那个方向前进。就如你所了解的那样,我们所尽力在做的是,使人在理论上像是畜群的护卫者一样。"

"是的。"

"所以让我们遵循同样的道路,使女人也以同样的方式出生 d
和培养,看看这对我们来说是否恰当。"

"怎么做?"他问道。

"你是否认为母看家狗应该与公看家狗一起分担护卫、狩猎以及公狗所要承担的任何别的职责?或者它们应该待在窝内,由于生育和照料小狗而不能从事这样的工作,而公狗承担所有看护畜群的工作?"

"它们应该分担每一种工作,"他说,"(不然)唯一的理由就 e
是我们把母狗看作是体力上较弱的:公狗是较强壮的。"

"如果你没有给任何两个不同的动物以同样的培养和教育,你能把它们用于同一个目的吗?"我问道。

"不能。"

"所以,如果我们要把女人用于男人一样的目的,那么我们必须用同样的方式去教育她们。"

'Yes.'

452a 'Now, the men were set cultural studies and physical exercise.'

'Yes.'

'So these two subjects had better be set the women too. Then there's the military training: we ought to put them through exactly what we put the men through.'

'That's a reasonable deduction from what you're saying,' he said.

'I suppose a lot of our suggestions would seem ludicrous and outlandish if they became practical realities,' I said.

'No doubt,' he said.

'Which of them do you think would be the most ludicrous?' I asked. 'Isn't it obviously the idea of having women exercising naked in the gymnasia along with the men—and not only young women, but older
b ones as well? I mean, there are old men who come to the gymnasia and are still fond of exercise despite their wrinkled flesh and ugly appearance.'

'Good heavens, yes!' he said. 'That would certainly be thought ludicrous, as things stand today.'

'Well,' I said, 'we've chosen the course of our argument, so we shouldn't let sarcastic jibes worry us. People would crack lots of jokes of all kinds if they were faced in practice with changes of this nature in physical and cultural education, let alone in how armour was worn and horses were ridden.'

c 'You're right,' he said.

'We've started out on this argument, however, so we must take the legislative rough with the smooth. We'll ask those wits not to do what they usually do, but to be serious for a change, and we'll remind them that until quite recently the Greeks used to regard it as shocking and ludicrous for *men* to be seen naked—in fact, in most foreign countries this is still the case. The Cretans were the first to exercise naked (followed by the Spartans), and when they started to do so, it was an

“是的。” 452a

“现在我们让男人学习文艺和进行体育锻炼。”

“是的。”

“所以最好也让女人学习这两门课。然后还有军事教育:我们应该对她们进行和男人完全一样的教育。”

“从你所说过的话来看,这是一个合情合理的推论。”他说。

“我想我们的很多想法如果变成现实的话,看起来会是奇怪而可笑的。”我说。

“毫无疑问。”他说。

“你认为其中的哪一个是最可笑的?”我问道,“显然不就是让女人赤身裸体地与男人一起在体育场上锻炼的想法——不光是年轻的女人,同样还有年老的女人? 我的意思是说,老年人虽然 b
满脸皱纹、相貌丑陋,但还是来到体育场上,热衷于锻炼。”

“天哪! 是的!”他说。“同样的事情放在今天看,那当然会被认为是滑稽可笑的。”

“那么,”我说,“我们已经选择进行我们的讨论,那么我们不应该让冷嘲热讽打扰我们。人们面对这种身体和文艺教育本性的变化,他们会造出很多笑话来,更不用说穿戴甲胄、骑马了。” c

“你说得对。”他说。

“然而我们已经开始讨论了,所以我们必须在法律上化险为夷。我们会要求那些聪明人放弃他们通常的做法,而认真对待变化,我们会提醒他们,直到最近希腊人才常常认为赤身裸体的男子是难堪而可笑的——实际上在许多别的城邦,情况还是这样的。克里特人是首先裸体锻炼的人,后来有斯巴达人,当他们开

d opportunity for the wags of the day to make fun of it all, don't you think?'

'Yes.'

'But when experience proved the superiority of nakedness to clothing in all these kinds of contexts, then superficial mockery waned in the light of what reasoned argument revealed to be best. It was shown to be inane to think anything ludicrous except badness, to try to raise a laugh by regarding as absurd the spectacle of anything except foolishness and badness, and also to seriously hold any standard of beauty except goodness.'

'Absolutely,' he said.

'The first thing we have to reach agreement on, then, is whether or not these proposals are viable, isn't it? And shouldn't we allow that there is room for doubting—whether the doubt is expressed hu-
453a morously or seriously—whether women do have the natural ability to co-operate with men in all their jobs, or in none, or in some but not others (in which case there's the further question of which category warfare belongs to)? Don't you think that this would be the best way for us to make a start and would probably lead to the best conclusion?'

'By far the best,' he said.

'Shall we voice their doubts between ourselves, then, on their behalf,' I asked, 'so that the opposite point of view is not left to fend for itself?'

b 'Why not?' he replied.

'So let's have them say, "You don't need external sceptics, Socrates and Glaucon. You yourselves asserted, right at the start of the founding of your community, that everyone had to do the one job for which his nature had equipped him."'

'Yes, I should say so. Of course we did.'

始这样做的时候，当时人们也嘲笑这种做法，你难道不这样认 d
为吗？”

“是这样想的。”

“但是当经验证明在所有场合下裸露比着装要好的时候，肤浅的嘲笑在理性论证为最善的事物前就消失了。这就证明这是一派胡言：不把邪恶看作可笑的，而把别的东西看作是可笑的，不去讥讽愚昧和邪恶，而试图嘲笑别的景象，将其看作是荒谬的，还
一本正经地坚持任何一种排除了善的美的标准。” e

“确实如此。”他说。

“那么我们首先要达成一致意见的是，这些提议是否可行，不是吗？难道我们不应该留有怀疑的余地——无论这怀疑是风趣地还是严肃地被提出来——无论女人是否具有与男人合作的天
生能力以从事他们所有的工作，或者什么都干不了，或能做某些 453a
事情而做不了另一些事情，（在这种情况下还有进一步的问题：战争属于哪一范畴）？你难道不认为这种方式对我们来说会是最好的开端，并且可能会得出最好的结论？”

“好极了。”他说。

“那么在我们中间是否要站在他们的立场上提出他们的怀疑，”我问到，“这样相反的观点就不会没有人替它辩护了？”

“为什么不呢？”他回答说。 b

“所以让我们替他们说：‘苏格拉底和格劳孔，你们不需要外在的怀疑。你们自己在建立城邦之初的时候就断言，每个人必须做适合其禀赋的工作。’”

“是的，我应该这么说过。我们当然断言过。”

'"And doesn't a woman's nature differ a great deal from a man's?"'

'Of course it does.'

'"So the members of each sex should properly be assigned dif-
c ferent work—work which suits their particular nature—shouldn't they?"'

'Of course.'

'"So your current proposal is bound to be incorrect, and you're contradicting yourselves with the claim that men and women should do the same jobs, despite the enormous differences between their natures." Can you defend our proposals against this accusation, Glaucon?'

'Hardly,' he replied, 'not without some preparation. What I'd do is ask *you* to come up with the response for us—so that's what I am doing.'

'I foresaw this accusation a long time ago, Glaucon,' I said, 'and plenty of other similar criticisms too. That's why I was afraid
d and didn't really want to get involved with regulations about what to do with wives and how to bring up children.'

'No, it certainly doesn't seem to be an easy task,' he remarked.

'No, it isn't,' I said. 'But it's like this: it makes no difference whether you fall into a . little pool or into the middle of the largest ocean—you're still swimming.'

'Yes.'

'So we'd better try swimming to safety out of this sea of argument, hoping for some improbable rescue like a dolphin picking us up.'

'I suppose so,' he said.

e 'Let's see if we can find a way out, then,' I continued. 'We maintain that different natures should do different work, and that men and women do have different natures; and now we're claiming that these different natures should do the same work. Is this what we're accused of?'

'Exactly.'

“‘女人的禀赋不是与男人禀赋有很大区别吗?’” c

“当然有很大区别。”

“‘所以各个性别的成员应该恰当地分配到不同的工作——适合他们特殊本性的工作——不应该这样吗?’”

“当然应该这样。”

“‘所以你们当前的建议必定是错误的,你们与男女应该做同样的工作的说法自相矛盾,而不管他们的禀赋存在巨大的差异。’格劳孔,你能为我们的建议而反驳这种指责吗?”

他回答说:“没有准备我几乎不能做出回答。我想请求你为我们做出回答——这就是我所做的。”

“格劳孔,我早已预见到这个指责了,”我说,“也预见了很多
其他类似的指责。这就是为什么我害怕并且不想真正地牵涉到 d
有关如何对待妻子、如何抚养孩子的法规的原因。”

“在我看来,这确实不是件容易事。”他说。

“不容易,”我说,“然而问题是这样的:无论你掉进小池塘还是掉进大海中央,这都没什么区别——你还是得游泳。”

“是的。”

“所以我们最好试着安全地游出这片辩论的海洋,希望有某些似乎不太可能的急救办法,比如海豚将我们托起。”

“我是这样想的。”他说。 e

“那么让我们来看看是否能找到一条出路,”我继续说,“我们坚持认为不同的禀赋应该做不同的工作,而男女确实具有不同的禀赋;而我们现在宣称这些不同的禀赋应该做同样的工作。这就是我们受到指责的地方吗?”

“正是。”

454a ‘You know, Glaucon, skill at disputation is a splendid thing,’ I said.

‘Why?’

‘Because a lot of people, I think,’ I replied, ‘find themselves unconsciously seduced by it: they think they're practising dialectic, not eristic. The reason for this is their inability to conduct the enquiry by dividing the subject-matter into its various aspects. Instead their goal is the contradiction of statements at the purely verbal level, and they converse with one another eristically, not dialectically.’

‘Yes,’ he said, ‘that's a common phenomenon. But does it have any relevance to our current situation?’

b ‘Nothing could be more relevant,’ I answered. ‘At any rate, we're in danger of unconsciously resorting to disputation.’

‘How?’

‘We're pursuing the idea that different natures should get different occupations with considerable vigour and eristic force at the verbal level, but we haven't spent any time at all enquiring precisely what type of inherent difference and identity we meant when we assigned different occupations to different natures and identical occupations to identical natures, and whether context makes any difference to what we said.’

‘No, we haven't looked into that,’ he said.

c ‘By the same token,’ I said, ‘we might as well ask ourselves, apparently, whether bald men and men with hair have the same nature or completely different natures. And suppose we agreed that they have completely different natures, then we might have bald shoemakers, and make hair disqualify people from being shoemakers, or vice versa.’

‘Which would be absurd,’ he said.

‘And the reason it would be absurd,’ I said, ‘is because earlier

“格劳孔,你知道,争论的技巧真是件了不起的东西。”我说。 454a

“为什么?”

“我想是因为有许多人,”我回答说,“发现他们自己毫无意识地受到它的引诱:他们以为自己在进行辩证,而不是争论。其原因是他们不能把主题划分为它的各个方面来进行探讨。相反,他们的目标是在纯粹字面层次上对陈述进行反驳,他们用争论术而不是辩证法相互进行交谈。”

“是的,”他说,“这是个很普遍的现象。但它与我们当前的情况有什么关系吗?”

“太有关系了,”我回答说,“不管怎么说,我们处于不知不觉 b
地诉诸于争论的危险中。”

“怎么说?”

“关于不同的禀赋应该从事不同的职业这一观念,我们花费了相当大的气力和辩论的智力,在文字层面上纠缠不清,但是我们却并没有花费任何时间来精确地查究一下:当我们将不同的职业分配给不同禀赋的人,以及同一职业分配给相同禀赋者时,我们所指的内在禀赋上的差别与同一是哪种类别的,以及是否语境上的不同才使得我们所说的产生若干差异。”

“我们没有考察过。”他说。

“同样,”我说,“我们似乎也可以问我们自己,秃头的人与长 c
头发的人是否具有同样的禀赋还是具有完全不同的禀赋。要是我们同意他们具有完全不同的禀赋,那么我们可能有秃头的鞋匠,而不让长头发的人成为鞋匠,或者相反。”

“这是荒谬的。”他说。

“之所以可笑,”我说,“其原因可能在于早先我们没有在绝对的

we weren't talking about identity or difference of nature in any abso-
d lute sense. We had in mind only that type of difference or similarity which is relevant to identity of occupation, didn't we? We meant, for example, that a man with a medical mind and a woman with a medical mind have the same nature. Don't you agree?'

'I do.'

'Whereas a male doctor and a male joiner have different natures?'

'Absolutely.'

'So if either the male or the female gender turns out to be better than the other gender at some profession or occupation, then we'll claim that this is an occupation which ought to be assigned to that gender. But if the only difference turns out to be that females bear off-
e spring, while males mount females, then we'll say that this doesn't yet bring us any closer at all to proving that men and women are different in the context we're talking about, and we'll continue to think that our guardians and their women should have the same occupations.'

'Right,' he said.

455a 'This is exactly what we'll require our opponent to explain to us next, then—for which of the professions or occupations which bear on the organization of a community are there inherent differences between men and women?'

'Yes, that would be a fair question.'

'And he might well copy what you said a few moment ago, and reply that it's hard to come up with an adequate response on the spur of the moment, but that research would make it easy.'

'Yes, he might.'

'Shall we ask our disputatious friend to accompany us, then, to see if we can prove to him that there is no occupation which bears on
b the administration of a community which belongs especially to women or to men?'

'Yes.'

意义上谈论禀赋的相同与差异。我们所考虑的只是那种与工作相关的差异和相同,不是吗？比如说,我们认为一个具有医生心智的男人和一个具有医生心智的女人具有相同的禀赋。你难道不同意吗?” d

“我同意。”

“而一个男医生和一个男木匠就具有不同的禀赋吗?”

“毫无疑问。”

“所以如果在某些职业或工作中,如果男性或女性表现得比对方更加优越,那么我们就会说,某种工作就应该指派给男性或女性。但如果差异只是女性生孩子而男性授精于女性,那么我们会说,这根本不能使我们证明在我们所讨论的情形下男女是 e 有差异的,我们还会认为卫士和他们的女人应该拥有同样的工作。”

“对的。”他说。

“那么这正是接下来我们要求我们的论敌向我们解释的——就与城邦的组织有关的职业或工作来说,男女在禀赋上有哪些差 455a 异呢?”

“这是个很好的问题。”

“他可能会像你刚才那样回答说,很难立刻就给出一个充分的答复,但加以探讨就会使答复比较容易。”

“是的,他可能会这样。”

“那么,我们就要求我们那些好争辩的朋友和我们一道,来看看我们是否能够证明,就一个城邦的管理而言,并没有什么职业是专门属于女性或男性的,我们可以这样做吗?” b

“是的。”

'"All right, then," we'll say to him, "here's a question for you. When you distinguish people as naturally competent or incompetent in a particular context, don't you mean that some people find it easy to learn that subject, while others find it hard? And that some people start to do their own broadly speaking original work in the subject after only a little study, while others can't even retain what they've learnt after even a lot of study and care? And that some people's bodies are sufficiently subservient to their minds, while others' are obstructive? Aren't these the features—there are more too—which enable you to
c define some people as naturally competent, and others as naturally incompetent?"'

'Indisputably,' he said.

''Well, do you know of any subject on earth in which men do not outclass women in all these respects?' Anyway, do we need to extend the conversation by discussing sewing, looking after pancakes, and boiling vegetables, which women are supposed to be good at, and where defeat makes them the most ridiculous creatures in the world?'

d 'You're right,' he said. 'The one gender is far superior to the other in just about every sphere. It may be that many women are better than many men at many things, but by and large it is as you say.'

'Therefore, my friend, there's no administrative job in a community which belongs to a woman *qua* woman, or to a man *qua* man,' I said. 'Innate qualities have been distributed equally between the two sexes, and women can join in every occupation just as much
e as men, although they are the weaker sex in all respects.'

'Yes.'

'So shall we assign the men all the work and leave the women nothing?'

'Definitely not.'

'The point being that some women may be good at medicine or

“我们会对他说:‘那么好吧,有个问题要问你。当你把人分为
禀赋上善于或不善于做某件事的时候,你指的不就是有些人觉得某
个东西学起来容易,而另一些人觉得很难?不就是说,一些人在某
个方面稍加学习即可开始做其宽泛意义上的初始工作,而其他人即
便经过很长时间的学习与照顾,甚至连记都记不住?不就是说,有
些人心灵手巧、身随心动,而其他人则是笨手笨脚、身为心碍?这 c
些——还有更多的——不就是使你对一些人禀赋上符合要求而
另一些人禀赋上不符合要求做出辨别的外在特征吗?’”

“毫无疑问。”他说。

“‘那么你是否知道世上有些事情男人在所有这些方面都超
不过女人?’不管怎么说,我们是否有必要将我们的讨论扩展到讨
论缝纫、烧饭、做菜上去,女人理所当然地擅长这些事情,而男人
超过她们则会使之成为世上最可笑的人。” d

“你说得对,”他说,“一种性别在所有领域要比另一种性别优越得多。许多女人可能在许多事情上比许多男人要优越,但总的来说,是你说的那样。”

“所以,我的朋友,没有任何城邦的管理工作因为女人在做而
属于女人,或因为男人在做而属于男人的。”我说,“内在的品质是
同样被分配给两性的,女人能像男人一样能参加所有的工作,虽
然她们在所有方面都是较弱的。” e

“是的。”

“由此我们是否要把所有工作都指派给男人,而让女人什么都不做?”

“肯定不是。”

“关键是有些女人可能擅长医术或音乐,即使别的女人并不

music, even if others aren't. That's what we'll say, I suppose.'

'Of course.'

456a 'And isn't it the case that some women may be good at sports or warfare, while others aren't?'

'I should say so.'

'And philosophically inclined or disinclined too? And some may be passionate, while others aren't?'

'Again, yes.'

'Some women may make good guardians, then, while others won't, since these were the innate qualities we selected as the marks of men who would make good guardians, weren't they?'

'They were.'

'Both women and men, then, have the same natural ability for guarding a community, and it's just that women are innately weaker than men.'

'I suppose so.'

b 'These are the women, then, who should be selected to live with the male guardians and to join them in guardianship. They are endowed with the natural ability to do so, and they are from the same stock as the male guardians.'

'Quite.'

'And the same occupations should be assigned to people with the same natures, shouldn't they?'

'Yes.'

'So we've come full circle back to where we were before. We're agreed that it isn't unnatural for the wives of our guardians to be set cultural studies and physical exercise.'

'Absolutely.'

'Our regulations were viable, then, and weren't just wishful thinking,

擅长。我想这就是我们会说的。”

“当然。”

“不是有这样的情况吗:有的女人可能擅长运动或战斗,而别的女人并不擅长?” 456a

“可以这么说。”

“是否有的女人也爱好或厌恶哲学? 有些可能有激情,而有些没有?”

“是的。”

“那么有些女人可能成为好卫士,而另一些不能,因为这些就是我们选出来作为男性好卫士标志的内在品质,不是吗?”

“是的。”

“那么,男人女人都同样具有保卫城邦的天赋才能,只是女人天生比男人弱而已。”

“我想是的。”

“那么,这些女人应该被挑选出来与男性卫士生活在一起并 b
参与他们的保卫之职。她们具有做这种工作的天赋才能,她们具有和男性卫士同样的禀赋。”

“很正确。”

“相同的工作应该被分派给具有相同禀赋的人,不是吗?”

“是的。”

“所以我们绕了个圈回到了前面的地方。我们同意,对我们卫士的妻子来说,学习文艺和体育锻炼并非是不自然的。”

“确实如此。”

“那么,我们的规定是可行的,并不是一厢情愿,因为它们合乎

c since they're compatible with nature. In fact, it is current practice, which contravenes this, which is apparently more likely to be unnatural.'

'So it seems.'

'Now, we were trying to discover whether our proposals were viable and for the best, weren't we?'

'Yes.'

'And we've concluded that they're viable, haven't we?'

'Yes.'

'So next we need to reach agreement on whether they're for the best, don't we?'

'Obviously.'

'Well, in order to make women good at guarding, we won't be providing them with a different education from the one that works for men, will we? After all, it's the same nature the educational system takes on in both cases.'

d 'Yes, it is.'

'Now, I wonder what you think about this idea.'

'Which one?'

'The notion that some men are better than others. Perhaps you think they're all the same?'

'Definitely not.'

'In the community we're founding, then, do you think the guardians or the shoemakers will prove to be the better people, when the guardians have been educated in the way we've described and the shoemakers have been educated in their craft?'

'I'm not going to treat that as a serious question,' he said.

'I see,' I said. 'And what about the rest of the citizen body?

禀赋。事实上，是当前的做法违反了自然，它们似乎是更不自然的。” c

“看来如此。”

“现在，我们试着来考察一下我们的建议是否可行，是否是最好的，怎么样？”

“好的。”

“我们已经得出结论，它们是可行的，不是吗？”

“是的。”

“所以接下来我们需要达成一致意见，这就是它们是否是最好的，不是吗？”

“显然。”

“好，为了使女人善于护卫，我们不会给她们提供与男人不同的教育，是吗？毕竟，在两种情况下教育体制所教导的是同样的禀赋。” d

“是的。”

“现在，我想知道你对这个想法是怎么看的？”

“哪个？”

“某些男人比其他男人要优秀的观点。也许你认为他们都是一样的？”

“肯定是不一样的。”

“那么，在我们建立的城邦里，当卫士以我们描述过的方式受到教育，鞋匠接受了他们的技术教育之后，你认为是卫士还是鞋匠会成为较优秀的男人？”

“我不会把那当作一个严肃的问题的。”他说。

“我明白了，”我说，“那么和其余的公民比呢？卫士将是最优秀 e

Will the guardians be the best?'

'By far the best.'

e 'And won't the women we're talking about be better than all the rest of the women?'

'Again, by a long way,' he said.

'Is anything better for a community than for it to engender women and men who are exceptionally good?'

'No.'

'And this is the effect of cultural studies and physical education
457a when they're employed as we have described, isn't it?'

'Of course.'

'In addition to being viable, then, the regulation we were making for our community was for the best as well.'

'Yes.'

'So the wives of the guardians ought to strip off; they'll be protected by goodness rather than clothes. They'll take part in warfare and whatever else guarding the community involves, and this will be their one and only occupation. However, they will receive lighter duties than the men, because of the weakness of their sex. Any man
b who treats the fact that women are exercising naked with goodness as their goal as a reason for laughter is "plucking laughter unripe"; we now appreciate that he has no awareness of what he's laughing at or what he's doing, since it's impossible, and will remain impossible, to improve on the idea that anything beneficial is commendable, and anything harmful is deplorable.'

'Absolutely.'

'So may we now claim to have escaped this first wave, as it were? We've discussed what legislation to enact where women are concerned and managed to avoid being completely swamped while decreeing

的吗?"

"是最优秀的。"

"我们所说的女人不也比所有其余的女人更加优秀吗?"

"也是要优秀得多。"他说。

"对一个城邦来说还有比产生非常优秀的男女更好的事情吗?"

"没有。"

"这就是受过我们所说的音乐和体育教育的结果,不是吗?" 457a

"当然是的。"

"那么我们为城邦所提出的规定不光是可行的,而且还是最好的。"

"是的。"

"所以卫士的妻子应该赤身裸体;她们会受到美德而非衣服的保护。她们参加战争以及其他城防事务,这是她们的一个工作并且是唯一的工作。然而,与男人相比,由于女性的柔弱,她们会得到较轻的职责。女人裸体操练,以美德为她们的目标,任何以此作为嘲笑理由的男人就是'采摘未熟之果';我们现在认 b
为他对自己的所笑所行毫无意识,因为现在不可能,将来也不可能对这种说法做改进:任何有益的事物是美好的,任何有害的事物是丑陋的。"

"毫无疑问。"

"所以现在我们可以说已经避过了这第一个浪头,好比是这样吗?关于妇女,我们讨论了需要建立什么法律,并设法避免了被彻底颠覆,同时还规定了我们的男女卫士须得分担他们所有 c

c that our male and female guardians have to share all their occupations. In fact, the argument was internally consistent in its claim that the proposals were both viable and beneficial.'

'It's a pretty sizeable wave you're escaping,' he remarked.

'You'll be saying it's pretty insignificant when you see the next one,' I said.

'I won't see it unless you tell me about it,' he said.

'It's legislation which follows from what we've just enacted and from all the laws we made earlier too, I think,' I said.

'But what is it?'

d 'That there's to be no such thing as private marriage between these women and these men: all the women are to be shared among all the men. And that the children are also to be shared, with no parent knowing which child is his, or child knowing his parent.'

'This is a far bigger wave than the first one,' he said, 'and its viability and value are far more likely to be doubted.'

'I don't see how its advantages can be called into question,' I said. 'If the sharing of wives and children is feasible, it's bound to be extremely valuable. I should think that most of the doubt will be concentrated upon whether or not it's viable.'

e 'No, there are plenty of reasons to be sceptical about both aspects,' he said.

'You mean I can't separate the two arguments?' I said. 'I was hoping I'd escape from one of them, by securing your agreement to the idea's advantages, and that I'd only be left with discussing its viability.'

'But you were caught escaping,' he said, 'and you have to justify both aspects.'

'I must pay the penalty,' I said, 'but I ask for a little bit of leniency: please let me indulge in some lazy thinking, as someone out

的工作。事实上，在说这个建议是既可行且有益的时候，论据和观点本质上是前后一致的。”

“你避过的可是个不小的浪头啊。”他说。

“当你看到下一个的时候，你就会说这个浪头并不大了。”我说。

“除非你告诉我，否则我看不见。”他说。

“我想，是一条从我们刚才建立的以及所有从我们早先建立的法律中推导出来的法律。”我说。

“是什么呢？”

“在这些男女之间没有私自婚姻这种事情：所有的男人共有 d
所有的女人。孩子也都是共有的，没有父母知道哪个孩子是他的，也没有孩子知道其父母。”

“这个浪头比前一个大得多，”他说，“其可行性和价值似乎更值得怀疑。”

“我并不认为其益处会受到怀疑，”我说，“如果共妻共子是可行的，那么这必定是非常有价值的。我想最大的怀疑会集中在它是否可行吧。”

“不，有很多理由对两方面怀疑。”他说。 e

“你的意思是说我不能把两个论证分开？”我说，“我本希望通过，使你同意这个想法的好处，我就能逃脱其中的一个，剩下的我只要讨论其可行性就行了。”

“但假设你逃跑被抓住了呢，”他说，“你必须对两个方面都作出解释。”

“我必须受罚，”我说，“但我请求开恩：请让我放纵自己懒于
思考，就像人们出去独自散步一样。你知道那样的人并不会困扰 458a

for a solitary stroll might well do. You know how someone like that doesn't bother with the prior question of how to fulfil his desires. He doesn't want to exhaust himself wondering whether or not their fulfilment is viable, so he just imagines that they've been fulfilled and then sorts everything else out and happily details the kinds of things he's going to do when they are realized—and so makes a mind that was al-
b ready lazy even lazier. Now, I'm feeling enervated myself at the moment, and I'd like to delay investigating the proposals'viability until later. On the assumption that they are viable, I'll now—with your permission—look into how the rulers will sort them out in practice and prove that nothing could be more advantageous to the community and to the guardians than their enactment. This is what we'll try to investigate together first, if you approve of my suggestion, and then we'll tackle the other issue later.'

'That's all right by me,' he said. 'Go ahead.'

'Well, in my opinion,' I said, 'if the rulers and their auxilia-
c ries live up to their names, then the auxiliaries will be prepared to carry out instructions, and the rulers will be prepared to give them instructions. These instructions will sometimes be in direct conformity with law, but sometimes— where we've left the possibility—they'll simply reflect our legal principles.'

'That sounds reasonable,' he said.

'Now, you are their legislator,' I said, 'and once the women have been through the same selection procedure as the men, you'll send the ones who match the men's innate qualities as closely as possible to join them. Since they share living-quarters and mess-halls and since none of
d them has any private property of this kind, they will coexist and commingle during their exercises and their educational programme in general, and consequently their instincts are bound to lure them into having sex with one another. Don't you think that's bound to happen?'

'I don't think it's logically necessary,' he replied, 'but the imperative is coming from the sex drive, and I suppose most people find the proddings of the sex drive far more influential and compelling than those of logic!'

于前一个如何满足他愿望的问题。他并不想殚精竭虑地去考虑得到满足是否可行,所以他只是设想它们已经得到满足,然后把别的事情安排起来,高高兴兴地详述当实现后他要想做的那些事情——这样就使得一个已经很懒的心灵更加懒散。此刻,我觉得自己无力,我想把对建议的可行性推迟到以后研究。假设它们是 b
可行的,现在我——在你的允许之下——将考察统治者会怎样在实行起来时安排它们,并且证明对于城邦和卫士来说,没有什么比他们的法规更有益的了。这是我们一起首先要试图加以考察的,如果你同意我的建议的话,那么我们会考察别的问题。"

"我同意,"他说,"继续吧。"

"好,在我看来,"我说,"如果统治者和他们的辅助者名副其实的话,那么辅助者会准备实践指示而统治者会准备给他们以指 c
示。这些指示有时是与法律直接相一致的,但有时——我们留了余地——他们自己斟酌我们的法律原则。"

"这听上去很有道理。"他说。

"现在你是他们的立法者,"我说,"一旦女人通过与男人同样的选举程序选出,你就把那些与男人的内在品质尽可能接近的女人派给男人并加入他们。因为他们同吃同住,因为他们当中没有人拥有任何这类的私有财产,所以一般而言,在他们的训练及其教育计划进行期间,他们共同生存并混合在一起,结果便是,他们的内在冲动必定会引诱他们彼此交媾。你难道不认为那是必然 d
会发生的吗?"

"我并不认为这在逻辑上是必然的,"他回答说,"但是这又是必然的,这种必然性来自于性欲的驱使,而且我猜想大多数人会认为,性欲冲动的激励比那些逻辑都更有势力,也更强烈而急迫。"

'They certainly do,' I said. 'The next point, Glaucon, is that in a community which is to be happy, undisciplined sex (or undisci-
e plined anything else, for that matter) is a profanity, and the rulers won't allow it.'

'That's because it's wrong,' he said.

'So obviously our next task is to ensure that marriages are as far removed from profanity as possible—which will happen if they contribute as much as possible towards the community's welfare.'

'Absolutely.'

459a 'So we need to ask how to maximize this contribution of theirs. Now, Glaucon, I've seen lots of hunting dogs and fine birds in your house, so I wonder whether you've noticed a particular aspect of their mating and procreation.'

'What?' he asked.

'The main point is this. Isn't it true that although they're all pedigree creatures, some of them prove to be exceptionally good?'

'Yes.'

'So do you breed from all of them indiscriminately, or do you take care to choose the outstanding ones as much as possible?'

'I choose the outstanding ones.'

b 'And of these, do you choose the youngest ones or the oldest ones or, wherever feasible, the ones in their prime?'

'The ones in their prime.'

'And wouldn't you expect the result of failure to follow this breeding programme to be the deterioration of your strain of birds and dogs?'

'Yes,' he said.

'Does a different principle apply to horses and other creatures, do you think?' I asked.

'It would be odd if it did,' he said.

“确实如此，”我说，“格劳孔，下一个要点是，在一个想要幸福快乐的城邦中，无节制的性欲（或就此而论任何其他无节制的东西），都是一种亵渎，而且管理者是不会允许的。” e

“那是因为它是不对的。”他说。

“所以显然我们下一个工作似乎就是，要保证婚姻尽可能地远离亵渎——这样就最可能有助于城邦得到幸福。”

“毫无疑问。”

“所以我们需要问的是，如何使它们的这种好处最大化。格 459a
劳孔，现在我在你家里看到很多猎犬和良种鸡，所以我想知道你是否留意过它们交配和生殖的特殊之处。”

“什么？”他问道。

“主要问题是这样的。虽然它们都是些纯种的动物，是否有一些显得格外优秀呢？”

“是的。”

“所以你把它们全部都不加区别地繁殖，还是关注并挑选最优秀的那些？”

“我挑选那些最优秀的。”

“在它们当中，你选择那些最年幼的还是最老的，或者要是可 b
能，选择正值壮年的那些？”

“正值壮年的那些。”

“不这样育种就会导致你的鸡和狗品种退化，你绝不希望有这样的结果吧？”

“是的。”他说。

“你认为不同的原则适用于马和其他动物吗？”我问道。

“如果这样的话可就奇怪了。”他说。

'My dear Glauconl' I exclaimed. 'We're going to need really exceptional rulers if the same principle applies to humans too.'

'Well, it does,' he said. 'What do you make of it?'

c 'That they'll be compelled to rely a great deal on medicines,' I said. 'As you know, we regard treating people whose bodies don't require medicine, but who are prepared to follow a diet, as within the competence of a less accomplished doctor; when medicines are called for, however, a more courageous doctor is evidently required.'

'This is true, but what are you driving at?'

'That the rulers will probably have to rely a lot on falsehood and deceit,' I said, 'to help their subjects. You'll remember our claim that lies and so on are useful as a type of medicine.'

d 'Yes, and there's nothing wrong with using them like that,' he said.

'Well, it occurs to me that this usage is particularly important in the domain of mating and procreation.'

'Why?'

'It follows from our conclusions so far that sex should preferably take place between men and women who are outstandingly good, and should occur as little as possible between men and women of a vastly inferior stamp. It also follows that the offspring of the first group should be brought up, while the offspring of the second group shouldn't. This is how to maximize the potential of our flock. And the
e fact that all this is happening should be concealed from everyone except the rulers themselves, if the herd of guardians is to be as free as possible from conflict.'

'You're quite right,' he said.

'So what we, as legislators, have to do is institute certain holidays and religious ceremonies, during which we'll bring the brides and the grooms together; and we'll have our poets

“我亲爱的格劳孔！”我大声说道，“要是把同样的原则也运用于人类，那我们就需要真正的高明的统治者了。”

“是的，”他说，“这事你是怎么看的？” c

“我们会不得不依赖大量的药物，”我说，“你知道，对于照料那些身体不需要药物又肯遵循饮食制度的人来说，我们认为这是在不那么高明的医生的能力范围之内的；然而当需要用药的时候，则显然需要一个更有勇气的医生。”

“对的，但你指的是什么意思？”

“统治者可能会不得不相当多地依靠谎言和欺骗以帮助被统治者，”我说，“你要记住我们的想法，即谎言等作为一种药物是有
用的。” d

“是的，那样使用谎言不是错的。”他说。

“那么，在我看来在结婚和生育方面使用谎言是尤其的重要。”

“为什么？”

“从我们上面的结论中得出，最好应该在最出色的男女之间发生性关系，而尽可能不让最差的男女发生关系。也可以推论说，第一个群体的后代应该得到抚养，而第二个群体的后代则不应该得到抚养。这就是如何使我们的群体的潜力最大化。并且所有这些正在发生的实情，除了统治者本人之外，其他的每一个
人都应该被隐瞒住，如果想要成群结队的卫士们尽可能地不要陷 e
入内讧的话，还必须这样做。”

“你说得非常正确。”他说。

“所以作为立法者，我们要做的就是规定某些节日和宗教仪式，在那期间我们把新娘新郎带到一起来；我们会让我们的诗人

460a compose suitable wedding-odes for them. We'll leave the quantity of marriages up to the rulers: they'll want to keep the number of men in the community more or less constant, bearing in mind wars and epidemics and so on, so as to do their best to avoid increasing or decreasing the community's size.'

'Right,' he said.

'We'd better set up a subtle lottery, then, so that those inferior men we spoke of blame chance and not the rulers every mating-time.'

'Definitely,' he said.

b 'And the main privilege and reward that any young men who are good at fighting or at some other activity ought to receive is the right to sleep with the women more frequently, so that as many as possible of the children are fathered by this kind of person, and there is at the same time a plausible reason for this happening.'

'Right.'

'Now, the officials whose job it is to take charge of any children who are born—and they could be men, women, or some of each, since positions of authority are open to both men and women equally, of course...'

'Yes.'

c 'Well, I suppose they'll take the children of good parents to the crèhe and hand them over to nurses (who live in a separate section of the community); and they'll find some suitable way of hiding away in some secret and secluded spot the children of worse parents and any handicapped children of good parents.'

'Otherwise our breed of guardians will become tainted,' he said.

'And they'll take care of the children's feeding by bringing the
d mothers to the crèhe when their breasts are full of milk, although they'll devise all sorts of stratagems to make sure that no mother recognizes her own child. If the mothers' supply of milk is inadequate, they'll bring in other women to supplement it. They'll take care that the mothers don't breast-feed for too long, and they'll assign sleepless nights and all the hard work to wet-nurses and nannies.'

为他们创作恰当的婚礼赞词。我们会把结婚的数量留待统治者 460a
去考虑;他们要保持城邦中的人口几乎维持不变,要考虑战争、疾病等等,这样他们就可以尽可能地避免城邦规模的扩大或缩小。"

"是的。"他说。

"那么,我们最好规定一个巧妙的抽签办法,这样我们所谓的低劣之人每次婚配的时候只能怪运气而不是统治者。"

"诚然是的。"

"任何善于战斗或别的活动的年轻人,所得到的主要特权和 b
奖赏,应该是与女人更频繁地同床的权利,这样这个人作为父亲就可以尽可能多地生孩子,同时这样做也是有令人信服的理由。"

"对的。"

"那么,官员的工作就是照管生下来的孩子——他们可以是男的或女的,或有男有女,因为官职当然是对男女同样开放的。当然……"

"是的。"

"那么,我想他们会把优秀的父母生的孩子送到育婴室去,并 c
把他们交给保姆,他们单独住在城邦的一个部分;对于那些低劣的父母生的孩子和任何优秀的父母生的残疾孩子,他们会找一些恰当的办法把他们藏在秘密而隐蔽的地方。"

"否则我们卫士的种族就会玷污。"他说。

"他们会把乳房有奶水的母亲带到育婴室,给孩子喂奶以照
看孩子,但他们设计了各种手段以确保没有母亲能认出她自己的 d
孩子。如果母亲的奶水供应不足,他们会带来别的女人提供补充。他们会注意不让母亲哺乳过久,他们会把守夜和其他所有麻烦的工作指派给奶妈和保姆。"

'You're making child-bearing very easy for the wives of the guardians,' he remarked.

'Which is only right and proper,' I said. 'But let's get on with the next item of our proposals. We said that the children's parents should be in their prime, didn't we?'

'True.'

e 'Do you agree that a woman is in her prime for twenty years or so, and a man for thirty years or so?'

'Which twenty or thirty years?' he asked.

'A woman can serve the community by producing children between the ages of twenty and forty, a man by fathering children from when he passes his peak as a runner's until the age of fifty-five.'

461a 'Yes, in both cases this is the period when they're in their physical and intellectual prime,' he said.

'Therefore, if the production of children for the community is encroached on by anyone too old or too young, we'll say that he has sinned against both gods and men by fathering a child who (if the matter goes unnoticed and the child is born) will not have been affected by the rites and prayers which the priestesses and priests and the whole community pray at each wedding-festival—for every generation of children to improve on their parents' goodness and value—but will instead have been born under the influence of darkness and dire
b lack of self-control.'

'Right,' he said.

'And even if a man's age doesn't exclude him from procreation,' I said, 'the same regulation will apply if he has sex with a woman of the right age when a ruler has not paired them. We'll declare the child he's trying to foist on the community a bastard, without standing or sanction.'

'Quite right,' he said.

“对于卫士的妻子来说,你使养育孩子变得很轻松了。”他评论说。

“这是唯一正确和恰当的,”我说,“不过让我们继续我们建议的下一个规划。我们说过孩子的父母应该是正值壮年,不是吗?”

“对的。”

“你同意精力最好的女子是二十岁左右而男的是三十岁 e
左右?”

“二十几或三十几?”他问道。

“女人在二十到四十岁时生孩子为城邦服务,男人作为孩子的父亲是从跑步最快的年龄到五十五岁。”

“是的,在这段时间两者都处于他们生理和智力的最旺盛时 461a
期。”他说。

“所以,如果为城邦生育孩子的事受到太年老或太年轻的人的侵犯,那么我们会说他作为孩子的父亲不光亵渎了诸神而且也亵渎了男人,如果事情没有被发觉而孩子却生下来了,那么孩子将得不到男女祭司和整个城邦在每个婚礼上所进行的祝福和祷告——祈求每一代孩子都胜过父母的美德和价值——相反他们
将在阴暗的、极度缺乏自制的影响之下被养育。” b

“对的。”他说。

我说:“即使一个男人的年龄允许其生育,如果当统治者没有让他们成婚,而他与一个适龄女子交媾,那么同样的法规也是适用的。我们会说他试图把一个没有身份或没有得到准许的私生子强塞给城邦。”

“非常正确。”他说。

'When the men and women get past the age for procreation, I imagine we'll release them and allow them the freedom to have sex with anyone they want—except that a man is forbidden to have sex with a
c daughter and her female offspring, and a mother and her female precursors, and a woman is forbidden to have sex with a son, a father, and their male descendants and precursors. But before we release them, we'll impress upon them the importance of trying their best to abort absolutely every pregnancy that occurs, and of ensuring that any baby born despite their efforts is not brought up.'

'Yes, that's a sensible proposal,' he said. 'But how are they to tell who are whose fathers and daughters and so on?'

d 'They won't be able to,' I said. 'However, a man will call any child born in the tenth month, and in the seventh month of course, after he participated in one of the wedding-ceremonies a son (if the child is male) or daughter (if female); they'll call him father and their children will be his grandchildren, who'll regard his generation as grandfathers and grandmothers, and who'll count anyone born in the period when their mothers and fathers were producing children as
e their sisters and brothers. The result will be what we were just saying: they'll avoid sex with one another. However, the law will allow brothers and sisters to sleep together, if the lottery turns out that way and the Delphic oracle has no objection.'

'You're quite right,' he said.

'So this is how your community's guardians will share women and children, Glaucon. We next need to have the argument confirm that this is basically in keeping with the constitution and that it is by far the best course of action. Isn't that the thing to do?'

462a 'Definitely,' he said.

'Shouldn't we initiate the enquiry by asking ourselves which factor, in our opinion, makes the most important positive contribution towards the organization of a community—and this is the factor a legislator has to aim for when he's making his laws—and which factor does the most harm? Then we should try to see whether these new proposals

“当男人女人过了生育的年龄，我想我们让他们解脱吧，让他们自由地与任何他们想要的人做爱——但男人禁止与女儿和她的女性后代、母亲以及女性长辈交媾，女人禁止与儿子、父亲、她 c
们的男性后代和长辈交媾。但在我们让他们解脱之前，我们要让他们记住重要的是每次怀孕一定要尽可能堕胎，以及无论他们付出多大的精力，任何这样生下来的孩子肯定是不能抚养的。”

“是的，这是个明智的建议，”他说，“但他们怎么辨认谁是谁的父亲和女儿等等？” d

“他们辨认不出，”我说，“然而，一个男人可以把任何在他参加了一个婚礼之后有十个月或七个月大的孩子称作儿子，如果是个男孩的话；或称作女儿，如果是个女孩的话；他们称他为父亲，他们的孩子将是他的孙子孙女，孙子孙女把他的一代人称作祖父祖母，他们把任何与他们父母生育孩子时同时出生的人称作兄弟姐妹。结果便是我们刚才说过的那样：他们要避免发生性关系。 e
然而，如果抽签得出并且德尔斐神谕不反对的话，那么法律会允许兄弟姐妹睡在一起。”

“你说得很对。”他说。

“格劳孔，所以这就是你们城邦的卫士共有妇女和儿童的方式。我们接下来需要证实这说法：这基本上是与政治制度相一致的并且是最好的做法。我们不就是要这样做吗？”

“确实如此。”他说。 462a

“我们不就应该以向自己提问来开始我们的探究：在我们看来，对于城邦的组织来说，什么因素具有最重要的正面作用——一个立法者制定他的法律时必须以这个因素为目的——什么因素是最有害的？然后我们应该尽力去考察这些新建议是否与善

of ours match the traces of the good factor and not of the harmful one.'

'Absolutely.'

b 'Could we describe anything as worse for a community, do you think, than something which tears it apart and destroys its unity? And could we describe anything as better for a community than something which binds it together and unifies it?'

'No, we couldn't.'

'And isn't it the sharing of feelings of pleasure and distress which binds a community together—when (in so far as it is feasible) the whole citizen body feels more or less the same pleasure or distress at the same gains and losses?'

'Absolutely,' he said.

'And isn't it, on the other hand, the non-sharing of these feelings which causes disintegration—when something happens to the community or some of its members and the attendant feelings range from depression to delight?'

c 'Naturally.'

'And doesn't this privatization of feelings happen when the members of a community are out of tune with one another when they use expressions like 'mine' and 'not mine', and likewise when they identify something as foreign?'

'Absolutely.'

'So the best-run community is the one in which as many people as possible use these expressions, 'mine' and 'not mine', to refer to the same things in the same respects. Yes?'

'Definitely.'

'And the one which approximates as much as possible to a single human being? I mean, when someone's finger is hurt, the whole federation, which encompasses body and mind in its span and forms a single organized system under its ruling part, is aware of the pain and
d feels it, as a whole, along with the injured part, and that's why we

的因素而不是与有害的因素的轨迹相一致。”

“确实如此。”

“对于一个城邦来说，你认为我们还能说出有什么事情比撕裂和破坏其统一的事情更坏的吗？对于一个城邦来说， b
我们还能说出有什么事情比使之结合和统一的事情更好的吗？”

“我们说不出。”

“不就是同甘共苦使城邦结为一体——就其是可行的而言，当公民整体都对于共同得失同甘共苦的时候？”

“毫无疑问。”他说。

“另一方面，不就是不共同分享这些情感而导致了分裂——当城邦中或某些成员身上发生了什么事情，随之而来的情感却哀乐不同的时候？” c

“自然如此。”

“当城邦中的成员使用像‘我的’、‘不是我的’这样的表达而变得相互不和谐的时候，同样当他们把某件东西看作是异己的时候，这种个体化的情感不就产生了？”

“毫无疑问。”

“所以在治理得最好的城邦中有尽可能多的人用‘我的’、‘不是我的’来指同样一些方面的同样一些事情，是吗？”

“诚然是的。”

“城邦尽可能地像一个人？我的意思是说，当某个人的手指受了伤的时候，由身体和心灵构成的并在其统治部分的管理下形成一个有机系统的整体，并与受伤的部分一起作为一个整体意识并感到了疼痛，这就是为什么我们说一个人伤了他的手指的原 d

say that the person has hurt his finger. And the same principle applies to any other part of a person, whether it's experiencing the discomfort of pain or the relief of pleasure.'

'Yes, I agree,' he said. 'And, to answer your question, yes—the more closely a community's organization approximates to this situation, the better run that community is.'

'So in this kind of community, any experience—whether good or bad—of any of its members will in all likelihood be regarded as its
e own experience, and the community as a whole will share the affected member's feelings of pleasure or pain.'

'Yes, that's bound to be the case in a well-regulated community,' he said.

'Now would be a good time', I said, 'for us to return to our community, and see whether it is the preeminent example of a community with the qualities we've just formulated, or whether some other community surpasses it.'

'Yes, we ought to do that,' he said.

463a 'All right. Now, our community—like every community—contains both rulers and commoners, doesn't it?'

'Yes.'

'Who all refer to one another as fellow citizens?'

'Of course.'

'But in other communities the commoners call the rulers something else besides "fellow citizens", don't they?'

'Yes, in most communities they call them "masters", and in democracies they call them just that—"rulers".'

'What about in our community? How will the general populace think of the rulers, apart from thinking of them as fellow citizens?'

因。同样的道理也适用于人的任何别的部分，无论经历痛苦的煎熬还是快乐的安慰。”

“是的，我同意，”他说，“对你的问题的回答是肯定的——一个城邦组织越接近这种情况，那个城邦就治理得越好。”

“所以在这样的城邦中，任何其成员的遭遇——无论是好的还是坏的——都会被看作是它自己的遭遇，整个城邦会共承其成 e
员的快乐或痛苦的感受。”

“是的，在一个治理得很好的城邦里情况必定是这样的。”他说。

我说：“现在对我们来说是回到我们的城邦的好时机，看看它是否是一个杰出的榜样，具有我们刚才说过的品质，或者是否有某个别的城邦超过了它。”

“是的，我们应该那样做。”他说。

“好吧。那么我们的城邦——像所有的城邦一样——包含了 463a
统治者和民众，不是吗？”

“是的。”

“他们都互称公民吗？”

“当然。”

“但在其他城邦中除了称统治者为‘公民’外还称呼他们别的，不是吗？”

“是的，在大多数城邦中称他们为‘君主’，在民主城邦中只称他们为‘统治者’。”

“在我们的城邦中呢？普通民众除了把统治者看作是公民外还怎么看待他们？”

b ‘As their protectors and defenders,’ he said.

‘And how will *they* regard the general populace?’

‘As their paymasters and quartermasters.’

‘In other communities how do rulers regard the general populace?’

‘As slaves,’ he said.

‘And one another?’

‘As fellow rulers,’ he said.

‘How do our rulers regard one another?’

‘As fellow guardians.’

‘Would you say that in other communities a ruler might regard some of his fellow rulers as friends and others as strangers?’

‘Yes, that commonly happens.’

c ‘And he regards and describes his friends as belonging to his circle, and the strangers as nothing to do with him?’

‘Yes.’

‘What about the guardians in your community? Could any of them regard or refer to a fellow guardian as a stranger?’

‘Certainly not,’ he said. ‘He'll be regarding everyone he meets as a brother or a sister, a father or a mother, a son or a daughter, a grandchild or a grandparent.’

‘Excellently put,’ I said. ‘But here's another question for you. As legislator, will you be obliging them only to label one another relatives,
d or also to make all their behaviour conform to these labels? Take their fathers, for instance: will they have to show their fathers all the usual respect and care and obedience due to parents, or else have both gods and men think the worse of them for their unjust and immoral behaviour? Will these be the traditions which every single

“看作他们的保护者和护卫者。”他说。 b

“他们怎么看待普通民众?”

“看作他们的纳税者和供应者。”

“在其他城邦中统治者如何看待普通民众?”

“看作是奴隶。”他说。

“相互之间呢?”

“共同统治者。”他说。

“我们的统治者相互怎么看待?”

“共同保卫者。”

“你是否会说,在别的城邦中,统治者可能把某些与他一同统治的人看作朋友,而把其他人看作外人?”

“是的,那是常情。”

“他是否把自己的朋友看作并说生成是属于他的圈子里的人,而把外人看作与他无关?” c

“是的。”

“你们城邦中的卫士怎么样呢? 他们当中有谁把共同保卫者看作或说成是外人?”

“当然不是,”他说,“他会把任何遇到的人看作兄弟或姐妹,父亲或母亲,儿子或女儿,孙子孙女或祖父母。”

“说得好,”我说,“但还有个问题要问你。作为一个立法者,你会迫使他们仅仅互称亲戚,还是要使得他们的所有行为与这些名称相符? 比如拿他们的父亲来说:他们是否必须对父亲表示出一般的尊敬和关心,并顺从他们的父母,要 d
不然诸神和人都会对他们的不正义和不虔诚的行为表示不满的?关于那些告知他们是父亲的人和所有别的亲戚,你们

citizen of your community will din into the ears of the children from their earliest years about the people they are told to regard as fathers and about all their other relatives, or will you have different traditions?'

e 'No, I'll have the ones you've mentioned,' he said. 'It would be ridiculous for them only to mouth these family labels without it affecting their behaviour.'

'So there's no community in which it's more likely that, when one of its members does well or badly, people will be in tune with one another in using the expression we mentioned, and will say, "The success is mine" or "The failure is mine."'

'That's absolutely true,' he said.

464a 'Well, didn't we say that when people hold this belief and use this expression they start to share feelings of pleasure and distress?'

'We did, and we were right.'

'Isn't it above all the members of our community, then, who will genuinely share and refer to the same thing as "mine"? And because they share in this way, they'll share feelings of pleasure and distress more than anyone else, won't they?'

'Much more.'

'And, apart from the general constitution of the community, it's the fact that the guardians share their women and children that is responsible for this, isn't it?'

'Yes, that's by far the most important factor,' he said.

b 'Now, our conclusion was that there is nothing better for a community than this sharing of feelings. We compared a wellrun community to a body, and pointed out what a body does in relation to the pleasure and pain of its parts.'

'Yes, and the conclusion was right,' he said.

'So we've demonstrated that the community's greatest benefit is due to the fact that its defenders share their women and children.'

'We certainly have,' he said.

城邦中的每个公民是否从小时候就耳濡目染,这些成了传统,或者你们有别的不同的传统?”

“没有,我有的是你提到过的那些,”他说,“对他们来说徒口 e
说说亲人之名而与他们的行为无涉,这会是可笑的。”

“所以没有城邦更会像是这样的了,当其成员境遇好或坏的时候,人们在使用我们说过的那些表述上异口同声,他们会说:‘成功是我的’或‘失败是我的’。”

“非常正确。”他说。

“那么,我们不是说过当人们具有了这个信念并使用这样的 464a
表述的时候,他们就开始分担快乐和忧愁的情感了吗?”

“我们说过,我们说得很对。”

“那么我们城邦中的公民不就尤其能够真正地分担同一件事物并把它看作是‘我的’?他们以这种方式分享,所以比其他人更能分担快乐和忧愁的情感,不是吗?”

“是更能体会。”

“除了城邦的根本制度之外,卫士共有他们的妻子儿女也是其中的原因,不是吗?”

“是的,这是最重要的因素。”他说。

“那么我们的结论就是,对于一个城邦来说,没有什么比这种 b
分享感情更好的了。我们把一个治理良好的城邦比作一个身体,并指出身体的反应与各个部分的快乐和痛苦相关。”

“是的,这结论很正确。”他说。

“这样我们就已经证明,城邦最大的幸福在于卫士共有他们的妻子儿女。”

“我们当然已经证明了。”他说。

'Moreover, this conclusion goes with what we were saying earlier. I mean, we did say that genuine guardians shouldn't own houses
c or land or anything, but should be given their food by others, as payment for their guarding, and should all eat together.'

'Right,' he said.

'Isn't it the case, as I say, that both our earlier proposals and the current ones increase the likelihood of their being genuine guardians, and prevent them tearing the community apart by using the expression "mine" to refer not to the same thing, but to various things? Different people call different things "mine" when they each have
d their own houses into which they pull anything they can keep out of the hands of others, and when they each have their own wife and children; and this situation introduces into the community the personal pleasures and pains of private individuals. Aren't they more likely to be genuine guardians if they all regard the same things as within their circle of interest, tend in the same direction, and feel pleasure and pain, as much as possible, under the same circumstances?'

'Absolutely,' he said.

'And won't trials and lawsuits against one another be almost non-existent, since they'll own nothing except their bodies and share eve-
e rything else? And consequently they'll be free of all the conflict that arises when people have money or children and relatives.'

'That's more or less inevitable,' he said.

'Lawsuits for assault or bodily harm won't be part of their moral code either, because we'll make it a moral obligation for people in any given age-group to defend themselves against their peers, which will force them to take care of their bodies.'

'Right,' he said.

“此外，这个结论与我们早先所说的也是一致的。我的意思是说，我们确实说过真正的卫士不应该具有自己的房子、土地或任何东西，但应该从其他人那里得到食物，作为担任卫士的报偿，并且所有人应该在一起饮食。” c

“对的。”他说。

“我说的不就是这个意思吗：我们早先和现在的建议使他们更像是真正的卫士，而防止他们通过使用‘我的’这种的表述，不是去指称同一个事物而指称不同的事物，从而把城邦撕得四分五裂？当他们各自拥有房子，把别人手中的东西往家里搬，并且各自拥有他们自己的妻子儿女的时候，不同的人就把不同的事物称 d
作‘我的’；这种情况就把个人各自的快乐和痛苦带到了城邦中。如果他们所有人都把同一件事物当作属于他们自己的利益，朝着同一个方向，尽可能地在同样的处境下同甘共苦，那么他们不就更像是真正的卫士吗？”

“毫无疑问。”他说。

“那么他们相互之间的官司和诉讼不就几乎不存在了吗？因为他们除了自己的身体和其他一切共有物之外，就什么都不拥有了。结果他们就会避免所有纠纷，当人们拥有金钱或孩子以及亲属时就会发生这些纠纷。” e

“差不多必定如此吧。”他说。

“行凶、殴打的诉讼也不会是他们道德法则的一部分，因为对于任何年龄的人来说我们会使之成为一种道德义务，即在同龄人中进行自卫，这能迫使他们关爱他们的身体。”

“对的。”他说。

465a ‘There’s something else that makes this regulation right too,’ I said. ‘If an angry person satisfies his rage like this, he’s less likely to escalate the matter into a major conflict.’

‘Yes.’

‘Now, we’ll have given older people authority over younger ones and made them responsible for disciplining them.’

‘Obviously.’

‘And it’s unlikely that younger people will ever try to assault or strike their elders (unless ordered to do so by the rulers), or show them disrespect in any other way. There are two guardians whose presence is enough to stop them—fear and respect. Respect will stop
b them laying hands on their parents, and they’ll be afraid of all the help any victim would get from people who regard themselves as his sons or brothers or fathers.’

‘Yes, that’s what would happen,’ he said.

‘So thanks to our legislation they’ll live together in perfect peace, don’t you think?’

‘Definitely.’

‘And because of their freedom from in-fighting, there is no danger of a rift ever forming between them and the rest of the community or within the rest of the community.’

‘No, there isn’t.’

‘For fear of sounding a discordant note, I hardly like even to
c mention the trivial mischiefs they’ll avoid. There’s how poor people have to flatter the rich; there are all the problems and worries they suffer while they’re having their children educated and because in order to support a household they’re forced to raise money by borrowing, by refusing to pay back debts, by doing whatever it takes to make an income—only to hand the accumulated money over to their wives and servants to spend on housekeeping. There are a number of different burdens one finds in this context, but they’re too obvious and demeaning to be worth mentioning.’

“还有别的原因使得这项法规成为合理的，”我说，“如果一个 456a
发怒的人像这样怒气得到了发泄，那么他便不大会将事情发展成为大的冲突。”

“是的。”

“那么我们会把管理年轻人的权力交给老年人，以便让他们有责任来管教年轻人。”

“显然。”

“年轻人似乎不会试图对年长者动武或殴打他们，或以任何别的方式对他们表示不敬，除非统治者命令他们这样做。只要有两个保护者在场就足以组织他们了——害怕和敬畏。敬畏会阻
止他们动手冒犯他们的父母，他们会害怕所有来自那些自认为是 b
其儿子、兄弟或父亲的对任何受害者的援助。”

“是的，是那么回事。”他说。

“所以由于我们的法规，他们会非常和平地生活在一起，难道你不这么认为吗？”

“毫无疑问。”

“由于他们没有内部的争斗，所以与城邦中的其余人之间，或在城邦的其余人之中就不会有形成分裂的危险。”

“不会有危险。”

“因为担心听到一种不和谐的语调，我甚至不想提到他们要避
开的琐碎的烦心事儿。那就是穷人如何不得不去巴结奉承富人；他 c
们遭受了各种问题和担忧，他们要使他们的孩子得到教育，为了养家糊口不得不以拒绝还债和干活赚些钱的方式筹钱——只是把积攒起来的钱交给他们的妻子和佣人花在家务上。在此，人们能发现有许多不同的重担，但它们都太粗浅低俗而不值得一提。”

'Yes, even a blind man could see them,' he said.

d 'So they'll avoid all these troubles, and they'll live more happily than any Olympic victor.'

'Why?'

'The happiness which people attribute to Olympic victors is due to a tiny fraction of what our guardians have. The guardians' victory is more splendid, and their upkeep by the general populace is more thorough-going. The fruit of their victory is the preservation of the whole community, their prize the maintenance of themselves and their children with food and all of life's essentials. During their lifetimes they are honoured by their community, and when they die they are
e buried in high style.'

'These are excellent prizes,' he said.

'Do you remember', I asked, 'that earlier someone or other
466a criticized us for failing to make the guardians happy because although they could take possession of the property of everyone in the community, they actually had nothing? We said we'd look into the matter later, if it was convenient, and that for the time being we were making our guardians guardians and making our community as happy as we could, and that it wasn't our intention to single out one particular group within the community and devise happiness just for them.'

'I remember,' he said.

'Well, since we now think that our auxiliaries live a far better
b and more rewarding life than any Olympic victor, we're hardly going to place it at the same level as the life of a shoemaker or any of our other urban or rural workers, are we?'

'I don't think so,' he answered.

'Nevertheless, the comment I made at the time is also fair in this context. If a guardian aims for the kind of happiness which is incompatible with his being a guardian—if the moderate, secure, and

“是的，甚至是瞎子也能看得见。”他说。 d

“所以他们会避免所有这些麻烦，他们会生活得比任何奥林匹克赛会的胜利者还要幸福。”

“为什么？”

“人们给予奥林匹克赛会胜利者的幸福是我们的卫士所拥有的一小部分。卫士的胜利更加光荣，他们得到普通民众的供养更加全面。他们胜利的成果使整个城邦得以保存，他们的奖励使他们自己以及他们孩子的食物和所有生活必需品都得到确保。在他们的一生中都受到他们城邦的尊敬，当他们死的时候也享有哀
荣备至的葬礼。” e

“这些是优厚的奖赏。”他说。

“你难道不记得吗，”我问道，“早先有些人批评我们说，我们
没有让卫士得到幸福，因为他们虽然可以拥有城邦中所有人的财 466a
产，但他们实际上什么都没有？我们曾说过在恰当的时候我们之后会对此事作考察的，但暂时我们要使我们的卫士和我们的城邦尽可能地幸福，我们的意图并不是在城邦中挑出某个特定的阶级并且把幸福只给他们。”

“我记得。”他说。

“那么既然现在我们认为我们的辅助者生活得比任何奥林匹克赛会的胜利者优越得多并且更加有益，那么我们就几乎不会把
他们的生活放在鞋匠或任何别的城乡劳动者生活的同一个层次 b
上，是吗？”

“我想不会。”他回答说。

“还有，我在当时所做的评论在这种情况下也同样适用。如果一个卫士以那种与其作为卫士不相称的幸福为目的——如果

outstanding lifestyle we've described is not enough for him and, under the influence of some idiotic and immature conception of happiness,
c he sets about exploiting his power to appropriate all the community's assets for himself, he'll start to appreciate how wise Hesiod was when he said that in a sense "half is more than a whole".'

'I'd recommend him to keep to the guardian's life,' he said.

'Do you agree, then,' I said, 'that the best course is for the men and women to receive the same education, share children. and co-operate in the guarding of the rest of their fellow citizens, as we've described? And do you agree that whether it involves staying within the community or going out to war, the women should help in the
d guarding and hunting, as female dogs do? They should share in everything as much as they can, and this will not only be the best course of action for them, but is also not incompatible with their nature, as com-pared with masculinity, and is the kind of partnership which nature intended for the two sexes?'

'Yes, I agree,' he said.

'Well, we still have to decide', I said, 'whether in fact, and under what circumstances; this sharing is viable among humans, as it is among other species.'

'I was just about to take you up on that very point,' he said, 'but you got in first.'

e 'Because it's obvious what they'll do about warfare, I suppose,' I said.

'What?' he asked.

'Men and women will Campaign together, and they'll also take any sturdy children with them to war, so that they see the work they'll
467a have to do when they become adults, just as the children of other kinds of work-men do. But the children won't just watch: they'll also act as apprentices and servants in all aspects of war, and look after their fathers and mothers. I mean, you must have noticed what happens in the case of other occupations—how the children of potters, say, spend a long time as apprentices and observers before getting

他不满足于我们所说的节制、安稳而高尚的生活方式，受到某些
愚蠢而幼稚的幸福观的影响，他开始利用他的权力为自己攫取城
邦的所有财富，他开始欣赏赫西俄德的聪明才智，因为他说过在 c
某种意义上‘一半比全部还多’。”

“我劝他保持卫士的生活。”他说。

“那么你是否同意，”我说，“对于男人和女人来说，最好的方
式就是接受同样的教育，共有孩子，共同保卫其他的公民，就像我
们说过的那样？你是否同意，无论是在城邦中还是出去打仗，女
人都应该像母狗一样帮助男人防卫和追杀敌人？他们应该尽可
能地在所有事情上都共同承担，这对他们来说不只是最好的行动 d
方式，而且也不违背他们的本性，这种伙伴关系是两性的本性所
要求的？”

“是的，我同意。”他说。

“喔，我们仍必须判定，”我说，“这种共同承担是否在事实上，以及在什么情况下，在人类中是可行的，一如在其他动物中。”

“我正好要提那一点了，”他说，“但你抢了先。”

“因为我想这明显就是，他们在战争中要做的事情。”我 e
说。

“什么事情？”他问道。

“男人和女人共同出发，他们还带上强健的孩子一起上战场，
这样孩子们就会看到他们成人以后必须要做的工作，就像别的匠
人的孩子一样。但孩子不只是观看：他们还要在战争的各个方面 467a
担当助手和勤杂工，还要照顾他们的父母们。我的意思是说，你
肯定注意到在别的工作中的状况——比如说制陶匠的孩子，在实

involved in any actual pottery.'

'Yes, I know.'

'And should potters take more care than the guardians over educating their children by familiarizing them and letting them observe their duties?'

'That would be ridiculous,' he said.

'Moreover, every creature fights better, anyway, when its offspring are around.'

b 'True. But Socrates, aren't they running quite a risk? If they fail, which is always a possibility in war, then they'll be responsible for their children being killed as well as themselves, and for the rest of the community finding it impossible to recover.'

'You're right,' I said. 'But the main point is: do you think they should be provided with a risk-free life?'

'Certainly not.'

'Well, if they have to face danger, shouldn't it be when the result of success will be an improvement in their conditions?'

'Obviously.'

c 'And do you think it hardly matters—not enough to compensate for the danger—whether or not the children who are to become soldiers when they're adults observe warfare and all It's entails?'

'No, it does make a difference, in the sense you're talking about.'

'It'll be best, then, if our primary objective is having the children observe warfare, but we also find ways to keep them safe. Right?'

'Yes.'

'Well, the chief point', I said, 'is that their fathers will know

际从事任何制陶工作之前要花很长时间做学徒观察制陶。”

“是的，我知道。”

“难道比起卫士，制陶匠应该花更多的心思让他们观察和熟悉他们的工作，以此去教育他们的孩子？”

“那是很可笑的。”他说。

“此外，每种动物当他们的孩子在身边的时候，无论如何都会更加善战。” b

“是的。但是，苏格拉底，他们不是在冒很大的风险吗？如果他们失败了，这在战争中总是有可能的，那么他们会让孩子们同他们一起都被杀害的，这对于城邦中的其余人来说，他们会觉得不可能再复兴了。”

“你说得对，”我说，“但主要问题是：你认为他们应该得到一个没有危险的生活吗？”

“当然不是。”

“如果他们不得不面对危险，那么胜利的结果不就会使他们有所长进吗？”

“显然。”

“还有，对于将来成人时要当战士的孩子们来说，是否让他们去观察战争及其全部的细节，你认为这几乎无关紧要——不足以 c
弥补危险带来的损失吗？”

“这在你所说的意思上是有区别的。”

“那么这样是最好的，即我们的初衷是让孩子观察战争，但我们还要设法保护他们的安全。对吗？”

“是的。”

“那么，”我说，“关键就是，他们的父亲知道所有人所共知

d all that can humanly be known about warfare, and will therefore be able to distinguish risky military ventures from safe ones.'

'That's likely,' he said.

'So they'll take them to the one kind and steer clear of the others.'

'Right.'

'And they'll not be putting second-rate supervisors in charge of them, but people who thanks to their experience and their age are qualified to act as guides and attendants.'

'Yes, that's the right thing to do.'

'Still, we're agreed that the unexpected often occurs.'

'Yes.'

'And that is why we'd better equip our children with wings from an early age, my friend, so that they can escape by flying away, if they have to.'

e 'I don't understand,' he said.

'We have to put them on horseback', I explained, 'from the earliest possible age, and they can go and watch campaigns only when they've been taught to ride. The horses they go on won't be excitable or aggressive, but will he the fastest and most manageable ones available. That's the best way for them to take stock of their work, and they'll have no difficulty in following the older people who are their guides to safety if necessary.'

'I think you're right,' he said.

468a 'What about warfare?' I asked. 'What attitudes do you want your soldiers to have towards themselves and towards the enemy? Do you think my ideas are correct or not?'

'Tell me them,' he said.

'Shouldn't anyone who deserts or discards his weapons or

的戎马之事,所以能够区分冒险的军事行动和安全的军事行动。" d

"似乎如此。"他说。

"所以在一种情况下他们会把孩子带去,而在另一种情况下他们不会把他们带去。"

"对。"

"他们不会让二流的军官去照管孩子们,而是交给那些其经验和年龄皆配得上担当领导者和看护者的人。"

"是的,那样做很对。"

"我们还是一致认为意外常常会发生。"

"是的。"

"我的朋友,这就是我们为什么必须一开始就给我们的孩子插上翅膀的原因,这样如果他们要是不得不逃跑的时候,他们就能飞一般地逃走。"

"我不明白。"他说。 e

"我们应该尽可能早地把孩子们放在马上,"我解释说,"只有当他们学会了骑马,他们才能去观看战斗。他们所骑的马不会激动或冲动,而是那种跑得快并且容易驾驭的马。这是估量他们工作的最好方式,要是有必要,他们就能毫无困难地在长者的带领下来到安全之地。"

"我想你说得对。"他说。

"那么战争呢?"我问道,"你想要你的战士对自己和敌人采取 468a
什么样的态度呢?你认为我的想法是正确的还是不正确的?"

"把你的想法告诉我吧。"他说。

"任何像那样逃跑、丢弃武器或做了任何类似怯懦之事的人

does anything cowardly like that be made an artisan or a farmer?' I asked.

'Yes.'

'And anyone who is taken alive by the enemy should be presented to his captors, and they can treat this catch of theirs in any way they choose.'

'Absolutely.'

b 'What about someone who distinguis heshimself for outstanding bravery? Shouldn't he first, before returning home from the campaign, be crowned with chaplets by each of his comrades-in-arms—the young men and the children—one by one? Is that a good idea, do you think, or not?'

'I think so.'

'And should they take him by the hand?'

'Yes, that too.'

'But I don't think you'll go so far as to agree with my next idea,' I said.

'What is it?'

'That he should kiss and be kissed by each of his comrades.'

'That's very important indeed,' he said. 'In fact, I'll add a rider
c to your regulation: for the duration of that campaign, no one he wants to kiss is allowed to refuse. This will make anyone who happens to be in love with a male or female comrade try harder to win the prize for bravery.'

'That's an excellent idea,' I said, 'because we've already said that a good man will be allowed to participate in a greater number of marriage ceremonies than others and that it will invariably be a good man rather than anyone else who is selected for them, so that as many children as possible are fathered by men of this type.'

'Yes, I remember,' he said.

'Moreover, Homer too approved of rewarding young men for their

不就应该让他们成为工匠或农民?”我问道。

“是的。”

“任何被敌人活捉的人应该被当作礼物送给捉住他的人,他们可以以任何他们所选择的方式来处置这个被他们俘虏的人。”

“毫无疑问。” b

“那么某些特别勇敢的人呢?从战场回来他不就首先应该是依次被他的每个战友——年轻人和孩子——戴上花冠,你认为这是否是个好想法?”

“我认为这是个好想法。”

“他们应该用手拉着他吗?”

“这也是应该的。”

“但我想你还不至于会同意我下一个想法。”我说。

“什么想法?”

“他应该亲吻每一个战友,并且也被他的每一个战友亲吻。”

“这确实非常重要,”他说,“事实上,我还要在你的规定之上再加上一条:在那战争期间,他想要亲吻谁,谁都不可以拒绝。这 c 会使任何正好与男性或女性战友相爱的人更是努力地赢取勇气的奖赏。”

“那是一个了不起的想法,”我说,“因为我们曾经说过,比起其他人,一个优秀的人应该被允许多多参加婚礼,并且总是挑选优秀的人而不是任何别的人来做这种事情,这样这种人就会成为尽可能多的孩子的父亲。”

“是的,我记得。”他说。

“此外,荷马也说过要奖励年轻人的美德。他说埃阿斯在战

d goodness. He said that for distinguishing himself in battle Ajax"was awarded the whole length of the chine" —this being an appropriate reward for vigour and valour because it's simultaneously a source of strength as well as a reward.'

'You're quite right,' he said.

'We'll let Homer be our guide in this matter, then,' I said. 'I mean, we too will use religious rites and so on as occasions for rewarding anyone who has displayed virtue not only with odes and the privileges we've been talking about, but also"with the seat of honour, with the best cuts of meat, and with goblets full of wine",so that we simultaneously give our virtuous men and women an opportunity for
e training as well as a reward.'

'That's an exceptionally good idea,' he said.

'All right. Now, what about those who die during the course of a campaign? In the first place, we must count anyone who dies a glorious death as a member of the golden caste,mustn't we?'

'Definitely.'

469a 'And we'll believe Hesiod when he says that after people of this kind die"they become pure deities attached to the earth, who in their goodness guard mortal men and keep them from harm". Right?'

'Yes, we will.'

'So won't we consult Apollo to find out how to lay to rest men of superhuman stature and what special things to do, and then bury them in the way he prescribes?'

'Of course.'

b 'And thereafter we'll regard their tombs as the tombs of deities, and we'll tend to them and worship there, won't we? And don't you think we should institute the same custom whenever anyone who during his lifetime was acknowledged to be exceptionally good dies of old age or whatever?'

'Yes, that's the right thing to do,' he said.

'Now, what attitude will our soldiers have towards their enemies?'

场上异常英勇，‘得到了全副脊肉的奖赏’——这是对他的精力和 d
英勇的一种恰当的奖励，因为这奖励同时又是力量之源。”

“你说得很对。”他说。

“那么我们让荷马在此事上来引领我们吧，”我说，“我的意思是说，我们会使用宗教仪式等等场合来奖励任何展示出德性的人，不光是用我们说过的赞美诗，而且还‘给以荣誉的席位，最好的肉以及斟满杯子的美酒’，这样同时给我们具有德性的男女一
个训练的机会以及奖赏。” e

“这是个非常好的想法，”他说。

“好吧。那么，那些在战争中死去的人呢？首先我们必须把任何荣耀地死去之人当作黄金种族的一员，难道不是吗？”

“毫无疑问。”

“我们会相信赫西俄德，他说在这种人死后，‘他们就成为附
于大地的神灵，以他们的美德保护终有一死之人，使他们远离伤 469a
害’。对吗？”

“是的，我们会相信。”

“所以我们不就要询问阿波罗，指点如何安葬这些超凡之人，做些什么特别的事情，然后按他说的方式埋葬他们？”

“当然。”

“从那以后我们就把他们的坟墓看作神灵的坟墓，我们会在
那里进行祭扫和敬拜，不是吗？你难道不认为我们应该对任何这 b
样的人采用同样的仪式：他们因年老或别的什么原因而去世的，其一生被认为是特别优秀的？”

“是的，这样做是对的。”他说。

“那么我们的战士对他们的敌人持有什么样的态度？”

'In what sense?'

'Takeen slavement first. Do you think it's right for communities of Greeks to enslave other Greeks? Shouldn't they do their best to prevent any other community from enslaving Greeks and make it the norm
c to spare anyone of Greek stock, for fear of themselves being enslaved by non-Greeks?'

'It's absolutely crucial that they spare Greeks,' he said.

'Not only should they not own Greek slaves themselves, then, but they should also advise other Greeks to follow their example.'

'Yes,' he said. 'That should encourage them to concentrate on non-Greeks and leave one another alone.'

'And what about the victors despoiling the dead? Taking their
d weapons is all right, but otherwise is it a good practice? I mean, doesn't it provide an excuse for cowards not to advance against an enemy who is still fighting, because they can make out that they're doing their duty by poking around among the corpses? This sort of looting has often in the past been the rum of armies.'

'I quite agree.'

'Plundering corpses seems mean and mercenary, don't you think? And treating the body of a dead person as an enemy, when the hostile element has flown off and only the instrument it once used for fighting remains, seems to indicate a womanly, petty mind. I mean, do you think there's any difference between this behaviour and that of
e dogs who, if they're hit with stones, get annoyed at the stones, but don't go anywhere near the person who threw them?'

'That's an absolutely perfect analogy,' he replied.

'So we'd better avoid the practice of plundering corpses and also preventing our opponents from recovering the bodies of their dead, don't you think?'

'Yes, we certainly should,' he said.

"在什么意义上说?"

"首先是奴役。你认为对希腊人的城邦来说,去奴役别的希腊人是正义的吗?他们不是应该力图防止任何别的城邦来奴役希腊人并把救助任何希腊人种族当作一个习俗,以防他们自己也被非希腊人奴役吗?" c

"救助希腊人是非常关键的。"他说。

"那么他们不仅不应当把希腊人当作自己的奴隶,他们还应该劝告别的希腊人也仿效他们。"

"是的,"他说,"应该鼓励他们去针对非希腊人而不相互发难。"

"胜利者剥取死者的东西又怎么样呢?拿走他们的武器就没错吗,抑或反之才是好的?我的意思是说,拿走武器,这不就给胆怯者提供了一个借口让他们不去追赶还在战斗的敌人,因为他们 d
好像把在死尸上乱逛当成了他们的职责?这种攫取战利品的行为过去常常断送了军队。"

"我非常同意。"

"你难道不认为剥取死尸的物品是卑鄙龌龊的?当敌人已散,只留下其曾用来作战的工具时还把死人的尸体当作敌人,这似乎是妇人的小心眼。我的意思是说,你是否认为这种行为与狗的行为有什么区别,如果狗被石头击中,他们就对石头怒气冲冲, e
但不敢靠近扔它的人?"

"这是个相当好的类比。"他回答说。

"所以我们应该避免剥取死人物品的行径,也应该防止我们的敌人取回他们死者的尸体,你难道不这么认为吗?"

"是的,我们当然应该这样做。"他说。

'And we won't be taking arms and armour to our temples as trophies either, especially if they came from Greeks, if we're the slighh-
470a test bit interested in being on good terms with other Greeks. We're more likely to be afraid of the possible pollution involved in robbing our kin of their weapons and taking them to a sacred site, except when the practice is divinely sanctioned.'

'You're quite right,' he said.

'What about devastating the land and burning the homes of Greeks? How will your troops behave towards their enemies?'

'I'd be glad to hear what you have to say about this,' he said.

'Well, I think they'll avoid both practices,' I said, 'and only steal the annual harvest. Shall I tell you why?'

b 'Yes, please.'

'I think that the fact that there are these two separate terms, war and conflict, is indicative of the existence of two things with separate distinguishing features. One of the two is an internal affair, within a single domain; the other is an external affair, crossing borders. "Conflict" refers to the hostility of an internal element, "war" to that of an external element.'

'No one could fault what you're saying in the slightest,' he said.

c 'I wonder if you'll find the next point just as sound. I maintain that Greeks are bonded to one another by internal ties of blood and kinship, but interact with non-Greeks as people who are foreign and live outside their domain.'

'That's right,' he said.

'When Greeks and non-Greeks fight, then, we'll describe this as warfare, and claim that they are natural enemies and that the term "war" should refer to this type of hostility. But when Greeks get involved in this kind of thing with other Greeks,

“我们也不会将武器与盔甲当作战利品带到神殿里去的，特别是假如它们是从希腊人那里得到的，而且如果我们稍微有点儿在乎与其他希腊人友好关系的话，我们就更不会那样做了。我们更担心的是夺取我们同胞的武器，把它们带到一个神圣的地方而可能造成的亵渎，除非这是神所准许的。” 470a

“你说得非常正确。”他说。

“毁坏希腊人的田地、烧毁其房屋又怎么样呢？你们的军队对他们的敌人会有什么反应？”

“我很高兴听听你对此的看法。”他说。

“好吧。我想他们两种做法都要避免，”我说，“而只是偷走他们的年收成。要我告诉你为什么吗？” b

“是的，请讲。”

“有两个不同的术语，战争和冲突，我想这一事实正说明了有两个具有完全不同特征的事物存在。其一是内部事务，在自己范围内；另一个是外部事务，跨越了边界，‘冲突’指的是内部因素的敌对，‘战争’指的是外部因素的敌对。”

“你说的话根本无可指摘。”他说。

“我想知道，你是否认为下一个的观点同样合理。我坚持认为希腊人之间通过血缘和亲属的内在关系而联系在一起，而与外邦、住在他们的领地之外的非希腊人发生交际关系。” c

“对的。”他说。

“那么，当希腊人与非希腊人开战的时候，我们就把这称作战争，称他们是天然的敌人，并且‘战争’这个词应该用来指称这种类型的敌对。要是当希腊人与别的希腊人之间发生了这种事情，那

we'll claim that they are natural friends, and that in a situation like
d this Greece is diseased and in conflict, and we'll maintain that the term "conflict" should refer to this type of hostility.'

'I for one agree with your view,' he said.

'Now that we've agreed what conflict is,' I said, 'imagine it happening, imagine a community divided against itself, and you'll see that, if each side devastates the other side's land and burns their homes, conflict comes across as an abomination and neither side can be regarded as patriotic, since if they were, they would stop short of ravaging their nurse and their mother. However, it seems reasonable
e for the winners to take the losers' crops, and it smacks of aiming for reconciliation rather than perpetual warfare.'

'Yes, there's far more compassion in this aim,' he said.

'Well, this community you're founding is going to be Greek, isn't it?' I asked.

'Of course,' he answered.

'And its members will be good, compassionate people, won't they?'

'Certainly.'

'Won't they feel warmth for their fellow Greeks? Won't they regard Greece as their own land and join all other Greeks in their common religious rites?'

'They certainly will.'

471a 'Then they'll regard any dissension between themselves and Greeks as conflict, since Greeks are their own people, and they won't even use the term "war" in this context, will they?'

么我们会把他们说成是天然的朋友，在这种情况下希腊得了病，发生了冲突，我们会坚持认为‘冲突’这个词应该指称这种类型的敌对。” d

“我完全同意你的看法。”他说。

“现在我们已经同意什么是冲突，”我说，“设想当它发生时，想象一下一个城邦自身分裂，你会看到，如果每一方毁坏另一方的土地、焚烧他们的家园，那么冲突看上去似乎是一种痛恨，没有任何一方可以被看作是爱国的，因为他们要是爱国的话，他们就会停止损毁他们的保姆和他们的母亲。[1] 然而胜利者夺取失败者的粮食却是有理由的，这意味着其目的在于和解而不是长久的 e
战争。”

“是的，以此为目的更有同情心。”他说。

“那么你正在建立的城邦将会是希腊，不是吗？”我问道。

“当然。”他回答说。

“其所有的成员都是善良的、有同情心的希腊人，不是吗？”

“当然。”

“他们不就会热爱他们的希腊同胞吗？他们不就会把希腊看作自己的土地并与所有其他希腊人一同举行公共的宗教仪式？”

“他们当然会的。”

471a
“他们会把任何他们自己与希腊人之间的不和当作冲突，因为希腊人是自己人，在这种情况下他们不会使用‘战争’这个词，是吗？”

---

〔1〕 指土地，参见414e。

'No.'

'So in times of dissension they'll be looking for reconciliation, won't they?'

'Yes.'

'So they won't be motivated by hatred, but by wanting to bring their opponents to their senses. As disciplinarians, then, rather than enemies, they won't punish their opponents with enslavement or death.'

'That's right,' he said.

'And as Greeks, they won't ravage Greece either, or burn homes, or conclude that the whole population of a given community—men, women, and children—is hostile to them, but only those few hostile people who were responsible for the dissension. All these rea-
b sons will make them unwilling to ravage their opponents' land or demolish their houses, since the majority of the population will be their friends; instead, they will see the dispute through until the point is reached when those who are innocent have suffered enough and they force the guilty few to pay for what they've done.'

'I agree that this is the attitude the members of our community ought to have towards their opponents,' he said. 'And they'll reserve for non-Greeks the treatment Greeks currently give one another.'

'Shall we include this rule among our regulations for the guardi-
c ans, then—that they are not to devastate land or burn houses?'

'Yes,' he said, 'and let's add that it and our earlier regulations are all good.'

“不会使用这个词的。”

“所以既然是不和，那么他们会寻求和解，不是吗?”

“是的。”

“所以他们不会被仇恨所驱使，而是使其对手恢复理性。那么作为执行纪律者而非敌人，他们不会用奴役或死亡来惩罚他们的对手。”

“对。”他说。

“作为希腊人，他们也不会蹂躏希腊，不会烧毁家园，总之，一个城邦中的所有人——男人、女人和孩子——都不会对他们怀有敌意，而只有那少数怀有敌意之人才是争端的罪魁祸首。所有这些理由都会使得他们不愿意损毁对方的土地或捣毁对方的房屋， b
因为大部分人是他们的朋友；相反，他们会一直作战直到那些无辜的人遭受了足够的伤害，而迫使少数有罪之人为他们的所作所为付出代价。”

“我同意这就是我们城邦的成员应该具有的对待对方的态度，”他说，“他们会把希腊人彼此相待的这种通行方式留给非希腊人。”

“那么我们是否把这条法律算作一条我们关于卫士的法律——他们不得毁坏土地或焚毁房屋?” c

“是的，”他说，“让我们补充说，这条以及我们早先的规定都是好的。”

[英 汉 对 照]

西方学术经典文库

理 想 国

REPUBLIC

[古希腊] 柏拉图 著
庞爔春 译
张云江 译校

(二)

九 州 出 版 社
JIUZHOUPRESS

CHAPTER 8

'I get the impression, though, Socrates, that this is the kind of topic where, if no one interrupts you, you'll forget that it is all a digression from a previous topic—that is, whether this political system is viable, and if so, how. I accept that all these practices, if realized, would be good for any community they were practised in, and I can
471d supplement your account: they are highly likely to fight well against enemy forces, in so far as they are highly unlikely to abandon one another, since they regard one another as brothers, fathers, sons, and call one another by these names; if women joined them on a campaign (whether their task was to fight alongside the men or to support them in the rear), they'd have the effect of terrifying the enemy and could come up as reinforcements in an emergency, and I'm sure this would make our militia completely invincible; and I can see all the domestic
e benefits they'd bring which you haven't mentioned. You can take for granted my agreement that the realization of the constitution would result in all these advantages and innumerable others as well; so you don't have to talk about the actual constitution any more. Let's just try now to convince ourselves that it is viable and to find out how it is via-
472a ble, and let's not bother with anything else.'

'I wasn't expecting you to ambush my argument like this,' I said. 'Can't you sympathize with my procrastination? Perhaps you don't realize that it was hard enough for me to escape from the first two waves, and now you're invoking the largest and most problematic of the set of three waves. When you see it and hear it, then you'll sympathize with me and see that it was perfectly realistic of me to have misgivings and qualms about proposing such a paradoxical idea for investigation.'

第八章

“但是,苏格拉底,我有这样的感觉,如果没有人打断你的话,你会忘记这完全离开了先前的主题,那就是:这个政治体制是否是可行的,如果可行,是如何可行的。我承认如果所有这些制度能够实现,那么在任何城邦中实施都会是好的,并且对你所说的,
我能做些补充:他们非常善于对敌作战,并且他们决不会相互抛 471d
弃,因为他们以兄弟、父亲和儿子相待,并且也互相称呼这些名称;如果女人与他们一起参战,无论她们的工作是与男人一起作战,还是在后方支援他们,她们对敌人具有震慑作用并且能够提供紧急支援,我确信这会使得我们的军队无往而不胜;我还注意到你没有提到的所有他们给城邦内部带来的好处。你会赞同我
的想法,这种制度的实现会带来所有好处以及别的数不清的好 e
处;所以你不必再讨论现实的制度了。现在让我们只是尽力使自己相信这是可行的,并且找出是如何可行的,让我们不要操心别的事情了。”

“我没预料到你会对我的论证做如此这般的伏击,”我说,“你 472a
不能同情我的犹豫之心吗?也许你没有意识到对我来说,逃离前两个浪头的困难已经足够大了,现在你又掀起一个三个浪头中的最大并且最成问题的浪头。当你看到并听到它的时候,你会同情我,会意识到我对提出这样一个要研究的悖论性的想法而持有怀疑和担心,完全是出于现实的考虑。”

'The more you say this kind of thing,' he said, 'the less likely
b we are to let you off discussing how this political system might be realized. Please don't waste any more time: just get on with it.'

'Well, the first thing we have to do,' I said, 'is remember that it's our search for the nature of morality and immorality that has brought us here.'

'All right,' he said. 'So what?'

'Nothing really. It's just that if we do discover what morality is, will we expect a moral man to be indistinguishable from it, and to be
c a perfect image of morality? Or will we be satisfied if he resembles it as closely as possible and participates in it more thoroughly than anyone else?'

'Yes, we'll be happy with that,' he said.

'Therefore,' I said, 'it's because we need a paradigm that we're trying to find out what morality is, and are asking whether a perfectly moral man could exist and, if so, what he would be like (and likewise for immorality and an immoral man). We want to be able to look at these men, to see how they stand as regards happiness and misery, and to face the inevitable conclusion about ourselves, that the more we resemble these exemplars, the more our
d condition will resemble their condition. In other words, the purpose of our enquiry is not to try to prove that perfect morality or immorality could ever actually exist.'

'True,' he said.

'Do you doubt an artist's competence if he paints a paradigmatically good-looking human being, and portrays everything perfectly well in the painting, but can't prove that a person like that could actually exist?'

'I certainly do not,' he protested.

'Well, aren't we saying that we're trying to construct a theoretical paradigm of a good community?'

'Yes.'

'Then do you doubt our competence as theoreticians in this context if we can't prove that a community with our theoretical constitution could actually exist?'

他说："你越是说这种事情，我们就越是不让你逃脱讨论这种政治制度是如何可能实现的。请不要再浪费时间了：就开始说说吧。" b

"好吧，我们必须要做的第一件事情，"我说，"就是记住我们要探求将我们的话题引导至此的正义与不正义的本质问题。"

"是的，"他说，"那又怎么样呢？"

"不怎么样。只是说如果我们发现了什么是正义，那么我们是否希望一个正义之人与正义毫无区别，并且就是正义的完美影像？或者，如果他尽可能地与之相像，并且比起任何别的人，他们 c
更多地分有正义，那么我们是否很满足呢？"

"是的，我们会为此感到很高兴。"他说。

"所以，"我说，"这就是为什么我们需要一个样板，以此我们试图发现什么是正义，探究真正的正义之人是否可能存在，如果存在又是什么样，对于不正义和不正义之人也是同样。我们想要能够观察这些人，看看他们是如何看待幸福和不幸的，并使我们面对关于自己的必然结论：我们越是像这些榜样，我们的处境就越是与他们的处境相似。换句话说，我们研究的目的不是试图去 d
证明真正的正义或不正义是否在现实中存在过。"

"对。"他说。

"如果一个艺术家依样画了个美人，在画中把所有的东西都画得很完美，但不能证明那样一个人的真实存在，那么你会怀疑他的能力吗？"

"我当然不会怀疑，"他反对说。

"那么，我们不是在试图建立一个好城邦的理论样板吗？"

"是的。" e

"如果我们不能证明我们理论上建构的城邦在现实中存在，那么在这种情况下你会怀疑我们作为理论家的能力吗？"

'Of course not,' he said.

'So that's how matters really stand,' I said. 'However, if for your sake I also have to apply myself to proving how and under what circumstances it might get as close as possible to viability, then although this is a different kind of argument, I must ask you to make the same concession as before.'

'What concession?'

473a 'Is it possible for anything actual to match a theory? Isn't any actual thing bound to have less contact with truth than a theory, however much people deny it? Do you agree or not?'

'I do,' he said.

'So please don't force me to point to an actual case in the material world which conforms in all respects to our theoretical construct. If we can discover how a community's administration could come very
b close to our theory, then let's say that we've fulfilled your demands and discovered how it's all viable. I mean, won't you be satisfied if we get that close? I would.'

'I would too,' he said.

'Next, then, I suppose we should try to discover and show what the flaw is in current political systems which stops communities being governed as well as we've described, and what the smallest change is which could enable a community to achieve this type of constitution. By the smallest change, I mean preferably a single change, but if that's impossible, then two changes, or at any rate as few as possible and the least drastic ones possible.'

c 'Absolutely,' he said.

'Well,' I said, 'I think there is a single change which can be shown to bring about the transformation. It's not a small change, however, or easy to achieve, but it is feasible.'

'What is it?' he asked.

“当然不能。”他说。

“所以事情实际上就是这样的，”我说，“然而，看在你的面子上，我也还必须致力于证明如何并且在什么条件下它可以尽可能地得以实现，这虽然是个不同的论证，但我必须请求你做出与先前同样的让步。”

“什么让步？”

“任何现实的东西有可能与理论相符合吗？比起理论，任何 473a
现实的东西不是必定与真理更加没什么关系，而不管人们如何地加以否认？你是否同意？”

“我同意。”他说。

“所以请不要强迫我在物质世界中指出一个现实的例子，能够在所有方面与我们的理论建构相一致。如果我们能发现一个城邦的管理如何与我们的理论非常地接近，那么就让我们说已经
满足了你的要求，并且发现了理论是如何全部可行的。我的意思是 b
说，如果我们接近了那样的程度，难道你还不满意？我是满意了。”

“我也会满意的。”他说。

“那么接下来我想我们应该试图去发现并表明当前的政治体制中的缺陷，它阻碍了城邦以我们说过的那种方式得到治理，表明最小的变化能够使得一个城邦实现这种类型的管理。我所谓的最小的变化最好指的是一个变化，但如果不行，那么就两个变动，无论如何越少越好，越小越好。”

“毫无疑问。”他说。 c

“好吧，”我说，“我想有一个变化被认为是能够带来变革。然而这不是一个最小的变化，也很难办到，但却是可行的。”

“是什么？”他问道。

'I'm now about to confront the difficulty which, in our image, is the largest wave,' I said. 'Still, it must be voiced, even if it's going to swamp us, exactly like a wave, with scornful and contemptuous laughter. Are you ready for me to speak?'

'Go ahead,' he said.

'Unless communities have philosophers as kings,' I said, 'or the
d people who are currently called kings and rulers practise philosophy with enough integrity—in other words, unless political power and philosophy coincide, and all the people with their diversity of talents who currently head in different directions towards either government or philosophy have those doors shut firmly in their faces—there can be no end to political troubles, my dear Glaucon, or even to human troubles
e in general, I'd say, and our theoretical constitution will be stillborn and will never see the light of day. Now you can appreciate what made me hesitate to speak before: I saw how very paradoxical it would sound, since it is difficult to realize that there is no other way for an individual or a community to achieve happiness.'

'What a thing to say, Socrates!' Glaucon said in response. 'This is quite an idea! Now that it's out in the open, you'd better expect hordes of people—and not second-rate people either—to fling off their clothes
474a (so to speak), pick up the nearest weapon, and rush naked at you with enough energy to achieve heroic feats. And if you don't come up with an argument to keep them at bay while you make your escape, then your punishment will be to discover what scorn really is.'

'And it'll all be your fault, won't it?' I said.

'I've no regrets,' he replied. 'But that doesn't mean I'll desert you: I'll defend you to the best of my ability. Goodwill and encouragement are my arsenal, and my answers probably suit you more than
b someone else's might. You can count on this assistance, so please try to win the sceptics round to your point of view.'

'You're providing such major support that I must make the ef

“在我们看来，我现在要面对最大的困难了，这是个最大的浪头，”我说，“虽然讥讽和鄙视的嘲笑正像那浪头一样要使我们倾覆，但我们还是必须要说出来。你准备听我说了吗？”

“说吧。”他说。

“除非城邦中有贤哲为王，”我说道，“或者当前为人称呼为王和统治者的人，恪守严格的道德规范来实践对智慧的热爱与追 d
求——换句话说，除非政治势力与对智慧的热爱相互一致，而且要把所有那些或偏向智慧、或偏向统治而方向不同、天分各异的人严格地拒斥在门外——否则，我亲爱的格劳孔，就会有数不尽的政治问题或甚至是整个人类的问题，我想说，我们的理论建构就会流产并且会不见天日。现在你知道是什么使得我先前犹豫 e
不想说了：我想这听起来是很矛盾的，因为人们很难意识到，对于个人或城邦来说，没有别的方法来实现幸福了。”

“苏格拉底，你说的是什么呀！”格劳孔回答说，“这是个什么样的想法啊！现在它会受到攻击，你最好等着一大批人——不是二流之人——即是说，他们会脱掉衣服，拿起手边的武器用全力 474a
赤膊向你冲过来以成就他们的英勇事迹。如果在你逃脱的时候，你拿不出论证阻挡他们而陷入困境，那么你会发现你会受到嘲笑的惩罚。”

“这全是你的错，不是吗？”我说。

“我并不为此感到愧疚，”他回答说，“但那并不意味着我会抛弃你：我会尽最大能力捍卫你。好意和勇气是我的武器，我的回答可能比别人的回答更加适合你。你可以把这当作帮助，所以请 b
尽力战胜围绕你观点的怀疑吧。”

“你所提供的是如此大的帮助，这样我就必须作出努力，”我

fort,' I said. 'Now, in my opinion, we'll never escape from the people you mentioned unless we offer them a definition of a philosopher so that it is clear what we mean by our rash claim that philosophers should have political power. When there's no doubt about what it is to be a philosopher, then a defence becomes possible, if we can show
c that some people are made to practise philosophy and to be political leaders, while others shouldn't engage in philosophy and should follow a leader.'

'The definition would be timely,' he remarked.

'All right. I wonder if this route leads to any kind of adequate clarification. Why don't you join me, and we'll see?'

'Lead on,' he said.

'I'm sure you're aware, without me having to remind you,' I said, 'that if the claim that someone loves something is to be accurate, he must undeniably love that thing as a whole, not just some aspects of it.'

d 'You've got to remind me, apparently,' he said, 'because I don't quite understand.'

'I'd have expected someone else to say that, Glaucon, not you,' I said. 'It's unlike an expert in love to forget that an amorous lover finds some pretext for being smitten and unhinged by every single alluring boy. They all seem to deserve his attention and devotion. I mean, isn't this how you and others like you behave towards good-looking young men? Don't you compliment a snub nose by calling it "pert", describe a hooked nose as "regal", and call one which falls
e between these two extremes "perfectly proportioned"? Don't you call swarthy young men "virile" and pallid ones "children of the gods"? And who do you think invented the term "honey-coloured"? It could only have been some lover glossing over and making light of a sallow complexion, because its possessor was in the alluring period of adolescence. In short, you come up with every conceivable excuse and
475a all kinds of terms to ensure that you can give your approval to every

说,“那么在我看来,我们永远都逃不过你说的那些人,除非我们给他们一个哲学家的定义,这样就能澄清我们匆忙的说法,说哲学家应该拥有政治权力说的是什么意思。当对哲学家是什么没有疑问的时候,然后辩护才是可能的,如果我们能够表明要使有些人从事哲学活动并且使之成为政治领导者,而别的人不应该从 c
事哲学活动并且不应该担任领袖。”

“这个定义是及时的。”他评论说。

“好吧。我想知道这条道路是否引向任何彻底的澄清。你为什么不加入我一起考察呢?”

“你带路吧。”他说。

我说:“我确信你不经我提示已经意识到,如果某人爱某物这样的说法是准确的话,那么不可否认,他爱的是作为整体的事物而不仅仅是它的某些方面。”

“你似乎还得提示我,”他说,“因为我不太明白。” d

“格劳孔,我本期望是别人才会那样说,而不是你,”我说,“要是爱者忘记了找一些被每个充满魅力的美少年吸引的理由,那么他似乎不像是一个爱情能手。所有美少年似乎都值得关注和倾心。我的意思是说,这不就是你和像你这样的人对年轻美貌的男子的反应吗?你难道不会恭维一个塌鼻子说它是‘精致’,把鹰勾鼻说成是‘高贵’,把处于这两个极端的中间者称作‘比例非常协调’?你难道不是把皮肤黝黑者称作‘有男子汉气概’,把皮肤白 e
皙者称作‘诸神之子’?你认为是谁发明了‘蜜一般的颜色’这个词语呢?这只可能是某个爱者用来掩盖苍白的面容并使之容光焕发,因为拥有这面容的人正处于青春焕发的时期。简而言之,你要拿出各种想得到的理由和各种词语以确保你能够把赞美给 475a

alluring lad.'

'If you insist on trying out your ideas of how lovers behave on me,' he said, 'you can have my assent, because I don't want to jeopardize the argument.'

'And haven't you seen people who are fond of drinking behave in exactly the same way?' I went on. 'They make all kinds of excuses for their devotion to wine of every kind.'

'Yes.'

'And I'm sure you've noticed that if ambitious people can't get
b the command of a whole army, they take a company; and if they can't win the respect of important and high-powered people, they're happy to be respected by lesser people. It's status in general which they desire.'

'Absolutely.'

'So tell me where you stand on this question. If in our opinion someone desires something, are we to say that he desires that type of thing as a whole, or only some aspects of it?'

'The whole of it,' he replied.

'So the same goes for a philosopher too: we're to say that what he desires is the whole of knowledge, not just some aspects of it. True?'

'True.'

'If someone fusses about his lessons, then, especially when he's
c still young and without rational understanding of what is and isn't good for him, we can't describe him as a lover of knowledge, a philosopher, just as we can't describe someone who is fussing about his food as hungry, as desiring food, and don't call him a gourmand, but a poor eater.'

'Yes, it would be wrong to call him anything else.'

'On the other hand, if someone is glad to sample every subject

予每个具有魅力的年轻人。”

“如果你坚持要在我身上试验你的想法，即爱者是如何表现的，”他说，“我是会同意你的，因为我不想破坏你的论证。”

“你难道没注意到爱喝酒的人也有同样的表现吗？”我继续说，“他们为喜欢喝各种酒而找出各种理由。”

“是的。”

“我确信你注意到有些人如果不能掌控整个军队，那么他们便掌控一个小队；如果得不到位高权重之人的尊敬，那么得到小 b
人物的尊敬他们也会很高兴。一般来说他们所渴望得到的就是权位。”

“毫无疑问。”

“所以告诉我你对这个问题的看法。如果在我们看来某人渴望某物，那么我们是否可以说他渴望这种作为整体的事物还是说只是它的一些部分？”

“事物的整体。”他回答说。

“所以对于哲学家来说也是一样：我们会说他渴望知识的整体，而不仅仅是它的某些部分。对吗？”

“对的。”

“那么如果有个人抱怨他的学业，尤其是当他还年轻、什么对他有益和什么对他无益没有加以理性地理解的时候，我们不能把 c
他说成是一个热爱知识的人或一个哲学家，就像我们不能把某个对食物挑三拣四的人形容为饥饿，或描述为迫切地需要食物，而且我们也不能称呼他是美食家，而只不过是一个可怜的食客罢了。”

“是的，把他称为别的什么也是错误的。”

“另一方面，如果有个人对各种知识都愿意涉猎一下，并且不

and eagerly sets about his lessons with an insatiable appetite, then we'd be perfectly justified in calling him a philosopher, don't you think?'

d 'Then a motley crowd of people will be philosophers,' Glaucon said. 'For instance, sightseers all do what they do because they enjoy learning, I suppose; and it would be very odd to count theatre-goers as philosophers, when they'd never go of their own accord to hear a lecture or spend time over anything like that, but they rush around the festivals of Dionysus to hear every theatrical troupe, as if they were getting paid for the use of their ears, and never miss a single festival, whether it's being held in town or out of town. Are we to describe all these people and the disciples of other amusements as philosophers? And

e what about students of trivial branches of expertise?'

'No,' I replied, 'they're not philosophers, but they resemble philosophers.'

'Who are the true philosophers you have in mind?' he asked.

'Sightseers of the truth,' I answered.

'That must be right, but what exactly does it mean?' he asked.

'It wouldn't be easy to explain to anyone else,' I said. 'But you'll grant me this, surely.'

'What?'

476a 'Since beautiful is the opposite of ugly, they are two things.'

'Of course.'

'In so far as they are two, each of them is single?'

'Yes.'

'And the same principle applies to moral and immoral, good and bad, and everything of any type: in itself, each of them is single, but each of them has a plurality of manifestations because they appear all over the place, as they become associated with actions and bodies and one another.'

'You're right,' he said.

知足地开始他的学习，那么我们完全有理由称他为哲学家，你难道不这么想吗？”

“那么各种各样的人都会是哲学家了。”格劳孔说，“比如说， d
我想所有爱看的人也包括在内了，因为他们喜欢学习；把看戏的人当作哲学家会是很奇怪的，他们从来不会主动地去听一场辩论或把时间花在任何那样的事情上，他们在酒神节上倒是到处乱跑，去听每场演出，似乎他们的耳朵被出租出去了，无论在城内还是在城外，他们从来不错过每个庆典。我们会把所有这些人以及别的娱乐活动的信徒当作哲学家吗？还有那些小技艺的学徒 e
们呢？”

“不会，”我回答说，“他们不是哲学家，但他们像哲学家。”

“在你看来谁是真正的哲学家？”他问道。

“看到真理的人。”我回答说。

“这肯定是对的，不过这到底是什么意思？”他问道。

我说：“当然在这一点上除了你会同意之外，向其他任何人解释可不容易。”

“什么？”

“因为美是丑的对立面，它们是两样东西。”

“当然。” 476a

“它们既然为二，所以各自为一？”

“是的。”

“同样的原则也适用于正义和不正义，善和恶以及所有其他类型的东西：就其自身而言，其每一个都是一，但其每一个又展示出多，因为它们处处与行动、形体及其相互之间有所关联。”

“你说得对。”他说。

'Well,' I continued, 'this is what enables me to distinguish the sightseers (to borrow your term) and the ones who want to acquire
b some expertise or other and the men of action from the people in question, the ones who are philosophers in the true sense of the term.'

'What do you mean?' he asked.

'Theatre-goers and sightseers are devoted to beautiful sounds and colours and shapes, and to works of art which consist of these elements, but their minds are constitutionally incapable of seeing and devoting themselves to beauty itself.'

'Yes, that's certainly right,' he said.

'However, people with the ability to approach beauty itself and see beauty as it actually is are bound to be few and far between, aren't they?'

c 'Definitely.'

'So does someone whose horizon is limited to beautiful things, with no conception of beauty itself, and who is incapable of following guidance as to how to gain knowledge of beauty itself, strike you as living in a dream-world or in the real world? Look at it this way. Isn't dreaming precisely the state, whether one is asleep or awake, of taking something to be the real thing, when it is actually only a likeness?'

'Yes, that's what I'd say dreaming is,' he said.

'And what about someone who does the opposite—who does
d think that there is such a thing as beauty itself, and has the ability to see it as well as the things which partake in it, and never gets them muddled up? Do you think he's living in the real world or in a dream-world?'

'Definitely in the real world,' he said.

'So wouldn't we be right to describe the difference between their mental states by saying that while this person has knowledge, the other one has beliefs?'

'Yes.'

'Now, suppose this other person—the one we're saying has be-

“那么，”我继续说，“这使得我能够把爱看的人——借你的词——想得到这样那样技艺的人和实干者，与我们所讨论的那些人，即真正意义上的哲学家相区分。” b

“你说的是什么意思？”他问道。

“看戏的人和爱看的人喜欢美妙的声音、颜色和形状，喜欢由这些元素构成的艺术作品，但他们的心灵在构成上不能看到并使自己热爱美本身。”

“是的，这当然是对的。”他说。

“然而，具有理解美本身，就其自身来领会美的人，必定是少之又少的，不是吗？”

“毫无疑问。” c

“所以那些视野局限于美的事物，而没有认识美本身的人，以及那些没能按着指引去获得关于美本身的知识之人，会让你觉得他们生活于梦境还是真实的世界之中？这样来看看。无论人们是睡着了还是醒着，梦幻是否正是一种把某物当作真实存在之物状态，而这实际上只是一个相似之物。”

“是的，我想说梦幻就是这样的。”他说。

“那些相反的人呢——他确实认为有美本身这样的东西，也具有认识分有美的事物的能力，而不会把它们相混淆？你认为他生活在真实的世界中还是生活在梦幻的世界中？” d

“当然是在真实的世界中。”他说。

“所以我们不就可以说他们的精神状态是不一样的，这种人具有知识而另一种人具有意见？”

“是的。”

“现在假设这另一种人——那种我们说具有信念而没有知识

liefs, not knowledge—were to get cross with us and query the truth of our assertions. Will we be able to calm him down and gently convince
e him of our point of view, while keeping him in the dark about the poor state of his health?'

'We really ought to,' he said.

'All right, but what shall we say to him, do you think? Perhaps this is what we should ask him. We'll tell him that we don't resent any knowledge he might have—indeed, we'd be delighted to see that he does know something—and then we'll say, "But can you tell us, please, whether someone with knowledge knows something or nothing?" You'd better answer my questions for him.'

'My answer will be that he knows something,' he said.

'Something real or something unreal?'

'Real. How could something unreal be known?'

477a 'We could look at the matter from more angles, but we're happy enough with the idea that something completely real is completely accessible to knowledge, and something utterly unreal is entirely inaccessible to knowledge. Yes?'

'Perfectly happy.'

'All right. But if something is in a state of both reality and unreality, then it falls between that which is perfectly real and that which is utterly unreal, doesn't it?'

'Yes.'

'So since the field of knowledge is reality, and since it must be incomprehension whose field is unreality, then we need to find out if
b there is in fact something which falls between incomprehension and knowledge, whose field is this inter—mediate, don't we?'

'Yes.'

'Now, we acknowledge the existence of belief, don't we?'

'Of course.'

的人——对我们发脾气并质问我们论断的真实性。我们是否能够让他安静下来,对他好言相劝让他信服我们的观点,并且让他知道自己处于不健康的状态?” e

“我们确实应该这样做。”他说。

“好吧,但你认为我们应该对他说什么呢?也许我们应该这样问他。我们会告诉他,我们对他可能有的知识并不讨厌——实际上,我们很高兴他知道些什么——那么我们会说:‘不过请你告诉我们,一个具有知识的人知道些什么呢?还是什么都不知道?’你最好能替他回答我的问题。”

“我的回答是他知道些什么。”他说。

“是存在的事物还是不存在的事物?”

“存在的,不存在的事物怎么是可知的呢?” 477a

“我们可以从更多的角度来考察事物,但我们很高兴有这样的想法,即完全存在的事物是完全可知的,完全不存在的事物是完全不可知的,是吗?”

“非常高兴。”

“好吧。但要是某个事物既处于存在又处于不存在的状态之中,那么它就在完全存在的事物和完全不存在的事物之间,难道不是吗?”

“是的。”

“所以由于知识的领域是存在,而不存在的领域必定是无知,那么我们需要找出事实上是否有某事物处于无知和知识之间,其领域就是这中间部分,不是吗?” b

“是的。”

“那么我们就承认了意见的存在,不是吗?”

“当然。”

'Is it a different faculty from knowledge, or is it the same?'

'Different.'

'Every faculty has its own distinctive abilities, so belief and knowledge must have different domains.'

'Yes.'

'Now, since the natural field of knowledge is reality—its function is to know reality as reality... Actually, I think there's something else we need to get clear about first.'

'What?'

c 'Shall we count as a distinct class of things the faculties which give human beings and all other creatures their abilities? By 'faculties' I mean things like sight and hearing. Do you understand the type of thing I have in mind?'

'Yes, I do,' he said.

'Let me tell you something that strikes me about them. I can't distinguish one faculty from another the way I commonly distinguish other things, by looking at their colours or shapes or anything like that, because faculties don't have any of those sorts of qualities for me
d to look at. The only aspect of a faculty I can look at is its field, its effect. This is what enables me to identify each of them as a particular faculty. Where I find a single domain and a single effect, I say there is a single faculty; and I distinguish faculties which have different fields and different effects. What about you? What do you do?'

'The same as you,' he said.

'Let's go back to where we were before, then, Glaucon,' I said. 'Do you think that knowledge is a faculty, or does it belong in your opinion to some other class?'

'I think it belongs to that class,' he said, 'and is the most powerful of all the faculties.'

e 'And shall we classify belief as a faculty, or what?'

"它是与知识不同的还是相同的官能?"

"不同的。"

"每个官能有其各自特殊的能力,所以意见和知识肯定拥有不同的领域。"

"是的。"

"那么由于知识的天然领域是存在——它的功能是认识作为存在的存在。事实上,我想还有另一些事情我们需要首先加以澄清。"

"什么?"

"我们是否应该把给予人类和别的动物以能力的官能当作一 c
类特殊的事物呢?'官能'指的是像看和听这样的东西。你明白我心里想说的那类事物了吗?"

"是的,我明白了。"他说。

"让我告诉你一些关于它们的、让我印象深刻的东西吧。我不能把一种官能与另一种官能相区分,就像我平时区分其他事物一样,通过考察它们的颜色、形状或别的诸如此类的东西,因为官能没有可以让我去考察的性质。我可以考察的官能的唯一一个方面是它的领域
和它的效果。这使得我把其中的每一个都当作特殊的官能。当我发 d
现有一个领域和一个效果的地方,我就说有一个官能;我把具有不同领域和不同效果的官能区别开来。你呢?你是怎么做的?"

"和你一样。"他说。

"那么让我们回到之前那个地方,"我说,"你是否认为知识是一种官能,或在你看来属于某个别的类型?"

"我认为它是属于那个类型的,"他说,"并且是所有官能中最有力的。"

"我们应该把意见当作一种官能还是什么?" e

'As a faculty,' he said. 'Belief is precisely that which enables us to entertain beliefs.'

'Not long ago, however, you agreed that knowledge and belief were different.'

'Of course,' he said. 'One is infallible and the other is fallible, so anyone with any sense would keep them separate.'

'Good,' I said. 'There can be no doubt of our position: knowledge and belief are different.'

478a 'Yes.'

'Since they're different faculties, then, they have different natural fields, don't they?'

'Necessarily.'

'The field of knowledge is reality, isn't it? Its function is to know the reality of anything real?'

'Yes.'

'And the function of belief, we're saying, is to entertain beliefs?'

'Yes.'

'Does it entertain beliefs about the same thing which knowledge knows? Will what is accessible to knowledge and what is accessible to belief be identical? Or is that out of the question?'

'It's ruled out by what we've already agreed,' he said. 'If different faculties naturally have different fields, and if both knowledge
b and belief are faculties, and different faculties too, as we said, then it follows that it is impossible for what is accessible to knowledge and what is accessible to belief to be identical.'

'So if it is reality that is accessible to knowledge, then it is something else, not reality, that is accessible to belief, isn't it?'

'Yes.'

'Does it entertain beliefs about what is unreal? Or is it also impossible for that to happen? Think about this: isn't it the

“当作一种官能，”他说，“正是意见才使得我们能够发表意见。”

“然而不久以前，你同意过知识和意见是不同的。”

“当然，”他说，“一个是不会发生错误的，另一个是可发生错误的，所以任何有理智的人都会把它们区分开的。”

“好，”我说，“我们的观点就没有疑问了：知识和意见是不同的。” 478a

“是的。”

“那么因为它们是不同的官能，所以它们具有不同的天然领域，不是吗？”

“必定如此。”

“知识的领域是存在，不是吗？其功能在于认识任何存在的事物的存在。”

“是的。”

“我们是否可以说意见的功能就是发表意见？”

“是的。”

“发表意见所说的，与知识认识的是否是同一个东西？可以认识的事物与可以形成看法的事物是相同的吗？或者说那是不可能的？”

“这已经被我们的共同看法排除了，”他说，“如果不同的官能天然地具有不同的领域，并且如果知识和意见都是官能，如同我们说过的那样也是不同的官能，那么就可以推出，可知的事物与 b
可以形成意见的事物是不可能相同的。”

“所以如果存在是可知的，那么是别的事物而不是存在可以形成意见，不是吗？”

“是的。”

“发表意见是关于存在的事物吗？或者说那样也是不可能的？想想看：发表意见的人心里是想着某样东西的，情况不就是

case that someone who is entertaining a belief is bringing his believing mind to bear on something? I mean, is it possible to have a belief, and to be believing nothing?'

'That's impossible.'

'In fact, someone who has a belief has some single thing in mind, doesn't he?'

'Yes.'

'But the most accurate way to refer to something unreal would be
c to say that it is nothing, not that it is a single thing, wouldn't it?'

'Yes.'

'Didn't we find ourselves forced to relate incomprehension to unreality and knowledge to reality?'

'That's right,' he said.

'So the field of belief is neither reality nor unreality?'

'No.'

'Belief can't be incomprehension or knowledge, then?'

'So it seems.'

'Well, does it lie beyond their limits? Does it shed more light than knowledge or spread more obscurity than incom-prehension?'

'It does neither.'

'Alternatively, does belief strike you as more opaque than knowledge and more lucid than incomprehension?'

'Considerably more,' he said.

d 'It lies within their limits?'

'Yes.'

'Then belief must fall between them.'

'Absolutely.'

'Now, didn't we say earlier that something which is simultaneously real and unreal (were such a thing to be shown to exist) would fall between the perfectly real and the wholly unreal,

这样的吗？我的意思是说，拥有空洞无物的意见是可能的吗？”

“不可能 。”

“事实上，有意见的人心里想着某个事物，不是吗？”

“是的。”

“但对不存在的事物的最准确的表述方式，是说它什么都不是，而不是说它是一个事物，不是吗？” c

“是的。”

“我们不是发现自己必须把无知与不存在联系起来，把知识与存在联系起来？”

“对。”他说。

“所以意见的领域既不是存在也不是不存在？”

“都不是。”

“那么，意见不可能是无知或知识？”

“看来如此。”

“那么它是否在它们的界限之外？它是否比知识更加明亮或比无知更加晦暗？”

“都不是。”

“那么你认为意见是否比知识更加晦暗而比无知更加明亮？”

“程度要深得多。”他说。

“它在界限之内吗？” d

“是的。”

“那么意见必定在它们两者之间。”

“毫无疑问。”

“那么，我们不是早先说过某些同时既存在又不存在的事物，要是这样的事物是被证明为存在的话，它们就处于完全存在与完

and wouldn't be the field of either knowledge or incomprehension, but of an intermediate (again, if such a thing were shown to exist) between incomprehension and knowledge?'

'Right.'

'And now we've found that what we call belief is such an intermediate, haven't we?'

'We have.'

e 'So the only thing left for us to discover, apparently, is whether there's anything which partakes of both reality and unreality, and cannot be said to be perfectly real or perfectly unreal. If we were to come across such a thing, we'd be fully justified in describing it as the field of belief, on the principle that extremes belong together, and so do intermediates. Do you agree?'

'Yes.'

479a 'Let's return, on this basis, to the give and take of conversation with that fine fellow who doesn't acknowledge the existence of beauty itself or think that beauty itself has any permanent and unvarying character, but takes the plurality of beautiful things as his norm—that sightseer who can't under any circumstances abide the notion that beauty, morality, and so on are each a single entity. What we'll say to him is, "My friend, is there one beautiful thing, in this welter of beautiful things, which won't turn out to be ugly? Is there one moral deed which won't turn out to be immoral? Is there one just act which won't turn out to be unjust?"'

b 'No, there isn't,' he said. 'It's inevitable for these things to turn out to be both beautiful and ugly, in a sense, and the same goes for all the other qualities you mentioned in your question.'

'And there are doubles galore—but they turn out to be halves just as much as doubles, don't they?'

'Yes.'

全不存在的事物之间，就既不是知识的领域也不是无知的领域，而是处于无知和知识的中间，如果这样的事物也被证明为存在的话？”

“对。”

“现在我们已经发现所谓的意见是这样一个中间者，不是吗？”

“我们已经发现了。”

“所以留给我们最后去发现的唯一事物似乎就是是否有什么 e
事物既存在又不存在，而不能说成是完全的存在或完全的不存在。要是我们发现了这样的事物，那么完全有理由把它说成是意见的领域，在原则上端点共属，中间也一样。你同意吗？”

“同意。”

“在这个基础之上让我们回到与那位好同伴的讨论上来，他 479a
不承认美本身的存在，或认为美本身没有任何永恒不变的特征，而是把繁多的美的事物当作他的标准——那位观赏者在任何情况下都不会接受这种说法：美、正义等等都是一种单一体。我们会对他这样说：‘我的朋友，在众多的美的事物中，难道没有一个美的事物会倒转为丑的吗？难道没有一个道德的行为会倒转为不道德的吗？难道没有一个正义的行动会倒转为不正义的吗？’”

“有的，”他说，“这对于这些事物来说是不可避免的：在某种 b
意义上它们既是美的又是丑的，对于你提到的所有其他性质也一样。”

“有双倍多的东西——但看上去是一半多，就像看上去有双倍多一样，不是吗？”

“是的。”

'And do things which are large, small, light, and heavy deserve these attributes any more than they deserve the opposite attributes?'

'No, each of them is bound to have both qualities,' he said.

'So isn't it the case, then, that any member of a plurality no more is whatever it is said to be than it is not whatever it is said to be?'

'This is like those double entendres one hears at parties,' he
c said, 'or the riddle children tell about the eunuch and his hitting a bat-they make a riddle by asking what he hit it with and what it was on —in the sense that the members of the plurality are also ambiguous: it is impossible to form a stable conception of any of them as either being what it is, or not being what it is, or being both, or being neither.'

'How are you going to cope with them, then?' I asked. 'Can you find a better place to locate them than between real being and unreality? I mean, they can't turn out to be more opaque and unreal than unreality, or more lucid and real than reality.'

d 'True,' he said.

'So there we are. We've discovered that the welter of things which the masses conventionally regard as beautiful and so on mill around somewhere between unreality and perfect reality.'

'Yes, we have.'

'But we have a prior agreement that were such a thing to turn up, we'd have to call it the field of belief, not of knowledge, since

“一些事物，它们可以是小的、大的、重的和轻的，同时，不是也更可以相反地是大的、小的、轻的和重的吗？”

“是，它们中的每一个必定具有两种性质。”他说。

“所以情况不就是这样的，被认为是存在的多个中的一个，并不比被认为是不存在的要多？”

“这就像是人们在宴会上听到的那些模棱两可的话，”他
说，“或者像是给儿童讲述的太监打蝙蝠的谜语[1]——他们 c
这样来问这个谜语，他用什么打，在什么东西上——在这个意义上说多个事物也是模棱两可的：不可能对其中的任何一个形成一个固定的看法，是存在还是不存在，是两者都有还是两者皆无。”

“那么你准备怎么对付它们？”我说，“除了把它们放置在存在与不存在之间，你还能找到更好的地方吗？我的意思是说，它们不可能比不存在更晦暗更不实在，或比存在更明亮更
实在。” d

“对的。”他说。

“所以我们已经找到了大量事物，一般人通常认为它们是美的等等，它们处在不存在与完全存在之间的某个位置。”

“是的，我们已经发现了。”

“但是我们之前已经同意要是有这样的事物出现，那么我们必定将之称作意见的领域，而不是知识，因为占据了某个不确定

[1] 这个谜语是这样的：一个男人（又不是男人）看见（又没看见）一只鸟（又不是鸟）停在一根树枝（又不是树枝）上，他用一块石头（又不是石头）去打它。谜底是一位太监瞥见一只蝙蝠停在一根芦苇上，他用一块石片去打它。

the realm which occupies some uncertain intermediate point must be accessible to the intermediate faculty.'

'Yes, we do.'

e 'What shall we say about those spectators, then, who can see a plurality of beautiful things, but not beauty itself, and who are incapable of following if someone else tries to lead them to it, and who can see many moral actions, but not morality itself, and so on? That they only ever entertain beliefs, and do not *know* any of the things they believe?'

'That's what we have to say,' he said.

'As for those who can see each of these things in itself, in its permanent and unvarying nature, we'll say they have knowledge and are not merely entertaining beliefs, won't we?'

'Again, we have to.'

480a 'And won't our position be that they're devoted to and love the domain of knowledge, as opposed to the others, who are devoted to and love the domain of belief? I mean, surely we haven't forgotten our claim that these others love and are spectators of beautiful sounds and colours and so on, but can't abide the idea that there is such a thing as beauty itself?'

'No, we haven't forgotten.'

'They won't think us nasty if we refer to them as "lovers of belief" rather than as philosophers, who love knowledge, will they? Are they going to get very cross with us if we say that now?'

'Not if they listen to me,' he replied. 'It's not right to get angry at the truth.'

'But the term "believers" is inappropriate for those who are devoted to everything that is real: they should be called philosophers, shouldn't they?'

'Absolutely.'

的中间点的领域必须由中间的官能来把握。”

“是的，我们同意。”

“那些能看到多样的美的事物而看不到美本身的人，那些别 e
人试图引领他们走向美本身而他们没有能力加以追随的人，那些能够看到诸多正义的行为而看不到正义本身的人，等等这样的人，我们应该把这些观看者称作什么呢？他们是否只发表意见而不认识任何他们所相信的事物？”

“我们必须这么说，”他说。

“至于那些能够看到每个这样的事物本身及其永恒本质的人，我们会说他们具有知识而不仅仅只有意见，不是吗？”

“我们肯定会这么说。”

“我们的观点不就是，与其他致力并热爱意见领域的人相反，他们致力并热爱知识领域？我的意思是说，我们当然没有忘记我们的主张，其他人热爱妙声美色等等，还有以妙声美色为可餐的
人，不会接受这样一种观念的，即有美自身这样的一种东西。这 480a
不就是我们的看法吗？”

“对，我们没有忘记。”

“如果我们把他们称作‘爱意见者’而不是爱知识的哲学家，他们不会认为我们冒犯了他们，是吗？如果我们现在那样说的话，他们是否会对我们生气？”

“如果他们不听我说的话，”他回答说，“对真理生气就不对了。”

“但对那些致力于所有实在事物的人来说，‘爱意见者’这个词是不恰当的：他们应该被称作哲学家，难道不是吗？”

“毫无疑问。”

484a ‘It’s taken a long and thorough discussion, Glaucon,’ I said, ‘and it’s not been easy, but we’ve now demonstrated the difference between philosophers and non-philosophers.’

‘A short discussion probably wouldn’t have been enough,’ he replied.

‘I suppose you’re right,’ I said. ‘Anyway, I think the conclusion would have been clearer if that had been the only subject we’d had to discuss, and there weren’t plenty of topics left for us to cover if we’re to
b see the difference between a moral and an immoral life.’

‘What’s the next issue for us to look into?’ he asked.

‘The next one’s the one that follows, of course,’ I replied. ‘Given that philosophers are those who are capable of apprehending that which is permanent and unvarying, while those who can’t, those who wander erratically in the midst of plurality and variety, are not lovers of knowledge, which set of people ought to be rulers of a community?’

‘What would be a sensible answer for us to give?’ he asked.

‘That the position of guardianship should be given to whichever set we find capable of guarding the laws and customs of a community,’ I said.

c ‘Right,’ he said.

‘I assume it’s clear whether someone who’s going to guard something should be blind or have good eyesight?’ I said.

‘Of course it is,’ he answered.

‘Well, imagine someone who really lacks the ability to recognize any and every real thing and has no paradigm to shed light for his mind’s eye. He has nothing absolutely authentic to contemplate, as painters do, and use as a reference-point whenever he needs to, and
d gain a completely accurate picture of, before establishing human norms of right, morality, and goodness (if establishing is what is required), and before guarding and protecting the norms that have already been established. Do you think there’s any difference between his condition and blindness?’

“格劳孔，这是个漫长而透彻的讨论，”我说，“这并不容易，但 484a
我们现在已经证实了哲学家与非哲学家之间的区别。”

“一个简短的讨论也许是不够的。”他回答说。

“我想你是对的，”我说，“无论如何，我想要是我们只讨论一
个主题，如果我们在考察正义的生活与不正义的生活之区别的时
候，没有涉及到那么多问题的话，那么结论将会是更加清晰的。” b

“接下来我们要考察的问题是什么呢？”他说。

“当然是循序渐进，”我回答说，“要是哲学家是那些能够认识永恒不变之事物的人，而那些不能认识。在多样的事物中迷失方向的人不是热爱智慧的人，那么哪些人应该是城邦的统治者呢？”

“我们怎么回答才是合理的呢？”他问道。

“卫士的职位应该给那些我们认为能够保卫城邦的法律和习
俗的人。”我说。 c

“对的。”他说。

“我想这是清楚的：一个要保护某物的人应该是瞎的，还是应该具有好眼力？”我说。

“当然很清楚。”他回答道。

“唔，设想有某人，他确实缺少认知全部实存事物的能力，而
且对其心灵的眼睛而言，他也没有样式或范例可以使事物清楚明
白地显示出来。他没有什么绝对真实的东西用来凝视，就像画匠
需要的时候就可以把它当作参照物，得到一个完全准确的图像， d
之后才确立人类的正义、道德和善良的规范（如果要求确立的
话），之后才能保护和捍卫那些已经确立起来的规范。你认为他
的处境与瞎子有什么区别吗？”

‘No, there’s hardly any difference at all,’ he said.

‘Is this the type of person you’d prefer us to appoint as guardians? Or shall we appoint those who can recognize every reality, and who not only have just as much practical experience as the others, but are also at least as good as them in every other respect?’

‘If they really are at least equal in every other sphere,’ he said,‘and since they are pre-eminent in the sphere you’ve mentioned, which is just about the most important one there is, then it would be ridiculous to choose anyone else.’

485a ‘So what we’d better explain is how a single person can combine both sets of qualities, hadn’t we?’

‘Yes.’

‘Well, right at the beginning of this argument we said that the first thing we had to grasp was what it is to be a philosopher, I’m sure that if we reached a satisfactory agreement on that point, we’d also agree that despite being a single person, he can combine both sets of qualities, and that philosophers are the only ones who should rule over communities.’

‘Why?’

b ‘Let’s start by agreeing that it’s natural for philosophers to love every field of study which reveals to them something of that reality which is eternal and is not subject to the vicissitudes of generation and destruction.’

‘All right.’

‘Moreover,’ I said,‘we can agree that they’re in love with reality as a whole, and that therefore their behaviour is just like that of ambitious people and lovers, as we explained before, in that they won’t willingly give up even minor or worthless parts of it.’

‘You’re right,’ he said.

“没有，几乎完全没有什么区别。”他说。

“你愿意我们把这种人任命为卫士吗？或我们应该任命那些能够认识每一种实在的人，他们不仅具有与别人一样丰富的实践经验，而且至少在所有别的方面也与别人一样优秀？”

他说：“如果确实至少在所有别的方面与人一样，并且因为最重要的是，在你提到过的那个方面他们最为优秀，那么选择别人就是可笑的。”

“所以我们最好解释一下，一个人如何才能把两方面的品性 485a
结合起来，不是吗？”

“是的。”

“好吧，在这个论证的一开头，我们说过我们首先要理解什么是哲学家。我确信要是我们对此取得令人满意的一致看法，那么我们也会同意尽管他是一个人，但他也能把两方面的品性结合起来，并且同意哲学家是唯一应该统治城邦的人。”

“为什么？”

“我们以同意下面的观念为论证的出发点，即对于哲学家而言，他们有一种天赋，热爱能向他们揭示出实存事物的每一处知
识领域，这些实存事物是永恒的，并且不受时代兴衰与成毁变迁 b
的影响。”

“对。”

“此外，”我说，“我们同意他们爱的是作为整体的存在，所以他们的行为正像是我们之前说过的爱荣誉者和爱者，因为即使是它的一小部分或一个没有价值的部分，他们也不愿放弃。”

“你说得对。”他说。

c ‘The next thing for you to think about is whether there's a further feature they must have, if they're going to live up to our description of them.’

‘What feature?’

‘Honesty—the inability consciously to tolerate falsehood, rather than loathing it, and loving truth.’

‘It makes sense that they should,’ he said.

‘It doesn't only make sense, my friend: a lover is absolutely bound to love everything which is related and belongs to his beloved.’

‘Right,’ he said.

‘Well, can you conceive of anything more closely related to knowledge than truth?’

‘Of course not,’ he replied.

d ‘Is it possible, then, for love of knowledge and love of falsehood to be found in the same nature?’

‘Definitely not.’

‘Then a genuine lover of knowledge will from his earliest years find nothing more attractive than truth of every kind.’

‘Indisputably.’

‘And we know that anyone whose predilection tends strongly in a single direction has correspondingly less desire for other things, like a stream whose flow has been diverted into another channel.’

‘Of course.’

‘So when a person's desires are channelled towards learning and so on, that person is concerned with the pleasure the mind feels of its own accord, and has nothing to do with the pleasures which reach the mind through the agency of the body, if the person is a genuine philosopher, not a fake one.’

e ‘Inevitably.’

‘He'll be self-disciplined, then, and not mercenary, since he's

“对你来说要考虑的下一件事情便是，如果他们想要做到跟我们的描述一样的话，他们是否还需要具有更多的品性。” c

“什么品性？”

“诚实——不能有意识地容忍错误，要厌恶错误并且热爱真理。”

“他们是应该这样做。”他说。

“我的朋友，这不仅仅讲得有道理：一个爱者绝对必定是爱所有与被爱者相关并且属于被爱者的事物。”

“对。”他说。

“那么你能想出什么比真理更接近知识的事物吗？”

“当然没有。”他回答说。

“那么在同一个本性中，是否有可能发现爱知识与爱错误？” d

“绝对不可能。”

“那么一个真正爱知识的人从他的早年起，就发现没有什么比每一种真理更具吸引力了。”

“毫无疑问。”

“我们知道，任何一个在某个方面具有强烈偏好的人，对于其他事物的欲望就相应地较少，就像水流被引向了另一个渠道。”

“当然。”

“所以当一个人的欲望被引向学习等方面，那个人关注的是使心灵感到自身和谐的快乐，而与那些通过身体的中介而达到心灵的快乐无关，如果这人是个真正的哲学家而不是一个假冒的哲学家的话。” e

“的确如此。”

“那么，他会自我约束，而不唯利是图，因为他本质上不会

constitutionally incapable of taking seriously the things which money can buy—at considerable cost—and which cause others to take money seriously.'

'Yes.'

486a 'And here's another point you'd better take into consideration, to help you distinguish a philosophical from a non-philosophical character.'

'What?'

'You must watch out for the presence of small-mindedness. Nothing stops a mind constantly striving for an overview of the totality of things human and divine more effectively than involvement in petty details.'

'Very true,' he said.

'When a mind has broadness of vision and contemplates all time and all existence, do you think it can place much importance on human life?'

'Impossible,' he said.

'So it won't find death terrifying either, will it?'

b 'Not at all.'

'Then a cowardly and small-minded person is excluded from true philosophy, it seems.'

'I agree.'

'Well now, take a person who's restrained and uninterested in money, and who isn't small-minded or specious or cowardly. Could he possibly drive hard bargains or act immorally?'

'No.'

'So when you're trying to see whether or not someone has a philosophical mind, you'll watch out for whether, from his earliest years, he shows himself to be moral and well mannered, or antisocial and uncouth.'

'Yes.'

重视可以用钱购买的东西——即便是花大钱买来的——而这些东西则会使得其他人深深陷入对金钱的迷恋之中。”

“是的。”

“为了帮助你区别哲学家和非哲学家的品性,这里还有一点 486a
你应该加以考虑。”

“什么?”

“你必须当心出现心胸狭窄。没有什么比陷入琐碎细节更能有效阻止心灵持续努力地总体观察人和神的事情全貌的了。”

“非常正确。”他说。

“当一个灵魂具有宽阔的眼界,对所有时代的所有存在都进行沉思,你认为他会把重心放在人类的生活上吗?”

“不可能。”他说。

“所以他也不会觉得死亡是可怕的,是吗?” b

“根本不可怕。”

“这么看来,胆小和心胸狭窄之人就被排除于真正的哲学之外。”

“我同意。”

“那么,比如说,一个人有克制力、对金钱不感兴趣,他并不心胸狭窄或懦弱。他是否有可能会是尖刻或行为不义呢?”

“不会。”

“所以当你想要观察某人是否具有贤哲的心灵,你就应该密切注意,从其早年起,他所表现出的行为举止是合乎道德、贤明谨慎的,还是无礼粗暴、笨拙粗俗的。”

“是的。”

c ‘And there’s something else you won’t forget to look out for as well, I imagine.’

‘What?’

‘Whether he’s quick or slow at learning. I mean, you wouldn’t expect someone to be particularly fond of something it hurt him to do and where slight gains were hard to win, would you?’

‘I’d never do that.’

‘What about if he’s incapable of retaining anything he’s learnt? Is there any way he can have room for knowledge, when he’s full of forgetfulness?’

‘Of course not.’

‘In the end, don’t you think, after all his thankless toil, he’s bound to loathe both himself and intellectual activity?’

‘Yes.’

d ‘So we’d better count forgetfulness as a factor which precludes a mind from being good enough at philosophy. We’d better make a good memory a prerequisite.’

‘Absolutely.’

‘Now, isn’t it the case that lack of culture and grace in someone can only lead him to lack a sense of proportion?’

‘Of course.’

‘And do you think that truth is closely related to proportion or to its opposite?’

‘To proportion.’

‘So we need to look for a mind which, in addition to the qualities we’ve already mentioned, has an inherent sense of proportion and elegance, and which makes a person instinctively inclined towards anything’s essential character.’

‘Of course we do.’

e ‘All right. Surely you don’t think that any of the interconnected qualities we’ve mentioned are at all inessential for a competent and

"我想还有些东西你也不要忘了加以观察。" c

"什么?"

"他学习起来是敏捷还是迟钝。我的意思是说,你不会希望一个人尤其喜欢做某项工作而付出很多,收效却甚微,是吗?"

"我不会的。"

"如果他记不住所学的又怎么办呢? 如果他非常健忘,有什么办法能让他为知识腾出点空间吗?"

"当然没有。"

"你难道不认为在他付出了所有无回报的苦力之后,他最终必定会讨厌自己和智力活动?"

"是的。"

"所以我们最好把健忘当作一个不足以使心灵从事哲学的因素而事先加以排除。我们最好把好记忆作为一个先决条件。" d

"毫无疑问。"

"那么情况难道不就是这样的:一个人缺乏和谐、优雅,只能把他引向缺乏分寸感吗?"

"当然。"

"你认为真理更接近于分寸还是其对立面?"

"接近分寸。"

"所以除了我们已经提到的品性之外,我们还需要寻找一个天生具有分寸感和优雅的心灵,它使一个人本能地导向任何事物的本质。"

"我们当然要这样做。"

"很好。对于一个有能力而完善的心智而言,要把握住实在, e
你确定不认为我们已经提到的那些相互关联的品质都是无关紧

complete mental grasp of reality?'

'No, they're absolutely essential,' he said.

487a 'Can you find any flaw, then, in an occupation like this, which in order to be competently practised requires the following inherent qualities in a person: a good memory, quickness at learning, broadness of vision, elegance, and love of and affiliation to truth, morality, courage, and self-discipline?'

'Not even Momus could criticize this occupation,' he replied.

'Now, aren't people who, thanks to their education and their age, have these qualities in full the only ones to whom you would entrust your community?'

b Adeimantus spoke up. 'Socrates,' he said, 'no one's going to take you up on this point; but that may be due to the fact that there's a particular experience which people who hear you speak on any occasion always have. They get the impression that, because they lack expertise at the give and take of discussion, they're led a little bit astray by each question, and then when all the little bits are put together at the end of the discussion, they find that they were way off the mark and that they've contradicted their original position. They're like unskilled backgammon players, who end up being shut out by skilled
c ones and incapable of making a move: they too end up being shut out and incapable of making an argumentative move in this alternative version of backgammon, which uses words rather than counters, since they feel that this is not necessarily a certain route to the truth. From my point of view, what I'm saying is relevant to our current situation. You see, someone might object that his inability to find the words to challenge you doesn't alter the evident fact that the majority of the people
d who take up philosophy and spend more than just their youth on it—who don't get involved in it just for educational purposes and then drop it—turn out to be pretty weird (not to say rotten to the core), and that the effect of this pursuit you're praising even on those of its practitioners

要的吧?”

“不,它们绝对是必不可少的。”他说。 487a

“那么你在这样的事业中是否还能发现什么缺陷,为了有能力实践这项事业,一个人必须天生具有以下品性:好的记忆,敏于学习,开阔的眼界,有风度,热爱并亲近真理、正义、勇敢和自制?”

“即使莫摩斯[1]对此也无可指责。”他回答说。

“那么,有些人由于他们的教育和年纪而完全具有了这些品性,你可以把你们的城邦托付给他们?”

阿狄曼图提高嗓门。“苏格拉底,”他说,“在这一点上没有人 b
会反驳你;但这也许是因为这样的事实,即那些在任何场合都经常听你讲述的人具有了一种特殊的感受。他们有这样的印象,因为他们缺乏问答讨论的专门技艺,他们被每个问题渐渐地引入歧途,当所有这些点滴最后在讨论末加起来的时候,他们发现他们犯了很大的错误,他们已经与原先的观点相矛盾了。他们就像没
有经验的棋手,最后被下棋能手围困住,一步都走不了:与下棋同 c
样,他们最后也被围困住,而这里使用的只是词语而不是棋子,他们一个论证都拿不出,因为他们感到这并非必然是一条理所当然通向真理的道路。在我看来,我所说的与我们当前的状况有关。你看有人会反对说,他没能找到话来反驳你,这也改变不了这个明显的事实,即大部分人学了哲学并且除了把年轻时代花在上面,还
花了更多的时间——他们并不是出于教育的目的而学习哲学后 d
放弃——使他们变得很怪异,更不用说坏到骨子里,那些被认为

〔1〕 莫摩斯:非难指责之神。

who are supposed to be particularly good is that they become incapable of performing any service to their communities.'

I responded by asking, 'Do you think this view is right?'

'I don't know,' he replied. 'But I'd be happy to hear what you have to say on the matter.'

'What you'd hear from me is that I think they're telling the truth.'

e 'Then how can it be right', he said, 'to say that there'll be no end to political troubles until philosophers have power in their communities, when we agree that philosophers are no use to them?'

'It'll take an analogy to answer your question,' I said.

'And you never use analogies, of course,' he said.

'What?' I exclaimed. 'It's hard enough to prove my point with-
488a out you making fun of me as well as forcing me to try. Anyway, here's my analogy: now you'll be in a better position to see how inadequate it is. I mean, what society does to the best practitioners of philosophy is so complex that there's no other single phenomenon like it: in order to defend them from criticism, one has to compile an analogy out of lots of different elements, like the goat-stags and other compound creatures painters come up with.'

'Imagine the following situation on a fleet of ships, or on a sin-
b gle ship. The owner has the edge over everyone else on board by virtue of his size and strength, but he's rather deaf and short-sighted, and his knowledge of naval matters is just as limited. The sailors are wrangling with one another because each of them thinks that he ought to be the captain, despite the fact that he's never learnt how, and can't name his teacher or specify the period of his apprenticeship. In any case, they all maintain that it isn't something that can be taught,
c and are ready to butcher anyone who says it is. They're for ever

是非常优秀的人通过你所赞美的事业而所产生的结果便是他们变得不能为他们的城邦提供任何的服务。”

我反问他说:“你认为这种观点是对的吗?”

“我不知道,”他回答说,“但我很乐意听听你对此事所要说的。”

“你从我这儿听到的就是,我认为他们说出了真理。”

他说:“当我们同意说哲学家对他们没用,而又说除非哲学家 e
统治他们的城邦,否则政治上的麻烦事就没有终日,这样说是对的吗?”

“可以用一个类比来回答你的问题。”我说。

“当然可以,但你是从不使用类比的呀。”他说。

“什么?”我惊讶地说,“要是没有你不但迫使我一试,而且还取笑我,那么要证明我的观点倒是很难了。不管怎么说,我的类
比是这样的:现在你会更清楚地看到它是多么不充分了。我的意 488a
思是说,社会与哲学实践者的关系是如此的复杂,以致没有其他像这样的情况了:为了替他们受到的批评而辩护,人们必须从大量不同的素材中拼凑出一个类比来,就像画匠画出的羊鹿和其他复合而成的动物。

“设想下面这种情况,在船队或一只船上,船长在体格和力量
上都要超过船上其他所有人,但他耳聋而且近视,他的关于航海 b
事务的知识很有限。水手们相互争吵,因为每个人都认为自己应该是船长,虽然他从没学过如何当船长,并且也说不出他的老师或确定他的学徒期。无论如何,他们都坚持说这并不是某种可以传授的东西,要是有任何人说是可传授的,他们就把他杀了。他
们总是簇拥在船长周围,恳求他,不择手段地要船长把掌舵权交 c

crowding closely around the owner, pleading with him and stopping at nothing to get him to entrust the rudder to them. Sometimes, if their pleas are unsuccessful, but others get the job, they kill those others or throw them off the ship, subdue their worthy owner by drugging him or getting him drunk or something, take control of the ship, help themselves to its cargo, and have the kind of drunken and indulgent voyage you'd expect from people like that. And that's not all: they think highly of anyone who contributes towards their gaining power by showing skill at winning over or subduing the owner, and describe
d him as an accomplished seaman, a true captain, a naval expert; but they criticize anyone different as useless. They completely fail to understand that any genuine sea-captain has to study the yearly cycle, the seasons, the heavens, the stars and winds, and everything relevant to the job, if he's to be properly equipped to hold a position of authority in a ship. In fact, they think it's impossible to study and acquire expertise at how to steer a ship (leaving aside the question of
e whether or not people want you to) and at the same time be a good captain. When this is what's happening on board ships, don't you think that the crew of ships in this state would think of any true cap-
489a tain as nothing but a windbag with his head in the clouds, of no use to them at all?'

'They definitely would,' Adeimantus replied.

'I'm sure you don't need an analysis of the analogy to see that it's a metaphor for the attitude of society towards true philosophers,' I said. 'I'm sure you take my point.'

'I certainly do,' he said.

'You'd better use it, then, in the first instance, to clarify things for that person who expressed surprise at the disrespect shown to philosophers by society, and try to show him how much more astonishing
b it would be if they were respected.'

'All right, I will,' he said.

'And that you're right to say that the best practitioner's of philosophy are incapable of performing any public service. But you'd better tell him to blame their uselessness on the others' failure to make use of them, rather than on the fact that they are accomplished philosophers.

给他们。有时他们恳求不成,而别人得到这个工作,他们就把那
些别的人杀了或把他们扔下船,对可敬的船长,他们利用药物或
醉酒或什么东西而使其屈服,控制了船,享用船上的货物,你可以
设想那样的人所进行的迷醉而放纵的航行。不仅如此:他们敬重
任何使用计谋赢得船长或使船长屈服而帮助他们夺取权力的人,
把这个人说成是了不起的水手、真正的船长和航海专家;而贬斥 d
任何无用之人。他们完全不懂得任何真正的航海家必须学习年
份周期、季节、天空、星辰、风以及所有与工作相关的东西,如果他
要配得上船上的领导地位的话。事实上,他们认为不可能学习和
获得如何掌舵的技艺,同时成为一个好船长,更不用说人们是否
想要你学习和获得掌舵的技艺了。当船上发生了这些事情之后, e
你难道不认为这样的船员会认为任何真正的船长无非就是过于
理想的唠叨鬼,对他们完全没有用处?” 489a

“他们肯定会这样想的。”阿狄曼图回答说。

“我确信你不需要对这个类比做一分析了,你可以看出这个比喻就是社会对哲学家的态度,”我说,“我确信你理解我的意思。”

“我当然理解。”他说。

“那么首先,你最好把它解释给那些对哲学家受到社会的鄙
视而惊讶的人,试图向他表明如果他们受到尊敬,那才是更令人
吃惊的。” b

“好吧,我会的。”他说。

“你可以这样说:最优秀的哲学实践者是不能够担任任何城邦工作的。但你最好应该让他把他们的无用归咎于别人没能使用他们,而不要归咎于他们是优秀的哲学家这个事实。我

I mean, it's unnatural for the captain to ask the sailors to accept his authority and it's unnatural for wise men to dance attendance on rich men; this story is misleading. The truth of the matter is that it makes no difference whether you're rich or poor: if you feel ill, you're bound to dance
c attendance on a doctor, and if you need to accept authority, you must dance attendance on someone in authority who is capable of providing it. If he is really to serve any useful purpose, it's not up to him to ask those under him to accept his authority. And you won't be mistaken if you compare present-day political leaders to the sailors in our recent tale, and the ones they call useless airheads to the genuine captain.'

'You're absolutely right,' he said.

'Under these conditions and circumstances, it's not easy for the best of occupations to gain a good reputation, when reputations are in
d the hands of people whose occupations are incompatible with it. But by far the worst and most influential condemnation of philosophy comes about as a result of the people who claim to practise it—the ones the critic of philosophy was talking about, in your report, when he described the majority of the people who take up philosophy as rotten to the core (although the best of them are merely useless). And I agreed that you were telling the truth, didn't I?'

'Yes.'

'Well, we've described the reasons for the uselessness of the good practitioners, haven't we?'

'We certainly have.'

'Shall we next describe why the corruption of most philosophers
e is inevitable, and try to explain why this shouldn't be blamed on philosophy either, if we can?'

'Yes.'

'Let's start our discussion by reminding ourselves of the fundamental points in our description of the kind of character a truly good-
490a person will inevitably have. If you remember, above all he was led by truth: if he didn't pursue truth absolutely and wholeheartedly, he was bound to be a specious impostor, with nothing whatsoever to do

的意思是说，船长恳求船员接受他的领导是不自然的，聪明人奉承富人也是不自然的；这些话都是会令人误解的。事情实际上是，无论你富有还是贫穷都没有区别：如果你觉得难受，你就必定要去请求医生，如果你需要接受统治，那么你必须请求能够运用权力的人。如果他确 c
实要服务于任何有用的目的，那么不是他去请求他的下属接受他的统治。如果你把现在的政治领导人比做我们刚才故事中的水手，把那些被称作空想者的人比做真正的船长，那么你是不会错的。”

“你说得非常正确。”他说。

“在这些情况和条件下，当名声掌握在那些职业与最高尚的职业不相容的人的手里的时候，那些高尚的职业要获得一个好名声可不容易。但对哲学的最坏和最有影响的诽谤来源于那些自认为在实践哲 d
学的人——他们就是在你的发言中所说的批评哲学的人，他们把从事哲学的大部分人说成是坏到了骨子里，（尽管其中优秀的人也不过是没有用处的）。我当时同意你的话是说得对的，不是吗？”

“是的。”

“那么我们也曾说过从事哲学的优秀之人之所以无用的原因，不是吗？”

“我们当然说过。”

“我们是否要说一说为什么最优秀的哲学家的堕落是不可避免的，并且如果我们可以的话，还试着解释一下为什么这不应该归咎于哲学家？” e

“是的。”

“我们回忆一下我们说过的那种真正优秀的人必须具有的基本品性，让我们以此开始我们的讨论。如果你记得的话，首先他要受真理的引领：如果他不绝对地全心全意地追求真理，那么他 490a

with true philosophy.'

'That's what we said.'

'Well, that in itself is diametrically opposed to current opinion about philosophers, isn't it?'

'It certainly is,' he said.

'Now, our response will be to point out that a genuine lover of
b knowledge innately aspires to reality, and doesn't settle on all the various things which are assumed to be real, but keeps on, with his love remaining keen and steady, until the nature of each thing as it really is in itself has been grasped by the appropriate part of his mind—which is to say, the part which is akin to reality. Once he has drawn near this authentic reality and united with it, and thus fathered intellect and truth, then he has knowledge; then he lives a life which is true to himself; then he is nourished; and then, but not before, he finds release from his love-pangs. Would this be a reasonable response for us to make?'

'Nothing could be more reasonable,' he said.

'And will he be the sort of person to love falsehood or will exactly the opposite be the case, and he'll loathe it?'

'He'll loathe it,' he said.

c 'I'm sure we'd insist that no array of evils could follow the leadership of truth.'

'Of course we would.'

'But rather, a character imbued with health and morality, and the self-discipline that accompanies them.'

'Right,' he said.

'Anyway, there's no need for us to have the whole array of the philosopher's characteristics line up all over again. I'm sure you remember how we found that philosophers naturally have courage, broadness of vision, quickness at learning, and a good memory. You interrupted by saying that although our argument was absolutely incontrovertible, it was still possibled for someone to leave arguments out of

必定会是个与真正的哲学没有任何关系的虚伪的江湖骗子。”

“那就是我们说过的。”

“那么这种看法与当前对哲学家的看法完全相反,不是吗?”

“当然。”他说。

“那么我们的回答指出真正爱知识的人天性上渴望实在,不
会在所有看上去似乎存在多种多样的事物上停留,而是继续前 b
进,他的爱依然强烈而不迟钝,直到每个确如其自身的事物的本质被他心灵的恰当部分——也就是那个与实在相类似的部分——所把握。一旦他接近真正的实在并与之结合,这样就生出了理性和真理,然后他就有了知识;然后他才能如其实际地生活;于是他的心灵得到滋养、提升;在这之后而非从前,他才能从爱欲之大患中得到解脱。我们所做的这个回答还过得去吧?”

“再有道理不过了。”他说。

“那么他会是那种热爱谬误的人吗? 或者恰好与之相反,也就是说,他会憎恶谬误吗?”

“他会憎恶谬误的,”他说。 c

“我确信我们会坚持不让经过装饰的罪恶追随在事实与真理的指引之下的。”

“我们当然会这样。”

“而我们宁愿真理的性质中充满健康与道德的气息,而且有自律与之共存。”

“对的,”他说。

“无论如何,我们没有必要再列举一遍哲学家具有的所有品性。我确信你记得哲学家本性地具有勇气、宽广的视野、敏于学习和优秀的记忆。你打断说,虽然我们的论证绝对是无可争议的,

b it and look at the actual people we were talking aout, and to conclude that while some philosophers are evidently merely useless, the majority of them are bad through and through. We're trying to uncover the reasons for their bad name, and so we're now up against the question why the majority are bad. That's why we brought the true philosopher's characteristics back in again and felt compelled to provide a clear statement of them.'

'True,' he said.

e 'What we have to do', I said, 'is see how this philosophical nature is corrupted and why it is often completely ruined, while immunity from corruption is rare—and these escapees are the people who get called useless, rather than bad. After that, we'll turn to pseudo-phil-
491a osophical natures and the kinds of people who take up the occupation which is proper to a philosophical nature, and we'll try to discern what it is in the make-up of their minds which drives them towards an occupation which is too good and too sublime for them, so that they commit a wide variety of offences and make everyone, all over the world, think of philosophy in the way you've mentioned.'

'What sources of corruption do you have in mind?' he asked.

'I'll do my best to explain,' I replied. 'I suppose it's indisputable that a fully philosophical nature—of the kind we've described,
b with the whole array of qualities we lined up not long ago—is a rare human phenomenon: there aren't going to be very many of them. Don't you agree?'

'Definitely.'

'Well, look how heavily these few people are outnumbered by powerful sources of corruption.'

'What are they, though?'

'The most astounding thing of all is that there isn't one of their commendable characteristics which doesn't ruin a mind which possesses it and cause a rift between it and philosophy. I'm talking about courage, self-discipline, and all the qualities we went through.'

但人们依然有可能不顾这些论证而考虑我们实际上所谈论的那些 d
人,并得出结论:显然一些哲学家不但没有用,而且其中的大多数坏透了。我们试图揭示出他们的坏名声的缘由,现在我们遇到了这个问题:为什么大多数人是坏的。这就是为什么我们重新提出真正哲学家的品性的原因,我们感到有必要对哲学家做一个清晰的阐述。”

“对的。”他说。 e

“我们必须要做的”,我说,“是要察看一下,这种哲学天性是如何被破坏掉的,还有为什么它会经常被完全地毁灭掉,而同时能够免于被毁的却很少——而这些逃脱者也便是被人称作无用而非坏蛋的人。之后,我们会转而考察虚假的哲学本性,对于那
种从事适合其哲学本性工作的人,我们会尽力区分出他们心灵的 491a
构成,它驱使他们追求一个对他们来说过好、过于崇高的职业,以致犯了各种各样的错误而使所有地方的所有人都把哲学看作你曾说过的那个样子。”

“你认为败坏的源泉是什么?”他问道。

“我会尽力解释的,”我回答说,“我想这一点是无可争议的:充分的哲学本性——我们说过的那种,我们刚才列举的所有品
性——是一种在人类中少有的现象:不会存在很多这样的人。难 b
道你不同意吗?”

“毫无疑问。”

“那么来看看有力的腐败之源是如何大大地超过少数人的。”

“它们是什么呢?”

“最令人惊骇的事情是,他们的那些令人赞叹的品性中,没有一个不在毁坏一颗拥有这些品质的心灵,并在它与哲学的追求之间造成了一种分裂。我说的是勇敢、自制和所有我们曾说过的品性。”

'It's not easy to make sense of this idea,' he said.

c 'And that's not all,' I said. 'Every single one of the acknowledged good things of life is a factor in its corruption and the rift—good looks, affluence, physical fitness, influential family relationships in one's community, and so on and so forth, I've cut the list short, because you can see what I'm saying.'

'I can,' he said. 'And I wouldn't mind hearing a more detailed explanation.'

'If you grasp the general principle of the matter,' I said, 'everything will fall into place and what I've already said will start to make sense.'

'What are you getting at?' he asked.

d 'We know', I said, 'that if any plant or creature, at the stage when it is a seed or a new growth, fails to get the right nourishment or weather or location, then the number of its deficiencies, in respect to properties it should have, is proportionate to its vigour. I mean, bad is the opposite of good, rather than of not-good.'

'Of course.'

'So I suppose it's plausible to think that a very good thing will end up in a worse state than a second-rate thing if the conditions of its nurture are less suited to its nature.'

'Yes.'

e 'Well, by the same token, Adeimantus,' I asked, 'won't we claim that if the most gifted minds are subjected to a bad education, they become exceptionally bad? I mean, do you imagine that horrendous crimes and sheer depravity stem from a second-rate nature, rather than from a vigorous one which has been ruined by its upbringing? Could significant benefit or significant harm conceivably proceed from innate weakness?'

'No, you're right,' he said.

'Now, in my opinion, if it receives a suitable education, the

“理解这个说法可不容易啊。”他说。

“不仅如此,”我说,“生活中每一个被认为是好的东西都是败 c
坏和分裂的原因——漂亮、富裕、健壮、城邦里强大的家族势力等等。仅举此几例,因为你能明白我说的意思。”

“我能明白,”他说,“我并不介意听听更详细的解释。”

“如果你把握了事情的总原则,”我说,“那么所有事情就一目了然了,我所说的话也会得到理解。”

“你说怎么理解?”他问道。

“我们知道,”我说,“如果任何植物或动物在种子或新生阶段 d
得不到恰当的养分、气候或环境,那么从它应该具有的品性来看,它越是强壮就具有越多的缺陷。我的意思是说,恶与善对立而不是与非善对立。”

“当然。”

“所以我们有理由这样认为,如果养分条件不太适合于其本性的话,那么一个优秀的事物所处的状态最终会比一个二流的事物更差。”

“是的。”

“那么,同样地,阿狄曼图,”我问道,“我们不是可以说如 e
果最有天赋的心灵受到坏的教育,那么它们也会变得非常坏吗?我的意思是说,你能设想巨大的罪行和纯粹的邪恶来源于一个二流的天赋,而不是来源于一个已经被它的教养毁了的强壮的天赋?可以设想天赋弱小的人能做的出巨大的好事或巨大的坏事吗?”

“不能,你说得对。”他说。

“那么在我看来,如果它接受了恰当的教育,那么我们所说的 492a
哲学天性必定会成长并趋向至善。然而,如果在不恰当的教育

492a philosophical nature we proposed is bound to grow and arrive at perfect goodness. However, if its germination and growth take place in an unsuitable educational environment, then without divine intervention its destination will inevitably be completely the opposite. Or do you follow the masses and believe that there are members of the younger generation who are corrupted by professional teachers, and that there are professional teachers who, despite being private citizens, can be a source of corruption to any degree worth mentioning? Don't you think, rather, that it is the very people who make this claim who are the most influential teachers, and who provide the most thorough
b education and form men and women of all ages into any shapethey want?'

'When do they do this?' he asked.

'When a lot of them huddle together on seats in the assembly or lawcourt or theatre,' I said, 'or when they convene for military purposes, or when there's any other general public gathering, and the boos and applause of their criticism or praise (excessive in both cases) of whatever is being said or done make a terrible din, and it's not only them—the rocks and their surroundings double the noise of
c their approval and disapproval by echoing it. In a situation like this, how do you think a young man's heart, as they say, will be affected? How can the education he received outside of this public arena stand up to it, do you suppose, without being overwhelmed by criticism or praise of this kind and swept away at the mercy of the current? Won't he end up just like them, with the same moral standards and the same habits as them?'

d 'He's bound to, Socrates,' he said.

'And we haven't yet mentioned the most irresistible pressure they bring to bear,' I said.

'What is it?' he asked.

'It's the concrete pressure these consummate professional educators apply when they turn to action, if their words have failed to indoctrinate someone. I mean, surely you're aware that they punish

环境中萌发和成长，如果没有神的介入，其结果就不可避免地会是完全相反的。或者你跟着民众去相信，年轻的一代被职业教师[1]所教坏，这些教师尽管是私人职业市民，但却足够成为一种败坏之源？你难道不认为恰恰是说这些话的人才是最有影响的教师，他们提供了最完善的教育，按他们想要的任何方式去塑造男女老少？” b

“他们在什么时候做这些事的？”他问道。

我说：“当他们中的许多人一起坐在议会、法庭或剧场里的时候，或当他们由于军事目的而集合的时候，或在其他任何公共集会中，而且无论是在说什么或做什么，他们批评的嘘声和赞扬的鼓掌喝彩声（在这两种情况下都是超过正常限度的）制造了一种可怕的喧闹，而且还不止这些——石柱和他们的环境通过回声，c
使他们赞成和反对的声音加倍响亮。在像这样的情况下，你想一个年轻人的心，就像他们说的那样，怎么不受影响呢？你想他在公共会场之外所接受的教育怎么经受得起，而不被这样的批评或赞美所征服，并且不被这洪水冲走呢？他最后不就像他们一样了，具有与他们相同的道德标准和相同的习惯？”

“这是肯定的，苏格拉底。”他说。 d

“我们还没有提到他们带来的最不可抗拒的压力。”我说。

“是什么？”他问道。

“如果他们的言辞不能说服某些人，这些高超的教育者就使用具体的压力，转而采取行动。我的意思是说，你当然认识到他

〔1〕 这里指苏格拉底这类私人教师，以收费形式传授知识。也称为智者，或诡辩家，但与另一种公众诡辩家不同，后者指那些在公共场所发表言论制造影响的政治性人物。

disobedience with forfeiture of rights, and with fines and death?'

'Yes, I'm certainly well aware of that,' he said.

'Can you think of any teacheR or any kind of privately received instruction with the strength to hold out against these pressures?'

e 'I think it's impossible,' he said.

'Yes, and it's extremely stupid even to try to be that kind of teacher,' I said. 'You see, it's quite impossible, as the present and the past show, for any educational programme to alter anyone's character, as far as goodness is concerned, contrary to the conditioning he receives in the public arena—by "anyone" I mean any human, of course, Adeimantus: as the proverb recommends, we'd better make
493a an exception of divinity. I mean, I can tell you that you'd be quite right to see God at work when anything does retain its integrity and fulfil its potential within current political systems.'

'That's what I think too,' he said.

'And I wonder whether you agree with me on a further point as well,' I said.

'What?'

'Even though they call it knowledge, every one of those private fee-charging individuals—the ones who are called sophists and are regarded as rivals by these educators we've been talking about—teaches nothing but the attitudes the masses form by consensus. Imagine that the keeper of a huge, strong beast notices what makes it angry, what
b it desires, how it has to be approached and handled, the circumstances and conditions under which it becomes particularly fierce or calm, what provokes its typical cries, and what tones of voice make it gentle or wild. Once he's spent enough time in the creature's company to acquire all this information, he calls it knowledge, forms it into a systematic branch of expertise, and starts to teach it, despite total ignorance, in fact, about which of the creature's attitudes and desires is commendable or deplorable, good or bad, moral or immoral. His usage

们用剥夺他们的权利、罚款和死刑来惩罚不服的人?”

“是的,我当然很清楚地认识到了。”他说。

“你能想出任何教师或任何私下接受的教导有力量与这些压力相抗衡吗?”

“我想这是不可能的。”他说。 e

“是的,试图要当那样的教师甚至都是极其愚蠢的,”我说,“你看看,就像过去和现在所表明的一样,这是几乎是不可能的:就美德而言,让任何教育去改变任何人的品性,这个品性与他在公共场合所接受的教育相反——我说的‘任何人’当然指的是任何人力,阿狄曼图:就像格言所说的,我们最好把神当作一个例
外。我的意思是说,我可以告诉你,在当前的政治体制中,要是有 493a
什么事物保持了它的正直,实现了它的潜能,那么你可以非常恰当地说你看到了神在发挥作用。”

“那也是我所想的。”他说。

“我想知道还有一点你是否也会同意我。”我说。

“哪一点?”

“即使他们将之称作知识,但每一个收取学费的私人教师——被称作诡辩家的人,被我们所谈过的教育者认为是竞争者的人——除了教授众人通过一致赞同所形成的意见之外什么都不教。设想一个巨大猛兽的饲养者,他注意的是什么会使野兽发怒,它欲求的
是什么,必须如何接近它、照管它,在什么样的条件或环境下它会变 b
得尤其地凶猛或温顺,什么激发它发出特定的声音,什么样的语调使它温顺或狂野。如果他花了一段时间与动物在一起从而获得了所有的信息,他把它称作知识,并将之形成一门系统的技艺,开始加以教授,而事实上对动物的哪些意向和欲求是高尚的,哪些是卑鄙

c of all these terms simply conforms to the great beast's attitudes, and he describes things as good or bad according to its likes and dislikes, and can't justify his usage of the terms any further, but describes as right and good things which are merely indispensable, since he hasn't realized and can't explain to anyone else how vast a gulf there is between necessity and goodness. Wouldn't you really and truly find someone like this implausible as a teacher?'

'Yes, I would,' he said.

'Well, do you think there's anything to choose between him and
d someone who's noticed what makes the motley masses collectively angry and happy and thinks he has knowledge—whether it's in the field of painting or music or government? I mean, whenever someone's relationship with the masses consists of displaying his composition (or whatever product it may be) or his political service to them, and giving them power over him—or rather, more power than they need have—then the proverbial necessity of Diomedes forces him to compose things of which they approve. Sometimes one of the sophists might argue that what the masses like coincides with what is genuinely good and fine, but this argument always comes across as utterly absurd, don't you think?'

e 'It always has and it always will, in my opinion,' he said.

'So, against this background, please remember what we were saying before. Is it possible for the masses to accept or conceive of the existence of beauty itself, rather than the plurality of beautiful things? Or anything in itself, rather than the plurality of instances of each thing?'

494a 'Not at all,' he said.

'It's impossible, then, for the masses to love knowledge,' I said.

'Yes, it is.'

'They're bound to run philosophers down, then, as well.'

的，哪些是善的，哪些是邪恶的，哪些是正义的，哪些是不正义的，他一无所知。关于所有这些词的用法，他仅仅是符合野兽的意向，他 c
按照野兽的喜好来描述事物的好坏，而不能进一步为他的这些词的用法说出道理来，而仅仅把必然的事物称作美的和善的，因为他没有意识到也不能向任何别的人解释必然者和善者之间的差距是多么巨大。你难道真的把如此不可信的人当作教师吗？”

“不会把他当作教师的。”他说。

“那么你认为他与以下这些人有什么区别，他们把喜怒哀乐混杂在一起并且认为他们具有知识——无论是绘画方面、音乐方 d
面还是统治方面？我的意思是说，如果有人与大众搞好关系，并向大众展示他的诗作或任何什么作品，或者为他们提供政治上的服务，并把他们置于自己之上——毋宁说这权力超过了他们的需要——那么格言中所说的狄奥墨德斯的必然性就迫使他创作取悦大众的东西。有时某个诡辩派的人可能会争辩说，大众所喜欢的是符合于真正的善和美的，但这种说法看上去似乎总是非常可笑的，你难道不这么想吗？”

“在我看来，过去总是这样，将来也会总是这样。”他说。 e

“所以在这个情境下，请记住我们之前所说的。对于群众而言，要接受或理解美自身的存在，而非美丽事物的那种多数状态的存在，你认为是可能的吗？或者说，接受、理解任何物自身，而
非每一事物实例的多数状态，这有可能吗？” 494a

“他们绝对不可能接受。”他说。

“那么民众就不可能爱知识。”我说。

“是不可能。”

“那么他们也必定会非难哲学家。”我说。

'That's inevitable.'

'And so are those individuals whose relationship with the masses consists of wanting to please them.'

'Obviously.'

'In this context, can you see how any innate philosopher will preserve the integrity of his nature, and consequently stay with the oc-
b cupation and see it through to the end? Look at it in the context of what we were saying earlier. We agreed that a philosopher has quickness at learning, a good memory, courage, and broadness of vision.'

'Yes.'

'From his earliest years, then, he'll outclass other children at everything, especially if he's as gifted physically as he is mentally, won't he?'

'Of course,' be answered.

'So when he grows up, his friends and fellow citizens will want to make use of him for their own affairs.'

'Naturally.'

c 'They'll be a constant presence, then, with their requests and courtesies, as they flatter him and try to get him on their side in anticipation of the influence that will one day be his.'

'Yes, that's what invariably happens,' he said.

'What do you imagine he'll do in this situation,' I asked, 'especially if he happens to come from a wealthy and noble family within a powerful state, and is also good-looking and well built? Don't you think he'll be filled with unrealizable hopes, and will expect to be capable one day of managing the affairs not only of Greece, but of the
d non-Greek world as well? In these circumstances, won't he get ideas above his station and puff himself up with affectation and baseless, senseless pride?'

'He certainly will,' he said.

'Now, suppose someone gently approaches him while he's in this frame of mind and tells him the truth—that he's taken leave of his senses

“这不可避免。”

“那些与民众的关系在于想要取悦民众的个人也是这样。”

“显而易见。”

“在这种情况下,你还能看到任何天生的哲学家会保持他的正直的本性,继而坚持事业而进行到底吗?看看我们之前说过的
那个情形吧。我们承认哲学家敏于学习,有好的记忆、勇敢以及 b
有宽广的视野。”

“是的。”

“从他的童年起,他就会在所有事情上都超过别的孩子,尤其是如果他在身体和灵魂上都具有天赋,不是吗?”

“当然。”他回答说。

“所以当他长大了,他的朋友和公民同胞都会为了他们自己的事务而想要使用他。”

“当然。”

“那么他们会经常请求他,向他献媚,他们预料到某一天他会 c
掌权,所以讨好他并且试图把他拉到他们的一边。”

“是的,这样的事情是难以避免的。”他说。

“在这种情况下,你想他会做什么呢?”我问道,“尤其是如果他恰好来自于一个强大的城邦中的一个富裕而高贵的家族,并且还英俊,具有好体格?你难道不认为他会充满不现实的希望,期望有一天不光能够管理希腊的事务,而且还能管理非希腊城邦的
事务?在这些条件下,他的想法不就是超出了他的身份,并且充 d
满了虚假做作和卑鄙无理的傲慢?”

“他当然会这样。”他说。

“现在,当他心情是这样时,设想有人轻轻地走过去告诉他真

and should try to dispel this inanity, but that he won't gain intelligence unless be works like a slave for it—do you think it's going to be easy for the message to penetrate all these pernicious influences and get through to him?'

'No, far from it,' he said.

e 'And', I went on, 'supposing his innate gifts and his affinity with the rationality of what's being said do enable him to pay attention at all, and he is swayed and attracted towards philosophy, what reaction would you expect from those others, when they think they're losing his services and his friendship? Won't they do and say absolutely anything to stop him being won over? And as for the person who's trying to win him over, won't they come up with all kinds of private schemes and public court-cases to stop him succeeding?'

'Inevitably,' he said.

495a 'What chance does this young man have of becoming a philosopher?'

'No chance, really.'

'So, as you can see,' I went on, 'we were right to say that it is, in fact, the actual ingredients of a philosophical nature which are in a sense responsible (given a pernicious educational environment) for someone being deflected from his occupation, and that the acknowledged good things of life—affluence and similar resources—are also responsible. Do you agree?'

'Yes,' he said. 'We were quite right.'

'There we are, then, Adeimantus,' I said. 'Those are the pow-
b erful factors which ruin and corrupt anyone who is, by nature, best suited for the best occupation—and such people are rare anyway, as we said. Moreover, these are the men who have the potential to do the greatest harm to communities and to individuals, and the greatest

话——他已经失去了理智，应该努力驱散这种糊涂的状态，但是，除非他像奴隶一般地为此付出劳动，否则不会获得理智——你认为这话会很容易地穿透所有这些有害的影响而使他明白吗？”

“不会，远非如此。”他说。

“而且，”我继续说，“假设他天资好，并且接受这番道理，使
他能够充分重视，并受到哲学的影响和吸引，那么其他人呢，当 e
他们认为他们正在失去他的服务与友谊的时候，你能猜想到他们的反应吗？难道他们绝对不会做任何事情、说任何话语来阻止他被拉走吗？而对于这个设法拉走他的人，难道他们不会想出各种各样的私密计划，并运用公开的法庭诉讼，来阻碍他成功吗？”

“这是不可避免的。”他说。 495a

“这个年轻人有可能成为一个哲学家吗？”

“事实上是不可能的。”

“所以就像你能看到的，”我继续说，“我们这样说是正确的，即事实上，正是构成哲学本性的实际因素，在某种意义上，是要对某人偏离其职业负责的（再加上特定的一种恶性教育环境），而且生活中公认的好东西——财富和类似的资源——也有责任。你同意吗？”

“是的，”他说，“我们完全可以这么说。”

“那么，阿狄曼图，我们讨论到了这一步了，”我说，“那些强大
的原因摧毁和败坏了任何其本性最适合那最高尚的职业的 b
人——这样的人，就如我们说的那样，无论如何都是少有的。此外，这些人是潜在地会给我们的城邦和个人带来最大害处的人，

good too, if that's the course they happen to take. An insignificant person, however, never has any effect of any significance on any individual or society.'

'You're quite right,' he said.

'So that's how the most appropriate people are deflected and
c desert philosophy, without consummating the relationship. They end up living a life which is inappropriate for them and which isn't true to their natures, and they leave philosophy, like an orphan with no relatives, to the mercy of others who aren't good enough for her, and who defile her and gain her the kind of tarnished reputation you say her detractors ascribe to her—for going about with people who are either worthless or obnoxious.'

'Yes, that's the usual view,' he said.

'And it's not unreasonable,' I said. 'You see, when the abandonment of this territory is noticed by others—inferior members of the human race—and when they also see how rich it is in renown and sta-
d tus, they behave like escaped convicts who take sanctuary in temples: they break away from their professions, with no regrets, and encroach on philosophy. In fact, they're the ones who do have some facility at their own paltry professions, because in spite of this treatment, philosophy still remains more prestigious than other occupations; and this prestige attracts a lot of people—immature people, who have been
e physically deformed by their jobs and work, and are mentally just as warped and stunted by their servile business. Don't you think that's inevitable?'

'It certainly is.'

'Do you think the impression they give', I went on, 'is any different from that of a small, bald metalworker who's come into some money? He's just got himself out of debtors' prison, he's had a bath and is wearing brand-new clothes and a bridegroom's outfit, and he's about to marry his master's daughter because she's hard up and has

要是乘着那潮流的话,[1]他们也是能带来最大益处的人。然而一个平庸的人对于任何个人或社会是没有任何重要的影响的。”

“你说得很对。”他说。

“所以那些最适合的人就这样偏离并放弃了哲学,而没有使他与哲学的关系取得成果。他们最终过着一种不适合他们的生活,而且这种生活对其本性而言也是非真实的,就这样他们离弃了哲学,使得哲学像一个孤儿一样没有了亲人,在其他那些对她不够好的人 c
面前伶仃孤苦、无依无助,而且这些人还玷污了她的纯洁,使她蒙受了如你所说的那些诽谤者归咎于她的那种败坏的名声——对人们散布说她是毫无价值的,或者说她是令人非常讨厌的。”

“是的,那是一般的看法。”他说。

“这些话很有道理,”我说,“你看看,当别人——人类中的一些低劣者——看到这块地被荒废了,当他们还看到里面充满了名誉和地位的时候,他们就像逃犯一样来到了神庙中的圣殿:他们毫不后悔地 d
逃离了他们的职业来侵蚀哲学。实际上,他们是在其微不足道的工作中具有某些本领的人,哲学尽管受到了这样的对待,但比起其他职业来还是保有更高的声誉;这个名声吸引了很多人——一些不完善的人,他们在身体上受到工作和劳动的破坏,在灵魂上受到低贱的工作的扭曲而得不到成长。你难道不认为那是不可避免的吗?” e

“当然不可避免。”

我继续说:“你认为他们所具有的形象与一个继承了一些钱的、矮小又秃顶的打铁匠有任何区别吗?他刚刚从债务之狱中放出来,洗了个澡,穿上了新衣服打扮得像个新郎,他就准备去娶师

〔1〕 参见485d。

no one to look after her.'

496a 'No, they're exactly the same, really,' he said.

'What sort of offspring are they likely to father, then? Second-rate half-breeds, don't you think?'

'Inevitably.'

'Now, when people who are unworthy of education force their presumptuous attentions on her, what sorts of ideas and thoughts do they produce, would you say? Isn't it perfectly appropriate to call them sophisms, and to claim that they are all illegitimate and lacking in true intelligence?'

'Absolutely,' he said.

b 'That leaves us with only a tiny number of people, Adeimantus,' I said, 'who have the right to consort with philosophy. A person of high character and sound education might fortuitously have been exiled, and so have remained true to his nature and faithful to philosophy by being out of the reach of corrupting influences; or occasionally a great mind is born in some backwater of a community and finds the politics petty and beneath him. And I suppose a few, because of their natural gifts, do have the right to find some other occupation demeaning and to turn from it to philosophy. Then there is also
c the bridle of our friend Theages, which can act as a curb: Theages was in all other respects well equipped to be deflected from philosophy, but he had to pamper his physical ailment and so he was curbed and prevented from taking up politics. It's not worth mentioning my own case—the communications I receive from my deity—because there's either very little or no precedent for the phenomenon.'

'When the few members of this band have glimpsed the joy and happiness to be found in mastering philosophy and have also gained a clear enough impression of the madness of the masses; when they've realized that more or less every political action is pernicious and that if someone tries to assist morality there will be no one to back him up
d and see that he comes out unscathed, but it would be like an encoun-

傅的女儿,因为她家境贫寒,没有人照顾她。”

“他们确实非常相像。”他说。 496a

“那么他们可能会生出什么样的后代来,你难道不认为是二流的杂种吗?”

“毫无疑问。”

“当那些不适合受教育的人把他们放肆的想法强加给哲学的时候,你说他们会产生出什么样的思想和观点来呢?不就可以非常恰当地称之为智术,可以说它们都是不合法的、缺乏真正理性的?”

“毫无疑问。”他说。

“阿狄曼图,留给我们的只有很少一些人了,”我说,“他们有权与哲学为伴。一个具有高贵的品性和完善教育的人可能有幸 b
被流放了,他没有受到腐败的影响,所以依然忠实于他的本性,忠实于哲学;或者有时一个伟大的心灵出生于一个城邦中的闭塞之地,不屑于城邦事物;我想有很少一些人由于他们天赋的本性而有权认为某些其他的职业是卑微的从而转向哲学;还有我们朋友塞亚革斯的缰绳,它们就像是一种束缚:塞亚革斯在所有其他方面他都完全可以背离哲学,但他还得关切他的身体上的疾病,所 c
以他受到了限制从而阻碍了他从事政治。我自己的情况就不值得一提了——我从神灵那得到启示——因为这种现象很少有过或从未有过。

“这个群体中的很少数成员见到在从事哲学时所发现的快乐和幸福,并且对民众的疯狂也有了清晰的认识;当他们认识到每个政治行动多多少少都是有害的,并且如果有人试图协助正义,如果没有人支持他并且使他免于受到伤害,那么这看上去像是人 d

ter between a human being and wild beasts; since he isn't prepared to join others in their immorality and isn't capable, all alone, of standing up to all those ferocious beasts, but would die before doing his community or his friends any good, and so would be useless to himself and to everyone else—once he has grasped all this with his rational mind, he lies low and does only what he's meant to do. It's as if he's taken shelter under a wall during a storm, with the wind whipping up the dust and rain pelting down; lawlessness infects everyone else he sees, so he is content if he can find a way to live his life here on earth without becoming tainted by immoral or unjust deeds, and to depart
e from life confidently, and without anger and bitterness.'

497a 'If he could do that,' he said, 'he'd really have done something with his life.'

'But he could do much more with his life', I replied, 'if he just lived in a suitable political system, which enabled him to develop more and to preserve the integrity of public business as well as his own affairs. Anyway, I think we've said enough about why philosophy has a bad name, and why it doesn't deserve it, unless you've got something to add.'

'No, I've nothing to add on this issue,' he said. 'But which contemporary political system do you think is suitable for philosophy?'

b 'Not a single one,' I replied. 'That's exactly what I'm critical of—that no current political system is good enough for a philosophical nature to grow in without getting modified and altered. It's like a seed which has been brought from its native land and planted in foreign soil: its vitality tends to become drained, and the species becomes absorbed into the dominant local variety. In the same way, this type of person can't retain his native qualities, but is deflected and assumes properties that don't really belong to him. If he comes across a
c political system with the same degree of excellence as his character,

类遇到了野兽；因为他并不愿意加入别人的不正义行为之中，但他没有能力独自抵抗所有这些凶猛的野兽，在给城邦或他的朋友带来任何好处之前，他就已经死了，所以对他自己和对任何别的人来说，他都是无用的——一旦他用他理性的心灵理解了这些，他就过着平静的生活，只做他想做的事情。这就像他在风卷起泥土、大雨滂沱的暴风雨中躲在墙下；他看到违法犯罪在其他人身上蔓延，所以如果他能在这个世上找到一种未被不正义或不正义的行为所玷污的生活，他就满意了。他就能够充满信心地、毫无 e
愤怒和痛苦地离弃生命。”

“要是他能这样做的话，”他说，“他一生实际上已经做了一些 497a
了不起的事情了。”

“但他用一生还能做更多的事情，”我回答说，“如果他生活在一个恰当的政治体制里，他就能得到更多的发展并能在城邦事务和他个人事务上保持正直。无论如何，我想关于为什么哲学具有坏名声以及为什么哲学不应得到这个名声的原因，我们已经说得够多的了，除非你还有什么要补充的。”

“没有了，在这个问题上我没什么要补充的了，”他说，“但你认为当前的政治体制中哪个适合哲学？”

“没有一个适合的，”我回答说，“那正是我所批评的——当前 b
的政治体制中没有一种能够让哲学本性不经修改和变动就可以得到成长的。这就像一颗当地的种子被播种到异乡的土地里：它的活力变得衰竭，这种品种被当地占主流的品种所取代。以这样的方式，哲学就不能保持它天生的品性，而是偏离了本性并具有了一些真正说来不属于它的品性。如果哲学遇到了一种与它的品性一样优秀的政治体制，那么其本性的神圣性就会显露出 c

then the divinity of the philosophical character will become apparent, as distinct from the humanity of all other natures and occupations. Now, your next question is obviously going to be what this political system is.'

'You've got me wrong there,' he said. 'I wasn't going to ask that, but whether the community we're founding and describing is the one you mean, or whether there's another candidate.'

'On the whole, it's our community,' I said. 'But there's an earlier point that needs repeating, that the community would have to con-
d tain an element which understands the rationale of the political system and keeps to the same principles which you as legislator followed when you made the laws.'

'Yes, that did come up,' he agreed.

'I didn't make it sufficiently clear, however,' I said, 'because I was worried about the objections you were raising which have shown how long and complicated an argument it takes to prove the point. And what we're still faced with is hardly the easiest part of the account.'

'What is it?'

'How a community can engage in philosophy and survive. I mean, great enterprises are always hazardous, and anything fine really is, as the saying puts it, difficult.'

e 'All the same,' he said, 'the account won't be complete until this point has been cleared up. So we'd better explore it.'

'The only thing that could stop us doing so is lack of ability,' I said. 'It won't be lack of will, and you'll be an eyewitness to my determination. Look at it now, in fact—and how I'm prepared to stick my neck out and say that our community should turn the current approach to philosophy upside down.'

'What do you mean?'

'At the moment,' I said, 'those who actually do engage in it are young men, scarcely out of childhood. In the interval before they
498a take up estate-management and moneymaking, they dabble in the most

来,而与人的其他天赋和职业完全不同,这些都属于人性。你接下来的问题显然就是这个政治体制是什么样的?”

“你搞错了,”他说,“我不是想问那个问题,而是我们建立并描述过的那个城邦是否就是你说的那个,或者是否还有另一个。”

“总的来说,它就是我们的城邦,”我说,“但有一个早先说过的要点需要重提一下,即,城邦必须包含这样的成员,他们理解政治体制的原则并且遵守你作为立法者立法时所遵循的同样的原 d
则。”

“是的,确实提到过。”他同意说。

“然而我说得还不够清楚,”我说,“因为我担心你提出的反对,这表明为了证明这个观点需要一个非常冗长而烦琐的论证。我们所面对的、要阐述的部分并非是最容易的。”

“是什么?”

“一个城邦如何能够既从事哲学又得以幸存。我的意思是说,伟大的事业总是有巨大的风险,如常言道,好事多磨嘛!”

他说:“在这个观点得到澄清之前,这个解释仍然没有结束。 e
所以我们最好对此加以探讨。”

“唯一能阻止我们这样做的事物是缺乏能力,”我说,“不是缺乏意志,你会亲眼看到我的决心。现在来考察一下,实际上,我是准备如何冒着风险说我们的城邦应该把当前从事哲学的方式给颠倒过来。”

“你是什么意思?”

“现在,”我说,“人们实际上从青年起就开始从事哲学,他们
还刚刚摆脱童年。在他们从事城邦管理和赚钱之前的这段时间 498a

difficult aspect of philosophy—the bit which has to do with rational argument—and then they drop it. And they are supposed to be the most advanced philosophers! After that, they count it as no mean achievement actually to accept an invitation to listen to a philosophical debate, since they think that philosophy should be merely an incidental occupation. And in old age they are—with a few exceptions—snuffed out more thoroughly than Heraclitus'sun, since they are never rekindled later.'

b 'Whereas they should do what?' he asked.

'Exactly the opposite. While they're young, they should be educated and should study philosophy in a way which suits their age. Their bodies are growing and developing during this period, and they should concentrate on getting them into a state where they minister to philosophy. In due course of time, when their minds are beginning to mature, they should put more effort into mental exercise; and when their physical strength starts to wane and they are too old to play a
c public part in the community or to serve in the militia, they should be allowed to roam free and graze at will, and to concentrate on philosophy, with everything else being incidental. This is the correct programme for people who are going to live a happy life and guarantee for themselves circumstances in the next world, after their death, which match the life they lived here.'

'You certainly give the impression of being wholehearted about this, Socrates,' he said. 'But I think most of the people who hear you express these views will be even more wholehearted about challenging them, since they won't be convinced in the slightest. And Thrasymachus will take the lead in this, I imagine.'

'Please don't cause trouble between me and Thrasymachus,' I
d said, 'when we've only just become friends—not that we were enemies before. I'll spare no effort until I've either won him and everyone else over to my point of view—or at least done something to prepare them in

里,他们接触到了哲学的最困难的部分——那个必须涉及到理性论证的部分——然后他们就放弃了哲学。他们就被认为是最优秀的哲学家了！以后,他们要是真的被邀请去听一次哲学辩论,他们就把这当作是件大的事情,因为他们认为哲学应该仅仅作为一个副业。他们到了老年——很少有例外的——比赫拉克利特的太阳熄灭得还要彻底,因为它们之后无法再次点燃。” b

“但是他们应该怎么办呢?”他问道。

“正好相反。当他们年轻的时候,他们应该受教育,应该以适合他们年龄的方式学习哲学。在这个时期,他们的身体正在成长和发育,他们应该集中精力使自己进入学习哲学的状态。随着年龄的增长,当他们的心智开始成熟的时候,他们应该在精神的锻炼上花更多的精力;而当他们的体力开始衰退的时候,他们就太老而不能在城邦里担任公职或服役了,应该允许他们自在逍遥, c
专门从事哲学,而别的所有事情都是副业。对那些想要过得幸福的人,保证他们死后的另一个世界中拥有与现世同样的生活,那么这就是正确的做法。”

“苏格拉底,在这一点上你给我的印象确实很热诚,”他说,“但是我想大多数听你这么说的人,会更加热诚地反对这些观点,因为他们一点都不会被说服。我想塞拉西马库斯会第一个反对。”

“请不要在我和塞拉西马库斯之间制造麻烦,”我说,“我们刚才已经成为朋友了——不是从前的敌人了。我将不遗余力直到 d
要么说服了他,要么说服了任何别的人相信我的观点——或至少为他们做些准备,万一他们将来投胎做人的时候又遇上这些

case they ever meet these arguments again in future incarnations!'

'You're thinking in the short term, then!' he remarked.

'It's nothing compared with eternity,' I responded. 'But I'm not at all surprised that most people find what I'm saying incredible: after
e all, it's never been within their experience. They're used to carefully assimilated phrases, rather than hearing words tumbling out without preparation as they are now. And they've never come across even a single case of a man who is, in both his actions and his words, as
499a perfectly identified and assimilated with goodness as is possible, and who is in a position of authority in an equally good community. Do you think they have?'

'Definitely not.'

'Then again, Adeimantus, they've not been adequately exposed to discussions which aren't dishonourable and mean, but are designed for a thorough and intense quest for the truth, for the sake of knowledge, and which are hardly on nodding terms with those subtleties and eristic tricks whose sole purpose, whether they occur during lawsuits or private conversations, is to increase the speaker's reputation and his chances of winning the argument.'

'No, they haven't,' he said.

b 'These are the reasons and considerations', I said, 'which led me earlier, despite my anxieties—since the truth left me no option—to claim that no community or political system, and by the same token no person either, could ever attain perfection until some accident forced those few philosophers (the ones who are currently called useless, rather than the ones who are called rotten) to take charge of a community whether or not they wanted to, and made the citizens obey them, or alter-
c natively until, thanks to divine providence, either current kings and rulers or their sons were gripped by authentic love for authentic philosophy. In my opinion, it's unreasonable to claim that either or both of these alternatives are impossible; if this were so, then we'd deserve to be ridiculed for our empty assertions, our wishful thinking. Don't you agree?'

争论！”

“那么你考虑的还不算长远。”他评论道。

“与永恒相比，这算不了什么，”我回答说，“不过大多数人觉得我所说的不可信，我完全不奇怪：这毕竟是他们从未经历过的。他们习惯于小心谨慎地理解话语，而不是像他们现在一样听毫无 e
准备的滔滔发言。他们甚至从未遇到过这样的人：他在他的言行举止都与至善尽可能地相符相称，他统治着一个同样善的城邦。 499a
你认为他们遇见过吗？”

“肯定没有。”

“那么再说，阿狄曼图，他们还从未受过讨论的充分浸染，这种讨论并非卑俗平庸的，它是为了获得知识，而用来进行真理的透彻精深探求的，它根本就不会认可那些巧伪之术或狡辩伎俩，那些东西的唯一目的在于提高说话者的声誉和他在争论中获胜的可能性，无论是在诉讼中还是在私人的谈话中。”

“是的，他们是还未得到过。”他说。

我说：“尽管我有所担心——因为真理让我别无选择——但
是这些理由和考虑使我先前就说没有一个城邦或政治体制达到 b
完美，同样也没有一个人能够达到完善，除非某些偶然迫使少数哲学家——是那些现在被称作是无用的人，而不是被称作败坏的人——不管他愿不愿意掌管了城邦，使公民们服从他，或者借助于神意，要么使当前的国王和统治者或他们的儿子真正爱上真正
的哲学。在我看来，没有理由说其中之一或两者都是不可能的； c
如果是这样的话，我们就应该由于我们空洞的主张和我们一厢情愿的想法而受到嘲讽。你难道不同意吗？”

'Yes.'

'So whether the outstanding practitioners of philosophy were compelled to take charge of a community at some point in the infinity of past time, or whether they are now being compelled to do so in
d some foreign land which lies far beyond the limits of our awareness, or whether they will be compelled to do so in the future, we are prepared to insist that the political system we've described either did or does or will exist, whenever it is that the Muse of philosophy gains control of a community. The point is that the compulsion is feasible, and we aren't talking about unrealizable theories—though we're the first to admit that it wouldn't be easy.'

'I agree,' he said.

'Most people don't, however, wouldn't you say?' I asked.

'I suppose so,' he said.

'Adeimantus,' I said, 'you really shouldn't condemn the mas-
e ses like that. They'll change their minds if you don't approach them argumentatively. You mustn't rub them up the wrong way while trying to remove their low opinion of intellectualism. You must show them who you mean by philosophers, and explain (as we did just now) what it takes to be a philosopher and what the pursuit involves, so
500a that they realize that you're not talking about the people they think of as philosophers. I mean, do you think that, even if they see things this way, they won't change their minds and adopt a different position? Do you think that someone open-minded and eventempered can get angry unless he's in the presence of anger, or can be resentful unless he's in the presence of resentment? I won't even let you reply before telling you my opinion: this kind of intransigence is a rare phenomenon, and the majority of people don't have it.'

'I agree,' he said, 'without hesitation.'

b 'Do you also agree that responsibility for the usual disparagement of philosophy is to be laid at the door of those gate-crashers who barge

“同意。”

“所以无论优秀的哲学实践者是否在遥远的古代的某个时候被迫掌管过城邦,或无论他们现在是否在我们所不知道的某个地方被迫这样做,无论他们是否在将来被迫这样做,我们会坚持我们说过的,即政治体制要么过去是存在的,要么现在是存在的,要么将来会存在,无论何时,都是哲学缪斯来统治城邦。关键是强制是可行的,我们不谈论不可实现的理论——虽然我们首先承认这并不容易。” d

“我同意。”他说。

“然而大多数人是不同意的,你不是这个意思吗?”我问道。

“我是这样想的。”他说。

“阿狄曼图,”我说,“你不应该那样贬斥民众。如果你不以争论的方式接近他们的话,他们是会改变他们的想法的。你在试图消除他们贬低理性的态度的时候绝不可以重蹈覆辙。你必须向他们解释你说的哲学家是什么意思,并且就像我们刚才那样解释是什么使其成为一个哲学家,哲学家追求的是些什么,这样他们就会意识到你不是在说他们所认为的哲学家。我的意思是说,你是否认为即使他们是这样看问题的,他们也不会改变他们的想法而接受一种不同的观点?你认为某个心胸开阔、温文尔雅的人要不是遇到了愤怒之事,他会发脾气吗,要不是遇到愤恨之事,他会愤恨吗?甚至不用你回答,我就会告诉你我的看法:这种不容让的现象是很少见的,大多数人都不会这样。” e 500a

他说:“我毫不犹豫地会同意。”

“你是否也同意:通常对哲学的轻视的原因在于,那些闯进他 b

in where they have no right to be, call one another names, behave offensively, and constantly gossip about people, which is a highly unphilosophical activity?'

'Definitely,' he replied.

'The point is, of course, Adeimantus, that someone whose mind really is fixed on reality has no time to cast his gaze downwards on to
c the affairs of men and to enter into their disputes (and so be infected with resentment and malice). His eyes are occupied with the sight of things which are organized, permanent, and unchanging, where wronging and being wronged don't exist, where all is orderly and rational; and he makes this realm the model for his behaviour, and assimilates himself to it as much as is feasible. I mean, don't you think that one's behaviour is bound to resemble anyone or anything whose company one enjoys?'

'Inevitably,' he said.

d 'So because a philosopher's links are with a realm which is divine and orderly, he becomes as divine and orderly as is humanly possible. Even so, he still meets with plenty of criticism from all quarters.'

'Absolutely.'

'Now, if a philosopher were compelled not to restrict his modelling to himself, but to work both publicly and in his private life to stamp men's characters with what he sees m that realm, do you think he'd make a poor artisan of self-discipline, morality, and in general of what it is to be, in ordinary terms, a good person?'

'Not at all,' he answered.

e 'And if people realize that what we're saying about him is the truth, will they still get angry at philosophers? Will they still doubt our claim that there is no way in which a community is going to be happy unless its plan is drawn up by artists who refer to a divine model?'

501a 'No, they won't get angry if they realize that,' he said. 'But how will these artists go about their work?'

们无权进入之地的不速之客，相互辱骂，行为不轨，常常与人说三道四，这全然不是哲学活动？”

“毫无疑问。”他回答说。

“阿狄曼图，关键是那些灵魂确实是关注于存在的人，当然就没有时间去把他的目光盯着人事并与充满敌意的人进行争吵，那 c
样的话就会受到愤恨与邪恶的影响。他的眼睛里充满了那些有序的、永恒不变的事物的形象，伤害和被伤害都不存在，有的都是有序和理性；他把这领域当作他行动的榜样，尽可能地使自己模仿它。我的意思是说，你难道不认为一个人的行为必定与任何他喜欢的人或物相像吗？”

“必定如此。”他说。

“因此，与神圣和有序的领域相关的一个哲学家，他会尽人之所能而变得神圣和有序。即使如此，他还是遇到了许多来自各方 d
的批评。”

“确实如此。”

“那么，如果一个哲学家被迫不仅要塑造他自己，而且还要在公共的和他的个人生活中，用他在那个领域看到过的东西来塑造人们的品性，你认为他会是一个自制、正义以及一般所谓的作为一个好人所应具有的品性方面的不合格的工匠吗？”

“绝不会。”他回答说。

“如果人们知道我们关于哲学家说的是真的，那么他们还会对哲学家生气吗？他们还会怀疑我们所说的——城邦决不会幸 e
福，除非描绘天上模型的艺术家描绘出了规划？”

“如果他们意识到了的话，他们就不会生气，”他说，“但这些艺术家怎么着手他们的工作呢？” 501a

'They must treat a community and people's characters like a painting-board,' I said, 'and their first job is to wipe it clean. This isn't a particularly easy thing to do, but you'll appreciate that the main way they differ from everyone else is in refusing to deal with an individual or a community, and not being prepared to sketch out a legal code, until they've either been given a clean slate or have made it so themselves.'

'Yes, and they're right,' he said.

'Next they'll make an outline of the constitution, don't you think?'

'Of course.'

b 'I imagine the next stage would involve their constantly looking this way and that as they work—looking on the one hand towards that which is inherently moral, right, selfdisciplined, and so on, and on the other hand towards what they're creating in the human realm. By selecting behaviour-patterns and blending them, they'll produce a composite human likeness, taking as their reference-point that quality which Homer too called "godly" and "godlike" in its human manifestation.'

'Right,' he said.

'And I suppose they'd rub bits out and paint them in again, un-
c til they've done all they can to create human characters which stand the best chance of meeting the gods' approval.'

'It should be a very beautiful painting, anyway,' he remarked.

'Well,' I asked, 'are we making any progress towards persuading those energetic opponents of ours, the ones you mentioned, that this is the kind of painter of constitutions we were recommending to them before? They got angry with him then, because we were putting political power in his hands, but are they rather more mollified now that they've heard our account?'

“他们必须把城邦和人的品性看作是一块画板，”我说，“他们的第一项工作就是把它擦干净。这并非是件特别容易的事，但你会发现他们与任何别的人的主要区别就在于，直到他们要么已经有了一块干净的画板，要么他们自己已经把它弄干净了，否则他们不会来处理个人或城邦事务的，也不会准备制定出法律。”

“是的，你说得对。”他说。

“接下来他们会制定出一个政治制度的纲要，难道你不这么想吗？”

“当然是这样想的。”

“我想在下一阶段，他们会经常在工作中左顾右盼——一方 b
面看看那些内在的正义、美、自制等等，另一方面看看他们在人类领域所创造的事物。通过选择行为模式并将其混合在一起，他们就会制造出来一种合成式的人类肖像，并将荷马所谓的‘神的’、‘似神的’的品质当作人类表现的参考点。”

“对的。”他说。

“我想他们应该擦干净之后将之重新画一遍，直到他们尽其
所能地创造了人的品性，这些品性是要最大可能地受到神的赞 c
许。”

“无论如何这应该是一幅非常美丽的画。”他评论说。

“那么，”我问道，“我们在说服那些你提到过的、极力反对我们的人时，是否取得了什么进展，说这些就是我们之前向他们推荐过的政治制度的画匠？当时他们对他很气愤，因为我们给他政治权力，但他们听了我们的解释后，他们现在是否温和一点了吗？”

'They'll be much less upset,' he said, 'if they've got any sense.'

d 'I mean, how could they have any reservations? Could they doubt that philosophers are lovers of reality and truth?'

'Hardly,' he said.

'But could they doubt the affiliation of the philosophical nature we described to excellence?'

'No, they couldn't doubt that either.'

'Well, could they argue against the idea that, under the right circumstances, this sort of person is more likely than anyone to become perfectly good and a consummate philosopher? Will our critic maintain that the other lot—the ones we ruled out—are more likely?'

'Of course not.'

e 'Will they stop getting cross at us, then, for saying that until philosophers gain political power, there'll be no end to troubles for communities or their citizens, and our fictional political system will never become a full-fledged reality?'

'They might be less upset,' he said.

'How about if we say that they are completely mollified and utterly convinced,' I suggested, 'rather than that they might be less upset? That should shame them into agreeing with us, if they can't do so for any other reason.'

502a

'All right,' he said.

'Even if we can assume, then, that we've convinced them of this point,' I said, 'will they still argue that there's no chance of the children of kings or rulers being born with the philosophical characteristics?'

'They couldn't do that,' he said.

“他们会温和得多的，”他说，“如果他们明白事理的话。”

“我的意思是说，他们还有什么没有说出来的疑虑吗？他们还能怀疑哲学家是爱真实和真理之人吗？” d

“几乎不能。”他说。

“但他们是否会怀疑我们说过的与哲学本性的亲近达到至善了？”

“不，他们也不会怀疑。”

“那么他们会反对这种想法吗，即在恰当的条件下，比起任何人，这种人更可能变得至善并成为优秀的哲学家？我们的批评者是否会坚持认为很多别的人——那些被我们排除的人——更有这种可能？”

“当然不会。” e

“那么在哲学家掌权之前，对城邦和它的公民来说有无尽的骚乱，我们构想的城邦体制也决不会完全实现的时候，他们是否不会生我们的气了？”

“他们火气可能会小一点。”他说。

我暗示说：“要是我们说他们完全平息下来了，全然信服了，
而不只是他们火气可能更小了又如何呢？羞耻心使他们与我们 502a
达成一致看法，如果没有任何别的理由使他们这样做的话。”

“对。”他说。

“即使假设我们已经让他们信服这个观点，”我说，“他们是否还会争辩说，君主或统治者的孩子是不可能生来就具有哲学家的品性的？”

“他们不会这样做了。”他说。

'Could they claim that these philosophical children of kings and rulers are absolutely bound to be corrupted? I mean, even we are ad-
b mitting that it's difficult for them to preserve their integrity, but is it plausible to argue that, out of all of them, not even a single one could ever, in the entire passage of time, remain unspoilt?'

'Of course not.'

'If even one remains uncorrupted', I said, 'in a community which is prepared to obey him, then that is enough: everything which is now open to doubt would become a full-fledged reality.'

'Yes, one would do,' he agreed.

'Because if he, as ruler, establishes the laws and practices we've described,' I went on, 'then it's surely not inconceivable that the citizens of the community will be prepared to carry them out.'

'Of course it isn't.'

'But is it unimaginable and inconceivable that others might agree with our point of view?'

c 'I don't think so,' he said.

'And our earlier discussion of the question whether our proposals are for the best (if they are feasible) was, in my opinion, adequate.'

'Yes, it was.'

'So what we've found by now is this, apparently: if our proposed legislation were actually to happen, it would be impossible to improve on it; and its realization may be difficult, but is not impossible.'

'Yes, that's what we've found,' he said.

"他们会说这些君主和统治者的具有哲学天赋的孩子必定会堕落吗？我的意思是说，即使我们承认对他们来说保持正直是困难的，但有谁可以确信地说，在所有时间里他们所有人当中难道没有一个人可以保持不败坏吗？" b

"当然没有人会这样说的。"

我说："如果有一个人在城邦中保持不堕落并使别人愿意服从于他，那么这就足够了：所有现在受怀疑的事物都将完全实现。"

"是的，一个就够了。"他同意说。

"因为如果他作为统治者建立了我们已经描述过的法律和规范，"我继续说，"那么城邦中的公民愿意实行，这并不是不可设想的。"

"的确不是不可设想的。"

"但是别的人可能会同意我们的观点，这是不可想象或不可置信的吗？"

"我不这样认为。"他说。 c

"我们先前讨论的问题——我们的建议如果是可行的话，那么是否是最好的——在我看来是充分的了。"

"是充分的了。"

"所以我们现在似乎已经发现了：如果我们所建议的法律确实可以实现，那么它就不可能改进了；[1]实现它可能是困难的，但并非不可能。"

"是的，这就是我们已经发现的。"他说。

---

[1] 即是说这种法律是最好的。

CHAPTER 9

'Well, it was quite a struggle, but we've completed that topic.
Next we'd better go on to the remaining issues. What will it take—
502d what studies and practices—for these preservers of our political system
to be a possibility? And at what ages should they undertake the vari-
ous subjects to be studied?'

'Yes, we ought to discuss these issues,' he agreed.

'So I gained nothing,' I said, 'when earlier I cleverly delayed
the awkward matter of their marital arrangements, and the topics of
procreation and what rulers to appoint. I was aware that the whole
truth about what rulers to appoint would arouse resentment and anger.
It didn't make any difference, though, because now I'm up against the
necessity of discussing these matters anyway. There's nothing more to
e say about women and children, but I've got to start all over again,
more or less, in exploring the question of the rulers. I'm sure you re-
member our claim that they have to demonstrate love of their commu-
503a nity while being tested in both pleasant and painful circumstances,
and make it clear that they won't shed this patriotism whatever ordeals
or fears they meet with, or whatever changing situations they endure.
Anyone who is incapable of retaining it is to be excluded, whereas an-
yone who emerges from every test without impurities (like gold tested
in fire) is to be made a ruler and given privileges and rewards in life
and in death. We spoke along those lines, but the discussion was
starting to deviate and hide itself, because it was afraid of broaching
b the matter we're now facing.'

'Yes, I remember,' he said. 'You're quite right.'

第九章

“好吧，这真是累人，不过我们已经完成了这个讨论。接下来我们最好继续剩下的问题。要使得我们的城邦制度成为可能，这些制度的保护者需要做些什么呢？学习些什么或从事些什么？ 502d
他们应该在什么年纪着手学习各门课程呢？”

“我们应该讨论一下这些问题。”他同意说。

“所以我没有取得什么进展”，我说，“我是说当我先前适当地搁置了他们婚姻的安排以及生育后代和指派统治者等那些尴尬而棘手的问题的时候。我曾认为关于指派什么样的统治者这整个真实问题会引起记恨与愤怒。然而这没有什么区别，因为无论如何我现在又不得不讨论这些问题。关于妇女和孩子没什么更多话要说 e
的，但在探讨统治者这个问题方面，我不得不多多少少重新来一遍。我确信你记得我们说过，当他们无论是在快乐还是困苦的环境中受到考验的时候，他们必须表现出热爱他们的城邦，并且无论他们遇 503a
到了严酷的考验还是恐惧，也无论他们忍受着什么样的变换的环境，必须保证他们不会放弃这种爱国心。任何不能保持爱国心的人都被淘汰，而任何经过所有锤炼而不留杂质之人，就像火中炼就的金子一样，他们必须被任命为统治者，给予他们特权，生时给予其尊容，死时给予其褒奖。我们说过这些话，但讨论开始离题并隐晦起来，因为担心触及我们现在所面对的问题。” b

“是的，我记得，”他说，“你说得非常对。”

‘I was too scared to make the reckless assertions that have now been expressed,’ I said,‘but now the presumptuous statement that if we are to have absolutely authentic guardians, then we must appoint philosophers, is out in the open.’

‘Yes, it is,’ he said.

‘Do you realize how few they'll be, in all likelihood? Consider the nature which, in our account, they have to have and how rare it is for its various parts to coalesce into a single entity: it usually ends up in bits and pieces.’

c “What do you mean?’ he asked.

‘People who are quick at learning, have good memories, and are astute and smart and so on, tend—as you know—not to combine both energy and broadness of mental vision with the ability to live an orderly, peaceful, and stable life. Instead, their quickness carries them this way and that, and stability plays no part at all in their lives.’

‘You're right,’ he said.

d ‘On the other hand, a sound and stable character, which makes people more dependable and slow to respond to frightening situations in battle, also makes them approach their studies in the same way. They're as slow to respond and to learn as if they'd been drugged, and they're constantly dozing off and yawning when they're asked to do anything intellectually arduous.’

‘True,’ he said.

‘But our claim is that a good and sufficient helping of both sets of qualities is a prerequisite for anyone to be allowed to take part in an authentic educational programme or to be awarded political office and power.’

‘Right,’ he said.

‘So it'll be a rare phenomenon, don't you think?’

“我当时太害怕以致没能说出现在这个大胆的主张,”我说,“但现在可以公开大胆地说,如果我们一定要拥有真正的卫士的话,那么我们必须委任哲学家。”

“是的。”他说。

“不知你认识到没有,可能性很大的情形便是,这类人会是多么地稀少?这是基于以下对哲学家天赋考虑而得出的一个判断,即在我们看来,要将哲学天赋各个不同的部分结合成一个单一的整体,那是何等罕见的一件事情啊,而他们则必须具有这种结合而成的单一的整体才行:这一整体通常会散落成片断和碎片而落空的。”

“你说的是什么意思?”他问道。 c

“有些人敏于学习、有好记忆并且灵巧聪明等等,他们——如你所知——不大会把力量和宽广的心灵视野以及有序、安宁、稳定的生活能力结合起来。相反,他们的敏捷带着他们团团转,稳定在他们的生活中毫无作用。”

“你说得对。”他说。

“另一方面,一个完善、稳定的品性使得人更加可靠并且不受战争中的骇人场面的惊吓,也能使他们以同样的方式进行学习。 d
但他们反应迟钝、懒于学习,他们就像麻木了一般,当他们要求去做什么繁重的脑力劳动的时候,他们就常常瞌睡、打哈欠。”

“对。”他说。

“而我们的主张是,对任何被允许参加真正的教育课程或授予城邦职务和权力的人来说,良好而充分地具有两方面的品性是一个必要的前提。”

“对。”他说。

“所以这种现象是罕见的,你难道不这么认为吗?”

'Of course it will.'

e 'It's not just a matter of testing someone in the ways we've already mentioned, then—by means of ordeals and fear and pleasure. There's a further point we omitted before, but are including now: we must give him plenty of intellectual exercise as well, so that we can see whether he is capable of enduring fundamental intellectual work,
504a or whether he'll cut and run as cowards do in other spheres.'

'Yes, we certainly ought to try to find that out,' he said. 'But what do you mean by fundamental intellectual work?'

'I'm sure you remember when, as a result of distinguishing three aspects within the mind, we defined morality, selfdiscipline, courage, and wisdom,' I said.

'If I didn't,' he said, 'then we might as well stop right now.'

'Do you also remember how we prefaced our discussion of those qualities?'

'How?'

b 'We said that it would take a different route, a longer one, to reach the best possible vantage-point and that they would be plainly visible to anyone who went that way, but that it was possible to come up with arguments which were in keeping with the kinds of discussions we'd already been having. You said that would do, and we proceeded at the time on that basis. I think the argument was defective, in terms of precision, but it's up to you to say whether you were happy with it.'

'Yes, I was happy enough with it,' he said, 'and so was everyone else.'

c 'But in these sorts of matters, my friend,' I said, 'anything which misses the truth by even a tiny amount is nowhere near "enough". Anything less than perfect is not up to the mark at all, though people occasionally think it's adequate and that they don't need to look any further.'

'Yes, a great many people feel this,' he said, 'because they're lazy.'

“当然是罕见的。”

“因此,这就不仅仅是要以我们说过的那种方式对某人加以检验的问题了,即不仅仅是通过严峻的考验和恐惧以及快乐加以考察这么一回事。这里还有一点我们之前遗漏了,但现在涵盖进了:我们也必须给予他大量的心智上的锻炼,这样我们就能考察他是否能够担负起基本的心智劳作,或者他是否像在别的领域里的懦夫一样匆匆溜走。” e 504a

“是的,我们当然应该试图加以考察,”他说,“但你说的基本的心智劳作指的是什么呢?”

“我确信你记得,当我们区分心灵的三个部分时,结果是我们定义了正义、自制、勇敢和智慧。”我说。

“如果我不记得,”他说,“那么我们还是马上停下来的好。”

“你也记得我们是如何开始讨论这些品性的吧?”

“如何开始的?”

“我们说过需要走一条不同的道路,一条更加漫长的道路,以达到至高点,任何走完这条路的人就能清楚地看见它们了,但拿出一个与我们已经讨论过的相应的证明是可能的。你说那就行了,于是我们就在这基础上前进了。我认为这种论证就其精确性而言是有缺陷的,但对它是否满意就要看你了。” b

“是的,我对它很满意了,”他说,“其他每个人也是满意的。”

“但是,我的朋友,对这种事情来说,”我说,“任何事物要是有一点点够不上真理那么就离‘足够’尚远。任何还不完善的事物就完全够不上标准,虽然人们时常认为这就足够了,他们不需要再进一步考察了。” c

“很多人都这样认为,”他说,“因为他们懒惰。”

'But it's a completely inappropriate feeling for a guardian of a community and its laws to have,' I said.

'I suppose so,' he said.

'Then a guardian had better take the longer route, Adeimantus,' I
d said, 'and put just as much effort into his intellectual work as his physical exercise. Otherwise, as we said a moment ago, he'll never see that fundamental field of study through to the end—and it's not just fundamental, but particularly appropriate for him.'

'Are you implying that morality and the other qualities we discussed are not the most important things there are—that there's something even more fundamental than them?' he asked.

'It's not only more fundamental,' I said, 'but it's exactly the kind of thing which requires viewing as a completely finished product, without skimping and looking merely at an outline, as we did just
e now. I mean, wouldn't it be absurd to devote extremes of energy and effort to getting as precise and clear a picture as possible of insignificant matters, and then not to think that the most important matters deserve the utmost precision too?'

'An excellent sentiment,' he said. 'But surely you don't expect to get away without being asked what this fundamental field of study of yours is, and what it is concerned with?'

'No, I don't,' I answered. 'Go ahead and ask your questions. In actual fact, you've not infrequently been told what it is, but it's ei-
505a ther slipped your mind for the moment, or you're intending to make trouble for me by attacking my position. I incline towards the latter alternative, since you've often been told that the most important thing to try to understand is the character of goodness, because this is where anything which is moral (or whatever) gets its value and advantages from. It can hardly have escaped your notice that this is my position, and you must know what I'm going to add: that our knowledge of goodness is inadequate. And you appreciate, I'm sure, that there's absolutely no point in having expert knowledge of everything else, but lacking knowledge of goodness, just as there isn't in having anything
b else either, unless goodness comes with it. I mean, do you think there's any advantage in owning everything in the world except good

“但对城邦以及法律的卫士来说,这是完全不恰当的想法。”我说。

“我也是这么认为的。”他说。

“那么,阿狄曼图,卫士最好走那条更漫长的道路,”我说,“在
灵魂的劳作中,他要付出和身体锻炼同样的努力。否则,就像我 d
们刚才说过的一样,他决不会把学习的基本领域进行到底的——
这不仅是基本的,而且是尤其适合于他的。”

“你是指正义以及我们所说的其他品性并不是最重要的事物吗?——还有什么比之更加根本的呢?”他问道。

“不只是有更加根本的,”我说,“它正是这样的事物,它需要
被看作是完整的成品,而不是像我们刚才那样大略地仅仅看看它
的轮廓。我的意思是说,在无关紧要的小事上投入极大的气力和
努力,以求理解得尽可能地精确和清晰,而同时并不认为那些最 e
重要的事物才值得最大的精确,这难道不荒谬吗?”

“说得很对,”他说,“但你休想希望逃脱这样的问题,即你学习的根本领域是什么,它与什么有关?”

“我不会逃的,”我回答说,“继续问你的问题吧。实际上,你
经常听我说它是什么,但你现在要么是忘记了,要么是存心找我
的麻烦,攻击我的观点。我倾向于认为是后一种可能,因为你多 505a
次听说要尽力去理解最重要的事物是善的理念,因为任何正义
(或无论什么)等事物都是从这得到它的价值和优点的。这就是
我的观点,这是你不会不注意的,而且你肯定知道我所要补充的:
我们关于善的知识是不够的。我确信你认识到,如果拥有其他每
一种事物的专门知识而缺乏善的知识,这是没什么用的,就像我
们拥有任何别的事物一样,除非有善相伴随,否则也是没有用的。
我的意思是说,拥有世上的任何事物就是没有善的事物,或理解 b

things, or in understanding everything else except goodness, and therefore failing to understand anything worth while and good?'

'I certainly don't,' he said.

'Now, it can't have escaped your notice either that the usual view of goodness is that it's pleasure, while there's also a more ingenious view around, that it's knowledge.'

'Of course it hasn't.'

'As you also know, however, my friend, the people who hold the latter view are incapable of explaining exactly what knowledge constitutes goodness, but are forced ultimately to say that it is knowledge of goodness.'

'And so to make complete fools of themselves,' he remarked.

c 'Of course they do,' I said. 'First they tell us off for not knowing what goodness is, then they talk to us as if we did know what it is. I mean, to say it's knowledge of goodness is to assume that we understand what they're saying when they use the term goodness.'

'You're absolutely right,' he said.

'What about the definition of goodness as pleasure? Aren't its proponents just as thoroughly misguided as the others? I mean, they too are forced to make a concession, in this case that there are bad pleasures, aren't they?'

'Certainly.'

'So their position ends up being that it is possible for a single thing to be both good and bad, doesn't it?'

'Naturally.'

d 'It's clear, therefore, that there's plenty of scope for serious disagreement where goodness is concerned. Yes?'

'Of course.'

'Well, isn't it also clear that whereas (whether it's a matter of doing something, or owning something, or having a certain reputation)

所有别的事情就是不理解善,从而不能理解任何有价值或善的事物,你认为这有什么好处吗?"

"我当然认为没什么好处。"他说。

"那么你不会没有注意到,一般看法认为善就是快乐,而也有一些高明一点的看法认为善就是知识。"

"我当然注意到了。"

"然而,我的朋友,你也知道,持后一种观点的人不能确切地解释是什么知识构成了善,最后就不得不说它就是善的知识。"

"他们这样使自己太可笑了。"他说。

"当然可笑,"我说,"他们起先指责我们不知道善是什么,然 c
后在与他们交谈时就好像我们知道了善是什么了。我的意思是说,说它是善的知识就假定了当他们使用'善'这个词的时候,我们理解他们所说的。"

"你说得非常正确。"他说。

"那么把善定义为快乐呢?主张这种说法的人不是也像别人一样受了误导?我的意思是说,他们不是也不得不承认,在这种情况下就有恶的快乐了,不是吗?"

"当然。"

"所以他们的最终观点就会是这样:一个事物可能既是善的又是恶的,不是吗?"

"当然。" d

"那么明显,牵涉到善的地方就有很多严重的分歧。是吗?"

"当然。"

"那么,这不也是明显的吗:无论是在做什么事情,或占有什么,或拥有某种名誉,人们通常偏爱正义和正确的外表,即使不牵涉到

people usually prefer the appearance of morality and right, even if there's no reality involved, yet no one is content with any possession that is only apparently good? It's the reality of goodness they want; no one thinks at all highly of mere appearance in this sphere.'

'Yes, that's perfectly clear,' he said.

'So here we have something which everyone, whatever their temperament, is after, and which is the goal of all their activities.
e They have an inkling of its existence, but they're confused about it and can't adequately grasp its nature or be as certain and as confident about it as they can about other things, and consequently they fail to derive any benefit even from those other activities. When something of this kind and this importance is involved, can we allow the best mem-
506a bers of our community, the ones to whom we're going to entrust everything, to be equally in the dark?'

'Certainly not,' he protested.

'Anyway,' I said, 'I imagine that anyone who is ignorant about the goodness of moral and right conduct would make a second-rate guardian of morality and right, and I suspect that no one will fully understand them until he knows about their relation to goodness.'

'Your suspicion is right,' he said.

b 'So the constitution and organization of our community will be perfect only if they are overseen by the kind of guardian who has this knowledge, won't they?'

'Necessarily,' he said. 'But Socrates, do *you* identify goodness with knowledge or pleasure, or with something else?'

'Just listen to him!' I exclaimed. 'It's been perfectly obvious all along that other people's views on the matter weren't going to be enough for you.'

'That's because I don't think it's right, Socrates,' he said, 'for
c someone who's devoted so much time to the matter to be in a position to state others' beliefs, but not his own.'

'But do you think it's right', I responded, 'for someone to talk as if he knew what he doesn't know?'

实在,而没有人满足于拥有任何仅仅表面上善的事物?他们想要的是实在的善;没有人会在这里赞扬仅仅是表面上善的事物。”

“是的,这非常明显。”他说。

“所以在这里我们有一些事物,无论每个人的品性如何,他们都在追求,这是他们所有行动的目标。他们微微地感觉到它的存在,
但他们为之迷惑而不能充分地把握它的本质,或像对别的事物一样 e
确信和肯定,他们最终甚至不能从别的活动中得到任何好处。当涉
及到这种重要事物的时候,我们能够让我们城邦中最优秀的成 506a
员——那些我们委以所有事物的人——同样蒙在鼓里吗?”

“当然不能。”他坚决地说。

“无论如何,”我说,“我想任何对于道德和正义的行为之善无知的人,会成为一个道德和正义方面的二流卫士,我猜想,没有人在他知道道德和正义这二者与善的关系之前,会完全理解道德和正义。”

“你的猜测是对的。”他说。

“所以只有当具有这种知识的卫士监督我们城邦的政治制度
和管理的时候,它才会完善,不是吗?” b

“那是必定的,”他说,“但是,苏格拉底,你把善与知识或快乐或别的什么事物相等同吗?”

“瞧你说的!”我大声说道,“别人对此事的看法一直都不会让你满意,这很明显。”

他说:“苏格拉底,那是因为我认为这样不合适,让一个在这个问
题上花了那么多的时间的人去表述别人的意见,而不是他自己的。” c

我回答说:“但你认为一个人能谈论他不知道的事物,就像他知道一样?”

‘Of course not,’ he said. ‘Not as if he knew, but as if he'd formed opinions—he should be prepared to say what he thinks.’

‘But aren't ideas which aren't based on knowledge always defective, in your experience?’ I asked. ‘The best of them are blind. I mean, don't people who have a correct belief, but no knowledge, strike you as exactly like blind people who happen to be taking the right road?’

‘Yes,’ he said.

‘Well, do you want to see things which are defective, blind,
d and deformed,’ I asked, ‘when you could be getting lucid, correct views from elsewhere?’

‘Socrates,’ said Glaucon, ‘please don't back away from the finishing-line, so to speak. We'd be happy with the kind of description of goodness that you gave of morality, selfdiscipline, and so on.’

‘So would I, Glaucon,’ I said, ‘very happy. But I'm afraid it'll be more than I can manage, and that my malformed efforts will make me ridiculous. What I suggest, my friends, is that we forget a-
e bout trying to define goodness itself for the time being, You see, I don't at the moment think that our current impulse is enough to take us to where I'd like to see us go. However, I am prepared to talk about something which seems to me to be the child of goodness and to bear a very strong resemblance to it. Would you like me to do that? If not, we can just forget it.’

‘Please do,’ he said. ‘You can settle your account by discussing the father another time.’

507a ‘I hope I can make the repayment,’ I said, ‘and you can recover the debt, rather than just the interest, as you are now. Anyway, as interest on your account, here's an account of the child of goodness. But please be careful that I don't cheat you—not that I intend to—by giving you a counterfeit description of the child.’

‘We'll watch out for that as best we can,’ he replied. ‘Just go ahead, please.’

‘First I want to make sure that we're not at cross purposes,’ I said, ‘and to remind you of something that came up earlier, though you've often heard it on other occasions as well.’

“当然不能，”他说，“不是说他知道，而是说他形成了意见——他应该乐意说说他的想法。”

“但按你的经验，脱离知识的想法不是总有缺陷的吗？”我问道，“其中最好的也是盲目的。我的意思是说，那些具有正确意见而没有知识的人，难道不让你觉得与盲人偶尔走对路非常类似吗？”

“是的。”他说。

我问道：“那么，当你可以从别处得到清晰、正确的观点的时候，你还想看那些有缺陷的、盲目的、歪曲的事物吗？” d

“苏格拉底，”格劳孔说，“我们说，请不要在终点线折回。你已经描述过正义、自制等等，对善也给出同样的描述，我们就满意了。”

“格劳孔，这样我也会很满意，”我说，“但我担心这超出我所能做的，笨拙的努力会使我很可笑。我的朋友，我建议我们暂且忘了试着去定义善自身。你看看，我想现在我们当下的力量还不 e
足以把我们带向我希望我们去的地方。然而，我愿意谈一谈那个在我看来似乎是善的孩子的事物，它与善非常相像。你愿意让我那样做吗？否则我们就把它忘了吧。”

“请说说吧，”他说，“你下次谈谈这位父亲，把债还清。”

“我希望我能还，”我说，“你也能收回贷款而不是像你现在一 507a
样只收利息。无论如何，这个对善的孩子的解释就是给你的利息。但请小心，不要让我把你们欺骗了——并不是我故意这样做——对孩子做了一个虚假的描述。”

“我们会尽可能地当心的，”他回答说，“你只管说吧。”

“我首先要确定的是，我们并没矛盾分歧，”我说，“而且还要提醒你们想起早前讨论的一些东西，尽管你们在其他场合也经常听到过它。”

'What?' he asked.

b 'As we talk,' I said, 'we mention and differentiate between a lot of beautiful things and a lot of good things and so on.'

'Yes, we do.'

'And we also talk about beauty itself, goodness itself and so on. All the things we refer to as a plurality on those occasions we also conversely count as belonging to a single class by virtue of the fact that they have a single particular character, and we say that the *x* itself is "what really is".'

'True.'

'And we say that the first lot is visible rather than intelligible, whereas characters are intelligible rather than visible.'

c 'Absolutely.'

'With what aspect of ourselves do we see the things we see?'

'With our sight,' he replied.

'And we use hearing for the things we hear, and so on for all the other senses and the things we perceive. Yes?'

'Of course.'

'Well, have you ever stopped to consider', I asked, 'how generous the creator of the senses was when he created the domain of seeing and being seen?'

'No, not really,' he said.

'Look at it this way. Are hearing and sound deficient? Do they
d need an extra something to make the one hear and the other be heard—some third thing without which hearing won't hear and sound won't be heard?'

'No,' he answered.

'And in my opinion', I went on, 'the same goes for many other domains, if not all: they don't need anything like this. Or can you

“是什么?”他问道。 b

“就如我们所说的,”我说,“我们提到并区分了许多美的事物和许多善的事物,如此等等。”

“是的,我们是这样做的。”

“我们也谈论过美自身、善自身等等。所有我们在那些场合当作‘多’的事物,我们也可以相反地把它们说成是:由于其具有单一的理念而属于一个类别,我们把其自身称作‘其所是’。”

“对的。”

“我们说第一类事物是可见的而不是可理解的,而理念是可理解的而不是可见的。”

“毫无疑问。”

“用我们的哪个部分来观看我们看到的事物?” c

“用我们的视觉。”他回答说。

“我们用听觉来听我们听到的事物,对于所有其他感觉和我们感知的事物都是这样。是吗?”

“当然。”

我问道:“那么你是否曾停下来想过,感觉的创造者在他创造看和被看领域的时候是多么费力?”

“确实没有想过。”他说。

“这样来研究。听觉和声音是不足的?它们是否需要另一个事物使一个能听,使另一个被听到——没有这个第三者,听觉就不会听到,声音就不会被听到?” d

“不需要。”

“在我看来,”我继续说,“对很多其他领域——如果不是所有领域——来说也是一样的:它们不需要任何像这样的事物。或者

point to one that does?'

'I can't,' he said.

'But do you realize that sight and the visible realm *are* deficient?'

'How?'

'Even if a person's eyes are capable of sight, and he's trying to use it, and what he's trying to look at is coloured, the sight will see
e nothing and the colours will remain unseen, surely, unless there is also present an extra third thing which is made specifically for this purpose.'

'What is this thing you're getting at?' he asked.

'It's what we call light,' I said.

'You're right,' he said.

508a 'So if light has value, then because it links the sense of sight and the ability to be seen, it is far and away the most valuable link there is.'

'Well, it certainly does have value,' he said.

'Which of the heavenly gods would you say is responsible for this? Whose light makes it possible for our sight to see and for the things we see to be seen?'

'My reply will be no different from what yours or anyone else's would be,' he said. 'I mean, you're obviously expecting the answer, "the sun".'

'Now, there are certain conclusions to be drawn from comparing sight to this god.'

'What?'

'Sight and the sun aren't to be identified: neither the sense itself
b nor its location—which we call the eye—is the same as the sun.'

'True.'

'Nevertheless, there's no sense-organ which more closely resembles the sun, in my opinion, than the eye.'

你能指出其一?”

“我不能。”他说。

“但你是否意识到视觉和可见领域是不足的?”

“怎么会?”

“即使一个人的眼睛具有看的能力,而且他力图去看,又他所力图看到的是有色彩的事物,但是如果不存在这二者之外的第三种事物,它是专门为看的目的而来的,那么视觉就什么也看不见,并且色彩也仍然看不到。” e

“你说的这个事物是什么?”他问道。

“这就是我们所说的光。”我说。

“你说得对。”他说。

“所以如果光有其价值,那么是因为它连接了视觉和被看见的能力,它肯定是存在的最有价值的连接。” 508a

“它当然有价值。”他说。

“你会说天上的哪位神是其原因? 谁的光使我们的视觉能够看见,使我们所看的事物被看到?”

“我的回答与你的或其他人的回答没有什么区别,”他说,“我的意思是说,你期望的回答显然就是‘太阳’。”

“现在,通过把视觉比作这神,就得出某些结论来了。”

“什么结论呢?”

“视觉与太阳不同:感觉本身和它所处的位置——我们称之为眼睛——都与太阳不同。” b

“对的。”

“然而在我看来,没有比眼睛更像太阳的感觉器官了。”

'The resemblance is striking.'

'Moreover, the eye's ability to see has been bestowed upon it and channelled into it, as it were, by the sun.'

'Yes.'

'So the sun is not to be identified with sight, but is responsible for sight and is itself within the visible realm. Right?'

'Yes,' be said.

'The sun is the child of goodness I was talking about, then,' I said. 'It is a counterpart to its father, goodness. As goodness stands
c in the intelligible realm to intelligence and the things we know, so in the visible realm the sun stands to sight and the things we see.'

'I don't understand,' he said. 'I need more detail, please.'

'As you know,' I explained, 'when our eyes are directed towards things whose colours are no longer bathed in daylight, but in artificial light instead, then they're less effective and seem to be virtually blind, as if they didn't even have the potential for seeing clearly.'

'Certainly,' he said.

d 'But when they're directed towards things which are lit up by the sun, then they see clearly and obviously do have that potential.'

'Of course.'

'Well, here's how you can think about the mind as well. When its object is something which is lit up by truth and reality, then it has—and obviously has—intelligent awareness and knowledge. However, when its object is permeated with darkness (that is, when its object is something which is subject to generation and decay), then it has beliefs and is less effective, because its beliefs chop and change, and under these circumstances it comes across as devoid of intelligence.'

“它们非常相像。”

“此外,眼睛看的能力是由太阳赋予的,并且就其自身而言是太阳赋予它的流射。”

“是的。”

“所以太阳不等于视觉,而是视觉的原因,并且其自身也在可见的领域之内。对吗?”

“是的。”他说。

“那么太阳就是我们所说的善之子,”我说,“它与它的父亲——善——很相像。就像善在可知领域中与理智和我们知道 c
的事物相关,太阳在可见的领域中与视觉和我们看到的事物相关。”

“我不理解,”他说,“我需要更多的详细说明。”

“如你所知,”我解释道,“当我们的眼睛直视那些其颜色不再沐浴于阳光之下而是在微弱的光线下的事物的时候,它们不那么清晰,看上去很模糊,就像我们的眼睛甚至没有看清事物的能力一样。”

“当然。”他说。

“但当我们的眼睛直视受阳光照耀的事物的时候,那么眼睛 d
就有能力看得清清楚楚。”

“当然。”

“那么你也是这样思考心灵的。当它的对象被真理和实在照亮的时候,那么它显然就有理智的认识和知识。然而,当它的对象处于黑暗笼罩的时候,即当它的对象屈从于生灭的时候,那么它便只具有意见,便是不那么清晰,因为这意见变动不定,在这些情况下它就看上去似乎是缺乏理智。”

'Yes, it does.'

e 'Well, what I'm saying is that it's goodness which gives the things we know their truth and makes it possible for people to have knowledge. It is responsible for knowledge and truth, and you should think of it as being within the intelligible realm, but you shouldn't identify it with knowledge and truth, otherwise you'll be wrong: for all
509a their value, it is even more valuable. In the other realm, it is right to regard light and sight as resembling the sun, but not to identify either of them with the sun; so in this realm it is right to regard knowledge and truth as resembling goodness, but not to identify either of them with goodness, which should be rated even more highly.'

'You're talking about something of inestimable value,' he said, 'if it's not only the source of knowledge and truth, but is also more valuable than them. I mean, you certainly don't seem to be identifying it with pleasure!'

'How could you even think it?' I exclaimed. 'But we can take our analogy even further.'

b 'How?'

'I think you'll agree that the ability to be seen is not the only gift the sun gives to the things we see. It is also the source of their generation, growth, and nourishment, although it isn't actually the process of generation.'

'Of course it isn't.'

'And it isn't only the known-ness of the things we know which is conferred upon them by goodness, but also their reality and their being, although goodness isn't actually the state of being, but surpasses
c being in majesty and might.'

'It's way beyond human comprehension, all right,' was Glaucon's quite amusing comment.

'It's your fault for forcing me to express my views on the subject,' I replied.

'Yes, and please don't stop,' he said. 'If you've left anything out of your explanation of the simile of the sun, then the least you

“是的。”

“那么，给予我们知道的事物以真理并使得人们具有知识的 e
事物，就是我所说的善的理念。它是知识和真理的原因，你应该把它当作是处于可知领域之内，而不应该把它与知识和真理相等同，否则你就是错的：在它们所有的价值中，善是更有价值的。在
另一个领域，可以恰当地把光和视觉看作与太阳很相似，但也不 509a
能把其中的任何一个与太阳等同起来；所以在这个领域可以恰当地把知识和真理看作是与善很相像，但是不能将其中的任何一个与善等同起来，善甚至应该被视作更高的。”

“你所说的事物具有无可估量的价值，”他说，“如果善不仅是知识和真理的源泉的话，那么善也比它们更具价值。我的意思是说，你肯定不会将其与快乐等同起来吧！”

“你怎么会那样想？”我大声说道，“但我们可以进一步考察一下我们的类比。”

“如何考察？” b

“我想你会同意，被看到的能力不只是太阳给予我们所见之事物的礼物，太阳还是它们产生、生长和养育的源泉，虽然太阳本身实际上并不是产生的。”

“当然不是。”

“不光是我们所知道的事物的可知性，而且它们的实在和存在都是由善所赋予的，虽然善实际上并不是处于实在中，而是在地位和能力上都超越实在。”

“阿波罗啊，这超越了人类的理解。”格劳孔非常滑稽地说。 c

“迫使我对这个问题说出我的观点，这是你的错。”我回答说。

“是的，请别停止，”他说，“关于太阳的比喻如果你还有任何

could do is continue with it.'

'There are plenty of omissions, in fact,' I said.

'Don't leave any gaps,' he said, 'however small.'

'I think I'll have to leave a lot out,' I said, 'but I'll' try to make it as complete as I can at the moment.'

'All right,' he said.

d 'So bear in mind the two things we've been talking about,' I said, 'one of which rules over the intelligible realm and its inhabitants, while the other rules over the visible realm—I won't say over the heavens in case you think I'm playing clever word-games. Anyway, do you understand this distinction between visible things and intelligible things?'

'Yes.'

'Well, picture them as a line cut into two unequal sections and, following the same proportion, subdivide both the section of the visible realm and that of the intelligible realm. Now you can compare the sections in terms of clarity and unclarity. The first section in the visi-
e ble realm consists of likenesses, by which I mean a number of things:
510a shadows, reflections (on the surface of water or on anything else which is inherently compact, smooth, and bright), and so on. Do you see what I'm getting at?'

'I do.'

'And you should count the other section of the visible realm as consisting of the things whose likenesses are found in the first section: all the flora and fauna there are in the world, and every kind of artefact too.'

'All right.'

'I wonder whether you'd agree,' I said, 'that truth and lack of truth have been the criteria for distinguishing these sections, and that the image stands to the original as the realm of beliefs stands to the realm of knowledge?'

b 'Yes,' he said, 'I certainly agree.'

东西要解释的话，那么至少你应该继续说下去。”

“实际上是有很多遗漏的。”他说。

“不要有任何的遗留，”他说，“不管有多么细小。”

“我想我不得不省略很多，”我说，“但现在我尽量说得完整些。”

“好。”他说。

“所以，请记住我们曾谈到过的两样事物，”我说，“其一统治 d
着可知领域及其居住者，而另一个统治着可见领域——我不说是天界，以免你认为我在玩耍巧妙的文字游戏。不管怎么说，你理解可见之物与可知之物之间的区别了吗？”

“是的。”

“那么用一条线来表示它们，把这条线截成不等的两段，按照同样的比例再划分可见的领域和可知领域两个部分。现在你可以依据清晰和不清晰来比较各部分。可见领域中的第一部分包
含影像，我指的是诸多事物：影像、水面或任何其他光滑、有光泽、 510a
内部致密的东西的反光，如此等等。你明白我说的意思吗？”

“我明白。”

“而且你可以将可见领域的其它部分认作是这样一种事物，即在可见领域的第一部分中是可以找到它们的肖像的：所有存在于世上的植物群与动物群，还有每一类人工制品等。”

“对的。”

“我想知道你是否会同意，”我说，“区分这些部分的标准在于是真实的还是欠缺真实的，而且影像之依赖于原物，一如意见领域之依赖于知识领域才能保持得住。”

“是的，”他说，“我当然同意。” b

'Now have a look at how to subdivide the section which belongs to the intelligible realm.'

'How?'

'Like this. If the mind wants to explore the first subdivision, it can do so only by using those former originals as likenesses and by taking things for granted on its journey, which leads it to an end-point, rather than to a starting-point. If it wants to explore the second subdivision, however, it takes things for granted in order to travel to a starting-point where nothing needs to be taken for granted, and it has no involvement with likenesses, as before, but makes its approach by means of types alone, in and of themselves.'

c 'I don't quite understand what you're saying,' he said.

'You will if I repeat it,' I said, 'because this preamble will make it easier to understand. I'm sure you're aware that practitioners of geometry, arithmetic, and so on take for granted things like numerical oddness and evenness, the geometrical figures, the three kinds of angle, and any other things of that sort which are relevant to a given subject. They act as if they know about these things, treat them as basic, and don't feel any further need to explain them either to them-
d selves or to anyone else, on the grounds that there is nothing unclear
about them. They make them the starting-points for their subsequent investigations, which end after a coherent chain of reasoning at the point they'd set out to reach in their research.'

'Yes, I'm certainly well aware of this,' he said.

'So you must also be aware that in the course of their discussions they make use of visible forms, despite the fact that they're not interested in visible forms as such, but in the things of which the visible forms are likenesses: that is, their discussions are concerned with what it is to be a square, and with what it is to be a diagonal (and so
e on), rather than with the diagonal (and so on) which occurs in their
diagrams. They treat their models and diagrams as likenesses, when

“那么考察一下如何来进一步细分属于可知领域的部分。”

“如何细分?”

“就像这样。如果心灵想要探究第一个小部分,那么它这样做只需把那些先前作为原物的东西当作影像来使用,研究必须从假定出发,达到一个结论而不是第一原则。然而如果想要探究第二个小部分,那么其行程要从假定出发,以便达到非假定的第一原则,这就像前面的一样与影像无关,但其方式是只使用理念并且完全使用理念。”

“对你所说的我不是很理解。”他说。

“如果我再说一遍,你就会明白了,”我说,“因为这个预备性的解释会使之更容易理解。我确信你知道从事几何、算术及这类 c
学问的人假设了奇数、偶数,几何图形,三种类型的角这类事物,以及任何其他与某个知识门类相关的事物。他们表现出似乎知道这些事物,把它们当作是根本的并且觉得没有进一步向自己或任何别的人解释的需要,因为关于它们没有什么是不清楚的。他
们将之当作接下来研究的第一原则,通过一系列的严密的推理最 d
后得出他们研究的结论。”

“是的,我当然清楚地意识到了这点。”他说。

“所以你肯定还知道,在他们的讨论过程中,他们利用的是可见的形状,尽管实际上他们对形状本身并不感兴趣,引起他们注意的是影像内在的事物,而可见的形状只是与它相仿的影像而已:更具体地说,他们讨论所关注的是使正方形成为正方形的东
西,还有使对角面成为对角面的东西(等等),而不是出现在他们 e
图形中的对角面(等等)。实际上,尽管这些事物自身是有影像的(指的是这些事物在水面上的阴影和倒影),他们却是将这些事物

these things have likenesses themselves, in fact (that is, shadows and reflections on water); but they're actually trying to see squares and so on in themselves, which only thought can see.'

511a 'You're right,' he said.

'So it was objects of this type that I was describing as belonging to the intelligible realm, with the rider that the mind can explore them only by taking things for granted, and that its goal is not a starting-point, because it is incapable of changing direction and rising above the things it is taking for granted. And I went on to say that it used as likenesses those very things which are themselves the originals of a lower order of likenesses, and that relative to the likenesses, the originals command respect and admiration for their distinctness.'

b 'I see,' he said. 'You're talking about the objects of geometry and related occupations.'

'Now, can you see what I mean by the second subdivision of the intelligible realm? It is what reason grasps by itself, thanks to its ability to practise dialectic. When it takes things for granted, it doesn't treat them as starting-points, but as basic in the strict sense—as platforms and rungs, for example. These serve it until it reaches a point where nothing needs to be taken for granted, and which is the starting-point for everything. Once it has grasped this starting-point, it turns around and by a process of depending on the things which depend from the starting-point, it descends to an end-point. It makes absolutely no use of anything perceptible by the senses: it aims for
c types by means of types alone, in and of themselves, and it ends its journey with types.'

'I don't quite understand,' he said. 'I mean. you're talking about crucial matters here, I think. I do understand, however, that you want to mark off that part of the real and intelligible realm which is before the eyes of anyone who knows how to practise dialectic as more clear than the other part, which is before the eyes of practitioners of the various branches of expertise, as we call them. The latter make the things they take for granted their starting-points, and al-

的样式与图形视为与水中阴影与倒影性质类似的一种影像；而他们真正想要领会的正方形之类，是在事物自身之内的，只有思想才能领会得到的。”

“你是对的，”他说道。 511a

“所以我描述的正是这一类型的感知对象，它们属于可知领域，附加条件是，心灵只有以理所当然地假定的方法才能探究它们，而且它的终点还不是一个出发点，因为它不能改变方向而上升至它理所当然地假定的事物之上。还有我过去说过的，它所使用的影像是这样一些事物，即它们自身又是一种更低层序影像的原物，而相对于影像而言，原物因其清晰明确还是值得关注与尊重的。”

“我明白了，”他说，“你说的是几何及其相关学科的对象。” b

“那么你是否明白我说的可知领域的第二个部分？就是那逻各斯凭本身的实践辩证法的能力而把握到的事物。当它假定某事物的时候，它并不是将之当作第一原则，在严格意思上是将之当作基础——比如说当作立足点和跳板。在它达到一个无须任何假设事物的点之前，它们是一直起作用的，这个点就是一切事物的第一原则。一旦人们把握了这个第一原则，它就反过来通过依据那从第一原则引出来的事物而下降到结论。完全不使用任何被感觉感知的事物：只通过理念本身达到理念本身，其行 c
程最后归结到理念。”

“我不是很理解，”他说，“我的意思是说，我想你在这里谈论的是很关键的事情。不过我确实明白了，一部分是任何知道如何实践辩证法之人眼前的实在与可知领域，另一部分是我们所谓的那些从事各种技艺之人眼前的领域，你是想把它们区分开来，前

though they inevitably use thought, not the senses, to observe what they observe, yet because of their failure to ascend to a starting-
d point—because their enquiries rely on taking things for granted—you're saying that they don't understand these things, even though they are intelligible, when related to a starting-point. I take you to be describing what geometers and so on do as thinking rather than knowing, on the grounds that thinking is the intermediate state between believing and knowing.'

'There's nothing wrong with your understanding,' I said. 'And you should appreciate that there are four states of mind, one for each of the four sections. There's knowledge for the highest section and thought for the second one; and you'd better assign confidence to the
e third one and conjecture to the final one. You can make an orderly progression out of them, and you should regard them as possessing as much clarity as their objects possess truth.'

'I see,' he said. 'That's fine with me: I'll order them in the way you suggest.'

514a 'Next,' I said, 'here's a situation which you can use as an analogy for the human condition—for our education or lack of it. Imagine people living in a cavernous cell down under the ground; at the far end of the cave, a long way off, there's an entrance open to the outside world. They've been there since childhood, with their legs and necks tied up in
b a way which keeps them in one place and allows them to look only straight ahead, but not to turn their heads. There's firelight burning a long way further up the cave behind them, and up the slope between the fire and the prisoners there's a road, beside which you should imagine a low wall has been built—like the partition which conjurors place between themselves and their audience and above which they show their tricks.'

'All right,' he said.

'Imagine also that there are people on the other side of this wall who are carrying all sorts of artefacts. These artefacts, human statu-
c ettes, and animal models carved in stone and wood and all kinds of
515a materials stick out over the wall; and as you'd expect, some of the people talk as they carry these objects along, while others are silent.'

者比后者更清晰。后者把假定当作他们的第一原则，虽然他们使
用思想而不是感觉来观察他们所考察的事物，然而因为他们不能
上升到第一原则——因为他们的研究依赖于假定——所以，即使 d
把它们与第一原则联系起来使它们是可知的，你也可以说他们不
理解这些事物。我想你会把几何学家之类的人所做的说成是理
智而不是理性，因为理智是介于意见和理性的中间状态。”

“你的理解没什么错的，”我说，“你应该认识到心灵的状态有
四种，每一个都与一个部分相应。理性是最高部分，理智是第二
部分；你最好把信念划作第三部分，猜测划作最后一个部分。你 e
可以依次给它们排一个序列出来，你应该视它们具有的清晰度以
及它们的对象持有真实性的程度来确定这个序列。”

“我明白了，”他说，“我同意：我会按你的建议把它们排序。”

“接下来，”我说，“你可以把这个情形当作对人类状态——受过 514a
我们教育的人和没有受过教育的人——的一个类比。设想一些生活
在地下洞穴的人；从洞穴底部有一条长长的通道通向一个向外面世界
敞开的入口。他们从小就在洞穴里，他们的腿和脖子被绑缚在一个地
方而被固定在那里，只允许他们向前看，而不允许回头。在他们身后 b
较远的高处有些燃烧的火光，在火与囚禁者之间的高处有一条路，你
应该设想路边已经筑了一堵矮墙——就像木偶演员在自己与观众之
间设的一道屏障，在这上面他们表演他们的戏法。”

“好吧。”他说。

“再设想这堵墙的另一边有人拿着各种人工制品。这些人工
制品，石质、木质和各种质地的雕刻的人像及动物模型，都高过这 c
堵墙；如你所预料的，在这些人中，有的人在拿着东西的同时在说 515a
话，而另一些人则不说话。”

'This is a strange picture you're painting,' he said, 'with strange prisoners.'

'They're no different from us,' I said. 'I mean, in the first place, do you think they'd see anything of themselves and one another except the shadows cast by the fire on to the cave wall directly opposite them?'

'Of course not,' he said. 'They're forced to spend their lives without moving their heads.'

b 'And what about the objects which were being carried along? Won't they only see their shadows as well?'

'Naturally.'

'Now, suppose they were able to talk to one another: don't you think they'd assume that their words applied to what they saw passing by in front of them?'

'They couldn't think otherwise.'

'And what if sound echoed off the prison wall opposite them? When any of the passers-by spoke, don't you think they'd be bound to assume that the sound came from a passing shadow?'

'I'm absolutely certain of it,' he said.

c 'All in all, then,' I said, 'the shadows of artefacts would constitute the only reality people in this situation would recognize.'

'That's absolutely inevitable,' he agreed.

'What do you think would happen, then,' I asked, 'if they were set free from their bonds and cured of their inanity? What would it be like if they found that happening to them? Imagine that one of them has been set free and is suddenly made to stand up, to turn his head and walk, and to look towards the firelight. It hurts him to do all this and he's too dazzled to be capable of making out the objects whose shadows
d he'd formerly been looking at. And suppose someone tells him that what he's been seeing all this time has no substance, and that he's now closer to reality and is seeing more accurately, because of the greater reality of the things in front of his eyes what do you imagine his reaction would be? And what do you think he'd say if he were shown any of the passing objects and had to respond to being asked what it was? Don't you think he'd

他说："你画的是一幅关于奇特囚禁者的奇怪图画。"

"他们与我们没什么区别，"我说，"我的意思是说，首先你认为他们除了看到火光投射到他们对面洞壁上的影像外，他们会看到自己和别人的任何什么东西吗？"

"当然看不到，"他说，"他们的头被迫一辈子都动不了。" b

"那么，那些被人举着前行的东西呢？他们不是也只能看到它们的影像吗？"

"当然。"

"那么，假设他们能相互交谈：你难道不认为他们会用他们的词语去谈论那些在他们面前进过的东西吗？"

"否则他们是不可设想的。"

"他们对面的囚所墙壁上的回声呢？当一个过路人说话的时候，你难道不认为他们必定会相信声音来自于移动的影像？"

"我对之非常确信。"他说。

"总之，"我说，"人工制品的影像构成了在这种处境下的人所 c
认识的唯一现实。"

"必定如此。"他同意说。

我问道："如果他们被解除了禁锢，矫正了迷误，你认为会发生什么呢？假如他们发现这样的事发生在自己身上又会怎么样呢？设想其中有一人解除了桎梏，突然站了起来，转过他的头，走动，朝火光那边看去。这些都会使他痛苦，他也会由于眼花缭乱而不能辨认出他以前看到其影像的那些事物。要是有人告诉他， d
他过去看到的都是不实在的，他现在看到的才接近于实在，也看得更加准确，因为在他眼前的是事物更大的实在——你想他是什么反应？如果向他展示所有移动的事物，并且问他这是什么，还

be bewildered and would think that there was more reality in what he'd been seeing before than in what he was being shown now?'

'Far more,' he said.

e 'And if he were forced to look at the actual firelight, don't you think it would hurt his eyes? Don't you think he'd turn away and run back to the things he could make out, and would take the truth of the matter to be that these things are clearer than what he was being shown?'

'Yes,' he agreed.

'And imagine him being dragged forcibly away from there up the rough, steep slope,' I went on, 'without being released until he's
516a been pulled out into the sunlight. Wouldn't this treatment cause him pain and distress? And once he's reached the sunlight, he wouldn't be able to see a single one of the things which are currently taken to be real, would he, because his eyes would be overwhelmed by the sun's beams?'

'No, he wouldn't,' he answered, 'not straight away.'

'He wouldn't be able to see things up on the surface of the earth, I suppose, until he'd got used to his situation. At first, it would be shadows that he could most easily make out, then he'd move on to the reflections of people and so on in water, and later he'd be able to see the actual things themselves. Next, he'd feast his eyes on the heavenly bodies and the heavens themselves, which would be eas-
b ier at night: he'd look at the light of the stars and the moon, rather than at the sun and sunlight during the daytime.'

'Of course.'

'And at last, I imagine, he'd be able to discern and feast his eyes on the sun—not the displaced image of the sun in water or elsewhere, but the sun on its own, in its proper place.'

'Yes, he'd inevitably come to that,' he said.

'After that, he'd start to think about the sun and he'd deduce that it is the source of the seasons and the yearly cycle, that the whole
c of the visible realm is its domain, and that in a sense everything which he and his peers used to see is its responsibility.'

'Yes, that would obviously be the next point he'd come to,' he agreed.

要他回答，那么你想他会说什么？你难道不认为他会不知所措，会认为他以前看到的事物比现在向他展示的事物更加实在？”

“更加实在。”他说。

“如果他被迫看那真实的火，难道你不认为那会伤了他的眼 e
睛？你难道不认为他会转身逃走，回到他看得清的事物中去，并且确实会认为那些事物比给他看的事物更加清晰？”

“是的。”他同意说。

我继续说：“设想他被硬拉着走上那条逶迤的陡坡，在他被拽到阳光下之前，不把他放开。这样对待他难道不会让他痛苦忧虑
吗？他一旦来到了阳光下，对那些现在被当作真实的东西，他一 516a
个都看不见，因为他的眼睛受不了阳光，是吗？”

他回答说：“他不会一下子就能看见的。”

“我想直到他习惯了这种情境之前，他是不会看见地面上的事物的。首先，他最容易辨认的是影像，然后他转而辨认出人和其他事物在水中的倒影，最后他能看见真实事物本身。接下来，他让他的眼睛在夜里尽情欣赏天体和天空本身，这比较容易：他
看星光与月光比看白天的太阳和阳光要容易。” b

“当然。”

“我想最后他能分辨和观看太阳了——不是水中或别的地方被置换了的影像，而是在其本来位置的太阳本身。”

“是的，他必然会走到那一步。”他说。

“在那之后，他开始思考太阳，并且他会推想太阳是四季和年岁周期的原因，整个可见世界都是它的领域，也是他和他的同伴
过去看到过的所有事物的原因。” c

“是的，这显然是他想要得出的下一个观点。”他同意说。

'Now, if he recalled the cell where he'd originally lived and what passed for knowledge there and his former fellow prisoners, don't you think he'd feel happy about his own altered circumstances, and sorry for them?'

'Definitely.'

'Suppose that the prisoners used to assign prestige and credit to one another, in the sense that they rewarded speed at recognizing the shadows as they passed, and the ability to remember which ones normally come earlier and later and at the same time as which other
d ones, and expertise at using this as a basis for guessing which ones would arrive next. Do you think our former prisoner would covet these honours and would envy the people who had status and power there, or would he much prefer, as Homer describes it, "being a slave labouring for someone else—someone without property". and would put up with anything at all, in fact, rather than share their beliefs and their life?'

e 'Yes, I think he'd go through anything rather than live that way,' he said.

'Here's something else I'd like your opinion about,' I said. 'If he went back underground and sat down again in the same spot, wouldn't the sudden transition from the sunlight mean that his eyes would be overwhelmed by darkness?'

'Certainly,' he replied.

'Now, the process of adjustment would be quite long this time, and suppose that before his eyes bad settled down and while he wasn't
517a seeing well, he had once again to compete against those same old prisoners at identifying those shadows. Wouldn't he make a fool of himself? Wouldn't they say that he'd come back from his upward journey with his eyes ruined, and that it wasn't even worth trying to go up there? And wouldn't they—if they could—grab hold of anyone who tried to set them free and take them up there and kill him?'

'They certainly would,' he said.

'Well, my dear Glaucon,' I said, 'you should apply this allegory, as a whole, to what we were talking about before. The region

“那么如果他回想起他原先居住的洞穴和那时的知识水平以及他先前遭囚禁的同伴，你难道不认为他会对变换的处境感到欣慰，替同伴们感到遗憾吗？”

“毫无疑问。”

“假设囚徒曾相互给予荣誉和赞扬，他们奖励那些人，他们能
很快地辨认出移动的影像，能记住一般是哪个先、哪个后、哪个与
另一个同时，并且擅长将之作为根据猜测下一个的出现。你认为 d
我们这个先前的囚徒会贪想这些荣誉并且羡慕那些在那里有地
位有权力的人吗，或者他会像荷马所说的那样更愿意‘做一个为
别人劳动的奴隶——一个没有家产的人’，实际上，他能够忍受任
何事情，就是不能与他们拥有同样的意见和生活？”

“是的，我想他宁愿经历任何事情也不愿意那样生活。”他说。 e

“我想听听你对另一些事的看法，”我说，“如果他回到了地下，再坐在同样的位置，从阳光中突然离开不就意味着他的眼睛因为黑暗而什么也看不见吗？”

“当然。”他说。

“那么，调整的过程会是很漫长的，要是在他的眼睛适应之
前，他什么都看不见的时候，他又与先前那些同样的囚徒比试辨 517a
别那些影像。他难道不会被耻笑吗？他们难道不会说他从上面
回来眼睛就坏了，甚至上到那里去的尝试都是不值得一提的？他
们难道不会——如果他们可以的话——抓住任何试图解救他们
并把他们带到上面去的人，并且把他杀了？”

“他们当然会的。”他说。

“那么，我亲爱的格劳孔，”我说，“你应该把这个比喻整个运
用到我们之前说过的事情上去。可见的区域相当于囚穴，那里的 b

which is accessible to sight should be equated with the prison cell, and the firelight there with the light of the sun. And if you think of the upward journey and the sight of things up on the surface of the earth as the mind's ascent to the intelligible realm, you won't be wrong—at least, I don't think you'd be wrong, and it's my impression that you want to hear. Only God knows if it's actually true, however. Anyway, it's my opinion
c that the last thing to be seen—and it isn't easy to see either—in the realm of knowledge is goodness; and the sight of the character of goodness leads one to deduce that it is responsible for everything that is right and fine, whatever the circumstances, and that in the visible realm it is the progenitor of light and of the source of light, and in the intelligible realm it is the source and provider of truth and knowledge. And I also think that the sight of it is a prerequisite for intelligent conduct either of one's own private affairs or of public business.'

'I couldn't agree more,' he said.

'All right, then,' I said. 'I wonder if you also agree with me in not finding it strange that people who've travelled there don't want to engage in human business: there's nowhere else their minds would ever
d rather be than in the upper region—which is hardly surprising, if our allegory has got this aspect right as well.'

'No, it's not surprising,' he agreed.

'Well, what about this?' I asked. 'Imagine someone returning to the human world and all its misery after contemplating the divine realm. Do you think it's surprising if he seems awkward and ridiculous while he's still not seeing well, before he's had time to adjust to the darkness of his situation, and he's forced into a contest (in a lawcourt or wherever) about the shadows of morality or the statuettes which cast
e the shadows, and into a competition whose terms are the conceptions of morality held by people who have never seen morality itself?'

518a 'No, that's not surprising in the slightest,' he said.

'In fact anyone with any sense,' I said, 'would remember that the eyes can become confused in two different ways, as a result of two different sets of circumstances: it can happen in the transition from light to darkness, and also in the transition from darkness to light. If

火光相当于太阳光。如果你把上升的行程和地面上事物的景象看作心灵上升到可知领域,那么你是不会错的——至少我不会认为你错,这想法正是我要你听的。然而只有神才知道这是否确实是正确的。无论如何,在我看来,最后看到的事物是——也不容易看见——可知领域中的善的理念;无论在什么情况下,看见善的理念 c
就使人们推论说,善是一切正义和美好事物的原因,在可见领域中它是光的创造者,是光之源泉,在可知领域中,它是真理和知识的源泉和提供者。我也认为在个人私事或公共事务中理性行为的前提条件是看见了善的理念。"

"我非常同意。"他说。

"那么,好吧,"我说,"我想知道你是否也同意我,觉得这并不奇怪,去过那里的人并不想介入人事:他们的心灵除了去高处之外无处可去——这并不奇怪,如果我们的比喻在这方面是正确的话。" d

"并不奇怪。"他同意说。

"那么这样呢?"我问道,"设想有人凝视了神圣的领域后回到了人世和所有的苦难之中。如果当他还看不清楚,还没有时间适应他所处环境的黑暗,就被迫(在法庭或别的什么地方)争论正义的影像或别的产生影像的偶像,辩论所用的词语是一些从未见过正义本身的人所拥有的正义概念,如果他这时看上去猥琐可笑, e
你是否觉得这很奇怪?"

"一点都不奇怪。"他说。

我说:"实际上任何有头脑的人都会记得,眼睛会以两种不同 518a
方式变迷茫,这是由两种不同的环境引起:从光亮到黑暗可以引起,从黑暗到光亮也会引起。当他注意到一个人的灵魂也会有这种迷糊的状态以致什么都辨认不出,如果他加以同样的考虑的

he took the same facts into consideration when he also noticed someone's mind in such a state of confusion that it was incapable of making anything out, his reaction wouldn't be unthinking ridicule. Instead, he'd try to find out whether this person's mind was returning from a mode of existence which involves greater lucidity and had been blinded by the unfamiliar darkness, or whether it was moving from relative ignorance to relative lucidity and had been overwhelmed and dazzled by the increased brightness. Once he'd distinguished between the two conditions and modes of existence, he'd congratulate anyone
b he found in the second state, and feel sorry for anyone in the first state. If he did choose tolaugh at someone in the second state, his amusement would be less a bsurd than when laughter is directed at someone returning from the light above.'

'Yes,' he said, 'you're making a lot of sense.'

'Now, if this is true,' I said, 'we must bear in mind that education is not capable of doing what some people promise. They claim to introduce knowledge into a mind which doesn't have it, as if they
c were introducing sight into eyes which are blind.'

'Yes, they do,' he said.

'An implication of what we're saying at the moment, however,' I pointed out, 'is that the capacity for knowledge is present in everyone's mind If you can imagine an eye that can turn from darkness to brightness only if the body as a whole turns, then our organ of understanding is like that. Its orientation has to be accompanied by turning the mind as a whole away from the world of becoming, until it becomes capable of bearing the sight of real being and reality at its most bright, which we're saying is goodness. Yes?'

d 'Yes.'

'That's what education should be,' I said, 'the art of orientation. Educators should devise the simplest and most effective methods of turning minds around. It shouldn't be the art of implanting sight in the organ, but should proceed on the understanding that the organ already has the capacity, but is improperly aligned and isn't facing the right way.'

'I suppose you're right,' he said.

'So although the mental states which are described as good generally

话，那么他的反应不会是不加思索地嘲笑。相反，他会尽力找出这个人的灵魂是否离开了一种具有比较光明的生存状态而被不熟悉的黑暗弄得看不见了，或者是从较无知转变到了较光亮并且被较强的光亮弄花了眼。一旦他区分了两种状态和生存的方式，那么他会向任何他发现处在第二种状态的人祝贺，而为任何 b
处在第一种状态的人感到遗憾。如果他想要讥笑那处在第二种状态的人，那么比起嘲笑那背离上面光亮处的人来说，他的这种取笑并不那么荒谬。"

"是的，"他说，"你说得很有道理。"

"那么，如果这是真的话，"我说，"我们必须记住，教育并不能做到某些人所保证的事情。他们说可以把知识灌输到原来没有知识的灵魂中去，就像他们把视力放到瞎了的眼睛中去。" c

"是的，他们是这样做的。"他说。

我指出："然而我们现在的论证表明，每个人的心灵中都有求知的能力。如果你能设想只有当整个身体转变时，眼睛才能从黑暗转向光明，我们的学习器官就像眼睛一样。其方向必定伴随着作为整体的心灵转离变动的世界，直至它变得能够观看实在的事物和最亮的实在，即我们所说的善。是吗？" d

"是的。"

"教育就应该是定向的技艺。"我说，"教育者应该设计简单而有效的方法使心灵得以转变。它不应该是在器官中培植视力的技艺，而应该照这样的理解进行，即：这器官已经有了这种能力，但没有得到恰当的调整，没有面对正确的方向。"

"我想你说得对。"他说。

"所以虽然所谓的善的心灵状态一般看来与好的身体状态相

e seem to resemble good physical states, in the sense that habituation and training do in fact implant them where they didn't use to be, yet understanding (as it turns out) is undoubtedly a property of something which is more divine: it never loses its power, and it is useful
519a and beneficial, or useless and harmful, depending on its orientation. For example, surely you've noticed how the petty minds of those who are acknowledged to be bad, but clever, are sharp-eyed and perceptive enough to gain insights into matters they direct their attention towards. It's not as if they weren't sharp-sighted, but their minds are forced to serve evil, and consequently the keener their vision is, the greater the evil they accomplish.'

'Yes, I've noticed this,' he said.

'However,' I went on, 'if this aspect of that kind of person is hammered at from an early age, until the inevitable consequences of
b incarnation have been knocked off it—the leaden weights, so to speak, which are grafted on to it as a result of eating and similar pleasures and indulgences and which turn the sight of the mind downwards—if it sheds these weights and is reoriented towards the truth, then (and we're talking about the same organ and the same people) it would see the truth just as clearly as it sees the objects it faces at the moment.'

'Yes, that makes sense,' he said.

'Well, doesn't this make sense as well?' I asked. 'Or rather, isn't it an inevitable consequence of what we've been saying that uned-
c ucated people, who have no experience of truth, would make incompetent administrators of a community, and that the same goes for people who are allowed to spend their whole lives educating themselves? The first group would be no good because their lives lack direction: they've got no single point of reference to guide them in all their affairs, whether private or public. The second group would be no good because their hearts wouldn't be in the business: they think they've been transported to the Isles of the Blessed even while they're still alive.'

'True,' he said.

似，即习惯和锻炼实际上确实培育了它们原来没有的东西，然而 e
思想——就如其表明的那样——无疑具有某些更加神圣的性质：
它决不丧失力量，其有用或无用、有益或有害都在于它的定向。
比如说，你肯定注意到那些被认为恶而聪明的人具有狭隘的心 519a
灵，目光敏锐并且对他们关注的事情具有充分的洞察力。这并不是说他们目光不敏锐，而是说他们的灵魂被迫服务于恶，结果是，他们的眼光越是敏锐，他们所造的恶就越大。”

“是的，我已经意识到了。”他说。

“然而，”我继续说，“如果那样的人在这个方面从小得到锤炼，直到肉身化的不可避免的后果得以去除——可以说就是这些
重负，它们由于贪吃和别的快乐和纵欲而植根于人们的身上，它 b
们使灵魂的目光向下看——如果它卸下这些重负并朝向了真理（而且我们所说还是这同一个器官、同一个人），那么它看到真理就会像看它现在所面对的事物那样清晰。”

“是的，说得有道理。”他说。

“嗯，这不是也很有道理吗？”我问道，“或者更可从我们已经说过的话中推出这样一个必然的结论，即没有修养的人，他对真理没有什么经验，那么也就无法胜任一个城邦管理者的责任，而
同样地，对于那些被允许尽其一生致力于自我修行的人而言，也 c
是不能胜任管理者的，是这样吧？第一群人不能胜任是因为其生活缺乏指导：在他们的所有事务中，无论是私事还是公事，他们都没有一个统一的控制点来引导他们。第二群人不会成为良好的管理者是因为其志不在此：甚至还在他们活在人世的时候，他们冥想自己已经欣喜若狂地进入到世外神岛了。”

“对。”他说。

'Our job as founders, then,' I said, 'is to make sure that the best people come to that fundamental field of study (as we called it earlier): we must have them make the ascent we've been talking about and see goodness. And afterwards, once they've been up there and
d had a good look, we mustn't let them get away with what they do at the moment.'

'Which is what?'

'Staying there,' I replied, 'and refusing to come back down again to those prisoners, to share their work and their rewards, no matter whether those rewards are trivial or significant.'

'But in that case,' he protested, 'we'll be wronging them: we'll be making the quality of their lives worse and denying them the better life they could be living, won't we?'

e 'You're again forgetting, my friend,' I said, 'that the point of legislation is not to make one section of a community better off than the rest, but to engineer this for the community as a whole. Legislators should persuade or compel the members of a community to mesh together, should make every individual share with his fellows the bene-
520a fit which he is capable of contributing to the common welfare, and should ensure that the community does contain people with this capacity; and the purpose of all this is not for legislators to leave people to choose their own directions, but for them to use people to bind the community together.'

'Yes, you're right,' he said. 'I was forgetting.'

'I think you'll also find, Glaucon,' I said. 'that we won't be wronging any philosophers who arise in our community. Our remarks, as we force them to take care of their fellow citizens and be their guardians, will be perfectly fair. We'll tell them that it's reasonable
b for philosophers who happen to occur in other communities not to share the work of those communities, since their occurrence was spontaneous, rather than planned by the political system of any of the communities in question, and it's fair for anything which arises spontaneously and doesn't owe its nurture to anyone or anything to have no interest in repaying anyone for having provided its nourishment. "We've bred *you*, however" we'll say, "to act, as it were, as the hive's leaders and kings, for your own good as well as that of the rest

“那么，作为缔造者，我们的工作，”我说，“就是要确保最优秀
的人达到学习的根本性领域（就像我们先前所称的那样）：我们必
须如同我们说过的那样使他们上升并看到善。之后，一旦他们到
达那里并且看够了，我们绝不可以让他们带着他们在那时的所做 d
而逍遥。”

“这是什么意思呢？”

“不让他们停留在那里，”我回答说，“而拒绝回来再下到那些囚徒那里去，拒绝承担囚徒们的工作、分享囚徒们的奖赏，而不管这些奖赏是微不足道的还是价值连城的。”

“但在那种情况下，”他反驳说，“我们会损害他们：我们会把他们较好的生活弄糟并否定了他们可能具有的一种较好的生活，不是吗？”

“我的朋友，你又忘记了，”我说，“立法的关键不是使城邦的 e
一个部分比另一个部分好，而是为作为整体的城邦谋幸福。立法
者应该说服或强制城邦的成员紧密团结起来，应该使每个人把他
能向共同幸福提供的利益与他的同伴分享，并且应该确保城邦拥 520a
有具备这能力的人；对于立法者而言，所有这些目标不在于让人
们去选择自己的方向，而是使他们用人来团结城邦。”

“是的，你说得对，”他说，“我忘记了。”

“格劳孔，我想你也发现了，”我说，“我们不会损害任何产生
于我们城邦的哲学家。我们迫使他们关心他们的同胞公民并成
为他们的卫士，这种说法是相当公正的。我们会告诉他们产生于
其他城邦中的哲学家有理由不分担那些城邦的工作，因为他们的 b
产生是自发的，而不是任何我们所谈到的城邦的政治体制设计出
来的。任何自发产生、其养育并不亏欠于任何人或物的事物有理
由不欠任何为它提供养育之人的情。我们会说：‘可以说，我们把

of the community. You've received a better and more thorough educa-
c tion than those other philosophers, and you're more capable of playing a part in both spheres. So each of you must, when your time comes, descend to where the rest of the community lives, and get used to looking at things in the dark. The point is that once you become acclimatized, you'll see infinitely better than the others there; your experience of genuine right, morality, and goodness will enable you to identify every one of the images and recognize what it is an image of. And then the administration of our community—ours as well as yours—will be in the hands of people who are awake, as distinct from the norm nowadays of communities being governed by people who shadow-box and fall out with one another in their dreams over who
d should rule, as if that were a highly desirable thing to do. No, the truth of the matter is this: the less keen the would-be rulers of a community are to rule, the better and less divided the administration of that community is bound to be, but where the rulers feel the opposite, the administration is bound to be the opposite."'

'Yes,' he said.

'And do you think our wards will greet these views of ours with scepticism and will refuse to join in the work of government when their time comes, when they can still spend most of their time living with one another in the untainted realm?'

e 'No, they couldn't,' he answered. 'They're fair-minded people, and the instructions we're giving them are fair. However, they'll undoubtedly approach rulership as an inescapable duty—an attitude which is the opposite of the one held by the people who have power in communities at the moment.'

521a 'You're right, Glaucon,' I said. 'You'll only have a well—governed community if you can come up with a way of life for your prospective rulers that is preferable to ruling! The point is that this is the only kind of community where the rulers will be genuinely well off

你们培养成蜂房中的领袖和王,既是为你自己好也是为城邦中其余之人好。你们得到的教育比那些别的哲学家更好更完善,在两个领域中你们都能发挥作用。所以你们当中的每个人必须轮流 c
下到城邦中的其余之人生活的地方,并习惯于在黑暗中观察事物。关键是一旦你们习惯了,你们就会比那里的其他人看事物要清楚得多;你们对于真正的正义、道德和善的体验会使你们辨别出每一个影像并且辨认出是什么事物的影像。那么我们城邦的管理——我们的和你们的——就会掌控在清醒之人的手中,而与当今城邦的规范不同,它们被这样的人统治着,这些人与影子搏斗,在梦中争吵谁应该统治,就好像那是最大的可欲之物。不,事情的真相是这样的:想做一个城邦的统治者的人越不急切地去统 d
治,那么城邦的管理就必定越好并且分歧越少,而有着相反感受的统治者的地方,其管理必定也是相反的。'"

"是的。"他说。

"你认为我们培养的人,当他们还能够在大多数时间相互住在受玷污的世界里的时候,对我们的观点会批评相待,会拒绝轮流参加管理工作吗?"

"不会,他们不会拒绝的,"他回答说,"他们是公正无偏之人, e
我们给他们的要求也是公正的。不过,他们无疑会把参与统治当作是一项不可逃避的责任——这种态度正好与当前城邦的掌权者所具有的态度相反。"

"格劳孔,你说得对,"我说,"如果你能拿出一种对你们将来 521a
的统治者来说有利统治的生活方式,只有那样你才能治理好城邦!关键是只有在这种城邦中,统治者才是真正富有的,不是物质上的,而是说他们拥有作为幸福之必要前提的财富——有德行

(not in material terms, but they'll possess the wealth which is a prerequisite of happiness—a life of virtue and intelligence), whereas if government falls into the hands of people who are impoverished and starved of any good things of their own, and who expect to wrest some good for themselves from political office, awell-governed community is an impossibility. I mean, when rulership becomes something to fight for, a domestic and internal war like this destroys not only the perpetrators, but also the rest of the community.'

'You're absolutely right,' he said.

b 'Apart from the philosophical life,' I said, 'is there any way of life, in your opinion, which looks down on political office?'

'No, definitely not,' he answered.

'In fact, political power should be in the hands of people who aren't enamoured of it. Otherwise their rivals in love will fight them for it.'

'Of course.'

'There's no one you'd rather force to undertake the guarding of your community, then, than those who are experts in the factors which contribute towards the good government of a community, who don't look to politics for their rewards, and whose life is better than the political life. Agreed?'

'Yes,' he said.

和有智慧的生活,而要是城邦落入那些贫穷而自身又缺乏任何好的事物的人手中,他们希望从官职中为自己捞得一些好处,这样就不可能有一个治理有序的城邦。我的意思是说,当统治权成为争夺对象时,像这样的内战不光毁了作恶之人,还毁了城邦中其余的人。”

“你说得很对。”他说。

我说:“除了哲学生活,在你看来还有什么样的可以轻视官职 b
的生活方式?”

“肯定没有了。”他回答说。

“事实上,政治权力应该掌握在不迷恋它的人手上。否则迷恋权力的对手就会为之而与他们开战。”

“当然。”

“那么没有人会被迫担任起保卫城邦的工作,除了那些管理者,他们懂得哪些因素有助于管好城邦,他们并不出于回报自我而来管理城邦,他们的生活比政治生活更好。同意吗?”

“是的。”他说。

CHAPTER 10

521c ' So would you like us to consider next how to produce people of this type in our community, and how to lead them up to the Light—like the people we hear about who rise from Hades to dwell among the gods?'

'Yes, of course I'd like us to do that,' he replied.

'Now, what we're dealing with here, it would seem, is not the spinning of a potsherd, but the reorientation of a mind from a kind of twilight to true daylight—and this reorientation is an ascent to reality, or in other words true philosophy.'

'Quite so.'

d 'We ought to try to see which intellectual pursuits can have this effect, then, oughtn't we?'

'Of course.'

'What intellectual pursuit, then, Glaucon, might attract a mind away from the realm of becoming and towards reality? Oh, something just occurred to me while I was speaking: we said that in their youth these people had to be warriors, didn't we?'

'Yes, we did.'

'Therefore, the area of study we're after must have an additional feature.'

'What?'

'It must be of value to men of war.'

'Yes, it certainly must,' he said, 'if possible.'

'Now, the education we've arranged for them so far consists of
e physical exercise and cultural studies.'

第十章

“所以你想让我们接下来考察一下如何在我们的城邦中造就 521c
这样的人，如何把他们向上带到光明——就像那些我们听到的从冥府上升到居住于诸神之中的人？”

“是的，我当然想那样做。”他回答说。

“我们现在所考察的看来并不是像翻贝壳游戏那么容易，而是使灵魂从朦胧的曙光重新转向真正的白日——这个转向就是上升到实在，或换句话说就是真正的哲学。”

“很对。”

“那么我们应该试图看看什么样的学问会有这种效果，不是吗？” d

“当然。”

“那么，格劳孔，什么样的学问能够吸引一个心灵脱离变化的领域而朝向实在呢？当我在说的时候，我想到了一些事情：我们说过这些人在年轻的时候必须是战士，不是吗？”

“是的，我们说过。”

“所以，我们正在寻找的学问必须有另一种性质。”

“是什么？”

“这对战士来说是有价值的。”

他说：“是的，要是有可能的话，就必定有价值。”

“那么迄今为止，我们为他们组织的教育包括体育锻炼和音
乐学习。” e

'Yes,' he said.

'And physical exercise is concerned with the world of coming into being and passing away, since its domain is physical growth and decay.'

'I suppose so.'

'So it isn't the area of study we're after.'

'No.'

522a 'What about the cultural education we described earlier?'

'But that merely complemented the physical exercise,' he said. 'I'm sure you remember that it trains the guardians by habituation: it doesn't produce knowledge, but harmony in the sphere of music, elegance in the sphere of rhythm, and other allied habits in the field of literature, whether the literature in question is fictional or closer to non-fiction. There's nothing in it which can lead a student towards the kind of goal you're after at the moment.'

b 'Your memory is very accurate,' I said. 'Thanks for reminding me: it's true that there's nothing like that in it. But then, what sort of intellectual pursuit *are* we after? I mean, all the professions seemed servile, somehow.'

'Of course they did. But if we exclude cultural studies, physical exercise, and the professional occupations, what else is there that anyone could study?'

'Well,' I said, 'if they're all we can take, then let's take something which applies to them all.'

'What?'

c 'For example, there's that everyday thing—one of the first things everyone has to learn — which all the modes of expertise, thinking, and knowledge make use of.'

'What are you getting at?' he asked.

'It's nothing special,' I said. 'It's the ability to distinguish one,

“是的。”他说。

“体育教育与生灭的世界有关,因为它影响身体的生长和衰退。”

“我想是这样的。”

“所以,它不是我们所寻找的学习领域。”

“不是。” 522a

“我们之前说过的音乐教育呢?”

“然而那仅仅补充了体育锻炼,”他说,“我确信你肯定记得它通过习惯而教育卫士:它并不产生知识,而是在音乐领域中产生和谐,在节奏领域中产生优雅以及在文学领域中产生另外相关的习惯,无论所谓的文学是虚构的还是较为真实的。其中没有什么是可以把一个学习者引向你现在寻求的这种目标的。” b

“你记得非常准确,”我说,“感谢你提醒我:其中确实没有那样的东西。然而我们所寻求的那种智力性职业是什么样的呢?我的意思是,所有的职业不知怎么的看上去都是卑从的。”

“它们当然如此。但要我们排除了音乐教育、体育锻炼和专业技艺之外,人们还能学习别的什么呢?”

“好吧,”我说,“如果它们就是我们能学习的全部内容,那么我们就学习一些能应用于它们全部的东西。”

“什么?”

“比如说,有一件日常的事物——每个人必须得学习的第一件事物——各种形式的专业技艺、思想和知识都会用得到它。” c

“你在说什么?”他问道。

“没什么特别的,”我说,“就是区分一、二、三的能力——简而

two, and three—in short, I'm talking about number and counting. I mean, isn't it the case that every branch of expertise and knowledge is bound to have some involvement with numbers and with counting?'

'Definitely,' he said.

'Even military expertise?' I asked.

'Yes, certainly. It has to,' he said.

'At any rate, tragedy after tragedy has Palamedes showing up
d Agamemnon's utterly ridiculous deficiencies as a military commander,' I said. 'Haven't you noticed how Palamedes claims that, once he'd invented counting, he deployed the troops at Troy and added up the ships and so on? The implication is that previously none of them had been counted, and Agamemnon's inability to count presumably means that he didn't even know how many feet he had. What sort of military commander do you think he was?'

'A peculiar one, I'd say, if there's any truth in this,' he replied.

'So our position will be—won't it? —that it's essential for a man of war to learn how to calculate and count,' I asked.

'He absolutely has to,' he said, 'if he's going to know anything at all about deploying troops, or rather, if he's even going to be a human being.'

'Now, there's an idea I have about this subject, and I wonder whether you share it,' I said.

'What is it?'

523a 'It rather looks as though it's one of the subjects we're after, which stimulate a student's intellect. But it also seems likely that no one makes correct use of its consummate ability to attract one towards reality.'

'What do you mean?' he asked.

'I'll try to clarify my point of view,' I said. 'In my mind, I distinguish between things which are and things which are not attractive in the way we're talking about. I'll try to get you to appreciate the

言之,我所说的是数字和计数。我的意思是说,事情不就是这样的吗:每一门技艺和知识必定多多少少与数字和计数相关?"

"毫无疑问。"他说。

"甚至是军事技艺?"我问道。

"是的,当然。必定相关。"他说。

"无论如何,帕拉墨得斯用一个个悲剧表现了阿伽门农作为 d
一个军事将领的非常可笑的缺陷,"我说,"你是否知道帕拉墨得斯发明了计数,他在特洛伊部署了军队并统计了船只等等?这意味着在这之前它们中没有一个被清点过,阿伽门农未能计数似乎意味着他甚至不知道他有多少步兵。你认为他是什么样的军事将领呢?"

"如果这是真的话,我想说他是一个特殊的将领。"他回答说。

"所以我们的立场是,对一个军人来说,学习计算和数数是必 e
要的,不是吗?"

"如果他想要知道任何关于部署军队的事情,他必须学习,"他说,"甚至作为一个人他也要学习。"

"那么,关于这个学问我有个想法,我想知道你是否也赞同。"我说。

"是什么?"

"它看起来像是我们寻找的学问之一,它激发学生的理解力。 523a
但似乎没有人正确地使用它的最大的能力去把心灵引向实在。"

"你说的是什么意思?"他问道。

"我会试图澄清我的观点的,"我说,"在我心里,按我们所说的方式,我区分了具有吸引力的事物和没有吸引力的事物。我也会试图让你理解这个区分,然后你告诉我你是否同意,这样我们

distinction as well, and then you can tell me whether or not you agree, so that we can be better placed to see how accurate my hunch is.'

'Yes, do explain,' he said.

'All right,' I said. 'I'm sure you'll see what I mean if I say that
b at the level of the senses, some things don't encourage the intellect to explore further, because the situation can be adequately assessed by the relevant sense, while other things can't help provoking an enquiring attitude, because sense perception fails to produce a sound result.'

'You're obviously talking about distant impressions and illusory paintings,' he said.

'No, you haven't quite got my point,' I said.

'What are you talking about, then?'

'In order to count as thought-provoking, in my opinion,' I explained,
c 'they have to produce contradictory sense-impressions at the same time; otherwise, they aren't thought-provoking. The impression sense-perception has to give of an object is that it is no more X than the opposite of X, however close or far away it is when you encounter it. An example will help you understand what I'm getting at. Here are three fingers, we'd say, the little finger, the second one and the middle one.'

'Yes,' he said.

'And please assume that I'm talking about seeing them from close range. Now, here's what I want you to think about.'

'What?'

'Well, each of them equally gives the impression of being a finger. There's no difference between them in this respect, and it doesn't matter whether the finger that's being looked at is in the middle or on
d either end, pale or dark, thick or thin, and so on and so forth. It's almost inconceivable that anyone's mind would feel impelled in any of these circumstances to think and try to come up with an answer to the question what a finger is, since sight has given the mind no grounds for supposing that the finger is at the same time the opposite of a finger.'

就能更好地看看我想法的准确性。”

“是的，你解释一下吧。”他说。

“好吧，”我说，“我确信你会明白我的意思的，如果我说在感觉的层次上，有些东西是不需要求助于思想进一步考察的，因为
这些情况通过相关的感官就得到充分的判断了，而别的东西不能 b
不需要激发起一种探究的态度，因为感觉不能得出可靠的结果。”

“你说的显然是远处的印象和画中的影像。”他说。

“不是，你还不是很理解我的意思。”我说。

“那么你说的是什么？”

“依我看来，为了能引起观念性的思考，”我解释说，“它们必须同时产生属于矛盾性质的或相互对立的感觉；否则就不会引发观念
性的思考。由感觉形成的模糊的观念、记忆所提供的一个认知对 e
象，当你与之相遇时，无论它是近还是远，都只能是‘X’与‘X’的相对，相反者，这样才能引发观念性的思考。举个例子可以帮助你理解我所说的。我们说这里有三个手指，小指、无名指和中指。”

“是的。”他说。

“请设想我所说的是从近距离来观看它们。现在，这就是我想让你去思考的。”

“什么？”

“其中的每一个看上去都是一个指头。在这个方面它们相互没
有什么区别，无论指头看上去在中间还是在两边，是白还是黑，是粗还 d
是细等等，这都没有什么关系。在这种情况下，任何人的心思如果感到有一种要去思考的推动力，而且还要对一根手指是什么的问题设法想出一种答案来，都是不可想象的事情，因为视觉并没有给心思提供一种根据或理由，可以假定手指同时是一根手指的相对、相反者。”

'That's right,' he agreed.

'So it makes sense to say that this situation doesn't provoke or arouse thought,' I said.

e 'Agreed.'

'What about the bigness or smallness of the fingers, however? Is what sight sees adequate in this case? Does it make no difference to it whether or not the finger it's looking at is in the middle or on either end? And doesn't the same go for touch and the fingers' thickness and thinness or hardness and softness? And the other senses also give inadequate impressions in this kind of situation, don't they? I mean, here's
524a how each sense works: the main point is that the sense into whose domain hardness falls is inevitably also the sense into whose domain softness falls; and the message it passes on to the mind is that, in its perception, the same thing is both hard and soft. True?'

'True,' he said.

'So isn't what happens in these situations that the mind inevitably feels puzzled about What this sense means by hardness, since it's saying that the same thing is soft as well? And when the sense that perceives weight reports that something heavy is light and that something light is heavy, isn't the mind bound to wonder what lightness and heaviness are?'

b 'Yes,' he said, 'because the messages it's receiving are strange and demand clarification.'

'It makes sense to suppose, then,' I went on, 'that these are the circumstances in which the chief thing the mind does is summon up calculation and thought to help it examine whether in any given case it's being informed about one object or two objects.'

'Of course.'

'And if there turn out to be two objects, then each of them is single and they're different from each other, aren't they?'

'Yes.'

'If each of them is single, then, and it takes two of them to make two, then it'll think about them as two separate objects. I mean,

"很对。"他同意说。

"所以有理由说这种情况并不激发或引起思考。"我说。 e

"同意。"

"但是手指的大和小又怎么样呢？在这种情况下，视觉所见到的就足够了吗？无论手指看上去在中间还是在两边，这有什么区别吗？对于触觉、手指的粗细软硬不也一样吗？在这种情况下，别的感觉也不能给出充分的印象，不是吗？我的意思是说，这就是每种感觉的运作方式：主要是硬所在领域的感觉必定也是软 524a
所在领域的感觉；它传达给灵魂的信号在感觉上同一件事物既是硬的又是软的。对吗？"

"对的。"他说。

"所以在这种情况下不就会发生这样的事情：心灵必定会对这种感觉所说的硬的含义感到迷惑，因为它说同一件事物既是硬的又是软的？当感知到重量的感觉报告说重的东西是轻的，轻的东西是重的，这时心灵不就必定想弄清轻和重是什么意思？"

"是的，"他说，"因为它得到的信息是陌生的，需要澄清。" b

我继续说："有理由假设在这种情况下心灵所要做的主要事情，就是运用算术和理性来帮助检查任何传来的信息是关于一个对象还是两个对象的。"

"当然。"

"如果出现了两个对象，其中每一个都是单一的并且相互不同，不是吗？"

"是的。"

"如果其中的每一个是单一的，那么理性就会把它们两个当作两个，把它们设想为两个分开的对象。我的意思是说，如果它

c if they were inseparable, it wouldn't be thinking about two objects: it would be thinking about one object.'

'Right.'

'However, in our current example sight sees both big and small as a kind of mixture, not as separate from each other. Yes?'

'Yes.'

'And in order to clarify the situation, the intellect is forced in its turn to look at big and small as distinct entities, not mixed together, which is the opposite of what sight does.'

'True.'

'And this, in outline, is why it occurs to us to ask what in fact bigness and smallness really are, isn't it?'

'Absolutely.'

'And that's how we come to distinguish what we call the intelligible realm from the visible realm.'

d 'You're quite right,' he said.

'So that's what I was getting at just now, when I was saying that some things are thought-provoking, and some things aren't. I define as thought-provoking the things which impinge upon our sense-perception along with their opposites, whereas I describe things which don't do that as incapable of arousing thought.'

'I understand now,' he said, 'and I agree.'

'All right, then. Which of these two categories do you think number—which is to say, oneness—belongs to?'

'I don't know,' he answered.

'Well, you can work it out from what we've already said,' I replied. 'If oneness is adequately seen (or grasped by any other sense)

e for what it is , then it doesn't have any power to attract towards

们不是分开的，那么理性就不会把它们当作两个对象：它会设想 c
为一个对象。"

"对。"

"不过在我们当前的这个例子中，视觉既看见大又看见小，它们是结合在一起的，而不是相互分开的。是吗？"

"是的。"

"为了澄清这种情况，理性必须把大和小作为单独的实体来加以考察，而不是混在一起，这与视觉所做的是相反的。"

"对。"

"概括地说，这就是为什么我们想到要问大和小实际上是什么的原因，不是吗？"

"毫无疑问。"

"这就是我们区分我们所谓的可知领域和可见领域的方式。"

"你说得很对。"他说。 d

"所以刚才当我说有些事物是引发思考的，有些事物不是引发思考的时候，我说的就是这个意思。我把那些与它们的对立物一起触动我们感觉的事物称为引发思考的，而把不是那样的事物称为不能引发思考的。"

"我现在理解了，"他说，"我同意。"

"那么好吧。你认为数——即是说'一'——属于这两类范畴中的哪一类？"

"我不知道。"他回答说。

"但你能从我们已经说过的话中推理出来，"我回答说，"如果'一'本身被看得清清楚楚或为任何别的感觉充分把握
了，那么它就没有任何力量去引向实在——就像我们所说的，手 e

reality—as a finger doesn't, we were saying. However, if it's never seen without its opposite simultaneously being seen, so that the impression it gives is no more of oneness than of the opposite, then evaluation becomes imperative and the mind has no choice but to be puzzled: it sets its thought-processes in motion, and casts about for an answer to the question what oneness itself actually is. And if this is what happens, then oneness is one of those subjects which guide and
525a turn people towards the contemplation of reality.'

'But that's exactly what seeing oneness does, in fact,' he said. 'We see the same thing simultaneously as one and as infinitely many.'

'And if oneness is like that,' I said, 'then number as a whole is as well.'

'Naturally.'

'Now, calculation and arithmetic are entirely concerned with number.'

'Certainly.'

'And they clearly guide one towards truth.'

b 'Yes, they're exceptionally good at that.'

'Then arithmetic is one of the subjects we're after, apparently. A man of war can't do without it, because he deploys troops, and a philosopher can't do without it, because he has to extricate himself from the world of becoming and make reality his field of operation, or else he'll never be able to reason and calculate.'

'True,' he said.

'And our guardians are, in fact, both warriors and philosophers.'

'Of course.'

'Therefore, Giaucon, we ought to provide for this subject in our legislation, and to persuade the people who are going to undertake our
c community's most important tasks to take up arithmetic. They

指没有任何力量去引向实在。然而，如果从未看到过它而不同时看到它的相反者，这样它给出的印象就是它与它的相反者都是'一'，那么就必须加以考察并且心灵只能困惑不解：它激发它的思考并寻求究竟什么是'一'自身这个问题的答案。如果这样的话，那么'一'就是那样的问题之一，那些问题将人们引向或使人们转向对实在的沉思。" 525a

"但实际上，这正是看到过'一'时所做的，"他说，"我们把同一件事物同时看作一和无限的多。"

"如果'一'是那样的话，"我说，"那么作为整体的数也是那样的。"

"自然。"

"那么计数与算术全是与数相关。"

"当然。"

"它们显然把人们引向真理。"

"是的，它们在那方面非常擅长。" b

"那么算术显然是我们寻找的学科之一。军人不能没有它，因为他要部署他的军队，哲学家不能没有它，因为他必须使他自己脱离可变世界去把握他工作的实在领域，否则他决不会推理和计算。"

"对的。"他说。

"我们的卫士实际上既是战士又是哲学家。"

"当然。"

"所以，格劳孔，我们应该把这个科目用我们的法律规定下来，说服那些将要承担我们城邦中最重要任务的人去学习算术。它们不应该浅尝辄止，而应该坚持学习，直到他们达到用灵魂 c

shouldn't engage in it like dilettantes, but should keep at it until they reach the point where they can see in their mind's eye what numbers really are, and they shouldn't study it as merchants and stallholders do, for commercial reasons, but for the sake of warfare and in order to facilitate the mind's turning away from becoming and towards truth and reality.'

'You're absolutely right,' he said.

d 'Now that arithmetic has been mentioned,' I said, 'it also occurs to me how neatly it fits in the context we're getting at, and how commonly it could be used by anyone who applies himself to it for intellectual rather than commercial purposes.'

'How?' he asked.

'Because it's particularly good at guiding the mind upwards—which is what we've been talking about—and forcing one to discuss numbers in themselves. It excludes the slightest hint, in a discussion, of numbers which have attendant visible or tangible material objects. I mean, I'm
e sure you're aware that the experts in the field pour scorn on any attempt to divide the actual number one and refuse to allow it. If you chop it up, they multiply it; they take steps to preserve one's oneness and to prevent it ever appearing to contain a multiplicity of factors.'

'You're absolutely right,' he said.

526a 'What do you think they'd say, then, Glaucon, if someone were to ask them, in surprise, "What are these numbers you're talking about? What numbers involve a oneness which fulfils your requirements, where every single unit is equal to every other unit, without even the smallest variation, and without being divisible in the slightest?"'

'I think they'd reply that the numbers they're talking about are only accessible to thought, and cannot be grasped in any other way.'

'So can you see, Glaucon,' I said, 'that it really does seem as
b though this subject is essential, since it apparently forces the mind to rely purely on intellectual processes and to aim for truth in itself?'

之眼能看见数实际上是什么的程度，他们不应该像商人或摊贩一样出于商业的原因来学习，而是应该为了战争，为了利于灵魂从变化中转向真理和实在。"

"你说得非常正确。"他说。

"既然已经提到了算术，"我说，"我也想到，它是多么符合我 d
们所谈的内容啊，对那些出于智识而不是商业目的而使用它的人来说，它常常是多么有用啊。"

"如何使用？"他问道。

"因为它尤其善于引导心灵向上——我们已经说过这个了——并迫使人们谈论数本身。在谈论中，对那些与可见或可触物体相伴随的最细微的提示也要排除。我的意思是说，我确信你意识到这方面的专家会对那些分割实在的数字'一' e
加以嘲笑并且拒不允许这样做。如果你把它分割开来，他们就使之增加；他们采取措施保护'一'，防止其看上去包含多个因素。"

"你说得非常正确。"他说。

"那么，格劳孔，你认为他们会说，如果有人惊讶地问他们： 526a
'你们说的这些数是什么？什么样的数包含有满足你们要求的'一'，每一个与另一个相同，甚至没有最细小的区别，一点都不可划分？'"

"我想他们会回答说他们所说的数仅仅只能用思想去把握而不能用任何别的方式去把握。"

"所以，格劳孔，你可以看到，"我说，"这门学科看来确实是重要的，因为它显然迫使心灵纯粹依靠理性的加工并且以真理本 b
身为目标？"

'Yes,' he said. 'It certainly does do that.'

'Now, have you ever noticed that people who are naturally good at arithmetic are also naturally quick at just about every subject? And that if you make slow-witted people learn and study arithmetic, then without exception they end up quicker than they used to be, even if they gain nothing else from it?'

'That's true,' he said.

c 'Moreover, I don't suppose it would be easy for you to find many subjects which require more effort from the student learning them.'

'No.'

'For all these reasons, then, this is a subject we'd better take seriously; we must have our best people study it.'

'I agree,' he said.

'That's the first subject dealt with, then,' I said. 'But in the second place, let's consider whether the subject which follows on its heels suits our purposes.'

'What subject do you mean?' he asked. 'Geometry?'

'Exactly,' I said.

d 'It obviously suits our purposes,' he said, 'because it has some military applications. You see, it does make a difference whether or not a person is good at geometry when he comes to organize an encampment, occupy territory, deploy an army over a narrow or wide extent, and form up troops in any other way in the course of a battle or while on the move.'

'Yes,' I said, 'but it hardly takes the whole of geometry and arithmetic to enable someone to cope with that kind of situation. What we have to consider is whether the more advanced aspects of geometry which constitute the bulk of the subject have any relevance in the context of smoothing the way towards seeing the character of goodness.
e And what we're saying is that anything is relevant in this context if it forces the mind to turn towards the realm where the most blessed part of reality is to be found, which the mind should do its utmost to see.'

“是的，”他说，“它当然是那样做的。”

“那么，你是否注意过那些天性善于算术的人往往也敏于学习每一门科目？如果你让反应迟钝的人学习和研究算术，那么他们最后会毫无例外地比以前更加敏捷，即使从中没有得到什么其他东西？”

“说得对。”他说。

“此外，我认为对你而言，要想发现许多要求学生比学习算术 c
时付出更多辛劳的科目，也是一件很不容易的事情呢。”

“不容易。”

“那么由于这些原因，我们最好严肃对待这门学科；我们必须让最优秀的人学习算术。”

“我同意。”他说。

“那么这是我们要学习的第一门课，”我说，“接下来，让我们来考虑下一门学科是否适合于我们的目标。”

“你说的是什么学科？”他问道，“几何学？”

“正是。”我说。

“这显然适合我们的目标，”他说，“因为它有一些军事上的用 d
处。你知道，当人们组织安营扎寨，占领土地，部署窄或宽队形的军队以及在战斗中或行进中以任何别的方式排列军队，一个人懂不懂得几何学，那的确是大不一样的。”

“是的，”我说，“但要使一个人应付那种情形几乎用不上整个
几何学和算术。我们必须考察的是，构成几何学大部分的较高级 e
的方面，在有助于顺利地看见善的特征方面是否有什么关系。我们所说就是任何与此方面相关的东西，它迫使灵魂转向实在的最神圣部分所在的领域，这是灵魂应该尽最大力气去观看的。”

'You're right,' he said.

'So if it impels the mind to see reality, it suits our purposes; but if it impels the mind to see the world of becoming, it does not.'

'Yes, that's what we're saying.'

527a 'Even people who know very little geometry', I said, 'won't dispute the fact that this branch of knowledge is quite different from how it is described by its practitioners.'

'In what sense?' he asked.

'They have a very absurd, if very inevitable, way of talking about geometry. They talk as if they were actually doing something and as if the point of all their theorems was to have some actual effect: they come up with words like "squaring" and "applying" and "adding" and so on,

b whereas in fact the sole purpose of the subject is knowledge.'

'Absolutely,' he said.

'And there's something else we'd better agree on.'

'What?'

'That this knowledge is of things which exist for ever, rather than of things which come into existence at some time and subsequently pass away.'

'There's no difficulty in agreeing to that,' he said. 'The objects of geometrical knowledge do exist for ever.'

'Therefore, Glaucon, geometry can attract the mind towards truth. It can produce philosophical thought, in the sense that it can reverse the misguided downward tendencies we currently have.'

'It's particularly effective at that,' he agreed.

c 'Then you'd better be particularly effective at telling the inhabitants of your Goodland to do their utmost not to dismiss geometry,' I told him. 'I mean, its by-products are not unimportant either.'

“你说得对。”他说。

“所以要是它推促心灵去观看实在，它便适合我们的目标；但要是它推促心灵去观看既成既灭的世界，它便不适合我们的目标。”

“是的，我们就是这样认为的。”

我说：“即使那些知道一点点几何学的人也不会争论这个事 527a
实，即这门知识与实践者所描述的非常不同。”

“在什么意义上？”他问道。

“他们以一种非常荒谬的方式——如果是不可避免的——谈论几何学。他们谈论时就像实际上正在做什么事一样，就像他们的所有定理的关键都在于具有某种实际的效果：他们使用像‘化方’、‘应
用’、‘添加’等等词语，而实际上这门学科的唯一目的就是知识。” b

“毫无疑问。”他说。

“我们对某些别的事情最好也达成一致吧。”

“什么？”

“这种知识是关于永恒存在的事物的，而不是关于在某时存在、接下来又消失的事物的。”

“同意这一点并没有什么困难，”他说，“几何知识的对象确实永恒存在。”

“所以，格劳孔，几何学能把灵魂引向真理。它能产生哲学思考，因为它能扭转我们现在所具有的被误导而向下的趋势。”

“在这方面特别有效果。”他同意说。

“那么你最好要非常有效地说服贵国的居民尽最大的努力不 c
要抛弃几何学，”我对他说，“我的意思是说，其附带的效果也并非不重要。”

'What are they?' he asked.

'There are the military ones you mentioned,' I replied, 'and also, as we know, people who've studied geometry are much more receptive than those who haven't to intellectual work in general; it makes absolutely all the difference in the world.'

'Yes, it certainly does,' he said.

'So shall we make this a second subject for the young people of our community to study?'

'Yes,' he said.

'And don't you think the third should be astronomy?'

d 'I do, anyway,' he said. 'I mean, it's not only farmers and sailors who need to be sensitive to the seasons, months, and phases of the year: it's just as important for military commanders as well.'

'You seem to be naïvely worried about what people will think of you,' I remarked. 'You don't want them to think you're recommending studies which have no practical benefit. It is, in fact, really hard for people to have confidence in the fact that studying this kind of subject cleans and re-ignites a particular mental organ which everyone has
e (while other occupations ruin it and blind it), and that this organ is a thousand times more worth preserving than any eye, since it is the only organ which can see truth. People who acknowledge this fact will be incredibly happy with your ideas, but all those people who are completely unaware of it will in all likelihood think you're talking rubbish, because, as they can see, this kind of study doesn't produce any worthwhile benefit of any other kind. So you'd better hurry up and decide which group of people you're addressing. Alternatively, you're not
528a really addressing either group: you're mainly framing your arguments for your own sake—which is not to say that you'd resent anyone else profiting from them as well.'

“它们是什么?”他问道。

“你提到的军事上的用途是一个,”我回答说,“还有就像我们知道的,一般而言,学过几何学的人比起那些没有进行过此类高智力活动的人,学习的接受能力是要强得多;这在根本上造成了完全的绝对不同的差别。”

“是的,当然。”他说。

“所以我们要把这当作我们城邦的年轻人要学习第二门学科吗?”

“是的。”他说。

“那么你难道不认为第三门学科应该是天文学吗?” d

“我确实是这么想的,”他说,“我的意思是说,不光是农民和水手需要对季节、月份和年的各个阶段敏感:这对将军来说也同样重要。”

“看来你在天真地担心人们对你的想法,”我说,“你不想让他们认为你推荐的学习是没有实际利益的。实际上确实很难让人们对这个事实抱有信心:学习这种学科可以清理和重新点燃每个人都具有的特别的心智器官(而别的工作却使之
毁坏和盲目),这个器官比任何眼睛要更值得保护,要重要上 e
千倍,因为这是唯一能看见真理的器官。承认这个事实的人无疑会为你的想法感到高兴,而所有那些完全没有意识到这个事实的人很可能会认为你所说的都是废话,因为就像他们所能看到的一样,这种学问不能产生任何别的有价值的好处。
所以你最好赶快决定你要对哪群人说话。或者,你并非真的 528a
是对某一群人说话:你主要是为自己而提出这些论证——这并不是说你讨厌别的任何人也从中受益。”

'That's what I'd prefer to do—talk, ask questions, and answer them chiefly for my own sake,' he said.

'Well,' I said, 'I'd like you to backtrack a bit. Just now we chose the wrong thing to follow geometry.'

'What do you mean?' he asked.

'We went straight from surfaces to solidity in circular motion,' I
b said, 'before we'd taken solidity on its own. The correct procedure is to go from the second dimension to the third—which is, of course, the domain of cubes and anything else with volume.'

'True,' he said. 'But I don't think this domain has been explored yet, Socrates.'

'There are two reasons for that,' I replied. 'First, no society respects it, and therefore its complexity makes people diffident about looking into it. Second, exploration isn't feasible unless the research is conducted under supervision, but a supervisor is unlikely to be found, and moreover, even if one were to be found, the current situa-
c tion is that the people doing the research in the field are so self-assured that they wouldn't listen to him. However, they would listen if a whole community treated the subject with respect and supervised it, and once research was undertaken with continuity and determination, then facts would be discovered. I mean, even under the current circumstances of its general disrespect and depreciation—at the hands of the researchers as well, since they can't explain what good it is—it still manages to be attractive enough to overcome all this opposition and to develop, and I wouldn't be surprised if discoveries were made.'

d 'Yes, it certainly is a particularly attractive subject,' he agreed. 'But please can you explain what you were getting at just now. You referred to geometry as the study of surfaces...'

'Yes,' I said.

“这是我更喜欢做的——谈话，提问，回答，主要都是为了我自己。”他说。

“那么，”我说，“我想要你稍稍退回去一点。在讨论几何学之后我们刚才选错了东西。”

“你说的是什么意思？”他问道。

我说：“在我们讨论立体本身之前就从平面径直去讨论进行
圆周运动的立体了。正确的做法应该从第二维到第三维——说 b
的当然是那些立体和别的、具有容积的东西的领域。”

“对的，”他说，“但是，苏格拉底，我想这块领域还没有被探索过。”

“之所以没有被探索过，有两个原因，”我回答说，“第一，没有
一个城邦尊重它，所以其复杂性使得人们很难去考察它。第二，研
究需要在指导下进行，否则探索是不可行的，但指导者似乎不大可
能找到，此外，即使找到了一个指导者，但在当前的状况下，这个领
域的研究者们太自信了，以至他们不会听从他的。然而，如果整个 c
城邦尊重这个学科并加以管理，那么他们就会听从，并且研究一旦
持之以恒地进行，那么事实真相就会被发现。我的意思是说，即使在当前这种受到普遍的轻视和贬低的环境下——也由于研究者不能解释善是什么——它依然具有足够的吸引力以克服所有种种障碍而得以发展，如果做出了什么发现，我不会大惊小怪的。”

“是的，这当然是一门非常具有吸引力的学科，”他同意 d
说，“但你能否解释一下你刚才所说的话。你说几何学是研究平面的……”

“是的。”我说。

'... and then at first you said that astronomy came next, but later you took this back,' he said.

'I was in a hurry to complete the discussion,' I explained, 'and that was slowing me down. Although investigation of three-dimensionality came next, the research in the field has made the subject
e so difficult to take seriously that I missed it out and put astronomy, which is solidity in motion, after geometry.'

'You're right,' he said.

'So let's make astronomy the fourth subject,' I said. 'on the understanding that, if a community were to underwrite the research, the branch of knowledge we're omitting at the moment would be available.'

'Yes, that sounds reasonable,' he said. 'And since you ticked me off just now for my crude endorsement of astronomy, Socrates, I'll
529a now give it the kind of endorsement you're after. I mean, I can't imagine anyone doubting that it forces the mind to look upwards and guides it from this realm to another realm.'

'It seems as though I'm the only one to doubt it, then,' I said. 'You see, I disagree.'

'On what grounds?' he protested.

'Because I think its current usage, in the hands of those who try to interest people in philosophy, is guaranteed to make people look downwards.'

'What do you mean?' he asked.

'I get the impression,' I said, 'that your conception of the study of things up on high is rather generous! It looks as though you'd
b think that the study of decorations on a ceiling by bending one's neck back, and the acquisition of information that way, makes use of the intellect rather than the eyes! You may be right, and I'm probably being simple-minded, but it's only a field of study which is concerned

“……一开始你说接下来的是天文学,可是后来你又返回来了。”他说。

我解释说:“我这样真是欲速则不达。虽然在平面几何之后接着应该研究立体几何,然而这个领域的研究使这门学科难以得到认真看待,以至我将之忽略了,在平面几何之后就去谈天文学了,它是讨论运动中的立体的。” e

“你说得对。”他说。

“所以让我们把天文学当作第四门学科吧,”我说,“假设如果城邦会承诺确保研究的话,那么我们现在忽略的这门知识就会是有用的。”

“是的,听上去很有道理,”他说,“苏格拉底,因为你刚才指出我对天文学粗鲁的赞同态度,现在我要以和你一致的方式来赞同天文学。我的意思是说,我不能想象有谁会怀疑天文学有推动人 529a
的心灵向上看的力量,并且引导心灵从此域进入彼域。”

“那么看来我似乎是唯一一个怀疑它的人了,”我说,“你知道,我不同意。”

“有什么理由吗?”他反驳道。

“因为我认为它的通行惯例,即由那些力图使人们对哲学发生兴趣的人来进行引导,就会保证使人们向下看的。”

“你说的是什么意思?”他问道。

我说:“我觉得,你对学习上面的东西的想法太宽泛了!你似乎认为抬起头来研究天花板上的装饰并以那样的方式获得信息, b
你以为这就是在使用理性而不是在使用眼睛!你也许是对的,我可能头脑简单,但这是唯一与非物质的实在相关的研究领域,我认为它能使心灵向上观看,我不会把通过直瞪瞪地向上观看或斜

with immaterial reality that I can regard as making the mind look upwards, and I wouldn't describe the attempt to study perceptible things by gawping upwards or squinting downwards as learning (since there's no knowledge involved in these cases); neither would I say that in these cases
c ses the mind is looking upwards rather than downwards, even if the studying takes place while lying on one's back on the ground or in the sea.'

'That's a fair comment," he said. "You're right to have told me off. But apart from how it's studied at the moment, then, how do you think astronomy should be studied, if studying it is to have some point in the context we're talking about?'

'Like this,' I replied. 'It may be that there's nothing in the visible realm which is more beautiful or less erratic than these decorations in the
d sky, but even so, since they're within the visible realm, they should be regarded as considerably inferior to true decorations, in respect of the beauty and precision of the movements which, in the realm of true number and all the true figures, genuine speed and slowness make relative to each other as they transport things which are not accessible to sight, but only to reason and thought. Don't you agree?'

'Definitely,' he said.

'Therefore,' I continued, 'we should use the heavenly decorations merely as illustrations to help us study the other realm, as we would if we were faced with exceptional geometrical figures drawn in fine detail by
e Daedalus or some other artist or painter. On seeing figures of this kind, an expert geometer would think that for all the beauty of their exe-
530a cution, it would be absurd seriously to expect an examination of them to reveal the truth about equals or doubles or some other ratio.'

'Of course it would be absurd,' he agreed.

'Don't you think that a genuine astronomer feels the same when he looks at the movements of the heavenly bodies?' I asked. 'He'll certainly think that the artist of the heavens has constructed them and all they contain to be as beautiful as such works could ever possibly be, but what about the ratio between night and day, between them and a month, between a month and a year? And what about the rela-
b tions of the heavenly bodies in general to these phenomena or to one

着眼睛向下观看而企图研究可感事物当作学习,因为在这些情况下不涉及到知识,即使仰卧在地上或海上学习,我也不会说心灵 c
正在向上观看而不是向下观看。”

“说得有理,”他说,“你批评得很好。但是除了现在的这种天文学的学习方式之外,如果在我们所说的这个情境下学习天文学还有些意义的话,那么你认为天文学应该怎么学习?”

“像这样学习,”我回答说,“可能是这样的,在可见的领域中没有什么比这些天空中的装饰更美或更正确,但即使是这样,因为它们是在可见领域中的,所以它们应该被看作远不及真正的装 d
饰,在美和运动的精确性方面,在真正的数和所有真正的形象领域中,真正的快和慢相互关联,就好像它们运载着不可被视觉看到的而只可被理性和思想看见的事物。你难道不同意吗?”

“毫无疑问是同意的。”他说。

“所以,”我继续说,“我们应该把天空的装饰仅仅当作说明图来帮助我们学习别的领域,我们就像面对一幅由戴达罗斯或某个其他匠人或画匠画的连细节都很精巧的几何图形。在看到这样 e
的图形的时候,几何学家会认为他们的作品非常精美,但一本正经地希望通过考察它们而去揭示关于相等、成倍或其他比例的真理,这就很荒谬了。” 530a

“这当然很荒谬。”他同意说。

“你难道不认为真正的天文学家在观看天体的运动的时候也有同样的感受吗?”我问道,“他当然会认为天匠已经建造了天体,它们包含的所有事物都是尽可能最完美的,但是黑夜与白天的比例、它们与月份的比例以及月份与年份的比例呢? 天体与这些现象或与别的天体之间的关系呢?把这些物质的可见事物看作是 b

another? Don't you think he'd regard it as ludicrous to suppose that these things are constant and unvarying, and never change in the slightest, when they're material and visible, and to devote all one's energy to discovering the truth about these things?'

'I agree,' he said, 'or anyway, I do when I hear your account.'

'So the way we'll do astronomy will be identical to the way we do geometry,' I said, 'since in both cases we'll be making use of matters that require elucidation. And if we don't ignore the heavenly
c bodies, we'll never be engaged in true astronomy, and we'll never develop rather than atrophy our mind's innate intelligence.'

'Your instructions will involve astronomers in a great deal more work than they're used to at the moment,' he remarked.

'Yes, and I think we'll be issuing further instructions of the same kind,' I said, 'if our legislation is to do any good. But are there any other suitable fields of study that you can think of?'

'Not just at the moment,' he replied.

d 'There are, however, several types of movement, I think,' I said. 'An expert would probably be able to give us a complete list, but even we can easily see two of them.'

'What are they?'

'In addition to the astronomical variety, there's one that complements it too,' I said.

'Which one do you mean?'

'The eyes are made for astronomy,' I said, 'and by the same token the ears are presumably made for the type of movement that constitutes music. If so, these branches of knowledge are allied to each other. This is what the Pythagoreans claim, and we should agree, Glaucon, don't you think?'

'Yes,' he said.

e 'Music is a difficult subject,' I said, 'so we'll consult the

恒常不变，最细微的变化也决不发生，而人们把所有的精力都投入到发现关于这些事物的真理中去，你难道不认为他会觉得这很荒谬吗？”

“我同意，”他说，“无论如何，我同意你的话。”

“所以我们研究天文学的方式要和我们研究几何学的方式一样，”我说，“因为在两种情况下，我们会利用要求说明的问题。如果我们不忽略天体，我们就绝不会从事真正的天文学，我们也绝不会发展我们心灵中的天赋理智而是使之萎缩。” c

“你的要求必将会使得天文学家的工作比现在多得多。”他说。

“是的，我想我们还会提出更多类似的要求，”我说，“如果我们的立法工作要有任何效用的话。不过，你还能想到任何别的恰当的学习领域吗？”

“现在还没想到。”他回答说。

“然而我想有几种运动的方式，”我说，“专家可能可以给我们 d
完整地列举出来，不过我们甚至也能很容易地看出其中的两种。”

“它们是什么？”

“除了天文学外，还有一种补充它的。”我说。

“你说的是什么意思？”

我说：“眼睛是为了天文学而造的，同样理由，耳朵是可能为了构成音乐的那种运动而造的。如果是这样的话，那么这些知识的门类是相互结合在一起的。这是毕达戈拉派的主张，并且我们也应该同意，格劳孔，你难道不这么想吗？”

“是这样想的。”他说。

我说：“音乐是一门很难的学科，所以我们要问一问毕达戈拉 e

Pythagoreans to find out their views, and to see if they've anything to add. But throughout we'll be looking after our own agenda.'

'Which is what?'

'To make sure that our wards don't set about learning any pointless aspects of music—any aspect which doesn't unfailingly fetch up at the place which (as we were just saying in the case of astronomy) ought to be the destination of all these subjects. Don't you realize that
531a people get music wrong too? They laboriously measure the interrelations between audible concords and sounds, which is as useless an activity as anything astronomers get up to.'

'Yes, they really make fools of themselves,' he said. 'They talk about 'concentrations' and bring their ears close to the source of the sound—as if they were trying to hear what the people next door were saying! And then some of them claim to be able to detect a further intermediate resonance and maintain that they've found the smallest possible interval, which should be used as the basis of measurement, while others dispute all this and claim that the notes in question are to all intents and purposes identical. But both camps rate their
b ears above their intellect.'

'You're talking', I said, 'about those excellent characters who make life hard for strings and torture them by twisting them on pegs. I don't want to push the image too far and mention how they strike the strings with a plectrum and challenge them, and how the strings refuse to talk and come up with specious pleas. So I'll drop the image and tell you that I wasn't thinking of those people, but the ones we were saying just now would explain music to us, because they act in the same way that astronomers do. They limit their research to the
c numbers they can find within audible concords, but they fail to come up with general matters for elucidation, such as which numbers form concords together and which don't, and why some do and some don't.'

'That's a superhuman task you're talking about,' he remarked.

派，听听他们的观点，看看他们是否有什么要补充的。但自始至终我们还是要遵循我们自己的议程。”

“是什么？”

“为了确保我们所训导的人不要试图去学习音乐的任何无意义的那些方面——任何方面，只要它不能可靠地行进至学习的最终目的地，就不该去学习（就像我们刚刚在天文学的例子中说过的一样），而这个目的地应该也是所有这些学科的目的地。你难 531a
道没有认识到人们在学习音乐时也犯错误了？他们费尽九牛二虎之力来测度听得见的和谐与声音之间的关系，这就像天文学家所做的事情一样，是一项无用的活动。”

“是的，他们确实很荒唐，”他说，“他们谈论四分音符，把他们的耳朵凑近音源——就好像他们在听邻人说话！然后其中的某些人声称能够进一步探听到中间的声音，并且坚持认为他们已经发现了最小的音程，这应该被当作一个基本的计量单位，而别人否认这一切，并声称那些正在讨论的音符实际上都是一样的。但双方都把他们的耳朵置于他们的理智之上。” b

我说：“你在说那些优秀的人物，他们费力地拷打琴弦，把它们绞在琴柱上。我并不想把这个比喻说得太远，说他们如何用弦拨敲打琴弦并拷问它们，琴弦如何拒绝言说并提出似是而非的抗辩。所以我抛弃了比喻而告诉你我并不在想那些人，而是那些我们刚才说过的人现在会向我们解释音乐，因为他们做的方式是和天文学家一样的。他们把他们的研究限于他们在可听见的和谐 c
中所发现的数，而未能说明整个问题，比如说哪些数形成和谐而哪些不能形成和谐，为什么有些可以而有些不可以。”

“你说的是一般人办不到的任务。”他说。

'But a useful one,' I said, 'if it serves the aim of trying to understand what morality and goodness are. In any other context, however, it's a pointless pursuit.'

'I suppose so,' be said.

d 'What I'd say', I continued, 'is that engaging in all the subjects we've been discussing has some relevance to our purposes, and all that effort isn't wasted, if the work takes one to the common ground of affinity between the subjects, and enables one to work out how they are all related to one another; otherwise it's a waste of time.'

'I suspect you're right,' he said. 'But you're talking about an awful lot of hard work, Socrates.'

'What?' I asked. 'The prelude is hard, you say? Don't you realize that this is all just the prelude to the main theme, which is the important subject? I mean, you surely don't think that being accomplished in these subjects makes one good at dialectic.'

'No, certainly not,' he answered, 'although it does happen sometimes—very occasionally—in my experience.'

'But don't you think the inability to explain anything, and to understand explanations, rules out the possibility of knowing any of the things we're saying are important?' I asked.

'Yes, I agree with you on this too,' he replied.

532a 'And isn't this exactly the theme which dialectic develops, Glaucon?' I asked. 'It may be an intelligible theme, but sight can be said to reflect it, when, as we were saying, it sets about looking at actual creatures, at the heavenly bodies themselves, and finally at the sun itself. Just as, in this case, a person ends up at the supreme point of the visible realm, so the summit of the intelligible realm is reached when, by means of dialectic and without relying on anything perceptible, a person perseveres in using rational argument to approach the true reality of things until he has grasped with his intellect
b the reality of g oodness itself.'

“但还是一个有用的任务，”我说，“如果其目的在于试图理解什么是正义和什么是善。然而在别的情况下，这是一个没有指望的追求。”

“我想是这样的。”他说。

“我要说的是，”我继续说道，“如果我们付出的努力能够将一个人带到学科间相关联之处的共同基础之上，而且能够使一个人发现这 d
些学科是如何彼此关联在一起的，那么进行我们已经讨论过的所有学科的研究、学习，才与我们的目的有所联系；否则就是浪费时间。”

“我想你是对的，”他说，“但是，苏格拉底，你说的是一项很繁重的工作。”

“什么？”我问道，“你说的是前奏很难吗？你难道没有意识到这仅仅是主题的一个前奏并且是重要的学科吗？我的意思是说，你当然不会认为精通这些学科就能使人擅长辩证法。” e

“不，当然不会，”他回答说，“虽然按我的经验，有时——非常少——也会有这种情况。”

“但你难道不认为没有能力解释任何事物并且理解这些解释，这就排除了认识我们所说的任何重要事物的可能性？”我问道。

“是的，在这一点上我也同意你。”他回答说。

“格劳孔，这不正是辩证法所要发展起来的主题吗？”我问道， 532a
“它可能是一个理智的主题，但视觉被认为是能够反映它的，当它就像我们所说的，从观看实在的动物开始，观看天体自身并最终观看太阳自身。在这个情况下，就像一个人最终达到了可见领域的顶点，同样，当一个人通过辩证法而不依赖于任何可感之物，并坚持使用理性的论证去接近真正事物的实在，直到用他的理智把握善本身的实在，那时他就达到了可知领域的巅峰。” b

'Absolutely,' he said.

'And this is the journey a practitioner of dialectic makes, wouldn't you say?'

'Of course.'

'And the prisoners' release from their bonds,' I went off, 'their reorientation away from shadows and towards figurines and firelight, their ascent out from under the ground into sunlight, their lingering inability to look in the upper world at creatures and plants and the light of the sun, rather than gazing at reflections in water and at
c shadows (shadows, that is, of real things, not the shadows of figurines cast by a light which, relative to the sun, is of the same order as the figurines)—just as, in this case, the most lucid part of the body is taken up to see the most lucid part of the material, visible realm, so the whole business of studying the areas of expertise we've been discussing has the ability to guide the best part of the mind upwards until it sees the best part of reality.'

d 'I'm happy with that,' he said, 'despite the fact that acceptance and rejection both seem to me to be problematic, from different points of view. However, we shouldn't let this be just a one-off discussion today, but should often return to the issue. So let's assume that our ideas are correct, and get on with discussing the actual main theme in as much detail as we did the prelude. So please tell us the ins and outs of the ability to do dialectic, and how many different
e types of it there are, and what methods it employs, since they'd presumably be the means of approaching that place which, once reached, is travellers' rest and journey's end.'

533a 'You won't be able to follow me there, my dear Glaucon,' I said, 'which is a pity, because there'd be no shortage of determination from me, and what you'd see there wouldn't be an image of what we're talking about: you'd see the truth itself—or that's what I think, anyway. I may be right, and I may be wrong—that's not for us to insist on at the moment; but we can state with confidence that there'd be something of the kind to be seen, don't you think?'

“毫无疑问。”他说。

“这就是辩证法的实践者所要做的旅行，你难道不会这么说吗？”

“当然会这么说。”

我继续说：“囚徒从桎梏中解放出来，他们从阴影重新转向小
塑像和火光，他们从地下上来到地面上的阳光下，他们还犹豫着
不能观看上面这个世界的动植物以及太阳光，而是凝视水中的倒
影和影像，这影像是由真实事物产生的，而不是火光所投下的小 c
塑像的影像，相对于太阳来说，它们还是处在与小塑像同样的层
次——在这种情况下，正如身体中最明白的部分被用来观看物质
和可见领域中最明亮的部分，同样我们讨论过的整个学习专业领
域的工作都具有这种指导心灵最善的部分向上，直到它看见实在
的最善部分的能力。” d

他说：“我对此很满意，虽然从不同的观点来看，在我看来接受和拒
绝两者都似乎是成问题的。然而，我们不应该仅仅在今天
讨论这个问题就算了，而应该常常回答这个问题。所以让我们假
设我们的想法是正确的，继续详细地讨论这个实在的主题，就像我们讨
论前奏时一样。所以请告诉我们从事辩证法的能力的详细情况，有几
种不同的辩证法，运用的是什么方法，因为它们可能是达到那个地方的 e
途径，一旦达到了那个地方也就是旅行的终点，旅行者就可以休息了。”

“我亲爱的格劳孔，你不能跟着我去那个地方，”我说，“这很 533a
可惜，这不是因为我缺乏决心，而是因为你会看到那里没有我们
所说的影像：你看到的是真理本身——或者无论如何，我是那样
想的。我可能是对的，我也可能是错的——此刻，这不是我们要
坚持的；但我们可以充满信心地说可以看到某类事物，你难道不
这么认为吗？”

'Of course.'

'And what about the idea that dialectic alone can elucidate these matters, to someone with experience in the subjects we've discussed, and that otherwise it's impossible?'

b 'Yes, we should state that confidently too,' he said.

'Anyway, what is indisputable in what we're saying', I said, 'is that dialectic is the only field of enquiry which sets out methodically to grasp the reality of any and every thing. All the other areas of expertise, on the other hand, are either concerned with fulfilling people's beliefs and desires, or are directed towards generation and manufacture or looking after things while they're being generated and manufactured. Even any that are left—geometry and so on, which we were saying do grasp reality to some extent—are evidently dreaming a-
c bout reality. There's no chance of their having a conscious glimpse of reality as long as they refuse to disturb the things they take for granted and remain incapable of explaining them. For if your starting-point is unknown, and your end-point and intermediate stages are woven together out of unknown material, there may be coherence, but knowledge is completely out of the question.'

'Yes, it is,' he agreed.

'So dialectic is the only field of enquiry', I went on, 'whose quest for certainty causes it to uproot the things it takes for granted in
d the course of its journey, which takes it towards an actual starting-point. When the mind's eye is literally buried deep in mud, far from home, dialectic gently extracts it and guides it upwards, and for this reorientation it draws on the assistance of those areas of expertise we discussed. It's true that we've often called them branches of knowledge in the past, but that's only a habit and they really need a different word, which implies a higher degree of clarity than belief has, and a higher degree of opacity than knowledge has. Earlier, we used
e the term "thought". But I don't suppose we'll quarrel about terminology when we're faced with matters as important as the ones we're looking into at the moment.'

'No, we won't,' he said, 'just so long as whatever term is used expresses the state of mental clarity.'

“当然是这样想的。”

“只有辩证法才能够向那些学习过我们所讨论的科目的人说明这些事物,否则是不可能的,这个想法怎么样?”

“是的,我们也应该充满信心地这么说。”他说。

我说:“不管怎么说,我们说辩证法是系统地把握任何事物和 b
每一个事物的实在的唯一研究途径,这并不是没有争议的。另一方面,其他的专业领域要么是关于满足人们的信念和欲望,要么是旨在生产和制造或照料那些生产或制造出来的东西。甚至任何其余的学科——几何学等等,我们说它们确实在某种程度上把握了实在——显然是在幻想实在。只要它们原封不动地使用它们假设的事物并且依然未能对之加以解释,那么它们根本不可能 c
有意识地瞥见实在。因为要是你的前提是未知的,你的结论和中间步骤由未知的材料构成,它们也许可以一致,但知识完全是不可能的。”

“是的,是这样的。”他同意说。

“所以研究辩证法是唯一的途径,”我继续说,“它对确定性的要求使其在它的旅程中脱离了假设的事物而朝向实在的第一原则。当灵魂的眼睛真的是深陷于泥潭,迷失了的时候,辩证法轻 d
轻地把它拉上来并且指导它向上,在我们讨论过的那些专业领域的帮助下它将重新定向。我们过去确实把它们称作知识的门类,这意味着它比意见的清晰程度更高,比知识的模糊程度也更高。我们之前使用‘理智’这个词。但我想当我们面对与现在正在考察的事情一样重要的事情的时候,我们不会为术语而争吵的。” e

“我们不会争吵的,”他说,“只要所使用的术语表达了心灵的清晰状态。”

'So the terms we used earlier will do,' I said. 'We'll call the
534a first section knowledge, the second thought, the third confidence, and the fourth conjecture; and the first pair constitute intellect (which is concerned with real being), the second pair belief (which is concerned with becoming). As being stands to becoming, so intellect stands to belief; and as intellect stands to belief, so knowledge stands to confidence and thought to conjecture. However, we'd better pass over the proportionate relations between the objects of intellect and belief, Glaucon, and the twofold division of each of the two realms—the domain of belief and the domain of intellect—if we want to avoid getting entangled in an argument which would be many times as long as the ones our discussion has already thrown up.'

b 'Well, I agree with everything else you've said, in so far as I can follow it,' he said.

'And don't you think that the ability to understand what it is to be any given thing, when someone else explains it, is indicative of a dialectician? And wouldn't you say that, in so far as anyone who lacks this ability is incapable of explaining anything to himself or to anyone else either, then he doesn't know anything?'

'Of course I would,' he answered.

'The same principle applies to goodness, then, as well. If someone is incapable of arguing for the separation and distinction of the character of goodness from everything else, and cannot, so to
c speak, fight all the objections one by one and refute them (responding to them resolutely by referring to the reality of things, rather than to people's beliefs), and can't see it all through to the end without his position suffering a fall—if you find someone to be in this state, you'll deny that he has knowledge of goodness itself or, in general, of anything good at all. Instead, if he does somehow manage to make contact with a reflection of goodness, you'll claim that the contact is due to belief, not knowledge. He dreams his current life away in a state of semi-consciousness, you'll say, and he'll never wake up here: he'll
d go to Hades, the place of total sleep, first. Agreed?'

“这样我们就满足于先前使用的术语吧，”我说，“我们把第一部分称作知识，把第二部分称作理智，把第三部分称作信念，把第四部分称作臆测；第一对构成理性（其关涉的是真实的存在），第 534a
二对构成意见（其关涉的是生成）。就像实在相对于生成，理性也相对于意见；就像理性相对于意见，知识也相对于信念，理智相对于臆测。不过，格劳孔，要是我们想避免卷入到这样的争论中去的话，我们最好略过理性对象和意见的比例关系以及两个领域中各自的二分——意见的领域和理性的领域，这个争论比我们已经进行过的讨论还要冗长很多倍。”

“好吧，就我能跟得上的范围来说，在所有你说过的其余事情 b
上，我都同意你。”他说。

“当别人解释任何一件事情的时候，他都能理解，你难道不认为这表明他是辩证法家？如果任何一个人缺乏向自己、向别人解释任何事情的能力，那么他便什么都不知道，你难道不会这样说吗？”

“我当然会这样说了。”他回答说。

“那么，同样的原则也适用于善。如果某个人不能论证善的理念与任何别的事物是不同的、分开的，也就是说，他不能一个个地抵抗所有的反对观点并反驳它们，即用事物的实在而不是用人们的意见去坚 c
定地回应他们，不能坚持到底而不使他的立场遭受挫折——如果你发现了有人处在这样的状况下，那么你会否认他具有善本身的知识，或者一般的说，他也根本不具有任何善的事物的知识。但是，在某种程度上，如果他能够触及到善的影像，那么你会说这种接触是属于意见而不是知识。你会说他现在的生活都在半意识的状态中梦想，他决不会在这里醒来：他首先就去了哈德斯，那长眠之地。同意吗？” d

'Yes, definitely,' he said. 'I'll certainly be making all of these claims.'

'Now, suppose your theoretical upbringing and education of your younger generation were to become a reality. I imagine you'd deny them power and crucial responsibility in the community if they were as irrational as surds.'

'Yes, I would,' he said.

'Will you include in your legislation, then, the ruling that a major part of the education they engage in must be the subject which will enable them to acquire particular expertise at the give and take of discussion?'

e 'I will,' he replied, 'if you join me.'

'Don't you think', I asked, 'that dialectic occupies the highest position and forms, as it were, the copestone of the curriculum? And that, if so, there's no subject which ought to occupy a higher position,
535a and therefore it completes our educational programme?'

'Yes, I agree,' he answered.

'All that remains for you to do,' I said, 'is distribute the subjects: to whom, and on what basis, shall we assign them?'

'Yes, that's obviously what we're left with,' he said.

'Well, do you remember what kind of people we chose as rulers, when we made our choice earlier?'

'Of course I do,' he answered.

'Now, on the whole,' I went on, 'the characteristics we should favour ought to remain the same, I suggest. I mean, we should prefer people with a high degree of reliability and courage, and also, within rea-
b son, people who are very good-looking. In addition, however, to being good and solid, we must also look for people with a natural talent for these studies.'

'What special qualities do you have in mind?'

'They must be sharp and quick at learning, Glaucon,' I said. 'You see, physical exercise is far less appalling to the mind than intense

“是的，毫无疑问，”他说，“我当然会做出所有这些断言。”

“设想一下你对你们的年轻一代理论上的培养和教育都变成了现实。我想如果他们像无理数一样是无理性，那么你不会把城邦中的权力和关键性任务交给他们了。”

“是的，我不会给他们的。”他说。

“那么你是否要立法使他们所接受的大部分教育必须是这样的学科，这门学科使他们能够获得在谈论中提问和回答的技艺？”

“我会的，”他回答说，“如果你和我一起的话。” e

我问道：“你难道不认为辩证法占据了最高的位置和形式，可以说是教育计划王冠上的宝石？如果是这样的话，没有一个学科可以占据一个更高的位置，所以是它完成了我们的教育计划？” 535a

“是的，我同意。”他回答说。

我说：“剩下所有你要做的就是分配科目：他们应该把它们以什么方式分配给谁？”

“是的，那显然是留给我们去做的。”他说。

“那么，你是否记得当我们之前做选择的时候，我们选了什么样的人作为统治者？”

“我当然记得。”他回答说。

我继续说：“那么，从总体上来说，我建议我们青睐的品质应该保持一致。我的意思是说，我们应该偏好那些最可靠、最勇敢并在合理的范围内也相当有风度的人。不过，我们不仅要求善且坚定，还必须寻找那些具有这些学习天赋的人。” b

“你心里想的是什么样的特殊品质？”

“他们在学习上必须敏捷，格劳孔，”我说道，“你明白，对于心灵而言，身体上的操练比起紧张的脑力劳动远算不上什么可怕的

intellectual work, since intellectual work is more exclusively mental. It belongs to the mind, rather than being shared with the body.'

'True,' he said.

c 'And we should also look for people who have good memories, are tenacious, and enjoy all kinds of work. Otherwise, there's no way that they'll be prepared to complete such a long course of intellectual study over and above all the hard work of the physical programme.'

'That's right,' he said. 'That'll take all the advantages nature can provide.'

'The problem nowadays, anyway,' I said, 'and the reason why philosophy has become devalued, is (to repeat ourselves): that its practitioners are people who aren't good enough for it. It should be practised by men of true pedigree, not by bastards.'

'What do you mean?' he asked.

d 'The main thing', I explained, 'is that the practitioner must not be hamstrung in his enjoyment of work, with half of him enjoying it and half of him not. That's what you get when someone enjoys exercising and hunting and all kinds of physical work, but doesn't enjoy using his mind or listening to lectures or undertaking research, and instead loathes working in all these contexts. Then there are also people who are hamstrung in their enjoyment of work by having the opposite attitude.'

'You're absolutely right,' he said.

'By the same token,' I continued, 'we'll call a mind handi-
e capped in the context of truth if, while loathing conscious lying (in that it not only finds it hard to stomach from itself, but also gets highly irritated when others do it), it happily puts up with unconscious lying and doesn't get irritated when its ignorance is exposed, but wallows in ignorance as cheerfully as any pig.'

'Absolutely,' he said.

536a 'And the same goes for self-control, courage, broadness of vision, and all the other aspects of virtue,' I said. 'It's particularly important to distinguish men of true pedigree from bastards in all these contexts. The inability to look at these qualities from every possible

事情,因为脑力劳动更多是专属于精神层面的。它属于心灵,而不为身体所分有。"

"对。"他说。

"我们也应该寻找一些具有好记性、百折不挠并喜爱各种工 c
作的人。否则他们决不会愿意除了身体锻炼的艰苦工作之外,还完成如此漫长的理性学习课程。"

"对,"他说,"那需要好好利用天赋所能提供的东西。"

我说:"无论如何,当前的问题和哲学为什么贬值的理由是——我们再说一遍——其实践者是那些还配不上哲学的人。应该由那些纯真者而不是杂劣者来实践哲学。"

"你说的是什么意思?"他问。

我解释说:"关键就是实践者决不可在他喜爱的工作中有所 d
偏废,一半喜欢这工作而一半不喜欢。你要知道,当某个人喜欢锻炼、狩猎以及各种体力劳动时,他便不喜欢使用他的心灵、不喜欢听讲或从事研究,并厌恶所有这些工作。还有些人以相反的方式偏爱他们喜欢的工作。"

"你说的非常正确。"他说。

"同样,"我继续说,"在真理的问题上我们将这样的心灵称作
是残疾的,他讨厌有意说谎,他难以忍受自己说谎,别人说谎也会 e
极大地激怒他,但他愉快地容忍无意的谎言,当暴露出无知的时候他也不会被激怒,而是像猪一样快乐地在无知中打滚。"

"毫无疑问。"他说。 536a

"对于自制、勇敢、眼界开阔以及所有别的方面的美德也是一样,"我说,"在所有这些情况下,尤其重要的是把真子与私生子区分开来。不能在各个可能的角度考察这些品质,会导致人们和城

angle leads people and communities to use crippled bastards for some purpose or other—as their friends, maybe, or as their rulers.'

'Very true,' he said.

b 'It's important for us to take precautions against all traps of this kind,' I said. 'If we bring people who are in perfect physical and mental condition to this lengthy study programme and course of training, and educate them in it, we'll have done nothing wrong even by the strictest standards of moral behaviour, and we'll be preserving the integrity of our community and political system. However, if we introduce people of any other kind to it, we'll not only achieve the opposite results, but we'll also increase the flood of ridicule which pours down on philosophy.'

'That would be disgraceful,' he said.

'Yes, it would,' I agreed. 'But it looks as though I'm open to ridicule myself at the moment.'

'In what respect?' he asked.

c 'I forgot that our tone has been light-hearted,' I answered, 'and I spoke with rather too much intensity. You see, while I was speaking, I looked at philosophy and saw how unjustly it has been dragged in the gutter. That made me cross, and I suppose I used the over-serious tone that I did because I felt a kind of rage.'

'Well, from my point of view as a member of the audience,' he said, 'it didn't strike me as excessive.'

'But from my point of view as the speaker,' I said, 'it did. Anyway, we should bear in mind that although our earlier selection procedure favoured old men, our present one rules them out. I mean, we
d shouldn't let Solon convince us that while growing old there is still plenty of scope for learning: in fact, there's more scope for running than for learning! In any given sphere, it's up to young people to work long and hard.'

'That's necessarily true,' he said.

邦处于某些理由或别的理由而使用跛足的杂劣者——作为他们的朋友,或者也许作为他们的统治者。"

"非常正确。"他说。

"对于我们来说,重要的是小心所有这类陷阱,"我说,"如果
我们让那些身体和灵魂都处于完善状态的人去参加这个冗长的 b
学习计划和训练课程并教育他们,那么,即使从最严格的道德行为规范来看,我们也没做错什么,我们维护了城邦和政治制度的完整。然而,如果我们选进了任何别的类型的人,那么我们不光会得到了相反的结果,而且也会使洪水般的嘲笑涌向哲学。"

"这是可耻的。"他说。

"是的,确实是可耻的,"我同意说,"但此刻我使自己看起来很可笑。"

"在什么方面?"他问道。

我回答说:"我忘了我们的语气是很轻松的,而我说得太过激 c
烈了。你知道,当我在说话的时候,我看着哲学,看到它受到不公正地对待。这让我发怒,我想我使用了过于严厉的语气,我这样做是因为我感到愤怒。"

"唔,不过从我作为一名听众的角度来看,"他说道,"它并没有使我感到有什么过分之处。"

"但在我看来,作为一名发言者,"我说,"这是过分的。无论如何,
我们应该记住,虽然我们先前的选举程序是有利于老人的,而我们现在
的选举程序却将他们排除在外。我的意思是说,我们不应该信服梭伦, d
他说人老了还能学习很多的东西:实际上,他们跑不了多少,更学不了多少! 在任何领域,应该是让年轻人去从事漫长而艰难的工作。"

"这肯定是对的。"他说。

'So it's while they're young that we should set them arithmetic, geometry, and the rest of the studies which are the essential preliminaries before taking up dialectic. But we shouldn't present the work as compulsory.'

'Why not?'

e 'Because an autonomous person should never learn a subject in a slavish fashion,' I explained. 'It's true that if physical work is performed under compulsion, the body isn't impaired, but compulsory intellectual work never remains in the mind.'

'True,' he said.

'So the educational environment in which you foster your youn-
537a ger generation, Glaucon,' I said, 'should be light-hearted rather than authoritarian. This will also help you to see what natural abilities every one of them has.'

'That's plausible,' he said.

'And do you remember', I continued, 'our assertion that the children should be taken on horseback to observe warfare and, if they can do so safely, should also be taken up to the front and given a taste of blood, as young dogs are?'

'Yes, I do,' he replied.

'Well, any of them who demonstrates a high degree of proficiency in his exercising, studying, and facing fear should be enrolled in a special unit,' I said.

'At what age, do you mean?' he asked.

b 'When they've finished with the basics of physical exercise,' I said. 'The point is that it's out of the question for them to do anything else during the period in question, which may last for two or three years, because exertion and exhaustion don't mix with intellectual work. Also, one of the crucial ways we'll be testing them will be by seeing what impression each of them gives during the period when they're concentrating on physical exercise.'

'Of course,' he said.

“所以当他们年轻的时候，我们就应该让他们学习算术、几何学和别的科目，它们是在学习辩证法之前重要的预备性科目。但我们不应该使学习成为强迫性的。”

“为什么不呢？”

“因为一个自律的人决不应该以被迫的方式学习一门学科，” e
我解释说，“真实情况是，如果体力劳动被强迫去完成，身体不会削弱，但是强制性的脑力学习是绝不会在心灵中留存东西的。”

“对的。”他说。

我说：“所以，格劳孔，你培养年轻一代的教育环境应该是轻
松的而不是专断的。这也会有助于你了解他们每个人所具有的 537a
天生的能力。”

“这似乎有道理。”他说。

我继续说：“你是否记得我们说过，孩子应该被放到马背上去观看战争，如果他们能够安全地做到，还应该把他们带到前线，让他们像幼犬一样尝尝血的滋味？”

“是的，我记得。”他回答说。

“他们当中任何在锻炼、学习和面对恐惧而展示出高度能耐的人，都应该被招募进一个特殊的团体。”我说。

“你指的是几岁？”他问道。 b

“当他们完成基本的体育锻炼以后，”我说，“关键是在这段时间里，他们不可能做任何别的事情，这段时间可能持续两年或三年，因为极度的劳作和疲累是与理性劳作不相容的。我们考察他们的重要方式就是在这段时间中，当他们集中于体育锻炼的时候，考察他们当中每个人的表现。”

“当然。”他说。

'After this period', I went on, 'a select group of the twenty-year-olds will receive promotion above the rest, and will be required to consolidate the subjects they were taught unsystematically as chil-
c dren until they gain an overview of the relationships these subjects have to one another and to reality.'

'Yes,' he said, 'it's only when this has occurred that one's learning has a secure foundation.'

'And it's also the main way of testing whether or not someone is naturally suited for dialectic,' I said, 'since the ability to take an overview is the distinguishing mark of a dialectician.'

'I agree,' he said.

'What you'll have to do, then,' I said, 'is look out for this quali-
d ty and try to see which of your people are particularly capable in this respect, and have staying power in their intellectual work, in warfare, and in their other duties. These are the ones who, once they're past the age of thirty, you must select from among the select and promote even further; and you must subject them to dialectical training, to try to see which of them is capable of letting go of vision and of sense perception in general, and can proceed to the realm of truth and reality itself. But you have to be very careful at this point, Glaucon.'

'Why?' he asked.

e 'Don't you realize how much harm occurs in the way dialectic is practised nowadays?' I said.

'What harm?' he asked.

'People become thoroughly rebellious,' I answered.

'They certainly do,' he said.

'Well, it's not a surprising state for them to get into, is it, do you think?' I asked. 'Can't you forgive them?'

'Why should I?' he asked.

“在这段时间过后，”我继续说，“一组精选出来的二十岁左右的人会得以提升到其余之人上面，他们被要求去巩固那些作为孩子时未被系统地教授的学科，直到他们对这些学科的相互关系以 c
及这些学科与实在的关系得到了一个概观。”

“是的，”他说，“只有这样人们的知识才能有一个牢靠的基础。”

“这也是检测一个人的天性是否适合于辩证法的主要方法，”我说，“因为能够把握一个概观是辩证法家的显著标志。”

“我同意。”他说。

我说：“那么你必须要做的就是注意这些品质，并试图找出哪些人在这方面是尤其具有能力的，在脑力劳作、战争以及其他职 d
责上，他们具有稳固的能力。一旦他们过了三十岁，你就必须把他们从精英当中选拔出来并再次加以提升；你必须让他们接受辩证法的训练，试图去考察他们当中有谁能够不用眼睛和一般的感官，并能够进入真理和实在本身的领域。但是，格劳孔，你在这一点上必须十分小心。”

“为什么？”他问道。

“你难道没有认识到，目前出现多少危害，妨碍了辩证法的实 e
践啊？”我说。

“什么危害？”他问道。

“人们变得十分顽劣，难以管束。”我回答说。

“他们确是如此。”他说。

“那么，你认为他们达到这种状态没什么奇怪的，不是吗？”我问道，“你能原谅他们吗？”

“我为什么应该原谅他们呢？”他问道。

538a ‘Here’s an analogy,’ I said. ‘Suppose an illegitimate child is brought up in affluent circumstances, in the midst of a large, powerful family with hordes of flatterers; and suppose that, when he grows up, he becomes aware that he isn’t the child of his self-styled parents, but can’t find out who his real parents are. Can you guess what his attitude would be towards the flatterers and towards his surrogate parents when he didn’t know that this wasn’t his rightful place, and then when he learnt the truth? Or shall I tell you what I suspect?’

‘Please do,’ he said.

b ‘I suspect’, I said, ‘that, before he learnt the truth, he’d be more inclined to respect his father and mother and the rest of the people he’d presumed to be his relatives than he would the flatterers, and less inclined to turn a blind eye to any need of theirs, and to do or say anything rebellious to them, and to disobey them in any important respect.’

‘That’s likely,’ he said.

‘However, once he’d become aware of the true state of affairs, I suspect he’d leave off giving them his respect and concern, and transfer his attention to the flatterers instead. He’d listen to them more
c than he did before, model his lifestyle on theirs, openly spend time with them, and not have the slightest interest in that father of his and the rest of his pseudo family—unless he’s inherently a person of high principles.’

‘Yes, that’s exactly what would happen,’ he agreed. ‘But how does this analogy apply to people who are exposed to rational arguments?’

‘Like this. From childhood, we’ve held certain views about moral and right conduct. These views formed the environment of our upbringing, we are subject to them as we are to our parents, and we obey them and respect them.’

‘True.’

d ‘Now, there are also enjoyable practices which run counter to

“打个比方，”我说，“假设一个养子在一个富裕的环境中被抚养大，生活在充满谄媚的有权有势的大家庭中；并且假设当他长 538a
大时，他意识到他不是自称其父母之人的孩子，但他找不出谁是他真正的父母。当他并不知道这不是他合法的处所，后来当他得知了真相的时候，你能猜测一下他对待谄媚者和对待他养父母的态度是什么样吗？或者要我告诉你我的猜测吗？”

“请讲。”他说。

“我想，”我说，“在得知真相之前，比起谄媚者来说，他会更倾向于尊重他的父母以及其他被他当作自己亲戚的人，而不大可能 b
对他们的需要漠不关心，任何言行都不大可能会违背他们，在任何重要方面也不会不听从他们的。”

“这很有可能。”他说。

“然而，他一旦认识到了事情的真相，我猜测他不再尊重他们，不再关心他们，而是把他的注意力转移到谄媚者身上。他听从他们更甚于以前，模仿他们的生活方式，公开地与他们在一起，对他的养父和他的家庭一点都不关心——除非他天性上就是一 c
个情操高尚的人。”

“是的，这很可能发生，”他同意说，“但这个类比如何适用于那些从事理性论证的人？”

“像这样，从小我们就有了某些关于道德和正义行为的看法。这些看法形成了我们的教育环境，我们服从它们，就好像我们服从我们的父母一样，我们遵守并尊重它们。”

“对的。”

“那么还有些令人愉快的习俗，它们与这种道德规范背道而 d

this moral code. These practices flatter and tempt our minds, but anyone with even a scrap of restraint doesn't give in, and continues instead to respect and obey those traditional views.'

'True.'

'Well, suppose', I went on, 'that the kind of person we're imagining is faced with a question like "What is right?" He answers that it consists in the conduct enjoined by the originator of his society's code, but the argument proves him wrong, and proves him wrong again and again, until he's battered into thinking that this code is no more right than wrong. Then the same happens with morality
e and goodness and all the qualities he used particularly to respect. What do you think the consequences of this are on his behaviour? What will happen to his respect and obedience?'

'He'll inevitably become more disrespectful and disobedient than he was before,' he said.

'Now, when he's changed his mind about what to respect and about his former familiar code,' I said, 'and at the same time can't discover the truth, where can he turn? Doesn't it only make sense to
539a think of him being seduced by the tempting lifestyle?'

'Yes,' he said.

'So he'll stop being law-abiding and become rebellious.'

'Inevitably.'

'People who are exposed to rational arguments, then,' I said, 'are quite likely to rebel and, as I suggested a moment ago, we should forgive them, don't you think?'

'Yes, and feel sorry for them,' he added.

'So if you want to avoid having to feel sorry for your thirty year-olds, then you must handle rational arguments with the utmost circumspection, mustn't you?'

'Yes, definitely,' he said.

b 'And one important precaution you can take is not to let them

驰。这些习俗向我们的心灵献媚并引诱我们的心灵,但任何有节制的人是不会屈服的,而是相反,他们会继续尊重和遵守那些传统的观点。”

“对的。”

“那么,假设,”我继续说,“我们所设想的那种人面对像这样的一个问题:‘正义是什么?’他回答说社会规范的缔造者所规定的行为是这样的,但论证却表明他是错误的,并且还一次次地证明他是错误的,直到他被驳倒并认为这种规范不比错误的事物更正确。对于正义、善以及所有他过去特别尊重的品质也都是这 e
样。你认为这会对他的行为造成什么样的结果?他会尊重和遵守吗?”

“他必定会变得不如以前尊重和遵守。”他说。

我说:“那么当他对什么应该尊重以及他对以前家庭信条改变看法时,同时又没能找到真理,他会转向什么地方呢?不就只能认为他受到那种具有蛊惑力的生活方式的引诱吗?” 539a

“是的。”他说。

“这样他就会不再守法并且变得难以管束。”

“肯定是这样的。”

我说:“那么从事理性论证的人很可能违反法律,就像我刚才所说的那样,我们应该原谅他们,你难道不是这样想的吗?”

“是这样想的,我为他们感到遗憾。”他补充说。

“所以如果你想避免为你那些三十岁的人感到遗憾的话,你必须非常小心地对待理性论证,不是吗?”

“是的,毫无疑问。”他说。

“你可以采取的一个重要的预防办法,即不让他们年纪轻轻 b

get wind of rational arguments when they're young, don't you think? I mean, I'm sure you've noticed how when adolescents get their first taste of argumentation, they abuse it and treat it like a game. They can't find any other use for it except disputation; they use knock-down arguments which they borrow from others to demolish people's positions. Like puppies, they love to tug away at anyone they come across and to tear his argument to shreds with theirs.'

'Yes, it's incredible,' he said.

'So before long—once they've demolished a lot of arguments
c and often had their own demolished as well—they find they've radically changed their minds about everything. And the result of this is that people take a dim view of them, and of philosophy in general.'

'You're absolutely right,' he said.

'An older person, however,' I went on, 'is hardly likely to succumb to this insanity: he'd sooner resemble someone who's willing to practise dialectic and look for the truth, than someone who trivializes everything with his game-playing and disputatiousness. His own be-
d haviour will be more moderate, and he'll increase, rather than decrease, dialectic's reputation.'

'Right,' he said.

'And hasn't the point of what we've been saying been to get rid of the current practice of letting absolutely anyone, even when entirely unsuitable, come to rational argumentation, and to ensure that it is only orderly and stable people who get involved in it?'

'Yes,' he said.

'Suppose, in order to complement the way physical exercise was approached, someone were to study, with constancy and concentration, nothing but rational argumentation for twice as many years as he
e devoted to physical exercise. Would that do?'

'Do you mean six years or four years?' he asked.

'Why don't you just make it five?' I suggested. 'You see, the

就去尝试理性的论证，你难道不这么想吗？我的意思是说，我确信你肯定注意到了，当年轻人第一次尝试了论证，他们就滥用论证并把它当作游戏。除了用来辩论之外他们找不出任何别的用处了；他们采用那些从别人那里借来的强有力的论证去批驳人们的观点。就像小狗一样，它们喜爱拖住路过它们的人，那些人就喜爱用他的论证去拖咬路过他们的人。”

“是的，肯定是这样的。”他说。

“所以不久——一旦他们批驳了很多论证，他们自己的论证也常常受到批驳——他们觉得自己对于所有事物的想法已经大 c
大改变了。结果人们便轻视他们，也轻视一般的哲学。”

“你说得很对。”他说。

我继续说：“而年纪大的人几乎不会屈从于这种疯狂：他宁可效仿那些愿意实践辩证法和追寻真理的人，而不去效仿那些通过游戏或争吵而把一切说得是小事情的人。他自己的行为会更加本分，并且他会提升而不是降低辩证法的名声。” d

“对的。”他说。

“我们所说的这些话的关键不就在于排除现在这样的做法，决不让任何完全不适合的人参加理性论证，而是确保只让那些有条理、稳健的人来参加讨论？”

“是的。”他说。

“设想一下，为了补充体育锻炼方式，一个人什么都不学，而是坚持不懈、专心致志地以两倍于他花在体育锻炼上的时间来学习理性的论证。这样可以吗？”

“你指的是六年还是四年？”他问道。 e

“你为什么不定为五年？”我建议道，“你知道，你要做的下一

next thing you have to do is make them go back down into that cave and force them to take charge of warfare and whatever other areas young people should be responsible for, so that they gain just as much practical experience as everyone else. Moreover, while they hold these positions of responsibility, you'd better test them to see whether they remain unmoved by all the various temptations they're exposed
540a to, or whether they go astray.'

'How long do you suggest for this?' he asked.

'Fifteen years,' I replied. 'Not all of them will reach their fiftieth year unscathed and with absolutely outsanding performances in every task they undertook and branch of knowledge they studied, but you can guide those who do to the climax of their lives. You must make them open up the beam of their minds and look at the all-em-bracing source of light, which is goodness itself. Once they've seen it, they must use it as a reference-point and spend the rest of their lives orde-
b ring the community, its members, and themselves. They take turns at this: they spend most of their time doing philosophy, but when their turn comes, then for the community's sake they become involved in its affairs and slog away at them as rulers. This is something they do as an obligation, not as a privilege. Because they have this attitude, they're constantly training others to follow suit, and once they've completed this process and have bequeathed guardianship of the community to others in their place, they depart for a new home in the Isles of the Blessed. And the community constructs public memorials and establishes ceremonies in their honour, and treats them (if the Delphic oracle
c gives its blessing) as deities, or otherwise as happy and godlike men.'

'You've created an image of the rulers which makes them as thoroughly attractive as a master sculptor makes his statues, Socrates,' he remarked.

'And there are female rulers too, Glaucon,' I said. 'Please don't think that what I've been saying doesn't apply equally to any women in the community with the required natural abilities.'

'That's right,' he said. 'Men and women will share everything equally, as we explained.'

件事情就是使他们下到洞穴里，并迫使他们负责指挥战争以及年轻人应该担负起的其他任务，这样他们就获得了与别人一样多的实践经验。此外，当他们担负起这些职责的时候，你最好要考察他们，看看他们是不为各种诱惑所动，还是误入歧途了。” 540a

“你认为这应该有多久?”他问道。

“十五年，”我回答说，“并不是所有人都能这样活到五十岁，他们没有经历磨难，在他们承担的每个工作中以及他们学习的每门知识中的表现极其出色，这样你可以引导那些人达到生命的巅峰。你必须使他们的心灵放出光芒，使之观看那包容一切的光源，即善自身。他们一旦看到了它，他们肯定会将之作为原型并把他们的剩余岁月用来管理城邦以及成员，还有他们自己。他们 b 轮流做这些事情:他们把大部分时间用来研究哲学，但轮到他们的时候，为了城邦，他们参与城邦事务，作为统治者他们不辞辛劳地工作。做这些事情是他们的义务而不是他们的特权。因为他们有这样的想法:经常培养别人以继承自己，一旦完成了这个程序并且把自己保卫城邦的职务留给别人后，他们就离开了，到世外神岛的新家去了。城邦树立起公共的纪念碑并设立纪念仪式来纪念他们，如果德尔斐神谕赐福的话，那么就把他们当作神来看待，否则就当作快乐的，和神一般的人来看待。” c

“苏格拉底，你已经塑造了一个统治者的形象，并使得它很吸引人，就像雕塑大师塑造了他的雕像。”他说。

“格劳孔，还有女性统治者，”我说，“请不要认为我所说的不能同样适合于城邦中的任何女人，她们具备所要求的天赋。”

“对的，”他说，“就像我们说明过的一样，男人、女人同等地分担一切。”

d ‘Well then, do you agree that our community and political system weren't just wishful thinking?’ I said. ‘The community may be difficult to realize, but it's feasible; the essential prerequisite, as we've insisted, is that genuine philosophers—one or more of them—wield power. They have to be born in a community, but grow up to regard the political rewards currently available to themas despicable, as
e mean and worthless. Instead, they have to find nothing more valuable than integrity and its rewards, and nothing more important and essential than morality, which they serve and foster as they take in hand every detail of their community.’

‘How do they go about this?’ he asked.

541a ‘First, they banish everyone over the age of ten into the countryside,’ I answered. ‘Then they take charge of the community's children and make sure that they're beyond the reach of existing conventions, which their parents adhere to, and bring them up under their own customs and laws, which are similar to the ones we were describing before. That's the quickest and simplest way for the community and political system we've been discussing to be established, to attain happiness, and to benefit the people among whom they occur.’

b ‘Yes, definitely,’ he said. ‘And I think you've given an excellent explanation of how our community would be realized, if it ever were.’

‘So is that it, then?’ I asked. ‘Have we finished discussing this community of ours and its human counterpart? I mean, I suppose it's obvious what kind of person we'll claim he has to be.’

‘Yes, it is,’ he said. ‘And, to answer your question, yes, I think we've finished.’

“好吧,那么你是否同意我们的城邦和政治制度并不仅仅是 d
一厢情愿的空想?”我说,“城邦可能难以实现,但并不是行不通的;就像我们曾坚持的一样,重要的前提条件就是真正的哲学家——他们中的一个或多个——掌权。他们必须是出生于这个城邦,但长大了却把当前城邦的荣誉看作是卑劣的、平庸的、没有价值的。与之相反,他们必须确定,没有什么比正直及其褒奖更有价值的了,而且还必须确定,没有比正义,亦即当他们承担起他们城邦的每一项指定的任务时他们都要服从与培养发展的东西, e
更重要与必需的了。”

“那么他们又该如何下手去做呢?”他问道。

“首先,他们把所有十岁以上的人送到乡下去,”我回答说,
“然后他们照看城邦的这些孩子们,确保他们不受现有习惯的影 541a
响——他们的父母就坚持这种习惯——在他们自己的习俗和法律下把他们抚养大,这与我们之前所说的相似。为了得到幸福,为了给城邦中的人们带来好处,那么对于那些我们讨论过的要加以建立的政治制度来说,这就是最快、最简便的方式。”

“是的,毫无疑问,”他说,“关于我们的城邦如何实现,如果它
曾实现过,我想你已经给出了一个完美的解释。” b

“那么就是这样了吗?”我问道,“我们是否已经讨论完了我们的这个城邦以及相应的人?我的意思是说,我想我们会提出那些人必须是什么样的,这一点是很清楚的了。”

“是的,它很清楚了,”他说,“而且,我想我们已经完成了对于你的问题的回答。”

CHAPTER 11

543a ‘All right, Glaucon. Now, we concluded that the best government of a community depends on sharing women, children, and education in all its aspects, and by the same token on peacetime and wartime functions being performed by women as well as by men, and on their kings being those who have proved outstanding at philosophy and warfare.’

‘Yes, we did,’ he agreed.

b ‘And we also agreed that, once they're in office, the rulers are to take the militia and settle them in the kind of quarters we described earlier—that is, where nothing is exclusive to any individual, but everything is shared. Furthermore, apart from their quarters being like this, we also drew some conclusions about their possession of property, as you may remember.’

‘I do,’ he said. ‘We thought that, contrary to current practice, none of them should own any property, but that as warriors and guardians they should be paid by everyone else an annual stipend for their guar-
c ding, consisting of the provisions appropriate to their duties, and that they should look after the community as a whole, as well as themselves.’

‘That's right,’ I said. ‘But now that we've finished with all that, let's try to resume our journey by recalling where we were when we took the side-turning that led us here.’

‘That's no problem,’ he said. ‘You were talking, much as you are now, as if your discussion of our community were complete. You were saying that you'd call good the kind of community you'd de-
d scribed at that point, and its human counterpart—even though, as it turns out, you were in a position to describe an even better community
544a and an even better person. Anyway, you claimed that, given the rightness of our community, all the rest were flawed, and you said,

第十一章

“好吧，格劳孔，现在，我们得出结论说，最好的城邦管理在于 543a
共有女人、孩子以及教育的所有方面，同样，无论在和平时代还是
在战争年代，工作由男人和女人分担，而他们的统治者就是那些
被证明在哲学和战争方面皆优秀的人。”

“是的，我们可以这么说。”他同意说。

“我们还同意，统治者一旦在职，他就要带领士兵去驻扎 b
在我们在前面描述过的那种营房里——就是说，在那里没有
什么东西是专属某个人的，所有东西都是共有的。除了他们
这样的营房，我们还得出过某些关于他们拥有财产的结论，你
也许还记得。”

“我记得，”他说，“与现在的做法相反，我们曾认为他们当中
没有一个人可以拥有任何财产，作为战士和卫士，别的所有人应
该向他们提供一笔年金，这包括与他们的职责相应的给养，而他 c
们应该保卫整个城邦和他们自己。”

“对的，”我说，“但既然那些事情我们都已经说过了，那么让我们回到我们所走的那个把我们带到这里的岔道口，以继续我们的旅程。”

“没问题，”他说，“你刚才就像现在一样在讨论，好像关于我
们城邦的讨论已经完成了。你把所描述的城邦以及相应的人称作
是好的——虽然你表明还可以把城邦和人描绘得更好些。无论如 d
何，你声称如果我们的城邦是正确的，那么所有其余的城邦都 544a

if my memory serves me well, that of these remaining political systems, four types would be worth mentioning, and that we ought to see where they and their human counterparts go wrong, so that we can decide whether or not the best person is also the happiest person, and the worst the unhappiest, which we can only do once we've seen all these types of human being and reached agreement as to which is best and which is worst. I had just asked which four political systems you
b had in mind, when Polemarchus and Adeimantus interrupted. You responded to them, and that's how the discussion reached this point.'

'Your memory is spot on,' I said.

'Why don't you resume your stance, then, as if you were a wrestler? I'll ask the same question, and you can have a go at saying what you were poised to say then.'

'I'll try,' I said.

'In fact, speaking for myself, I really would like to hear which four political systems you had in mind,' he said.

c 'I should be able to tell you that without any difficulty,' I said, 'since the ones I mean are recognized political systems with names. There's that popular favourite, the Cretan and Spartan system; the second one, which is also the second most popular, is the thoroughly rotten system known as oligarchy; then next there's democracy, oligarchy's adversary; and the fourth, the ultimate political disease, which leaves all the rest behind, is noble dictatorship. Can you think of any other type of po-
d litical system which counts as a distinct variety? I mean, there are autocracies and monarchies which can be bought, and other political systems (to be found among both Greeks and non-Greeks) which equally fall somewhere among the ones I've mentioned.'

'Yes, there are all sorts of odd systems one hears about,' he remarked.

'Well, do you appreciate that there are bound to be as many types of human being as there are of political system?' I asked. 'Or do you imagine that political systems somehow come into being from oak or from rock, rather than from the characters of the communities'

是错误的。如果我的记忆还很好的话，那么其余的政治制度中还有四
种是值得一提的，我们应该考察一下它们本身以及相应的人在什么地
方出了错，这样我们就可以断定最善的人是否也是最幸福的人，最恶
的人是否也是最不幸福的人；只有当我们考察了所有类型的人并一致
同意哪些是最善的，哪些是最恶的之后，我们才能这样做。当玻勒玛
库斯和阿狄曼图插嘴的时候，我刚问了你心里想的是哪四种政治制
度。你回答了他们，这就是讨论如何延续到了现在。” b

“你记得很准。”我说。

“那么你为什么不像一个摔跤手一样再来一回合呢？我会问
你同样的问题，你可以试着说说你当时想说的话？”

“我会尽力的。”我说。

“实际上，就我本人而言，我真的想听听你心里所想的四种政
治制度。”他说。

“我应该能够毫无困难地告诉你，”我说，“因为我所指的是由名字 c
标明的政治制度。有受到广泛赞扬的克里特、斯巴达体制；第二种也是
较为受欢迎的，即以寡头制闻名，完全腐坏了的制度；接下来的是民主
制，与寡头制相反；第四种是最后的政治病害，其严重远远超过所有其余
的制度，那便是贵族的僭主制。你还能想到任何别的类型的政治制度
作为一个特殊的类别吗？我的意思是说，独裁制和可以买来的君主制， d
以及别的政治制度（能在希腊人和非希腊人当中找到），它们同样地分
布于我提到过的那些人当中。”

“是的，人们是听到过各种各样奇怪的制度。”他说。

“那么，你知道有多少种政治制度就必定有多少种类型的人
吗？”我问道，“或者你认为政治制度以某种方式来源于木头或石
头，而不是来源于城邦中居住者的品性？如果这种品性压倒了

inhabitants? If one type of character outweighs the rest, so to speak,
e then don't you think it draws all the other types with it?'

'Yes, that's the only possible way in which political systems arise,' he agreed.

'So if there are five types of society, then any given individual should also have one of five kinds of mental trait.'

'Naturally.'

'Now, we've already described the individual counterpart to aristocracy, and no one could fault our claim that it's a person of goodness and morality.'

545a 'Yes, we have.'

'So next we'd better describe the inferior kinds of person—the competitive and ambitious person who corresponds to the Spartan system, then the oligarchic, democratic, and dictatorial types. This will enable us to see which of them is the least moral; we can then contrast him with the most moral type, and that will complete our enquiry into how absolute morality compares with absolute immorality in respect of the happiness or unhappiness they entail for people who possess them. Then we'll be in a position either to follow Thrasymachus and pursue immorality, or to follow the argument which is developing
b at the moment and pursue morality. Do you think that's what we'd better do?'

'Yes, most definitely,' he said.

'Well, we started off by looking at characteristics as they manifested in societies, before turning to individuals, on the grounds that this would make it easier for us to see them. So we'd better continue by looking first at the "ambitious" political system—I can't think of
c another familiar word for it: perhaps we should call it 'timocracy' or "timarchy". We'll examine its human counterpart, by comparing him with it; then oligarchy and an oligarchic person; next we'll look at democracy and try to form an impression of a democratic person; and in the fourth place we'll turn our attention to dictatorial government of a community and then we'll look at a dictatorial temperament. Don't you think this is how we should try to gain the competence to assess the

其余的品性,那么可以这么说,你难道不认为是它牵引着所有别 e
的类型吗?"

"是的,这是政治制度得以产生的唯一一种可能方式。"他同意说。

"所以如果有五种类型的社会,那么任何既定的个人也应该具有五种精神特质中的一种。"

"那是自然。"

"那么,我们已经描述过相应于贵族制的个人,没有人可以指责我们的说法,即这个人是善的和正义的。"

"是的,我们已经描述过。" 545a

"所以接下来我们最好考察一下较差类型的人——争强好胜、贪求名誉的人相应于斯巴达体制,然后是寡头、民主分子和僭主。这样能够使我们看清楚他们当中谁是最不正义的;然后我们可以将他与最正义的那类人做比较,看看拥有绝对的正义和绝对的不正义而必然带来的幸福或不幸福,将两者进行比较,那样我们就完成我们的研究了。以后我们要么同意塞拉西马库斯,跟随他追求不正义,要么跟随现在
提出的论证去追求正义。你认为我们是否最好这样做呢?" b

"是的,确定无疑。"他说。

"那么让我们在转而考察个人之前,先来考察一下展示在社会中的品性,因为这会使我们容易看清楚。所以我们先来考察一下'热爱名誉'的政治制度——我想不出另一个熟悉的词语来称呼它:也许我们应该称它为'荣誉政体'或'荣誉统治'。我们会通
过比较而考察相应的人;然后是寡头政体和寡头;接下去我们会 c
考察民主制并试图描述一下民主式的个人;其四,我们会把我们的注意力转向僭主统治的城邦,然后我们会考察独裁者的性情。你难道不认为这样我们就应该具有了判断我们面前的问题的能力

matter before us?'

'Yes, that's a perfectly reasonable way to go about the investigation and the assessment,' he replied.

'All right, then,' I said. 'Let's try to account for the transition from aristocracy to timocracy. I suppose this much is straightforward—
d that all political change is due to the actual power-possessing members of society themselves, when conflict arises among them. Even if there are very few of them, instability is out of the question as long as they're of one mind. Yes?'

'Yes.'

'How, then, Glaucon,' I asked, 'will change become a feature of our community? How will conflict arise between and among the auxiliaries and the rulers? Perhaps you'd like us to imitate Homer and pray for the Muses to tell us "how conflict first occurred", and to have them speak in a pompous and highfalutin fashion, using the kind of
e semi-serious tone one uses when teasing and making fun of children.'

'What do you mean?'

546a 'Something like this. Hard though it may be for a community with this structure to undergo change, yet everything that is born must die, and so even this kind of structure will not last for ever, but will fall apart. This is how it will happen. Fertility and infertility are not restricted to plants: surface-dwelling creatures also periodically experience both mental and physical fertility and infertility, each time their cycles complete a revolution. Short-lived creatures have short cycles, long-lived ones the opposite. Where the human species is concerned, despite the cleverness of the people you've trained to be in charge of your community, they'll still fail to catch the times of fertili-
b ty and barrenness, although they supplement the evidence of their senses with rationality. They'll mistime things and produce children when they shouldn't.

'Now, a divine creature's cycle is defined by a perfect number; but a human creature's number is the smallest one in which increases

了吗?”

“是的,这种研究和评判的方式非常有道理。”他回答说。

“那么好吧,”我说,“让我们试图解释一下从贵族制到荣誉政体的转变吧。我想这是很显然的——当在实际掌权的社会成员内部发生冲突的时候,所有这些政治上的变动都因为他们自身的 d
缘故。即使只有很少数人,只要他们团结一心,动乱就是不可能的。是吗?”

“是的。”

“那么,格劳孔,”我问道,“我们的城邦如何发生变动呢?辅助者和统治者之间的冲突怎么会发生呢?也许你想要我们模仿荷马祈求缪斯女神告诉我们‘第一次冲突是怎么发生的’,并且让她们使用逗弄孩子时的半严肃的语调以骄傲自大的方式说 e
出来。”

“你说的是什么意思?”

“有点像是这样。让具有这种结构的城邦发生变动是很困难 546a
的,但是一切皆有生有灭,所以即使是这样的结构也不会永存,而是会解体的。它是这样发生的。生育期和不育期并不局限于植物:生存在地面上的动物也周期性地经历灵魂和身体上的生育期和不育期,每个周期就结束一次变化。活得短的动物周期短,活得长的动物周期长。至于人类,尽管你培养出来管理城邦的人具有聪明才智,虽然他们用理性弥补了感官知觉,但他们还是不能 b
够把握生育期和不育期的时间。他们在一些事情上会做得不合时宜,在不应该生育孩子的时候却生育了孩子。

“神圣产物的周期是由完美的数来规定的,但人类的数是一个最小的数,在其中蕴涵着潜在的和实现潜在的增加,这从相似

entailing potential and realized potential gain three intervals and four terms from among the causes of similarity and dissimilarity, and from among the things that increase and decrease, and so make everything
c mutually conformable and rational. The base numbers involved—3 in relation to 4, along with 5—produce two harmonies when they are increased three times. One harmony is made up of a factor squared, times a hundred times itself; the other harmony is in a sense made up of equal factors, but in a sense of unequal factors-one factor being 100 of the numbers from the rational diagonals of 5, each diminished by I (or 100 of the numbers from the irrational diagonals of 5, each diminished by 2), and the other factor being 100 of the cubes of 3.'

'The geometrical number produced is responsible for this area—
d for the quality of children born—and when your guardians are unaware of this, they pair men and womend sexually on the wrong occasions, and the resulting children will not be naturally gifted or fortunate. It may be that the preceding generation will choose only the best of these children for office, but all the same they won't be as good as they should be, and when they in turn inherit their fathers' positions of authority, despite being guardians they'll begin to neglect us: they'll underrate the importance of cultural studies, and then of physical exercise, and consequently the young people of your community will become rather uncultured. As a result, the next generation of rulers to be appointed will not be particularly good at guarding, in the sense that they won't be so good at assessing those castes of Hesiod's
e and yours—the castes of gold and silver, of copper and iron. Iron will
547a get all mixed up with silver, copper with gold; discrepancy and discordant incongruity will occur, and they always breed hostility and antagonism, wherever they occur. It has to be admitted that "this is the lineage" of conflict, whatever the circumstances of its occurrence on any given occasion.'

'Yes, we'll endorse their opinion,' he said.

'We have to,' I said. 'They are the Muses, after all.'

和不相似以及从增加与减少的事物中获得三级四项,这样使得一切成为相互和谐和富有理性的。所说的这些基本数字——三比四,和五一起——当它们乘三次时就产生出两个和 c 谐。其一是由相等的因子乘以自身的一百倍构成;另一个在某种意义上说是由相等的因子构成,而在另一种意义上说是由不相等的因子构成——一个因子是从有理数对角线五所得出的数字的一百倍,每一个减去一,或者从无理数对角线五得所出的数字的一百倍,每一个减去二,另一个因子是三的立方的一百倍。

"如果产生的几何数是这件事的原因——出生的孩子质量的原因——当你们的卫士没有意识到这一点的时候,他们让男女在错误的时候发生性关系,那么生出来的孩子就不具 d 有天赋或是不幸的。前辈可能会只在这些孩子中选择最好的去任职,但他们仍旧不如应该的那样优秀。当轮到他们继承他们父辈的权位时,尽管他们是卫士,但开始忽视我们了:他们会低估音乐教育的重要性,然后是低估体育锻炼的重要性,结果你们城邦的年轻人会变得相当没有教养。结果,被委任的下一代统治者会变得尤其不善于防卫,因为他们不善于鉴别那些赫西俄德和你们的种族——金种、银种、铜种和铁种。 e
547a 铁与银都混杂在一起,铜与金都混杂在一起;不一致、不和谐、不协调便产生了,每当它们产生时,就经常会发生敌对和对抗。不管在什么条件和环境下发生,都必须承认为'这是血统'的冲突。"

"是的,我同意她们的看法。"他说。

"我们必须同意她们的看法,"我说,"她们毕竟是缪斯。"

b ‘What are they going to say next?’ he asked.

‘Once conflict has been born,’ I said, ‘the two castes start to pull in different directions. The iron and copper caste incline towards business and want to possess land, houses, gold, and silver. The gold and silver caste, on the other hand, don’t feel in need of money: thanks to their innate wealth, they tend to be temperamentally attracted towards goodness and the traditional ways. Because of the tension and antipathy between them, they compromise by agreeing to assign
c themselves land and houses for private ownership, and at the same time they subjugate their former friends and wards, whom they used to guard, and make them their dependants and slaves, while they take responsibility for warfare and for guarding themselves against them.’

‘Yes, I think that’s the cause of the transition,’ he agreed.

‘And wouldn’t this political system fall between aristocracy and oligarchy?’ I asked.

‘Yes.’

‘Anyway, that’s how the transition will take place. But once it
d has taken placc, how will the community be governed? Perhaps the answer’s obvious: won’t it in some respects take after both oligarchy and the system which preceded it (since it falls between them), and in other respects have its own distinctive features?’

‘Yes,’ he answered.

‘Now, there’ll be respect for the rulers, and its militia won’t get involved in any businesses like farming and manufacture, but will have arranged common mess-halls for themselves and will devote themselves to physical exercise and to training for war. In all these respects, it’ll reflect the political system which preceded it, won’t it?’

‘Yes.’

e ‘On the other hand, there’ll be reluctance to choose men of knowledge for political office, since the only intellectuals within the community by then will be complex characters, lacking in robust directness. The community will incline towards the greater directness of passionate types, who are by their natures more suited for war than for

“她们接下去要说什么？”他问道。 b

“一旦产生了冲突，”我说，“两个等级就开始走向不同的方向。铜铁等级爱好商业并想拥有土地、房屋和金银。另一方面，金银等级认为不需要金钱：由于他们内在的财富，他们在性情上容易受到善和传统方式的吸引。因为他们之间存在着紧张关系和相互的厌恶之情，两个等级选择了互相让步以解决分歧，同意将土地、房屋分配在他们自己私人名义下，与此同时，他们使其原 c
来的朋友和受保护者屈从，这些人原本是他们要加以卫护的，但当他们承担起战争的责任，并为了保卫自己而与之处在敌对状况时，这两个等级就使之成为了自己的附庸及苦工。”

“是的，我认为这就是转变的原因。”他同意说。

“这种政治制度不就介于贵族制和寡头制之间吗？”我问道。

“是的。”

“无论如何，转变就是这样发生的。但一旦发生了，城邦怎么来管理呢？也许答案显然是这样的：它不就在某些方面像寡头制 d
和那种在它之前的制度一样，因为它介于两者之间，而在另一些方面又具有它独特的特点？”

“是的。”他回答说。

“那么，在那里，统治者会受到尊重，其士兵不用从事如务农和手工制作类的任何事务，而是为他们自己安排公共食堂并参加身体锻炼和军事训练。在所有这些方面都反映着它之前的政治制度，不是吗？”

“是的。”

“另一方面，选择那些拥有知识的人来担任城邦的职位会有 e
些犹豫，因为那时城邦中的聪明人的品性是混杂的，不坚强并缺乏正直。城邦偏爱那种较为直率而充满激情的人，他们在本性上

peace; it will value the ruses and stratagems which war entails, and
548a will spend all its time on warfare. Most of these sorts of features will be peculiar to it, won't they?'

'Yes.'

'Furthermore,' I went on, 'the members of this kind of community will share with people under oligarchies a craving for money. they'll have a fanatical respect for gold and silver—but a furtive respect, because they'll have storerooms and vaults in their homes where they can put them and hide them away, and they'll also have surrounded their homes with walls, for all the world as if their houses were private dens within whose confines they can extravagantly spend
b their money on their wives and anyone else they choose.'

'True,' he said.

'But because they value money and aren't open about possessing it, they'll actually be mean about it—although they'll be happy to satisfy their craving by spending other people's money. They'll pluck their pleasures in secret, hiding away from the law like children running and hiding from their father. The background to all this will be the fact that their education will have been forced on them, rather than finding willing ears, and this will be due to their neglect of the authentic Muse—and of her companions, reason and philosophy—and to their placing
c more value on physical exercise than on cultural studies.'

'You're talking about a political system which is a thorough mixture of good and bad,' he remarked.

'Yes, it is a mixture,' I agreed, 'but thanks to the predominance of the passionate element, there's only one aspect which particularly stands out—all its competitiveness and ambition.'

'Yes, that's extremely noticeable,' he said.

'So much, then,' I said, 'for the origin and nature of this political system. I assume than a verbal sketch of the outline of the system
d will do, rather than filling in all the details, since even a sketch will enable us to see where the extremes of human morality and immorality

更适合于战争而不是和平；他们崇尚战争所需的战术策略，并把他们的所有时间都花在战争上。大多数这些特征都为这种城邦 548a
所特有，不是吗？”

“是的。”

“此外，”我继续说，“这类城邦的成员和寡头制下的民众一样都贪图金钱。他们对金银有一种疯狂的敬慕——但却是一种暗暗的敬重，因为他们在家里有储藏室和地下室用来存放金银，把它们藏起来，他们的家四面有围墙，无论如何，他们的房子是他们的巢穴，在里面他们把大量的时间花在他们的妻子和任何别的宠 b
幸者身上。”

“对的。”他说。

“但是因为他们看重金钱而又不能公开地占有，实际上他们在金钱上是很吝啬的——但他们会很高兴花别人的钱来满足自己的欲望。他们偷偷地享乐并躲避法律，就像小孩逃跑躲避他们的父亲一样。所有这些都在于这样的事实，即他们的教育是强加于他们的，而不是由他们自愿的，这是由于他们忽视了真正的缪斯女神——以及她们的伴侣，理性和哲学——而把他们的重点放在了体育锻炼上而不是音乐学习上。” c

“你所说的政治制度是完全混合了善与恶。”他说。

“是的，是混合的，”我同意说，“但由于激情的成分占了主导，只有一个方面突出出来——那就是好胜和爱荣誉。”

“是的，这非常明显。”他说。

“那么，”我说，“这种政治制度的起源和本性就说那么多了。我认为用词语勾勒一下这个体系的纲要就够了，而不用详述所有的细节，因为即使是概述也能够让我们看清最正义和最不正义的 d

lie, and it would take for ever to go through every possible political system and human characteristic in minute detail.'

'Yes, that's right,' he said.

'What about the person who corresponds to this political system, then? What's his background? And What's he like?'

'I think he'd approximate pretty closely to Glaucon here,' said Adeimantus, 'with his competitiveness.'

e 'Maybe he would in this respect,' I said, 'but there are traits he has which do not resemble any of Glaucon's, I think.'

'Which ones?'

'He's bound to be more obstinate,' I said, 'and to have spent less time on cultural studies. He'll approve of culture, however, and
549a he'll enjoy listening to lectures, even though he won't be any good at speaking himself. This kind of person will treat slaves harshly (rather than finding them beneath consideration, which is the attitude of a properly educated person), but he'll be gentle with those he likes. He'll be excessively submissive to authority, and ambitiously eager for authority himself. He'll regard military achievements as qualifying someone for political office, rather than ability at speaking and so on, and he'll be fond of sports and hunting.'

'Yes,' he said, 'because these are the characteristics of the political system we've been describing.'

'Now, as a young man,' I continued, 'a person of this type will
b disdain money, but the older he gets, the more he'll welcome it at every opportunity, don't you think? This is because his mercenary side will have come to the fore, and because his attitude towards goodness will be tainted, thanks to his lack of the best guardian.'

'What guardian is that?' asked Adeimantus.

'A mind which combines reason and culture,' I replied. 'it's only when this resides in someone throughout his life that his goodness is kept intact.'

'You're right,' he said.

人了,而要详述每个可能的政治制度以及细说人类品性,这将是漫长的。”

“是的,你说得对。”他说。

“那么与这种政治制度相应的人呢?他有什么样的背景?他是什么样的性格呢?”

“我想会非常近似格劳孔,”阿狄曼图说,“具有好胜心。”

“也许在这方面是很像的,“我说,“但是我想他还有其他特征 e
与格劳孔一点都不像。”

“什么特征?”

我说:“他一定更加固执并且在音乐学习上花较少的时间。然而他会赞同音乐教育,也乐于听讲,虽然他本人不善言谈。这
样的人对待奴隶是很严厉的,而不是觉得自己有受过恰当教育之 549a
人的优越感,但是对那些他喜欢的人则会是很和蔼的。他对待权威会非常恭顺,自己也雄心勃勃地渴望权威。他会把军事上的成就而不是能说会道等等的能力作为一个人胜任城邦职务的条件,他喜爱体育和狩猎。”

“是的,”他说,“因为这就是我们描述过的政治制度的特征。”

“那么,作为一个年轻人,”我继续说,“这样的一个人会轻视金
钱,但是他年纪越大,他就越会在每一机会中对金钱都欢喜接受,你 b
难道不这么认为吗?这是因为他贪财的一面展露出来了,并且由于他缺少最好的防卫而使他对待善的态度也受到了败坏。”

“那是什么样的防卫?”阿狄曼图问道。

“一个结合了理性和音乐的心灵,”我回答说,“只有当它存留于某人一生时,他的善才能得以保全。”

“你说得对。”他说。

'So that's what a timocratic person is like in his youth,' I said. 'And he is the counterpart to the kind of community we've been talking about.'

c 'Yes.'

'As for his background,' I went on, 'it's something like this. As a young man, he's the son of a father who is good, but who lives in a badly governed community and therefore steers clear of status and office, and lawsuits and all that kind of involvement in public affairs, and is happy to be discounted and consequently to avoid all the nuisance of involvement.'

'Yes, but how does this produce a timocratic type?' he asked.

'It all starts', I explained, 'when he hears his mother complai-
d ning that her husband doesn't have political power, and that this is why she is snubbed by all the other women. Then she sees that he isn't especially interested in money, and plays no part in the fighting and mudslinging that occur in private lawsuits or in political situations, and doesn't get worked up about all that kind of thing; she also notices that he's always minding his own business, and doesn't overrate her (not that he underrates her either). All this makes her cross and she tells him that his father isn't a real man, and that he's too nonchalant, and goes on and on with all the usual complaints women routinely come up with in these kinds of circumstances.'

e 'Yes, there are plenty of these typical complaints,' said Adeimantus.

'As you know, then,' I continued, 'even the supposedly loyal servants of this sort of man whisper the same kinds of things to his sons, and if the servants notice that a young man's father is failing to prosecute someone who owes him some money or is wronging him in some other way, they encourage the son to make sure that he gets even with all these people when he's an adult, and to be more of a man
550a than his father. Outside of the house, the young man hears and sees more of the same sort: he notices that people who mind their own business are regarded by the rest of the community as stupid and are despised, while those who don't are respected and admired. So, when the young man hears and sees all this, and also listens to what his

“一个爱荣誉的年轻人就是这样的,”我说,“他与我们说过的那种城邦相对应。”

“是的。” c

“至于他的背景,”我继续说,“有些像这样:作为一个年轻人,他是一个好父亲的儿子,但这位父亲生活在一个治理不善的城邦中,所以他没有地位和官职,不参与诉讼和所有那样的公共事务,他很高兴放弃一些权力,最终免于介入所有这些麻烦事中。”

“是的,但这如何造就了一个爱荣誉的人呢?”他问道。

我解释说:“起初当他听到母亲抱怨说她的丈夫没有政治权力,以为这就是为什么她受到所有别的女人冷落的原因。然后当 d
她看到他尤其不对金钱感兴趣,并且不参与私人诉讼或政治场合的争斗与中伤,对所有那样的事情他都提不起劲来;她还注意到他总是不问世事,而且不恭维讨好她(当然也不轻视贬低她)。所有这些都使她很生气,她告诉儿子,说,他的父亲不是个真正的男人,说他过于出世,还有女人们在这种场合通常唠唠叨叨提出来的所有一般的抱怨。” e

“是的,是有许多这样的抱怨。”阿狄曼图说。

我继续说:“那么,就如你所知的那样,这种人的仆人似乎被认为是忠诚的,但还是会向主人儿子们悄悄地说这类事情。如果这些仆人注意到了年轻人的父亲没有控告欠他钱或以别的方式损害他的人,他们就鼓励主人的儿子长大后一定要报复所有这些人,要比他的父亲更像一个男人。在家外,年轻人听到、 550a
看到更多同样的事情:他注意到那些不问世事的人被城邦中其余的人看作是愚蠢的并且受到鄙视,而那些相反的人则受到尊重和仰慕。这样,当这个年轻人听到和看到所有这些事

father has to say, and sees his way of life from close quarters and compares it with the alternative, he is pulled in two directions: his fa-
b ther irrigates and nurtures his rational mind, while everyone else nurtures the desirous and passionate parts of his mind. Now, he isn't a bad person, but he's been exposed to some bad influences, so he resolves these contrary impulses by reaching a compromise: he transfers authority within himself to the intermediate part of himself—the competitive and passionate part—and so he becomes a supercilious, ambitious man.'

'I think you've described his background perfectly,' he said.

c 'So There's our second political system and our second type of person,' I said.

'Yes,' he agreed.

'Next, to paraphrase Aeschylus, shall we "tell who else has been deployed, to stand before which community"—or rather, shall we keep to our plan and speak of the community first?'

'Yes,' he said.

'I think that oligarchy would follow the kind of political system we've described.'

'But what kind of constitution do you mean by oligarchy?' he asked.

'A political system which is based on property value,' I re-
d plied, 'so that the rich have political power, and the poor are exclude from government.'

'I see,' he said.

'Hadn't we better explain the initial transition from timarchy to oligarchy?'

'Yes.'

'But even a blind man could see how it happens,' I said.

'How?'

'The downfall of timarchy is brought about by trying to keep that

情,还听到他父亲所不得不说的话,并且近看过他的生活方式并将之与别人做过比较的时候,他便受到两个方向的牵引:他的父亲浇灌并培育他的理性灵魂,而别人培育他灵魂中的欲望和激情 b 部分。他并不是一个坏人,而是受到某些坏的影响,所以他决定调和这些对立的力量:他把自身的权威转让给他自己的中间部分——好胜而又充满激情的部分——这样他就变成了一个高傲而又热爱荣誉的人了。”

“我想你已经完美地描述了他的背景。”他说。

“我们的第二种政治制度和我们的第二种类型的人就是这样 c 的。”我说。

“是的。”他同意说。

“接下来,我们是否要像埃斯库罗斯所说的那样‘在别的城邦面前谈论别的人’——或者还是按照我们的计划先来讨论城邦?”

“先讨论城邦。”他说。

“我想接着那种我们描述过的政治制度的就是寡头制。”

“但你说寡头制指的是一种什么样的制度?”他问道。

我回答说:“一种基于财产价值的政治制度,富人就拥有政治权力,而穷人则被排除在城邦管理之外。” d

“我明白了。”他说。

“我们不是最好应该解释从荣誉政治到寡头制的最初转变吗?”

“是的。”

“即使一个盲人也能看清这是怎么发生的。”我说。

“如何发生?”

“试图填满我们说过的储藏室——人们用来存放他们黄金的

storeroom we spoke of—the one people have for their gold—full up. You see, first people invent ways to spend their money and they subvert the laws for this purpose, in the sense that they and their wives refuse to obey them.'

'That makes sense,' he said.

e 'Next, I suppose, everyone starts to look at everyone else with envy, and that becomes the normal attitude.'

'That's likely.'

'And then', I said, 'they get more and more involved in making money; and the higher they rate money, the lower they rate goodness. I mean, isn't the difference between wealth and goodness analogous to them each lying in one of the pans of a pair of scales and constantly tending in opposite directions?'

'It certainly is,' he said.

551a 'So if wealth and wealthy people are admired in a community, then goodness and good people are despised there.'

'Obviously.'

'Now, you cultivate what you admire, whatever it may be, and ignore what you despise.'

'Yes.'

'So eventually they stop being competitive and ambitious, and become acquisitive and mercenary instead. They acclaim and admire anyone rich, and make it easy for him to gain political power, but they despise anyone poor.'

'Yes.'

'They then enact the legislation which is the distinctive feature of an oligarchic political system, in which they ordain a certain amount of
b money—a larger amount if the oligarchy is more of an oligarchy, a smaller amount if it is less of one—and announce that only those whose property attains the ordained value shall play a part in government. They either use force of arms to get this legislation passed, or they've

地方——就会导致荣誉政体的垮台。你知道人们首先想方设法地挥霍金钱,还为此颠覆法律,他们和他们的妻子都拒不遵守法律。”

“说得有道理。”他说。

“接下来,我想,所有人都开始以嫉妒的目光看待任何别的 e
人,这成为了惯常态度。”

“这很有可能。”

“那么,”我说,“他们变得越来越深地陷于赚钱;他们越是看重金钱,就越是看轻善德。我的意思是说,财富与善德的区别,不就像是把它们各自放在天平的秤盘上,总是趋向不同的方向吗?”

“当然是的。”他说。

“所以如果财富和富人在城邦中受到尊重,那么善德和善德 551a
之人就在那里受到鄙视。”

“显然。”

“那么,你实践你所尊重的,而不管它是什么,忽视你所鄙视的。”

“是的。”

“所以他们最终会不再好胜并爱好荣誉,而是变得贪恋钱财。他们赞美并尊重富人,使他易于获得政治权力,而鄙视穷人。”

“是的。”

“那么他们就制定法律,这法律具有寡头政体的显著特征,它
规定了一定数量的金钱——寡头制程度越高的地方这个数额就 b
越大,寡头制程度越低的地方这个数额就越小——并且宣布只有那些财产达到规定数量的人才能从政。他们要么使用武力来使这

already used fear to make this kind of constitution a *fait accompli*. Do you agree?'

'Yes.'

'So that's more or less how it comes to be established.'

'Yes,' he said, 'but what kind of system is it? We said it was
c flawed—what are these flaws?'

'You should start by thinking about its distinctive feature,' I said. 'I mean, what do you think it would be like if ships' captains were appointed in this way, because of the value of their property, and poverty ruled someone out even if he was a better captain?'

'Then people would have terrible voyages,' he said.

'And does the same go for positions of authority in other spheres?'

'I'd say so.'

'Except political power?' I asked. 'Or does it also apply to political power?'

'It applies there above all,' he said, 'because it's the most dif-
d ficult and important kind of power there is.'

'That's the first major mistake oligarchy makes, then, apparently.'

'So it seems.'

'Well, here's another flaw, and I wonder if it's any less serious.'

'What is it?'

'That a community of this kind can't be single: it's inevitably divided into the haves and the have-nots. They may live in the same place, but they're constantly plotting against one another.'

'No, that's certainly just as serious a flaw,' he said.

'Another deplorable feature is that they'd probably be incapable of going to war against an enemy. They could either arm the populace at large, in order to use them in the war—but that would inevitably

项法律得以通过,要么使用恐吓来确立这种法律。你同意吗?”

“是的。”

“寡头制可以说是这样被建立起来的。”

“是的,”他说,“但这是一种什么样的制度?我们说它是有缺陷的——这些缺陷是什么呢?” c

“你应该先想想它明显的特征,”我说,“我的意思是说,你认为这是否像是通过这种方式来指派一个船长,就因为他们有钱有财,即使某人是一个较好的船长,他也因为财产而被排除在外了。”

“那么人们的航行就很可怕了。”他说。

“对于其他领域的权职也同样吗?”

“我想是这样的。”

“除了政治权力?”我问道,“或者也是适用于政治权力的?”

“它尤其适用于政治权力,”他说,“因为它是最困难并且是最重要的一类政治权力。”

“那么这显然是寡头制所做的第一个主要错误。” d

“看来是这样的。”

“那么,还有一个缺陷,我想知道它是否不那么严重。”

“是什么?”

“这样的城邦肯定不是单个的:它必定被分成有产者和无产者。他们可能生活在同一个地方,但他们常常相互算计对方。”

“这当然是一个严重的缺陷。”他说。

“另一个可悲的特点就是,他们可能去打仗反对敌人。或者他们为了进行战争而利用民众并大规模地武装他们——但那又

e give them more cause for fear than the enemy; or they could avoid using the populace, and then, when it came to actual fighting, they'd be revealed as true oligarchs! At the same time their mercenary nature makes them unwilling to levy a war-tax.'

'That's no good.'

'Then there's something we've been expressing disapproval of all
552a along—the fact that in this kind of political system people won't stick to a single occupation, but will be farmers, businessmen, and soldiers at the same time. Do you think that's the right way to go about things?'

'No, I certainly don't.'

'Now, would you agree that this is the first political system to admit the ultimate evil?'

'What are you getting at?'

'It's possible for someone to sell everything (and for someone else to acquire his property) and continue to live in the community without being one of its limbs—without being a businessman or a manufacturer, or in the cavalry or the heavy infantry. He'd be classified instead as impoverished and destitute.'

'Yes, this is the first system it could happen in,' he agreed.

b 'Anyway, that kind of thing isn't ruled out by an oligarchy, otherwise we wouldn't find both excessive affluence and utter poverty at the same time.'

'Right.'

'Now what do you think about this? Did the person we're imagining actually benefit his community in the respects we're considering while he was well off and was spending his money? Or is it true to say that he was only a pseudo-ruler, and that in reality he didn't rule over the community or serve it in any capacity, but merely consumed whatever he could lay his hands on?'

不可避免地成为他们害怕的更大的原因,更胜于害怕敌人;或 e
者他们不利用民众,那么当实际发生战争的时候,他们就成了真正的寡头了!同时他们贪恋金钱的本性使得他们不愿意支付战争税。"

"这不好。"

"有一些事情是我们一直反对的——在这样的政治制度中,
人们不会固守一个工作,而是同时既做农民、商人又做军人。你 552a
认为这种做事方式对吗?"

"我当然认为是不对的。"

"那么你是否同意这种政治制度是首先允许这最大的罪恶存在的呢?"

"你说的是什么意思?"

"一个人有可能卖光一切,别人可能获得他的财产,他还继续生活在城邦中而不作为其一部分——不是作为商人或手工匠人,也不是作为骑兵或步兵,而是作为一个穷困的人。"

"是的,这种情况可能最先发生在这个政治制度中。"他同意
说。 b

"无论如何,这样的事情不会为寡头制所排除,否则我们就不会同时发现极度的富裕和极度的贫穷了。"

"对。"

"那么关于这点你怎么想?我们所说的富人在花钱的时候,从我们所考察的几个方面看,可以认为这实际上有利于城邦吗?或者应该说他仅仅是一个假冒的统治者,实际上他并不统治城邦或具有任何服务于城邦的能力,而仅仅是消耗他能碰触到的任何东西?"

'Yes, that's right,' he said. 'He wasn't an authentic ruler: he
c was nothing but a consumer.'

'Shall we describe him as a drone, then?' I asked. 'His home is equivalent to the cell in a honeycomb where a drone is born, and he becomes the bane of his community as a drone becomes the bane of the hive.'

'I like that idea, Socrates,' he said.

'Now, the first variety of drones, Adeimantus—the ones with wings—have been denied stings by God. The second variety, however—the ones that go on foot—fall into two categories: some of them are stingless, but some have terrifying stings, don't they? The stingless ones end up in their old age as beggars, while everyone who's designated a criminal started life as one of the drones with stings.
d Yes?'

'True,' he said.

'It obviously follows,' I said, 'that any community where you can find beggars also has thieves, pickpockets, temple-robbers, and perpetrators of similar crimes concealed somewhere about the place.'

'Yes, obviously,' he agreed.

'Well, don't you find beggars in communities which are governed by oligarchies?'

e 'Yes,' he said, 'just about everyone except for the rulers!'

'Isn't the implication of what we're saying that these communities also contain plenty of criminals with stings,' I asked, 'who are deliberately and forcibly repressed by the authorities?'

'Yes, it is,' he said.

'And we're claiming that the presence of these criminals is a direct result of lack of education, bad upbringing, and a bad political system?'

'We are.'

'There you are, then. That's what a community is like when it's

“是的，这很对，”他说，“他并不是一个真正的统治者：他仅仅 c
是一个消费者。”

“那么我们是否可以称他为雄蜂？”我问道，“他的家相当于雄蜂出生的蜂窝，他变成了他城邦的祸害，就像雄蜂变成了蜂房的祸害。”

“苏格拉底，我喜欢这种说法。”他说。

“那么，阿狄曼图，神已经为第一类有翅膀的雄蜂去掉了螫针。然而第二类——用脚走路的那类——分为两种：他们当中有些是没有螫针的，但有些具有可怕的螫针，不是吗？那些没有螫针的人最后他们老了便成了乞丐，而任何专干坏事的人则开始过
一种有螫针的雄蜂生活。是吗？” d

“对的。”他说。

我说：“那么显然可以推论出，任何你能发现乞丐的城邦，在那里也必然掩藏着小偷、扒手、抢劫神庙的盗贼以及犯类似罪行的为非作歹的人。”

“是的，显然如此。”他同意说。

“那么，在由寡头统治的城邦中，你难道没有发现乞丐吗？”

“发现了，”他说，“除了统治者，我发现了所有人！” e

“这不就暗示我们所说的这些城邦也充满了带有螫针的罪犯，”我问道，“他们受到当权者的严密而严格的控制？”

“是的。”他说。

“我们说这些罪犯的出现是直接由缺乏教育、不良的培养以及坏的政治制度引起的？”

“我们可以这么说。”

“那么，当一个城邦由寡头统治的时候，就是这样的，那些就

governed by an oligarchy, and those are its major flaws—though there may be more.'

"That all sounds about right,' he said.

553a 'So much, then,' I concluded, 'for our description of the kind of political system which uses property value as a criterion for rulership, and which is called 'oligarchy'. Next, we'd better look at the background and nature of its human counterpart.'

'Yes.'

'The transition from a timocratic person to an oligarchic one invariably happens as follows, wouldn't you say?'

'How?'

'When a child is born to a timocratic man, he initially looks up
b to his father and follows in his footsteps. Later, however, he sees him suddenly wrecked on some political reef, and watches as his father and all his property are washed overboard. His father might have been a military commander or held some other important position, and then have ended up in court as a result of sycophants making trouble for him, and been put to death or exiled or deprived of his citizenship and had all his property confiscated.'

'Yes, that's not at all impossible,' he said.

'The effect of seeing and experiencing all this, Adeimantus, and
c of losing his property, is (I should think) that the son gets afraid and immediately tosses ambition and his passionate side headlong from the throne they'd been occupying in his mind. Laid low by poverty, he turns to tawdry commercial activities, and gradually accumulates wealth by thrift and hard work. Don't you think that under these circumstances he'd install his desirous and mercenary side on that throne? Don't you think he'd make it his internal equivalent of the Persian king, and deck it out with tiaras and necklaces and scimitars?'

'I do,' he said.

d 'While his rational and passionate aspects, I imagine, are made

是它主要的缺陷——虽然可能有更多。”

“所有这些听起来都很恰当。”他说。

我总结说:“那么我们对于这种政治制度的描述就到这里吧, 553a
这种政治制度把财产价值作为统治权的标准,这就叫做‘寡头制’。接下来,我们最好考察一下与此相应的人的背景和本性。”

“是的。”

“你难道不会说,从爱好荣誉的人到爱好钱财类型的人的转变,常常是这样发生的?”

“怎么样?”

“当一个爱好荣誉的人生了一个孩子的时候,这个孩子一开
始尊重他的父亲并效法他。然而,之后他看到他父亲突然在政治 b
上触了礁,并看到他父亲和他的所有财产统统落了空。他的父亲可能是一个军事将领或担任别的某个要职,而最后阿谀奉承之人找他麻烦,把他送上了法庭,或被处死,或被流放或剥夺公民身份,并且他的所有财产也被充公了。”

“是的,这是很有可能的。”他说。

“阿狄曼图,那个儿子看到并经历了这一切,失去了财产,我想其结果便会使他变得胆怯并马上动摇了在他们心目中占据皇
冠宝座的荣誉心和激情。他羞于贫穷,他转而从事华而不实的商 c
业活动,并渐渐地通过偷窃和苦干而积累了财富。你难道不认为在这些条件下,他会把欲望和贪恋金钱的那一部分奉为神圣?你难道不认为他会把它作为心中的波斯王,并用冠冕、项链和月形刀做装饰?”

“我是这么想的。”他说。

“我想他的理性和激情的部分被迫在王的脚下折节为奴。他 d

to sit on the ground on either side of the king's feet in abject servitude. The only calculations and researches he allows his rational mind to make are concerned with how to start with a little money and increase it, the only admiration and respect he allows his passionate side to feel are for wealth and wealthy people, and he restricts his ambition to the acquisition of money and to any means towards that end.'

'There's no transition so quick or so complete in its effects', he remarked, 'as when a young person becomes mercenary instead of ambitious.'

e 'So do you think we've found our oligarchic type?' I asked.

'Well, he does evolve from the type who corresponds to the political system from which oligarchy evolves.'

'Let's see if he has similar characteristics, then.'

'All right.'

554a 'The first point of similarity is the supreme value he places on money, wouldn't you say?'

'Of course.'

'Then there's the fact that he's thrifty and hard-working. He satisfies only those of his desires which are essential, and suppresses all the rest (he thinks they're pointless), so as not to incur any further expenses.'

'Yes.'

'He's rather ascetic,' I said. 'He tries to make a profit out of every situation, and he's a hoarder—an attribute which is commonly admired in people. Aren't these the characteristics of the person who
b corresponds to the political system we've been describing?'

'I'd say so,' he said. 'At any rate, money is the be-all and end-all for that community as well as for him.'

'It's because he never bothered about his education, I suppose,' I said.

'Yes. I think so,' he replied. 'Otherwise, he wouldn't have

允许他的理性的灵魂所做的唯一计算和研究,就是有关于如何开始赚钱致富,允许他的激情部分只尊重和敬慕财富和富人,他把他的荣誉心限于赚钱以及任何致富之道。”

他说:“一个青年变得贪财而不是变得爱好荣誉,在其效果上没有比这个转变更迅速或更彻底的了。”

“所以你是否认为我们已经找到了我们寡头类型的人?”我问 e
道。

“他确实是从与那种政治制度相对应类型的人转变而来,从那种政治制度中演变出寡头制。”

“那么让我们看看他是否具有类似的品性。”

“好吧。”

“第一个相似点就是他特别看重金钱,对吗?” 554a

“当然。”

“然后还有一点就是他很节俭和勤劳。他只满足自己基本的需要,压制其余所有他认为无益的欲望,这样就不至付出任何更多的代价。”

“是的。”

“他相当节制,”我说,“在每个场合他都试图获取利益,他是个囤积者——这个品性通常为人所称赞。这些人的品性不就与
我们已经描述过的政治制度相应吗?” b

“我想说是这样的,”他说,“无论如何,对于城邦和对于他来说,金钱就是最重要的东西。”

“我料想这是因为他从来就不为他的教育费过心思。”我说。

“是的,我想是这样的,”他回答说,“否则他就不会把盲人

thought so highly of a blind person and made him the leader of his troupe.'

'Good point,' I said. 'Now, what about this? Don't you think we should say that his lack of education engenders within him drone-
c like desires—some in the beggarly mode, some in the criminal mode—which are forcibly and deliberately repressed, on the whole?'

'I certainly do,' he replied.

'Do you know where you'll find these people behaving like criminals?' I asked.

'Where?' he asked.

'When they're entrusted with the guardianship of orphans, and when similar easy opportunities for wrongdoing come their way.'

'True.'

'This makes it clear that it's only because some remnant of decency makes them forcibly repress their evil desires that they have a reputation for fair dealing in other contexts. And they repress these desires not because they're convinced that they should, or because
d they've use reason to tame them, but because they have no choice and because they're afraid—afraid for the rest of their property. Do you agree?'

'Yes, definitely,' he said.

'But when it's a case of them spending someone else's money, Adeimantus,' I went on, 'then, I swear, the drone-like desires most of them contain will be exposed.'

'Yes,' he said, 'I couldn't agree more.'

'So internal conflict will characterize this kind of person: he isn't single, he's divided into two. His condition is simply that his

看得如此之高并把他作为演剧的主角。”

“说得好，”我说，“那么，这又怎么样呢？你难道不认为我们应该说，他的缺乏教育使他内心产生了雄蜂一样的欲望——有些如像乞丐，有些如像罪犯——总的来说，这些欲望还是受到严厉 c
而严密的压制？”

“我当然是这样想的。”他回答说。

“你可知道在哪里你会发现这些像罪犯一样行动的人吗？”我问道。

“在哪里呢？”他问。

“当他们受委托照看孤儿的时候，当有类似很容易犯罪的机会来到他们面前的时候。”

“对的。”

“这就清楚了，只是因为其心中某些残余的名节规矩，才使得他们强制性地压制住了他们罪恶的欲望，这样他们才会在其他场合有了公平交易的好名声。而他们压制这些欲望，并不是因为他 d
们确信他们应该这样做，或者是因为他们用理性驯服了这些欲望，而是因为他们别无选择，是因为他们害怕——害怕失去他们剩余的财产。你同意这样的说法吗？”

“是的，毫无疑问。”他说。

“阿狄曼图，当他们有机会花别人的钱的时候，”我继续说，“那么，我发誓，他们大多数人具有的雄蜂一般的欲望就会暴露出来。”

“是的，”他说，“我完全同意。”

“所以内心的冲突是这类人的典型特征：他不是单一的，而是分成两个。他的状况就是这样的，总的来说他较善的欲望控制着

e better desires by and large control his worse ones.'

'True.'

'That is why, in my opinion, although this sort of person gives a better impression than lots of people do, he still comes nowhere near true goodness, which requires mental unity and harmony.'

'I agree.'

'Moreover, because he's mean about money, he doesn't put
555a himself personally on the line and strive to win some political victory or generally to gain public recognition for good deeds. He's reluctant to spend money for the sake of prestige or for anything else like that which involves rivalry against others, because he's afraid of waking up desires which would require him to spend money and of summoning up their assistance in a competitive situation. So he fights in true oligarchic fashion, with just a few parts of himself, and he's usually defeated—but rich.'

'That's right,' he said.

'So we have no reason now to doubt the correspondence between
b a community governed by an oligarchy and a mean, mercenary type of person, do we?' I asked.

'None at all,' he said.

'Next, I suppose, we'd better try to see how democracy starts, and what its characteristics are once it exists. That will help us identify the corresponding individual, and then we can assess his merits, relative to those of the other types.'

'Yes, that would be in keeping with what we've been doing so far,' he said.

'Don't you think,' I said, 'that the transition from oligarchy to democracy is a result of people being insatiably greedy for what they've come to accept as good—that they ought to get as rich as they possibly can?'

'In what sense?'

他的较恶的欲望。” e

“对的。”

“在我看来,这就是为什么虽然这样的人给人的印象比很多人给人的印象要好,但他依然并不接近真正的善,这需要灵魂上的整一与和谐。”

“我同意。”

“此外,因为他对于金钱很吝啬,所以他并不敢付出代价去争取赢得某些政治上的胜利,或者说去获得大家对于善行的认可。 555a
他不情愿为了名誉而花钱,或在任何别的东西上花钱去参与反对别人的竞争,因为他担心激起要求他花钱的欲望,也担心在竞争的场合唤起它们的帮助。所以他仅仅拿出他的一小部分钱财进行寡头式战斗,他通常是被打败的——但却富有。”

“对的。”他说。

“所以我们现在没有理由去怀疑寡头制统治的城邦与吝啬、贪财的那种人是相对应的,是吗?” b

“毫不怀疑。”他说。

“接下来,我想,我们最好试图考察一下民主制是如何起源的,以及一旦它产生出来后所具有的品性。这可以帮助我们辨认出相应的个人,然后我们就可以联系那些别的类型以评判他的品格。”

“是的,这与我们目前所做的是一致的。”他说。

“你难道不认为,”我说,“从寡头制到民主制的转变就是由那些人造成,他们对那些他们认为是好的东西——他们应该尽可能地变富有——贪得无厌?”

“什么意思?”

c ‘The way I see it is that because political power within the community depends on the possession of wealth, the rulers aren't disposed to curb by legal means the undisciplined elements of the younger generation, to prevent them from spending their money and ruining their estates, because this enables them to buy up those estates and to loan money at interest, and so get even richer and gain even more public standing.’

‘Hhat's extremely plausible.’

‘We need no further evidence, then, for the impossibility of the citizen body of a community simultaneously rating affluence highly and
d being adequately self-disciplined: they are bound to neglect either one or the other.’

‘Yes, that's clear enough,’ he said.

‘Now, the negligent sanctioning of indiscipline which occurs within oligarchies has been known in the past to reduce men of some calibre to poverty.’

‘It certainly has.’

‘There they squat in the community, I imagine, equipped with their stings—and with weapons. Some are in debt, some have lost their citizenship, some are enduring both these hardships. In their hatred of the people who have acquired their property, they long for
e revolution, and plot against them and everyone else as well.’

‘True.’

‘But their targets, stooped businessmen that they are, appear not to notice. They continue to inject the venom of money into any remaining member of the community who submits to them, they continue to collect compound rates of interest, the offspring of the loan, and
556a they continue to fill the community with drones and beggars.’

‘Of course they do,’ he said.

‘Nor do they show any inclination to extinguish the blaze of this kind of trouble’, I went on, ‘by banning indiscriminate usage of

“我是这样理解的，因为城邦中的政治权力依靠所拥有的财 c
产，统治者就不愿意通过法律措施来阻止年轻一代中的不守法因素，不愿意阻止他们挥霍钱财，毁坏他们的产业，因为这能够使得他们购买那些产业并放贷款以收取利息，这样他们就变得愈加富有，得到更多的公众声誉。”

“这是很有可能的。”

“那么我们并不需要更多的证明来说明对于城邦中的公民团体来说，是不可能既看重富裕又充分自制：他们必定要么忽略这
个，要么忽略另一个。” d

“是的，这是足够明白的了。”他说。

“人们认为过去寡头制中对不守法的纵容已使某些有才能的人变得贫穷。”

“当然是这样的。”

“我想他们蹲在城邦中，以他们的螯针作为武器。有些人负债累累，有些人失去了公民身份，有些人遭受了这两种困苦。他们憎恨那些剥夺他们财产的人，他们渴望革命，并密谋反对那些
人，也反对其他每一个人。” e

“是的。”

“但是他们阴谋反对的目标，即那些卑躬屈膝的巨商富贾们，看起来好像并没有注意到这一点。他们继续将金钱带来的怨恨之毒液注入到城邦中被迫屈从他们淫威的其余成员的身中，他们继续驴打滚似的聚集金钱利息带来的暴利，那是借贷的产物，而
且他们还继续在城邦中增添无所依靠的懒汉及乞丐。” 556a

“他们确是这样做的。”他说道。

“而且他们也没有任何的意向表明”，我继续说，“他们愿意通

one's assets or by some alternative legislation which gets rid of behaviour of that sort.'

'What alternative legislation?'

'It's not as effective as the first option, but it does force the members of a community to cultivate goodness. I mean, if there were
b a rule to the effect that most categories of voluntary contract should be entered upon at the lender's own risk, then the pursuit of money within the community would become less shameless, and fewer evils of the kind we've been talking about would develop.'

'Considerably fewer,' he said.

'As things are, however,' I said, 'it's thanks to the rulers of the community—for all the kinds of reasons we've been describing—that their subjects are in the state they're in. Meanwhile, they make themselves and their families... well, their children never know what it's like to work, physically or mentally, so they become spoilt and too
c soft and lazy to resist pleasure and pain, don't they?'

'Of course.'

'And they themselves ignore everything except making money: there's nothing to tell between them and the poor in terms of how little attention they pay to goodness, is there?'

'No, there isn't.'

'So this is the basis on which the rulers and their subjects meet one another, as they walk in the streets or come together under any circumstances—for a show, say, or as fellow sailors or fellow soldiers on a campaign. Even in the teeth of danger, they eye one another; but there's
d no way that the poor are despised by the rich in this situation. Poor people tend to be lean and sun-tanned, and when they stand in the battle-line next to the rich with their indoor pallor and plentiful extra flesh, they notice their breathlessness and utter ineptitude. Don't you think they'll conclude that it's their own cowardice that has allowed the rich to get rich, and they'll get together in private and tell one another,
e "They're ours for the taking. There's nothing to them"?'

过禁止财产自由处置,或者通过颁布可替代前办法的法令,来熄灭这团烦乱的烈焰啊。"

"什么可替代的法令呢?"

"它没有前一种方法有效,但它也能迫使城邦中的成员去培养善德。我的意思是说,如果有一条规定,通过它做到,大多数种类的非官定契约,其风险由贷方自己承担,那么城邦中嗜金如命而不知羞耻的风气就会变得较少,而我们刚才谈论过的诸种罪恶也就少有增长。"

"会少很多的。"他说。

"然而在目前情况下,由于城邦统治者的原因——由于我们说过的所有原因——他们的臣民就处于这样的状态之中。同时,他们使自己和他们的家人……生活优越,他们的孩子从不知道体力和心灵的工作是什么样的,这样他们被宠坏了,过于软弱、懒惰而不能抵制快乐和痛苦,不是吗?" c

"当然。"

"他们自己除了赚钱,其余的一概不管:从他们很少注意善德这一点上来说,他们与穷人没有什么区别,是吗?"

"是没什么区别。"

"所以这便是一个基础,在其上,统治者和他们的被统治者相遇,无论当他们在街上还是在任何别的情况下的集会——比如说参加庆典或同是水手或同是行军中战士。甚至在抗拒危险当中,他们彼此相视;在这种场合穷人绝不会被富人看不起。穷人大都 d
是消瘦而黧黑的,而当他们站在战斗队列中,旁边是富家子弟,因不惯户外运动而脸色苍白,身上堆着胖嘟嘟的赘肉,穷人还注意到他们气喘吁吁,简直连话都说不出来。你难道不认为他们会得出结论说,正是由于他们自己的怯懦才让富人变得富有,他们私下聚会的时候也会相互说:'他们是依靠穷人的。他们什么都没有'?" e

'I'm sure that's what they do,' he said.

'Now, it takes only a slight external influence to push an unhealthy body towards illness, and sometimes nothing external need be involved at all for the body's elements to start fighting one another. Likewise, a community which is in a similarly unhealthy state needs only a slight pretext—one party might bring in reinforcements from an external oligarchy, or the other from an external democracy—to fall ill and start fighting with itself, and sometimes no external influence at all is needed for conflict to begin. Do you agree?'

557a 'Definitely.'

'So democracy starts, in my opinion, when the poor members of the community are victorious. They kill some of the rich, they expel others, and they give everyone who's left equal social and political rights: in a democratic system governmental posts are usually decided by lot.'

'Yes,' he said, 'that's how democracy is founded, but it might not involve force of arms: fear might have been used to drive their enemies away.'

b 'All right,' I said, 'but what kind of constitution is it? What's a democratic political system actually like? I mean, this is how we'll learn about the corresponding democratic individual, obviously.'

'Obviously,' he agreed.

'Well, in the first place, the members of the community are autonomous, aren't they? The community is informed by independence and freedom of speech, and everyone has the right to do as he chooses, doesn't he?'

'That's the claim, anyway,' he answered.

'And given this right, then clearly every individual can make for himself the kind of life which suits him.'

'Clearly.'

c 'I should think, then, that there'd be a wider variety of types

“我确信他们会这么做的。”他说。

“在这些情况中,就像一个不健康的身体,只要一点点外在的影响,就会使之生起病来,而有时候还并不需要什么外在因素的参与,身体的各个部分就开始彼此违和了。同样,处于类似不健康状态的城邦只需一个小小的借口——一个党派可能从寡头制外部引进支援,另一个党派可能从民主制外部引进支援——城邦就生病了并且开始内战,有时完全不需要外部的影响就会产生冲突。你同意吗?”

“当然同意。” 557a

“所以在我看来,当城邦中的穷人胜利的时候,民主制就产生了。他们杀死一些富人,并把其余的敌人驱逐出去,他们赋予所有剩下的人以同等的社会和政治权力:在民主制中,官职通常是由抽签决定的。”

“是的,”他说,“民主制就是这样建立起来的,它可能并不使用军事力量:通常可能使用恐吓把他们的敌人赶走。”

“对的,”我说,“但这是一种什么样的制度呢?民主政体通常 b
是什么样子的呢?我的意思是说,很显然,我们知道与民主制相对应的个人就是这样的。”

“显然是的。”他同意说。

“那么首先,城邦中的成员是自主的,不是吗?城邦的特征不就是独立和言论自由并且每个人有权做他想做的事情,不是吗?”

“总之,应该是这么说的。”他回答说。

“如果是这样的话,那么每个人为自己选择那种适合于他的生活方式。”

“显然。”

“那么,我应该认为比起任何别的社会,这个社会具有更加多 c

of people in this society than in any other. '

'Of course there would. '

'It's probably the most gorgeous political system there is,' I continued. 'Its beauty comes from the fact that it is adorned with every species of human trait, as a cloak might be adorned with every species of flower. And I suppose', I added, 'that plenty of people would find it highly attractive, just as women and children are attracted by the sight of colourful variety. '

'Yes, a great many would,' he said.

d 'It's a good place to look for a constitution, Adeimantus, as well,' I said.

'Why?'

'Because it's so open that it contains every type of political system there is. For anyone wanting to construct a community, as we were a short while ago, a visit to a democratically governed community is essential, to help him choose the kind he likes. It's a sort of general store for political systems: you can visit it, make your choice, and then found your community. '

e 'Yes, I suppose it would be easy to find samples,' he said.

'You're not forced to hold political office in this kind of community,' I said, 'even if you'd be good at it; you're not forced to be a subject either, unless you want to. You don't have to go to war when there's a war on, or to keep the peace when everyone else is, if peace isn't to your liking. Then again, even if you're legally forbidden to
558a play a part in governmental or judicial procedures, you can still do both, if you feel like it. Isn't this an extraordinarily pleasant way to spend one's life, in the short term?

'Yes, probably,' he said, 'but not in the long term'

'And what about the exquisite calmness of some condemned criminals? I'm sure it's within your experience of this kind of society how people who've been sentenced to death or exile still stay on and

样类型的人。”

“当然有更多的类型。”

“这可能是最绚丽多彩的政治制度了，”我继续说，“它的美来自于这样一个事实，就像各种不同的花装点着衣服，各种不同人的品性装点着城邦。我想，”我补充说，“很多人会觉得这非常吸引人，就像女人和孩子受到色彩斑斓的景象吸引一样。”

“是的，有很多人会这样想。”他说。

“阿狄曼图，这里也是寻找一种制度的好地方。”我说。 d

“为什么？”

“因为这里非常开放，包含各种各样的政治制度。对于任何想要建立一个城邦的人来说，就像我们不久前一样，考察一下民主式管理的城邦是必要的，以帮助他选择喜欢的那一种。这是政治制度的大市场：你可以去看看，做出你的选择，然后再建立你的城邦。”

“是的，我想会很容易就找到一个样板的。”他说。 e

“你并不是被迫在这种城邦中担任官职的，”我说，“即使你会很擅长做官；你也并不是被迫作为被统治者的，除非你愿意。当战争发生的时候，你也不必参战，或者所有别的人处在和平的时候，你可以不必保持和平，如果和平不为你所喜欢的话。同样，如果你即使在法律上不许你参与管理或审判程序，如果你喜欢，你依旧可以参与两者。简而言之，以这种方式生活不是非常快乐 558a
吗？”

“也许是的，”他说，“但长远看来却不是。”

“那么某些被判了刑的罪犯满不在乎的样子又怎么样呢？我确信你对这样的社会肯定有些经验：那些已经被判死刑或流放

go about their daily business in full view of everyone. No one cares or notices as they roam around, as invisible as the dead.'

'Yes, this is not uncommon,' he said.

b 'One could hardly call this system's attitude towards the principles we took seriously when we were founding our community pedantic—"flexible" and "high-handed" would be more accurate. We said that no one could be good (short of having been born with really exceptional talents), unless even his childhood games had taken place within a good environment and his way of life had been the same. This political system, however, arrogantly spurns all of that, and doesn't care what kinds of provenance people had before coming to
c government; as long as someone claims to be sympatheti to the general populace, he is honoured within this political system.'

'A very vulgar way of going about things,' he commented.

'So these are democracy's features—these and others like them,' I said. 'It looks as though it's an enjoyable, lax, and variegated kind of political system, which treats everyone as equal, whether or not they are.'

'Yes, this is all perfectly familiar,' he said.

'Now, what do you think the corresponding private individual is like?' I asked. 'I suppose we'd better start by considering his background, as we did in the case of the political system.'

'Yes,' he said.

'Here's my idea. Any son born to that mean, oligarchic charac-
d ter would, I imagine, be brought up by his father to behave in the same way.'

'Naturally.'

'So he too would forcibly control his desires for any pleasures which involve spending money rather than making it—that is, for the pleasures which have been classified as unnecessary.'

'Obviously he would,' he agreed.

'Shall we start by defining what we mean by necessary and unne-

的人还继续留在城邦里，在所有人眼前从事他们平常的工作。没有人看到或在意他们，他们就像看不见的亡灵一样在漫游。”

“是的，这并没有什么不寻常的。”他说。

“人们几乎不能把这种制度对待我们建立城邦时庄严提出的 b
原则之态度称作是迂腐的——‘灵活’和‘专横’可能更加准确。我们说若是天生确实缺乏极好的天赋，那么没有人可以成为善人，除非他在一个好的环境中参加儿童游戏并且同样生活在一个好的环境当中。然而这种政治制度傲慢地摒弃所有这些，并且也不关心从事管理的人之前是来源于哪一种类型；一个人只要宣称
对人民大众抱有好感，那么他就在这种政治制度中受到尊重。” c

“这种做事方式是非常粗俗的。”他评论说。

“所以这些和其他类似的特点就是民主制的特征，”我说，“这看起来像是令人愉悦的、松散而花哨的政治制度，它平等地对待所有人，无论他们是否平等。”

“是的，大家对此都很熟悉。”他说。

“那么你认为相应的个人是什么样子的？”我问道，“我想我们最好先来考察一下他的背景，就像我们在考察政治制度时一样。”

“是的。”他说。

“我的想法是这样的：我想吝啬的寡头人物生的儿子被他父
亲抚养大，其行为方式也和他父亲一样。” d

“自然。”

“所以他也会竭力控制住他对快乐的欲望，这关涉到花钱而不是赚钱——即那些被认为是不必要的快乐。”

“他显然会这样的。”他同意说。

“那么，我们是否一开始就要定义必要和不必要的欲望指的

cessary desires, then?' I asked. 'We don't want our conversation to be shrouded in obscurity.'

'Yes, let's,' he replied.

e 'Wouldn't it be right to describe as necessary any desires which we're incapable of stopping, and any whose satisfaction is beneficial to us? I mean, both these categories of desire are essential to human nature, wouldn't you say?'

'Definitely.'

559a 'We'd be right to think of them in terms of necessity, then.'

'Yes.'

'What about desires which can be dispensed with (given training from childhood onwards) and whose presence certainly does no good, and may even do harm? Wouldn't we be right to call them unnecessary?'

'Yes, we would.'

'Shall we find an example of each type, so that we can get a rough idea of their nature?'

'We'd better.'

'Don't you think the desire for eating (provided it doesn't go be-
b yond what's required for a healthy physical condition), the desire simply for bread and savouries, is a necessary one?'

'Yes, I do.'

'In fact, the desire for bread is necessary in both senses: it's beneficial, and it's impossible for a living creature to stop it.'

'Yes.'

'Whereas the desire for savouries is necessary only as an aid towards physical fitness.'

'Yes.'

是什么？”我问道，“我们不想我们的讨论被笼罩在模糊之中。”

“是的，就让我们这样做吧。”他回答说。

“我们不是可以恰当地把任何我们不能阻止的欲望以及任何
满足了对我们有益的欲望称作的必要的吗？我的意思是说，你难 e
道不会说这两类欲望是人性所需要的吗？”

“毫无疑问会这样说。”

“那么我们从必要性来思考它们，就是对的。” 559a

“是的。”

“有些欲望是可以消除的（从孩童之前就加以训练的话），而且有这些欲望肯定没什么好事，甚至还可能带来危害，这些欲望又怎么样呢？我们不就可以恰当地称它们为不必要的吗？”

“是的，我们可以。”

“我们是否要为每一种找个例子，这样对于它们的本性就能有一个大致的概念？”

“我们最好这样做。”

“要是食欲并不超出一个健康身体所要求的，那么你难道
不认为食欲以及单纯的对于面包和美食的欲望也是必要的
吗？” b

“是的，我是这样想的。”

“实际上，对于面包的欲望在两种意义上都是必要的：它是有益的，并且生物是不可能阻挡这欲望的。”

“是的。”

“然而仅仅有助于身体健康而言，对于美食的欲望也是必要的。”

“是的。”

'What about the desire for more food than this, however, or for a varied diet? It can usually be eliminated by the habit of restraint, learnt young in life, and it's harmful to both the body and the mind
c (in the context of intelligence and self-discipline), so we wouldn't be wrong to call it unnecessary, would we?'

'No, that would be perfectly correct.'

'Shall we say that unnecessary desires involve spending money, while necessary desires help one work and therefore make money?'

'Of course.'

'And doesn't the same principle apply to the desire for sex, and desire in general?'

'Yes.'

'So, to put this in the context of a distinction we drew earlier, the type of person we've been calling a drone is overflowing with these pleasures and desires, and is ruled by the unnecessary ones, whereas
d the mean, oligarchic type is ruled by the necessary ones. Right?'

'No doubt about it.'

'Let's return, then, to the transition from the oligarchic type to the democratic one,' I said. 'It seems to me that it invariably happens as follows.'

'How?'

'When a young person, whose upbringing has been as uncultured and mean as we were saying a short while ago, tastes the drones' honey and starts to associate with ferocious, dangerous beasts who are capable of arranging for him pleasures of every conceivable kind, form, and description—that, I suggest, is how the transition begins
e from an internal oligarchic state to a democratic one.'

'It's almost inevitable,' he said.

'Now, we found that the transition occurs at a political level when one party is helped by like-minded reinforcements from outside. In the same way, doesn't our young man change when one of

“那么对于比这更多食物的欲望或对于各种菜的欲望呢？这通常通过年轻时学习的节制习惯而得以去除，它对身体和灵魂中的理性和自制力都是有害的，所以我们称它为‘不必要’是不会错的，是吗？” c

“是不会错，这样说非常正确。”

“我们是否要说不必要的欲望包括花钱，而必要的欲望帮助人们工作，由此有助于他们赚钱？”

“当然。”

“同样的原则不也适用于性欲和一般的欲望吗？”

“是的。”

“所以把这个放到他们之前所做的区分中来看，我们称之为雄蜂类型的人充满了这些快乐和欲望，他们被不必要的欲望支配着，而吝啬的寡头类型的人被必要的欲望支配着。对吗？” d

“毫无疑问。”

“那么，让我们回来看看从寡头式的人物向民主式的人物的转变，”我说，“在我看来是这样发生的。”

“怎样？”

“当一个年轻人所受的教育是我们不久前说过的那种没教养而又吝啬的教育时，他尝到了游手好闲的甜头，而且开始与那些凶恶而危险的人面兽心的家伙们为伍，他们能够为他安排每一种 e
可以想象到的花样百出的享乐——我这么看，他内心主张寡头政治的思想向主张民主政治的思想的转变，就是这样开始的。”

“这几乎是不可避免的。”他说。

“现在我们发现了当一个党派得到外部同情者的支援，这时城邦就发生变动。以同样的方式，当我们年轻人的某个部分受到

his aspects is supported from outside by desires of the same persuasion and breed?'

'Absolutely.'

'And if his oligarchic aspect is reinforced in response to this threat, as a result of his being scolded and ticked off by his father or
560a by the rest of his relatives, I should think the upshot would be conflict and counter-conflict, an internal civil war.'

'Of course it would.'

'Sometimes, I imagine, the democratic aspect is routed by the oligarchic aspect, and some of his desires are killed or expelled. This happens when inhibitions are implanted in the young man's mind, and he puts his life in order again.'

'Yes, that sometimes happens,' he said.

'Then later, I suppose, the father's ignorance of how to bring up
b his child leads to other desires, of the same breed as the exiled ones, growing up and becoming plentiful and powerful.'

'Yes, that tends to happen,' he said.

'They draw him back to his old associates, and these secret liaisons result in the birth of a horde of them.'

'Of course.'

'In the end, I suppose, they seize the fortress in the young man's mind and find it deserted: it holds no information of value, no sound habits and true ideas—none of the sentinels and guardians which best protect the minds of men who find favour in God's sight.'

c 'Yes, they are by far the best,' he agreed.

'So false and specious ideas and thoughts charge up the hill and occupy the young man's fortress instead of these sentinels.'

'I'm sure you're right,' he said.

外部具有同样追求的欲望的支援和培养时,他不就变化了?”

“毫无疑问。”

“如果由于受到他父亲或别的亲戚的指责和告诫,他的寡头性一面通过这种威胁而得到了加强,那么我应该认为结果会是一 560a
场内心的斗争,冲突与压制冲突。”

“当然会是这样的。”

“有时我认为民主性方面会屈服于寡头性方面,他的一些欲望被抹杀或驱逐了。当禁令重新植根于年轻人心灵的时候,他的生活又恢复了秩序。”

“是的,有时会发生。”他说。

“那么之后,我想他父亲疏忽了如何教育孩子,这导致另外的
欲望,与那些被驱逐的欲望是同一类,它们成长起来并增多增 b
强。”

“是的,这有可能发生。”他说。

“它们把他拉回到他的老伙伴那里,这些秘密关系导致一大堆欲望的产生。”

“当然。”

“最后,我想,它们把年轻人心灵中的堡垒占领了并发现里面空无一物:没有有价值的知识,没有良好的习惯,没有真正的理想——这样的哨兵和卫士一个都没有,它们是神所宠爱之人的心灵的最好保护人。”

“是的,它们是最好的。”他同意说。 c

“所以错误虚假、似是而非的观念与思想乘虚而入,并替代了这些守卫者而占据了年轻人的心灵堡垒。”

“我确信你说得对。”他说。

'Then he returns to those lotus-eaters and lives with them openly. If his relatives send reinforcements for the mean part of his mind, those specious ideas shut the gates of the royal fortress within him. Not only do they not let these reinforcements in, but they also refuse to
d accept any mediation by older people from outside the family. Once they've won the war, they denounce inhibition as simple-mindedness, deprive it of rights, and send it out into exile; they call self-control "cowardice", drag its name in the gutter, and then expel it; they perpetuate the view that moderation shows lack of style and that frugality is stinginess, and then, with the help of a horde of futile desires, they banish them beyond their borders.'

'They certainly do.'

'Once they've taken over the mind of the neophyte, and purged
e and purified it for the great mysteries, they next waste no tune before recalling from exile insubordination, disorder, extravagance, and uninhibitedness. They parade them in glory, with chaplets on their heads and with a full complement of attendants. They sing the praises of these qualities and gloss over their true nature: they call insubordination "erudition", disorder "freedom", extravagance "magnifi-
561a cence", and uninhibitedness "courage". Isn't this,' I asked, 'more or less how a young person exchanges conditioning by necessary desires for the permissiveness and laxity of unnecessary, futile pleasures?'

'Yes, you've explained it very well,' he said.

'From then on, I imagine, he spends as much money, effort, and time in his life on unnecessary pleasures as on necessary ones. With luck, however—and if he doesn't overdo the high life—and if, when he's older and the main disturbance has passed, he allows the
b exiles back to some extent and doesn't succumb utterly to the invaders, then he finds a way of life which involves a balance of pleasures. He submits to every passing pleasure as its turn comes to hold office, as it were, until it has been satisfied, and then submits to the next one, and so on. He doesn't deprive any pleasure of its rights, but

“然后他回到那些吃忘忧果(落拓枣)的人当中去,公开地和他们生活在一起。如果他的亲人为他心灵中的节俭部分增援,那么这些错误虚伪的思想就会在他里面关上心灵王国堡垒的城门。它们不光不让援军进入,也拒绝来自家族之外老人的任何调解。
一旦它们赢得战争,它们就会把禁令贬斥为头脑简单,剥夺其权 d
力并把它驱逐出去:它们将自制称为‘怯懦’,将自制之名拖入粗俗肮脏的阴沟中肆意凌辱,然后将其驱逐;它们视以下观念为永恒的思想,即适度是不够体面的表现,而节俭是小气,于是在一群琐细欲望的帮助下,它们将适度、节俭等美德都驱逐出境。”

“他们当然是这样做的。”

“一旦它们接管了新归入者的灵魂,并且为了伟大的神话它们将
灵魂清空扫净,接下来,它们便马不停蹄地召回流放在外的傲慢、放 e
纵、奢侈和无耻。它们在容光中游行,头上戴着花冠,站满了观看者。它们赞美这些品性并掩饰他们真正的本性:它们把傲慢称作‘博学’,把放纵称作‘自由’,把奢侈称作‘慷慨’,把无耻称作‘勇敢’。不是这样吗,”我问道,“或多或少地,一个年轻人就是这样从受必要欲望所支配,而改换为被不必要的、无益的快乐的恣意享受所支配的吗?”

“是的,你已经解释得很清楚了。”他说。

“我想,从此以后他会把一生的金钱、精力和时间都花在不必要的享乐上,与花在必要快乐上的一样多。然而,幸运的话——如果他做得不是太过分的话——如果当他老了的时候摆脱了主
要的烦扰,那么他就会让被驱逐者在一定程度上得以返回,不会 b
完全屈从于入侵者,然后他就会找到一种生活方式,它包含了各种快乐的平衡。可以这么说,他屈从于每个瞬间即逝的欲望的轮流执政,直到它满足得到为止,然后再屈从于下一个欲望,如此等

tends all of them equally.'

'Yes.'

'And', I continued, 'he refuses to listen to—to let into his fortress—the truth of the idea that there are differences between pleas-
c ures. Some are the result of fine, good desires, and these are worth cultivating and valuing; but some are the result of bad desires, and these are to be curbed and kept down. He denies this, however, and insists that they are all alike and of equal value.'

'Yes, I quite agree,' he said. 'That's his attitude, and that's what he does.'

'So that's how he lives,' I said. 'He indulges in every passing desire that each day brings. One day he gets drunk at a party, the next day he's sipping water and trying to lose weight; then again, he
d sometimes takes exercise, sometimes takes things easy without a care in the world, and sometimes he's apparently a student of philosophy. At frequent intervals, he gets involved in community affairs, and his public speaking and other duties keep him leaping around here, there, and everywhere. If military types arouse his admiration, he inclines towards the military life; if it's businessmen, he's all for business. His lifestyle has no rhyme or reason, but he thinks it enjoyable, free, and enviable and he never dispenses with it.'

e 'You've given a perfect description of an egalitarian,' he said.

'Yes,' I said, 'and I think he's also multi-hued and multi-faceted, as gorgeous and varied a patchwork as that community is. His way of life can be admired by many men and women, because he contains examples of so many political systems and walks of life.'

'Yes, he does,' he agreed.

562a 'I suggest, then, that we designate this type of individual the counterpart to democracy and assume that we'd be correct to call him the democratic type.'

'I agree,' he said.

'All that's left for us to do, then,' I said, 'is describe the

等。他并不剥夺任何快乐的权力，而是平等地对待它们。”

“是的。”

“并且，”我继续说，“他不认为有不同的快乐这种说法的真实性，他也不打开他的堡垒。有些来于自好的，善的欲望，这些值得培养和 c 赞赏；而有些来自于坏的欲望，这些要加以束缚和压抑。然而他否认这些，却还坚持说它们都是类似的并且具有同等的价值。”

“是的，我非常同意，”他说，“这就是他的态度和所作所为。”

“所以他就是这样生活的，”我说，“他沉溺于每天带来的一次又一次的如过眼云烟般的渴求之中。今天他聚众酗酒，明天他又会去喝清水而设法减肥；然而又是这样，有时锻炼身体，有时游手好 d 闲，有时似乎又研究起哲学来。他经常参加城邦的事务，由于公共演说和别的任务，这使他跳到这儿跳到那儿，所有地方都走遍。如果军人引起他的仰慕，他就喜欢军事化的生活；如果商人引起他的仰慕，那么他就去做商人。他的生活方式没有节奏、缺乏理性，但他认为这种生活是令人愉悦的、自由的、令人羡慕的，他决不会将之摒弃。”

“你对平等主义者做了非常好的描述。”他说。 e

“是的，”我说，“我想他也是多姿多彩、八面玲珑的人，如同那种城邦一样，像是一个华丽而多样的大杂烩。他的生活方式受到很多男女的仰慕，因为他包含了如此多样的政治制度和生活方式的样板。”

“是的，他确实包含了那么多样板。”他同意说。

“那么我认为我们可以把这样的个人与城邦相对应起来，并 562a 且我们可以正确地称他为民主政治的典型代表。”

“我同意。”他说。

“对于我们来说，所有剩下要去做的，”我说道，“就是描述最

political system and the individual which are the ultimate in excellence—dictatorship and the dictator.'

'Exactly,' he said.

'All right, then. How does dictatorship begin, Adeimantus? I mean, apart from the fact that we can be pretty certain that it evolves out of democracy.'

'Yes, that's clear.'

b 'I wonder whether dictatorship evolves out of democracy in more or less the same way that democracy evolves out of oligarchy.'

'How is that?'

'There is something', I said, 'which the members of an oligarchy have come to accept as good, and which is the *raison d'être* of oligarchy. This is wealth, isn't it?'

'Yes.'

'And it is insatiable greed for wealth—being too busy making money to pay attention to anything else—which causes its downfall, we found.'

'True,' he said.

'So what I'm wondering is whether democracy's downfall is also brought about by insatiable greed for what it defines as good.'

'What's that, do you think?'

'Freedom,' I replied. 'I'm sure you've been in a community with a democratic government and heard them claim that there is nothing finer than freedom, and that this is why democracy is the only suitable environment for a free man.'

'Yes, one hears the claim repeatedly,' he said.

'so, to complete the question I was about to ask a moment ago,' I said, 'is it insatiable greed for freedom and neglect of everything else which causes this political system to change and creates the need for dictatorship?'

'How would it do that?' he asked.

完善的政治制度和最完善的个人——僭主制和僭主。”

“正是。”他说。

“那么好吧。阿狄曼图,僭主制是如何起源的?我的意思是说,显然,我们确信它是从民主制演化而来。”

“是的,那很显然。”

“我想知道僭主制从民主制演化而来的方式是否多多少少地与民主制从寡头制演化而来的方式相似。” b

“怎么相似?”

我说:“寡头制中的成员把某些东西当作善,这也是寡头制存在的理由。这就是财富,不是吗?”

“是财富。”

“我们认为对财富的无止境的贪求——过分地忙于赚钱而不顾任何别的事情——导致了它的垮台。”

“对的。”他说。

“所以我们想知道的是,民主制的垮台也是对那些被认为是善的东西的无止境地贪求造成的。”

“你认为那是什么?”

“自由,”我回答说,“我确信你肯定去过民主式管理的城邦并听到过他们说没有什么比自由更好的了,这就是为什么民主制是 c
唯一适合于自由人的环境的原因。”

“是的,多次听到过这种说法。”他说。

“所以,说完我刚才想问的问题吧,”我说,“对自由的无止境的贪求,忽视了所有别的东西,这导致了这种政治制度的变动并造成了对专制的需要,是不是呢?”

“这是怎么回事呢?”他问道。

'In its thirst for freedom, a democratically governed community
d might get leaders who aren't any good at serving wine. It gets drunk on excessive quantities of undiluted freedom, and then, I suppose, unless the rulers are very lenient and keep it provided with plenty of freedom, it accuses them of being foul oligarchs and punishes them.'

'Yes,' he agreed, 'that's what it does.'

'Then those who obey authority have abuse heaped on them,' I said, 'and are described as voluntary slaves, nonentities; admiration and respect are given to people who, in both their private life and in public, behave like subjects if they're rulers, and behave like rulers if they're subjects. isn't it inevitable that a community of this kind will
e take freedom as far as it can go?'

'Of course.'

'Equally inevitably, my friend,' I said, 'lawlessness seeps into everyone's homes; ultimately, even animals are infected.'

'Can you explain this for us?' he asked.

'For instance,' I said, 'the pursuit of freedom makes it increasingly normal for fathers and sons to swap places: fathers are afraid of their sons, and sons no longer feel shame before their parents or stand in awe of them. And it starts to make no difference whether one is a citizen or a resident alien, or even a visitor from abroad: everyone is
563a at the same level.'

'Yes, that happens,' he said.

'Those are the most important cases,' I said, 'but there are others. In these circumstances, for example, teachers are afraid of their pupils and curry favour with them, while pupils despise their teachers and their attendants as well. In short, the younger generation starts to look like the older generation, and they turn any conversation or action into a trial of strength with their elders; meanwhile, the older members of the community adapt themselves to the younger ones,
b ooze frivolity and charm, and model their behaviour on that of the young, because they don't want to be thought disagreeable tyrants.'

“对于自由的渴望会使一个民主式管理的城邦让某些根本不善于祭酒之人当上领导人。我想城邦喝了过多的浓烈的自由之 d
酒会醉倒,除非统治者们非常仁慈并提供充分的自由,否则他们会被指责为愚蠢的寡头并惩罚他们。”

“是的,”他同意说,“就是这样的。”

我说:“而那些服从权威的人受到侮辱并且被说成是甘心为奴、一文不值;如果统治者表现得像被统治者,而被统治者表现得像统治者,人们就会对于这些在公共和私人生活中都如此这般的人给予仰慕和尊重。这样的城邦不就必然会把自由推向极端?” e

“当然。”

“我的朋友,”我说:“无法纪必定还同样渗透到每个人的家里去;最终甚至还影响到动物。”

“你能给我们解释一下吗?”他问道。

“比如说,”我说,“对自由的追求使父亲与儿子交换地位越来越正常:父亲害怕他的儿子,在父母面前儿子也不再感到羞愧或敬畏。公民或外来的居住者甚至外来的来访者之间开始没有什么区别了:所有人都是同等的。” 563a

“是的,事实是这样的。”他说。

“这些是最主要的情况,”我说,“然而还有别的情况。比如说在这样的情况下,老师害怕他们的学生并讨好他们,而学生也鄙视他们的老师以及他们的保育员。简而言之,年轻一代开始充当长辈,他们竭力与老一辈分庭抗礼;同时城邦中的老者顺着年轻人,表现得轻浮和具有魅力,模仿年轻人的行为,因为他们不想被 b
认为是讨厌的专制者。”

'Right,' he said.

'The peak of popular freedom for this community is reached', I continued, 'when male and female slaves have as much freedom as the people who bought them. And I almost forgot to mention the extent to which men and women meet as autonomous equals.'

c 'Why don't we just do what Aeschylus suggests,' he said, 'when he asks, "Shall we voice what we were poised to say?"'

'All right,' I said. 'This is what I have to say. If you hadn't seen it, you'd never believe how much more freedom pets have in this community compared with any other. The dogs really do start to resemble their mistresses, as the proverb says, but so do horses and donkeys as well, in the way they learn to strut about with absolute freedom, bumping into anyone they meet on the road who doesn't get
d out of the way. And everything else is just as saturated with freedom.'

'You're telling me my own dream,' he said. 'I often experience just that on my way out of town.'

'Taking all this into consideration,' I said, 'the long and short of it is that the minds of the citizens of a democracy become so sensitive that they get angry and annoyed at the slightest hint of enslavement. Do you know what I mean? And they're so worried about the possibility of anyone having authority over them that they end up, as
e I'm sure you're aware, taking no notice of the laws either, whether written or unwritten.'

'Yes, I'm well aware of that,' he said.

'So there, I think,' I said, 'you have the fine, vigorous shoot from which dictatorship grows.'

'No one could deny its vigour,' he said. 'But what's the next stage?'

'The same sickness that infected oligarchy and caused its demise', I said, 'erupts in democracy too, but in a more widespread and virulent form, because of its openness, and reduces it to slavery. In fact, it's a general principle that overdoing anything leads to a huge compensatory shift towards the opposite: seasons, plants, and bodily health are all subject to this principle, and political systems are par-

“对的。”他说。

我继续说:“当男女奴隶与购买他们的人一样具有自由的时候,民众的自由在这个城邦就达到了顶峰。噢,我几乎忘了提一下,在这种范围内男女都能得到自主平等。”

“我们为什么不像埃斯库罗斯所说的那样,”他说,“他问道, c
‘我们是否可以畅所欲言?’”

“好吧,”我说,“这就是我想要说的。如果你没有亲眼目睹过,那么你决不会相信这个城邦中的宠物都要比其任何别的城邦中的宠物自由地多。就像谚语说的那样,狗确实开始像和它们的主人一样了,马和驴也同样,它们学会毫无顾忌地大摇大摆地走
路,遇到挡路的人它们就撞上去。别的一切都充满了自由。” d

“你向我讲述的是我的梦境,”他说,“我在城外路上常常遇到。”

“总起来考虑,”我说道,“概括的意思是,民主制下公民的思想变得如此敏感,只要有一点点被奴役强制的迹象,他们就会愤怒、焦躁。你知道我说的是什么吗?我确信你意识到了,他们担心别人有可能去统治他们,以致他们最后也无视法律,无论是成
文的还是未成文的。” e

“是的,我很清楚地意识到了。”他说。

“所以在这儿,我想,”我说道,“你就发现了一条精壮的根,专政独裁之僭主制便是从这条根上萌芽生长起来的。”

“没有人会否认它的强壮,”他说,“但下一个阶段呢?”

“使寡头制受感染并导致它灭亡的同样疾病,”我说,“也存在于民主制中,但是由于它的开放性而以更加广泛和致命的形式爆发出来,并导致了奴役。实际上,这个大原则就是物极必反:季节、植物、身体的健康都是遵循这个原则的,而政治制度就是一个特别

564a ticularly good examples of it.'

'That sounds plausible,' he said.

'In other words, it's plausible to claim that excessive freedom, at both the individual and the political level, can only change into excessive slavery.'

'Exactly.'

'It makes sense, then,' I continued, 'to say that dictatorship is bound to arise out of democracy—from what, I take it, is the peak of freedom to the most severe and savage form of slavery.'

'Yes, it does,' he agreed.

'But that wasn't the point of your question, I think,' I said. 'You wanted to know what the sickness is which proliferates in a de-
b mocracy as well as in an oligarchy, and reduces it to slavery.'

'That's right,' he said.

'Well,' I said, 'I've already mentioned that breed of lazy, extravagant people and how they're divided into leaders or followers, depending on the degree to which they possess courage. They're the ones we said were like drones—the leaders with stings, the followers stingless.'

'Yes, that's right,' he said.

'Well, the presence of these two kinds of drone,' I said, 'throws any political system into chaos, as phlegm and bile do in the case of the body. The ability to look a long way ahead and take precautions against them is a sign of a good doctor and legislator, just as
c much as it is a sign of a skilful bee-keeper. Ideally, they should try to prevent their birth; but if they've already been born, they should try to eradicate them as quickly as possible, cells and all.'

'Yes, You're absolutely right,' he said.

'Now, we'll never be in a position to make the assessment we want without a clear enough view,' I said. 'Here's a move that'll help.'

'What move?'

好的例子。” 564a

“这看来是有道理的。”他说。

“换句话说，无论是在个人层面上还是在城邦的层面上，都有理由说过度的自由只能演变成过度的奴役。”

“正是这样的。”

我继续说：“那么有理由说僭主制必定产生于民主制——我认为从民主自由的顶峰发展出了最严酷、最野蛮的奴役形式。”

“是的，它确是如此。”他同意说。

“但是我想这不是你问题的关键点，”我说，“你想知道的是，在民主制和寡头制中蔓延并导致它们奴役的疾病是什么样的。” b

“说得对。”他说。

“那么，”我说，“我已经提到过那种懒惰奢侈之人，以及他们是如何依据自己所具有勇气的多少而被划分成领导者和追随者的。他们就是我们说过的雄蜂——领导者是有螫针的雄蜂，追随者是没有螫针的雄蜂。”

“是的，这说得很对。”他说。

“那么这两类雄蜂的出现会给任何政治制度造成混乱，就像身体中的黏液和胆汁造成混乱一样。能够长远地预见并防范他们，是一个好医生和好立法者的标志，就像是一个有经验的养蜂 c
人的标志一样。最好他应该力图阻止它们出生；但如果它们已经生出来了，那么他应该力图尽快地根除它们，连同巢穴彻底铲除。”

“是的，你说得非常正确。”他说。

“那么我们没有看清楚之前我们决不能作出判断，”我说，“这个步骤会有帮助的。”

“什么步骤？”

'Let's assume that there are three distinct components to a demo-
d cratically governed community—as in fact there are. First, its openness allows the drone element to develop within it, and in this respect it resembles an oligarchy.'

'True.'

'But this element is far more vigorous in a democracy than an oligarchy.'

'Why?'

'In an oligarchy it isn't given any respect and is excluded from political office, so it never gets a chance to flex its muscles and become strong. In almost all democracies, however, it is the leading element: its most vigorous members make speeches and do things, while the rest settle in a buzzing swarm around the rostra and prevent
e anyone presenting alternative points of view, and consequently the government of a democratic community is almost entirely in the hands of this element.'

'Yes, indeed,' he said.

'Now, the second element is constantly being propagated by the inhabitants.'

'What is it?'

'Although everyone is trying to make money, it's invariably the most disciplined people who do best financially.'

'That's likely.'

'They're a rich source of honey for the drones, I should think: it's very easy for them to siphon it off from there.'

'Well, it's hardly possible to siphon it from the have-nots,' he remarked.

'And this element, the drones'fodder, is called the moneyed class.'

'That sounds about right,' he said.

565a 'The third element would be the general populace—the smallholders, who don't spend all their time on politics and don't have a great deal of property. They form the largest section of the population,

“让我们设想一个民主式管理的城邦中有三个不同的成
分——就当它们实际存在吧。首先,其开放性允许雄蜂的自身内 d
部得到发展,在这个方面它像寡头制。”

“对的。”

“但这个成分在民主制中要比在寡头制中强劲得多。”

“为什么?”

“在寡头制中它得不到任何尊重,也得不到官职,所以它决无机会得到锻炼以变得强盛。然而几乎在所有的民主制中,它是一个主导的成分:最强有力的成员演讲做事,而其余的人则叽叽喳喳地集结成群,不让任何人发表不同的观点,
结果便是,民主制城邦的管理权几乎全部掌握在这样的人手 e
上。”

“确实是这样的。”他说。

“从居住者中经常会产生第二种成分。”

“是什么?”

“虽然每个人都在试图赚钱,但最有节制的人必定也最会赚钱。”

“这很有可能。”

“那里有大量的蜂蜜供给雄蜂,我应该认为它们很容易从中吸食。”

“嗯,从穷人身上几乎不可能吸食什么。”他说。

“这种所谓的喂养雄蜂的成分就是富人阶级。”

“这听起来很有道理。”他说。

“第三种成分就是一般的民众——这些小农并不把所有时间 565a
花在政治上,也没有大量的财产。他们构成了人口的大部分,当他

and when they gather in one spot they are the most authoritative group in a democracy.'

'True,' he said. 'But they tend not to gather very often, unless there's honey to be gained.'

'And they always get it,' I said. 'Those champions of theirs do their very best to rob the rich and distribute the trivial amounts they don't keep for themselves to the general populace.'

b 'Yes, that's how they get their honey,' he said.

'Their victims are forced to defend themselves, I suppose, by making speeches to the people and acting wherever possible.'

'Of course.'

'And then they're accused by the democratic leaders of plotting against the people and of being oligarchs, even if revolution is the last thing on their minds.'

'Of course.'

'Ultimately, when they realize that the populace at large is out to wrong them, not because it really wants to, but because in its ignorance it's been misled by the lies and slanders of their opponents,
c then—and only then—they do in fact willy—nilly become oligarchs. It's not that they really want to, but the drones'stings inject this poison into their systems as well, to grow inside them.'

'That's undeniable.'

'And the result is that the two sides turn to arraignments, lawsuits, and trials about each other's conduct.'

'Yes.'

'And aren't the people always given to setting up a particular individual as their special champion, who under their caring nurture grows to a prodigious size?'

'Yes, they do tend to do that.'

d 'It's clear, then,' I said, 'that this champion is the only possible

们集合起来的时候，就形成了民主制中最有权威的团体。”

“对的，”他说，“但是他们并不常集会，除非他们有蜂蜜可以获得。”

“他们常常得到甜头，”我说，“他们当中的头头想尽办法去抢劫富人，把他们不要的蝇头小利分给一般民众。”

“是的，他们就是这样得到甜头的。”他说。 b

“我想那些受害者不得不通过向人们演讲以及采取任何可能的行动来保护自己。”

“当然。”

“之后他们受到民主派领导人的指控，说他们策划反对民众，被指控为寡头，即使他们心里最不喜欢的就是革命。”

“当然。”

“最终当他们意识到广大民众试图伤害他们，不是因为民众真的想伤害他们，而是因为他们的无知，他们受到了自己反对者的谎言和毁谤的误导，那时——仅仅是那时——他们在实
际上才很不愿意地变成了寡头。他们并不真的愿意成为寡 c
头，而是雄蜂的螫针把螫毒也刺进了他们的体制并在其中生长。”

“这是不可否认的。”

“结果就是双方对彼此行为进行指责、诉讼和审判。”

“是的。”

“人们不总是喜欢把一个特别的个人推为他们特殊的领头人，他在他们的培植下逐渐变得伟大?”

“是的，他们确实爱那么做。”

“那么这一点是清楚的，”我说，“这个领头人是唯一可能的根 d

root from which any dictatorial shoot that appears is bound to have grown.'

'Perfectly clear.'

'So what makes a champion change into a dictator? Isn't it obviously when a champion starts to behave in the same way as what the stories tell us happens to people in the sanctuary of Zeus Lycaeus in Arcadia?'

'What's that?' he asked.

'That anyone who tastes even a single morsel of human entrails mixed in among those of other sacrificial offerings is bound to become a wolf. Haven't you heard this story?'

e 'Yes, I have.'

'Doesn't the same thing happen to a champion of the people? Suppose the masses are more or less totally under his thumb and he feels no compunction about shedding the blood of a fellow citizen; suppose he trumps up the usual charges against someone, takes him to court, and murders him, thereby eliminating a human life; suppose on his tongue and in his unholy mouth is the taste of the blood of a
566a kinsman, and he turns to demanding banishment and death, and to hinting at the cancellation of debts and the reassignment of land. Isn't it unalterably inevitable that this man will next either be assassinated by his enemies or change into a wolf instead of a human being—that is, become a dictator?'

'It's absolutely inevitable,' he agreed.

'And he's the one who stirs up conflict against the propertied class.'

'Yes.'

'Now, he might be exiled and return to his home country in spite of his enemies. If so, then he comes back as a complete dictator, doesn't he?'

'Obviously.'

b 'Alternatively, his enemies might not be able to arouse enough hostility against him to have him exiled or executed, so they start to

源,从中必定长出任何类似专制的萌芽。”

“非常清楚。”

“那么是什么使得领头人演变成为僭主呢?很明显,当一个斗士开始像我们听说过的故事,也就是在阿卡狄亚的吕克亚宙斯圣殿中,发生在人们身上的故事一样,以其中同样的方式行事时,他不就变成了一个僭主了吗?”

“那是什么故事?”

“任何人,哪怕他只是品尝了一口混在其它祭品中的人的内
脏,就必定会变成狼。你没有听说过这个故事吗?” e

“是的,我听过。”

“民众的头儿不也同样吗?设想民众多多少少都受他的支配,对于使别人流血并不感到懊悔;设想他用一般的指控来诬告某人,把他带到法庭,将其谋害,以此草菅人命;设想在他的舌头和邪恶的嘴巴上沾着同胞的血,他还转而命令将别人流放或处
死,指示取消债款和分发田地。接下来,这样的人不就不可避免 566a
地要么被敌人谋杀,要么由人变成了一只狼——就是说,变成了一个僭主了?”

“这肯定是不可避免的。”他同意说。

“他是一个激起冲突以反对富人阶级的人。”

“是的。”

“那么他可能被放逐了却又不管他的敌人的反对而回到他的祖国。如果是这样的话,那么他完全是作为一个僭主回来的,不是吗?”

“显然。”

“或者,他的敌人们不足以引起对他的敌意以驱逐他或杀害 b

try to find a secret way to assassinate him.'

'Yes, that's the usual course of events,' he said.

'And then, at this stage, every dictator comes up with the notorious and typical demand: he asks the people for bodyguards to protect him, the people's defender.'

'Yes,' he agreed.

'And because they're afraid for his safety, and at the same time optimistic about their own future, they give him his bodyguards, I'm sure.'

c 'That's right.'

'This is when anyone wealthy, whose wealth has made him suspected of being opposed to democracy, acts in accordance with the oracle given to Croesus and "flees beside the pebbly Hermus without delay and without worrying about Cowardice".'

'Yes, because he won't get a second chance to worry,' he said.

'And if he's caught, he'll be put to death,' I added.

'Inevitably.'

d 'Now, that champion obviously doesn't "lie sprawled in his vastness over a vast area", but topples numerous others and stands firm on the chariot of the state, a complete dictator now, instead of a champion.'

'That's bound to be the case,' he said.

'How happy do you think he is?' I asked. 'And how happy is the community which contains a creature of this sort? Shall we talk about this?'

'Yes, let's,' he said.

'In the early days,' I said, 'in the first period of his supremacy, he greets everyone he meets with a smile. He claims not to be a
e dictator, makes a lot of promises to his closee associates and in his public speeches, rescinds debts, gives land to the people and to his supporters, and poses as an altogether amiable and gentle person,

他,所以他们开始试图找一种秘密的方式去谋杀他。”

“是的,这种事是常常有的。”他说。

“然后在这个阶段,每个僭主都会提出典型的声名狼藉的要求:他要求卫队保护他这个民众的保卫者。”

“是的。”他同意说。

“因为他们担心他的安全,同时对他们自己的未来抱有乐观态度,我确信他们会给他卫队的。”

“对的。” c

“当任何富人因其财富使他被嫌疑反对民主制,他就必须按照克娄苏得到的神谕行事并且‘沿着多石的赫尔墨斯河岸逃跑,不要停留,不要担心懦弱’。”

“是的,因为他再也没有第二次机会担心了。”他说。

“如果他被捉住了,他就会被处死。”我补充说。

“必定会被处死。”

“那么,这个领头人显然不是‘张开长大的身体躺在大地上’,
而是打倒了许多别的人,稳稳地站在城邦的战车上,现在完全成 d
了一个僭主而不是领头人。”

“情况必定是这样的。”他说。

“你认为他有多幸福?”我问道,“拥有这种人的城邦有多幸福?对此我们是否要谈论一下?”

“是的,让我们讨论一下吧。”

“在早期,”我说,“在他当政的初期,他遇到任何人总
是抱以笑容。他声称不会成为一个独裁者,对他的密友许 e
下诸多诺言,在公共演说中豁免债务,把土地分发给民众和他的支持者,并且总是表现成一个和蔼、温和的人,

doesn't he?'

'Inevitably,' he said.

'Meanwhile he is, I imagine, settling his differences with some of his exiled enemies, and killing others. Once that threat is a thing of the past, he turns to provoking warfare, so as to keep the people in need of a leader.'

'Yes, that's likely.'

567a 'And also, wouldn't you say, so as to tax them and make them poor, so that they're forced to concentrate on their daily business and have less time to plot against him?'

'Obviously.'

'And also, I think, to find a plausible way of killing people he suspects of entertaining notions of freedom, and of consequently being likely to resist his authority: he simply makes sure that the enemy get their hands on them. Don't you agree? All of these reasons guarantee that a dictator must constantly he provoking wars, mustn't he?'

'He has to.'

'Now, these actions of his will probably be resented by the citizens of his community, won't they?'

b 'Of course they will.'

'And some—they'll have to be the bravest—of those who helped him on his way and who are in positions of power will speak their minds to him, as well as to one another, and will criticize what's going on, won't they?'

'I should think so.'

'So a dictator has to eliminate the lot of them—or else relinquish power—until there's no one of any value left among either his friends or his enemies.'

'Obviously.'

不是吗？”

“必定如此。”他说。

“同时，我想他会和某些被他放逐的敌人调停矛盾，并杀掉其他不合作者。一旦威胁与危险成为过去的事情，他便转而挑起冲突，如此一来，便使得大众继续不断地需要一个领导者。”

“是的，这很有可能。”

“而且，他挑起冲突，如此一来，他也便可以向人民征税，而使 567a
他们贫穷，这样大众便被迫奔走谋生，也就没有时间密谋反对他了，难道你做不出这样的判定吗？”

“还有，我想，有些人对自由观念的趣味有所觉察，从而可能会反抗他的淫威，为了找到一个看似有道理的杀死这些人的理由：他愚蠢地坚信是敌人假手于这些人来反抗自己的。你难道不同意吗？所有这些动机都保证一个独裁者必须不断地挑起冲突与祸乱才行，他也是必须如此吧？”

“他肯定会的。”

“那么他的这些行为可能会遭到城邦中公民的反对，不是吗？” b

“他们当然会反对的。”

“他们中的有些人——他们肯定是最勇敢的人——在他通往掌权的道路上帮助过他，并且现在正掌有权力，他们会对他说出自己的想法以及相互议论，还会批评所发生的事情，不是吗？”

“我想应该是这样的。”

“所以一个僭主必须除掉他们中的很多人——否则就是把权力拱手让人——无论是他的朋友还是他的敌人，任何有用无用的人一个都不留。”

“显而易见。”

'He has to keep a sharp eye out, then, for anyone with cour-
c age, self-confidence, intelligence, or wealth. He has no choice in the matter: he's bound to treat them as enemies and to intrigue against them, until he's purged the community of them. That's the nature of his happy state.'

'A fine purge that is,' he remarked.

'Yes,' I said, 'and quite different from a medical purge of the body. Doctors remove the worst and leave the best; he does the opposite.'

d 'He has to, if he's to retain power, apparently,' he said.

'He's caught in an enviable dilemma, then,' I said, 'which requires him to choose between sharing his life with people who are, on the whole, second-rate, and who hate him, or not living at all.'

'That's right,' he said.

'Now, the greater the resentment felt by the citizens of his community at his conduct, the larger and more reliable his bodyguard will have to be, won't it?'

'Of course.'

'Well, who can he rely on? Where will he get his soldiers from?'

'Swarms of them will wing their way to him as if by magic,' he said, 'if he offers them the payment they want.'

e 'You wouldn't be talking about drones, by any chance, would you?' I asked. 'Drones of all different shapes and sizes from abroad?'

'You've understood me perfectly,' he said.

'But who can he rely on from his own community? Do you think he'd...?'

'What?'

'... steal slaves from his citizens, emancipate them, and include them among his bodyguard?'

“那么。他必须保持目光的敏锐，看出谁具有勇气，谁具有自
制，谁具有智慧，谁具有财富。在这些事情上他别无选择：他必定 c
要把他们当作敌人并且还要谋害他们，直到他把他们从城邦中清
除干净为止。这就是他的幸福状态的本质。”

“这种清除真是妙啊。”他说。

“是的，”我说，“这与医学上对身体的清洗是很不同的。医生清除最坏的，保留最好的；他却相反。”

“如果他想保住权力，那么他显然必须这么做。”他说。

“那么他就处于一个令人羡慕的二难之中，”我说，“这要求他 d
作出选择，要么与那些总的来说不大有价值的人以及憎恨他的人
生活在一起，要么就是死。”

“对的。”他说。

“那么他城邦中的公民对他的所作所为越是感到怨恨，他的卫队就必须越是庞大和可靠，不是吗？”

“当然。”

“那么他能够依靠谁呢？他到哪里去找他的士兵呢？”

他说：“如果他向他们支付想要的薪水，那么他们就会魔术般地成群地向他涌来。”

“你说的不正巧是雄蜂，是吗？”我问道，“从外邦来的各种不
同样子和大小的雄蜂。” e

“你已经完全理解我了。”他说。

“但他能依靠城邦中的什么人呢？你认为他……？”

“什么？”

“……从他的居民那里偷窃奴隶，释放他们并把他们招募进他的卫队？”

'He undoubtedly would,' he replied. 'He could surely rely on them more than on anyone else.'

568a 'Dictatorship is certainly an enviable thing, then,' I said. 'Look at the friends he has and the people he can depend on, once he's killed all his previous associates.'

'Yes, well, that *is* the kind of person he keeps company with,' he said.

'These companions of his, these newly created citizens, form his circle of admiring friends, while decent people avoid him like the plague, don't they?'

'Of course they do.'

'It's not surprising', I said, 'that tragedy in general is thought to be a clever affair and Euripides is taken to be the most outstanding tragic playwright.'

'Why?'

'Because with his penetrating mind he's already expressed this i-
b dea: "Dictators are clever because of the clever company they keep," he says. He was obviously referring to the clever people we've been saying form a dictator's circle.'

'He also eulogizes dictatorship in a number of ways,' he added, 'by calling it "godlike", for instance. And he's joined in this by all the other poets.'

'And it's precisely because tragic poets are clever', I said, 'that they'll forgive us (and others with a similar political system) for refusing to allow them into our society, on the grounds that they sing the praises of dictatorship.'

c 'I expect the gifted ones will forgive us, anyway,' he said.

'They can tour around other communities instead, where they'll attract huge audiences and use the beauty, carrying-power, and persuasiveness of the voices of the actors they hire to convert them to dictatorship or democracy.'

'Yes.'

'And that's not all. They'll be paid and acclaimed for doing this.

“毫无疑问他会这样做的，”他回答说，“他肯定会依靠他们，更甚于依靠别的任何人。”

我说：“一旦他杀了所有他先前的朋友之后，看看他这些朋友 568a
和他所依靠的民众，那么当僭主当然是一件令人羡慕的事情。”

“是的，与他为伴的就是这样的人。”他说。

“这些陪伴他的人，这些刚刚成为公民的人构成了敬慕他的朋友圈子，而高尚的人像逃避瘟疫一样逃避他，不是吗？”

“他们当然是这样做的。”

“这并不奇怪，”我说，“悲剧一般被认为是件聪明活儿，欧里庇得斯被认为是最杰出的悲剧作家。”

“为什么？”

“因为他用他敏锐的头脑说过这样的想法，他说：‘僭主是聪
明的，因为他以聪明人为伴。’他指的显然是我们所说的构成僭主 b
圈子的聪明人。”

“他还以很多方式歌颂过僭主，”他补充说，“比如说，他把僭主形容为‘神一般的’。他与所有别的诗人一起赞美僭主。”

“正是因为悲剧诗人是聪明的，”我说，“所以他们会原谅我们（以及其他和我们有着类似政治制度的人）的做法，即不允许他们进入我们的城邦，因为他们歌颂僭主制。”

“我想那些明智之人无论如何都会饶恕我们的。”他说。 c

“相反他们会周游别的城邦，在那里他们吸引了大批观众，利用他们雇佣演员的美妙、有力而有说服力的嗓子，使他们转向僭主制或者民主制。”

“是的。”

“这还不是全部。他们会得到报偿并为此得到赞扬。大多数

They'll get the most from dictatorships, and somewhat less from democracies; and then the higher up our scale of political systems they go, the more the acclaim will die away, as if it were short of breath
d and unable to continue.'

"Yes.'

"But we digress,' I said. 'we'd better return to that army which a dictator possesses, in all its splendour, size, variety, and inconstancy, and discuss how he'll maintain it.'

'He'll obviously use up any wealth the community's temples have,' he said, 'whenever his victims' money runs out, so that he won't have to tax the people too much.'

e 'What about when there's no longer enough in the temples?'

'He and all the men and women who hobnob with him will obviously be maintained by his father's wealth,' he said.

'I see,' I said. 'You're implying that the general populace, which is the dictator's father, will keep him and his companions.'

'They'll have little choice in the matter,' he said.

'What do you mean?' I said. 'Suppose the people get annoyed with him and tell him it's wrong for a son in his prime to be kept by a father, and that, on the contrary, the son should be keeping the fa-
569a ther; suppose they tell him that the purpose of their giving him life and power was not for them to be dominated, now that he's grown up, by their own slaves and for them to support him and their slaves and all the rest of the riff-raff, but so that he could be their champion in freeing them from the dominion of the rich and the so-called gentlemen of their community; suppose they now behave like a father throwing his son out of the home, along with his freeloading friends, and they order him to leave the community, and to take his companions with him. What would happen then, do you think?'

报偿和赞扬是从僭主制中得到的，少部分是从民主制中得到的；然后他们在我们的政治制度的梯子上爬得越高，其名声也就越下降，他们似乎喘不过气来，不能继续攀登了。” d

“是的。”

“但我扯远了，”我说，“我们最好回到僭主所拥有的军队上去，这整个是一支花里胡哨、人员众多、多样混杂、变化不定的军队，我们讨论一下他是如何维护它的。”

“每当花光了被他打败之人的钱，他显然会用光城邦中神庙的所有财富，”他说，“这样他就不会向民众征太多的税。”

“那么当神庙中的钱再也不够的时候呢？” e

“他以及所有与他一起的男女食客显然要由他父亲的财富来供养。”他说。

“我明白了，”我说，“你指的是作为僭主之父的一般民众要供养僭主以及他的一帮子人。”

“在这件事上他们几乎没有什么选择。”他说。

“你说的是什么意思？”我说，“假设民众对他发怒并告诉他说，正当壮年的儿子还要父亲供养是不对的，而是反过来，儿子应
该供养父亲；还对他说，他们给予他生命和权力，并不是等他长大 569a
使他们受自己奴隶的压迫，也不是支持他和他们的奴隶以及所有其余的乌合之众，而是，这样做他就能成为他们的领导人，把他们从富人以及他们城邦中所谓的上等人的压迫中解放出来；假设他们现在的行为像是一个父亲把他的儿子以及他的狐朋狗友赶出家门一样，他们命令他带上他的同伴一起离开城邦。那么你认为会发生什么呢？”

'Then it'll certainly take hardly any time for the people to find
b out what sort of creature they've fathered, cared for, and nurtured to maturity,' he said. 'And they'll soon see that the people they're trying to expel are the stronger party.'

'What?' I exclaimed. 'Do you mean that the dictator will be unscrupulous enough to lay hands on his father—to respond to a difference of opinion with physical violence?'

'Yes,' he said, 'once he's deprived his father of his weapons.'

'In other words,' I said, 'a dictator is guilty of the crime of father-beating, and is no comfort to his father in his old age. This, it turns out, is what dictatorship is and would be acknowledged to be. And, as the saying goes, the people would escape the smoke of being
c the slaves of free men only to fall into the fire of having slaves as their masters. They exchange considerable, and even excessive, freedom for the worst and harshest kind of enslavement—enslavement to slaves.'

'Yes, this is exactly what happens,' he agreed.

'In that case,' I said, 'it would be reasonable for us to claim that we've done enough to explain how dictatorship evolves out of democracy, and what it's like as a fully fledged entity. Yes?'

'Yes, we've certainly done enough,' he said.

571a 'All there is left for us to do', I said, 'is study an actual dictatorial person, to try to see how he evolves out of the democratic type, what he's like once he does exist, and whether his life is happy or unhappy.'

'Yes, that's right,' he said.

'Well, there's still a deficiency to remedy, I think,' I said.

'What?'

'I don't think we've finished distinguishing the various kinds of desires or finding out how many different kinds there are. And as long as this job remains unfinished, our enquiry will be veiled in obscurity.'

b 'But it's not too late, is it?' he asked.

“那么民众肯定不用费什么时间就能看出他们生育、看护和养育大的是一种什么样的动物了，”他说，“他们很快就会发现他们试图要驱逐的人是更强大的一方。” b

“什么？”我惊讶地说，“你的意思是说僭主会肆无忌惮到对付他的父亲——以暴力对待不同的意见？”

“是的，”他说，“一旦他剥夺了他父亲的武装之后。”

“换句话说，”我说，“僭主犯有伤父之罪并且虐待他年老的父亲。这就证明了僭主制是什么东西以及它会被认为是什么样的东西。就像谚语说的那样，才离熏烟，更落火坑，人们刚摆脱作为自由人的奴隶，他们作为奴隶的主人却又受到了奴隶的奴役。他们用相当大的、甚至 c
是过分的自由换取了最坏、最严酷的奴役——受他们奴隶的奴役。”

“是的，所发生的正是这样的。”他同意说。

“在那种情况下，”我说，“僭主制是如何从民主制演变而来的，以及它作为一个完全羽翼丰满的实体又是什么样子的，我们有理由说我们对此已经解释得够多的了。是吗？”

“是的，我们当然已经说得够多的了。”他说。

“所有留待我们去做的，”我说，“就是研究一个现实的僭主， 571a
力求考察一下他是如何从民主式的人物演变而来，一旦他确实存在了，会是什么样的？他的生活是幸福的还是不幸福的。”

“是的，这样做是对的。”他说。

“那么我认为还有不足需要弥补。”我说。

“什么？”

“我想我们没有区分各种欲望，也没有找出有多少种不同的欲望。只要这项工作还未完成，我们的研究就还是被笼罩在晦暗之中。”

“但这不是太晚，不是吗？”他问道。 b

'No. The thing about them I want to have out in the open is that some of the unnecessary pleasures and desires strike me as lawless. We probably all contain these pleasures and desires, but they can be kept under control by convention and by the co-operation of reason and the better desires. Some people, in fact, control them so well that they get rid of them altogether or leave only a few of them in a weakened state, but they remain stronger and more numerous in others.'

c 'What pleasures and desires are you thinking of?' he asked.

'The ones that wake up while we're asleep,' I replied. 'When all the rest of the mind—the rational, regulated, controlling part—is asleep, then if the wild, unruly part is glutted with food or drink, it springs up and longs to banish sleep and go and satisfy its own instincts. I'm sure you're aware of how in these circumstances nothing is too outrageous: a person acts as if he were totally lacking in moral principle and unhampered by intelligence. In his dreams, he doesn't stop at trying to have sex with his mother and with anyone or anything
d else—man, beast, or god; he's ready to slaughter anything; there's nothing he wouldn't eat. In short, he doesn't hold back from anything, however bizarre or disgusting.'

'You're quite right,' he said.

'On the other hand, I imagine, when someone who's self- disciplined and who keeps himself healthy goes to sleep, he's made sure that his rational mind is awake and has eaten its fill of fine ideas and arguments, which he's brought to an agreed conclusion within himself. Since he hasn't either starved or over-indulged his desirous part,
e it can settle down to sleep and not bother the best part of him with its feelings of pleasure or pain, and consequently the best part is free to
572a get on with the enquiries it carries out all by itself, when it is secluded and untarnished by anything else, and to try to fulfil its impulse for perceiving something in the past or present or future that it doesn't

“不太晚。我想要弄清楚的事情是，有些不必要的快乐和欲望给我的印象是不合法的。我们可能都有这些快乐和欲望，但它们可以通过法律，通过与理性的合作以及通过较好的欲望而得到控制。实际上，有些人将它们控制得很好以致将它们完全根除了或者只留下一些微弱的残余，而在另一些人身上却留下得更强更多。”

“你所想的是什么样的快乐和欲望？”他问道。 c

“那些在我们睡眠时活跃起来的快乐和欲望，”我回答说，“当心灵的其余所有部分——理性的、受过教化的、起控制作用的部分——睡眠的时候，如果野性的、狂放不羁的部分吃饱喝足了，它就跳起来希望赶走睡眠以满足自己的本能。我确信你知道在这样的情况下没有什么会是过于暴虐：一个人的行为就像他完全失去了道德原则，不受理智的控制。在他梦中，他不会阻止试图与
他的母亲以及任何别的人或物——男人、兽或神——交媾；他敢 d
杀害任何东西；没有什么他不敢吃的。简而言之，他对任何事情都不会退缩，无论有多么古怪或令人反感。”

“你说得非常正确。”他说。

“另一方面，我想当一个自制并健康的人去睡觉的时候，他要确信自己理性的心灵是清醒的，并且已用美好的理念和论证将之喂饱，并在自身达成一致的结论。因为他既没有让他的欲望部分
挨饿又没有过分地放纵他的欲望部分，它就能安静下来睡觉，并 e
且也不会用快乐或痛苦的感觉来打扰他至善的部分，结果至善的
部分就能自己自由地从事探究，当它与任何别的事物隔绝起来不 572a
受它们干扰的时候，它就会试图去满足研究过去、现在或未来的未知事物的冲动。他也使他的激情部分安静下来，不会由于生某人的气而在情感受到干扰的状态中去睡觉。换句话说，他使自己

know. He's also calmed down his passionate part and doesn't go to bed in an emotionally disturbed state because he's been angry with someone. In other words, he's quietened down two aspects of himself, but woken up the third—the one in which intelligence resides—and that's how he takes his rest; and, as you know, in this state he can maximize his contact with the truth and minimize the lawlessness of
b the visions he sees in his dreams.'

'I'm sure you're absolutely right,' he said.

'Now, we've wandered rather far from the main course of the argument, but the point I'm trying to get across is this: every one of us—even someone who seems very restrained—contains desires which are terrible, wild, and lawless, and this category of desire becomes manifest during sleep. Do you agree? Do you think I have a point?'

'Yes, I do agree.'

c 'Well, remember the nature of the democratic man, as we described him: his formative childhood upbringing was by a skinflint of a father who valued only desires which helped him make money, and despised alL the unnecessary ones with their frivolity and frippery, wasn't it?'

'Yes.'

'But then he fell in with a more elegant crowd, consisting of people who indulge in the desires we've just been describing, and his dislike of his father's meanness drove him to all kinds of outrageous behaviour, and to modelling himself on them. However, he was essentially better than these corrupters of his, and since he was being pulled in both directions, he found between the two ways of life a
d compromise in which he drew on each of them to a reasonable extent, in his opinion, and lived a life which wasn't miserly, but at the same time wasn't lawless either. And that's how he made the transition from being oligarchic to being democratic.'

'Yes, that's what we thought earlier, and it still seems valid,' he said.

'Now imagine', I said, 'that our democratic type has grown older and has a son who's been brought up, in his turn, in his father's ways.'

'All right.'

的两个部分安静下来，而唤醒第三个部分——即理智所在的部分——他就是这样得到休息的；就像你所知道的那样，在这种状态下，他能最大限度地接触真理并最小限度地接触他梦境中的不合法的景象。” b

“我确信你肯定是对的。”他说。

“现在我们已经离论证的主题太远了，但我想要说的要点是这样的：我们当中的每一个人——甚至那个人看起来是非常具有自制力的——拥有这些可怕的、野性的和不合法的欲望，这种欲望在睡觉的时候显现出来。你同意吗？你认为我说得有道理吗？”

“是的，我确实同意。”

“那么，记得我们描述过的那种民主式人物的本质吧：他的童年成长发展期的教养来自一个吝啬的父亲，他只看重有助于他赚 c
钱的欲望，而鄙视所有轻浮无用的不必要的欲望，不是吗？”

“是的。”

“但他与更优雅的人群交往，这个群体由沉溺于我们刚才描述的那些欲望的人构成，他对他父亲吝啬的厌恶使他做出各种各样无法无天的举动，并还使自己模仿他们。然而他在本质上比那些教唆他的人好，并且因为他受到两个方向的牵引，所以在两种生活方式中发现了一种折中之道，他按他的看法对两者以合理的程度做出了调和，他的生活并不寒酸，但同时也并非不合法。他 d
就是这样从寡头派转变成为民主派。”

“是的，我们早先是这么想的，现在看来还是有效的。”他说。

我说：“现在设想一下，我们民主式的人物长大了，有了一个儿子，这个儿子还是以他父亲的方式被抚养大。”

“好吧。”

'And imagine that the same thing happens to him as happened to his father: he's attracted by complete lawlessness (although the peo-
e ple who are advertising it to him call it complete freedom), his father and his family in general reinforce the desires he settled on as a com promise , and others reinforce his lawless side . When these black magicians, these creators of dictators, realize that there's only one way they're going to gain control of the young man, they arrange matters until they implant in him a particular lust, to champion the rest of his desires which are too idle to do more than share out anything that
573a readily comes their way. And don't you think this kind of lust is exactly like a great, winged drone?'

'Yes, that seems to me to be a perfect description of it,' he said.

'Then the rest of the desires buzz in a swarm around their champion, reeking of incense and perfumes, laden with garlands, overflowing with wine, and offering all the indulgent pleasures that go with that kind of social life. Under their caring nurture, he grows to his fullest extent and gains a sting whose poison is unfulfilled longing. This inner champi-
b on now takes frenzy for his bodyguard and runs amok. If he finds that the person contains any apparently good beliefs or desires which still cause him to feel shame, he kills them and banishes them, until he's purged the person of self-discipline and imported frenzy in its place.'

'That's a perfect description of a dictatorial type's evolution,' he said.

'And isn't this also the kind of reason why lust is traditionally called a dictator?' I asked.

'I suppose so,' he said.

'Now, there's something dictatorial about a drunken person's arrogance too, isn't there, Adeimantus?' I asked.

c 'Yes, there is.'

'And people who are insane and mentally disturbed try to dominate the gods, let alone other human beings, and expect to be able to do so.'

“设想发生于他父亲的同样的事情也发生于他的身上:他受到完全违法的东西吸引,虽然教唆他的人称之为完全的自由,他的父亲和 e
他的家人一般支持他折中的欲望,而别人支持他违法的一面。当这些邪恶的巫师,这些独裁者的教父,认识到他们只有一个办法才能获得对这个年轻人的控制时,他们便想方设法,直到在他身上移植入一种特殊的强烈欲望,由此支持推动他身上其他的欲望,后者因为过于懒散以至于所能做的不过是均分到手的任何东西。你难道不认为这种 573a
渴欲正像一只庞大而有翅的雄蜂吗?”

“是的,在我看来这样的描述非常好。”他说。

“然后,其他的欲望便嗡嗡作声地簇拥在它们的这个领头者周围,香雾弥漫,花团绵簇,美酒充盈,并供奉所有与那种社交生活相配的纵欲。它在它们的悉心养育下渐臻至壮,并获得一枚螫针,其毒性就是难填的欲壑。这个内心的领头者因它的卫士而变得疯狂起来,胡作非为。如果它发现这个人还含有任何好的、还能使他羞愧的信念或愿 b
望,那么它就会杀灭它们并驱逐它们,直到把这个人的自制清除干净并引进疯狂以代之。”

“这是关于僭主式人物转变的非常好的描述了。”他说。

“是不是因为同样的理由,使强烈的欲望在传统上被称作暴君呢?”我问道。

“我想是这样的。”他说。

“那么,阿狄曼图,一个醉酒之人的傲慢中也有暴君成分,不是吗?”我问道。 c

“是有的。”

“并且那些患有精神病的人以及心思混乱的人都试图对诸神施加影响,更不用说其他人类了,而且他们还期望真的能够做到这一点。”

'Yes,' he agreed.

'so strictly speaking, Adeimantus,' I said, 'the dictatorial type is the result of someone's nature or conditioning—or both—making him a drunken, lustful maniac.'

'Absolutely.'

'So that's how the dictatorial type evolves, apparently. Now, what's his life like?'

d 'At the risk of sounding like a tease,' he said, 'it's you who'll have to tell me.'

'All right,' I said. 'I think he proceeds to give himself over to feasting and revelry, parties and prostitutes, and all the activities which typically indicate that the dictator lust has taken up residence within a person and is in complete control of his mind.'

'Yes, that's bound to happen,' he agreed.

'Every day and every night, terrible desires with prodigious appetites branch out in large numbers from the main stem, don't they?'

'Yes, they do.'

'So his income is soon exhausted.'

'Of course.'

e 'And then he starts borrowing and working his way through his estate.'

'Naturally.'

'And when there's nothing left, his young brood of desires is bound to clamour long and loud. He's driven by the stinging swarm of his desires (and especially by lust, the captain of the bodyguard the
574a others form) to run amok—to see if there's anyone he can steal anything from by deceit or by force. Yes?'

'Definitely,' he said.

'He has no choice: he can either filch from every available source, or be racked with agonizing pains.'

“是的。”他同意说。

“所以，阿狄曼图，严格地说来，”我说，“僭主式的人物是由天性或环境而造成的——或两者——使他成为一个酗酒成性、念婪好色的疯狂之人。”

“毫无疑问。”

“所以僭主式的人物似乎就是这样演变出来的。那么，他的生活是什么样的呢？”

“听起来似乎要被嘲笑，”他说，“应该是你来告诉我了。” d

“好吧，”我说，“我想他接下去就是投身于宴饮、狂欢、聚会和嫖娼，所有这些活动都典型地表明强烈欲望这个暴君已经占据了一个人并且完全控制了他的灵魂。”

“是的，这是必定会发生的。”他同意说。

“每日每夜，可怕的、有着巨大胃口的欲望从主干上大量地生发出来，不是吗？”

“是的。”

“所以他的收入很快就花光了。”

“当然。”

“然后他就开始借钱并靠他的房产艰难度日。” e

“自然。”

“当什么都不剩下的时候，他刚出现的欲望必定要大声长呼。他被一大批欲望的螫针逼得发狂，尤其是被作为由其他欲望形成的卫士之首的色欲逼得发狂——看看是否可以通过欺骗或暴力从某些人中偷得些什么东西。是吗？” 574a

“毫无疑问。”他说。

“他别无选择：他要么可偷的都偷，要么忍受剧痛的折磨。”

'Agreed.'

'Now, every passing pleasant sensation he feels takes precedence over the ones which are in the past and steals from them, so by the same token he expects to take precedence over his parents, despite being younger than them, and to steal from them, in the sense of appropriating his father's property once he's exhausted his own. Yes?'

'Of course,' he agreed.

b 'And if his parents refused to hand it over to him, he'd initially resort to obtaining money from them on false pretences, wouldn't he?'

'Absolutely.'

'And if that didn't work, he'd turn to robbery with violence?'

'I think so,' he said.

'If his elderly parents resisted and fought back, Adeimantus, do you think he'd be circumspect and hesitant about doing anything dictatorial?'

'No, I don't hold out much hope for the parents of someone like this,' he said.

'Would he really beat up his mother, who's cared for him for years, Adeimantus, and whom he could never have lived with-out, for the sake of his latest dispensable girlfriend, whom he's just fallen
c in love with? Would he really beat up his aged, indispensable father, who may not be much to look at any more, but whose affection has lasted for so many years, for the sake of his latest alluring, but dispensable, boyfriend? Would he honestly let his parents be dominated by them, if he had them all living together in the same house?'

'Yes, he certainly would,' he said.

'What a happy thing it is, then,' I exclaimed, 'to be the parent of a dictator!'

“是的。”

“他感受到的每个瞬间即逝的快乐感觉超过了原先的快乐并且还劫夺了它们,所以出于同样的原因他也希望超过他的父母并且劫夺他们,虽然比他们年轻,但一旦他花完了自己的钱就去夺取他父亲的财产。是吗?”

“当然。”他同意说。

“如果他的父母拒绝给他,那么他就会首先想办法敲诈他们, b
不是吗?”

“毫无疑问。”

“如果那样不奏效,那么他是否会着手强行夺取?”

“我想是这样的。”他说。

“如果他年迈的父母拒绝并进行反抗的话,阿狄曼图,你认为他会小心谨慎并犹豫着是否要使用任何暴力吗?”

“不,像这种人的父母,我想不出来还能有什么希望。”他说道。

“阿狄曼图,你认为他真的会为一个最近才爱上的可有可无的女朋友而去打他的母亲吗?这位母亲照顾他多年,没有她,他
就肯定活不了。你认为他真的会为了一个新认识的很有魅力但 c
却可有可无的娈童而去打他年迈的不可缺少的父亲吗?这位父亲或许因为年迈而照顾不过来许多事情了,但他的慈爱已经持续多年。如果其父母与美妾娈童同居一个屋檐下的话,那么他就真得忍心让美妾娈童对父母吆三喝四、颐指气使吗?”

“是的,他肯定会这么做,”他说道。

“那么那是一件多么幸福的事情啊,”我大声说道,“成为一位僭主的父母!”

我大声叫道说:“那么做僭主父母是一件多么幸福的事情啊!”

'That's right,' he agreed.

d 'What happens when there's none of his parents' property left, but a large number of pleasures have gathered together in a swarm within him? Won't he first turn his hand to a bit of burglary or to mugging travellers late at night, and then try emptying out a temple? At the same time a gang of beliefs which had until recently been suppressed, but now form lust's bodyguard, come to his assistance to enable him to overpower all the views about good and bad behaviour he'd been brought up to hold and which he'd assumed to comprise morality. This gang consists of attitudes which had formerly—during the period when there was still a democratic government within him, and
e he was still subject to the laws and to his father—broken free only at night, while he was asleep. Once he's under the dictatorship of lust, however, his constant waking state is one that was formerly rare and restricted to dreams: there's no form of murder, however vile, that he isn't willing to commit; there's nothing he won't eat, no deed he isn't ready to perform. Lust lives within him like a dictator, with no regard
575a for law and convention. It uses its absolute power to influence the person in whom it lives, as an autocrat influences his community, to stop at nothing as long as the result is the perpetuation of itself and the pandemonium it generates. Some of this pandemonium is the result of bad company, and has therefore been introduced from outside; the rest is the result of the person's own practice of the same bad habits, and so has been released and set free internally. Don't you think this is how he lives?'

'Yes,' he said.

'Now, if people of this kind form a small proportion of a
b community's population, while the rest are self-disciplined,' I said, 'then they leave and serve in the bodyguard of a dictator somewhere else, or as mercenaries in some war or other. But if they occur in a time of peace and stability, they stay in their community and commit lots of trivial crimes.'

“对啊。”他同意说。

“当父母的财产所剩无几,而大量的欲望却群聚在他心里的 d
时候会发生什么呢?他难道不首先转变为盗贼或者抢劫夜行者,然后就是洗劫神庙?同时,有大群直至最近都还被压制的意见现在变成了色欲的卫士,辅助他以使他能够统治所有他从小培养起来加以坚守的善恶行为的信念,他认为其中包含了正义。这些意见由一些见解所构成,这些见解以前——在这个阶段,他心里还是有一个民主式的管理并且还是服从于法律和他父亲
的——是当他在睡觉的时候才被释放出来。然而,一旦他处在 e
强烈欲望的统治之下,他清醒的状态就变成了以前那种罕见的、局限于睡梦的状态:非常恶劣,没有什么罪恶是他不愿意去犯的;没有什么是他不会吃的,没有什么行为是他不会做的。在他
心中的强烈欲望就像一个暴君,毫不顾法律和习俗。强烈欲望 575a
利用它绝对的权力去影响那个它所寄生的人,就像一个独裁者影响他的城邦一样,只要所产生的结果是,它自身以及它所制造的欲望炼狱永久存在,那么他便无休止地什么坏事儿都敢做。这欲望炼狱中有一些是其邪恶伙伴造成的,因此是从外面进来的;剩下的则是个人自身同样恶癖习行的结果,因而是自内释放出来的,在其内心是不受约束的。你不认为这就是他的生活吗?”

“是的。”他说。

“那么,如果这样的人是城邦人口中的少数,同时其余的人又
是有自制的,”我说,“那么他们就会离开,到别的地方去做僭主的 b
卫士,或者在某个战争中去做雇佣兵。但是如果他们遇上了和平稳定的时期,他们便待在他们的城邦中并会犯很多常见小罪。”

'What sort of crimes do you mean?'

'They're thieves, burglars, pickpockets, muggers, temple robbers, kidnappers; if they have any ability at public speaking, they might be sycophants, and they're the kind of people who commit perjury in court and take bribes.'

c 'Yes, these are trivial crimes, as long as there aren't many people committing them,' he said. 。

'Anything trivial is only trivial in comparison with something important,' I went on, 'and all these crimes are (as the saying goes) well wide of the mark of dictatorship in the effect they have on how rotten and unhappy a community is. In fact, it's when these people and their followers start to form a significant proportion of a community's population, and realize how many there are of them, that they—assisted by the folly of the people—become the ones to whom the dictator we discussed owes his origin: he is simply whichever one
d of them has the greatest and most thriving dictator in his own mind.'

'Yes, that's likely,' he agreed. 'Dictatorship would come most naturally to him.'

'There's no problem if they're happy to defer to him, but if the community refuses to submit, then, if he can, it'll be his fatherland's turn for the same punishment he inflicted on his mother and father before. He'll bring new friends in from abroad and, for all her longstanding care, he'll make sure that his motherland (as the Cretans call their country) and fatherland are kept and maintained—in a state of enslavement to these new friends of his. After all, that's how the desire of this sort of person is fulfilled.'

e 'Yes, it is, absolutely,' he said.

'Now, don't people of this sort behave like dictators in their private lives even before they gain political power?' I asked. 'Take their relationships with others, for instance. They either go about with people who flatter them and are ready to carry out their every whim, or they're deferential themselves, if they want something from someone. As long as that's the case, there's nothing they wouldn't do to make
576a him believe they're his friends, but once they've got what they want,

“你指的是什么样的罪行呢?”

“他们做小偷、强盗、扒手、劫匪、偷盗神庙之人和拐骗犯;如果他们具有一点公共演说的能力,那么他们可能就是告密者,他们会是这样一种人,在法庭上做伪证并收受贿赂。”

“是的,只要没有很多人犯,那么这些就是小恶。”他说。 c

“任何小事之所以只是小事是与大事比较而言,”我继续说,“就像谚语说的那样,从造成城邦中的腐败和不幸福的效果而言,所有这些罪恶还远不及僭主制。实际上,当这些人和他们的追随者开始构成了城邦中绝大部分人口的时候,他们意识到有多么庞大,他们——加上民众的愚昧——变成了我们讨论过的僭主的起源:他就是那样一个在其心中有一个最强大的暴君的人。” d

“是的,这很有可能,”他同意说,“僭主制会非常自然地来到他身上。”

“如果民众乐于听从他,那么就没有什么问题,但是如果城邦拒绝接受他,那么如果他有能力的话,他也会像以前伤害他的父母一样惩治他的祖国。他从外邦带来新的朋友,他会确保那长久照顾他的母邦——就像克里特人称呼他们的城邦一样——和父邦维持在一种处于他的这些新朋友的奴役状态中。毕竟,这种人的欲望就是这样得到满足的。”

“是的,肯定是这样的。”他说。 e

“那么,这种人即使在获得政治权力之前,在他们的私人生活中,其行为不也像暴君一样吗?”我问道,“比如拿他们与别人的关系来说,他们要么与奉承他们的人来往并愿意实行他们每一个怪念头,要么当他们有求于人的时候,他们自己就很恭顺了。只要是在那种情况下,为了让人相信他们是他的朋友,他们就什么都 576a

they're distant again.'

'Definitely.'

'They never have any friends, then, throughout their lives: they can only be masters or slaves. Dictatorial people can never experience freedom and true friendship.'

'No.'

'We couldn't exactly call them reliable, could we?'

'Of course not.'

'And, assuming that our earlier conclusions about the nature of
b morality were correct, we'd have to say that there's no one more immoral than them.'

'Well, our earlier conclusions are right,' he said.

'In short, then,' I said, 'the worst type of person is one whose waking life resembles the dreams we discussed.'

'Yes.'

'He's the product of absolute power falling into the hands of an inherently dictatorial person, and the longer he spends as a dictator, the worse he becomes.'

Glaucon took over the job of talking with me, and said, 'Yes, that's bound to happen.'

会做,而一旦他们得到了自己想要的东西,他们就又疏远了。”

“毫无疑问。”

“那么他们一生中绝不会有任何朋友:他们只能是主人或者奴隶。专制之人绝不会体会到自由和真正的友谊。”

“不会体会到的。”

“我们完全不会称他们为可靠之人,是吗?”

“当然不会称他们为可靠之人。”

“假设我们先前的关于正义本质的结论是正确的话,那么我们不得不说没有比他们更不正义的人了。” b

“我们先前的结论是正确的。”他说。

“简而言之,”我说,“最恶的一类人就是那些清醒时的生活与我们讨论过的睡梦相似的人。”

“是的。”

“他是绝对权力落入一个天生暴君之手的产物,他作为一个暴君时间越久,他就变得越恶。”

格劳孔接过与我交谈的任务,说道:“是的,那是必定会发生的。”

CHAPTER 12

576c ‘Now,’ I continued, ‘won’t we find that the worst person is also the unhappiest person? And won’t we find—whatever most people think—that it’s the most enduring and thorough dictator who has the most enduring and thorough un-happiness?’

‘Yes,’ he said, ‘that’s inevitable.’

‘Now, isn’t it the case’, I asked, ‘that a dictatorial person is the counterpart of a community which is ruled by a dictator, and a democratic person corresponds to a community with a democratic government, and so on for the rest?’

‘Of course.’

‘So we can compare the state of goodness and the happiness of one type of community with another and apply the results to their corresponding human types, can we?’

d ‘Of course.’

‘How does the state of goodness of a community which is ruled by a dictator compare, then, with that of the one we described first, with its kings?’

‘They’re at opposite ends of the scale,’ he answered. ‘One is the best type of community, the other is the worst.’

‘I don’t need to ask which is which,’ I said, ‘because it’s obvious.

But now what about their happiness and unhappiness? Would you come up with the same estimate, or a different one? We shouldn’t be

第十二章

“那么，”我继续说，“我们难道不会觉得最恶的人也就是最不幸福的人吗？难道我们不会觉得——无论大多数人是怎么想的——担任时间最长并且最独裁的人拥有的是最长久而彻底的不幸福。” 576c

“是的，”他说，“那是必然的。”

“那么情况不就是这样的，”我问道，“一个专制者与暴君统治的城邦相对应，而一个民主者与民主式管理的城邦相对应，对于其余的也一样吗？”

“当然。”

“这样我们就能比较一种形态的城邦与另一种形态城邦中的善与幸福的状态，并且把结果应用于与它们相对应类型的人，是吗？”

“当然。” d

“那么如何把僭主独裁统治的城邦中善的状态和我们最先描述过的由王政统治的城邦中的善做一比较呢？”

“它们是正好相反，”他回答说，“一个是最好类型的城邦，另一个是最坏类型的城邦。”

“我用不着追究哪个最好哪个最坏了，”我说，“因为这很显然。但是他们的幸福和不幸福呢？你的评价是一样的呢还是不一样？我们不应该仅通过对一个人，即暴君，或直接构成他圈子

rushed into a decision by our impressions of just one person, the dictator himself, or by the few people who constitute his immediate circle. We should visit the community and see all the sights, immerse
e ourselves thoroughly in it and look everywhere, and then express an opinion.'

'That's a good suggestion,' he said. 'And everyone would see that a community under a dictator is as unhappy as any community can be, while a community under kingship is the happiest one possible.'

'And suppose I were to make the same suggestion as regards
577a their human equivalents too,' I said. 'Would that be a good suggestion? I'd be expecting someone to come up with his assessment of their happiness and unhappiness only if be has the ability to gain insights into a person by using his mind to take on that person's characteristics. Rather than childishly looking from the outside and being won over by the ostentatious facade a dictator presents to the outside world, he should be capable of insight. Suppose we found someone who's not only this good at assessment, but who has also lived in close proximity with a dictator, and has been an eyewitness to what goes on inside a dictator's house and how he treats the various members of his household, because these are the best circumstances for seeing a dictator
b stripped of his pompous clothing; and suppose he'd also seen how a dictator reacts to the risks involved in political life. Would I be right to claim that we should all listen to what this person has to say? Should we ask him to draw on all this firsthand experience to tell us how a dictator fares, as regards happiness and unhappiness, compared with our other types?'

'Yes, that would be a very good idea as well,' he said.

'Shall we pretend, then', I said, 'that *we* are expert assessors, and have in the past met dictators? Otherwise, there'll be no one to answer our questions for us.'

'Yes, let's.'

'All right, then,' I said, 'here's how you'd better proceed with
c the enquiry. You should bear in mind the equivalence between community and individual and submit them one after another to a

的那少部分人的印象来匆忙地作出决定。我们应该拜访一下城邦,考察所有的景象,考察所有地方,使我们自己透彻地了解它 e
后,然后才能发表意见。”

“这个建议很好,”他说,“所有人都能看到僭主统治的城邦是最不幸福的城邦,而王政统治的城邦是最幸福的。”

“设想一下对于与这些城邦相对应的人来说,我也同样
建议,”我说,“这会是个好建议吗?我希望只有当一个人能 577a
够使用他的心灵去考察人的品性而获得对他的洞见之后,这个人才能评判他们的幸福和不幸福。而不是像孩子一样观看外表而被僭主向外部世界所呈现出来的华美外表所迷惑,他应该具有洞察能力。设想我们发现一个人不光是善于评判,而且还与僭主朝夕相处,目睹过僭主家中发生的事情,以及他是如何对待家中不同成员的,因为这是剥去外衣观看僭
主的最好环境;设想他也还看到过僭主在牵涉到政治生活的 b
危机时是如何反应的。我是否可以正确地说,我们应该对这个人的讲述洗耳恭听?我们是否应该要求他从所有这些一手经历中告诉我们,与别的类型的人相比,僭主是幸福的还是不幸福的?”

“是的,这也会是一个非常好的想法。”他说。

“那么我们是否要自称为专业评判员并且在过去见到过僭主?否则,就没有人为我们回答我们的问题了。”

“是的,就让我们这样做吧。”

“那么好吧,”我说,“让我们继续这样来研究吧。你应该记 c
住城邦与个人是相对应的,要一个个地仔细考察;然后你才能描述

detailed examination; then you'll be in a position to describe the attributes either or both of them have.'

'What attributes?' he asked.

'Starting with a community,' I said, 'do you think a community which is ruled by a dictator is free or oppressed?'

'It's impossible to imagine a more complete state of oppression,' he replied.

'But some of its members are evidently free and are doing the oppressing.'

'Yes,' he said, 'but they're the minority. Wretched servitude, with no civil rights, is pretty much the universal condition of the citizen body—certainly of the truly good elements.'

d 'Given the correspondence between individual and community,' I said, 'then isn't his structure necessarily identical? Oppression and servitude must pervade his mind, with the truly good parts of it being oppressed, and an evil, crazed minority doing the oppressing.'

'Necessarily,' he agreed.

'Well, do you think a mind in this condition is free or enslaved?'

'Enslaved, I'd say—definitely.'

'Then again, a community which is enslaved and ruled by a dictator is hardly ever free to do what it wants, is it?'

'I quite agree.'

e 'What about a mind which is ruled by an inner dictator, then? Treating the mind as a single whole, it'll hardly ever be free to do what it wants, will it? It'll constantly be subject to the overpowering whims of its lust, and this will make it highly inconsistent and fickle.'

'Of course.'

'And would a community under a dictator be poor or well off?'

'Poor.'

其中的一个或两者所具有的性质。”

“什么性质?”他问道。

“先说城邦,”我说,“你认为一个由僭主统治的城邦是自由的还是受压迫的?”

“那是一个难以想象的更彻底受压迫的状态。”他回答说。

“但有些成员显然是自由的并且正在行使压迫。”

“是的,”他说,“但他们是少数。不幸的、没有公民权的奴役是全体公民的普遍状态,他们当然是一些真正优秀的成员。”

“如果个人与城邦是相对应的,”我说,“那么他的构成不 d
也必然是一样的吗?压迫与奴役必定充满他的灵魂,灵魂中真正善的部分受到压迫,而恶的部分,这疯狂的少数派行使着压迫。”

“必定如此。”他同意说。

“那么你认为处于这种状态的灵魂是自由的还是受奴役的?”

“受奴役的,我可以确定无疑地说。”

“那么还可以说,一个受到奴役的并由僭主统治的城邦几乎不能自由地做它想要做的事情,是吗?”

“我非常同意。”

“那么一个内心由僭主统治的心灵怎么样呢?如果把这个心 e
灵当作一个整体,那么它几乎不能做它想要做的事情,是吗?它常常会屈从于其强烈欲望占支配地位的怪念头,这会使得它极度地矛盾冲突和反复无常。”

“当然。”

“僭主统治的城邦是贫穷的还是富裕的?”

“贫穷的。”

578a ‘So a person with a dictatorial mind is bound to be in a constant state of poverty and need.’

‘Yes,’ he agreed.

‘Now, isn’t fear ever-present in communities and individuals of this sort?’

‘It certainly is.’

‘Is there any other community, do you think, where you’d come across more moaning, complaining, grievances, and hardships?’

‘No, definitely not.’

‘Would you come across more of them in any other type of individual, do you think? Or has the limit been reached with this dictatorial type and the frenzy caused by his desires and lusts?’

‘Of course it has,’ he said.

b ‘I imagine all this was the kind of evidence which led you to conclude that the community is as unhappy as any community can be.’

‘Do you disagree?’ he asked.

‘Not at all,’ I replied. ‘But what does the same evidence lead you to think about a dictatorial person?’

‘That he is far unhappier than any of the other types,’ he answered.

‘Now you’ve made a claim I do disagree with,’ I said.

‘Why?’ he asked.

‘I don’t think he’s that outstandingly unhappy,’ I said.

‘Who is, then?’

‘I should think you’d agree that here’s an even more miserable person than the one we’ve been discussing.’

‘Who?’

“所以一个拥有僭主心灵的人必定常常会处于贫穷和不满足 578a
的状态。”

“是的。”他同意说。

“那么这样的城邦和个人不是总是有畏惧?”

“当然有。”

“你认为在任何别的城邦你会遇到更多的呻吟、抱怨、不满和困苦吗?”

“不,当然不会。”

“你认为在任何别的类型的个人当中能遇到更多这样的情况吗? 或者说这种僭主的形态和由他的欲望和色欲产生的疯狂已经达到了极限吗?”

“当然达到了极限。”他说。

“我想所有这些都可以作为证明而使你得出结论说,这种城 b
邦是最不幸福的城邦。”

“你不同意吗?”他问道。

“完全同意,”我回答说,“但同样的证据使你对僭主式的人物怎么看?”

“他比别的任何类型的人更加不幸福得多。”他回答说。

“现在我不同意你的说法。”我说。

“为什么?”他问道。

“我认为他不是最为不幸福的。”我说。

“那么谁是最不幸福的?”

“我想你应该会同意说还有比我们曾讨论过的人更加不幸的人?”

“谁?”

c ‘A dictatorial person who can’t remain a private citizen all his life,’ I said, ‘but has the misfortune to end up, by force of circumstance, as an actual dictator.’

‘If I’m to be consistent with our earlier argument,’ he said, ‘I have to admit that you’re right.’

‘Yes,’ I said, ‘but it’s important for us not to rely on assumptions in these sorts of cases. We’re looking into the most important issue there is—which kind of life is good, and which is bad—so we must conduct a really thorough investigation, and I think I see how to proceed.’

‘You’re quite right,’ he said.

‘Well, I wonder what you’ll make of my idea that we should start the investigation by bearing in mind the following points.’

d ‘Which ones?’

‘Every single wealthy citizen in a community owns a lot of slaves. In this respect—that they have a number of people under their control—they resemble dictators; the only difference is that dictators control larger numbers of people.’

‘That’s right.’

‘Well, do you appreciate that these slave-owners aren’t in a state of fear? They aren’t afraid of their slaves, are they?’

‘What reason would they have to be?’

‘None,’ I answered. ‘But do you realize why?’

‘Yes. it’s because behind every single citizen is the community as a whole.’

e ‘Exactly,’ I said. ‘Now, imagine that a man who owns fifty or more slaves is plucked by some god from his community—wife, children, and all—and deposited in some isolated spot along with all his property, especially his slaves. There are no other free men around

“一个僭主式的人物不会一生总是一个普通公民，”我说，“最 c
终由于环境所迫而不幸成为一个实在的僭主。”

“如果我要与我们前面的论证保持一致的话，”他说，“那么，我必须承认你是对的。”

“是的，”我说，“但在这些情况下，重要的是我们不能依靠假设。我们考察的是最重要的问题——什么样的生活是善的，什么样的生活是恶的——所以我们必须进行一项真正彻底的研究，我想我知道应该是这样进行的。”

“你说得非常正确。”他说。

“那么，我想知道你是如何理解我的想法的，我认为我们的研究首先应该记住以下几点？” d

“哪几点？”

“城邦中每一个富裕的公民都拥有很多奴隶。在这个方面——他们支配了很多人——他们与僭主相似；唯一的区别就是僭主支配的人数更多。”

“对的。”

“那么你认为这些奴隶主不是处于畏惧之中吗？他们不害怕他们的奴隶，是吗？”

“他们有什么理由害怕呢？”

“没什么理由，”我回答说，“但你知道为什么吗？”

“是的。这是因为在每个公民个人背后有整个城邦。”

“正是，”我说，“那么设想一个拥有五十个或更多奴隶 e
的人和他的妻子、孩子以及所有人被某个神撵出城邦，和他的所有财产尤其是和他的奴隶一起被安置在某个偏僻的地方。没有别的自由人在他旁边帮助他。他是否会害怕他的

to help him. Would he be afraid of his slaves killing him and his family? And if so, how frightened do you think he'd be?'

'He'd be absolutely terrified, I expect,' he replied.

579a 'What he'd have to do, then, despite their being his slaves, is immediately get on the right side of some of them, make them extravagant promises, and give them their freedom, whatever misgivings he may have. In fact, he'd end up being dependent on the goodwill of his servants, wouldn't he?'

'It's either that or be killed,' he said, 'so he doesn't really have a choice.'

'And what do you think would happen if this god also surrounded him with a lot of neighbours in nearby settlements, and these neighbours of his couldn't abide anyone presuming to be anyone else's master, and punished with extreme severity any case they came across of this kind of oppression?'

b 'He'd be in an even worse trap,' he said, 'with all those enemies hemming him in on every side.'

'Well, is there any difference between this and the prison a dictator finds himself in, because of all the fears and lusts his nature, as we've described it, makes him liable to? He may be greedy for new experiences, but he's the only person in the community who can't travel abroad or see all the sights every other free man longs to see. Instead, he lives like a woman, buried indoors most of the time, re-

c senting any of his fellow citizens who go abroad and see something worth while.'

'Absolutely,' he said.

'So these are the kinds of troubles which swell the harvest of evils reaped by the individual who, in your recent assessment, is as unhappy as anyone can be—the dictatorial type, whose bad government is restricted to himself—when he can't remain a private citizen all his life, but is forced by some misfortune to take on the government of others, despite his inability to control even himself. This is

奴隶杀了他和他的家人呢？如果这样的话，那么你认为他会有多么害怕？”

“我料想他会非常害怕的。”他回答说。

“那么他必须要做的便是，尽管这些人是他的奴隶，不管他可能心存怎样的疑虑，他也要立即巴结他们中的一些人，向他们许 579a
下漫天的诺言，并给予他们自由。实际上，他最终要依靠他的奴隶的善意，不是吗？”

“要么那样做，要么被杀死，”他说，“所以他确实没有选择。”

“如果这位神还在他周围让很多邻人住在他附近，他的这些邻人不能容忍任何人成为任何别的人的主人，并且一旦他们遇到这样的压迫，他们就要处以最严厉的惩罚，你认为这样的话会发生什么呢？”

“他的处境就会更糟，”他说，“所有这些敌人从各个方面攻击 b
他。”

“那么，就像我们曾描述过的那样，由于僭主的本性使他依赖于所有畏惧和强烈欲望，这与他发现自己处于囚笼，有什么区别吗？他也许渴望新的经历，但他是城邦中唯一不能出城旅行或观看别的自由人想看的所有景象的人。相反，他生活得像个女人，大多数时间都在室内，憎恶任何到户外观赏值得一看之物的同城居民。” c

“绝对如此。”他说。

“这种混乱增加了个人所犯的罪恶，在你最近的评判中，你把这些人作为最不幸福的人——僭主类型的人，其糟糕的管理局限于他自身——当他不再一生都作为一个普通公民的时候，为某种不幸所逼迫而去统治别人，而他甚至没有能力控制他自己。这就

like someone ill with spastic paralysis being forced to enter the public arena and spend his life competing as an athlete against others or fighting in wars.'

d 'That's a perfect analogy, Socrates,' he said. 'You're quite right.'

'There's nothing but misery in a dictator's life, then, is there, Glaucon?' I asked. 'You thought you'd identified the worst life possible, but there's even more hardship in his, isn't there?'

'Definitely,' he said.

'The truth of the matter, then, even if people deny it, is that a real dictator is actually a real slave—judging by the extent of his obsequiousness and servitude—and a flatterer of the worst kinds of people.
e ple. His desires are completely insatiable as well: any expert observer of the totality of the mind can see that a dictator is actually never fulfilled and is therefore poor. Moreover, fear pervades his whole life, and he's convulsed with constant pains. This is what he's like, if his condition resembles that of the community he rules over—and it does, doesn't it?'

'Yes, it does,' he agreed.

580a 'And we haven't finished with his attributes yet: there are also all the ones we mentioned earlier, which he's not only bound to have, but bound to have even more thoroughly than before because of being in office. He's resentful, unreliable, immoral, friendless, and unjust; and he gives room and board to every vice. And the result of all this is not just the extreme wretchedness of his own condition: these attributes of his also rub off on people who come near him.'

'That's beyond all reasonable doubt,' he said.

'All right, then,' I continued. 'Now is the time for you to play the
b part of the judge with overall authority and reveal your verdict. Of the five types—regal, timocratic, oligarchic, democratic, and dictatorial—which comes first, in your opinion, in the contest of happiness? Which

像强迫一个神经瘫痪者参加公共竞技,作为一个运动员去与别人竞技或去打仗。" d

"苏格拉底,这是个非常好的类比,"他说,"你很对。"

"那么,格劳孔,僭主的生活中只有不幸,是吗?"我问道,"你认为你看到了最坏的生活,但在他的生活中甚至还有更多的不幸,不是吗?"

"毫无疑问。"他说。

"那么,即使人们会否认,但事实的真相是,一个真正的僭主实际上就是真正的奴隶——从他的奉承与奴性上来看——并且是巴结最坏那类人的人。他的欲望也是完全得不到满足的:任何 e
善于观察心灵整体的人,能够看到僭主实际上是决不会得到满足的,由此他是贫穷的。此外,他的整个生活中充满着恐惧,并且经常因疼痛而抽搐。他就像是这样的,如果他的状态像他统治的城邦的状态,他确实是这样的,不是吗?"

"是的。"他同意说。

"我们还没说完他的特征:还有一些是我们之前提到过 580a
的,他肯定不光拥有这些特征,甚至由于掌了权,比起以前就必定更是拥有这些特征。他愤恨、不可靠、不道德、不友善、不正义,他孕育了各种罪恶。所有这些导致的结果不光是他自己极度悲惨的状况,他的特征还使得他周围的人也成为最为悲惨的人。"

"这不会受到理性的怀疑。"他说。

"那么好吧,",我继续说,"那么现在你应该作为法官,握有最大的权威说出你的判决。五种类型当中——王者型的、爱荣誉型 b
的、寡头型的、民主型的、僭主型的——在你看来,在幸福比赛中

comes second? You'd better grade all five of them.'

'It's an easy decision to make,' he said, 'because the order in which they made their entrance, like troupes of dancers on a stage, corresponds to how I rate them. That's my estimate of where they come on the scale of goodness and badness, and of happiness and unhappiness.'

'Shall we hire a town crier, then,' I asked, 'or shall I be the one to proclaim that the son of Ariston has judged the happiest person
c to be the best and most moral person—that is, the person who possesses the highest degree of regal qualities and who rules as king over himself? And that he has also judged the unhappiest person to be the worst and most immoral person—that is, the person who possesses the highest degree of dictatorial qualities and rules as completely as possible as a dictator over himself and his community?'

'You make the announcement,' he said.

'And can I add a rider that this is so whether or not their condition is hidden from the eyes of gods and men?' I asked.

'You can,' he said.

d 'All right, then,' I said. 'That's the first proof, but I wonder how the second one strikes you.'

'What is it?'

'I think the correspondence between the three classes into which the community was divided and the threefold division of everyone's mind provides the basis for a further argument,' I said.

'What argument?'

'It seems to me that each of the three mental categories has its own particular pleasure, so that there are three kinds of pleasure as well. The same would also go for desires and motivations.'

'What do you mean?' he said.

'We found that one part is the intellectual part of a person,

谁是第一？谁是第二？你最好把五个都排一下位置。”

“这个决定是很容易做的，”他说，“因为就像舞台上的歌队一样，他们入场的顺序与我评价他们的方式相对应。我就是这样评价他们的善恶次序以及幸福与不幸的次序的。”

“那么，我们是要雇佣一个街头宣告员呢，”我问，“还是我来宣布，阿里斯同的儿子已做出判决说，最幸福的人就是最好和最正义的人——就是那些最大程度地拥有王者品性以及作为王而 c
统治自己的人？他同时也作出判决说，最不幸福的人就是最坏和最不正义的人——就是那些最大程度地拥有僭主品性以及完全作为僭主来统治自己和城邦的人？”

“你做出了宣判。”他说。

“我是否能够补充说，无论他们的状况是否不被诸神和人看见都是这样的？”我问道。

“你可以这么说。”他说。

“那么好吧，”他说，“这是第一个证明，但我想知道你对第二 d
个证明有什么看法。”

“是什么？”

“我想城邦中分成的三个阶层与每个人灵魂中的三分的对应关系，这为进一步的论证提供了基础。”我说。

“什么论证？”

“在我看来，心灵中的三个范畴中的每一个都有其自身特殊的快乐，这样也就有三种快乐。对于欲望和动机也是一样。”

“你说的是什么意思？”他说。

“我们发现一个部分是人的理性部分，另一个部分是激情的

another is the passionate part, and the third has so many manifestations that we couldn't give it a single label which applied to it and it
e alone, so we named it after its most prevalent and powerful aspect: we called it the desirous part, because of the intensity of our desires for food, drink, sex, and so on, and we also referred to it as the mercenary part, because desires of this kind invariably need money for their fulfilment.'

581a 'And we were right,' he said.

'What if we said that what it enjoys, what it cares for, is profit? This would be the best way for us to clarify the issue for ourselves: we could keep our references to this part of the mind concise, and call it mercenary and avaricious. Would that description hit the mark?'

'I think so,' he said.

'And isn't our position that the passionate part always has its sights set wholly on power, success, and fame?'

'Yes.'

b 'So it would be fair for us to call it competitive and ambitious, wouldn't it?'

'Perfectly fair.'

'And it's patently obvious that our intellectual part is entirely directed at every moment towards knowing the truth of things, and isn't interested in the slightest in money and reputation.'

'Certainly.'

'So we'd be right to call it intellectual and philosophical, wouldn't we?'

'Of course.'

'Now, sometimes this intellectual part is the motivating aspect of
c one's mind: sometimes—as circumstances dictate—it's one of the other two. Yes?'

部分，第三个部分具有多样的表现，以致我们不能给予其一个单一的名称，一个适用于它并且只适用于它的名称，所以我们用最普遍、最有力的那个方面来命名它：我们把它称作 e
是欲望部分，因为我们对于饮食、性等等的欲望很强烈，我们也把它称作贪财的部分，因为这种欲望必定需要钱来使它们得到满足。” 581a

“我们是对的。”他说。

“那么要是我们说它所欢喜和关心的是利益又怎么样呢？对于我们来说，这是澄清问题的最好方式：为了使我们对心灵的这个部分的指称保持简明，我们称它为贪财爱利。这样的描述准确吗？”

“我想是的。”他说。

“我们的看法不就是激情部分总是整个地盯着权力、成功和名誉？”

“是的。” b

“所以我们可以恰当地称之为好胜和雄心勃勃的部分，不是吗？”

“非常恰当。”

“很明显，我们的智性部分每时每刻都全神贯注于认识事物的真理，毫不关心金钱和名誉。”

“当然。”

“所以我们可以正当地称之为智性的或哲学的，不是吗？”

“当然。”

“那么，有时智性部分是人心灵的驱动部分；有时——由于受制于条件——另外两者中的一个是驱动部分。是吗？” c

'Yes,' he said.

'Which is why we're also claiming that there are three basic human types—the philosophical, the competitive, and the avaricious.'

'Exactly.'

'And it also explains why there are three kinds of pleasure as well, one for each of the human types, doesn't it?'

'Yes.'

'Now, I'm sure you're aware', I said, 'that if you were to approach representatives of these three types one by one and ask them which of these ways of life was the most enjoyable, they'd each swear
d by their own way of life, wouldn't they? A money-minded person wouldn't think that respect or learning, and their pleasures, were anywhere near as important as making money, unless there was also a profit to be made out of them, would he?'

'True,' he said.

'Then again, an ambitious person would regard enjoyment of money as vulgar,' I continued, 'and would think that only some concomitant respect could redeem enjoyment of intellectual activities from being an impractical waste of time, wouldn't he?'

'Yes,' he agreed.

e 'What about a philosopher?' I asked. 'How do you think he rates other pleasures compared with knowing the truth of things and with constantly employing his intellect and feeling that kind of pleasure? Doesn't he think they miss the mark by a long way? Doesn't he describe them as necessary, in the strict sense that, apart from intellectual pleasures, he needs only those which are unavoidable?'

'We can be perfectly certain about that,' he replied.

'Now, when people are arguing about the various pleasures which accompany aspects of themselves,' I said, 'and even about the

“是的。”他说。

“这也是为什么我们说有三种基本类型的人——哲学家、好胜者和贪利者——的原因。”

“正是。”

“这也解释了为什么有三种类型的快乐，并且每一种都与人的类型所对应的原因，不是吗？”

“是的。”

“那么，我确信你意识到了，”我说，“如果你研究三种类型的代表，逐一询问这些生活方式中哪一种是最快乐的，他们每人都发誓说这是他们自己的生活方式，不是吗？一个想着赚钱的人认为尊重或学习的快乐根本比不上赚钱重要，除非从中也有利可图，是吗？” d

“对的。”他说。

“那么再者，一个爱荣誉的人会把金钱的快乐当作是庸俗的，我继续说，“而且还会认为智性活动是一种不切实际的浪费时间，只有由此换来的他人恭敬与尊重才能弥补这一损失，他不是这样认为的吗？”

“是的，”他同意道。

“那么爱智慧的哲人呢？”我问道。“你怎么想？他将其它感 e
官快乐与通晓、了悟事物实相的快乐进行比较，与不断地投入其思维和直感于这种通晓研究工作的那种快乐进行比较，他不会认为他们大大地错失过人生的目标了吧？在严格的意义上而言，除了智性的快乐而外，他不会将那些感官快乐描述为必不可少的，而他所需要的感官之乐，也只是那些不可避免的而已，是吧？”

“我们对此是能够完全肯定的。”他回答说。

“那么当人们争论伴随他们自身各个方面的各种快乐，”我

kind of life one should lead, and when the only criterion they're using is where a way of life comes on the scale of pleasure and distress,
582a rather than on the scales of right and wrong or good and bad, then how can we know who has truth on his side?'

'I really couldn't tell you,' he said.

'Well, look at it this way. What does it take to make a good decision? Doesn't it take experience, intelligence, and rationality? Aren't these the best means of reaching a decision?'

'Of course,' he said.

'All right, then. Which of the three men has had the greatest exposure to all the pleasures we've mentioned? Do you think the avaricious type understands the truth of things and has therefore had more
b experience of intellectual pleasure than a philosopher has of the pleasure of moneymaking?'

'There's a world of difference,' he replied. 'From his earliest years onwards a philosopher has inevitably experienced both the other kinds of pleasure; there's never been any reason, however, for an avaricious person to experience the sweetness of intellectual pleasure and it remains unfamiliar to him—in fact, even if he wanted to get a taste of it, he'd find it difficult.'

'In other words,' I commented, 'a philosopher's experience of both intellectual and moneymaking pleasures puts him in a better position than an avaricious person, anyway.'

'A far better position.'

c 'And how does he compare with an ambitious person? Is he more familiar with the enjoyment of respect than an ambitious person is with the enjoyment of intelligence?'

'But anyone can get respect: it's a result of attaining one's objective,' he said. 'Respect is showered on people for their wealth, their courage, and their intelligence: all three types are familiar with what it's like to enjoy being respected, at any rate. But only a philosopher can have found out by experience what it's like to enjoy contemplating reality.'

d 'As far as experience is concerned, then,' I said, 'it's a philosopher who's in the best position to make a decision.'

说，“甚至争论人应该过哪种生活时，还有当人们对生活方式采用的唯一的评判标准是快乐与痛苦的，而不是正确与错误 582a
或善良与邪恶的时候，我们又怎样才能知道真理在谁哪一边呢？”

“我确实说不出来。”他说。

“那么这样来看看。凭什么做出正确的判断呢？难道不是凭经验、理性和推理吗？这些不是做出判断的最好方式吗？”

“当然。”他说。

“那么好吧。三种人中的哪一种对我们提到过的所有快乐最具有经验？你认为贪利者理解事物的真理，由此他对智性之乐的经验比哲学家对赚钱之乐的经验还多吗？” b

“天差地别，”他回答说，“从早年起，哲学家就必定要体验另外两种快乐；然而对于贪利者来说，根本没有理由去体验智性乐趣的甜美，这种甜美对他来说一直是陌生的——实际上，即使他想要尝一下它，他会觉得那样是很困难的。”

“换句话说，”我评论道，“无论如何，哲学家对智性和赚钱之乐的体验，使他比贪利者处于更有高的地位。”

“高得多。” c

“与爱荣誉者相比怎么样呢？他是否对尊重之乐的熟悉更胜于爱荣誉者对智性之乐的熟悉？”

“但任何人都能得到尊重：这是达到某人目标的结果，”他说，“人们由于财富、勇气和智性而得到尊重：无论如何，三种类型的人对于受尊重的快乐是什么样都很熟悉。但只有哲学家才能通过经验发现沉思实在的快乐是什么样的。”

“那么就经验而言，”我说，“哲学家最有资格做出评判。” d

'By far the best position,' he agreed.

'And he's the only one who'll be in a position to combine experience and intelligence.'

'Naturally.'

'Moreover, the resources for making a decision are available only to a philosopher, not to an avaricious or an ambitious person.'

'What resources?'

'We did say that decisions require rational argumentation, didn't
e we?'

'Yes.'

'And rational argumentation is a particularly important resource in this context.'

'Of course.'

'Now, if money and wealth were the best means of making decisions, then the likes and dislikes of the avaricious type would necessarily be closest to the truth.'

'Yes.'

'And if prestige, success, and courage were best, it would be the likes and dislikes of the ambitious, competitive type. Yes?'

'Obviously.'

'But since it takes experience, intelligence and rationality... ?'

'Then it's the philosophical type, with his appreciation of ration-
583a ality, whose tastes are closest to the truth,' he said.

'Of the three kinds of pleasure, the most enjoyable, then, is that which belongs to the intellectual part of the mind; one's life becomes most enjoyable when this part of the mind is one's motivating force.'

'Of course,' he said. 'I mean, when a thoughtful person recommends his own way of life, he ought to be taken seriously.'

'Which way of life—which pleasure—comes second, in his

“是最有资格的。”他同意说。

“他是唯一的能够把经验和智性结合在一起的人。”

“自然。”

“此外，只有哲学家才拥有做评判的资源，而贪利者和爱荣誉者则没有。”

“什么资源？”

“我们确实说过评判需要理性论证，不是吗？”

“是的。”

“在这种场合，理性论证是一个尤其重要的资源。”

“当然。”

“那么，如果金钱和财富是做出评判的最好手段，那么为贪利者所喜欢和不喜欢的就必然最接近真理了。” e

“是的。”

“如果名誉、成功和勇气是最好的手段，那么为爱荣誉者和好胜者所喜欢和不喜欢的就必然更接近真理了。是吗？”

“显而易见。”

“但是既然要以经验、理性和推理为标准呢……？”

“那么就是喜欢推理的爱智者那一类人，他们的喜好更接近于真理了。”他说。

“因此，在三种快乐中，最让人快乐的是属于心灵的智性部分 583a
的那一种；当心灵的这个部分成为一个人的驱动力量的时候，他的生活就变得最快乐了。”

“当然，”他说，“我的意思是说，当一个富于思想的人向别人推荐自己的生活方式时，他应该受到别人的认真对待。”

“在他的评判中，哪种生活方式——哪种快乐——是第二

assessment?"

'Obviously the pleasure which accompanies the military, ambitious life, since it differs less from his own way of life than the moneymaking one does.'

'Apparently, then, the way of life pursued by the avaricious type comes last, in his estimate. Yes?'

'Of course,' he said.

b 'That makes it two, then, one after another: immorality has twice been defeated by morality. In Olympic fashion, here's the third round—for Zeus the Saviour and Zeus of Olympus. I wonder whether you agree that only the philosopher's pleasure is true and pure, while the others are illusory; I seem to remember having heard some clever fellow or other expressing this idea. And in fact this would be the most important and serious fall of the whole competition.'

'It certainly would. But what are you getting at?'

c 'I'll find out, if you'll help my investigation by answering my questions,' I said.

'Go ahead,' he said.

'All right,' I said. 'Pain is the opposite of pleasure, wouldn't you say?'

'Yes.'

'And is there a state which involves no pleasure or pain?'

'Yes, there certainly is.'

'It's an intermediate state in which the mind isn't active in either of these ways, isn't it? What do you think?'

'I agree,' he said.

'Now, can you remember what people say when they're ill?' I asked.

位的呢?”

“显然是伴随军队的雄心勃勃的生活而来的那种快乐了,因为比起赚钱的生活方式来,它和他自己的生活方式差别更小些。”

“那么在他的评判中,贪利者所追求的生活方式显然排在最后。是吗?”

“当然。”他说。

“那么接连两次:不正义已经被正义打败了。按照奥林匹克 b
赛会的方式,还有第三回合——献给救世主宙斯和奥林匹亚的宙斯。我想知道你是否同意只有爱智者的快乐是真实的、纯一的,而其他人的快乐是虚幻的;我似乎记得某个聪明人说过这样的想法。实际上这在整个比赛中可能是最重要、最严重的失败。”

“当然是的。但你说的是什么意思?”

“如果你回答我的问题来帮助我的研究,那么我会搞明白 c
的。”我说。

“继续吧。”他说。

“好吧,”我说,“痛苦是快乐的对立面,难道你不会这样说吗?”

“是对立面。”

“是否有一种状态既没有快乐又没有痛苦?”

“是的,确实有。”

“它是一种中间状态,在这里,心灵不是处于两种方式的任一活动中,不是吗? 你是怎么想的?”

“我同意。”他说。

“那么你是否记得人们生病的时候会说些什么?”我问道。

'What?'

'They claim that health really is the most pleasant thing in the
d world, but that they didn't appreciate the fact until they got ill.'

'Yes, that's familiar,' he said.

'And you're aware that when people are in great pain they say that the most pleasant thing in the world would be for the pain to end.'

'Yes.'

'And you've come across all sorts of other situations, I should think, in which people are feeling pain and claim that there is nothing more pleasant than the remission and absence of pain. It's not pleasure whose praises they sing in these situations.'

'That's because under these circumstances remission does become pleasant and desirable, I suppose,' he remarked.

e 'And it follows that when someone stops feeling pleasure, the remission of pleasure will be painful.'

'I suppose so,' he said.

'So the intermediate state, as we called it a moment ago—the state of inactivity—will at different times be both pleasure and pain.'

'So it seems.'

'Is it possible for anything to be both of two things if it is neither of those two things?'

'I don't think so.'

'Now, the mental feelings of pleasure and pain are both activities, aren't they?'

'Yes.'

584a 'And didn't we just find that the state which involves no pain or pleasure is actually a state of *inactivity* which falls between the

“什么？”

“他们说健康确实在世上最快乐的事了，但是在他们生病之前他们是不会认识到这个事实的。” d

“是的，通常是这样的。”他说。

“你知道当人们处于极大的痛苦中的时候，他们会说世上最快乐的事情就是结束痛苦。”

“是的。”

“我想你应该遇见过其他各种情况，在那些情况下人们感到痛苦，并说没有比免除和摆脱痛苦更快乐的事情了。在这些情况下，他们赞扬的不是快乐。”

“我想那是因为在这些情况下，免除了痛苦就是快乐的，而且是为人所渴望的。”他说。

“这可以推论说，当一个人不再感到快乐的时候，快乐的减弱 e
就会是痛苦的。”

“我想是这样的。”他说。

“所以这中间状态，就像我们刚才所称谓的那样——不动的状态——在不同的时候可能既是快乐的又是痛苦的。”

“看来如此。”

“如果任何一个事物两者皆不是，那么它是否可能两者皆是呢？”

“我想不行。”

“那么灵魂对于快乐和痛苦的感觉都是活动，不是吗？”

“是的。”

“我们刚才不是发现不牵涉到痛苦或快乐的状态，确实是处 584a

two?'

'Yes, we did.'

'How can it be right, then, to regard absence of pain as pleasant, or absence of pleasure as painful?'

'It can't be.'

'There's no reality here, then, just some superficial effect,' I said. 'Inactivity merely appears pleasant and painful on those occasions, because it's being contrasted respectively with pain and with pleasure. These appearances aren't reliable in the slightest: they're a kind of deception.'

'Yes, that *is* what the argument suggests,' he said.

b 'Well, I'd like to show you pleasures which aren't products of pain,' I said. 'I'm worried about the possibility of your currently regarding all pleasure as the cessation of pain, and all pain as he cessation of pleasure, and thinking that this is how things are.'

'Where shall I look?' he asked. 'What pleasures are you talking about?'

'If you'd care to consider the enjoyment of smells,' I replied, 'you'd see particularly clear examples, though there are plenty of other cases too. The point is that there's no preceding feeling of pain, and yet you can suddenly get an incredibly intense pleasure at a scent, which also leaves no distress behind when it's over.'

'That's true,' he said.

c 'So we'd better resist the notion that pure pleasure is escape from pain, and pure pain is escape from pleasure.'

'Yes.'

'All the same,' I went on, 'I dare say that most so-called pleasures—the most intense ones, anyway—which reach the mind through the body are of this kind: in some way or other they involve escape from pain.'

'True.'

于两者之间的不动状态吗?”

“是的,我们发现了。”

“那么没有痛苦就是快乐,或没有快乐就是痛苦,这种看法怎么可能是正确的呢?”

“不可能正确。”

“因而这里并无真实性,而只是表面效果,”我说,“在那些情况下,因为平静不动是分别与痛苦和快乐作比较,所以它仅仅是看起来快乐和痛苦的。这些表面现象一点都不可靠:它们是一种欺骗。”

“是的,这是论证所表明的。”他说。

“那么,我想让你看看那种不是痛苦之产物的快乐,”我说, b
“我担心的是,你现在可能把所有的快乐都当作是痛苦的停止,把所有的痛苦都当作是快乐的停止,并且还认为事实就是这样的。”

“你叫我往哪里看?”他问道,“你说的是什么样的快乐?”

“如果你愿意考虑一下嗅觉的快乐,”我回答说,“你会非常清楚地看到几个例子,虽然还有许多别的情况。关键是之前没有痛苦,然而突然你对一个香味感到难以想象强烈的快乐,当这个香味过去之后也不留下什么痛苦。”

“对的。”他说。

“所以我们最好抵制这种想法:真正的快乐是脱离了痛苦,真 c
正的痛苦是脱离了快乐。”

“是的。”

“同时,”我继续说,“我胆敢说,大多数所谓的快乐——无论如何,那些最强烈的快乐——那些通过身体达到灵魂的快乐是这样的:它们在某种程度上都是脱离了痛苦。”

“对的。”

'And doesn't the same go for anticipatory pleasure and distress, which happen before the event as a result of expectations?'

'Yes.'

d 'Do you know what they're like—what the best analogy for them is?' I asked.

'What?' he answered.

'You know how things can be high, low, or in between?' I asked.

'Yes.'

'Well, someone moving from the bottom of anything to the middle is bound to get an impression of upward motion, isn't he? And once he's standing at the halfway point and look-ing down to where he travelled from, then if he hasn't seen the true heights, he's bound to think he's reached the top, isn't he?'

'Yes, I'd certainly have to agree with that,' he said.

e 'And if he retraced his steps, he'd think—rightly—that he was travelling downwards, wouldn't he?' I asked.

'Of course.'

'And all these experiences of his would be due to his ignorance of the true nature of high, middle, and low, wouldn't they?'

'Obviously.'

'So would you think it odd for people who have never experienced truth, and who therefore have unreliable views about a great many subjects, to be in the same position where pleasure, pain, and the intermediate state are concerned? They not only hold the correct
585a opinion that they are feeling pain, and do in fact feel pain, when they move into a state of pain, but they're also certain about the satis-

“对于预期的快乐和痛苦而言不也是一样吗？这些是作为一种期望的结果，先于事情而发生的。”

“是一样的。”

“你认为它们是什么样的——对于它们，最好的类比是什么？”我问道。 d

“什么呢？”他回答说。

“你知道事物怎样才能是高的、低的，或是处于中间的吧？”我问道。

“是的。”

“那么，某个从事物的底部上升到中间的人必定会有上升运动的印象，不是吗？一旦他站在中间点向下看自己的来处，那么如果他没有看到过真正的高度，他也必定会认为自己达到了顶点，不是吗？”

“是的，我当然同意。”他说。

“如果他往后退，他有理由认为他在向下运动，不是吗？”我问道。 e

“当然。”

“他的所有这些感觉都在于对真正的高、中间和低的本质的无知，不是吗？”

“显而易见。”

“所以你是否会对那些从来没有体验过真实之道的人感到奇怪呢？他们因为没有这种体验，所以对于非常多的领域或事物的见解也都是不可靠的，对于我们讨论的快乐、痛苦以及中间状态 585a
的见解亦然。当他们进入一种痛苦状态时，他们倒还持有一种正确见解，即他们正在感受痛苦，而且实际上也真的是在感受痛苦，不但如此，当他们从痛苦中离开而进入一种不苦不乐的中间状态

faction and pleasure they feel when they move away from pain and into the intermediate state. But they're being misled: there's no difference between people who've never experienced pleasure comparing pain with absence of pain, and people who've never experienced white comparing black with grey.'

'No, I don't find this at all odd,' he replied. 'In fact, I'd be far more surprised if it didn't happen.'

'Here's something for you to think about,' I said. 'Aren't hun-
b ger, thirst, and so on states in which the body is lacking something?'

'Naturally.'

'While stupidity and unintelligence are states in which the mind is lacking something?'

'Yes.'

'So food and intelligence are the sources of satisfaction in these cases?'

'Of course.'

'Is it the case that the more real something is, the more it can be a source of true satisfaction? Or is it the less real it is?'

'Obviously it's the more real it is.'

'Well, is reality present in a purer form in things like bread, drink, savouries, and food in general, do you think, or in things like
c true belief, knowledge, intelligence, and in short in all the things that constitute goodness? Here's another issue to help you decide. There are objects which never alter, never perish, and are never deceptive, and which are not only like that in themselves, but are found in an environment which is also like that; on the other hand, there are objects which are constantly altering and are perishable, and which are not only like that in themselves, but are found in an environment which is also like that. Which class of objects, do you think, contains a higher degree of reality?'

时,他们竟也确信自己感受到了满足与快乐。但是他们误入歧途了:那些从未体验过真正快乐的人,将痛苦与痛苦的缺乏相提并论,那些从未看见过白色的人,则将黑色与灰色相提并论,这两种人没什么区别。”

“不,我并不觉得有什么奇怪的,”他回答说,“实际上,如果不是这样的话,我反而会觉得更为奇怪的。”

“还有些事情需要你思考,”我说,“饥渴等等不是身体缺少某 b
种东西的状态吗?”

“自然。”

“同时,愚蠢和无智也是心灵缺少某种东西的状态吗?”

“是的。”

“所以在这些情况下,食物和智性是快乐的源泉?”

“当然。”

“情况是否是这样的:某物越是实在,它就越是可以作为快乐的源泉?或者越不实在就越是可以作为快乐的源泉?”

“显然越是实在就越是可以作为快乐的源泉。”

“那么你认为纯粹形式的实在出现在像面包、饮料、美味和一般的食物这些事物中呢?还是出现在像真正的意见、知识、智性以及简而言之一切构成善的事物之中呢?这里还有一个例子可以帮助你做出决定。有一些事物从不变化,从不腐朽,决不欺骗, c
不光存在于自身具有这种性质的事物中,还存在于与之相似的周围事物中;另一方面,有一些事物,它们常常变化并且是可朽坏的,它们不光存在于在自身具有这种性质的事物中,还存在于与之相似的周围事物中。你认为哪类事物包含有较高程度的实在?”

'The class of objects which never alter is far superior in this respect,' he replied.

'And isn't the reality of that which never alters just as knowable as it is real?'

'Yes.'

'And just as true?'

'Again, yes.'

'If it were less true, it would be less real as well, wouldn't it?'

'Necessarily.'

d 'To sum up, then, the kinds of things which tend to the body are less true and less real than the kinds of things which tend to the mind. Yes?'

'Yes, certainly.'

'And don't you think the same goes for the body, compared to the mind?'

'I do.'

'Is it the case, then, that an object which is satisfied by more real things, and which is itself more real, is more really satisfied than an object which is satisfied by less real things, and which is itself less real?'

'Of course.'

'Therefore, assuming that being satisfied by things which accord with one's nature is pleasant, an object which is really satisfied more (that is, by more real things) would be enabled more really and truly
e to feel true pleasure, while an object which comes by less real things would be less truly and steadily satisfied and would come by a less dependable and less true version of pleasure.'

'That's absolutely inevitable,' he agreed.

586a 'It turns out, then, that people to whom intelligence and goodness are unfamiliar, whose only interest is self-indulgence and so on,

“永恒不变的那类事物在这方面优越地多。”他回答说。

“永恒不变的事物的实在性，不是与它是真实的一样是可知的吗？”

“是的。”

“同样地真实？”

“同样是的。”

“如果不那么真实，那么也就没那么实在，不是吗？”

“必然如此。”

“那么总的来说，照看身体的那类事物比照看心灵的那类事 d
物更少真实和实在。是吗？”

“确实是。”

“那么，你不认为，与心灵相比，身体也更少真实和实在吗？”

“我是这样认为的。”

“那么在这样的情况下，一个事物得到更为实在的事物之充实，于是它自身也更为实在，与一个得到较少实在的事物之充实，于是自身也较少实在的事物相比，它更为充实，是吗？”

“当然。”

“所以假设得到与某人本性一致的事物的充实是快乐的，一个事物确实受到更多的充实，即更加实在的事物的充实，那么就会使人更实在、更真实地感到真正的快乐，而一个
事物来自于不那么实在的事物，它便不会那么真实和稳定地 e
得到充实，并且得到的是一种不那么可靠、不那么真实的快乐。”

“这肯定是不可避免的 。”他同意说。

“那么可以看到，那些没有经验过智性和善的人，他们的兴趣 586a

spend their lives moving aimlessly to and fro between the bottom and the halfway point, which is as far as they reach. But they never travel any further towards the true heights: they've never even looked up there, let alone gone there; they aren't really satisfied by anything real; they don't experience steady, pure pleasure. They're no different from cattle: they spend their lives grazing, with their eyes turned down and heads bowed towards the ground and their tables. Food and sex are their only concerns, and their insatiable greed for more and
b more drives them to kick and butt one another to death with their horns and hoofs of iron, killing one another because they're seeking satisfaction in unreal things for a part of themselves which is also unreal—a leaky vessel they're trying to fill.'

'Socrates,' Glaucon declared, 'you've given an inspired and perfect description of the life most people lead.'

'Isn't it also inevitable that the pleasures they're involved with are, in fact, combinations of pleasure and pain, mere effigies of true pleasure? Like those illusory paintings, the pleasure and pain are viv-
c id only because of the contrast between them, and their intensity is therefore no more than apparent. They impregnate people with an insane lust for the pleasure they offer, and these fools fight over them, as the Trojans in Stesichorus' story, out of ignorance of the truth, fought over the mere apparition of Helen.'

'Yes, something like that's bound to be the case,' he said.

'What about the passionate part of the mind? Won't the situation be more or less the same for anyone who brings its desires to a successful conclusion? He's either ambitious, in which case he's motivated by resentment and seeks satisfaction in status; or he's competitive, in which case he relies on force and seeks satisfaction in suc-
d cess; or he's bad-tempered, in which case he resorts to anger and seeks satisfaction in an angry outburst. But none of these involve

只在于自我放纵等等,他们的生活花在从底部到他们所能达到的中部的漫无目的的徘徊上。但是他们决不能再向真正的高度前进:他们甚至从没有向上看过,更不用说前往那里了;他们确实没有被任何实在的事物所充实;他们没有经验过稳固与纯粹的快乐。他们与牛没什么区别:他们的生活就是吃草,他们的眼睛朝下,他们的头朝着土地和他们的餐桌。他们关心的只是食物和交媾,他们对于更多东西的无止境的贪求驱使他们用铁的角和蹄相互踢撞致死,杀了一个又一个,因为他们在不实在的事物中寻求 b
满足一个自身也是不实在的部分——他们试图灌满的是一个漏水的容器。"

"苏格拉底,"格劳孔说,"你对大多数人的生活做了一个给人启发的、完美的描述。"

"他们所拥有的快乐实际上不也必定是快乐和痛苦的混合,而仅仅是真正快乐的影像吗?就像那些产生幻觉的绘画,快乐和痛苦之所以是鲜明的是因为两者的对比,所以不 c
过是表面上很强烈。他们给人们注入对他们提供的快乐的疯狂欲望,那些愚人为之争斗,就像斯特昔科鲁故事中的特洛伊人一样,由于不知真相,他们仅仅为了海伦的幻影而开战。"

"是的,事情必定是这样的。"他说。

"灵魂中的激情部分又怎么样呢?对于任何想让他的欲望得到满足的人来说,情况不是多多少少同样的吗?要是他是爱好荣誉的,在这种情况下,他受到愤恨的激发而寻求得到地位;要是他是好胜的,在这种情况下,他就会依靠强力以寻求得到胜利;要是他是暴躁的,在这种情况下,他就诉诸于怒气,在怒气的爆发中寻 d

reason and intelligence.'

'Again, yes, something like that's bound to be the case,' he said.

'All right, then,' I said. 'Shall we confidently state that, where avarice and competitiveness are concerned, any desire which succeeds in attaining its objective will get the truest pleasure available to it when it is guided by truth, which is to say when it follows the
e leadership of knowledge and reason in its quest for those pleasures to which intelligence directs it? And shall we add that the pleasures it gets will also be the ones which are particularly suitable for it—that is, if suitability and benefit coincide?'

'Well, they do coincide,' he said.

'It follows that when the whole mind accepts the leadership of the philosophical part, and there's no internal conflict, then each part can do its own job and be moral in everything it does, and in particu-
587a lar can enjoy its own pleasures, and thus reap as much benefit and truth from pleasure as is possible for it.'

'Exactly.'

'When one of the other two parts is in control, however, it not only fails to attain its own pleasure, but it also forces the other parts to go after unsuitable, false pleasures.'

'Right,' he agreed.

'Now, the further removed something is from philosophy and reason, the more it'll have an effect of this kind.'

'Certainly.'

'And aren't things separated from law and order to the same extent that they're separated from reason?'

'Obviously.'

b 'And didn't we find that it's the lustful, dictatorial desires which are the furthest removed from law and order?'

'We certainly did.'

'While the regal, restrained desires are closest to them?'

'Yes.'

求满足。但是没有一个是与理性和智性有关的。”

“是的,事情也必定是这样的。”他说。

“那么好吧,”我说道。“我们是否应该确信地说,与贪利和好胜相关的、成功达其目的的任何欲望,只有在真实之引导,也就是说,当欲望跟随知识与理性的引导,去追求智性所指的那些快乐, e
它才会获得最真实可享的快乐?而且我们是否应该补充说,它所获得的快乐,也是特别适合它的——也就是说,如果适合性与有益性是相互符合的话?”

“是的,它们确实是相互符合的。”他说。

“由此可以推论出,当整个心灵接受了爱智部分的领导,没有内部的冲突,那么每个部分都各司其职,在它所做的所有事情上都是正义的,尤其是它能享受自己的快乐,这样就能从快乐中获得很多的利益和真实。” 587a

“正是如此。”

“然而当另外两个部分之一起控制作用的时候,不光是不能得到它自己的快乐,而且还迫使别的部分追求不恰当的错误的快乐。”

“对的。”他同意说。

“那么越是远离爱智与理性,就越是有这种效果。”

“当然。”

“与法律和秩序分离的事物不就是与理性分离吗?”

“显而易见。”

“我们不是发现色欲和暴君的欲望离法律和秩序最远吗?” b

“我们当然发现了。”

“而王者的受节制的欲望是否最接近法律和秩序?”

“是的。”

'The more of a dictator a person is, then, the greater the distance between him and pleasure which is both true and suitable; the more of a king a person is, the shorter the distance.'

'Necessarily.'

'It follows that there is no life less enjoyable than a dictator's, and no life more enjoyable than a king's.'

'No doubt about it.

'Do you know, in fact, how much less enjoyable a dictator's life is than a king's?' I asked.

'No. Please tell me,' he replied.

'There are three kinds of pleasure, apparently, and one of them is genuine, while two are spurious. A dictator, in his flight from law
c and reason, crosses over into the land beyond the spurious pleasures and settles down with his bodyguard of slavish pleasures. Perhaps the best way to describe the extent of his degeneration, which isn't all that easy to describe, is as follows.'

'How?' he asked.

'The dictator occupies the third place in the series which starts with the oligarchic type, since the democratic type comes in between them.'

'Yes.'

'So the pleasure he beds down with is also, assuming the truth of our earlier conclusions, a reflection three places away from oligarchic pleasure. Yes?'

'Yes.'

'Moreover, counting from the regal type (and assuming that ar-
d istocracy and kingship belong to the same category), it's the oligarchic type's turn to come third.'

'Yes.'

'It follows', I said, 'that a dictator's distance from true pleasure is, in numerical terms, triple a triple.'

“那么一个人越是成为僭主独夫，他与真实而合适的快乐之间的距离就越大；一个人越是成为王者，这距离就越短。”

“毫无疑问。”

“可以推论出，没有比僭主的生活更不快乐的生活了，也没有比王者的生活更快乐的生活了。”

“对此毫无疑问。”

“你是否知道实际上僭主的生活比王者的生活不快乐多少呢?”我问道。

“不知道，请告诉我吧。”他回答说。

“显然有三类快乐，其中的一种是真的，两种是假的。一个僭主，从律法和理性逃开，跨进了虚假快乐的领地，与他的奴隶般的 c
快乐卫士一起定居下来。也许描述他堕落程度的最好方式——这很难描述——是以下这样的。”

“怎么样的?”他问道。

“在以寡头派为开始的系列中，僭主处在第三级，因为民主派处于他们之间。”

“是的。”

“假如我们前面的结论是真实的，那么他所享有的快乐，也是在寡头派的快乐之下第三级处的一种虚像呢。是吗?”

“是的。”

“从王者那里算起——假设贵族制与王政属于同一个范畴——寡头派转而是第三级。” d

“是的。”

“可以推论出，”我说，“按数字计算，僭主离真正快乐的距离有九级。”

'I suppose so.'

'So it appears', I said, 'that the reflection which constitutes a dictator's pleasure is a plane number based on the quantity of the linear number.'

'Yes, definitely.'

'And the extent of the distance can be expressed as a square and a cube.'

'It can by a mathematician, anyway,' he said.

e 'So suppose you wanted to put it the other way round and state how far a king is from a dictator in terms of the truth of pleasure, the completed multiplication would show that his life is 729 times more pleasant than a dictator's. And a dictator is that much more wretched than a king.'

588a 'You've had to spout some complex mathematics,' he remarked, 'to describe the difference, in terms of pleasure and distress, between the two men—the moral one and the immoral one.'

'Yes, but I'm right,' I said, 'and it's a number which suits lives, assuming that days, nights, months, and years are related to lives.'

'Well, they certainly are,' he said.

'Now, if this is how decisive a victory a good, moral person wins over a bad, immoral one on the field of pleasure, just think how infinitely more resounding his victory will be on the field of elegance and propriety of life, and of goodness.'

'Yes, that's absolutely right,' he said.

b 'All right,' I said. 'At this point in the argument, let's remind ourselves of the original assertion which started us off on our journey here. Wasn't it someone saying that immorality was rewarding if you were a consummate criminal who gave an impression of morality? Wasn't that the assertion?'

'Yes, it was.'

'Well, now that we've decided what effect moral and immoral conduct have,' I said, 'we can engage him in conversation.'

“我想是这样的。”

“所以看来，”我说，“构成僭主快乐的虚像是基于直线数量的平面数。”

“是的，毫无疑问。”

“距离还能通过平方和立方加以表达。”

“无论如何，数学家能够表达出来。”他说。

“所以假设你要反过来说，要根据真正的快乐说出王者离僭 e
主有多远，复杂的乘法会显示他的生活比僭主的生活快乐 729 倍。僭主的生活比王者的生活悲惨得多。”

“你很快就做出了复杂的计算，”他说，“依据两个人——正义
之人和不正义之人——的快乐和痛苦描述了两者的区别。” 588a

“是的，但我是正确的，”我说，“假设日、夜、月、年与生活相关，那么这个数字是适合于生活的。”

“它们当然是适合于生活的。”他说。

“那么，如果在快乐的方面，善的、正义之人决定性地胜过了恶的、不正义之人。想一想，在礼仪、生活礼节和善的方面，他的胜利肯定是更加巨大的。”

“是的，肯定是这样的。”他说。

“好吧，”我说，“论证到这个地方，让我们提醒一下自己最初 b
的论断，我们的旅程是从那里开始到这里的。不是有人说过，如果你是个十恶不赦的罪犯而给人正义的印象，那么不正义是有益的吗？难道不是那个论断吗？”

“是那个论断。”

“那么，既然我们已经判定了正义和不正义的行为所造成的结果，”我说，“我们就能与他进行对话了。”

'What shall we say?' he asked.

'Let's construct a theoretical model of the mind, to help him see what kind of idea he's come up with.'

'What sort of model?' he asked,

c 'Something along the lines of those creatures who throng the ancient myths,' I said, 'like the Chimera, Scylla, Cerberus, and so on, whose form is a composite of the features of more than one creature.'

'Yes, that's how they're described,' he said.

'Make a model, then, of a creature with a single—if varied and many-headed—form, arrayed all around with the heads of both wild and tame animals, and possessing the ability to change over to a different set of heads and to generate all these new bits from its own body.'

d 'That would take some skilful modelling,' he remarked, 'but since words are a more plastic material than wax and so on, you may consider the model constructed.'

'A lion and a man are the next two models to make, then. The first of the models, however, is to be by far the largest, and the second the second largest.'

'That's an easier job,' he said. 'It's done.'

'Now join the three of them together until they become one, as it were.'

'All right,' he said.

'And for the final coat, give them the external appearance of a single entity. Make them look like a person, so that anyone incapable of seeing what's inside, who can see only the external husk, will see a single creature, a human being.'

e 'It's done,' he said.

'Now, we'd better respond to the idea that this person gains from doing wrong, and loses from doing right, by pointing out to its proponent that this is tantamount to saying that we're rewarded if we indulge

“我们要说什么呢?”他问道。

“让我们建立一个心灵的理论模型来帮助他看看提出了什么样的想法。”

“什么样的模型?”他问道。 c

“某些根据那些集中了古代神话的动物而塑造的东西,”我说,“就像喀迈拉、斯库拉、刻耳柏洛斯等等,其形体复合了不止一种动物的特征。”

“是的,传说是这样的。”他说。

“那么做一个单一形式的动物模型——如果是复合的并且具有多个头——周围长满了野兽和驯服动物的头,还能变成不同的头,也能从自己的身体里长出所有这些新的头来。”

“那需要某些塑造的技巧,”他说,“但因为词语是比蜡之类的 d
东西更容易塑造的材料,所以你可以认为模型已经造好了。”

“那么接下来要塑造的两座模型就是狮子和人的模型。然而第一座要造得最大,第二座造得次大。”

“这是个简单的工作,”他说,“造好了。”

“现在把这三者结合在一起,直到它们成为一个,就像怪物所是的那样。”

“好吧,”他说。

“至于最后的皮毛,要给它敷上一个单一实体的外表。使它们看起来像一个人,这样任何看不到里面景象的人,当他只看到外壳,就会把它当作一个单一的动物,一个人。” e

“造好了。”他说。

“那么,我们最好回应这样的想法:人们做错事有所得,做对事却无所得,并且向主张这话的人指出,这就等同于说,如果我们

and strengthen the many-sided beast and the lion with all its aspects,
589a but starve and weaken the man, until he's subject to the whims of the others, and can't promote familiarity and compatibility between the other two, but lets them bite each other, fight, and try to eat each other.'

'Yes, that's undoubtedly what a supporter of immorality would have to say,' he agreed.

'So the alternative position, that morality is profitable, is equiva-
b lent to saying that our words and behaviour should be designed to maximize the control the inner man has within us, and should enable him to secure the help of the leonine quality and then tend to the many-headed beast as a farmer tends to his crops—by nurturing and cultivating its tame aspects, and by stopping the wild ones growing. Then he can ensure that they're all compatible with one another, and with himself, and can look after them all equally, without favouritism.'

'Yes, that's exactly what a supporter of morality has to say,' he agreed.

c 'Whichever way you look at it, then, a supporter of morality is telling the truth, and a supporter of immorality is wrong. Whether your criterion is pleasure, reputation, or benefit, a supporter of morality is right, and a critic of morality is unreliable and doesn't know what he's talking about.'

'I quite agree: he doesn't in the slightest,' he said.

'But he doesn't mean to make a mistake, so let's be gentle with him. Here's a question we can ask him, to try to win him over: "My friend, don't you think that this is also what accounts for conventional standards of what is and is not acceptable? Things are acceptable
d when they subject the bestial aspects of our nature to the human—or it might be more accurate to say the divine—part of ourselves, but they're objectionable when they cause the oppression of our tame side under the savage side." Will he agree, do you think?'

放纵和加强多面野兽和狮子的所有方面,却让人饥饿、虚弱,直到他服从于另外两个为所欲为的怪念头,并且不能使另外两者更加熟悉和相容,而是让它们互相厮咬打斗并试图将对方吃掉,那么这样就对我们有利。” 589a

“是的,赞成不正义的人无疑会这么说。”他同意说。

“所以另一种主张正义有益的观点等同于说,我们的言行应该是为了最大地控制内在于我们的人,应该使他能够确保得到狮子品性的帮助,然后照看好多头野兽,就像一个农民照看他的庄稼一样——培育和照料它的温顺面而阻止狂野面的生长。这样他就能确保与人与己都能和睦相处,他能够毫无偏心地、平等地照看他们。” b

“是的,赞成正义的人正是会这样说的。”他同意说。

“那么无论你以什么方式来看,支持正义的人说的是正确的,而支持不正义的人说的是错误的。无论你的标准是快乐、名誉还是利益,正义的支持者是对的,而正义的批评者是不可靠的,他不知道自己在说什么。” c

“我非常同意:他根本就不知道。”他说。

“但他并不是故意犯错的,所以让我们和蔼地对待他。我们可以问他一个问题来试图说服他:‘我的朋友,你难道不认为这也解释了习俗标准,这些标准是关于什么是可接受的,什么是不可接受的?当事物使我们本性中的兽性部分受制于人性部分——更准确地说是神圣者——那么这些事物是可接受的;但当它们使我们的温顺面遭受野蛮面的压迫,那么它们就是不可接受的。’你认为他会同意吗?” d

'Well, I'll be recommending him to,' he answered.

'So what follows from this argument? Can there be any profit in the immoral acquisition of money, if this entails the enslavement of
e the best part of oneself to the worst part? The point is, if there's no profit in someone selling his son or daughter into slavery—slavery under savage and evil men—for even a great deal of money, then what happens if he cruelly enslaves the most divine part of himself to the vilest, most godless part? Isn't unhappiness the result? Isn't the dead-
590a ly business he's being paid for far more terrible than what Eriphyle did when she accepted the necklace as the price for her husband's death?'

'Yes, by a long way,' Glaucon said. 'I mean, I'll answer on behalf of our supporter of immorality.'

'Now, do you think the reason for the traditional condemnation of licentiousness is the same—because it allows that fiend, that huge and many-faceted creature, greater freedom than it should have?'

'Obviously,' he said.

'And aren't obstinacy and bad temper considered bad because
b they distend and invigorate our leonine, serpentine side to a disproportionate extent?'

'Yes.'

'Whereas a spoilt, soft way of life is considered bad because it makes this part of us so slack and loose that it's incapable of facing hardship?'

'Of course.'

'And why are lack of independence and autonomy despised? Isn't it still to do with the passionate part, because we have to subordinate it to the unruly beast and, from our earliest years, get the lion used to being insulted and to becoming a monkey instead of a lion—and all for the sake of money and to satisfy our greed?'

“好吧,我会推荐他这样做的。”他回答说。

“那么可以从论证中推论出什么呢?不正义地得到钱财会有什么利益呢,如果这还必然包含着使人最善部分受到最恶部分的奴役?关键是,如果一个人把他的儿子或女儿出卖为奴而无利可 e
图——受野蛮和邪恶之人的奴役——即使得到了一大笔钱,那么如果他残酷地使最神圣的部分受最邪恶、最猥亵部分的奴役会怎么样呢?结果不就是不幸吗?比起厄律斐勒接受了项链而以她丈夫的死为代价来说,在这个致命的交易中,他所得到的支付不
是可怕得多吗?” 590a

“是的,太可怕了,”格劳孔说道。“我的意思是,我会代表那些不义论的支持者回答的。”

“那么你是否认为传统上放纵受到谴责也是同样的理由,因为它让邪恶、巨大而多面的动物具有比其应该有的自由更大的自由?”

“显而易见。”他说。

“固执和暴躁被认为是不好的,因为它们使我们的狮性和蛇
性面得到夸大和加强,到了失衡的程度?” b

“是的。”

“娇宠和柔弱的生活方式被认为是不好的,因为它们使得我们的这个部分如此松弛和柔弱以致不能够面对困苦?”

“当然。”

“为什么缺乏独立性和自立受到鄙视?这不还是与激情的部分有关,因为我们不得不使之屈从于暴虐的野兽,从早年起就使狮子习惯于受侮辱而变成了一只猴子而不是狮子——这都是为了金钱和为了满足我们的贪欲?”

c ‘Yes.’

‘What about mundane, manual labour? Why do you think it has a bad name? Isn't it precisely because there's an inherent weakness in the truly good part of the person which makes him incapable of controlling his internal beasts, so that all he does is pander to them, and all he can learn is their whims?’

‘I suppose that's right,’ he said.

‘The question is, how can a person in this condition become subject to the kind of rulership which is available to a truly good person? By being the slave, we suggest, of a truly good person, whose
d divine element rules within him. But we're not suggesting, as Thrasymachus did about subjects, that his status as a subject should do him harm; we're saying that subjection to the principle of divine intelligence is to everyone's advantage. It's best if this principle is part of a person's own nature, but if it isn't, it can be imposed from outside, to foster as much unanimity and compatibility between us as might be possible when we're all governed by the same principle.’

‘You're right,’ he said.

e ‘It's also clear’, I continued, ‘that this is the function of law: this is why every member of a community has the law to fall back on. And it explains why we keep children under control and don't allow them their freedom until we've formed a government within them, as
591a we would in a community. What we do is use what is best in ourselves to cultivate the equivalent aspect of a child, and then we let him go free once the equivalent part within him has been established as his guardian and ruler.’

‘Yes, that's clear,’ he said.

‘Is there any conceivable argument, then, Glaucon, which will enable us to claim that immorality or licentiousness is rewarding, when the result of any kind of shameful behaviour may be a richer

"是的。" c

"普通的手工劳动怎么样呢？你为什么认为这个职业名声不好呢？这不正是因为人真正善的部分的内在虚弱使得他不能够控制他内部的野兽，以致他所做的一切都是在迎合它们，他所学的都是它们的怪念头？"

"我想是这样的。"他说。

"问题是，一个处于这种状态的人如何受真正善的人的统治？我们说，作为真正善的人的奴隶，其神圣部分在其内部统治着他。但我们并不是如塞拉西马库斯所说的那样，被统治者的身份应该 d
给他带来危害；我们说服从神圣的理性原则对每个人都是有好处的。如果这个原则是一个人自己本性的一部分，那么这就最好了，但如果它不是本性的一部分，那么能够从外部强加给它，当我们都受同一个原则的管理的时候，就在我们之间产生最大的一致和融洽。"

"你是对的。"他说。

"这也是清楚的，"我继续说，"这就是法律的功能，这就是为 e
什么我们城邦中的每个成员都有法可依。这解释了为什么我们要管教孩子，不给他们自由，直到我们在他们中建立起管理为止，
就像我们在城邦中建立起管理一样。我们所做的就是利用我们 591a
自己身上最善的部分去培育孩子身上相应的部分，一旦孩子身上相应的、作为其卫士和统治者的部分建立起来了，我们才让他们自由。"

"是的，这很明白。"他说。

"那么，格劳孔，当任何可耻行为的结果也许是使人变得更加富有或更加强大，当然也是使人变成一个更坏的人时，你想象

or otherwise more powerful person, but is certainly a worse person?'

'No, there isn't,' he replied.

b 'And how can it be profitable for a person's immorality to go unnoticed and unpunished? The consequence of a criminal getting away with his crimes is that he becomes a worse person. If he's found out and punished, however, then his bestial side is tamed and pacified, his tame side is liberated, and in short his mental state becomes as good as it can be. And, in so far as the mind is a more valuable asset than the body, it's more important for the mind to acquire self-discipline, morality, and intelligence than it is for the body to become fit, attractive, and healthy.'

'You're absolutely right,' he said.

c 'Then anyone with any sense will put all his energies, throughout his life, into achieving this goal. In the first place, he'll value only those intellectual pursuits which have the effect we've described on the mind, and regard any others as trivial, won't he?'

'Obviously,' he said.

'In the second place,' I went on, 'there's more to his attitude towards the care and condition of his body than simply the fact that he won't give himself over to bestial and irrational pleasure and make that the whole point of his life. He won't, in fact, be interested in physical health and he won't take the pursuit of physical fitness, health,
d and beauty seriously unless they also lead to self-discipline. We'll find him, throughout his life, attuning his body in order to make music with his mind.'

'Yes, that's exactly what it takes to be a true virtuoso,' he said.

'And won't the same attunement and harmony guide his acquisition of money? He's hardly going to be swayed by the usual standards of happiness and amass an inexhaustible pile of money, along with its inexhaustible troubles, is he?'

'I don't think so,' he said.

有什么论证使我们能够声称不正义或放纵是有利的?”

“没有这样的论证。”他回答说。

“一个人的不正义没有被人注意到、没有受到惩罚,这对他来
说有什么好处吗?一个罪犯逃脱了他的罪行的结果就是他变成 b
了一个更坏的人。然而如果他被发现了并且受到了惩罚,那么他的兽性面就被驯化、平服了,他的温顺面得到了自由,简而言之,他的心灵处于最善的状态。只要心灵是比身体更有价值的东西,那么比起身体变得健壮、有吸引力和健康,更重要的是心灵获得自制、正义和智性。”

“你说得非常准确。”他说。

“那么任何有理智的人会毕生把他的所有精力用于实现这个 c
目标。首先他只会重视对心灵会产生我们说过的那些效果的智性追求,而轻视别的东西,不是吗?”

“显而易见。”他说。

“其次,”我继续说,“在对身体的关爱和状况方面,他不会醉心于兽性和无理性的快乐,并将之作为生活的全部。实际上他不会对身体的健康感兴趣,不会严肃地追求身体的强壮、健康和美,除非它们能够引向自制。我们发
现他在其整个生活中都在调整他的身体以使他的心灵和 d
谐。”

“是的,这正是一个真正的音乐家所要做的。”他说。

“不也是同样的协调与和谐指引他赚钱吗?他几乎不会受惯常的幸福标准的摆布而积聚大量的财富,却伴随着无穷的麻烦,是吗?”

“我想他不会这样做的。”他说。

e ‘What he'll do, however,’ I said, ‘is keep an eye on his own inner society and watch out for trouble brewing among its members, caused by his having either too much or too little property. He'll stick to this guiding principle as much as possible, and increase and decrease his assets accordingly.’

‘Exactly,’ he agreed.

592a ‘And the same consideration will also guide his attitude towards honours. He won't hesitate to accept and experience those which will, in his view, make him a better person, but in his private life as well as in public life he'll avoid those which he thinks would cause the downfall of his established constitution.’

‘If that's what's important to him,’ he said, ‘he's unlikely to have anything to do with government.’

‘Actually,’ I said, ‘he certainly will, in his own community. But I agree that he probably won't in the country of his birth, short of divine intervention.’

‘I see,’ he said. ‘You mean that he will in the community we've just been founding and describing, which can't be accommodated anywhere in the world, and therefore rests at the level of ideas.’

b ‘It may be, however,’ I replied, ‘that it is retained in heaven as a paradigm for those who desire to see it and, through seeing it, to return from exile. In fact, it doesn't make the slightest bit of difference whether it exists or will exist anywhere: it's still the only community in whose government he could play a part.’

‘Yes, I suppose so,’ he said.

“然而，”我说，“他要做的就是关注自己的内心城邦，注意由于他拥有过多或过少的财富而在城邦成员中引起的那些麻烦。他会尽可能地遵守这个指导原则，并相应地增加或减少他的财产。” e

“正是。”他同意说。

“同样的考虑也会指导他对待荣誉的态度。他不会犹豫着接受和经历那些在他看来能使他更加完善的东西，但在他私人生活和公共生活当中，他会避免那些他认为会导致他建立起来的体制垮塌的东西。” 592a

“如果那对他来说是最重要的话，”他说，“那么他就不大可能参与任何政事。”

“实际上，”我说，“在他自己的城邦里他一定会的。但我同意在他出生的城邦可能不会，除非有神来介入。”

“我明白了，”他说，“你的意思是在我们刚才建立和描述过的城邦中他是会的，这个城邦在世界上的任何地方都是不存在的，所以停留于理想的层面上。” b

“但是，或许是那样的，”我回答说，“它作为一个原型，为着那些渴望看到它并透彻地看清它，渴望从异乡流浪中返回的人们，而存留在天上。实际上，无论它是于何处存在，或是将要于何处存在，根本没有一点儿差别：理想国仍旧是他能在其政事中扮演一个角色的唯一的城邦。”

“是的，我想是这样的。”他说。

CHAPTER 13

595a ‘You know,’ I said, ‘the issue of poetry is the main consideration—among many others—which convinces me that the way we were trying to found our community was along absolutely the right lines.’

‘What are you thinking of?’ he asked.

‘That we flatly refused to admit any representational poetry. I
b mean, its total unacceptability is even clearer, in my opinion, now that we've distinguished the different aspects of the mind.’

‘How is it clearer?’

‘Well, this is just between ourselves: please don't denounce me to the tragic playwrights and all the other representational poets. But it looks as though this whole genre of poetry deforms its audience's minds, unless they have the antidote, which is recognition of what this kind of poetry is actually like.’

‘What do you mean? What do you have in mind?’ he asked.

‘It's fairly clear’, I said, ‘that all these fine tragedians trace their lineage back to Homer: they're Homer's students and disciples,
c ultimately. And this makes it difficult for me to say what I have to say, because I've had a kind of fascinated admiration for Homer ever since I was young. Still, we should value truth more than we value any person, so, as I say, I'd better speak out.’

‘Yes,’ he said.

‘And you'll listen to what I have to say, or rather respond to any questions I ask?’

‘Yes. Go ahead and ask them.’

第十三章

“你知道，”我说，“诗歌问题是主要要考虑的问题——在许多 595a
别的问题当中——这使得我相信我们建立城邦的道路是肯定沿着准确的路线走的。”

“你认为是什么样的？”他问道。

“我们断然拒绝承认任何模仿性的诗歌。我的意思是说，在我看来，既然我们已经区分了心灵的不同部分，那么完全不接受
模仿性诗歌是很清楚的了。” b

“说得更清楚一些呢？”

“好吧，这只是我们私下说说，请不要向悲剧作家和所有别的模仿性诗人告发我。看起来整个诗歌体裁都扭曲了听众的心灵，除非他们有解毒剂，能辨认出诗歌的真实面目。”

“你说的是什么意思？你心里是怎么想的？”他问道。

“非常清楚，”我说，“所有优秀的悲剧诗人都把族谱追溯到荷马：他们最终是荷马的学生和门徒。这使得我难以说出
我必须要说的话，因为我从小就对荷马有一种强烈的敬意。 c
我们还是应该看重真理更甚于看重任何人，所以，就如我所说的那样，我想说出来。”

“是的。”他说。

“你听我不得不说的话，还是回答我问的任何问题？”

“继续吧，问吧。”

'Can you tell me what representation basically is? You see, I don't quite understand its point myself.'

'And I suppose I do!' he said.

'It wouldn't surprise me if you did,' I said. 'Just because a
596a person can't see very well, it doesn't mean that he won't often see things before people with better eyesight than him.'

'That's true,' he said. 'All the same, I'd be too shy to explain any views I did have in front of you, so please try to come up with an answer yourself.'

'All right. Shall we get the enquiry going by drawing on familiar ideas? Our usual position is, as you know, that any given plurality of things which have a single name constitutes a single specific type. Is that clear to you?'

'Yes.'

'So now let's take any plurality you want. Would it be all right
b with you if we said that there were, for instance, lots of beds and tables?'

'Of course.'

'But these items of furniture comprise only two types—the type of bed and the type of table.'

'Yes.'

'Now, we also invariably claim that the manufacture of either of these items of furniture involves the craftsman looking to the type and then making the beds or tables (or whatever) which we use. The point is that the type itself is not manufactured by any craftsman. How could it be?'

'It couldn't.'

'There's another kind of craftsman too. I wonder what you think of him.'

'What kind?'

c 'He makes everything—all the items which every single manufacturer makes.'

“你能否告诉我模仿根本上是什么？你知道，我自己不是很理解这一点。”

“难道我认为自己理解了！”他说。

“如果你理解了，这不会让我惊讶的，”我说，“仅仅因为一个人不能看得很清晰，这并不意味着他不能常常在那些具有比他视 596a
力更好的人之前看到事物。”

“对的，”他说，“但在你面前我仍然太胆怯，而不敢解释任何观点，所以请拿出你自己的答案吧。”

“好吧。我们利用熟悉的观念来进行探究吧，可不可以？就像你知道的，我们通常的观点是，任何具有多数性的事物，我们只用一个单一名称称呼它时，这类事物便含有一种单一性的特殊形式或理念。你明白吗？”

“当然明白。”

“所以现在让我们列举出你想要列举的多样性事物来。比如说，你是否会让我们说有许多床和桌子？” b

“当然。”

“但这两件家具仅仅包含两个理念——床的理念和桌子的理念。”

“是的。”

“那么我们必定会说，制作两件家具中的任何一件，都要求匠人观看理念，然后制作出我们使用的床或桌子或别的东西。关键是理念本身不是由任何匠人制作的。它怎么可能是制作出来的呢？”

“不可能。”

“还有另一种匠人。我想知道你对他是怎么看的。”

“哪种？” c

“他制造一切——任何单个匠人制作的所有物品。”

‘He must be extraordinarily gifted.’

‘Wait: you haven’t heard the half of it yet. It’s not just a case of his being able to manufacture all the artefacts there are: every plant too, every creature (himself included), the earth, the heavens, gods, and everything in the heavens and in Hades under the earth—all these are made and created by this one man!’

d “He really must be extraordinarily clever,’ he said.

‘Don’t you believe me?’ I asked. ‘Tell me, do you doubt that this kind of craftsman could exist under any circumstances, or do you admit the possibility that a person could—in one sense, at least—create all these things? I mean, don’t you realize that you yourself could, under certain circumstances, create all these things?’

‘What circumstances?’ he asked.

‘I’m not talking about anything complicated or rare,’ I said. ‘It doesn’t take long to create the circumstances. The quickest method, I
e suppose, is to get hold of a mirror and carry it around with you everywhere. You’ll soon be creating everything I mentioned a moment ago—the sun and the heavenly bodies, the earth, yourself, and all other creatures, plants, and so on.’

‘Yes, but I’d be creating appearances, not actual real things,’ he said.

‘That’s a good point,’ I said. ‘You’ve arrived just in time to save the argument. I mean, that’s presumably the kind of craftsman a painter is. Yes?’

‘Of course.’

‘His creations aren’t real, according to you; but do you agree that all the same there’s a sense in which even a painter creates a bed?’

‘Yes,’ he said, ‘he’s another one who creates an apparent bed.’

597a ‘What about a joiner who specializes in making beds? Weren’t we saying a short while ago that what he makes is a particular bed, not the type, which is (on our view) the real bed?’

‘Yes, we were.’

“他必定是具有超常的天赋。”

“等一下:你还只听到一半呢。他不光能够制作所有的人工制品,还能制作所有的植物、动物,包括他自身,还有大地、天空、诸神以及天空中的一切,还有地下冥府里的一切——所有这些都是由这一个人制作和创造的!”

“他确实必定是超常的聪明。”他说。 d

“你难道不相信我吗?”我问道,“告诉我,你是否怀疑在任何条件下这种匠人都可存在,或者你是否承认有这种可能性,即一个人能够——至少在某种意义上说——创造所有这些东西? 我的意思是说,难道你没有意识到在某些条件下你自己能够创造出所有这些东西?”

“什么条件?”他问道。

“我说的不是什么复杂或稀罕的事情,”我说,“你不用花很长时间去创造这些条件。我想最快的方法就是拿着一面镜子并随处都带在身上。你会很快就创造出我刚才提到的所有事物—— e
太阳、天空、大地、你自己以及所有别的动物、植物等等。”

“是的,但我创造的是影子而不是实在的真实事物。”他说。

“这点很好,”我说,“你及时地挽救了论证。我的意思是说,这类匠人大概是画匠,是吗?”

“当然。”

“按你的说法,他的创造不是真实的,但你是否仍然同意画匠在某种程度上说也创造了床?”

“是的,”他说,“他是又一个创造床之影子的人。”

“专事制作床的木匠怎么样呢? 我们刚才不是说他制作的是 597a
一张特殊的床,而不是理念,这在我们看来才是真正的床?”

“是的,我们说过。”

'So if there's no reality to his creation, then it isn't real; it's similar to something real, but it isn't actually real. It looks as though it's wrong to attribute full reality to a joiner's or any artisan's product, doesn't it?'

'Yes,' he said, 'any serious student of this kind of argument would agree with you.'

'It shouldn't surprise us, then, if we find that even these products are obscure when compared with the truth.'

'No, it shouldn't.'

b 'Now, what about this representer we're trying to understand? Shall we see if these examples help us?' I asked.

'That's fine by me,' he said.

'Well, we've got these three beds. First, there's the real one, and we'd say, I imagine, that it is the product of divine craftsmanship. I mean, who else could have made it?'

'No one, surely.'

'Then there's the one the joiner makes.'

'Yes,' he said.

'And then there's the one the painter makes. Yes?'

'Yes, agreed.'

'These three, then—painter, joiner, God—are responsible for three different kinds of bed.'

'Yes, that's right.'

c 'Now, God has produced only that one real bed. The restriction to only one might have been his own choice, or it might just be impossible for him to make more than one. But God never has, and never could, create two or more such beds.'

'Why not?' he asked.

"所以如果在他的创造中没有实在性,那么它就不是实在的,它类似于实在的事物,但实际上不是实在的。看来把全部实在性归于木匠或任何匠人的造物是错误的,不是吗?"

"是的,"他说,"任何认真从事这种论证的学生都会同意你的这种说法。"

"那么如果我们发现即使这些产品比起真理来还是模糊不清的话,我们也不应该惊讶。"

"不,不应该惊讶。" b

"那么我们试图理解的这个模仿者怎么样呢?我们要看看这些例子是否对我们有帮助吗?"我问道。

"我同意。"他说。

"我们有三张床。第一张是实在之床,我想我们会说它是神工的产物。我的意思是说,还有谁能够造呢?"

"当然没有别人能造。"

"然后是木匠制作的床。"

"是的。"他说。

"然后是画匠制作的床。是吗?"

"是的,同意。"

"画匠、木匠和神三者制作了三种床。"

"是的,对的。"

"现在,神制作的只是一个实在之床。或者是神有他自己的选择,或者是对他而言制作超过一个之上的实在之床是不可能 c
的,所以就限于只有一个。而神从来没有也绝不能创造出两个或更多的实在之床来的。"

"为什么不呢?"他问道。

'Even if he were to make only two such beds,' I said, 'an extra one would emerge, and both the other two would be of that one's type. It, and not the two beds, would be the real bed.'

'Right,' he said.

d 'God realized this, I'm sure. He didn't want to be a kind of joiner, making a particular bed: he wanted to be a genuine creator and make a genuine bed. that's why he created a single real one.'

'I suppose that's right.'

'shall we call him its progenitor, then, or something like that?'

'Yes, he deserves the name,' he said, 'since he's the maker of this and every other reality.'

'What about a joiner? Shall we call him a manufacturer of beds?'

'Yes.'

'And shall we also call a painter a manufacturer and maker of beds and so on?'

'No, definitely not.'

'What do you think he does with beds, then?'

e 'I think the most suitable thing to call him would be a representer of the others' creations,' he said.

'Well, in that case', I said, 'You're using the term "representer" for someone who deals with things which are, in fact, two generations away from reality, aren't you?'

'Yes,' he said.

'the same goes for tragic playwrights, then, since they're representers: they're two generations away from the throne of truth and so are all other representers.'

'I suppose so.'

'Well, in the context of what we're now saying about representation, I've got a further question about painters. Is it, in any given

“即使他仅仅制作了两张这样的床，”我说，“另一张就会出现，那么另两张就会以它为理念。这样就是它，而不是那两张床是实在的床。”

“对的。”他说。

“我确信神意识到了这一点。他不想成为那种制造某一特定 d
床的木匠，他想成为真正的创造者并制作出真正的床。这就是为什么他创造独一的实在的床。”

“我想这是对的。”

“那么我们是否要称呼他为创造主或类似的称呼？”

“是的，他配得上这个名字，”他说，“因为他是这个以及别的一切实在的制作者？”

“那么木匠呢？我们是否要称呼他为床的制作者？”

“是的。”

“我们是否也要称呼画匠为床之类东西的制作者和制造者呢？”

“不，肯定不行。”

“那么你认为他与床有什么关系呢？”

“我想最合适他的称呼就是别人所造的东西的模仿者。”他说。 e

“那么在那种情况下，”我说，“你把‘模仿者’这个词用来称呼那些与实际上和实在隔了两级远的东西打交道的人，不是吗？”

“是的。”他说。

“那么对于悲剧作家也是同样的，因为他们是模仿者，他们与真理的宝座隔了两级远，对于所有别的模仿者也是一样的。”

“我想是这样的。”

“那么就我们现在讨论的模仿来说，我还有个关于画匠的问

598a instance, the actual reality that they try to represent, or is it the craftsmen's products?'

'The craftsmen's products,' he said.

'Here's another distinction you'd better make: do they try to represent them as they are, or as they appear to be?'

'What do you mean?' he asked.

'I'll tell you. Whether you look at a bed from the side or straight on or whatever, it's still just as much a bed as it ever was, isn't it? I mean, it doesn't actually alter it at all: it just appears to be different, doesn't it? And the same goes for anything else you can mention. Yes?'

b 'Yes,' he agreed. 'It seems different, but isn't actually.'

'So I want you to consider carefully which of these two alternatives painting is designed for in any and every instance. Is it designed to represent the facts of the real world or appearances? Does it represent appearance or truth?'

'Appearance,' he said.

'It follows that representation and truth are a considerable distance apart, and a representer is capable of making every product there is only because his contact with things is slight and is restricted to how they look. Consider what a painter does, for instance: we're saying that he doesn't have a clue about shoemaking or joinery, but
c he'll still paint pictures of artisans working at these and all other areas of expertise, and if he's good at painting he might paint a joiner, have people look at it from far away, and deceive them—if they're children or stupid adults—by making it look as though the joiner were real.'

'Naturally.'

'I think the important thing to bear in mind about cases like this, Glaucon, is that when people tell us they've met someone who's mastered every craft, and is the world's leading expert in absolutely

题。在任何情况下,他们试图模仿的是真实的实在还是匠人的造物?” 598a

“是匠人的造物。”他说。

“你最好再做另一区分:他们试图模仿它们自身还是它们的影像?”

“你说的是什么意思?”他问道。

“我会告诉你的。观看一张床,无论从侧面看,从正面看还是别的方向看,这还是床自身,不是吗?我的意思是说,它真的完全没有改变吗:它只是看上去不同,不是吗?对于任何别的你说得出的事物也是一样的。是吗?”

“是的,”他同意说,“看上去不同,但实际上是一样的。”

“所以我想要你仔细地想一想,在任何情况下,绘画涉及的是 b
下列的哪一种。它旨在模仿实在世界的事实还是模仿影像?它模仿的是影像还是真实?”

“影像。”他说。

“可以推论出,模仿术与真实是相差很远的,模仿者仅仅由于对事物有一点点了解并限于它们的表象就能够制造出任何物品。想一想,比如说画匠做了什么:我们说他并不懂制鞋或木工,但他还是能够画出这门技艺或所有别的技艺方面的工匠肖像,如果他善于绘画,那么他也许可以画一个木匠,使 c
这个木匠看上去似乎是真实的,让人们在远处观看,欺骗他们这些儿童或笨人。”

“自然。”

“格劳孔,我想在像这样的情况下,要记住的一件重要事情便是,当人们告诉我们说他们遇到过一个人,他精通所有技艺,在每

d every branch of human knowledge, we should reply that they're being rather silly. They seem to have met the kind of illusionist who's expert at representation and, thanks to their own inability to evaluate knowledge, ignorance, and representation, to have been so thoroughly taken in as to believe in his omniscience.'

'You're absolutely right,' he said.

'Now, we'd better investigate tragedy next,' I said, 'and its guru, Homer, because one does come across the claim that there's no
e area of expertise, and nothing relevant to human goodness and badness either—and nothing to do with the gods even—that these poets don't understand. It is said that a good poet must understand the issues he writes about, if his writing is to be successful, and that if he didn't understand them, he wouldn't be able to write about them. So we'd better try to decide between the alternatives. Either the people who come across these representational poets are being taken in and are failing to appreciate, when they see their products, that these
599a products are two steps away from reality and that it certainly doesn't take knowledge of the truth to create them (since what they're creating are appearances, not reality); or this view is valid, and in fact good poets are authorities on the subjects most people are convinced they're good at writing about.'

'Yes, this definitely needs looking into,' he said.

'Well, do you think that anyone who was capable of producing both originals and images would devote his energy to making images, and would make out that this is the best thing he's done with his life?'

b 'No, I don't.'

'I'm sure that if he really knew about the things he was copying in his representations, he'd put far more effort into producing real objects than he would into representations, and would try to leave behind a lot of fine products for people to remember him by, and would dedicate himself to being the recipient rather than the bestower of praise.'

个人类的知识门类中，他肯定是世上的一流专家，我们应该回答 d
说他们是相当蠢笨的。他们似乎遇上了善于模仿术的魔术师一类人，由于他们不能鉴别知识、无知和模仿，他们就完全被欺骗了，以致相信那类魔术师是无所不知的。”

“你说得非常准确。”他说。

“那么接下来我们最好考察一下悲剧，”我说，“以及它的倡导者荷马，因为有人确实听说过没有专门技艺，没有什么与人类的 e
善与恶相关的事情——甚至没有什么与神相关的事情——是这些诗人不懂得的。据说一个好诗人必须理解他所写的事情，如果他的写作要获得成功，如果他不理解他所写的事情的话，那么他就不能把它们写出来。所以我们最好在两种可能中作一评断。要么是人们遇到了模仿诗人的人，看到他们作品的时候受了骗，不能识别出这些作品与实在之间隔了两层，也没有认识到，创造这类作品，当然是不用掌握关于真实的知识的(因为他们创造的是 599a
影像而非真实)；要么这种观点是有根据的，并且实际上，优秀的诗人，在大多数人们都相信他们擅长写作的主题上是权威者。”

“是的，这肯定需要加以考察。”他说。

“那么你认为任何既能制造原物又能制造影像的人，会把他的精力投入到制造影像中去吗，他会把这当作他生活中最好的事情吗？” b

“不，不会的。”

“我确信如果他真的了解他用模仿术所模仿的事物的话，他会把更多的精力投入到制造实在的事物上去，而不是投入到模仿术中去，并且会试图为人们留下许多精良制品来纪念自己，他会使自己成为一个赞美的接受者而不是给予者。”

'I agree,' he said. 'He'd gain a lot more prestige and do himself a great deal more good.'

c 'Well, let's concentrate our interrogation of Homer (or any other poet you like) on a single area. Let's not ask him whether he can tell us of any patients cured by any poet in ancient or modern times, as Asclepius cured his patients, or of any students any of them left to continue his work, as Asclepius left his sons. And even these questions grant the possibility that a poet might have had some medical knowledge, instead of merely representing medical terminology. No, let's not bother to ask him about any other areas of expertise either. But we do have a right to ask Homer about the most important and
d glorious areas he undertakes to expound—warfare, tactics, politics, and human education. Let's ask him, politely, "Homer, maybe you aren't two steps away from knowing the truth about goodness; maybe you aren't involved in the manufacture of images (which is what we called representation). Perhaps you're actually only one step away, and you do have the ability to recognize which practices—in their private or their public lives—improve people and which ones impair them. But in that case, just as Sparta has its Lycurgus and communities of all different sizes have their various reformers, please tell us
e which community has you to thank for improvements to its government. Which community attributes the benefits of its good legal code to you? Italy and Sicily name Charondas in this respect, we Athenians name Solon. Which country names you?" Will he have any reply to make?'

'I don't think so,' said Glaucon. 'Even the Homeridae themselves don't make that claim.'

600a 'Well, does history record that there was any war fought in Homer's time whose success depended on his leadership or advice?'

“我同意，”他说，“他所得到的声誉会大得多并且对自己的好处也多得多。”

“那么我们仅在一个领域集中于向荷马或任何别的你喜欢的诗人提问。让我们不要问他是否能告诉我们在古代或当 c
代任何诗人是否能治好任何病人，就像阿斯克勒庇俄斯治好他的病人一样，或者他们当中的任何人留下某些学生继续他们的工作，就像阿斯克勒庇俄斯留下他的儿子们一样。这些问题甚至也承认了诗人拥有某些医学知识的可能性，而不是仅仅模仿医学术语。也不要麻烦问他任何别的专业技艺领域方面的问题。但关于荷马所要解释的最重要、最光辉的事情——战争、策略、政治和人的教育，我们确实有权利问。让
我们礼貌地问他：‘荷马，也许你距离知道善的真相并没有两 d
层之隔，也许你并不从事我们所谓的模仿术的影像制造。也许你实际上只隔一层，你确实有能力辨认出哪些活动——在他们的私人生活和公共生活中——对人们有益，哪些对人们有害。但在那样的情况下，就像斯巴达拥有莱喀古斯以及所有不同规模的城邦拥有他们各自不同的改革者一样，请你告诉我们，哪个城邦感激你改善了他们的管理？哪个城邦把好
的法律制度带来的理由归功于你？意大利和西西里归功于卡 e
隆达斯以示尊敬，我们雅典人归功于梭伦。哪个城邦归功于你呢？’荷马有什么要回答的吗？”

“没什么要说的，”格劳孔说，“即使荷马的追随者自己也不会那样说。”

“那么是否有历史记载说有什么荷马时代的战争的胜利是依 600a
靠他的领导或建议？”

'No.'

'Well then, are a lot of ingenious inventions attributed to him, as they are to Thales of Miletus and Anacharsis of Scythia? I mean the kinds of inventions which have practical applications in the arts and crafts and elsewhere. He is, after all, supposed to be good at creating things.'

'No, There's not the slightest hint of that sort of thing.'

'All right, so There's no evidence of his having been a public benefactor, but what about in private? Is there any evidence that, during his lifetime, he was a mentor to people, and that they used to
b value him for his teaching and then handed down to their successors a particular Homeric way of life? This is what happened to Pythagoras: he wasn't only held in extremely high regard for his teaching during his lifetime, but his successors even now call their way of life Pythagorean and somehow seem to stand out from all other people.'

'No, There's no hint of that sort of thing either,' he said. 'I mean, Homer's associate Creophylus' cultural attainments would turn out to be even more derisory than his name suggests they are, Socrates, if the stories about Homer are true. You see, Creophylus is said to have more or less disregarded Homer during his lifetime.'

c 'Yes, that is what we're told,' I agreed. 'But, Glaucon, if Homer really had been an educational expert whose products were better people—which is to say, if he had knowledge in this sphere and his abilities were not limited to representation—don't you think he'd have been surrounded by hordes of associates, who would have admired him and valued his company highly? Look at Protagoras of Abdera, Prodicus of Ceos, and all the rest of them: they can use their exclusive tuition to make their contemporaries believe that without them in

“没有。”

“那么是否有许多精巧的发明归功于他,就像归功于米利都的泰勒斯和司奇提亚的阿那卡尔西斯?我指的是那种在工艺、技艺和其他地方有实际用途的发明。毕竟他被认为是善于创造事物的。”

“没有,那样的东西一件都没有。”

“好吧,这样就没有证据表明他能带来公共利益,那么在私人方面呢?是否有什么证据表明在他的一生中,他是人们的导师并且人们重视他的教导,之后把一种特殊的荷马式的生活方式传给 b
他们的继承者?毕达哥拉斯就是这样的:在他的一生当中,不光他的学说受到极高的尊重,甚至他的继承者现在还把他们的生活方式称作是毕达哥拉斯式的,并且在某种程度上似乎比所有别的人优越。”

“不,根本没有那种事情,”他说,“苏格拉底,我的意思是说,荷马的朋友克瑞奥菲鲁斯[1]的文化造诣甚至比他的名字所暗示的更加可笑,如果关于荷马的故事是真实的话。你知道,据说克瑞奥菲鲁斯在荷马在世时就多多少少有点看不起他了。”

“是的,我们听说过,”我同意说,“但是,格劳孔,如果荷马真 c
的是一位教育专家,他的产物就是较优秀的学生——这就是说,如果他有这方面的知识并且他的能力并不局限于模仿术——你难道不认为他早已被大群的朋友包围,他们会赞美他并且高度重视他的陪伴?看看阿布德拉的普罗泰戈拉和开奥斯的普罗狄科以及所有其余的人:他们利用他们的收费教学使同时代的人相信,

---

〔1〕 字面意思是“吃肉氏族的人”。

charge of their education they won't be capable of managing their own
d estates, let alone their communities, and they're so appreciated for this expertise of theirs that their associates almost carry them around on their heads. So if Homer or Hesiod had been able to help people's moral development, would their contemporaries have allowed them to go from town to town reciting their poems? Wouldn't they have kept a tighter grip on them than on their money, and tried to force them to stay with them in their homes? And if they couldn't persuade them to do
e that, wouldn't they have danced attendance on them wherever they went, until they'd gained as much from their teaching as they could?'

'I don't think anyone could disagree with you, Socrates,' he said.

'So shall we classify all poets, from Homer onwards, as representers of images of goodness (and of everything else which occurs in their poetry), and claim that they don't have any contact with the truth? The facts are as we said a short while ago: a painter creates an
601a illusory shoemaker, when not only does he not understand anything about shoemaking, but his audience doesn't either. They just base their conclusions on the colours and shapes they can see.'

'Yes.'

'And I should think we'll say that the same goes for a poet as well: he uses words and phrases to block in some of the colours of each area of expertise, although all he understands is how to represent things in a way which makes other superficial people, who base their conclusions on the words they can hear, think that he's written a really good poem about shoemaking or military command or whatever else it is that he's set to metre, rhythm, and music. It only takes these
b features to cast this powerful a spell: that's what they're for. But when the poets' work is stripped of its musical hues and expressed in plain words, I think you've seen what kind of impression it gives, so you know what I'm talking about.'

要是没有他们掌管教育，他们就不能管理自己的家庭，更不用说管理城邦了，他们是如此地敬慕专业技艺以致他们的朋友几乎将 d
他们扛在肩上了。所以如果荷马或赫西俄德有助于人们道德的发展，同时代的人还会让他们颠沛流离吟唱他们的诗歌吗？人们不就会紧紧地把他们留住，更甚于留住金钱，并且试图迫使他们住在自己家里吗？如果人们不能够说服他们那样做的话，人们不就会追随他们，无论他们去哪里，直到人们从他们的教导中得到 e
尽可能多的东西？"

"苏格拉底，我想任何人都会同意你的。"他说。

"所以我们要不要把所有自荷马以来的诗人都划为善德（以及其他每一种出现于他们诗歌中的事物）的影像的模仿者，并且说他们根本不了解真实？正如我们不久前所说的，事实是这样的：画匠创造出一个虚幻的鞋匠来，不光他不知道任何制鞋的事情，连他的观众也不知道。他们的结论仅仅是依据他们看见的颜 601a
色和形状。"

"是的。"

"我认为我们应该会说，对于诗人来说也是一样的：他使用词语和短语勾勒出每个专业领域的颜色，虽然他所知道的一切就是如何模仿事物，通过这种方式使得别的肤浅之人，即那些把自己的结论基于他们所听到的词语的人，认为他们使用音步、韵律和曲调确实写出了关于制鞋、军事指挥和任何别的事物的诗歌。仅用这些特性就产生了有着强大力量的咒语，而这是他们所追求的。但当诗人的作品去掉了音色，用平实的词语表达出来的时 b
候，我想你早已知道这会是什么样子的，所以你明白我说的是什么了。"

'I do,' he said.

'Isn't it', I asked, 'like what noticeably happens when a young man has alluring features, without actually being good- looking, and then this charm of his deserts him?'

'Exactly,' he said.

'Now, here's another point to consider. An image-maker, a re-
c presenter, understands only appearance, while reality is beyond him. Isn't that our position?'

'Yes.'

'Let's not leave the job half done: let's give this idea the consideration it deserves.'

'Go on,' he said.

'What a painter does, we're saying, is paint a picture of a horse's reins and a bit. Yes?'

'Yes.'

'While they're made by a saddler and a smith, aren't they?'

'Yes.'

'Does a painter know what the reins and the bit have to be like? Surely even their makers, the smith and the saddler, don't know this, do they? Only the horseman does, because he's the one who knows how to make use of them.'

'You're quite right.'

'In fact, won't we claim that it's a general principle?'

'What?'

d 'That whatever the object, there are three areas of expertise: usage, manufacture, and representation.'

'Yes.'

'Now, is there any other standard by which one assesses the goodness, fineness, and rightness of anything (whether it's a piece of equipment or a creature or an activity) than the use for which it was

“我明白。”他说。

我问道:“所发生的事情显然不就像是这样的:一个年轻人具有诱人的魅力,而实际上并不好看,之后这种魅力弃他而去?”

“正是。”他说。

“那么还有一点要加以考虑。影像的制作者,模仿者只知道外表而不知道实在。这不就是你的观点吗?” c

“是的。”

“让我们不要半途而废,让我们对这个想法给予应有的考察。”

“继续吧。”他说。

“我们说,一个绘画者所做的,是绘一幅马的缰绳和嚼子的画。是吗?”

“是的。”

“而它们是由制造马具的人和铁匠制作的,不是吗?”

“是的。”

“画匠知道缰绳和嚼子应该是什么样的吗?即使它们的制作者,铁匠和制造马具的人肯定也不知道这个,是吗?只有骑马的人才知道,因为他知道如何使用它们。”

“你说得很对。”

“实际上,我们不是会说这只是个一般的原则吗?”

“什么?”

“无论什么东西,有三个专业技艺的领域:使用、制造和模仿。” d

“是的。”

“那么人或自然除了有用而创造之外,是否还有任何别的标准,通过这些标准人们评判任何事物的善、美和正当,无论是一件

made, by man or by nature?'

'No.'

'It's absolutely inevitable, then, that no one knows the ins and outs of any object more than the person who makes use of it. He has to be the one to tell the manufacturer how well or badly the object he's using fares in actual usage. A pipe-player, for example, tells a pipe-maker which of his pipes do what they're supposed to do when actually

e played, and goes on to instruct him in what kinds of pipes to make, and the pipe- maker does what he's told.'

'Of course.'

'So as far as good and bad pipes are concerned, it's a knowledgeable person who gives the orders, while the other obeys the orders and does the manufacturing. Right?'

'Yes.'

'Justified confidence, then, is what a pipe-maker has about goodness and badness (as a result of spending time with a knowledgeable person and having to listen to him), while knowledge is the

602a province of the person who makes use of the pipes.'

'Yes.'

'Which of these two categories does our representer belong to? Does he acquire knowledge about whether or not what he's painting is good or right from making use of the object, or does he acquire true belief because of having to spend time with a knowledgeable person and being told what to paint?'

'He doesn't fit either case.'

'As far as goodness and badness are concerned, then, a representer doesn't have either knowledge or true beliefs about whatever it is he's representing.'

'Apparently not.'

'How nicely placed a poetic representer is, then, to know what he's writing about!'

'Not really.'

器具还是动物或行为?”

“没有。”

“那么必定是这样的:没有人比使用者更了解任何事物的细节。他应该把他在实际使用的事物的好坏告诉制造者。比如说,笛子表演者告诉笛子制作者当实际使用的时候,他的笛子应该具有什么样的表现,进而指导他制作什么样的笛子,而笛子的制作 e
者按他所说的去做。”

“当然。”

“所以就笛子的优劣而言,有知识的人给出指示而别的人按指示去制作,对吗?”

“是的。”

“那么笛子制作者所具有的是关于笛子优劣的被证实为正确的信念(这是花时间和有知识的人在一起并且须听从他而得的结果),而笛子的使用者所本有的则是知识。” 602a

“是的。”

“我们的模仿者属于这两类中的哪一类?他是不是从使用物品中获得了关于其画作好坏的知识呢,还是因为他不得不和有见识的人相处,他们告诉他该画什么,从而获得了正确信念?”

“他两种情况都不符合。”

“那么就优劣来说,模仿者关于他所模仿的任何事物都不具有知识或正确的意见。”

“显然没有。”

“那么一个诗人的模仿者,居然知道他正在写的是什么,这是何等美妙的替代啊!”

“实在是不妙。”

b 'No, because all the same, despite his ignorance of the good and bad aspects of things, he'll go on representing them. But what he'll be representing, apparently, is whatever appeals to a large, if ignorant, audience.'

'Naturally.'

'Here are the points we seem to have reached a reasonable measure of agreement on, then: a representer knows nothing of value about the things he represents; representation is a kind of game, and shouldn't be taken seriously; and those who compose tragedies in iambic and epic verse are, without exception, outstanding examples of representers.'

'Yes.'

c 'So the province of representation is indeed two steps removed from truth, isn't it?' I said.

'Yes.'

'But on which of the many aspects of a person does it exert its influence?'

'What are you getting at?'

'Something like this. One and the same object appears to vary in size depending on whether we're looking at it from close up or far away.'

'Yes.'

'And the same objects look both bent and straight depending on whether we look at them when they're in water or out of it, and both concave and convex because sight gets misled by colouring. Our mind obviously contains the potential for every single kind of confusion like
d this. It's because illusory painting aims at this affliction in our natures that it can only be described as sorcery; and the same goes for conjuring and all trickery of that sort.'

'True.'

'Now, methods have evolved of combating this—measuring, counting, and weighing are the most elegant of them — and consequently

“不,因为尽管他仍然不知道事物好的方面和坏的方面,但他继续模仿它们。他所模仿的东西显然还是吸引了大量无知的听众。” b

“自然。”

“那么关于这几点我们似乎已经达成了相当合理的一致:模仿者对他所模仿的事物没有什么有价值的知识;模仿是一种游戏,不应该认真对待;那些以抑扬格和史诗格创作悲剧的人毫无例外地都是典型的模仿者。”

“是的。”

“所以模仿术确实是与真实隔着两层,不是吗?” c

“是的。”

“但它对人的多个部分中的哪一个施加影响?”

“你说的是什么意思?”

“是这样的:同一个物体看上去大小有变化,这在于我们是从近处看还是从远处看。”

“是的。”

“同一个物体看上去既是弯的又是直的,这在于我们看的时候,它是在水中还是不在水中;物体看上去既是凹的又是凸的,是因为视觉受到颜色的误导。我们的心灵显然含有各种像这样的混乱的可能性。这是因为令人产生幻觉的绘画的目的,就是在我 d
们的本性中制造混乱苦恼的状况,就此而言,它只能被称作是一种巫术;而施妖术以及诸如此类的所有欺骗手段都是一样的。”

“对的。”

“现在已经发展出对抗这些的方法——量、数和称是其中最好的方法——结果可以终止似是而非的大小、数和重量对我们的

of ending the reign within us of apparent size, number, and weight, and replacing them with something which calculates and measures, or even weighs. Right?'

'Of course.'

e 'And this, of course, is the job of the rational part of the mind, which is capable of performing calculations.'

'Yes.'

'Now, it's not uncommon for the mind to have made its measurements, and to be reporting that x is larger than y (or smaller than it, or the same size as it), but still to be receiving an impression which contradicts its measurements of these very objects.'

'Yes.'

'Well, didn't we say that it's impossible for a single thing to hold contradictory beliefs at the same time about the same objects?'

'Yes, we did, and we were right.'

603a 'So the part of the mind whose views run counter to the measurements must be different from the part whose views fall in with the measurements.'

'Yes.'

'But it's the best part of the mind which accepts measurements and calculations.'

'Of course.'

'The part which opposes them, therefore, must be a low-grade part of the mind.'

'Necessarily.'

'Well, all that I've been saying has been intended to bring us to the point where we can agree that not only does painting—or rather representation in general—produce a product which is far from truth, but it also forms a close, warm, affectionate relationship with a part of
b us which is, in its turn, far from intelligence. And nothing healthy or authentic can emerge from this relationship.'

'Absolutely,' he said.

'A low-grade mother like representation, then, and an equally low-grade father produce low-grade children.'

'I suppose that's right.'

主宰，取而代之的是计数、计量甚或称重，对吗？”

“当然。”

“这当然是心灵中的理性部分的工作，它能够完成计算。” e

“是的。”

“那么常见的是心灵做了测量并报告说，一物比另一物大，或比它小或一样大，但得到的印象却是与对这些物体的测量相反。”

“是的。”

“嗯，我们不是说过，对于单一事物来说，不可能就这些相同的物体同时持有相互矛盾的看法？”

“是的，我们说过，而且我们是对的。”

“所以心灵中其观点与测量相悖的部分，必定不同于心灵中 603a
其观点与测量一致的部分。”

“是的。”

“但心灵的最优良部分会接受测量与计算的。”

“当然。”

“所以与它们对立的部分必定是心灵中的低贱部分。”

“必然。”

“那么我所说的一切都意在于使我们对这一点达成一致：不光是绘画——或一般的模仿术——制作出的制品远离真理，而且还与我们的一个部分形成了紧密、热情和密切的关系，而这个部分是远离理性的。在这种关系中不会产生健康和真正的事物。” b

“毫无疑问。”他说。

“那么像模仿术这样的低贱母亲和同样低贱的父亲生出低贱的孩子。”

“我想这是对的。”

‘Does this apply only to visual representation,’ I asked, ‘or to aural representation as well—in other words, to poetry?’

‘I suppose it applies to poetry as well,’ he said.

‘Well, we'd better not rely on mere suppositions based on paint-
c ing,’ I said. ‘Let's also get close enough to that part of the mind which poetic representation consorts with to see whether it's of low or high quality.’

‘Yes, we should.’

‘We'd better start by having certain ideas out in the open. We'd say that representational poetry represents people doing things, willingly or unwillingly, and afterwards thinking that they've been successful or unsuccessful, and throughout feeling distressed or happy. Have I missed anything out?’

‘No, nothing.’

d ‘Well, does a person remain internally unanimous throughout all this? We found that, in the case of sight, there's conflict and people have contradictory views within themselves at the same time about the same objects. Is it like that when one is doing things too? Is there internal conflict and dissent? But it occurs to me that there's really no need for us to decide where we stand on this issue now, because we've already done so, perfectly adequately, in an earlier phase of the discussion, when we concluded that, at any given moment, our minds are teeming with countless thousands of these kinds of contradictions.’

‘That's right,’ he said.

e ‘Yes,’ I said. ‘But that earlier discussion of ours was incomplete, and I think it's crucial that we finish it off now.’

‘What have we left out?’ he asked.

‘If a good man meets with a misfortune such as losing a son or something else he values very highly, we've already said, as you know, that he'll endure this better than anyone else.’

“这适用于视觉上的模仿,”我问道,“还是听觉上的模仿,换句话说,是否适用于诗歌?”

“我想也是适用于诗歌的。”他说。

“那么我们最好不要仅仅依赖于基于绘画的假设,”我说,“让
我们也靠近心灵中与诗歌模仿相一致的部分,看看它是低贱的还 c
是高尚的。”

“是的,我们应该这样做。”

“我们最好从某些清楚的观念开始。我们要说,模仿性的诗歌模仿人们自愿地或不自愿地行事,和在事后思考他们是成功的还是不成功的,以及感受到痛苦还是快乐。我说漏了什么吗?”

“不,没有。”

“那么,在所有这些当中,一个人内心保持一致吗?就视觉来
说,我们发现存在着冲突并且人们自身对于同一个事物同时有相 d
矛盾的看法。当人们行事的时候是否也是一样的?是否有内部冲突和异议?但在我看来,现在我们确实没有必要判定我们在这个问题上的立场,因为我们在早先的讨论中已经充分地讨论过了,我们总结说,我们的心灵在任何时候都充满了无数这样的矛盾。”

“对的。”他说。

“是的,”我说,“但我们早先的讨论是不完整的,我想现在我
们应该把它结束了。” e

“我们遗漏了什么?”他问道。

“如果一个好人遇上了厄运,比如说他失去了某个他非常珍爱的儿子或别的什么东西,如你所知,我们说过他会比别的任何人都更能承受得住。”

'Yes.'

'But here's something for us to think about. Will he feel no grief, or is that impossible? If it's impossible, is it just that he somehow keeps his pain within moderate bounds?'

'The second alternative is closer to the truth,' he said.

604a 'But now I've got another question for you about him. Do you think he'll be more likely to fight and resist his distress when his peers can see him, or when he's all alone by himself in some secluded spot?'

'He'll endure pain far better when there are people who can see him, of course,' he said.

'When he's all alone, however, I imagine he won't stop himself expressing a lot of things he'd be ashamed of anyone hearing, and doing a lot of things he'd hate anyone to see him do.'

'That's right,' he agreed.

'Isn't it the case that reason and convention recommend resist-
b ance, while the actual event pushes him towards distress?'

'True.'

'When a person is simultaneously pulled in opposite directions in response to a single object, we're bound to conclude that he has two sides.'

'Of course.'

'One of which is prepared to let convention dictate the proper course of action, isn't it?'

'Can you explain how?'

'Convention tells us, as you know, that it's best to remain as unruffled as possible when disaster strikes and not to get upset, on the grounds that it's never clear whether an incident of this nature is good

“是的。”

“但我们还有点什么得想一想。他不会感到悲痛呢，还是说不悲痛是不可能的？如果是不可能的，那么他设法把他的痛苦保持在适度的范围之内，这样做妥当吗？”

“第二种方式更接近真实。”他说。

“但现在关于他，我还有另一个问题要问你。你认为，是当他 604a
的同伴看着他的时候还是当他在一个隐蔽的地方独处的时候，他更可能抵抗和忍住他的痛苦？”

“当然是有人看着他的时候他更能忍住痛苦。”他说。

“然而当他一个人的时候，我想他不会阻拦自己说出很多羞于让任何人听到的话，并做出很多他讨厌任何人看到他做的事情。”

“对的。”他同意说。

“情况难道不是这样的：理性与习惯劝慰他克制，而实际的事
情却把他推向痛苦？” b

“对的。”

“当一个人对于单一的对象同时被拉向相反的方向，我们必定可以得出结论：他有两面。”

“当然。”

“其中之一就是准备让习惯指导他自己的行动过程，不是吗？”

“你能说明一下如何指导吗？”

“如你所知，习惯告诉我们，当遇到灾难的时候，最好尽可能地保持平静，不要变得急躁，因为总还是不清楚这样的事情是好是坏，悲观对待也于事无补，人类生活当中没有哪些方面是值得

or bad, that nothing positive is gained by taking it badly, that no aspect of human life is worth bothering about a great deal, and that grief
c blocks our access to the very thing we need to have available as quickly as possible in these circumstances.'

'What do you have in mind?' he asked.

'The ability to think about the incident', I replied, 'and, under the guidance of reason, to make the best possible use of one's situation, as one would in a game of dice when faced with how the dice had fallen. When children bump into things, they clutch the hurt spot and spend time crying; instead of behaving like that, we should con-
d stantly be training our minds to waste no time before trying to heal anything which is unwell, and help anything which has fallen get up from the floor—to banish mourning by means of medicine.'

'Yes, that's the best way to deal with misfortune,' he said.

'Now, our position is that the best part of our minds is perfectly happy to be guided by reason like this.'

'That goes without saying.'

'Whereas there's another part of our minds which urges us to remember the bad times and to express our grief, and which is insatiably greedy for tears. What can we say about it? That it's incapable of listening to reason, that it can't face hard work, that it goes hand in hand with being frightened of hardship?'

'Yes, that's right.'

e 'Now, although the petulant part of us is rich in a variety of representable possibilities, the intelligent and calm side of our characters is pretty well constant and unchanging. This makes it not only difficult to represent, but also difficult to understand when it is represented, particularly when the audience is the kind of motley crowd you find crammed into a theatre, because they're simply not acquainted with the experience that's being represented to them.'

605a 'Absolutely.'

烦心的，而且在这样的情况下，悲哀还会堵塞我们通向尽快得到 c
我们所需之物的通道。”

“你心里想的什么呢?”他问道。

“对突发事件进行考虑的能力”，我回答说，“有了这种能力，就能在理性的指导下，尽最大可能地利用好个人的处境，就像一个人在一场掷骰子赌输赢的游戏中，当他面对着已经落下的骰子的点数决定怎
么办一样。当孩子撞到了东西，他们就用手紧紧捂住伤痛处哇哇大哭 d
不停；我们不应该这样做，我们应该坚持不懈地训练我们的心灵，不要在设法治愈任何无药可治的东西上花费时间，而要帮助跌倒的任何东西重新从地上站起来——通过这种‘药’来消除悲痛与忧伤。”

“是的，这是对待不幸的最好方法。”他说。

“那么，我们的观点是，我们心灵中的最善的部分完全乐意受这样的理性的指导。”

“毫无疑问。”

“而我们的心灵中还有另一个部分，它迫使我们记住悲痛并表达我们的悲伤，还对眼泪有无止尽的贪求。我们对它能说什么呢？它不能听从理性，不能面对艰难的工作，它和对艰难苦痛的畏惧结合在一起，是吗?”

“是的，很对。”

“那么，虽然我们不冷静的部分充满了各种可模仿的可能性， e
但我们性格中理性和冷静的部分总是恒常不变的。这使得它不光难以模仿，而且模仿了也难以理解，尤其当听众是那些你看到的涌进剧场的乌合之众时更是如此，因为他们不熟悉向他们呈现的感情。”

“毫无疑问。” 605a

'Evidently, then, a representational poet has nothing to do with this part of the mind: his skill isn't made for its pleasure, because otherwise he'd lose his popular appeal. He's concerned with the petulant and varied side of our characters, because it's easy to represent.'

'Obviously.'

'So we're now in a position to see that we'd be perfectly justified in taking hold of him and placing him in the same category as a painter. He resembles a painter because his creations fall short of truth,
b and a further point of resemblance is that the part of the mind he communicates with is not the best part, but something else. Now we can see how right we'd be to refuse him admission into any community which is going to respect convention, because now we know which part of the mind he wakes up. He destroys the rational part by feeding and fattening up this other part, and this is equivalent to someone destroying the more civilized members of a community by presenting ruffians with political power. There's no difference, we'll claim, between this and what a representational poet does: at a personal level, he establishes a bad system of government in people's minds by gratifying their irrational side, which can't even recognize what size things are—
c an object which at one moment it calls big, it might call small the next moment—by creating images, and by being far removed from truth.'

'Yes.'

'However, we haven't yet made the most serious allegation against representational poetry. It has a terrifying capacity for deforming even good people. Only a very few escape.'

'Yes, that is terrifying. Does it really do that?'

'Here's my evidence: you can make up your own mind. When Homer or another tragedian represents the grief of one of the heroes,
d they have him deliver a lengthy speech of lamentation or even have him sing a dirge and beat his breast; and when we listen to all this, even the best of us, as I'm sure you're aware, feels pleasure.

“那么显而易见的是，模仿性的诗人与心灵的这个部分无关：他的技巧不是用来取悦它的，因为否则的话，他会失去对民众的吸引力。他关心的是我们性格中暴躁多变的部分，因为这容易模仿。”

“显而易见。”

“所以我们现在可以看到，我们完全有理由把他捉住并
把他与画匠归为一类。他像是一个画匠，因为他的作品缺乏
真实，另一个相似点在于，他所交流的不是心灵的最优秀的 b
部分而是别的部分。现在我们能够看清楚了，我们不让他进
入任何城邦是多么正确，这是尊重习惯，因为现在我们知道
了他唤醒的是心灵的哪一个部分。他通过养育、催肥另一个
部分而毁坏理性的部分，这相当于危害城邦中的较有教养的
成员，而去把政治权力交给无赖恶棍。我们会说这与模仿性
诗人所做的事情没有什么区别：在个人的层面上，他在人们
的心灵中通过满足其非理性的部分建立起了一个恶的管理
体制，它不能辨别事物的大小——一个物体在此刻它称之为 c
大的，在另一刻它可能称之为小的——通过制造影像和远离
真实。”

“是的。”

“然而，我们对于模仿性的诗歌还没有做出最严厉的控告。它甚至有一种腐蚀优秀之人的可怕能力。只有很少人能逃脱。”

“是的，很可怕。它真的会那样吗？”

“这是我的证据，你可以自己做出判断。当荷马或别的悲剧
作家模仿英雄的痛苦，他们让他发表冗长的哭诉，甚至让他唱哀 d
歌并捶打他的胸膛；当我们，甚至是我们当中的最优秀的人听到

We surrender ourselves, let ourselves be carried along, and share the hero's pain; and then we enthuse about the skill of any poet who makes us feel particularly strong feelings.'

'Yes, I'm aware of this, of course.'

'However, you also appreciate that when we're afflicted by trouble in our own lives, then we take pride in the opposite—in our ability to endure pain without being upset. We think that this is manly be-
e haviour, and that only women behave in the way we were sanctioning earlier.'

'I realize that,' he said.

'So,' I said, 'instead of being repulsed by the sight of the kind of person we'd regret and deplore being ourselves, we enjoy the spectacle and sanction it. Is this a proper way to behave?'

'No, it certainly isn't,' he said. 'it's pretty unreasonable, I'd say.'

'I agree,' I said, 'and here's even more evidence.'

606a 'What?'

'Consider this. What a poet satisfies and gratifies on these occasions is an aspect of ourselves which we forcibly restrain when tragedy strikes our own lives—an aspect which hungers after tears and the satisfaction of having cried until one can cry no more, since that is what it is in its nature to want to do. When the part of us which is inherently good has been inadequately trained in habits enjoined by reason, it re-
b laxes its guard over this other part, the part which feels sad. Other people, not ourselves, are feeling these feelings, we tell ourselves, and it's no disgrace for us to sanction such behaviour and feel sorry for someone who, even while claiming to be good, is over-indulging in grief; and, we think, we are at least profiting from the pleasure, and there's no point in throwing away the pleasure by spurning the whole poem or play. You see, few people have the ability to work out that we ourselves are bound to store the harvest we reap from others: these

所有这些的时候,我确信你会意识到他们会感到愉快。我们投降了,让我们被说服吧,分担英雄的痛苦吧;然后我们就热爱上了诗人的技巧,他们使我们感受到这些特别强烈的感情。”

“是的,我当然意识到这一点了。”

“然而你也知道,当我们在自己的生活中遇到不幸的时候,我们会为相反的行为感到骄傲——我们能够毫不烦乱地忍住痛苦。我们认为这是男子汉的行为,而只有女人才会有像我们刚才容忍的那种方式的行为表现。” e

“我知道到了。”他说。

“所以,”我说,“不是对看到这种我们为之感到遗憾的人感到厌恶和反感,而是欣赏并赞同这种表演。这种行为方式是恰当的吗?”

“不,当然不恰当,”他说,“我想说这很没道理。”

“我同意,”我说,“这里甚至还有更多的证明。” 606a

“什么?”

“想想这个:在这些场合,诗人讨好和满足的是我们的这样一个部分,当我们自己生活中遇到灾难的时候,我们就强行压制这个部分——这个部分渴望眼泪和痛哭以求发泄直到不再哭为止,因为这是它本性所要求去做的。当我们的内在善的部分没有充分地受到习惯和理性的训练,它放松了对这另一个部分即感到悲伤的部分的监管。另一些人,不是我们,感到了这些情感,我们对 b
自己说赞同这样的行为没什么不光彩的,也不必为那些宣称为好人却过多地放任于悲哀的人感到遗憾;我们认为我们至少可以从快乐中获得好处,没必要通过拒绝所有诗歌或戏剧而把快乐抛弃。你知道,很少人能够理解,我们自己必定会储藏从别人那里

occasions feed the feeling of sadness until it is too strong for us easily to restrain it when hardship occurs in our own lives.'

c 'You're absolutely right,' he said.

'And doesn't the same go for humour as well? If there are amusing things which you'd be ashamed to do yourself, but which give you a great deal of pleasure when you see them in a comic representation or hear about them in private company—when you don't find them loathsome and repulsive—then isn't this exactly the same kind of behaviour as we uncovered when talking about feeling sad? There's a part of you which wants to make people laugh, but your reason restrains it, because you're afraid of being thought a vulgar clown. Nevertheless, you let it have its way on those other occasions, and you don't realize that the almost inevitable result of giving it energy in this other context is that you become a comedian in your own life.'

'Yes, that's very true,' he said.

d 'And the same goes for sex, anger, and all the desires and feelings of pleasure and distress which, we're saying, accompany everything we do: poetic representation has the same effect in all these cases too. It irrigates and tends to these things when they should be left to wither, and it makes them our rulers when they should be our subjects, because otherwise we won't live better and happier lives, but quite the opposite.'

'I can't deny the truth of what you're saying,' he said.

e 'Therefore, Glaucon,' I went on, 'when you come across people praising Homer and saying that he is the poet who has educated Greece, that he's a good source for people to learn how to manage their affairs and gain culture in their lives, and that one should structure the whole of one's life in accordance with his precepts, you ought

607a to be kind and considerate: after all, they're doing the best they can. You should concede that Homer is a supreme poet and the original tragedian, but you should also recognize that the only poems we can

收获来的东西;这些场合滋养了悲悯之情,以至于当困苦发生在我们自己的生活中的时候,它就会变得过于强烈而使我们不容易制服它。”

“你说得很对。”他说。 c

“对于幽默不也是同样的吗?如果你自己羞于去做那些逗乐的事情,那么当你观看喜剧表演或私下听到笑话的时候,是什么给了你那么多的快乐?那时你不觉得它们很讨厌、令人反感,那么这不正是与在我们谈到悲伤的情感所没谈到的行为相同吗?你的一个部分想要使人们发笑,而你的理性则克制住它,因为你担心被认为是一个粗俗的小丑。然而,在其他场合你则任其自便,你没有意识到,在这些场合,给予其力量而带来的几乎不可避免的结果就是,你在自己生活中成了一个喜剧演员。”

“是的,这很对。”他说。

“对于爱欲、愤怒和所有欲望以及快乐和痛苦的情感,我们说 d
它们是伴随着我们所做的一切的:诗歌的模仿在所有的情况下也具有同样的效果。当情感应该留待枯萎的时候,诗歌却浇灌、照料这些情感,当它们应该受我们统治的时候,诗歌却使它们成为我们的统治者,这样我们就不会生活得更好、更幸福,而是相反。”

“我不得不承认你说得是对的。”他说。

“所以,格劳孔,”我继续说,“当你遇见人们称颂荷马,说他是 e
教育希腊的诗人,在学习管理他们的事务和生活教育方面,他对人们来说是一个好榜样,人们应该按照他的教导来安排人们的全部生活,这时,你应该友好而体贴,毕竟他们尽力了。你应该承认 607a
荷马是一个高超的诗人,是第一个悲剧作家,但你也应该知道,我

admit into our community are hymns to the gods and eulogies of virtuous men. If you admit the entertaining Muse of lyric and epic poetry, then instead of law and the shared acceptance of reason as the best guide, the kings of your community will be pleasure and pain.'

'You're quite right,' he agreed.

b 'So,' I said, 'since we've been giving poetry another hearing, there's our defence: given its nature, we had good grounds for banishing it earlier from our community. No rational person could have done any different. However, poetry might accuse us of insensitivity and lack of culture, so we'd better also tell her that there's an ancient quarrel between poetry and philosophy. There are countless pieces of evidence for this enmity between them, but here are just a few: there's that "bitch yelping and baying at her master"; there's "featu-
c ring prominently in the idle chatter of fools"; there's "control by a crowd of know-alls"; there are those whose "subtle notions" lead them to realize that they do indeed have "notional incomes". All the same, we ought to point out that if the kinds of poetry and representation which are designed merely to give pleasure can come up with a rational argument for their inclusion in a well-governed community, we'd be delighted—short of compromising the truth as we see it, which wouldn't be right—to bring them back from exile: after all, we know from our own experience all about their spell. I mean, haven't *you* ever fallen under the spell of poetry, Glaucon, especially when the spectacle is provided by Homer?'

d 'I certainly have.'

'Under these circumstances, then, if our allegations met a poetic rebuttal in lyric verse or whatever, would we be justified in letting poetry return?'

'Yes.'

'And I suppose we'd also allow people who champion poetry because they like it, even though they can't compose it, to speak on its

们只允许赞美诸神和具有美德之人的诗人进入我们的城邦，如果你让抒情诗和史诗的快乐缪斯进入城邦的话，那么你们城邦的王就不是以法律和大家都接受的理性，而是以快乐和痛苦作为最好的指导。”

“你说得很对。”他同意说。

“这样，”我说，“由于我们又一次审问了诗歌，所以我们有了 b
辩护：鉴于其本性，我们有很好的理由尽早地将之驱逐出我们的城邦。任何理性之人的做法没有什么不同的。然而诗歌可能指责我们迟钝、没文化。所以我们最好还要告诉她，古时就有诗与哲学之争。有无数的证据表明它们之间的敌对，这里仅仅是一小
部分：有‘对主人吠叫的母狗’；有‘痴人闲扯中的大人物’；有‘被 c
饱学之士支配的人’；还有那些拥有‘缜密概念’的人使他们意识到自己确实在‘概念上有所收获’。我们仍然应该指出，如果这种仅仅旨在产生快乐的诗歌和模仿，能拿出理性的证明来说治理得良好的城邦需要它们，那么我们会很高兴地——如果不让我们所领悟到的真理出面来解决双方的分歧，那就不对了——把它们从流放中带回来，毕竟，我们在自己的体验中知道它们的所有魅力。格劳孔，我的意思是说，你难道没有为诗歌的魅力所折服，尤其是
当荷马提供了这些剧情？” d

“我当然为之折服。”

“那么在这样的情况下，如果我们的指控在抒情诗或别的什么地方遇到了诗歌的反驳，我们是否会被说服让它们回来呢？”

“是的。”

“而且我想，对于人们，他们尽管不创作诗歌但却因为喜欢诗歌而拥护它，我们要允许他们用散文写作去表达，去试图证明诗

behalf in prose, and to try to prove that there's more to poetry than mere pleasure—that it also has a beneficial effect on society and on
e human life in general. And we won't listen in a hostile frame of mind, because we'll be the winners if poetry turns out to be beneficial as well as enjoyable.'

'Of course we will,' he agreed.

'And if it doesn't, Glaucon, then we'll do what a lover does when he thinks that a love affair he's involved in is no good for him: he reluctantly detaches himself. Similarly, since we've been condi-
608a tioned by our wonderful societies until we have a deep-seated love for this kind of poetry, we'll be delighted if there proves to be nothing better and closer to the truth than it. As long as it is incapable of rebutting our allegations, however, then while we listen to poetry we'll be chanting these allegations of ours to ourselves as a precautionary incantation against being caught once more by that childish and pervasive love. Our message will be that the commitment appropriate for an important matter with access to the truth shouldn't be given to this kind of poetry. People should, instead, be worried about the possible
b effects, on one's own inner political system, of listening to it and should tread cautiously; and they should let our arguments guide their attitude towards poetry.'

'I couldn't agree more,' he said.

'You see, my dear Glaucon,' I said, 'what's in the balance here is absolutely crucial—far more so than people think. it's whether one becomes a good or a bad person, and consequently has the calibre not to be distracted by prestige, wealth, political power, or even poetry from applying oneself to morality and whatever else goodness involves.'

'Looking back over our discussion,' he said, 'I can only agree with you. And I think anyone else would do the same as well.'

歌不仅仅是快乐——还对社会以及一般的人类生活有益。我们不会以敌视的心态去听他们说的,因为如果诗歌被证明是有益并 e
且是令人愉快的,那么我们就是胜利者。”

“我们当然会的。”他同意说。

“格劳孔,如果它做不到,那么我们就会像一个爱人发现他的爱情于他无益时所做的那样:只好不情愿地离开了。同样,既然我们受到我们美好社会的调教,终于使我们对这种诗歌怀有深情爱意,那么,如果有证明说没有什么比诗歌更好、更接近真理的了,我们会很高兴。然而只要它不能反驳我们的断言,那么当我 608a
们听到诗歌的时候,我们就要对着自己不停地述说我们的这些断言,作为一种预防咒语,以免再被那种幼稚而具有渗透性的热爱揪扯住。我们要明说的是,与达至真实这一重要事务相应的使命,是不应该交给诗歌的。相反,人们在倾听诗歌的时候应该担心它对人们内在政治制度可能造成的效果;他们应该让我们的论 b
证指导他们对待诗歌的态度。”

“我非常同意。”他说。

“你知道,我亲爱的格劳孔,”我说,“这儿的这个悬而未决的问题是绝对至关重要的——比人们想到的要重要的多。这关系到一个人是变成一个好人还是一个坏人,从而是否具有不受名誉、财富、政治权势诱惑的品质,甚至不受诗歌的诱惑,不把它本身应用于正义及其他任何的善。”

“回顾我们的讨论,”他说,“我完全同意你的说法。我想其他任何人也会同样同意的。”

CHAPTER 14

608c ‘But, you know,’ I said, ‘we haven’t discussed the most substantial rewards and wages which goodness entails.’

‘You mean there’s more?’ he said. ‘they must be stupendous, if they’re bigger than the ones we’ve already talked about.’

‘How can anything grow big in a short span of time?’ I asked. ‘I mean, a complete lifetime, from childhood to old age, is tiny compared with the whole of time.’

‘It’s nothing at all,’ he agreed.

‘Well then, don’t you think that anything immortal should con-
d cern itself with the whole of time, rather than with such a short extent?’

‘Yes, I do,’ he said. ‘But what are you getting at?’

‘Don’t you realize that our mind is immortal and never dies?’ I asked.

He looked straight at me in surprise and said, ‘No, I certainly don’t. Are you in a position to claim that it is?’

‘Certainly,’ I said. ‘So are you, I’d say. I mean, it’s a relatively straightforward subject.’

‘Not to me, it isn’t,’ he replied. ‘But I’d be glad to hear what you have to say on this “relatively straightforward subject”!’

‘All right,’ I said.

‘Go on, then,’ he said.

第十四章

“但你知道，”我说，“我们还没有讨论过善所包含的最大的奖 c
励和报偿。”

“你的意思是说有更大的？”他说，“它们一定是大得惊人，如果它们比我们曾说过的还要大的话。”

“任何事物在一段短短的时间里怎么能够长大呢？”我问道，“我的意思是说，从小到老的整个一生与整个时间相比是渺小的。”

“那是根本算不上什么的。”他同意说。

“那么你难道不认为任何不朽的事物应该与整个时间相关而
不是与这么短的一段时间相关？” d

“我认为应该和整个时间相关，”他说，“但你是怎么理解的？”

“你难道没有意识到我们的心灵是不朽的、绝不死亡的？”我问道。

他直瞪瞪惊讶地看着我说：“不，我当然不知道。你是这么主张的吗？”

“毫无疑问，”我说道。“我要说你也应该如此。我的意思是说，这是一个相对简单明了的问题。”

“对我来说可不是这样，”他回答说。“但是我很乐意听一听，关于这个‘相对简单明了的问题’，你会说些什么！”

“好吧。”我说。

“那么继续说吧。”他说。

'You acknowledge the existence of good and bad, don't you?' I asked.

'Yes.'

e 'I wonder if your conception of them is the same as mine.'

'What is that?'

'Badness always manifests in destruction and corruption, while goodness always manifests in preservation and benefit.'

'I agree,' he said.

'Now, would you say that there are things which are good and
609a bad for a given object? For example, ophthalmia is bad for eyes, illness for the body as a whole, blight for corn, rot for wood, rust for bronze and iron—as I say, nearly every object has some specific thing to afflict it, which is bad for it.'

'I agree,' he said.

'Isn't it the case that whenever one of these objects is afflicted by its affliction, it deteriorates, and ultimately decomposes and perishes?'

'Of course.'

'Therefore, any given object is destroyed by its specific affliction
b and defect; apart from this, there's nothing else that can destroy it, because goodness is never destructive, and neither is anything which is intermediate between good and bad.'

'Of course,' he said.

'Suppose that we come across something, then, which is certainly subject to the degenerative action of its defect, but which cannot be decomposed and destroyed by it. Won't we immediately realize that we're faced with something which, by its very nature, is indestructible?'

'I should think we would,' he replied.

'Now, is there anything which makes a mind bad?' I asked.

'Yes, definitely,' he said. 'All the things which have cropped up in the course of our discussion—immorality, lack of self-control,

“你承认存在善和恶,不是吗?”我问道。

“是的。”

“我想知道你对它们的理解是否与我的相同。” e

“是什么样的?”

“恶总是展示于破坏和腐化中,而善总是展示于保存和利益中。”

“我同意。”他说。

“那么你是否认为,对于一个特定的事物来说有善有恶?比
如说,眼炎对于眼睛来说是恶的,疾病对于整个身体来说是恶的, 609a
枯萎病对于谷物来说是恶的,腐烂对于木材来说是恶的,生锈对
于铜铁来说是恶的——就如我所说,几乎每个事物都有某些特定
的损害它、对它来说是恶的东西。”

“我同意。”他说。

“情况不是这样的吗:每当这些事物中的一个受到恶的扰乱,那么它就会变坏并最终腐化消亡?”

“当然。”

“所以任何事物都是被特定的恶和缺陷所损毁;除此之外没
有什么别的东西能够使它损毁,因为善绝不是破坏性的,并且任 b
何处于善和恶之间的东西也不是破坏性的。”

“当然。”他说。

“那么设想我们发现了某个由于其恶而屈从于腐化的事物,但它不能为之腐化和损毁。我们不就直接可以看到我们所面对的是本性上不可毁坏的事物吗?”

“我想我们可以看到。”他回答说。

“那么有什么事物使心灵变恶吗?”我问道。

“是的,肯定有的,”他说,“所有那些出现在我们的讨论中的

c cowardice, and ignorance.'

'Well, do any of these defects cause it to decompose and perish? Be careful now: we don't want to fall into the trap of thinking that when an immoral person is stupid enough to have his crimes found out, this is an instance of his being destroyed by his mental defect—in this case, by his immorality. No, here's how to proceed. You know how illness, which is a body's defect, wastes and ruins a body, until it is actually annihilated; and you know how all the objects we mentioned a moment ago are brought to a state of annihilation when they're taken o-
d ver and afflicted by their specific defect, with its destructive power. Yes?'

'Yes.'

'All right, let's apply the same line of argument to the mind. When immorality (or some other kind of defect) occupies a person's mind, does its presence and occupancy cause his mind to deteriorate and decay, and does it eventually bring his mind to death and cause it to separate from the body?'

'No, it doesn't do that,' he said.

'On the other hand,' I said, 'it doesn't make sense to think that anything could be destroyed by some other object's defect, rather than by its own.'

'No, it doesn't.'

e 'You see, Glaucon,' I continued, 'I want you to appreciate that a body does not, in our view, have to be destroyed by some defect or other in its food—staleness or mouldiness or whatever. No, we'll explain any instance of bad food making a body deteriorate by saying that the *cause* of the body's destruction was its specific defect, illness, and that the food was the *reason* it became ill. But since a body and food are quite different from each other, we'd better resist the temptation to
610a say that a body is destroyed by bad food—that is, by something else's defect—unless it engenders the body's specific defect.'

'You're quite right,' he said.

事物——不正义、缺乏自制、懦弱和无知。” c

“那么这些恶会导致它腐化消亡吗？现在请小心，我们不要落入思想的圈套：当一个愚蠢的不正义之人犯罪被发现了，就把这说成是被他灵魂的恶给毁了——在这种情况下就是被他的不正义所毁。不是的，我们应该这样说，你知道疾病（它是身体的缺陷）是怎样耗费和毁坏身体，直到真的消灭身体的；你知道所有我们不久前提到的事物，当它们被特定的恶以其毁灭性的力量占有并感染的时候，是如何被带向灭亡的，是吗？” d

“是的。”

“好吧，让我们把同样的论证思路应用于心灵。当不正义或某些别的类型的恶占据了一个人的心灵的时候，它的出现和占领会导致他心灵的败坏和腐化并最终把他的心灵带向死亡，导致它与身体的分离吗？”

“不，不是那样的。”他说。

“另一方面，没有理由认为任何事物可以被某些别的事物的恶所毁灭而不被它自己的恶所毁灭。”

“没有理由。”

“你看啊，格劳孔，”我继续说，“我想要你注意，在我们看来身 e
体是不会被食物中的某种不良缺陷或别的什么——腐烂或发霉或无论什么——毁灭的。不是的，任何坏的食物导致身体的变坏，我们会解释说，身体毁坏的原因是其特定的不良缺陷，即疾病，而食物是生病的理由。但是因为身体与食物彼此是非常不同的，所以我们
最好抵制住诱惑，不说身体是被坏的食物所毁——就是说，是被他 610a
物的不良所毁——除非它产生了身体中特定的不良。”

“你说得很对。”他说。

‘By the same token,’ I went on,‘if a bad physical state can't cause a bad mental state, we'd better not claim that a person's mind is destroyed (unless its own special defect is present) by a defect from elsewhere: that would be an instance of one thing being destroyed by something else's defect.’

‘Yes, that makes sense,’ he agreed.

‘We've got a choice, then. We can either prove this idea of ours
b wrong, or (in the absence of such proof) we have to say that no fever,
no illness of any kind, and no injury either—not even chopping the
whole body up into the tiniest possible pieces—has the slightest de-
structive effect on the mind. In order for us to accept that it does,
someone would have to demonstrate that these physical afflictions
cause an increase in immorality and injustice in the mind. But we
should refuse to accept the assertion that the mind or anything else is
destroyed if its own specific defect doesn't occur, and it's just a case
c of one thing providing an environment for something else's defect to
occur.

‘But no one will ever prove that death makes a dead person's mind more immoral,’ he said.

‘Someone might venture to tackle our argument head on, howev-
er,’ I said,‘and might try to avoid having to concede the mind's im-
mortality by claiming that a dying person degenerates and becomes
less moral. In that case, I suppose, if our opponent was right, we'd
have to deny our current claim that the *cause* of death for immoral
people is other people administering justice, while immorality is the
reason they do so. Instead, we'd have to claim that immorality is as
d fatal as a disease for anyone who possesses it; that people who con-
tract it die of it, because it is in its nature to kill; and that the speed
at which it kills them depends on the extent of their immorality!’

‘Yes, and if immorality is fatal to its possessor,’ he added, ‘then it obviously gives him no cause for alarm, since it'll put an end to all his troubles. No, I'm sure we're more likely to find that, on the

“同样,”我继续说,“如果一个恶的身体状态不能造成恶的心灵状态,那么我们最好不要说一个人的心灵被别的地方的恶所毁坏,除非出现了自己特定的恶,那样的话就是一个事物被另一个事物的恶所毁坏。”

“是的,这很有道理。”他同意说。

“那么我们有一个选择。我们或者证明我们的这种观点是错误的,或者如果缺乏这样的证据,那么我们必须说,热病、任何种 b
类的疾病,以及伤害——更不用说碎尸万段——都没有对心灵造成一点点的损害。为了让我们承认它能够造成伤害,人们必须证明这些身体上的痛苦能增加心灵中的不德与不义。但是我们应当拒绝接受这样的论断,即心灵或任何别的事物自身不产生特定的缺陷,它们却会受到毁坏。情况只是这样的:一个事物为别的某事物的缺陷的产生提供了环境。” c

“但没有人会证明死亡使得死者的心灵变得更加不正义。”他说。

“然而也许有人冒险继续抓住我们的论证不放,”我说,“并且可能试图通过声称一个垂死之人堕落了并变得不正义了而避免不得不承认心灵不朽。在这种情况下,我想如果我们的对手是对的,那么我们不得不否认我们现在的主张,即不正义之人死亡的原因在于别的执掌司法的人,而不正义是他们这样做的理由。相反,我们不得不主张,不正义对于任何拥有不正义的人来说都像疾病一样致命;感染不正义的人就死于不正义,因为不正义的本 d
性就在于杀害,其杀人的速度取决于他们不正义的程度!”

“是的,如果不正义对于拥有不正义的人来说是致命的,”他补充说,“那么它显然不会使他惊慌,因为它会结束他的所有麻烦。相反,我确信我们更可能发现不正义,如果可能的话,杀死的

e contrary, immorality kills other people, if it can, not its possessor. In fact, an immoral person even gains quite a tot of vitality from it, and restless vigour as well. In other words, the impression it gives is that it's found a billet a long way from being fatal.'

'You're right,' I said. 'Now, since we've found that the mind can't be exterminated by its specific defect and destroyed by its specific affliction, it's hardly likely that a defect which is designed for the destruction of something else is going to destroy the mind—or anything else, for that matter, except whatever it's designed for.'

'Yes, that's hardly likely,' he agreed.

611a 'It cannot be destroyed, then, by any defect specific to itself, or any defect specific to anything else. It plainly follows that it must exist for ever. And if it exists for ever, then it is immortal.'

'Yes, inevitably,' he agreed.

'So much for that, then,' I said. 'Now, if this is so, you'll appreciate that there must always be the same minds in existence. None of them can be destroyed, so their number cannot decrease; and it can't increase either, because any additional immortal entity of any kind would have to come, as I'm sure you realize, from a mortal entity, and therefore everything would eventually become immortal.'

'You're right.'

'But that's too implausible an idea for us to believe,' I said.

b 'And we'll also find it hard to believe that, in essence, the mind is the kind of thing to be pervaded by internal diversity, inconsistency, and dissension.'

'What do you mean?' he asked.

'That something is unlikely to be immortal if it's a compound, formed imperfectly from diverse parts,' I replied. 'But that's what we found the mind to be not long ago.'

'Yes, that would make immortality improbable.'

是别人而不是拥有不正义的人。实际上一个不正义的人甚至从中获得很多活力和无穷的精力。换句话说,它给人的印象是它已经建立了一个远离死亡的壁垒。” e

“你说得对,”我说,“因为我们发现心灵的特定的不良缺陷并不能杀死心灵,并且特定的痛苦不能毁灭心灵,那么旨在毁灭他物的不良缺陷更不可能去毁坏心灵——或就这点而言,更不会毁坏别的任何东西,除了任何它旨在毁坏的东西。”

“是的,那是几乎不可能的。”他同意说。

“那么,任何自身特定的不良缺陷或任何他物特定的不良缺 611a
陷都不能使之毁坏。这显然可以推论出,它必定是永恒存在的。如果它是永恒存在的话,那么它就是不朽的。”

“是的,这是必定的。”他同意说。

“那么关于那点就谈这些吧,”我说,“如果是这样的话,那么你会注意到存在的必定总是同样的灵魂。它们当中没有一个会被毁灭,所以它们的数目不会减少,也不会增加,因为我确信你知道,任何增加的不朽之物都是来源于可朽之物,由此最终一切都会变得不朽的了。”

“你说得对。”

“但我们不能相信这个太不可信的想法,”我说,“因为我们觉得很难相信心灵实质上是一个内部充满多样、不一致和矛盾的东西。” b

“你说的是什么意思?”他问道。

“一个事物如果是复合的、由多个部分不完善地组织在一起,那么它不太可能是不朽的,”我回答说,“但我们不久前发现灵魂就是这样的。”

“是的,这样就会使得不朽成为不大可能的。”

'Well, the immortality of the mind would seem to have been conclusively proved by the argument we've just been through, and by our other arguments as well. What we have to do, however, is try to see what the mind is really and truly like, when it's not deformed by its association with the body and with other evils (which is how we've been looking at it so far). We should try to see what it's like when it's
c untainted, and we'll have to rely on reason to get a clear enough view of that. You'll find that its beauty is greatly enhanced, and you'll gain far more insight into cases of morality and immorality, and all the qualities we've been discussing. Our current ideas about the mind are true, in so far as they correspond to what we can see of it at the moment; but the condition in which we're observing it is like that of Glaucus the sea-deity. If people were to see Glaucus, it would be
d hard for them to discern his original state any more, because some of the original parts of his body have been knocked off, some have been worn away and generally deformed by the waves, and other things—shells, seaweed, and stones—have grown on him, so that his appearance is quite different from what it used to be, and he looks altogether more like a monster. Similarly, when we look at the mind too, its condition, as we see it, is the result of countless malign influences. What we have to do, Glaucon, is look in a different direction.'

'Where?' he asked.

e 'We should take note of the fact that it is attracted towards wisdom, and consider what it is related to and the affiliations it desires, given that it is of the same order as the divine, immortal, and eternal realm. And we should consider what would happen to the mind if the *whole* of it allowed this realm to dictate its direction, and if this impulse carried it out of its current underwater location, and all the
612a stones and shells were broken off—all the accretions of earth and rock (since earth is its food) which currently grow uncontrollably in large numbers all over it because it indulges in the pleasures which

“好吧，我们刚才的论证以及我们别的论证都已经最终证明心灵是不朽。然而我们所要做的是试图考察一下，心灵在其没有与身体以及别的不良缺陷——至此我们还是这样来考察心灵的——结合在一起而扭曲的时候，心灵真真切切是什么样的。我们应该试图考察一下当其未受污染的时候是什么样的，我们必须依靠理性以对灵魂形成一个足够清晰的看法。c
你会发现，它的美得到大大的提升，你会对正义和不正义以及所有我们讨论过的品质获得更加深远的洞见。我们关于心灵的看法是正确的，只要它们与我们此刻看到的相一致，但我们现在观看的状况就像观看海神格劳科斯一样。如果人们想要
观看格劳科斯，他们会难以进一步辨认出他原来的样子，因为 d
他身体的原初的某些部分已经掉落，某些部分已经被海浪磨损并大体上改变了形状，还有一些别的东西——贝壳、海草和石块——都长在他身上，这样他的外观与过去的样子大为不同，他看上去更像是一个怪物了。同样当我们来观看灵魂的时候，我们看到的状态是受到无数恶的影响的结果。格劳孔，我们必须要做的就是朝别的方向看看。”

“哪里？”他问道。

“我们应该注意一下灵魂受到智慧吸引这个事实，鉴于它与 e
神圣、不朽和永恒的领域处于同一层次，考虑一下它与智慧的关系以及它所渴求的亲近关系吧。我们应该考虑一下，如果它整个地允许这个领域指导它的方向，如果这个力量把它从现在的水底
打捞出来并除去了所有石块和贝壳——由于土是它的食物，因为 612a
它放纵于那些人们说是能带来幸福的快乐，所以所有这些土和石的增加物现在不可遏制地到处大规模繁殖，这时我们就可以考察心

men say bring happiness. Then we'd be able to see what it's really like—whether it is manifold or uniform, or what its true nature and condition is. Anyway, I think we've given a reasonable account of what happens to it and the forms it assumes in human life.'

'Definitely,' he said.

'Now,' I said, 'haven't we succeeded in refuting all the charges
b that were mentioned? In particular, haven't we avoided praising the respects in which morality is rewarding and enhances a person's reputation, which is what you all said Hesiod and Homer did, and discovered that, when morality and the mind are both taken just in themselves, there's nothing better for the mind than morality, and that a person ought to behave morally whether or not he owns Gyges' ring, and whether or not he owns Hades' helmet as well a magical ring?'

'You're quite right,' he said.

'Surely, then, Glaucon,' I said, 'no one will mind if, as an appendix, we now go on to assign rewards to morality and virtue in
c general, and describe all the various ways in which men and gods remunerate morality during a person's lifetime and after his death?'

'Of course they won't,' he said.

'Now, you incurred a debt in the course of our discussion. Are you going to pay me back?'

'What debt?'

'I allowed you a moral man with a reputation for immorality, and an immoral man with a reputation for morality. You were asking for this concession to be made, for the sake of argument, because even though it might in fact be impossible for the true state of affairs not to be known by gods and men, you thought it would still

灵是什么样的了。然后我们就能看清它真的是什么样了——无论其真正本性和状态是复合还是单一的或别的什么样子。无论如何，我想我们已经对心灵的状态和它在人们生活中所具有的形式做了一个合理的解释。”

“毫无疑问。”他说。

“现在，”我说道，“我们不是已经成功地证明，所有提到的指责都是错误的吗？特别是，我们不是也已经避开了对尊敬的颂扬了吗？据说他人的尊敬是对正义的奖赏，并能增进某
个人的名望，你们都说这是赫西俄德与荷马的所作所为，而且 b
我们还发现，当正义与心灵都能接受的就是它们自身的时候，对于心灵而言，没有比行持正义更好的事情了，如此说来，一个人应该行为正义，而无论他是拥有吉格斯的戒指，还是戴着冥王哈德斯的帽子还有那枚魔戒，都应该如此，难道不是吗？”

“你说的非常正确，”他说道。

“那么可以肯定的是，格劳孔，”我说，“没有人会介意下面的 c
做法的吧，即如果作为一种附属品，我们现在继续把奖赏分派给普通意义上的正义和美德，并描述一下，在一个人生前死后的那段时间内，诸神是如何以各种不同的方式对其德行尽酬劳之能事的。”

“他们当然不会介意的。”他说。

“那么你在讨论过程中所欠的债呢？你准备还给我吗？”

“什么债？”

“我曾允许你说，一个正义之人拥有一种不义的名声，而一个不义之人却拥有正义的名声。出于论证，你们曾要求做出这个让步，因为虽然对于诸神和人来说，他们是不可能不知道真相的，

help us compare and assess morality and immorality on their own terms. Do you remember?'

d ' Of course I do,' he said.

'Well, our assessment *has* been made,' I said, 'and so I am now, on behalf of morality, asking you for a favour in return: I want us to agree, along with everyone else, that morality does have the reputation it enjoys among gods and men. We've found that actually being moral entails benefits, and that those in whom morality is genuinely present are not gaining a false impression of morality, so if you grant me this favour, morality can also collect the prize for its reputation and gain the benefits it bestows on its possessors.'

'It's a fair request,' he said.

e 'Well, the first idea I want to redeem from you', I said, 'is that the gods don't notice what these two characters are like. All right?'

'Yes, we'll repay that debt,' he said.

'Now, if they're both known to the gods, then the one must be in the gods' favour and the other must be their enemy, as we agreed at the beginning too.'

'True.'

'Now, I'm sure we'll agree that everything the gods have to give
613a will happen, in as beneficial a way as possible, to the person who's in their favour (unless he's already owed some unavoidable harm as a result of a former misdemeanour).'

'Yes.'

'If a moral person appears to be in a bad way, then, we're bound to assume that his poverty or illness or whatever will eventually be good for him, whether this happens during his lifetime or after it. The point is that the gods never neglect anyone who is prepared to devote himself to becoming moral and, by practising virtue, to assimi-
b late himself to God as much as is humanly possible.'

'Yes, it doesn't seem likely that he'd be neglected by God, when he resembles him,' he remarked.

但你认为这样有助于比较和判明正义自身和不正义自身。你记得吗?” d

“我当然记得。”他说。

“好,既然我们已经做出了评判,”我说,“那么现在我代表正义要求你回报:我要求我们以及所有别的人都同意,正义享有人和诸神的荣誉。我们已经发现真正的正义必定包含利益,并且那些真正具有正义的人得到的不是一个虚假的正义影像,所以如果你同意帮我这个忙的话,那么正义之人也能收获名誉的褒奖,并获得给予拥有正义之人的利益。”

“这是一个正当的要求。”他说。 e

“那么我要从你那儿收回的第一个想法就是,”我说,“诸神并没有认为两者是相同的。对吗?”

“是的,我们会还这个债的。”他说。

“那么,如果他们两者都为诸神所知,那么一个必定为诸神所宠爱而另一个必定是诸神的敌人,就像我们起先同意过的那样。”

“对的。”

“那么我确信我们同意诸神所予的一切会最有益于他们所宠 613a
爱的人(除非他由于先前的错误行为已经欠下了某些不可免除的处罚)。”

“是的。”

“因此,如果一个正义之人看上去不好,那么我们一定要认为他的贫困、疾病或别的什么最终会有益于他,无论这是发生在他生前还是死后。关键是诸神决不会忽视任何愿意投身于成为正义,并且通过尽人力所及地实践美德以使自己接近于神的人。” b

“是的,当他与神相似的时候,看起来他就不会为诸神所忽视。”

'Now, we have to suppose that an immoral person is in the opposite situation, don't we?'

'Definitely.'

'Anyway, these are the kinds of prizes that a moral person would get from the gods.'

'That's what I think, at any rate,' he said.

'What about from men?' I asked. 'In all honesty, isn't it true that clever criminals are exactly like those runners who do well on the way up the track, and then flag on the way back? They sprint away at
c the beginning, but end up being jeered off the track, and have to beat a hasty retreat with their ears on their shoulders and without winning any chaplets. Genuine runners, however, complete the course and earn themselves rewards as well as chaplets. Isn't that the usual outcome in the case of moral people? Aren't they acclaimed, and rewarded as well, at the end of every activity and transaction they're involved in, and at the end of their lives?'

'Yes, they certainly are.'

'You're not in a position to object if I make the same claims a
d bout moral people that *you* made about immoral people, then, are you? I'm going to claim that moral people can, in later life, have political power in their own communities if they want, can marry women from any families they want, can have their children marry whomever they want, and so on. Everything you said about immoral people I am now claiming applies to moral people. On the other hand, my position as regards immoral people is that, even if they get away with it when they're young, at the end of the race they're found out. Their old age is made miserable by the jeering insults of strangers and countrymen
e alike; they're flogged and they undergo the punishments you rightly described as coarse ... and then they'll be tortured on the rack, and they'll have their eyes burnt out... well, you'd better imagine that I've given you the whole list of the torments they suffer. Anyway, as I say, please see if you have any objections to all this.'

'No, I don't,' he said. 'What you're saying is perfectly fair.'

“那么我们认为不正义之人的处境必定是相反的，不是吗？”

“毫无疑问。”

“无论如何，这些就是一个正义之人能够从诸神那得到的奖赏。”

“不管怎么说，我就是这样想的。”他说。

“那么从人这里又得到什么呢？”我问道，“实话说，难道不是
这样的：聪明的罪犯正像是那些在去的路上跑得很快而在回来的
时候却步行的跑步运动员？他们一开始奋力奔跑，但最后却受到
嘲笑而被撵出跑道，不得不把耳朵耷拉在肩膀上，没有得到任何 c
花冠，而退下场来。然而真正的跑步运动员跑完整个路程，为自
己赢得奖励和花冠。正义之人的结局一般不也是这样的吗？在
每个他们所参加的活动和交往中以及在他们生命的终点时，他们
不是都能得到喝彩和奖励吗？”

“是的，他们当然能得到。”

“你不反对我把你描述不正义之人的说法用来描述正义之
人，是吗？我会说，正义的人在晚年时，如果愿意就能在自己的城 d
邦中拥有政治权力，与任何家庭中他们中意的女人结婚，他们的
孩子可以和任何他们想要的人结婚，如此等等。你关于不正义之
人的所有说法，我现在都说成是正义之人的。另一方面，我对于
不正义之人的观点是这样的：即使他们在年轻的时候侥幸逃脱，
但在赛跑的终点会被发现的。他们的老年受到外邦人和本邦人
的嘲笑辱骂而很可怜，他们受到鞭笞并经受你正当地称之为粗暴 e
的惩罚。然后这些人会折磨拷问他，还会烙他的眼睛。你可以设
想我已经给你说了他们遭受的所有折磨。无论如何，就像我说的
一样，请考虑一下你对于所有这些是否有什么要反驳的。”

“不，没有，”他说，“你所说的非常公正。”

'So in addition to the benefits which stem from morality in itself,'
614a I said, 'those are the kinds of prizes and rewards and trophies which a moral person comes by during his lifetime from gods and men.'

'They're wonderful,' he said, 'and well founded.'

'Actually they're nothing,' I said. 'they are few and insubstantial compared with what our two characters will meet after their death. I'd better explain: we owe it to both of them to do so, and if I don't, the debt won't be repaid in full.'

'Please do,' he said. 'There's hardly anything I'd rather hear a
b description of.'

'Well, I'm not going to tell you the kind of saga Alcinous had to endure,' I said. 'Endurance will be my theme, however—that of brave Er the son of Armenius, who was a Pamphylian by birth. Once upon a time, he was killed in battle, and by the time the corpses were collected, ten days later, they had all putrefied except his, which was still in good shape. He was taken home and, twelve days after his death, just as his funeral was about to start and he was lying on the pyre, he came back to life. Then he told people what he'd seen in the other world.

'He said that his soul left his body and went on a journey, with
c lots of other souls as his companions. They came to an awesome place, where they found two openings next to each other in the earth, and two others directly opposite them up in the sky. There were judges sitting between the openings who made their assessment and then told the moral ones to take the right-hand route which went up and through the sky, and gave them tokens to wear on their fronts to show what behaviour they'd been assessed for, but told the immoral ones to take the left-hand, downward route. These people also had tokens,
d but on their backs, to show all their past deeds. When Er approached, however, the judges said that he had to report back to mankind about what goes on there, and they told him to listen and observe everything that happened in the place.

'From where he was, he could see souls leaving, once they'd

“所以除了那些源于正义本身的利益之外，”我说，“这些就是一个正义之人在他的生活中从人和诸神那得到的各种奖励、报偿 614a
和奖品。”

“它们是令人羡慕的，”他说道，“也是有根有据的。”

“实际上它们还算不上什么，”我说道，“与我们说到的这两类人，在其死后所要遇见的情形相比较，这些奖惩都太微不足道了。我是要好好进行解释的：我们要将奖惩按照他们两种人的所作所为，该归谁的就归谁，如果我不这样做，那么债就不会全部还清。”

“请解释吧，”他说，“几乎没有比这个说明我更愿意听的了。” b

“好吧，我想要对你讲述的故事不是阿尔喀诺俄斯不得不忍受的故事，”我说，“然而坚忍将是我的主题——那是有着潘斐利亚人血统的阿尔美纽斯之子，勇敢的厄尔的故事。有一次在战斗中，他被杀了，十天后当人们来收尸的时候，唯有他的尸体没有腐烂，依然形状完好。他死后十二天被运回家，正当他躺在火葬柴堆上开始火化的时候，他复活了。然后他告诉人们他看见了另一个世界。

“他说他的灵魂离开了他的身体，与许多别的灵魂结伴继续旅行。他们来到一个令人敬畏的地方，他们发现在地上有两个挨 c
着的洞口，与之正对着的有另外两个在天上的洞口。判官就坐在洞口之间，他们做出判决，然后吩咐正义之人走右手边向上通向天空的路，让他们把标记戴在前面以标明他们那些受过判决的行为，而命令不正义之人走左手边向下的道路，这些人也戴着标记，但是戴在后背以标明所有他们做过的事情。不过当厄尔走近的时候，判官说他必须把那里发生的事情回去告诉人类，他们吩咐 d
他倾听和观看所有发生在那个地方的事情。

“从他所在的那个地方，他看到判决过的灵魂离开了，进入天

been judged, by one or the other of the two openings in the sky and in the earth, and he noticed how the other two openings were used too: one was for certain souls, caked in grime and dust, to arise out of the
e earth, while the other was for other, clean souls to come down out of the sky. They arrived periodically, and he gained the impression that it had taken a long journey for them to get there; they were grateful to turn aside into the meadow and find a place to settle down. The scene resembled a festival. Old acquaintances greeted one another; those who'd come out of the earth asked those from the heavens what had happened to them there, and were asked the same question in return.
615a The tales of the one group were accompanied by groans and tears, as they recalled all the awful things they'd experienced and seen in the course of their underworld journey (which takes a thousand years), while the souls from heaven had only wonderful experiences and incredibly beautiful sights to recount.

'It would take ages to tell you a substantial proportion of their tales, Glaucon, but here's a brief outline of what Er said. Each individual had been punished—for every single crime he'd ever committed, and for every person he'd ever wronged—ten times, which is to
b say once every hundred years (assuming that the span of human life is a hundred years), to ensure that the penalty he paid was ten times worse than the crime. Take people who had caused a great many deaths, by betraying a country or an army, and people who had enslaved others or been responsible for inflicting misery in some other way: for every single person they had hurt, they received back ten times the amount of pain. Conversely, the same principle applied to the rewards people received for their good deeds, their morality and
c justice. Things are different, however, for those who die at birth or shortly afterwards, but what he told me about them isn't worth mentioning. However, he did tell a story about the even greater rewards and penalties for observance and non-observance of the proper behaviour towards gods and one's parents, and for murder with one's own hand.

'He said that he overheard someone asking someone else where Ar-

上的洞口或进入地上的洞口，他也注意到了另外两个洞口的用
处：一个洞口是给某些灵魂的，这些灵魂风尘仆仆地从地下上来，
而另一个洞口是给另一些灵魂的，这些干净的灵魂从天上下来。
他们姗姗到来，给人的印象就是他们经过长途跋涉来到那里，他 e
们很高兴来到一片草地找到一个地方坐下。场面就像是一个节
日。熟人互致问候，那些来自地下的灵魂询问那些来自天上的灵
魂那里的情况，那些来自天上的灵魂反过来也问那些来自地下的
灵魂同样的问题。当从地下来的人们回想起他们经历过的，以及
在其地下行程中（一趟可就是一千年啊）目睹到的所有可怕而艰 615a
难的事情时，一群人不禁涕泪涟涟，哭成一片，而那些从天上来的
灵魂叙述的则只有令人羡艳的经历以及美不胜收的景物。

“格劳孔，讲述他们所说的大部分故事会花很多时间，但厄尔
所说的大致如此：每个人都要受到——对于每个他曾犯的罪，对
于每个犯罪的人——十倍的惩罚，这就是说，假设一个人的寿命
有一百岁，那么他必须每百年都要忍受十倍于他罪行的惩罚。比 b
如说，背叛了城邦或军队而造成了大量死亡的人，奴役别人或以
别的方式造成了别人遭受痛苦的人：对于每一个他们伤害过的
人，他们都受到十倍痛苦的惩罚。反过来，同样的道理也适用于
由于他们的善行、他们的道德和正义而受到的报偿。然而对于那
些出生时就死了或出生不久就死了的人是不一样的，但他对我所 c
说的关于他们的话就不值得一提了。不过，他的确讲述过有关以
下方面的故事，即对诸神与其父母遵从适当行为举止者予以重
奖，而对诸神及其父母不遵从适当的行为举止者，还有亲手非法
杀人者予以更大的惩罚。

“他说他听说过某人问另一人说阿狄埃乌斯王在哪里。一千

diaeus the Great was. (A thousand years earlier, this Ardiaeus had been the dictator of a certain city-state in Pamphylia, and is said to have committed a great many abominable crimes, including killing his aged father and his elder brother.) The person who'd been asked the
d question replied, "He's not here, and he never will be. One of the terrible sights we saw was when we were near the exit. At last, after all we'd been through, we were about to come up from underground, when we suddenly caught sight of Ardiaeus. There were others with him, the vast majority of whom had been dictators, while the rest had committed awful non-political crimes. They were under the impression
e that they were on the point of leaving, but the exit refused to take them. Whenever anyone whose wickedness couldn't be redeemed tried to go up, or anyone who hadn't been punished enough, it made bellowing sounds. Fierce, fiery-looking men were standing there," he went on, "and they could make sense of the sounds. These men simply grabbed hold of some of the criminals and took them away, but they placed fetters on Ardiaeus' wrists, ankles, and neck, and others
616a got the same treatment; then they threw their prisoners to the ground and flayed them, and finally dragged them away along the roadside, tearing them to pieces on the thorny shrubs. They told any passers-by that they were taking them away to hurl them into Tartarus, and explained why as well."

'He added that of all the various terrors they experienced there, the worst was the fear they each felt that, as they started their ascent, they'd encounter the bellowing sound, and that there was nothing more gratifying than hearing no sound and making the ascent.

'So much for Er's description of the penalties and punishments,
b and the equivalent rewards. They spent seven days in the meadow, and on the eighth day they had to leave and go elsewhere. On the fourth day after that they reached a place from where they could see a straight shaft of light stretching from on high through the heavens and the earth; the light was like a pillar, and it was just like a rainbow in colour, except that it was brighter and clearer. It took another day's travelling to reach the light, and when they got there they were at the
c mid-point of the light and they could see, stretching away out of the heavens, the extremities of the bonds of the heavens (for this light

年前,阿狄埃乌斯曾是潘斐利亚某个城邦的暴君,传说他犯下了大量骇人的罪行,包括杀死他年老的父亲和他的长兄。那个被问问题的人回答说:'他现在不在这里,他也绝不会来这里。其中一 d
个可怕的景象是我们在出口处看到的。最终我们毕竟过来了,我们要从地下出来了,那时我们突然看到阿狄埃乌斯。还有别人和他在一起,其中大多数曾经是暴君,而其余人犯的可怕罪行则与城邦无关。他们在印象中似乎要离开了,但出口是拒绝他们离开 e
的。每当任何罪不容赦的人或任何还未受够惩罚的人试图向上走的时候,出口就会发出吼声。有一些样子凶猛的人站在那里,'他继续说,'他们能听懂这些声音。他们抓住某些罪犯,将其带走,但他们给阿狄埃乌斯的腕、踝和脖子加上镣铐,在其他各处也加上枷锁;然后他们把罪犯推翻在地,痛打他们,最后沿着路边拖 616a
着他们,用荆条把他们抽得体无完肤。他们告诉所有过路人,他们会将罪犯们扔到塔塔洛斯并解释为什么会这样。'

"他补充说在他们经历的各种恐惧中,他们感到最可怕的就是当他们上来的时候遇到的吼声,没有什么比走上来而不听到吼声更庆幸的事情了。

"对于处罚和惩罚以及相应的报偿的描述就是这些。他们在草地上待了七天,第八天他们必须离开去别处了。那以后的第四 b
天他们来到一个地方,从那里他们可以看见一束笔直的光柱从天空上贯穿至大地,这光像是柱子,正像是彩虹,只是更加明亮、更加清澈。又花了一天的旅程,他们触及到了光,当他们到达那里的时候,他们处在光的中间,他们能够看见连结天空的自天而降的光束的末端(因为这光把诸天连结在一起,像战船的龙骨从下 c
面 支撑起战船一样,这束光也这样支撑起整个旋转体)。这光从

binds the heavens together, and as the girth that underpins a trireme holds a trireme together, so this light holds the whole rotation together), while stretching down from the extremities was the spindle of Necessity, which causes the circular motion of all the separate rotations.

'The spindle's stem and hook are made of adamant, while its
d whorl consists of various substances, including adamant. In appearance, the whorl basically looks like whorls here on earth, but, given Er's description, one is bound to picture it as if there was first a large hollow whorl, with its insides completely scooped out, and with a second, smaller one lying snugly inside it (like those jars which fit into one another), and then, on the same arrangement, a third whorl, a fourth one, and finally four others. For he said that there were eight
e concentric whorls in all, and that their circular rims, looked at from above, formed a solid surface, as if there were just a single whorl attached to the stem, which was driven right through the middle of the eighth whorl.

'The circle which constituted the rim of the first whorl, the one on the outside, was the broadest; next broadest was the rim of the sixth whorl; third was the rim of the fourth whorl; fourth was the rim of the eighth whorl; fifth was the rim of the seventh whorl; sixth was the rim of the fifth whorl; seventh was the rim of the third whorl; and eighth was the rim of the second whorl. The rim of the largest whorl was spangled; the rim of the seventh whorl was brightest; the rim of
617a the eighth whorl gained its colour by reflecting the light of the seventh one; the rims of the second and fifth whorls were more yellow than the rest, and were almost identical in hue; the third was the whitest; the fourth was reddish; the sixth was white, but not as white as the third.

'Now, although the rotation of the spindle as a whole was uniform, nevertheless within the motion of the whole the seven inner circles moved, at regular speeds, in orbits which ran counter to the direction of the whole. The seven inner circles varied in speed: the eighth was the fastest; then second fastest were, all at once, the sev-
b enth, sixth, and fifth; the third fastest seemed to them (Er said) to be the fourth, which was in retrograde motion; the fourth fastest was

必然之纺锤的末端降下来，它推动所有独立的螺旋进行圆周运动。

“纺锤的基部和挂钩是由坚固材料制造的，而它的碗拱是各种材料制成的，包括坚固材料。表面上，这个碗拱看上去与人间的碗拱基本相似，但根据厄尔的描述，人们必定把它设想成首先 d
有一个中空的大碗拱，第二个也是中空的，稍小，紧紧地放在它里面，就像那些一个套在另一个里面的罐子，然后以同样的排列方式还有第三个、第四个以及还有另外四个。因为他说一共有八个同心碗拱，从上看，它们的圆形边缘形成一个坚实的表面，就像是 e
一个碗拱附着于一个基部，光直接穿过第八个碗拱的中心。

“构成第一个碗拱边缘的圆，即外边的那个是最宽的；次宽的是第六个碗拱的边缘；第三的就是第四个碗拱的边缘；第四的就是第八个碗拱的边缘；第五的就是第七个碗拱的边缘；第六的就是第五个碗拱的边缘；第七的就是第三个碗拱的边缘；第八的就是第二个碗拱的边缘。最大的碗拱边缘颜色驳杂；第七个碗拱的边缘是最明亮的；第八个碗拱的边缘通过反射第七个碗拱的光而具有颜色；第二个和第八个碗拱的边缘比其余的更黄，几乎具有 617a
同样的颜色；第三个碗拱的边缘是最白的；第四个碗拱的边缘是红色的；第六个碗拱边缘是白色的，但是没有第三个那么白。

“那么，虽然整个纺锤的圆周运动是单一的，但在整个运动的内部有七个匀速圆周运动，在其轨道上运动方向与整体的运动方向相反。七个内部圆周运动的有不同的速度：第八个是最快的；次快的是第七个、第六个和第五个，它们一起运动；厄尔说第三快的在他们 b
看来是第四个，它进行着向后的运动；第四快的是第三个；第五快的是第二个。纺锤在必然女神的膝上旋转。纺锤的每个圆周都是作

the third, and the fifth fastest was the second. The spindle was turning in the lap of Lady Necessity. Each of the spindle's circles acted as the vehicle for a Siren. Each Siren, as she stood on one of the circles, sounded a single note, and all eight notes together made a single harmonious sound.

c 'Three other women were also sitting on thrones which were evenly spaced around the spindle. They were the Fates, the daughters of Necessity, robed in white, with garlands on their heads; they were Lachesis, Clotho, and Atropos, accompanying the Sirens' song, with Lachesis singing of the past, Clotho of the present, and Atropos of the future. Clotho periodically laid her right hand on the outer circle of the spindle and helped to turn it; Atropos did the same with her left hand to the inner circles; and Lachesis alternately helped the outer circle

d and the inner circles on their way with one hand after the other.

'As soon as the souls arrived, they had to approach Lachesis. An intermediary arranged them in rows and then, once he'd taken from Lachesis' lap lottery tokens and sample lives, stepped up on to a high rostrum and said, "Hear the words of Lady Lachesis, daughter of Necessity. You souls condemned to impermanence, the cycle of birth followed by death is beginning again for you. No deity will be assigned to

e you: you will pick your own deities. The order of gaining tokens decides the order of choosing lives, which will be irrevocably yours. Goodness makes its own rules: each of you will be good to the extent that you value it. Responsibility lies with the chooser, not with God."

'After this announcement, he threw the tokens into the crowd, and everybody (except Er, who wasn't allowed to) picked up the token that fell beside him. Each soul's position in the lottery was clear once he'd picked up his token. Next, the intermediary placed on the ground in

618a front of them the sample lives, of which there were far more than there were souls in the crowd; every single kind of human and animal life was included among the samples. For instance, there were dictatorships (some lifelong, others collapsing before their time and ending in poverty, exile, and begging), and also male and female versions of lives of

为一个塞壬[1]的载具而运转，每个塞壬都站在一个圆周上，发出一个音符，所有八个音符一起构成一个和谐的音调。

“另外三个女人也坐在围绕着纺锤的等距的宝座上。她们是必 c
然的女儿，她们是命运三女神[2]，她们身着白袍头戴花环。她们是拉刻西斯、克罗托、阿特洛波斯，伴随着塞壬的歌声，拉刻西斯唱过去，克罗托唱现在，阿特洛波斯唱未来。克罗托不时地把右手放到纺锤圆周的外面帮助它旋转；阿特洛波斯用她的左手放到内圈帮助纺锤旋转；拉刻西斯两手交替着帮助外圈和内圈旋转。 d

“当灵魂到达的时候，他们必须靠近拉刻西斯。一个使者把他们排成队，然后他从拉刻西斯膝上抓了阄和生活模式，登上一座高坛，说道：‘请听必然的女儿，拉刻西斯女神之意。诸一日之灵魂，你们的生死轮回又要开始了。不会把神指派给你，而是你选择自己的神。抓阄的次序决定了你选择生活的次序，这生活必 e
定是你的。善有其自身的规则：你们当中每个人依你们对美德的重视而成为善。责任在于选择者，而不是神。’

“宣布了这些之后，他把阄撒向大家，每个人捡起落在自己身边的阄（除了厄尔，不允许他去捡）。拾起的人对签中的每个灵魂的地位就明白了，接下来使者放在他们面前地上的是各种生活模 618a
式，比人群中的灵魂多得多，这些模式包括了人和动物的每种生活。比如说有僭主（有些终生在位，另一些中途垮台最终受穷、流放和乞讨），还有男女名流的生活，有因体形美的，有因貌美的，有

〔1〕 塞壬，希腊神话中的女海妖。她们用美妙的歌声诱惑船只上的海员，从而使船只在岛屿周围触礁沉没。

〔2〕 命运三女神：拉刻西斯、克罗托和阿特洛波斯，希腊神话中三位掌握人类命运的女神。其中拉刻西斯专司命运之索，克罗托是命运之线的纺织者，阿特洛波斯是命运之线的切割确定者。

b fame for one's physique, good looks, and general strength and athlet-
icism, or for one's lineage and the excellence of one's ancestors; and
there were lives which lacked these distinctions as well. Temperament
wasn't included, however, since that inevitably varies according to
the life chosen; but otherwise there was every possible combination of
qualities with one another and with factors like wealth, poverty, sick-
ness, and health, in extreme or moderate amounts.

'Now, it looks as though this is an absolutely critical point for a
c person, my dear Glaucon. And that is why every single one of us has
to give his undivided attention—to the detriment of all other areas of
study—to trying to track down and discover whether there is anyone
he can discover and unearth anywhere who can give him the compe-
tence and knowledge to distinguish a good life from a bad one, and to
choose the better life from among all the possibilities that surround
him at any given moment. He has to weigh up all the things we've
been talking about, so as to know what bearing they have, in combi-
nation and in isolation, on living a good life. What are the good or
d bad results of mixing good looks with poverty or with wealth, in con-
junction with such-and-such a mental condition? What are the effects
of the various combinations of innate and acquired characteristics such
as high and low birth, involvement and lack of involvement in poli-
tics, physical strength and frailty, cleverness and stupidity, and so
on? He has to be able to take into consideration the nature of the
mind and so make a rational choice, from among all the alternatives,
e between a better and a worse life. He has to be in a position to think
of a life which leads his mind towards a state of increasing immorality
as worse, and consider one which leads in the opposite direction as
better. There's no other factor he'll regard as important: we've already
seen that this is the cardinal decision anyone has to make, whether he
does so during his lifetime or after he's died. By the time he reaches
619a Hades, then, this belief must be absolutely unassailable in him, so
that there too he can resist the lure of afflictions such as wealth, and
won't be trapped into dictatorship or any other activity which would
cause him to commit a number of foul crimes, and to suffer even
worse torments himself. Instead, he must know how to choose a life
which occupies the middle ground, and how to avoid either extreme,
as much as possible, in this world and throughout the next. For this is
how a person guarantees happiness for himself.

因身体通常强壮和体育训练的，或因优秀的家族和祖先的；还有 b
一些没有这样优秀品质的生活。然而性格不包括在内，因为它必定是随着所选择的生活而变化的；但另外也有各种组合的可能，品性与品性混合，还与各种因素，如财富、贫穷、疾病、健康以极端或折中的方式混合。

“我亲爱的格劳孔，看来现在对一个人来说是非常关键的时刻。这就是为什么我们当中的每一个人都心须专注于——而无
利于所有别的学习领域——试图追踪并发现是否有人能够发现 c
或发掘任何给他能力和知识以区别善的生活和恶的生活，并在任何时候从他身边的所有可能性中选择最善的生活。他必须衡量我们说过的一切，这样就能知道它们一起或单独地对善的生活所产生的影响。美貌混合着贫穷或结合着富裕，还结合着这样或那
样的灵魂状态，会有什么样的善的或恶的结果？各种先天的与后 d
天习得的品性的组合，如出生高贵和卑贱，参与或不参与政治，身体强壮或虚弱，聪明或愚笨等等的结合会有什么效果？他必须能够考虑灵魂的本性并从所有的可能中，在较善的生活与较恶的生活中作出一个理性的选择。他必须能够把一种使他的灵魂导向
增加不正义状态的生活看作是较恶的，而把导向相反方向的生活 e
看作是较善的。他不会重视别的因素的：我们已经看到这是任何人都要作出的关键决定，无论是在他生前还是在他死后。那么当他抵达哈德斯之处时，在他心中的这个信念绝对是牢不可破的，这样
他才能真正抵制住诸如财富之类的惹人烦恼的诱惑，还有其他会导 619a
致他犯下邪恶罪行、使其自身遭受更恶劣折磨的活动。相反，他必须知道如何去选择一种行乎中道的生活，如何尽可能地在今生、来世避免偏激与过分。因为这样才能保证他自身的幸福。

b 'Anyway, according to the report the messenger from the other world delivered on the occasion I'm talking about, the intermediary continued: "Even the last to come forward will find an acceptable life, not a pernicious one, if he chooses wisely and exerts himself during his lifetime. The first to choose should take care, and the last need not despair."

'Er said that no sooner had the intermediary fallen silent than the person whose turn was first stepped up and chose the most powerful dictatorship available. His stupidity and greed made him choose this life without inspecting it thoroughly and in sufficient detail, so he didn't notice that it included the fate of eating his own children and
c committing other horrible crimes. When he took the time to examine his choice, he beat his breast and wept, but he didn't comply with the intermediary's earlier words, because he didn't hold himself responsible for his afflictions; instead he blamed fortune, the gods, and anything rather than himself. He was one of those who had come out of the heavens, since he'd spent his previous life in a well-regulated community, and so had been good to a certain extent, even though it
d was habituation rather than philosophy that had made him so. In fact, those who had come from the heavens fell into this trap more or less as often as the others, since they hadn't learnt how to cope with difficult situations, whereas the majority of those who had come out of the earth didn't rush into their decisions, because they knew about suffering from their own experiences as well as from observing others. That was one of the main reasons—another being the unpredictability of the lottery—that most of the souls met with a reversal, from good to bad or vice versa. The point is this: if during his lifetime in this world a person practises philosophy with integrity, and if it so hap-
e pens, as a result of the lottery, that he's not one of the last to choose, then the report brought back from that other world makes it plausible to expect not only that he'd be happy here, but also that he'd travel from here to there and back again on the smooth roads of the heavens, rather than on rough underground trails.

'It was well worth seeing, Er said, how particular souls chose

“总之,在我正在谈论的这个场合,据从其它世界来的使者所做的叙述云,神使继续说道:‘即使是最后一个前来的人,如果他明智地进行选择,并在其一生中尽心尽力,也会找到一种合意而非有害的生活。第一个选择的人应该小心,最后一个选择的人不用绝望。’ b

“厄尔说道:使者刚说完,轮到第一的人就迫不及待地走向前选择了最强大的僭主。他的愚蠢和贪婪使他未经从细节上充分而彻底地考察便选择了这样的生活,所以他没有注意到这种生活
包含着吃他自己的孩子和犯下其他可怕罪行的命运。当他有时 c
间对他的选择作一考察的时候,他捶胸痛哭,然而他并没有按照使者早先说过的话去做,因为他并没有准备要对他自己的痛苦负责;相反,他责备命运、诸神以及任何别的东西,而不是责备他自己。他是那些来自天上的人之一,因为他的前世是在一个治理良好的城邦中度过,所以从某种程度上来说,他是善的,虽然他的善是由
于他的习惯而不是哲学使然。实际上,那些来自天上的人多多少 d
少与别人一样落入陷阱,因为他们不知道如何应对困境,而那些大多数来自地下的人没有匆匆地作出决定,因为他们从自己的经历中以及对别人的观看中知道了苦难。这是一个主要的理由——另一个理由是抓阄的不可预见性——使得大多数灵魂遇上了互换,由善变恶或反过来。关键是:如果一个人在这个世界
中一生忠实地实践哲学,并且抓阄时又碰巧不是最后一个选择, e
如果是这样的话,那么从另一个世界带来的消息会使得他相信他不仅可以期望今世的幸福,而且从此世到彼世的来回中,走的也是平坦的天国之路而不是崎岖的地下之路。

“厄尔说,颇值得一看的是个别灵魂选择他们生活的原因;所

620a their lives; the sight was by turns sad, amusing, and astonishing. Their choice was invariably dictated by conditioning gained in their former incarnation. For instance, he said he saw the soul which had once belonged to Orpheus choose the life of a swan; because women had killed him, he hated everything female, and wanted to avoid a female incarnation. He saw Thamyras choose a nightingale's life, while
b a swan and other songbirds opted for change and chose to live as human beings. The soul which was twentieth in line picked the life of a lion; it was Ajax the son of Telamon, and he didn't want a human incarnation because he was unable to forget the decision that had been made about the armour. The next soul was that of Agamemnon: again, his sufferings had embittered him against humanity, and he chose instead to be reborn as an eagle. About halfway through, it was the turn of Atalanta's soul, and she caught sight of a male athlete's life: when she noticed how well rewarded it was, she couldn't walk on
c by, and she took it. After Atalanta, Er saw the soul of Epeius the son of Panopeus becoming a craftswoman; and later, towards the end, he saw the soul of Thersites the funny man taking on a monkey's form. As the luck of the lottery had it, Odysseus' soul was the very last to come forward and choose. The memory of all the hardship he had previously endured had caused his ambition to subside, so he walked around for a long time, looking for a life as a non-political private citi-
d zen. At last he found one lying somewhere, disregarded by everyone else. When he saw it, he happily took it, saying that he'd have done exactly the same even if he'd been the first to choose. And the same kind of thorough exchange and shuffling of roles occurred in the case of animals too, as they became men or other animals—wild ones if they'd been immoral, tame ones otherwise.

'When the souls had all finished choosing their lives, they approached Lachesis in the order the lottery had assigned them. She gave each of them the personal deity they'd selected , to accompany them

看到的景象是,令人遗憾、使人发笑和让人感到惊奇的选择纷至 620a
沓来、轮流上演。他们的选择总是不变地被其前生获得的习性所
支配。例如,他说他看见一个曾属于奥菲斯的灵魂选择了一只天
鹅的生活;因为妇人们杀了他,他痛恨一切具有妇人特征的东西,
想要避免生于妇女。他看到萨弥拉斯选择了夜莺的生活,而一只
天鹅或别的鸣禽选择互换,而选择了人的生活。队列中的第二十 b
号灵魂选择了狮子的生活;忒拉蒙之子埃阿斯不想成为人,因为
他不能忘记那场关于盔甲的判决。下一个灵魂是阿伽门农的:同
样,他的苦难使他痛恨人类,由此他选择再生为一只鹰。进行到
大约一半的时候,轮到了阿特兰塔的灵魂,她看到了男运动员的
生活:当她注意到他们受到了丰厚的奖赏,她不能错过,她就选择
了这种生活。在阿特兰塔之后,厄尔看到帕诺培乌斯之子厄培乌
斯要变成一个女匠人;之后,在近末尾处,他看到一个滑稽的人忒 c
耳西忒斯的灵魂套上了猴子的形体。由于抓阄的运气,奥德修斯
的灵魂是最后一个走向前作选择的。对于所有先前他经受的苦
难的记忆使他的雄心壮志得以平息,所以他到处走了很久,寻找
一种不参与政治的普通公民的生活。最后他在一个地方发现了
一个,它没有受到别人的注意。当他看见它的时候,他高兴地将
它捡起,说即使他是第一个作出选择的话,他还会选择同一个的。 d
在动物中也发生同样彻底的转变和角色转换,它们变成人或别的
动物——如果它们之前是不正义的,那么就变成为野性的,否则
就变成温顺的动物。

“当所有的灵魂选择好了他们的生活后,他们按签子上所写的次序走到拉刻西斯面前。她给他们每人一个他们所选择的私神陪伴他们一生,作为他们的卫士并完成他们所作的选择。每个

e throughout their lives, as their guardians and to fulfil the choices they had made. Each deity first led its soul to Clotho, to pass under her hand and under the revolving orbit of the spindle, and so to ratify the destiny the soul had chosen in the lottery. Then, once a connection had been made with her, the deity led the soul to Atropos and her spinning, to make the web woven by Clotho fixed and unalterable. Afterwards, the soul set a fixed course for Lady Necessity's throne and
621a passed under it; once it was on the other side, and when everyone else had joined it there, they all travelled through terrible, stifling heat (since no trees or plants grew in that place) to the Plain of Oblivion. Since the day was now drawing to a close, they camped there by the River of Neglect, whose waters no vessel can contain.

'Now, they were all required to drink a certain amount of water, but some were too stupid to look after themselves properly and drank more than the required amount. As each person drank, he forgot eve-
b rything. They lay down to sleep, and in the middle of the night there was thunder and an earthquake. All of a sudden, they were lifted up from where they were, and they darted like shooting stars away in various directions for rebirth. As for Er, although he hadn't been allowed to drink any of the water he had no idea what direction he took, or how he got back to his body, but he suddenly opened his eyes and found that it was early in the morning and that he was lying on the funeral pyre.

'There you are, then, Glaucon. The story has made it safely through to the end, without perishing on the way. And it might save
c us too, if we take it to heart, and so successfully cross the River of Oblivion without defiling our souls. Anyway, my recommendation would be for us to regard the soul as immortal and as capable of surviving a great deal of suffering, just as it survives all the good times. We should always keep to the upward path, and we should use every means at our disposal to act morally and with intelligence, so that we may gain our own and the gods' approval, not only during our stay here on earth, but also when we collect the prizes our morality has

神首先引导着它的灵魂到克罗托处，在她的手掌下通过，并在纺锤旋转的范围内来批准灵魂在抓阄中选定的命运。然后，一旦与 e 她已建立起了一种关系，神就会引领灵魂到阿特洛波斯及其纺织处，使得克罗托所纺的命运之织物固定而无法变更。之后，灵魂就会顺着一条固定的道路走到必然女神的王座下，并从下面通过；一旦它来到另一边，与所有别的灵魂在那里一起会合，他们就 621a 都踏上旅途，经过可怕而令人窒息的闷热来到遗忘平原（因为那个地方没有树或植物）。由于白天将要结束，所以他们在遗忘之河边扎营，其水没有什么容器可盛。

"那时他们都被要求喝一定量的水，但有些人太蠢了以至不能恰当地照看好自己，喝水超过了要求的量。每个喝了这水的人就忘记了一切。他们躺下睡觉，在半夜雷声隆隆，地动山摇。突 b 然，他们从所处的地方被提起，他们像流星一样被投向各个方向以获重生。至于厄尔，虽然他没有被允许去喝一滴水，但他也不知道自己是从哪个方向还有用了何种方式才回到自己身体的，然而他只知道突然睁开眼睛就发现是在清晨了，而且他正躺在火葬的柴堆上呢。

"格劳孔，就是这样了。这个故事被从头至尾完好无损地保存下来，没有亡佚。如果我们相信它，那么它可能救助我们，这样就能成功地渡过遗忘之河而不玷污我们的灵魂。不管怎么说，我 c 的劝告是，我们要把灵魂看作是不朽的并且能够从许多痛苦中幸存下来的，就像它总能从所有好时运幸存下来一样。我们应该总是保持向上的道路，我们还应当在行使由我们做主的每一种手段时行为合乎正义，而且要以智慧的方式去做，这样，不管我们是待在尘世，还是在收集我们的正义为自己所赢得的奖赏时（恰似获

earned us, which will be just as extensive as the rewards victorious
d athletes receive from all quarters. And then, both here and during the
thousand-year journey of our story, all will be well with us. '

胜的运动员从各个地方获得的奖赏一样多),我们或许才能得到
自己以及诸神的赞许。于是,在此世以及在我们的故事所说的千 d
年旅程中,我们都会诸事安顺。”

译者后记

《理想国》一般被认为是柏拉图中期的哲学作品，以下我准备谈谈柏拉图的对话录和《理想国》的现有中文译本及这个英译本，以期对读者阅读这个译本有所帮助。

一、关于柏拉图的对话录

柏拉图（约公元前427年－前347年）是著名的古希腊哲学家，他写下了许多哲学对话录，并且在雅典创办了知名的学院。柏拉图是苏格拉底的学生，也是亚里士多德的老师。苏格拉底和柏拉图的学说主要保存在柏拉图的对话录中。

（一）柏拉图对话录分期：

柏拉图对话录写成的确切时间不可确知。不过，依据现代语言学的理论，对话录里潜藏的语言信息已经可以列出一个大略的年代表。这些对话录通常被分类为三个明显不同的时期，少数作品则被视为是在过渡期写成的，另外有一些则难以分类。将柏拉图著作翻译为德文的神学家弗里德里希·施莱尔马赫（Friedrich Schleiermacher）可能是第一个将柏拉图著作区分为三个时期的人，不过，他当时提出的排列顺序与现代学者提出的相当不同，且较倾向于以哲学理论而非年代分类，他宣称这样分类更符合柏拉图一生中的哲学思想发展。施莱尔马赫将对话录区分为：

奠基期：《斐德罗篇》、《吕西斯篇》、《普罗泰戈拉篇》、《拉凯斯篇》、《卡尔米德篇》、《欧绪弗洛篇》、《巴曼尼得斯篇》。

转变期：《高尔吉亚篇》、《泰阿泰德篇》、《美诺篇》、《欧绪德谟篇》、《克拉底鲁篇》、《智者篇》、《政治家篇》、《会饮篇》、《斐多篇》、《斐勒布篇》。

巅峰期:《理想国》、(《克里底亚篇》、《蒂迈欧篇》、《法律篇》)。

最后在括号里的三篇对话录则是未被施莱尔马赫翻译的部分,虽然其他未列出的十篇对话录(包括《伊安篇》等)也被翻译了,但都被施莱尔马赫视为伪作。最后,施莱尔马赫主张《申辩篇》或者包括了《克力同篇》是苏格拉底的真实对话、而由柏拉图记载的。

英国的 Lewis Campbell 是第一个率先使用文体学证明以时期来划分柏拉图著作是可行的学者。

不过,许多以年代分类的排序依然具有很大的争议。现代学者通常同意的排序是如同以下的:

早期对话录:苏格拉底的角色都出现在这些对话录中,他们也都被视为真正代表了历史角度上的苏格拉底;因此这些对话录也被称为苏格拉底对话录。它们大多都是由苏格拉底讨论一个主题的对话构成的,通常是和伦理有关,并且有一个人担任贸然挑战苏格拉底的角色。在经过一系列的对话后,苏格拉底会证明那些对话者对于辩论主题本身根本一无所知。这些对话录将结局交于读者决定谁才正确,这使得这些对话录具有"间接"的教学功能。这段时期也包括了一部分与苏格拉底的受审判和死刑有关的情节。这个阶段的作品包括:《申辩篇》、《克力同篇》、《卡尔米德篇》、《拉凯斯篇》、《吕西斯篇》、《欧绪弗洛篇》、《美涅克塞努篇》、《小希庇亚篇》、《伊安篇》。

接下来几篇则被视为过渡期或转型期的对话录:《高尔吉亚篇》、《普罗泰戈拉篇》、《美诺篇》。

中期对话录:到了早期对话录的后期,柏拉图笔下的苏格拉底在对话录中会开始公开一些他的问题的答案,或者提出正面的原则,这些通常被视为是柏拉图首次试图提出的自己的观点。这些原则中第一个出现的是,宣称美德是一种智慧,同时没有人是自愿为恶的,这也有可能是苏格拉底自己的观点。中期的对话录最特殊之处在于提出了知识是来自于理解那些不会变动的“理念”,同时对话也试着研究那些理念。而灵魂的不朽,和有关正义、美、真理的特定原则也在这段时期开始出现。《会饮篇》和《理想国》被视为是柏拉图中期对话录的最重要部分。

这个阶段的作品包括:《欧绪德谟篇》、《克拉底鲁篇》、《斐多篇》、《斐德罗篇》、《会饮篇》、《理想国》、《泰阿泰德篇》、《巴曼尼得斯篇》。

晚期对话录:《巴曼尼得斯篇》里出现了一系列对于“理念”理论的批判,这被广泛视为是象征柏拉图抛弃了这个理论。一些最近的研究(如 Meinwald,1991 年)挑战了这种说法,因为在其余的对话录中,理念论并没有就此消失,而只是换了一副面貌,以不同形式或类型的事物来象征它们。苏格拉底也依然在晚期对话录中保持重要角色。晚期对话录中新出现了一种特殊的辩证法,被称为“聚集和分割”,最值得注意的是例子是《智者篇》和《政治家篇》,并且在《斐德罗篇》里第一次公开展现。“聚集和分割”辩证法可以这样简单描述:对话者试图分辨事物间的共通点和差异点,以检验一个想法是否是事实。《智者篇》里的一些段落指出了这便是哲学家应该做的事,而且甚至在早期对话录中也是这样的。

从晚期的对话录中可以看出柏拉图思想的成熟,对于许多早期对话录中讨论到的议题,柏拉图都透露了他的答案。晚期的作品被公认为是相当艰深而且具挑战性的哲学作品,与早期的对话录相比较,晚期的作品通常更为严肃而且具逻辑性,但也经常对于问题的解答持保留态度,而与早期作品有所不同。

这个阶段的作品包括:《智者篇》、《政治家篇》、《斐勒布篇》、《蒂迈欧篇》、《克里底亚篇》、《法律篇》。

(二)关于《理想国》

《理想国》的篇名是 Politeia,其含义包括公民的条件与义务、公民政治生活、政府组织形式等,也就是一般意义上所谓的政治。促使柏拉图写《理想国》的两个可能的原因是雅典在伯罗奔尼撒战争中的失败和苏格拉底的死。雅典在伯罗奔尼撒战争中失败后,雅典的政治极为动荡,“三十僭主”推翻了民主政治,实施了一系列暴政,但八个月后被推翻。在《理想国》中,柏拉图对僭主制的批判可以说是直接来源于此。苏格拉底被处死,其罪名是败坏青年以及引入并信奉新神而不信奉城邦公认的神。这两件事对柏拉图的影响很大,他在“第七封信”中说:“我们的城邦已经不依传统的原则和法律行事了,要建立一种新的道德标准是极为困难的,再说法律和习惯正在以惊人的速度败坏着。”他看出“所有现存的城邦无一例外治理得不好”,他决心继承老师的使命,思考从根本上“如何改革这个制度”,并坚信“只有正确的哲学才能使我们分辨什么对社会和个人来说是正义的东西”。这正是《理想国》的主旨。

《理想国》是通过苏格拉底与其他对话者之间的对话并围绕“什么是正义”这个主题而展开的。涉及的主要内容包括“关于正义问题的论辩,批判当时的正义观”;“城邦国家的起源和理性神的问题”;“理想国家的社会体制和治国原则”;“哲学王和理念论”;“灵魂转向和教育以及辩证法”;“各种不同政体的比较”;“艺术的本性和社会功用(诗与哲学之争)”以及著名的“线喻”、“日喻”和“洞喻”。柏拉图在本书中详细论述了政治理论和正义的本性。他认为政治哲学是基于人的灵魂的,而人的灵魂可以分为三个部分,即理智的部分、激情的部分和欲望的部分。同样对于城邦来说也有三个部分,即统治者、卫士和一般的劳动者,他们分别对应于灵魂的三个部分。一个完善的城邦就是统治者在卫士的帮助下统治劳动者,从而形成一个正义的城邦。

在此,译者仅仅是想为读者指明一般学界所认为的《理想国》讨论的主题,并不想通过后记的形式将自己的观点先行加于读者,希望读者从自身的实际情况出发,通过自己的仔细阅读去发现问题和思考问题。

二、关于现有的中译本及这个英译本

已出版的中文译本有:

1.《理想国》吴献书译;

2.《理想国》段至诚译;

3.《理想国》刘勉,郭永刚译;

4.《理想国》郭斌和,张竹明译;

5.《柏拉图全集》王晓朝译;

6.《柏拉图对话集》王太庆译,本书只译出部分章节。

我在翻译过程中借鉴了4、5、6三个译本,它们对我的翻译工作帮助很大,如果没有前辈努力所取得的成就,本人的重译工作是不可想像的。在此向译界前辈深表谢忱。由于本书是英汉对照本,所以在翻译过程中译者力求英语与汉语之间语序上的对应,以便读者对照阅读。同时,希望读者能从上述译本中吸收精华。另外,本译文中一定存在不当甚至错误之处,也希望读者不吝赐教。

此外,关于这个英译版本的分章。《理想国》原本用希腊文抄写在纸莎草纸上,分成10个部分,每部分约5米长,所以后来大多数《理想国》的校勘者和译者把全书分成10卷。也有少部分译者依据自己的理解把原文划分若干章节,以帮助读者对各部分增进理解,这个英译本就属这种情况。但这种做法的不足是往往会把译者个人的想法加于读者,所以请读者自己明辨。

庞爔春

2006年7月

《西方学术经典文库》(第一辑)

功利主义	[英]约翰·斯图亚特·穆勒
诗学·诗艺	[古希腊]亚里士多德 [古罗马]贺拉斯
经济发展理论	[美]约瑟夫·阿洛伊斯·熊彼特
经济学原理	[英]阿尔弗雷德·马歇尔
国民财富的性质与原理	[英]亚当·斯密
联邦党人文集	[美]亚历山大·汉密尔顿
就业、利息与货币通论	[英]约翰·梅纳德·凯恩斯
尼各马可伦理学	[古希腊]亚里士多德
道德情操论	[英]亚当·斯密
君主论	[意]尼科洛·马基雅弗利
新教伦理与资本主义精神	[德]马克斯·韦伯
古代法	[英]亨利·萨姆奈·梅因
第一哲学沉思集	[法]勒内·笛卡儿
查拉图斯特拉如是说	[德]弗里德里希·威廉·尼采
哲学研究	[英]路德维希·维特根斯坦
实践理性批判	[德]伊曼努尔·康德
社会契约论	[法]让·雅克·卢梭
理想国	[古希腊]柏拉图
心理学原理	[美]威廉·詹姆斯
精神现象学	[德]威廉·弗里德里希·黑格尔
神圣者的观念	[德]鲁道夫·奥托
小逻辑	[德]威廉·弗里德里希·黑格尔

论人类不平等的起源	[法]让·雅克·卢梭
道德形而上学基础	[德]伊曼努尔·康德
人性论	[英]戴维·休谟
政府论	[英]约翰·洛克
论法的精神	[法]查尔斯·路易斯·孟德斯鸠
代议制政府	[英]约翰·斯图亚特·穆勒
英国法与文艺复兴	[英]弗雷德里克·威廉·梅特兰
法律社会学基本原理	[奥]尤根·埃利希
论美国民主	[法]夏尔·阿列克西·德·托克维尔
原始社会的结构和功能	[英]A. R. 拉德克利夫-布朗
政治学	[古希腊]亚里士多德
罗马帝国编年史	[古罗马]科尔涅里乌斯·塔西佗
普通语言学教程	[瑞士]费尔迪南·德·索绪尔
货币哲学	[德]格奥尔格·西梅尔
法理学讲演录	[英]约翰·奥斯丁
思想录	[法]布莱兹·帕斯卡
利维坦	[英]托马斯·霍布斯
意识形态与乌托邦	[德]卡尔·曼海姆
忏悔录	[古罗马]圣·奥古斯丁
西太平洋上的航海者	[英]布罗尼斯拉夫·马林诺夫斯基
历史学:理论和实际	[意]贝内德托·克罗齐
逻辑哲学论	[英]路得维希·维特根斯坦